The SAGE Handbook of

Innovation in Social Research Methods

The SAGE Handbook of

Innovation in Social Research Methods

Edited by

Malcolm Williams

and W. Paul Vogt

Los Angeles • London • New Delhi • Singapore • Washington DC

First published 2011

SAGE Publications Ltd
1 Oliver's Yard
55 City Road
London EC1Y 1SP

SAGE Publications Inc.
2455 Teller Road
Thousand Oaks, California 91320

SAGE Publications India Pvt Ltd
B 1/I 1 Mohan Cooperative Industrial Area
Mathura Road, Post Bag 7
New Delhi 110 044

SAGE Publications Asia-Pacific Pte Ltd
33 Pekin Street #02-01
Far East Square
Singapore 048763

Library of Congress Control Number: 2010925768

British Library Cataloguing in Publication data

A catalogue record for this book is available from the British Library

ISBN: 978–1–4129–4648–3

Typeset by GLYPH International Pvt. Ltd., Bangalore, India
Printed in Great Britain by MPG Books Group, Bodmin, Cornwall
Printed on paper from sustainable resources

Contents

Acknowledgements

We thank Chris Rojek for the original idea for this volume and the excellent dinners he bought us. Thanks too to Jai Seaman at SAGE for her advice and patience throughout the project. We began asking colleagues throughout the world to say what they thought was currently innovatory in social research methods and we would like to thank them for their helpful and imaginative ideas.

List of Contributors

Claire Alexander is Reader in Sociology at the London School of Economics. Her research interests are in the area of race, ethnicity, masculinity and youth identities, particularly in relation to ethnography. Her main publications include *The Art of Being Black* (OUP, 1996) and *The Asian Gang* (Berg, 2000). She is co-editor of *Beyond Difference* (Ethnic and Racial Studies, July 2002), and *Making Race Matter: Bodies, Space and Identity* (Palgrave, 2005) and editor of *Writing Race: Ethnography and Difference* (Ethnic and Racial Studies, May 2006). She is co-director, with Dr Joya Chatterji, of an AHRC-funded research project (2006–2009) on 'The Bengal Diaspora: Bengali Settlers in South Asia and Britain'.

Ariel M. Aloe is Assistant Professor, Graduate School of Education, University at Buffalo – SUNY. He specializes in research synthesis, quantitative methods and teacher quality.

Paul J. Baker is Emeritus Distinguished University Professor at Illinois State University. He is trained in the field of sociology and has spent the past 25 years teaching aspiring administrators to think about the organizational complexities of schools. His special research interest is local responses to the continuous mandates for improvement from state and federal agencies. He has published numerous articles in various professional journals – *American Journal of Sociology, The Sociological Quarterly, American Sociologist, Research in Higher Education, Educational Leadership, Planning and Changing, Change Magazine* and *Journal of Education for Students at Risk.*

Betsy Jane Becker is Mode L. Stone Distinguished Professor of Educational Statistics and coordinator of the program in Measurement and Statistics in the College of Education at Florida State University, where she has been on faculty since Fall 2004. Becker's current research is funded by the National Science Foundation. Her methodological work involves the study of methods for synthesizing correlation matrices and regression slopes. She is also conducting syntheses of studies of teacher knowledge and teacher qualifications. Becker is past president of the Society for Research Synthesis Methodology, and a Fellow of the American Statistical Association.

Ivano Bison is Assistant Professor of Sociology at the University of Trento (Italy). He was Visiting Professor at the Department of Sociology, Madison, Wisconsin (2004) and at the Department of Sociology, University of Emory, Atlanta, Georgia (2006). His research interests include social stratification, life courses intergenerational disparities, inter- and intra-generational career mobility, educational inequalities, transition from school to work, poverty and gender disparities. He is currently teaching graduate and doctoral level courses in categorical data analysis and methodology and survey design at the University of Trento.

Antony Bryant is currently Professor of Informatics at Leeds Metropolitan University, Leeds, UK. His initial studies and his PhD were in the social and political sciences. He later completed a Masters in Computing, followed by a period working as a Systems Analyst and Project Leader for a commercial software developer. He has written extensively on research methods, being Senior Editor of *The SAGE Handbook of Grounded Theory* (Sage, 2007) – co-edited with Kathy Charmaz with whom he has worked extensively within the area of Grounded Theory and research methods in general. He has developed and taught a wide range of post-graduate courses in South Africa, Malaysia and China. He is currently ASEM Professor at the University of Malaya and Visiting Professor at the University of Amsterdam. His current research includes investigation of the ways in which the Open Source model might be developed as a feature of the re-constructed financial sector in the wake of the economic meltdown.

David Byrne is Professor of Sociology and Social Policy at Durham University. Previously he has worked as both an academic and in community development. His books include *Complexity Theory and the Social Sciences* (1998) and *Interpreting Quantitative Data* (2002). His major empirical research interest is in the consequences of deindustrialization for places and people and in the nature of social exclusion on a global basis. He is also keenly interested in the development of methodological perspectives and methods as tools which can be used in the application of social science to real social problems and sees case-based methods as having enormous potential in this context.

James Carpenter is a Reader in Medical and Social Statistics at the London School of Hygiene and Tropical Medicine (University of London). His methodological research interests include statistical methods for the analysis of partially observed data, multilevel modeling, meta-analysis and bootstrap methods.

Kathy Charmaz is Professor of Sociology and Director of the Faculty Writing Program at Sonoma State University in which she helps faculty with their scholarly writing. She has written, co-authored or co-edited eight books including *Developing Grounded Theory: The Second Generation, The Handbook of*

Grounded Theory (with Antony Bryant) and *Health, Illness, and Healing: Society, Social Context and Self,* as well as two award-winning books, *Constructing Grounded Theory: A Practical Guide Through Qualitative Analysis* and *Good Days, Bad Days: The Self in Chronic Illness and Time.* She also publishes in the areas of social psychology and writing for publication.

Kathleen M. T. Collins is an Associate Professor in the Department of Curriculum and Instruction at the University of Arkansas at Fayetteville. To date, she has published more than 60 research articles, book chapters and encyclopedia chapters and presented more than 70 research papers at international, national and regional conferences. In addition, she has made several invited addresses to faculty and students on the topic of mixed research. Dr Collins' interests are in research methodological issues as they pertain to mixed research, special populations and the identification and assessment of literacy problems of post-secondary students.

Wendy Dyer is a Senior Lecturer in Criminology at Northumbria University. Her research interests are in the area of innovative approaches to the exploration of large and complex datasets, and mental health and crime. Her main publications include *Single-Case Probabilities* (co-authored with Malcolm Williams, in D. Byrne and C. Ragin (eds), *The Sage Handbook of Case Based Methods.* Sage, 2009) and *The Psychiatric and Criminal Careers of Mentally Disordered Offenders Referred to a Custody Diversion Team in the United Kingdom* (*International Journal of Forensic Mental Health*, 2006, Vol. 5(1), pp. 15–28). She has coordinated the Prison and Offender Research in Social Care and Health (PORSCH) North East network since its inception in 2005 and has been awarded funding for various projects exploring the health and social care of offenders.

Rosalind Edwards is Professor in Social Policy and Director of the Families and Social Capital Research Group at London South Bank University. Her main research interests are family lives and family policy, and she is currently working on a qualitative longitudinal archiving study of children's sibling and friend relationships as part of the Timescapes consortium, and a comparative feasibility study exploring qualitative secondary analysis of family and parenting across sources and timeframes. Recent publications include: *Sibling Identity and Relationships: Sisters and Brothers* (with L. Hadfield, H. Lucey and M. Mauthner, Routledge, 2006), *Assessing Social Capital: Concept, Policy and Practice* (edited with J. Franklin and J. Holland, Cambridge Scholars Press, 2007) and *Researching Families and Communities: Social and Generational Change* (ed., Routledge, 2008). She is founder and co-editor of the *International Journal of Social Research Methodology* (with J. Brannen).

Susan E. Embretson is Professor of Psychology at the Georgia Institute of Technology. Her interests span psychometric methods, item response theory, cognition and intelligence and quantitative methods. Her main research program is integrating cognitive theory into psychometric models and test design, which has led to the possibility of automatic item generation. She has served as President of the Psychometric Society, the Society for Multivariate Experimental Psychology and Division 5 in the American Psychological Association (APA). She received the 1997 Outstanding Technical Contribution Award from the National Council on Educational Measurement and the 2001 Distinguished Scientific Contributions Award from Division 5 in APA for her research.

Roberto P. Franzosi is Professor of Sociology and Linguistics at Emory University. Franzosi's main interests have been in the study of conflict and violence (Italian postwar strikes, rise of Italian fascism, lynching in American Jim Crow South). He has also had a long-standing interest in issues of language and measurement of meaning. He is the author of several articles and four books: *The Puzzle of Strikes: Class and State Strategies in Postwar Italy* (Cambridge University Press, 1994), *From Words to Number: Narrative, Data, and Social Science* (Cambridge University Press, 2005), *Content Analysis* (Sage, 2008), and *Quantitative Narrative Analysis* (Sage, 2010).

Dianne C. Gardner is an Associate Professor of Educational Administration and Foundations at Illinois State University. Her scholarship foci include adult professional learning for instructional renewal in schools and assessment and evaluation in elementary, secondary and higher education. She is a former urban early childhood special education speech and language specialist and teacher educator at Alverno College in Milwaukee. She now teaches doctoral seminars on organizational leadership and received her PhD from the University of Wisconsin-Madison in higher and adult education leadership.

Giampietro Gobo is Associate Professor of Methodology of Social Research and Evaluation Methods, and Director of the centre ICONA (Innovation and Organizational Change in the Public Administration) at the University of Milan. He has published over 50 articles in the areas of qualitative and quantitative methods. His books include *Doing Ethnography* (Sage, 2008, under translation in Arabic), *Qualitative Research Practice* (Sage, 2004: co-edited with C. Seale, J.F. Gubrium and D. Silverman) and *Collecting Survey Data. An Interviewee-Centred Approach,* (Sage, 2010: with Sergio Mauceri). He is currently undertaking projects in the area of workplace studies (call centres, medic emergency dispatch centres, air traffic control rooms).

Elizabeth Griffiths is an Assistant Professor in the Department of Sociology at Emory University. She received her PhD in 2007 from the Department of Sociology at the University of Toronto. Her current research focuses on spatiotemporal variations in urban homicide, diffusion processes, the role of social disorganization and routine activities theories in explaining crime, homicide in public housing, and the relationship between household structure and victimization risk. Her research has been published in journals such as *Criminology*, *The Journal of Research in Crime and Delinquency* and *Social Problems*.

Lynne Haeffele is a former high school teacher and state education agency administrator. She is now a senior researcher in the Center for the Study of Education Policy at Illinois State University. Her research projects and published works include studies of teacher distribution, high-poverty/high-performing schools, college readiness, college student transfer and school/university partnerships. Her contractual work includes studies of state education governance, program evaluations, charter school development and peer review for the US Department of Education.

Martyn Hammersley is Professor of Educational and Social Research at the Open University. He has carried out research in the sociology of education and the sociology of the media. Much of his work has been concerned with the methodological issues surrounding social enquiry. He has written several books including: *Reading Ethnographic Research* (Longman, 1991), *What's Wrong with Ethnography?* (Routledge, 1992), *The Politics of Social Research* (Sage, 1995), *Taking Sides in Social Research* (Routledge, 1999), *Educational Research, Policymaking and Practice* (Paul Chapman, 2002) and *Questioning Qualitative Inquiry* (Sage, 2008).

Douglas D. Heckathorn is Professor of Sociology at Cornell University. He arrived at Cornell in 1999, after nine years of service as Professor of Sociology and Economics at the University of Connecticut. Dr Heckathorn received his PhD in Sociology from the University of Kansas (1974). He is the editor of *Rationality and Society.* Dr Heckathorn's intellectual interests lie in formal sociological theory, policy analysis, social psychology and quantitative methods, which he applies to an eclectic set of substantive foci including AIDS prevention research, collective action and jazz. His solo- and co-authored articles on these topics have recently appeared in *Poetics, Sociological Focus, Social Problems, American Sociologist, American Sociological Review,* and *Rationality and Society.* He is currently working on several interrelated projects. The first analyzes collective action and norm emergence using formal theories to specify the reciprocal relationship between choice and structure. A recent extension of that project analyzes aggregate social exchange across macrosocial categories, including race and ethnicity, gender, age and economic status, to analyze quantitatively both social structure and the power differentials encoded in those structures. He also continues collaborating with Robert Broadhead on HIV prevention research targeting active drug injectors. Finally, a methodological project uses a form of incentive-driven chain-referral sampling in combination with simulation and analytic methods to draw statistically representative samples of hidden populations, such as jazz musicians, active drug injectors and the homeless.

John H. Hitchcock's PhD was in Educational Psychology with a concentration in research methods (Albany State University of New York, 2003). He is an Assistant Professor in the Educational Studies Department in the College of Education at Ohio University. Dr Hitchcock's research focuses on the development and evaluation of interventions for special needs populations and culturally appropriate psychological assessment. In addition to working on the Sri Lankan research program described in this book, Dr Hitchcock is involved with several projects funded by the US Department of Education and the development of conceptual pieces dealing with advancements to mixed methods research design and program evaluation.

Ian Rees-Jones is Professor of Sociology at Bangor University. He has published extensively in the field of medical sociology addressing health inequalities, chronic illness and medical decision making. His research spans the historical sociology of health, medicine and welfare. His current research focus is on inequalities and social change and he leads an ESRC-funded project utilizing Multiple Correspondence Analysis to map changes in social space and lifestyles since the 1970s using the British Regional Heart Study. Recent books include *Consumption and Generational Change, The Rise of Consumer Lifestyles* (Transaction Publishers, 2009) and *Ageing in a Consumer Society: From Passive to Active Consumption in Britain* (Policy Press, 2008). He is also co-author with Paul Higgs of *Medical Sociology and Old Age: Towards a Sociology of Health in Later Life* (Routledge, 2009).

Rex B. Kline is an Associate Professor of Psychology at Concordia University in Montréal, Canada. Since earning his PhD in psychology, his areas of research and writing have included the psychometric evaluation of cognitive abilities, child clinical assessment, structural equation modeling, the preparation of students for conducting independent research and usability of engineering in computer science. He lives with his wife and two children in Alexandria, Canada.

Nancy L. Leech is an Assistant Professor at the University of Colorado Denver. Dr Leech is currently teaching masters and PhD level courses in research, statistics and measurement. Her area of research is promoting new developments and better understandings in applied qualitative, quantitative and mixed methodologies. To date, she has published more than 35 articles in referred journals and two books: *SPSS for Basic Statistics: Use and Interpretation* and *SPSS for Intermediate Statistics: Use and Interpretation*, both published by Taylor and Francis. Dr Leech has made more than 30 presentations at regional, national and international conferences.

Gayle Letherby is Professor of Sociology at the University of Plymouth. Gayle researches and writes in a variety of areas including reproductive and non/parental identity; working and learning in higher education; crime and deviance and travel mobilities. She is also interested in all things methodological, particularly the politics of the research process and product. Publications focusing on methodological concerns include *Feminist Research in Theory and Practice* (Open University, 2003), *Extending Social Research: Application, Implementation, Presentation* (Open University, 2007, edited with P. Bywaters), 'Have Backpack Will Travel: Auto/biography as a mobile methododology' in B. Fincham, M. McGuinness and L. Murray *Mobile Methodologies* (Palgrave).

Peter Martin is a Research Fellow at the Centre for Comparative Social Surveys at City University, London, where he is part of the team that coordinates the European Social Survey. He holds a postgraduate degree in Psychology from the University of Bremen, Germany, an MSc in Social Research Methods and Statistics and a PhD in Sociology from City University. His interests include mixed methods research, survey methodology, sequence analysis, contemporary racial attitudes and theories of racism.

Peter Martin is a PhD candidate in Sociology at City University, London, where he has conducted a mixed methods study to investigate the methodological intricacies of survey research on racism and related attitudes. He holds a postgraduate degree in Psychology from the University of Bremen, Germany and an MSc in Social Research Methods and Statistics from City University. He has also worked as a research assistant in life course psychology, as a research consultant and as a visiting lecturer in social research methods. His interests include mixed methods, survey methodology, sequence analysis, contemporary racial attitudes and moral action.

Heather H. McIntyre has an MS in industrial-organizational psychology from Virginia Polytechnic Institute and State University and is currently in the doctoral program for quantitative psychology at Georgia Institute of Technology. Her primary research interests centre on the modeling of cognitive response styles and strategies in personality testing via explanatory IRT as well as mixture and hybrid models. In particular, the conjoint use of item response and item response time data for these purposes is under investigation, as well as within-individual variation in response strategies during testing.

Bonnie Kaul Nastasi (PhD School Psychology, Kent State University, 1986) is Associate Professor in the Department of Psychology at Tulane University. Dr Nastasi's research focuses on development and evaluation of culturally appropriate assessment and intervention approaches to promote mental health and reduce health risks such as STIs/HIV. She has worked in Sri Lanka since 1995 on the development of school-based programs to promote children's and adolescent's psychological well-being, and is currently directing a multi-country study, with partners in 10 countries, to examine psychological well-being of children and adolescents. She is President-elect for Division 16 (School Psychology) of the American Psychological Association.

Anthony J. Onwuegbuzie is Professor in the Department of Educational Leadership and Counseling at Sam Houston State University. He teaches courses in qualitative, quantitative and mixed research. Dr Onwuegbuzie writes extensively on qualitative, quantitative and mixed methodological topics, having numerous articles and book/encyclopedia chapters published representing all three research paradigms/approaches. He has published more than 200 refereed journal articles and 30 book/encyclopedia chapters. He has made more than 450 presentations and keynote addresses at regional, national and international conferences. Dr Onwuegbuzie has received numerous outstanding paper awards. He serves as editor of *Educational Researcher* and co-editor of *Research in the Schools*.

Geoff Payne (AcSS) is Emeritus Professor of Sociology, University of Plymouth, where he was for many years Dean of Social Sciences. A former President of the British Sociological Association, his research has been mainly in the fields of social stratification, particularly social mobility and sociological methods. Recent publications include *Key Concepts in Social Research,* 2nd edn (Sage, 2010), *Teaching Quantitative Methods* (Sage, 2010, with Malcolm Williams) and *Social Divisions*, 3rd edn (Palgrave Macmillan, 2011). He currently teaches research methods in the School of Geography, Politics and Sociology, Newcastle University.

Keenan A. Pituch is an Associate Professor of quantitative methods in the Educational Psychology Department at the University of Texas at Austin. Graduate courses he has taught include correlation and regression, univariate and multivariate analysis of variance, hierarchical linear modeling and structural equation modeling. His research interests include multilevel modeling, mediation analysis, growth curve modeling and evaluation methodology as applied to large-scale educational experiments. His scholarship has appeared in journals such as *Educational Research and Evaluation, Journal of Experimental Education* and *Multivariate Behavioral Research*. He earned his PhD in Research Design and Statistics from Florida State University in 1997.

Ian Plewis joined the University of Manchester as Professor of Social Statistics in 2007 having previously worked at the Centre for Longitudinal Studies, Institute of Education, University of London since 1999 where he was Professor of Longitudinal Research Methods in Education and where he now holds a visiting professorship. His research interests are in the design and analysis of longitudinal studies, multilevel models and educational inequalities. He is a former editor of Series A of the *Journal of the Royal Statistical Society* ('Statistics in Society') and has published widely in both methodological and substantive journals.

Charles C. Ragin holds a joint appointment as Professor of Sociology and Political Science at the University of Arizona. For the past two decades his work has focused primarily on broad issues in methodology, especially the challenge of bringing some of the logic and spirit of small-*N* case-oriented research to the study of medium-sized and large *N*s. His books include *The Comparative Method* (University of California Press, 1987), *What Is a Case?* (with Howard S. Becker; Cambridge University Press, 1992), *Fuzzy-Set Social Science* (University of Chicago Press, 2000), *Configurational Comparative Methods* (with Benoit Rihoux; Sage, 2008) and *Redesigning Social Inquiry* (University of Chicago Press, 2008).

Donald B. Rubin , John L. Loeb Professor of Statistics, Department of Statistics, Harvard University, is an Elected Fellow/Member of the American Statistical Association, Institute of Mathematical Statistics, International Statistical Institute, American Association for the Advancement of Science, American Academy of Arts and Sciences, U.S. National Academy of Sciences, Honorary Member of the European Association of Methodology, and Corresponding (foreign) Fellow of the British Academy. He has authored/co-authored over 350 publications (including 10 books) and has made important contributions to statistical theory and methodology, particularly in causal inference, design and analysis of experiments and sample surveys, treatment of missing data and Bayesian data analysis. For many years he has been one of the mostly cited authors in mathematics in the world (ISI Science Watch). He has received many awards in statistics: the Samuel S. Wilks Medal, Parzen Prize for Statistical Innovation, the Fisher Lectureship, the George W. Snedecor Award, Mitchell Prize (twice), Statistician of the Year for both the Boston and Chicago Chapters of the ASA. He also has been Editor or Associate Editor of many statistical journals.

Garrett Andrew Schneider is a PhD candidate in sociology at the University of Arizona. His interests include the sociology of punishment, political economy, social theory and the logic of case-oriented research. His recent research includes a study of the politics of mandatory minimum sentencing and the evolution of federal banking regulation in the US over the course of the twentieth century.

John R. Slate is a Professor in the Department of Educational Leadership and Counselling at Sam Houston State University. With 25 years of higher education experience, he has won several university and state awards for educational research and has over 500 research publications and presentations. Dr Slate's research interests lie in the use of mixed method research and in analyzing state and national educational databases. He is currently teaching courses in basic and advanced statistics as well as working with doctoral students on addressing school reform issues. He serves on the editorial board of *Educational Researcher* and as co-editor of *Research in the Schools*.

Laura M. Stapleton is an Associate Professor of Quantitative Psychology in the Department of Psychology at the University of Maryland, Baltimore County and teaches graduate courses in intermediate statistics, structural equation modeling and measurement. Her research interests include multilevel latent variable models and the analysis of survey data obtained under complex sampling designs. Her scholarship in these areas has appeared in journals such as *Structural Equation Modeling, Multivariate Behavioral Research*, and *Educational and Psychological Measurement* and numerous book chapters. She earned her PhD in Measurement, Statistics and Evaluation from the University of Maryland in 2001.

Mike Thelwall is Professor of Information Science and leader of the Statistical Cybermetrics Research Group at the University of Wolverhampton, UK. He is also Visiting Fellow of the Amsterdam Virtual Knowledge Studio, a Docent at Åbo Akademi University Department of Information Studies and a research associate at the Oxford Internet Institute. He has published 152 refereed journal articles, 7 book chapters and 2 books including *Introduction to Webometrics*. He is an Associate Editor of the *Journal of the American Society for Information Science and Technology* and sits on eight other editorial boards.

Emma Uprichard is a Lecturer in Social Research Methods at the Department of Sociology at the University of York, UK. Her research interests revolve around the methodological challenge of studying the complex social world and include childhood, cities, time, food, research methods and methodology, and complexity theory.

Cyprian Wejnert completed his PhD in Sociology at Cornell University in 2009. His research interests include sampling methodology, social networks, hidden populations and HIV prevention. He is currently aiding the Centers for Disease Control and Prevention with HIV prevention research among at risk groups and has recently published in *Social Networks, Sociological Methodology,* and *Sociological Methods and Research.*

Richard D. Wiggins joined the Institute of Education, University of London as Head and Chair of Quantitative Social Science in 2007. His methodological interests include the longitudinal analysis of secondary data, mixed methods, survey design, attitude measurement and sampling methodology, evaluation research and policy analysis. Substantive research covers the exploration of structure and agency in the context of ageing, poverty, physical and mental health and well-being as well as cross-national differences in health and quality of life. More recently, he has been working on multilingual capital using administrative data sources for London's school population.

W. Paul Vogt is Emeritus Professor of Research Methods and Evaluation at Illinois State University where he has won both teaching and research awards. He specializes in research methodology and the design of program evaluations – particularly issues surrounding choice of methods and integrating multiple methods of investigation. His publications include: *Dictionary of Statistics and Methodology* (3rd edn, Sage, 2005); *Quantitative Research Methods for*

Professionals (Allyn & Bacon, 2006); *Tolerance and Education: Learning to Live with Diversity and Difference* (Sage, 1997); *Education Programs for Improving Intergroup Relations* (co-edited with Walter Stephan, Teachers College Press, 2004); *Selecting Research Methods,* 4 edited vols., (Sage, 2008); *Data Collection,* 4 edited vols., (Sage, 2010).

Malcolm Williams is Professor and Director of the School of Social Sciences at Cardiff University, where he joined in 2010. Prior to this he was Professor of Social Research Methodology at the University of Plymouth. He is the author/editor of several books on method and methodology, including *Science and Social Science* (Routledge, 2000), *Making Sense of Social Research* (Sage, 2003) and *Philosophical Foundations of Social Research* (Sage, 4 volume collection, 2006). He is the author of many scientific papers in areas such as probability theory, objectivity, representation and empirical work in household transitions, measurement of homelessness and social research pedagogy. He is joint editor of *Methodological Innovations Online*.

Introduction

Innovation in Social Research Methods

Malcolm Williams and W. Paul Vogt

One person's innovation is another's travesty and anyone with an interest in method can easily name their top ten innovations. To produce a volume on methodological innovation is to inevitably call forth a variety of views on whether the methods contained therein are the most innovatory, or indeed innovatory at all. The choice is inevitably somewhat subjective, though this does not necessarily mean it is without reasoning. The choice of methods and their implied underlying methodologies and epistemologies, in this volume, partly arises from the editors' own interests and positioning, but also from listening to what others thought to be innovatory. If a method, or even school of methods, is not represented and this itself stimulates debate, then arguably such absence might advance the development of social research. Nevertheless we would hope the chapters here will encourage methodological reflection as well as debate.

The aim of this volume is to survey where social research method 'is at' at the present time and where it may be going in the future. Some of the approaches will be familiar, even very familiar, to readers and some will be unfamiliar – and may even seem quirky. Some will be very much more evolved and have longer histories than others. In the chapters where the approaches with longer histories are featured, the authors set out what they regard as the current state of their development. There is a fashion in method which may be shaped by many things (we go on to discuss some of these below) and some innovations are of huge historical importance in social research, whilst others of possibly equal utility will not be taken up, or will quietly disappear. Finally, some innovations disappear as *innovative methods* because they have become part of the researcher's standard repertoire. Examples include structural equation modelling, multi-level modelling, qualitative case analysis and grounded theory. Yet these four are all still under rapid development and whilst new developments in these are discussed in the chapters that follow, they have all become standard items in the researcher's toolkit. The innovation lies more in developments within the method, than the method itself.

For this volume we asked the authors to risk some 'futurology'. Where do they think the approach, the method or technique they write about is going? Some have been bold in their predictions, some more cautious. If we had undertaken this task five years ago, how many of the chapter topics would have been the same and if we undertook this task five years from now, would our choices be the same? The answer in both cases would likely be the 'some'. Indeed some of the chapters in the current volume are not themselves specific approaches, but review developments in their methodological foundations. Other approaches, for example 'feminist methodology' or 'causal analysis' have been around a long time (particularly the latter) and a betting person would surely feel comfortable that they will continue to feature in discussions of methodological innovation, but even this is not certain.

Whilst it seemed clear that the aforementioned topics would inevitably be included, there was some discussion amongst the editors on other topics. Some were reluctantly not included; others were not included because their leading practitioners, or developers, were unable to write a chapter for the volume. Most of our choices arose from a consultation with social researchers internationally, conducted via an email circular. Where a topic was mentioned by several people, we thought it as a likely candidate for inclusion. We should perhaps say at this point, that the inclusion of a topic does not mean that both or either of the editors endorse the approach or technique, but we nevertheless accept that its innovation will shape method or methodological thinking.

THE SOCIAL CONSTRUCTION OF RESEARCH METHODS

The method of no discipline is inevitable, though there is an inevitable symbiosis between method and discipline. The character of the discipline and its problematic will influence the methods it uses. This is the received wisdom: that the topics a discipline tackles and the difficulties in answering the questions that arise, will determine the methods chosen. For example, we can trace the development and use of experimental and quasi-experimental method in US sociology and social policy to the evaluative demands of the Headstart Programme in the 1960s (Oakley, 2000: 198). Similarly, the increasing insistence on randomized controlled trials as the only 'gold standard' can be largely traced to the US Government Performance and Results Act of 1993 (see Vogt et al. in this volume).

But this can occur in the other direction. A method (or methodological approach) will shape the discipline. Again, in sociology, the 'cultural turn', particularly in European sociology, has changed the character of the discipline fundamentally. The topics and the questions asked are driven by (or one might say limited by) the methodological possibilities and starting positions. For many sociologists for example, through the 1980s and 1990s, quantitative methods and the logic of prediction and explanation were ruled out by an 'anti-scientism', or 'anti-positivism' that saw only an idiographic basis for sociology.[1] For a large number of social researchers this left only the methods of interpretation as legitimate (Payne et al., 2004). In British sociology some of the key topics of the 1970s were traditionally sociological and included stratification, community and conflict, but by the 1990s they were much more likely to be concerned with individual identity or performance.[2] In a content analysis of two years output of leading British sociology journals (in 2002/3) it was found that only 6% used quantitative methods at all (Payne et al., 2004). In the cultural turn (or indeed prior to this) it is not suggested that topic drove method, or indeed vice versa, but the net methodological result (in Europe at least) was to limit methodological possibility. The shift to interpretive, or humanistic methods, did have some beneficial effects. For example, the development of observational methods, biography, autobiography/autoethnography led to questions of the 'positioning' of the researcher and the subsequent development of a reflexivity of method (Ellis, 1997). However every dog will have its day and one can detect a shift back to explanatory sociology and the embracing of a 'methodological pluralism' (Payne and Payne, 2004). Indeed had this volume been produced five years ago, a chapter on 'reflexivity' would have been a likely candidate for inclusion and there had been some innovatory writing in the area (May, 1999). Its absence does not indicate that sociologists (and indeed other social scientists) are no longer 'reflexive', but rather that it has to a great extent entered the methodological mainstream and little innovatory work is being done.

The cultural turn has not been absent in the US, and conversely there have been some very good quantitative methodological developments in Europe, but it must be said that it is in the US where most of the advances in quantitative methods have taken place. Here one occasionally hears the complaint that these developments have led to an almost exclusively quantitative approach in some disciplines, for example criminology. And one study of publication outlets for the cultural or ethnographic turn found that most of these publications appeared in specialist outlets rather than in the discipline's general leading journals (Culyba et al., 2004).

SOCIAL RESEARCH NOW

Despite these divergences in methods favoured by national social research communities, the landscape of research is probably more conducive to innovation than it has been for the past quarter century. The output of social research, and arguably the methodological quality of that output, is greater than it has ever been. How do we account for this? There may be a number of interrelated reasons:

- The end of the 'science' or 'paradigm' wars (or at least their relegation to largely irrelevant skirmishes).
- The development of mixed methods approaches (or more generally methodological pluralism).
- Technological developments, particularly fast computing.
- Statistical and scientific developments more generally.
- Greater publishing opportunities.

Let us briefly review these as follows.

The paradigm wars and the post war settlement

What became known as the 'paradigm wars' have been acclaimed to be over (Guba and Lincoln, 1994),[3] however whilst this assertion is correct so far, as there has been a big reduction, even disappearance, of adversarial academic production (as we indicated above in respect of the preponderance of particular methods in localities), the wars have left their mark. The 'styles' of social research that have been the post war legacy make a difference to the position and status of social research and certainly to its component disciplines. And there still remains a lingering tendency among some researchers when they analyze qualitative data to believe that it is necessary to begin by saying something negative about positivism – a dead horse if ever there was one.

The paradigm wars were a contest of 'world views' in how we can know the social world. They were a contest between a scientific and a humanistic perspective, positivism versus anti-positivism, quantitative versus qualitative and were fought from the late 1960s until the early 1990s. Yet the conflict had its roots in a much older and fundamental quarrel about how we can know the social world, that went back a century or more to the dispute between emergent rationalist science and conservative romanticism (Manicas, 1987). In economics and sociology this was manifested in the German *Methodenstreit* (methodological conflict) of the late nineteenth century and continued in sociology through the 1920s and 1930s, to some extent manifested in the rivalry between the Columbia and Chicago Schools (Bannister, 1987).[4] These disputes were as much about what humans are like, as they were about how we could come to know them. In the human sciences they led to parallel methodological traditions: the idiographic humanist tradition that arose through the hermeneutics of deep religious study and concentrated on the revelation of deep meanings and the nomothetic, which followed the reasoning of the emergent natural sciences (Williams, 2000a). In social research these fundamental epistemological divergences underlay qualitative and quantitative methods respectively. The former emphasized knowing through accessing meaning, sometimes hidden meanings, whilst the latter placed emphasis on measurement. The protagonists in the 'paradigm wars' insisted on the epistemological exclusivity of one or the other of these. There is a huge literature on the battles and skirmishes of what was, in the end, a pointless and damaging episode in social research.[5] The damage lay in the impression of disciplines lacking purpose or direction and in Europe (mainly) culminated in postmodernism. Its nihilism and relativism rendered social research, in the way it had been hitherto understood, as pointless. Where it had a particular hold on the academic community, the damage to the credibility of social science amongst policy makers remains.

The pointlessness of the paradigm wars is thrown into sharp relief when one looks at the powerful emergence of mixed method approaches (more of which below) and the ability of researchers to combine sophisticated understandings with rigorous measurement. Arguably the protagonists forgot their social science history. Weber, in his reasoning for combining understanding with causal explanation, noted that only mathematics could claim to be purely nomothetic in its reasoning, with all other sciences requiring some level of interpretation or understanding (Weber, 1978: 23), an insight reiterated by Karl Popper, when he reminded us of the inescapable nature of theoretical assumptions (Popper, 1959: 106–11). Conversely, understandings without explanations failed to convince, or at least the denial of the inevitability of causal language or generalizations in qualitative research produced fairly obvious logical and performative contradictions (Hammersley, 2008; Payne and Williams, 2005).

Anti-positivism and even postmodernism, though damaging to credibility nevertheless challenged some long held shibboleths around value neutrality and assumptions about the simple linearity of data. Arguably these challenges opened social research to the influences of complexity science, realism and feminism. The former has yet to make important methodological inroads (though see David Byrne's and Emma Uprichard's chapters in this volume), possibly because the methodological and technical sophistication needed for complexity modelling have only been developed in a few isolated areas, such as Gilbert and Troitzsch (2005), Smith and Stevens (1997) and Casetelani and Hafferty (2009).[6] Realism (itself often closely associated with complexity approaches), on the other hand, has been directly or indirectly influential in several areas of work, some of which are represented in this volume (Byrne, Dyer, Rees-Jones, Ragin and Schneider, Uprichard). Realism (to use an over used description) might be seen as the methodological 'third way', combining a commitment to scientific explanation to an ontology that emphasizes both the 'real' character of social phenomena, with the inevitability of our need to know it through a description. In practice this has lead to a few important methodological developments, for example case based approaches such as those of Charles Ragin or the middle range realism of Ray Pawson (2000), but mostly in how we reason and theorize data (see Carter and New, 2004). Realism is ecumenical about method, because to successfully know reality it calls on both interpretation and explanation. Though realism is far from dominant in social research, it does demonstrate how an ontology of the social world can live comfortably with both the idiographic and the nomothetic.

In practice, although the fighting is largely over and a *de jure* methodological tolerance may be the outcome, there remain three methods groupings, only one of which truly embraces a spirit of methodological ecumenism: thus we have those researchers still primarily working in the scientific, or naturalist tradition and conversely those who exclusively work in the humanist or interpretivist tradition. In this volume one can see clearly the sophistication of developments in each approach, but one nevertheless has a sense of two unconnected epistemologies. The third group and they too are represented here, work with methods that have an element of both explanation and interpretation. Let us be clear, we do not say any one of these approaches is wrong, or better, but rather they emphasize the peculiarly epistemologically divided nature of social research. Such division is absent in the natural sciences and very much less pronounced in the arts and humanities. However, whilst we do not advocate that every social statistician learn discourse analysis, or every ethnographer learn multi-level modelling, we do believe that true methodological innovation requires a flourishing of naturalistic, humanistic and mixed approaches. And even when the demands of increasing specialization make it difficult or impossible for an individual researcher to master more than one research tradition, teams of researchers may do so, and *a fortiori,* entire disciplines certainly can.

Mixed methods and methodological pluralism

Mixed methods and methodological pluralism are not one and the same. Though the latter term is not in widespread use, we think it is a useful term to distinguish a methodological attitude from particular strategies that 'mix' methods. Thus 'pluralism' refers to overall output, not to an individual's plurality of methods (Payne and Payne, 2004: 149). A researcher may use only one method, or may use more than one method, but the decisions underlying methodological choice are not restricted by some prior epistemological commitment, but rather as a result of selecting the best method for the task in hand. And pluralism can encompass additional types of methodological integration – those that do not cross the quantitative-qualitative divide. For example, combining interviews, observations and document analyses in an ethnographic case study (all 'qualitative') can be excellent practice, as can integrating statistical techniques such as structural equation modelling and multi-level modelling (see the chapters by Kline, and Pituch and Stapleton (this volume)).

Nevertheless, as Tashakkori and Teddlie (1998: 17) note, mixed methods usually combine quantitative and qualitative approaches and they claim that 'mono methods' conducted by 'purists' and 'pure' designs are becoming increasingly rare. Though this is possibly an overstatement, it is certainly the case that larger studies, or research programmes, will combine more than one method, which may be qualitative and quantitative. The methods themselves might be applied sequentially, in parallel, may be of equivalent weight or status, or may differ. It is, for example, increasingly common to employ qualitative exploratory strategies, through say focus groups or field interviews, prior to survey design and conversely use the methods the other way around to develop or further clarify survey findings, or those based on secondary data.

Such strategies are unremarkable and not necessarily innovative, but what is more interesting are the truly hybrid approaches, that at the level of data collection or analysis incorporate measurement, interpretation and explanation. A very good example of this kind of hybrid strategy has been developed by Roberto Franzosi (2004, and in this volume) and the team effort described by Hitchcock and Nastasi (in this volume). The emergence of software such as NVIVO, compatible with SPSS, or Ragin's custom made QCA software (see Ragin and Schneider, this volume) have practically facilitated hybrid developments.

Pluralism has begun to move us away from thinking that designs are 'qualitative' or 'quantitative' and instead, much more fruitfully, thinking of design as the means by which a study will collect data (Vogt, 2007: 6; de Vaus, 2001). So, designs may be experimental, longitudinal, cross sectional or case study. An overall research programme design may incorporate more than one of these and within these particular designs one may utilize more than one method and that method may be quantitative, qualitative – or indeed itself 'hybrid'. The importance of methodological pluralism and mixed methods is less that such designs have pragmatic added value (though this is crucial) and more that they open an epistemological space that allows us to think about research problems unencumbered by prior conceptions of what constitutes legitimate social enquiry.

A glimpse of a radical new future of data collection and analysis can be found in a paper entitled *The Coming Crisis of Empirical Sociology*. In this Mike Savage and Roger Burrows (Savage and Burrows, 2007) argued that sociology and perhaps social science in general were in danger of falling behind methodologically. Whereas sociology had championed and thrived on the social survey and the in-depth interview, the era of 'knowing capitalism', the advances made in the collection and analysis of routine transactional data threatens to make obsolete, or at least marginalize, these more traditional methods. The term 'knowing capitalism' (Thrift, 2005) is characterized as, 'where circuits of information proliferate and are embedded in numerous kinds of information technologies' (Savage and Burrows, 2007: 886). The transactional data comes in many forms: from purchases, loyalty cards, etc. and the physical location of individuals from GPS, cell phone signals, etc. Savage and Burrows openly acknowledge that their paper was a polemic, but their key point seems to us to be very valid. It is both a challenge and an opportunity to be able to develop analytic methods that can access and analyze such vast amounts of data, but also to do this ethically. Whilst they may be right that more traditional methods based on the sample survey or interview may have only specialist use in the future, it would seem nevertheless that many of the analysis strategies and applications discussed in this volume rise to these challenges. The embracing of this new world of information technology and data collection is the ultimate methodological pluralism.

Technological developments

We touched on the possibilities for hybrid methods afforded by the development of NUDIST and NVIVO, but these software packages are only two of a vast and increasing range of software available to social researchers. Without doubt, these and the accompanying development of hardware and fast computing have revolutionized social research. We could have written this last sentence ten years ago and it would have been equally true, but in the last ten years there has been an exponential growth in computing power, software and platforms for the latter. Indeed, arguably, the last ten years in social research have witnessed more technological advances than in the previous several decades.

Two examples illustrate this.

Development of SPSS

In the early 1990s the use of SPSS became viable on freestanding personal computers and by the mid-1990s SPSSx and SPSSpc were being superseded by SPSS for Windows. Although this was lamented by many researchers who preferred to write syntax themselves in programme files, the 'drag and drop' menus and the user friendly data files revolutionized access to data analysis. With the most basic instructions, newcomers to SPSS could be entering data, defining and labelling variables, running frequencies and crosstabs and simple descriptive statistics in just hours, or indeed, minutes. Some saw this as a dangerous development that encouraged data dredging and all sorts of other undisciplined activities, but this 'democratization' also got apprentice researchers exploring data much more quickly. In terms of output, if maybe not quality, a graduate student could produce more output in an afternoon than Lazarsfeld could in month! SPSS for Windows was so simple the only impediment to good research were the research skills themselves and the limits of imagination. This example illustrates how technology has eased the entry of apprentice researchers into research and the way in which increased output has been facilitated.[7] SPSS itself is now moving into the territory intimated by Savage and Burrows, by developing applications, such as predictive analysis software, and those that can link SPSS to data and text mining.[8]

The rise of freeware for data analysis

A kind of democratization even more dramatic than the ease of use provided by menu-driven software is the free availability of increasing numbers of the most advanced software packages. Not only can anybody use it because it is easy to use, anybody can own it, because it is free. Methodological innovators not only create new methods, but they often provide free software for implementing the innovations. We have already mentioned Charles Ragin's Qualitative Comparative Analysis software. Roberto Franzosi's Quantitative Narrative Analysis software (called PC-ACE) is also freely downloadable. A third example is an easy to use program for missing data analysis called AMELIA developed by Gary King and colleagues in 2001. Originally available on King's website, it is now accessible through the R collection. As a final example, the two best-known programs for

Bayesian analysis are both freeware: *winBUGS* is available at http://www.mrc-bsu.cam.ac.uk/bugs; bayesm is part of the R package and is available at http://www.r-project.org. The reader will have noted the mention of 'R' in the last two sentences. R is the mother of all statistical freeware. In the judgement of many researchers it is superior to most or all commercially available packages, and the community of users enhances the package rapidly. It is not too incautious to predict that within a decade R will become the default choice of most quantitative analysts in the social sciences.

In addition to these manifestly social science applications, the possibilities of more generic open access web applications such as BlogPulse (http://www.blogpulse.com/) have yet to be widely exploited. Mike Thelwall has used data from the latter site (which measures internet blog postings) to show when and to what extent contemporary events (e.g. the evolution debate, the later career and death of Michael Jackson) impact on public debate (see this volume, Thelwall (2009) and Hookway (2008)).

Statistical and scientific developments

Until the 1960s the modal research project in the social sciences was comprised of a small number of cases and an even smaller number of variables. Often, a single researcher would make the observations and collect the data. The number of variables and observations in a case study could be bigger, but at the cost of a very small number of cases. Methods of quantitative analysis were designed with such 'small-*N*' studies in mind. The chief analytic concern was to reduce the dangers of overgeneralizing from a small sample – from whence the focus on statistical inference and the rise of the ubiquitous *p*-value.

Today, typical economists, political scientists, or sociologists work with huge data sets, data sets that they themselves have not collected. Concern with statistical significance has diminished (not disappeared by any means) if for no other reason than that with very large sets it can be hard to find a relationship that is *not* statistically significant, that fails to meet the minimum threshold of ($p < .05$). Today, social scientists who collect their own data often tend to fall into two camps: experimentalists, especially in psychology, and researchers collecting qualitative data using interviews, observations, or other ethnographic techniques. But the model quantitatively oriented sociologist, economist, or political scientist does not generate data, as an interviewer or experimenter would, but rather seeks the data from one of numerous secondary data archives. For example, 85 research articles were published in the *American Sociological Review* in 2007 and 2008. Of these, 71 or (83%) were written using archival data. A handful of these articles were based on historical archives, but apart from those few exceptions, authors mainly drew their data from government sponsored surveys or from census data. The availability of these kinds of data sources fundamentally alters the nature of research and the kinds of questions that can be asked. When researchers have thousands of cases and are able to examine dozens of variables, the nature of research changes from the artisanal activity it was a few decades before. And the relevant statistical tools do too. In general, the emphasis has shifted from estimating the likelihood that a particular finding could have occurred by chance (null hypothesis testing) and toward assessing the adequacy of large complex models.

The reinforcing interactions of the growth in computing power, the increase in the number and scope of data archives, and the development of statistical theory have transformed quantitative social science in many ways, most of which are touched on in the chapters that follow. Multi-level modelling (MLM)[9] is a compelling example. Most problems in the social sciences are in fact multi-level or contextual problems. For example, how can one estimate the separate effects on students' learning of their classrooms, their schools and their neighbourhoods? Each of these variables is a level nested inside another (students in classrooms, classrooms in schools, schools in neighbourhoods). Using traditional techniques, one cannot measure the separate effects of these levels without violating assumptions of independence of observations and measurements, because they involve statistical models of parameters that vary at different levels (Snijders and Bosker, 1999; Goldstein, 2003; Raudenbush and Bryk, 2002). Multi-level modelling has solved a long intractable set of problems. Access to this crucial but very sophisticated technique has been facilitated by software development; indeed, MLM is for all intents and purposes impossible without statistical software. Perhaps the best known of these is Raudenbush and Bryk's HLM package. But freeware options exist too. One of the best of these, offering both free downloadable software MLWIN (to UK based academics) and staged tutorials, is the University of Bristol Centre for Multi-Level Modelling at http://www.cmm.bristol.ac.uk/. And, not surprisingly, excellent options for fitting multilevel models exist in R as well.

Our second example of the fecund interaction of advances in computer hardware linked to innovations in statistical theory and software is structural equation modelling (SEM).[10] Like multi-level modelling, structural equation modelling is 'case hungry', and like MLM, SEM is generally inappropriate for use in small-*N* research. SEM is a set of statistical methods for testing causal models especially when the variables in the models raise measurement problems because they are latent and cannot be observed directly. Because many social science variables are latent constructs that have to be inferred from observable indicators (democracy, intelligence, ethnocentrism, program quality and so on) and because most social scientists have an interest in causal relations among variables, the role of SEM methods in modern quantitative research is great. SEM unites the techniques of factor analysis with those of regression and path analysis to combine a measurement model with a structural model. To assess the value of complex causal models SEM uses goodness of fit indices, which indicate how well the data fit the specified model.

Multi-level modelling and structural equation modelling are the two best known examples of recent transformations of quantitative analysis in the social sciences made possible by the troika of the rapid development of huge data archives, astonishingly fast computing and statistical techniques to take advantage of them.[11] While the two continue to develop separately, they are also being integrated in innovative ways by, for example, incorporating latent-variable measurement components into MLM and hierarchical elements into SEM. These kinds of promising developments are described in two chapters in this volume (by Kline and by Pituch and Stapleton).

Publishing opportunities

In the mid-twentieth century social research was a slow process. The comparatively primitive data collection and analysis technologies slowed the production process and the means to publicize results; discussing methods and their developments was limited by the relatively few journals and books. In her book *The History of Sociological Research Methods in America 1920–1960* (Platt, 1996), Jennifer Platt lists all of the sociological methods textbooks published between 1918 and 1959, in the US. There were 23 of them (the first ever published in 1918)! But, presumably, there were nevertheless enough avenues available to satisfy the publishing requirements of researchers.

Between the 1960s and the 1980s the publication of research methods texts grew steadily, but it was only in the 1990s that the exponential growth occurred. By far the biggest publisher has been Sage publications. They published their first methods book in 1970 and by 2010 their catalogue listed 1,023 titles in research methods and evaluation. They have published work by many of the late twentieth century 'greats' amongst social researchers, including Donald Campbell, Lee Cronbach and Michael Quinn-Patten (Cresswell, 2009). Their Quantitative Applications in the Social Sciences (QASS) series has more than 100 titles on basic statistics, measurement, and software applications. The Sage methods catalogue is now so large that an internal market between titles in very similar areas (particularly introductory texts) now exists.

We are not aware of any studies of the relationship between the growth of methods publishing (particularly that geared to specialist applications and techniques), software development and subsequent methodological development, but it is a reasonable hypothesis that some degree of symbiosis between these now exists.

Journal output has also grown rapidly, virtually all journals publish online and a number of journals (Sociological Research Online (http://www.socresonline.org.uk/), Methodological Innovations Online (http://www.methodologicalinnovations.org/)) only publish online. The development of online publishing and archiving of journals (particularly in JStor) has made output available faster and at the researcher's desk. Not only the output, but increasingly the data and the codes researchers have used to analyze it are available online as a routine part of the publication process; this democratizing aces to data is quite widespread in economics and seems underway in sociology (Freese, 2007). Search engines, such as Google Scholar, Web of Science, etc., have speeded up literature searches and consequently a researcher working in a particular area can complete a review of developments in that area in a matter of hours, whereas prior to online publishing and search engines, knowledge of developments was a hit and miss affair, with researchers often working on methodological developments, ignorant of similar work by other researchers.

At the time of writing, as we noted above, there are divergences in the kind of developments found in different jurisdictions, but these differences may erode. US output is equally accessible to researchers in Europe and vice versa, for example. Equally researchers in different parts of the world can easily collaborate. The present volume (and other similar volumes) is testimony to this. Virtually, the entire editing process was conducted electronically and indeed this is now the default means of production for such projects.

Finally, the possibilities for real time debate about methods is only just being exploited. Anecdotally, it would seem that the level of interpersonal communication by email about methods issues is quite high (see for example, the *Radical Statistics* discussion list in the UK at http://www.radstats.org.uk/).

Are there limits to this revolution? Whilst there are apparently no technological limits, there may be limits to the amount of output the market will sustain and indeed one suspects that often there is quite a lot of similarity in the output of the book market in particular. The other limit must be cognitive: how much new knowledge do researchers have the capacity or time to absorb? One outcome of this may be a narrowing of specialisms. The days of the social researcher with a working knowledge of several methods and a wide range of techniques may be limited. Instead social researchers may begin to specialize much more in the manner of natural scientists (Williams, 2000a). And indeed as we have already noted, working in teams with other specialists is the most likely path to functioning methodological pluralism.

METHODOLOGICAL FUTURES

In this introduction we have sketched out some of the factors that, we believe, have shaped methodological innovation in the last few decades. Individual chapters show methodological and technical possibilities, but for them to be realized there has to be an appetite for their use. This 'appetite' is stimulated or sated by a complex interplay of historical, social and technical conditions. The interrelationship between these is a true complex system in which a relatively minor change in initial conditions will bring about huge changes in outcome. Thus, the kind of 'futurology' about a particular method or technique is proposed on the basis of holding other historical, technical and social variables constant. A review of these at present reveals contradictions and puzzles.

For example, why is social research so little influenced by complexity approaches, when work using methods derived from these is well advanced in other sciences of complex systems, such as biology and meteorology? One could propose hypotheses about the conservatism of the General Linear Model (Byrne, 2002: chapter 2), or possibly the general lack of scientific sophistication in social research. Similarly, quantitative case based approaches (as opposed to frequency based ones) are, as yet, relatively underdeveloped. A common criticism of these approaches is their lack of equivalence of significance levels or testing. Yet the adoption of the frequency theory of probability, that underpins frequency approaches, in the nineteenth century was not an historic or technical inevitability. A propensity theory was, before this time, an equally likely candidate (Gillies, 2000: chapter 2). In quantitative social research one can detect a Kuhnian 'normal science' that has been good enough (good enough to attract funding and scholars that is) to continue to solve puzzles.

But to continue the Kuhnian analogy: Savage and Burrows' 'kite flying' article (cited above) may presage a revolution, which renders irrelevant technical advances in many anticipated areas. The concern must be that our efforts may be no more than to produce the social research equivalent of the Ford Edsel![12]

Whether we face revolution or evolution, we cannot ignore the wider social world in shaping the demand for and the reception of what we produce. At the time of writing one can detect a tension in this matter. The recession of 2008/9 produced a massive increase in government borrowing and the subsequent need in the following years to reduce that deficit. This has consequences for social research that may be negative or positive (and even both at the same time!). Negatively, budget reductions will impact on funding to academia and in turn threaten methodological development. In the UK, for example, much of the methodological advancement in recent years (and some of it is represented in this volume) has come from programmes funded from within the National Centre for Research Methods and its predecessors (http://www.ncrm.ac.uk/), itself funded by the Economic and Social Research Council, the social research funding body of government. Outside of academia most social research is conducted within government departments, or within independent/quasi-independent research units. What they all have in common is their reliance on government funding and the risks to their activity in its absence. Yet funding cuts across the public sector, combined with weaker performing economies, often has the unintended consequence of increasing demand for social research to counter the social problems that this produces. In the US, the Great Depression, can be seen as the midwife to what was a golden age of social research in the 1930s (Madge, 1963). What may change is what is funded and how it is funded. The 'what' could be small-scale diagnostic research, action research or evaluations, none of which would stretch the current capacity of our methodological knowledge and of course, such research is often vulnerable to political manipulation for short term gain (see Beals, 2006: 96). The phenomenon of 'quick and dirty' research, often conducted on a shoe string by private sector companies, is well known to the research community.

Indeed it may well be the private sector that dams and saves us! Market research is arguably leading the way in methodological advancement and at least some of the innovation we see in the current volume began life in that sector. Primarily it is market driven and well funded, a combination that may be the best motor for technological advancement, but whether those technologies will equally serve the needs of social development is uncertain. Furthermore, the 'quality' spread in market research ranges from great sophistication[13] to poor quality research with small or opportunistic samples conducted with few resources. Opportunistic web-based surveys or polls, telephone calls or mailings from direct sales organizations masquerading as market research are a threat to the integrity of market research.

One might cite other variables that will shape methodological development and some of these are discussed in this volume: For example, how we train future researchers and the resources that this commands, how we communicate our research findings. Greater sophistication produces greater challenges in data presentation to lay audiences (who may well fund or commission research). For example, how do the press report our findings and how can we help them to do this task better (Commission on the Social Sciences in Britain, 2003)? What are the challenges and opportunities of social networking sites? Finally and most importantly, our traditional methods of the social survey and the interview rely on public participation, but this is very much under threat. Can we improve response, particularly in those social groups or geographical areas where it is so poor? And if not, can we handle none response, or use imputation in more sophisticated ways (see Carpenter and Plewis in this volume)?

NOTES

1 Here we refer to sociology, but the cultural turn pervaded most social science disciplines.

2 Chris Rojek and Brian Turner (2000) coined the term 'decorative sociology' to describe 'the privileging of theory and textual approaches in social and cultural analysis over more traditional forms of analytic sociology.

3 It is nice irony that the end of the paradigm wars and the claim that they were in any case overstated, came from two of the key protagonists. Seven years earlier Guba (1987: 31) maintained that rival paradigms preclude each other in the way that belief in a flat world precludes belief in a round one.

4 This rivalry was not always as straight forward as a rivalry between Columbia as scientific and Chicago as humanist as both Robert Bannister 1987: 223–5 and Hammersley, 1989: chapter 6 note. Herbert Blumer's stance, for example, was anti positivist, but not anti scientific. Similarly Robert MacIver, who was at Columbia, was likewise an advocate of a scientific, but not positivist approach (Williams, 2008).

5 Ann Oakley's autobiographical account of her own methodological development demonstrates the depth of feeling on both sides of the 'wars' and particularly the criticism she faced when she advocated the use of quantitative methods in feminist research, in the late 1990s (Oakley, 1999)

6 The Smith and Stevens paper was published 13 years ago (in a volume containing reports of other social science studies using chaos/complexity approaches), but somewhat surprisingly there has been a relative dearth of empirical work employing complexity approaches, despite the plethora of papers advocating or anticipating its use. The Castellani and Hafferty book, though published in 2009 (12 years later), continues to promote complexity as a frontier approach in sociology. Gilbert and Troitszch's work in simulation is well known is sociology and its analogous disciplines, but similarly empirical work is relatively rare.

7 At the time of writing the long held hegemony of SPSS is under challenge from STATA (see http://www.stata.com/ Accessed 29/01/10).

8 See interview with Oliver Jouve SPSS Vice-President, Corporate Development http://www.analyticbridge.com/profiles/blogs/interview-spss-olivier-jouve (accessed 29/01/10). In 2009 SPSS was sold to IBM and has been rebranded as PASW (Predictive Analysis Software), but continues to be marketed under the SPSS logo and website. http://www.spss.com/ (accessed 29/01/10)

9 Multi-level modeling (MLM) goes under several names. Many refer to it as Hierarchical Linear Modeling (HLM) in part because of a pioneering software program. Economists tend to call it mixed effects models or random effects models. MLM is probably the clearest and most generic label.

10 Structural equation modelling is sometimes referred to as confirmatory factor analysis or as LISREL after the earliest practical software for conducting it.

11 Another set of innovatory techniques that illustrate the development of large-*N*, computer intensive statistical techniques is Markov Chain Monte Carlo (MCMC) simulation methods.

12 The Ford Edsel was an automobile produced by the Ford Motor Company between 1957 and 1959. It is a name synonymous with the failure of technological and marketing ambition to be attuned to public demand. It was one of Ford's most technologically advanced vehicles, one of its heaviest and one with the highest fuel consumption. It was launched at a time when the public were moving to lighter and more economical vehicles.

13 See for example papers published in the *International Journal of Market Research* http://www.ijmr.com/ (accessed 20/01/2010).

REFERENCES

Bannister, R. (1987) *Sociology and Scientism: The American Quest for Objectivity 1880–1940.* Chapel Hill, NC. University of North Carolina Press.

Beals, R.L. (2006) *Politics of Social Research.* New Brunswick, NJ: Transaction Publishers.

Carter, B. and New, C. (eds) (2004) *Making Realism Work: Realist Social Theory and Empirical Research.* London: Routledge.

Castellani, B. and Hafferty, F. (2009) *Sociology and Complexity Science: a New Field of Enquiry.* New York: Springer.

Commission on the Social Sciences in Britain (2003) *Great Expectations: the Social Sciences in Britain* (the 'Rhind Report'). London.

Cresswell, J. (2009) *How Sage Has Shaped Research Methods: a Forty Year History.* Thousand Oaks, CA: Sage.

Culyba, R.J., Heimer, C.A. and Petty, J.C. (2004) 'The ethnographic turn: Fact, fashion, or fiction?' *Qualitative Sociology,* 27(4): 365–89.

de Vaus, D. (2001) *Research Design in Social Research.* London: Sage.

Ellis, C. (1997) 'Evocative ethnography: Writing emotionally about our lives'. In W. Tierney and Y. Lincoln (eds) *Representation and the Text: Reframing the Narrative Voice.* Albany: State University of New York Press, pp. 115–42.

Franzosi, R. (2004). *From Words to Numbers: Narrative, Data, and Social Science.* Cambridge: Cambridge University Press.

Freese, J. (2007) Replication standards for quantitative social science: Why not sociology? *Sociological Methods & Research,* 36(2): 153–72.

Gilbert, N. and Troitzsch, K. G. (2005) *Simulation for the Social Scientist,* 2nd edn. Maidenhead: Open University Press.

Gillies, D. (2000) *Philosophical Theories of Probability.* London: Routledge.

Goldstein, H. (2003). *Multilevel Statistical Models.* London: Arnold.

Guba, E. (1987) 'Naturalistic evaluation'. *New Directions for Program Evaluation,* 34, 23–43.

Guba, E. and Lincoln, Y. (1994) 'Competing paradigms in qualitative research'. In N. Denzin and Y. Lincoln (eds) *Handbook of Qualitative Research.* Thousand Oaks CA: Sage.

Hammersley, M. (1989) *The Dilemma of Qualitative Method: Herbert Blumer and the Chicago School.* London: Routledge.

Hammersley, M. (2008) 'Causality as conundrum: The case of qualitative inquiry'. *Methodological Innovations Online,* Vol 23. http://erdt.plymouth.ac.uk/mionline/public_html/viewissue.php?id=6 (accessed 29/01/2010).

Heshusius, L. and Ballard, K. (eds) (1996) *From Positivism to Interpretivism and Beyond: Tales of Transformation in Educational and Social Research.* New York: Teachers' College Press.

Hookway, N. (2008) 'Entering the blogosphere: Some strategies for using blogs in social research'. *Qualitative Research,* 8(1): 91–113.

Madge, J. (1963) *The Origins of Scientific Sociology.* London: Tavistock.

Manicas, P. (1987) *A History and Philosophy of the Social Sciences.* Oxford: Blackwell.

May, T. (1999) 'Reflexivity and sociological practice'. *Sociological Research Online*, vol. 4, no. 3. http://www.socresonline.org.uk/socresonline/4/3/may.html (accessed 29/01/2010)

Oakley, A. (1999) 'Paradigm wars: some thoughts on a personal and public trajectory'. *International Journal of. Social Research Methodology*, (2)3: 247–54.

Pawson, R. (2000) 'Middle range realism'. *Journal of European Sociology*, XLI(2): 283–325.

Payne, G. and Williams, M. (2005) 'Generalisation in qualitative research'. *Sociology,* 39(2): 295–314.

Payne, G. and Payne, J. (2004) *Key Concepts in Social Research.* London: Sage.

Payne, G., Williams, M. and Chamberlain, S. (2004) 'Methodological pluralism in British sociology'. *Sociology,* 38(1): 153–64.

Platt, J. (1996) *A History of Sociological Research Methods in America 1920–1960.* Cambridge: Cambridge University Press.

Popper, K. (1959) *The Logic of Scientific Discovery.* London: Routledge.

Raudenbush, S.W. and Bryk, A.S. (2002) *Hierarchical Linear Models: Applications and Data Analysis Methods*, 2nd edn. Thousand Oaks, CA: Sage Publications.

Rojek, C. and Turner, B. (2000) 'Decorative sociology: towards a critique of the cultural turn'. *The Sociological Review*, 48(4): 629–48.

Savage, M. and Burrows, R. (2007) 'The coming crisis in empirical sociology'. *Sociology,* 41(5): 885–899.

Smith, T. and Stevens, G. (1997) 'Biological foundations of social interaction: Computational explorations of nonlinear dynamics in arousal-modulation. In R. Eve, S. Horsfall and M. Lee (eds) *Chaos, Complexity and Sociology.* Thousand Oaks, CA: Sage.

Snijders, T.A.B. and Bosker, R.J. (1999) *Multilevel Analysis: An Introduction to Basic and Advanced Multilevel Modeling.* Thousand Oaks, CA: Sage.

Tashakkori, A. and Teddlie, C. (1998) *Mixed Methodology: Combining Qualitative and Quantitative Approaches.* Thousand Oaks, CA: Sage.

Thelwall, M. (2009) *Introduction to Webometrics: Quantitative Web Research for the Social Sciences.* San Rafael CA: Morgan and Claypool.

Thrift, N. (2005) *Knowing Capitalism.* London: Sage.

Vogt, W.P. (2007) *Quantitative Research Methods for Professionals.* Boston: Pearson.

Weber, M. (1978).'The nature of social action'. In W. Runciman (ed.) *Weber: Selections in Translation.* Cambridge: Cambridge University Press.

Williams, M. (2000a) *Science and Social Science: An Introduction.* London: Routledge.

Williams, M. (2000b) 'Social research: The emergence of a discipline?' *International Journal of Social Research Methodology,* 3(2): 157–66.

Williams, M. (2008) 'MacIver on causation'. *Journal of Scottish Thought,* 1(1): 67–88.

PART 1

The Social Context of Research

Introduction

Malcolm Williams and W. Paul Vogt

The recent and mainly welcome plethora of methods writing, helping and advising us toward better technical competence, should not lead us to ignore the importance of the social context of social research itself. The knowledge social researchers produce is done so in a world of commitments. These commitments are those of the respondents/informers themselves and those of the researchers. Were it the case that we could separate those two spheres of existence, social research would be a more straightforward activity. However, researchers are seekers of knowledge in one context and citizens in another. Conversely, researchers do not have a monopoly on the generation of social knowledge, but rather citizens themselves may generate insights within a context, or beyond that context. Moreover, citizens may be oppressed or disadvantaged and these characteristics will shape their knowledge acquisition. Almost always researchers will begin from a position of material and cultural privilege and some would say that this changes the power relations and the nature of knowledge thus produced. Social research takes place in a flux of moral relations.

This is far from a new insight and can be traced back to the writings of John Stuart Mill who recognised that the subject matter of (what he called) the moral sciences was morality itself. However Mill and the positivist philosophers that followed him, of the Comtean, Durkheimian and Logical kind, were optimistic that the methods of science themselves would lead us to a morality that was self evidently and universally true. This perspective was remarkably resilient in the idea of value freedom that was a key tenet of the positivist social research in much of the twentieth century. Perhaps, more implicitly, it survived as a regulatory ideal in après or post-positivist quantitative research. Unlike the nineteenth century positivists who believed that method could lead to moral verities, the supporters of value freedom believed that method could and should be separate from morality. Thus, the first position is one that we can derive an ought from an is and the second that we must separate ought from is.

Three of the four chapters in Part 1 are concerned in one way or another with questions of the relationship between 'ought and is' and the fourth chapter is concerned with the causal outcomes of the reality that I have described as the moral flux.

Two dilemmas faced the editors when considering contributions to a part on the social context of research. The first was whether there should be such a part. Would there, for example, be chapters on the social context of organic chemistry in a volume given over to methodological advances in that discipline? Some would say that this is just the trouble with social research; it spends too much time examining itself. But social research is not organic chemistry. Its methods aim to capture social reflection, and in qualitative research at least, are shaped by such reflection. Methodological innovation is inextricably linked to context. Indeed in this volume the innovation deployed is shaped by or arises out of particular social context.

Having decided to include such a part, we were faced with a second dilemma, that of what or who to include. The literature in this area is vast, as are the numbers of producers of that literature. One principle did guide us, that the chapters should be conducive to the methodologically pluralist approach of the volume, that is they should not be narrowly partisan toward particular epistemological positions. Beyond that it became an issue of what particular ideas or thinking were innovative in some key areas. Consequently, objectivity, causality, feminism and what might be termed the 'starting conditions' for research were finally chosen as areas in which there was something new to say that would complement the rest of the volume. In each of these areas there is a very large literature, but specifically in social research there has not been much new thinking in recent years. Discussions of objectivity are muted or oblique, especially in the post-science war period, so as not to offend either of the former protagonists. Indeed, as Martyn Hammersley observes in his chapter, discussions of objectivity have been eclipsed by those of reflexivity. At least in the case of feminism some of the insights and innovations of earlier years have been absorbed and there is less talk of 'malestream' research than there once was. Indeed one of those insights has itself been reflexivity. Causation has continued to attract interest in the philosophy of science and philosophy of the social sciences, but in social research itself, probabilistic causation manifested as causal analysis, counterfactual analysis, etc. has become an epistemological done deal, with only realists proposing wholly new ways of approaching the methodology, as opposed to the method.

Despite 'calls to reflexivity' it is rare that we acknowledge the conditions of production of research knowledge. Reflexivity is so often an abstract concept, as Martyn Hammersley puts it 'autobiographical excavation', that it is meant to reveal ones value position. Somehow reflexivity becomes quality control, but how good are our data and how does this relate to training, career or the culture of peer review in academia – what might be termed 'the relations of production', an important and often ignored area that Geoff Payne takes up in this volume.

Part 1 begins with a chapter by Martyn Hammersley in which he reconceptualises objectivity. He begins by examining its narrow use in the positivist tradition which sees it as isomorphic with subjectivity, the former equating with methods which will lead to truth about the world and the latter as personal or group values which will diminish objectivity, so consequently should be eliminated. It is this narrow objectivism that has been an easy target for sceptics from a number of post-positivist perspectives including postmodernism and feminism.

The former have been especially influential in qualitative research and have abandoned any form of objectivity as a search for truth in favour of constructionist approaches to research accounts that do not privilege one set of findings over another, because this is a matter that is not decidable and it is said, such privileging is arbitrary. This inevitably leads to the abandonment of social science as science (in any sense of that word) and ethnography in particular (according to James Clifford) becomes and should become indistinguishable from fictional accounts.

Feminists have criticised objectivity on the grounds that it is an androcentric concept that privileges male forms of knowledge and consequently produces mistaken accounts of the world. Standpoint feminists, in response, have argued that knowledge is always from a perspective, but some perspectives can provide better knowledge than others. The standpoint of women, because it is one of oppression, produces more authentic accounts of the world. As Hammersley points out (and many feminists now accept) this is very problematic for a number of reasons, particularly the core one of why should oppression produce better knowledge? Surely the oppressor in attaining and maintaining his position will have become very knowledgeable about particular things. However, as Hammersley notes, there is much to learn from these critiques. Feminism teaches us that the answer we get will depend a lot on the questions we ask. Historically, Western society have been dominated in the public sphere by men who have asked particular questions. These questions and the knowledge acquired has been male so far that they advance forms of technology which perpetuate hegemony through war and forms of social organisations, that exclude or diminish the role of women. There is no Archimedean point, no place where we can ask neutral questions, they are always socially situated.

Some critics of objectivity replace this with reflexivity and indeed reflexivity as some form of personal auditing of one's perspective and subjectivity has become very influential, particularly in qualitative research. As Hammersley puts it

> . . .'reflexivity' here is the attempt to make explicit all the assumptions, value commitments, feelings, etc. which went into, or which underpin, one's research, how it originated and progressed, etc., so that readers can understand the path by which the conclusions were reached.

Nevertheless, even though reflexivity is a valuable tool we cannot do without some form of objectivity. As he goes on to say 'Without a viable conception of objectivity it seems unlikely that social science can flourish or even survive'. Yet, objectivity as a more broadly conceived epistemic virtue is both necessary and possible.

Hammersley asks us to focus on what objectivism, standpoints and reflexivity have in common 'that error can derive from the individual and social characteristics of the researcher, and that there are ways of minimising this threat'. A commitment to enquiry is an

> epistemic virtue that is designed to counter one particular source of potential error: that deriving from preferences and preconceptions associated with commitments that are external to the task of knowledge production – in other words, those that relate to the various goals any researcher has as a person, citizen, etc.

Enquiry as 'epistemic virtue' is, of course, not enough to guarantee good research as Geoff Payne persuasively argues. Payne's chapter explores the relationship between discipline (in this case sociology) and the conditions of production of research and shows how it is often the case that sociological reasoning is often compromised by methodological shortcomings and these are, at least in part, the result of a lack of reflection on what we do.

> Our collective research quality could benefit from reviewing the process through which people end up as researchers, and how 'junior' researchers become involved in carrying out projects often with little awareness of what really goes on in data capture, what informants are doing when we research them, or how the data captured and analysed with our sophisticated techniques actually relate to theoretical questions.

He illustrates this by examining anonymised examples of research papers rejected by leading journals. As he notes such output comprises a large part of that of sociology (and presumably other disciplines), where journal rejection rates can be very high. The methodological shortcomings Payne describes afflict both qualitative and quantitative research. Each often involves 'over claiming', the former through generalising social processes from specific local examples, the latter through poor selection of data sets, or a failure to recognise the limitations of those datasets. This second problem is all but endemic in secondary analysis, where sophisticated statistical techniques often disguise poor operationalisation or variable selection.

Payne's chapter is a cautionary tale. Innovation is not always about technique, but actually may be much more mundane and about our own professional development as researchers and disciplinary and interdisciplinary relations. Many of these problems Payne describes stem from a complacency about methods within disciplines and a culture which does not place them at the heart of what we do, or what we teach. Payne concludes his chapter with a call for greater humility and a reflection on 'what we know and how we know'.

It is a rare thing that a methodological approach is so successful that it is less visible or discussed than it once was. Arguably this has been the case for feminist methodology, though as Gayle Letherby points out, one seeks a particular feminist method or methods in vain, despite the belief that it is associated with qualitative methods. Certainly it was true that many feminist researchers did embrace qualitative approaches on the grounds that much of quantitative research used to be androcentric in its theorisation, assumptions and analyses, but really this was much more to do with the possibility of qualitative methods (especially the in-depth interview) allowing the voice of the interviewed to come through more clearly and authentically. Placing the researched at the heart of the research enterprise was a prerequisite if social research was to be used as a tool to overcome sexism in society.

As we have noted above, the legacy of this was reflexivity and the questioning of value freedom in research, an approach which has become mainstream. Indeed as Letherby cites Sue Wise as saying, the notion of 'mainstream' itself is now difficult to sustain and rather it is a matter of centres and peripheries in disciplines and indeed one might add interdisciplinarity. Whilst it is true that the myth of quantitative equals male and qualitative equals female has been persistent, it is equally true that feminists have embraced problem-centred methodological approaches placing them in the vanguard of methodological pluralism.

The strength of feminist approaches that have led to such pluralism is that they have emerged from a long epistemological gestation (though as Letherby notes, this process is not without its critics, even within feminism). The consequence of this has been a thoroughgoing questioning of the 'relations of production' of knowledge and a recognition that all knowledge is from some or other social perspective. Letherby's own contribution to this epistemological auditing has been the concept of 'theorised subjectivity', which

> relies on a recognition that, while there is a 'reality' 'out there', the political complexities of subjectivities, and their inevitable involvement in the research/theorising process make a definitive/final statement impracticable.

An examination of ones subjective position is however possible and desirable, particularly that as researchers we occupy a position of intellectual privilege. Whilst the specifics of methodological debate within feminism may draw on atypical methods or approaches, that the foregoing has a feel of familiarity to most social researchers is an indication of the interpolation of feminist methodological insights into the practice of research. One might speculate that whilst feminism will continue to influence how we do research, the concept of a feminist methodology may well eventually disappear.

Feminism's contribution to social research was for a long time controversial and even (as Letherby notes) a contributor to the 'paradigm' wars. Conversely, for several decades causality has simply divided those in social research into those who believe in it and those who don't, so in a sense it too had a role in the paradigm wars. But these wars are over and even the former nonbelievers are mostly prepared to accord a limited role to causal reasoning in the social world. Those who believed in causality all along were mostly located in the neo-empiricist 'causal analysis' tradition, which whilst immensely productive (see Rubin in this volume), was just one way of approaching causality in social research. As Nancy Cartwright remarked of the concept 'one word, many things': Two 'movements', realism and complexity, have challenged some of our starting conditions for thinking about causality in social research. David Byrne, in his chapter, challenges us to think about causality quite differently by coming at it 'backwards', that is starting from effects, not causes. Whilst 'experiments' in social research are rarer than they once were, they are making a come back in policy-based research, emulating the 'gold standard' (*sic*) of the randomised control trail (RCT). Perhaps just as importantly, the same logic of the search for elegant (Byrne would say simplistic) causes underpins the *post hoc* survey analysis. The idea of simple causation has been challenged by realism and complexity theory, the starting points for Byrne's chapter. He argues instead for the development of comparative method to aid us develop retrodictive accounts of complex social causality. Through a case study example he demonstrates how this can be done by using existing quantitative and qualititative methods in combination as ways of comparing multiple cases in order to establish multiple and complex causal processes. He does this through a case study example of 'effects' in the development of the post industrial city, in this case Leicester, in England.

Byrne's chapter, in so far as it is not about the 'relations of production' of research is different from the other three. Yet what is fascinating is that if we begin with a theorised narrative of what caused (what he describes as a 'system state') one might argue that a necessary condition is a reflexive stance, something each of the previous authors discuss as a key contextual issue. Moreover, Byrne's approach effectively dissolves the quantitative–qualitative divide in thinking about causality by incorporating both narrative and number in causal attribution.

1

Objectivity: A Reconceptualisation

Martyn Hammersley

In recent times, the word 'objectivity', like 'truth' and 'reality', has come to be interpreted by some social scientists as referring to a fiction, and is treated by most commentators with great caution or avoided altogether. The uncertain status of the word is sometimes signalled by it being placed within inverted commas. While these do not always indicate sneering rejection (Haack, 1998: 117), they are usually intended to distance the writer from any implication that what the word refers to actually exists, or at least to suggest that there is doubt about it.[1] In this chapter I want to examine the reasons why objectivity is found problematic, and I will also try to develop a clearer understanding of what function the concept might usefully serve in the context of social inquiry.

UNCERTAINTY ABOUT OBJECTIVITY

There are several reasons for current scepticism about objectivity. Part of the problem is that the words 'objective' and 'subjective' can be interpreted in a variety of ways, and these need to be distinguished. Daston and Galison (2007: 29–35) have outlined their complex semantic history, suggesting that, over time, they have reversed their meanings.[2] They were introduced into Scholastic philosophy in the fourteenth century, at which point 'objective' meant 'things as they appear to consciousness' (in other words, objects of thought) whereas 'subjective' meant 'things as they are in themselves' (in other terms, subjects with attributes). Kant modified this usage, so that 'objective' came to refer to the 'forms of sensibility' that structure our perceptions, by contrast with the subjective, that is the empirical, content that is poured into these vessels by the Ding-an-sich, thereby generating our perceptions and cognitions. Post-Kantian usage involved a further twist: 'objective' came to refer to what belongs to nature or to reality independently of our subjective experience of it. In these terms, a judgement can be said to be objective if it corresponds to an external object, and as subjective if it does not. The other side of the same conception of objectivity is the assumption that there is an objective, 'external' world in the sense that things exist and have the character they do irrespective of our beliefs or wishes about them; though, confusingly, there may also be an 'internal' subjective world in which things exist in this sense too. Daston and Galison go on to document different versions of this late modern conception of objectivity, one appealing to the idea of truth-to-nature, another to the possibility of mechanical reproduction, a third to trained judgement – and these are almost as different from one another as they are from Scholastic usage.[3]

Given this confusing history, it is perhaps not surprising that the concept of objectivity should be found troublesome today. Within the context of social science we can identify several, by no means isomorphic, contrasts that often participate in how the terms 'subjective' and 'objective' are intended, or interpreted, on particular occasions:

1 Mental versus physical
2 Internal as against external
3 Private rather than public
4 Implicit versus explicit
5 Judgement as against mechanical procedure
6 Idiosyncratic rather than shared or intersubjective
7 Variable versus stable or fixed
8 Particular rather than universal
9 Dependent as against independent
10 Relative rather than absolute
11 Erroneous versus true.

In much of the usage these various distinctions are blended together. All this reflects the continuing influence of a particular conception of objectivity that emerged within social inquiry most influentially during the early twentieth century, and one that has come to be questioned by many social scientists today. This is frequently given the label 'positivist'. However, this term is misleading, because of the range of (almost entirely negative) ways in which it is now used. For this reason, it seems better to employ a different label, and the one I will use here is 'objectivism'.[4]

OBJECTIVISM AND ITS ERRORS

Objectivism treats the word 'objectivity' as having a single sense, in which all the different meanings listed earlier are combined. In particular, the substantive senses of 'subjective' and 'objective' – referring to the mental versus the physical, the inner versus the outer, etc. – are generally treated as isomorphic with the epistemic sense of these two terms – as referring to the false and the true. Objectivism amounts to a particular conception of the nature of scientific inquiry, how it should be pursued, and what it produces. Its starting point is the idea that we are often led into error by false preconceptions and preferences that result in our tending to see or find what we expected or wished rather than what is true. In short, subjective factors of various kinds are treated as leading to conclusions being subjective rather than objective, in the sense that they reflect our errors rather than the world. Subjectivity is believed to bias inquiry, deflecting us from the truth that we would otherwise discover. From this it is concluded that we must engage in inquiry in a manner that is unaffected by our personal and social characteristics (prior beliefs, values, preferences, attitudes, personality traits, etc.), or at least that minimises their influence.

Several strategies are proposed for avoiding subjective error. One is that we should restrict ourselves to what is directly observable, and what can be inferred logically or via calculation from given data. Of course, there is an important sense in which nothing is directly observable with absolute certainty, so this tends to turn into the idea that researchers should only rely upon the sort of observational capabilities that every human being has, or that anyone could be easily trained to employ, rather than on specialised forms of intuition or connoisseurship.[5] More broadly, there is the idea that we must commit ourselves to a research design that specifies in procedural terms what will be done through all stages of the process of inquiry, not just in data collection, but also in drawing conclusions from the data. And this plan must then be followed as closely as possible. Thereby, it is argued, the inquiry process can be standardised and rendered transparent, eliminating the effects of idiosyncratic, subjective factors; an ideal that is sometimes referred to as procedural objectivity (Eisner, 1992, see also Newell 1986).

Such proceduralisation is viewed by objectivism not only as of value in itself, in that it minimises error deriving from subjectivity, but also as facilitating the use of checks on the accuracy of observation and inference, so that one investigator's findings can be compared with those of others. Of course, such comparisons had long been recognised as a means of assessing validity, but objectivism claims that if researchers use quite different approaches, reflecting their personal characteristics, then it is impossible to determine who is right and what the source of any discrepancy is. However, so it is argued, if multiple investigators use the same method their findings will be comparable.

In one version of objectivism, the very use of procedures designed to eliminate subjectivity is taken as itself constituting objectivity, and as defining what counts as objective, or scientific, knowledge. In other words, from this point of view, knowledge or truth is simply whatever conclusions are reached via such proceduralised inquiry. This nominalist version was influential in some strands of US psychology and sociology during the second quarter of the twentieth century, under the influence of Bridgman's operationism and elements of logical positivism.

However, most interpretations of objectivism have tended to treat proceduralised inquiry as achieving objectivity because, by eliminating subjective factors, it allows the objective voice of the world to speak through the research. In other words, it enables us truly to capture the make-up of the world, as consisting of distinct objects belonging to types that have essential characteristics defined by law-like relations. This might be labelled realist objectivism. However, the distinction between this and its nominalist counterpart is sometimes hard to draw, and it is probably of little significance in practice.

Some serious problems have been identified with objectivism. These can be outlined as follows:

1 While it is true that we may be led astray by subjective factors (whether conceived of as mental, inner, inexplicit, particular or whatever), it is also the case that we are inevitably dependent upon personal knowledge, capabilities and motivations in producing any evidence or conclusions. For instance, we cannot avoid relying upon our senses in making observations, and these are in important respect, of subjective, culturally constituted and cannot be separated from expectations or habits. Nor is it possible to reduce them entirely to the following of explicit procedures (Polanyi, 1958). Much of the same applies to the processes of inference involved in producing evidence from data and drawing conclusions from it. Here, we cannot operate entirely in the manner of a calculating machine, we cannot avoid employing assumptions, ampliative inference and imagination.
2 It is also important to recognise that research necessarily depends upon subjective commitments of various kinds. Even in the case of objectivism, researchers must be committed to following procedures carefully, and this is a personal characteristic as well as a social one. I will argue later that research requires a range of epistemic virtues, of which objectivity is itself one.
3 It may be true that evidence coming from the use of ordinary everyday perceptual capabilities is less open to potential error than that which relies upon specialised knowledge and skills; or, at least, that it is easier to check the results. However, this does not mean that reliance solely on those capabilities is more likely to lead to sound knowledge of the kind desired. What needs to be observed may not be accessible to ordinary capabilities, so that the questions we are addressing cannot be resolved by appeal to evidence of this sort. Similarly, drawing the kind of conclusions required, in a sound manner, will also often depend upon specialised knowledge and skills.
4 Subjective factors are not the only source, and certainly not the only cause, of error in observation and reasoning. For example, we may accurately note how the sun rises in the sky each morning, but to describe it as moving over the earth is still an error. Similarly, we may correctly document the similarities between two pieces of rock and infer, on the basis of their easily observable characteristics in comparison with other types of object, that they must have been produced by a common causal process when, in fact, one rock is igneous while the other is a product of sedimentation. In other words, we may employ careful observation and uncontroversial modes of inference yet still reach false conclusions. It could even be that the questions we are asking are based on false assumptions, the effect we are seeking to explain may not exist, our hypotheses may be misconceived, and so on.
5 It is never possible to ensure that different researchers will apply a procedure in exactly the same way, however closely it is specified. This is particularly true in social research because here much depends upon how the people being studied respond to the procedures employed. It is not just the behaviour of the researcher that must be standardised but theirs too. Moreover, it is in the nature of human social interaction that the actions of each side will be shaped by the other. Objectivism requires that people be presented with the stimulus field that is implied by the relevant procedure, but since what they experience will depend partly on their background

expectations, cultural habits, interactions with the researcher and so on, there is always considerable danger that what they *actually* experience will be rather different from what was *intended*; and may vary among them. For example, even if experimental subjects are all presented with the same instructions they may interpret them in discrepant ways, and behave differently as a result; whereas, had they interpreted them in the same way, their behaviour would have been the same. Similarly, two subjects may interpret the instructions differently and as a result produce the same type of response; whereas, had they interpreted the instructions in the same way, their behaviour would have been different.

6 Following a procedure will not *always* improve the quality of the observation or reasoning. This is because any procedure relies on assumptions, and these could be false. Furthermore, applying a procedure may rule out the use of some personal capability that is essential if the required type of observation is to be made, or if error arising from use of the procedure in particular circumstances is to be detected. Procedures and guidelines can serve a useful function in reminding us of what needs to be taken into account, but they can also result in our failing to notice what could be important in particular cases. There are issues too about what is and is not measurable by means of fixed procedures, which relate to the nature of the world being investigated. Some have argued that social phenomena are complex, in the technical sense that they are systems subject to influence by a potentially unlimited number of variables, and 'the influence of particular factors is variable according to the relationships that they enjoy with others at any moment in time' (Radford, 2007: 2). This raises questions about the viability of procedural objectivity in social science.

7 For all the reasons outlined above, the fact that two or more observers using the same procedure agree in their observations, or that two or more analysts using the same procedure come to the same conclusion in working with the same data, does not in itself indicate that their reports are true, even where they have operated independently of one another. Instead, their work may be affected by errors, including those built into the procedure itself, that lead them in the same, false direction.

There are also problems that arise specifically with what I have called realist objectivism. This portrays knowledge as in some sense representing, reflecting or reproducing reality, in such a way that there is a correspondence between the account produced and the object(s) to which it refers. There is a danger of being misled by metaphor here. In the face of visual metaphors of picturing, or even those of mapping or modelling, it is essential to remember that any body of knowledge consists of answers to some set of questions, and that many different questions can be asked about any specific set of objects, producing different knowledge about them. While there cannot be contradictory knowledge about the same set of objects, there can certainly be a very wide range of knowledge claims made about them. This suggests that it is false to assume that we are dealing with a world made up of objects, each having a finite set of features, that can be exhaustively 'represented'. What objects are identified and what features they have will depend partly on the questions we ask about the world. This seems to rule out the ontology assumed by realist objectivism.

While it is probably true that most social scientists have never adhered completely to objectivism, much methodological thought and research practice has been strongly affected by it. Indeed, it continues to have some influence even today – especially among quantitative researchers and in the context of research methods training courses. At the same time, the problems with objectivism have led many social scientists, especially qualitative researchers, to reject it completely. Indeed, a few have attacked, or abandoned, the concept of objectivity itself, while others have sought to fundamentally reconstruct it.

REACTIONS AGAINST OBJECTIVITY

Radical critics of objectivity sometimes start from the claim that, despite researchers' commitment to it, systematic error has operated across social science. For example, Hawkesworth writes:

> A significant proportion of feminist scholarship involves detailed refutations of erroneous claims about women produced in conformity with prevailing disciplinary standards of objectivity. (Hawkesworth, 1994: 152)

Much of the same sort of argument has been put forward by other radical critics, focusing on other sorts of bias: relating to social class divisions, ethnicity, sexual orientation, and so on. What makes their criticisms radical is that the problem is held to stem not from social scientists being insufficiently objective but rather from the concept of objectivity itself.

These radical critics have tended to focus their attack upon particular elements of objectivism that they believe have served to disguise bias. For example, they have sometimes seen objectivity as requiring that research be entirely value-free, in the sense that it should not be dependent upon or influenced by any value commitments at all. On this basis they argue that objectivity is impossible, and any claim to have achieved it ideological (see Williams, 2005). Similarly, critics often take objectivity to require the elimination from research of all passion and personal involvement. In these terms, it is presented as requiring researchers to turn themselves into robots without feeling. And, given that this is undesirable, objectivity is rejected for this reason too. A related criticism is that objectivity implies that researchers must separate themselves from all inherited assumptions, from the particular circumstances in which they are located and from their other background characteristics, so as to adopt a universalistic 'view from nowhere'. Again, the impossibility and/or undesirability of this is used as a basis for denouncing any commitment to objectivity.

In the face of these criticisms, it is important to emphasise that what are being rejected are key elements of objectivism, and that by no means all interpretations of 'objectivity' make these impossible or undesirable demands upon researchers. For example, in its original Weberian form the notion of value freedom was more sophisticated than its critics usually recognise. Weber acknowledged that there are constitutive ('theoretical') values guiding research, notably true, and that other ('practical')values are involved in defining relevant phenomena for investigation, even though he insisted that bias from practical value commitment is a persistent danger (see Bruun, 2007; Keat and Urry, 1975: chapter 9). Similarly, objectivity does not require the suppression of all passion or personal involvement in research, or the pretence that it is possible to step outside of one's social location and background assumptions; what the term refers to is the effort to prevent these things leading us into factual error. There is also sometimes a failure to distinguish between objectivity as achievement and objectivity as ideal or goal. It is one thing to say that we can and should try to be objective, quite another to say that we can ever *be* objective, or know that we have objective knowledge, in some absolute sense. Nevertheless, approximating the ideal of objectivity is of value in pursuing knowledge, since it reduces the chances of error, even if we can never fully eliminate it.

However, the most fundamental attacks on objectivity challenge the very concepts of truth, knowledge and error on which any interpretation of that concept relies, amounting to a sceptical rejection of traditional notions of inquiry.

Abandoning objectivity

There are critics who reject objectivity because they deny the possibility and desirability of knowledge, as conventionally understood (see, for instance, Lather, 2007). Also involved here may be the idea that objectivity amounts to a form of inauthenticity, an attempt (inevitably futile) to produce knowledge that does not reflect the distinctive personal characteristics, or unique social location of the investigator. What is required, instead, it is argued, is that any account be explicitly presented as a *construction*, rather than claiming to represent the object(s) to which it refers. Moreover, it should be a construction that openly acknowledges the fact that it draws on particular resources in particular circumstances, for particular purposes. What is also demanded is recognition that there can always be other, and contradictory, accounts of any scene; with choice amongst these being in an important sense undecidable or arbitrary.

This sceptical approach denies that it is possible for us to escape the influence of our social identities and locations, or that it is desirable for us to try to do this; *and it insists that this undermines any possibility of knowledge*. Closely related is the argument that any claim to objectivity is naïve or deceitful, that the idea of gaining knowledge of a world that is independent of our beliefs about it is an illusion. Furthermore, not only are all claims to knowledge necessarily constructions or socio-historical products, but so too are all means of assessing these. In place of the possibility of knowledge, we are faced with potentially irreconcilable *claims* to knowledge or beliefs. And it is suggested that the only grounds for evaluating these, at best, are ethical, political, or aesthetic.[6]

While this kind of scepticism is currently quite influential, sometimes travelling under labels like 'relativism' and 'postmodernism', we should note that it is unsustainable in practical terms: we cannot live without relying on the concepts of knowledge and truth. Indeed, even to argue for scepticism involves claiming to know that knowledge is not possible. Moreover, while actively generating doubt about what we take for granted may occasionally be of value, so as to remind ourselves of the fallibility of whatever we believe we know, this does not require denying the possibility of knowledge. And the idea that knowledge claims cannot be evaluated epistemically but can and should be assessed in ethical, political, or aesthetic terms amounts to a failure to follow through the logic of sceptical arguments. These apply in much the same way to claims about what is good or right as to claims about what sorts of things exist in the world, what characteristics and powers they have, and so on.

Re-specifying objectivity

Other critics of objectivity, rather than abandoning the concept, have set out to respecify it in very different terms. I will outline two broad approaches of this kind here; though there are different versions of each, and the two are sometimes combined.

(a) It is quite common today, especially amongst qualitative researchers, for a commitment to reflexivity to be seen as, in effect, a substitute for objectivity. What is meant by 'reflexivity' here is the attempt to make explicit all the assumptions, value commitments, feelings, etc. which went into, or which underpin, one's research, how it originated and progressed, etc., so that readers can understand the path by which the conclusions were reached.[7] This idea was anticipated by Myrdal (1969) in *Objectivity in Social Research*, though it seems unlikely that he envisaged it as implying the sort of autobiographical excavation that it has sometimes induced on the part of qualitative researchers, culminating for example in various forms of auto-ethnography (Ellis and Bochner, 2000). Interestingly, here an ideal of transparency is shared with procedural objectivity. Moreover, the commitment to reflexivity often seems to involve two forms that parallel the two versions of objectivism. There are some who see reflexivity as a process of research auditing (Lincoln and Guba, 1985; Schwandt and Halpern, 1988; Erlandson et al. 1993). This involves treating it as an instrumental requirement designed to allow error to be recognised and rectified. The argument is that, for the findings of research to be trustworthy, it must be possible for an auditor to retrace the path of the researcher, checking the premises on which each step of the analysis depended. By contrast, in what is now probably the most influential version, reflexive transparency is treated as of value in itself, rather than being designed to allow readers to determine whether the researcher 'went wrong' in reaching the conclusions they did; even less is the idea that it will allow readers to replicate the study. From this point of view, all accounts of the world are relative to, or are reflections or expressions of, how they were produced, most notably who was involved in producing them. Given this, it is taken to be incumbent upon social scientists to display this fact, and to show the particular manner in which their own accounts were generated.

While there is something to be learned from both these notions of reflexivity, they encounter serious difficulties. While financial audits are by no means unproblematic, by comparison with the assessment of research they are very straightforward indeed. Assessing the validity of research findings involves making judgements about their plausibility and credibility (Hammersley, 1997); it is not merely a matter of ensuring that the required information has been provided and that it 'adds up'. There is a great deal of room for disagreement in judgements about the cogency of arguments and evidence. One reason for this is that research is not founded upon data whose meaning and validity are given. Moreover, the concept of research auditing seems to imply that research proceeds by inference from data to conclusions in a relatively linear way, so that each step in the process can be checked. This does not match how research is actually, or could be, done; as is illustrated in the huge collection of 'natural histories' of research now available (Hammersley, 2003). Moreover, it is not clear that readers always need the sort of very detailed and extensive background information, about the researcher and the research process, that this version of reflexivity demands: we need to know the evidence supporting the main knowledge claims, and to be provided with sufficient information about the research process to assess likely threats to validity, but more than this can be an encumbrance.

The constructionist version of reflexivity amounts to relativism, of a personalist kind: the notion of validity or truth is transposed into a form of personal authenticity. Contradictory accounts of the world are to be tolerated, so long as their proponents are tolerant of others' accounts; in other words, so long as they refrain from claiming that their own views are true in any sense beyond 'honestly believed'. Indeed, it is sometimes implied that there is no other ground for judging the value of accounts of the world than in terms of their degree of reflexivity, including their recognition of their own constructed and particularistic character. The notion of social science as systematically developing knowledge is abandoned here (see Eisenhart, 1998). It is also important to note that this kind of reflexivity is an unending, indeed an unachievable, task. This is partly because there is no limit to what could be included in a reflexive account, as regards personal background, cultural history or epistemological assumptions. There is also the problem that, presumably, any reflexive account must itself be explicated if it is to facilitate full reflexivity, this explication in its turn also requires reflexive excavation, and so on *indefinitely*.

(b) A rather different strategy for re-specifying objectivity is what has come to be labelled 'standpoint theory' or 'standpoint epistemology'. Standpoint theorists reject the idea, central to objectivism, though not to all conceptions of objectivity, that the background perspectives and orientations of the researcher are necessarily a source of error that must be eliminated or suppressed. More importantly, they argue that some particular social location or identity within society can facilitate discovery of the truth about it, and may even be essential to this; whereas other locations or identities are viewed as involving serious epistemic blockages. In other words, it is claimed that those occupying a particular type of social position have privileged access to the truth. Moreover, this is often taken to include normative as well as factual truths: namely, knowledge about how the world ought to be, what is wrong with how things are, and what ought to be done.

An influential model for standpoint theory is Marx's claim that, once the capitalist system has become established, the working class are in a uniquely privileged position to understand its mode of operation. Here, Marx is sometimes portrayed as relying upon a philosophical meta-narrative similar to that of Hegel, who had portrayed history as a process of dialectical progress towards true knowledge, and the realisation of all human ideals. In the Marxist version: 'the self-understanding of the proletariat is simultaneously the objective understanding of the nature of society' (Lukacs, 1971: 149).

Various other arguments have been employed by Marxists to bolster, or substitute for, this metaphysical meta-narrative. One appeals to a notion of cultural lag: it is claimed that the ideas of any dominant class were forged in the past but later become obsolete because of changed circumstances. Alongside this, it is also sometimes argued that once in power a class no longer has a motive to understand society; indeed, it may even be motivated to misrecognise the character of the society, in order to rationalise its own dominance. In short, it will seek to deny or explain away unpleasant truths about the social relations over which it presides. By contrast, so the argument goes, the subordinate class has a strong motive to understand the real nature of society in order to gain power for itself, and it will have no motive for refusing to recognise the defects of existing society. Indeed, members of it are likely to develop a 'double consciousness', recognising the true nature of the society even while paying lip service to the official myths about it.[8]

The most influential recent exponents of standpoint theory have been among feminists (see Harding, 2004). Generally speaking, they have not relied upon a metaphysical meta-narrative. They have argued that because women are subjected to oppression and/or marginalised within patriarchal societies they are better able than men to understand the nature of those societies, in particular, to recognise forms of sexist prejudice and discrimination.

However, there are some serious problems with standpoint epistemology, and it has been subjected to criticism even by several Marxists and feminists (see, for example, Bar On, 1993). The first issue concerns with whether the warrant or rationale for epistemic privilege on the part of the subordinated or marginalised group is true. The Marxian–Hegelian meta-narrative is open to doubt; indeed, it is less than clear what would count as strong evidence for or against it. The other sorts of warrant, relying on a social psychology of oppressor and oppressed, are less problematic in this sense, but they tend to be put forward without much evidence supporting them. And, while they have some plausibility, as with many such theories there are competing arguments that are equally convincing. For example, even if we adopt the simplistic assumption that society is composed of a single set of oppressors and oppressed groups, it could plausibly be argued that the oppressors must have gained considerable knowledge about the nature of the society in course of achieving power, knowledge that is not available to the oppressed, and whose value could be durable. Moreover, they may have substantial motivation to seek further knowledge and understanding in order to sustain, and perhaps even expand, that power. What seems likely is that the two groups may have access to rather different sorts of knowledge, but this does not epistemically privilege one side or the other in any general sense. Similarly, while the marginalised may escape the effects of the dominant ideology, this does not guarantee that they will therefore 'see reality clearly'. Knowledge is not produced by gaining direct contact with the world, through immediate perception. Rather, cognitive work is required that draws on cultural resources. Whether or not any particular marginalised group, or sections amongst them, have access to the necessary resources and are able to engage in this cognitive work is an open question. Furthermore, it is not beyond the bounds of possibility that they may generate their own ideology or myth in order to reconcile themselves to their position, as Nietzsche argued had been the case in the development of Christianity as a 'slave morality'. From this point of view, it would be unwise to privilege just any set of ideas that is at odds with mainstream views in Western societies, especially when these may include fundamentalist religions and nationalist creeds of various kinds.

A second problem with standpoint epistemology concerns how any particular standpoint theory is to be assessed. Crudely speaking, there are two options here, one of which undermines standpoint theory itself while the other is circular and therefore cannot provide support. The first tries to assess the warrant for epistemically privileging one category of person on the basis of the evidence available, without assuming that any one evaluator of that evidence is better placed to do this than any other by dint of their social identity or location. But even if this evaluation were to support the particular standpoint theory, there is an important sense in which it would simultaneously have undermined it. This is because it amounts to founding standpoint theory on, or justifying it in terms of, a competing epistemology. So the question would arise: if we can determine whether or not a particular standpoint theory is true or false without relying upon the standpoint of the well-placed evaluator, why would we need to draw upon a distinctive standpoint for evaluating substantive claims to knowledge? The other option would be, of course, to insist that only those whom a particular standpoint theory treats as epistemically privileged can judge its validity. But this is circular, and therefore can provide no support.

The final problem concerns how we are to identify who does and does not belong to the epistemically privileged category of person.[9] Once again, because of circularity, this cannot be resolved by reliance on the standpoint theory itself, but must be decided in more mainstream epistemological terms. Again, though, if the latter serves for this purpose, why not for others? Even putting this aside, there is the possibility, recognised by many standpoint theorists, that some members of the epistemically privileged category may have inauthentic perspectives, for example, because their views have been shaped by the dominant ideology or by sectional interests. Examples would include women who reject feminism. The problem here concerns how any judgement of inauthenticity can be justified, given that anyone placed by one commentator on the wrong side of the membership line could themselves draw the line in a different place; and it is unclear how there could be any nonarbitrary resolution to this dispute. Another problem of a similar kind arises from the way in which the boundaries of different categories of oppressed or marginalised groups intersect. If multiple types of oppression or marginalisation are accepted – for example centering on gender, social class, sexual orientation, 'race'/ethnicity and disability – then how are these to be weighed in relation to one another in determining who speaks with epistemic privilege and who does not, or whose voice is more true and whose is less so? Again this looks like an irresolvable problem within the terms of standpoint epistemology.

It is worth noting that the various alternatives to objectivism I have discussed are incompatible with one another. Reflexive auditing and standpoint theory retain the concepts of truth and knowledge, whereas postmodernist scepticism and constructionist reflexivity do not.[10] At the same time, the first two positions involve quite different notions of what is necessary for sound knowledge to be produced from one another. Despite this, elements of these approaches – especially constructionist reflexivity and standpoint theory – are sometimes combined. An example is Harding's notion of 'strong objectivity' (Harding, 1991, 1992, 1993, 1995). She argues that evaluation criteria must take into account both who is putting forward the knowledge claim and its implications for what is taken to be the goal of inquiry, which extends beyond the production of knowledge to bring about emancipation. She criticises, what she sees as, the weak objectivity that has operated within natural and social science, claiming that it has failed to challenge the patriarchal, and other oppressive, assumptions that she believes pervade Western societies, and social research itself. So Harding argues that greater reflexivity is required than what weak objectivity generates: much more of the background assumptions and institutional structures of social scientific work must be exposed to scrutiny. She claims that conventional forms of both natural and social science are shot through with the ideological assumptions that come naturally to the white, middle-class men who predominate among researchers. It is the task of strong objectivity to challenge these. Moreover, she regards engagement with the perspectives of those who are oppressed or marginalised as essential for stimulating this process. It is not that their concerns or views should be accepted at face value, but rather that these people are in the best position to identify the normalising assumptions that operate within mainstream society, and that bias conventional research.

It is worth noting how Harding's position relates to the criticisms of the two approaches outlined above. The notion of strong objectivity places limits on reflexivity, since what needs to be exposed is defined by a comprehensive social theory about the current nature of Western society and its social divisions, and about the sorts of bias that these are likely to generate. So, there is no longer the problem that achieving reflexivity is an unending task. As regards standpoint theory, she avoids the criticism that adopting the perspective of the oppressed or marginalised may involve taking over false assumptions on their part, since she recognises that epistemic privilege cannot be treated as automatically leading to the truth. However, there are still serious problems with her position. The most important concerns the epistemic status of the comprehensive social theory about social and epistemic inequalities on which she relies. She simply takes its validity for granted, yet many social scientists would dispute it; and, in particular, the claim that it encompasses the only, or the main, source of systematic error operating on social research. Furthermore, dismissing these critics' arguments on the grounds that they (or some of them) are white, middle-class males would be circular. As this indicates, the fundamental dilemma of standpoint epistemology remains.

RECONCEPTUALISING OBJECTIVITY

In my view, neither objectivism nor currently influential reactions against it provide us with a satisfactory basis for the concept of objectivity, though there is much to be learned from them. We need a more subtle approach that identifies what is wrong with, and also what was right with, objectivism. The solution that objectivism proposes – and even its diagnosis of the problem – may have been wrong, but it was nevertheless a response to a genuine concern. This is about the threats to validity that stem from the background assumptions, preferences, commitments, etc. of the researcher. At the same time, in light of the problems identified with objectivism, it no longer makes sense to try to preserve a coherent sense of the word 'objective' as simultaneously applying to the inquirer, the mode of inquiry, the conclusions reached and the phenomena to which those conclusions relate. A more specific meaning must be given to the term.[11]

As a starting point, we should focus on the core idea – common to objectivism, audit reflexivity and standpoint theory – that error can derive from the individual and social characteristics of the researcher, and that there are ways of minimising this threat. Of course, we do not need to, and should not, assume that research can operate without reliance upon personal or socio-cultural capabilities and motivations. Similarly, we should not imply that preconceptions and preferences always lead to error, and that they never help us to understand the truth. Rather, the focus of any concept of objectivity must be on protecting the research process from the negative effects of these 'subjective' characteristics. At the same time considering contra standpoint theory and Harding's 'strong objectivity', we cannot rely on a prior, supposedly comprehensive theory to tell us where sources of error might lie and whom they will affect. There is no well-validated, exclusive theory of this kind available, and none may be possible. Rather, we should draw on the full range of ideas about how errors *could be* generated, from whatever directions. And we must assess their likelihood in particular cases, and take precautions against and check them, as far as is possible.

In order to make any progress in reconceptualising objectivity, we probably need to differentiate among the ways in which error arising from 'subjectivity' can arise, and treat it as designed to counter just one of these. I propose that it is treated as being concerned solely with error resulting from preferences, and the preconceptions associated with them, deriving from substantive commitments *that are external to the pursuit of knowledge*.[12] In these terms, objectivity amounts to continually being on one's guard against errors caused by preferences and preconceptions coming from this source.

Motivated bias, of the kind I am suggesting objectivity should be conceptualised as being designed to minimise, arises, primarily, from the fact that all researchers have additional identities and roles, which are concerned with different sorts of goal from research itself. Moreover, there will be overlap in areas of concern between research and these other roles. One effect is that researchers may believe that they already know the answers to questions that are, from a research point of view, still open to doubt; or they may be too easily persuaded of some things and too resistant to considering or accepting others. In other words, there may be a tendency to opt for or against particular possibilities because of false prior assumptions or preferences (for example inferences from evaluative views about particular people, places, situations, etc.); or there may be a temptation to fill gaps in data in ways that are false or at least speculative. Moreover, these tendencies may be increased by a sense of urgency or disquiet, for example by anger over injustice or fear of change.

Each of the various roles that we play involves not only distinctive goals but also relevancies and assumptions about the nature of pertinent aspects of the world, why they are how they are, how they ought to be and so on. In performing any one role we foreground what is taken to be appropriate and necessary to it and background the rest. While we cannot and probably should not completely suppress what is relevant to other roles, at the same time the assumptions and preferences associated with these latent roles can interfere negatively with how effectively we play what is our main role on any particular occasion. Objectivity is designed to minimise such negative interference, and the notion applies to other roles as well as to that of researcher (see Gouldner, 1973; Williams, 2005, 2006a, b). For example, in selecting candidates for admission to an educational institution, recruiting them to employment, or ranking them in terms of priority for medical treatment, there is usually a requirement of objectivity. Objectivity, in this general sense, requires that all, *and only*, the considerations relevant to the task must be taken into account. Any other matters, however significant they may be from the point of view of other roles, or in terms of our own personal convictions, should be put on one side or downplayed.[13]

So, in place of the very broad interpretation of 'objectivity' associated with objectivism, I suggest that we interpret the term more narrowly. Given this, there are several sorts of 'subjective' error that lie outside the scope of objectivity as I have defined it here. One is error that derives from the failings of our perceptual and cognitive capabilities, or from misuse of them. Also excluded is what we might call wilful bias (see Hammersley and Gomm, 2000). This is the knowing committal, or risking, of systematic error in the service of some goal other than the production of knowledge, whether this is a propagandist misusing and even inventing evidence in order to support some cause or the lawyer or advocate deploying genuine evidence to make the best case possible for a preconceived conclusion. In the context of research, such wilful bias is, I suggest, best conceptualised as stemming from a lack of proper commitment to inquiry or to its rational pursuit, in favour of commitment to other goals. Of course, I am not suggesting that these other goals, or these ways of pursuing them, are in themselves illegitimate. After all, inquiry can be subordinated to other activities (Hammersley, 2004). However, a key feature of *academic* research, in my view, is that it should not be subordinated to any other task.

I suggest that we see objectivity as one, among several, epistemic virtues that are essential to research.[14,15] Other epistemic virtues include a commitment to truth and truthfulness (Williams, 2002), intellectual sobriety (a determination to follow a middle way between over-caution or excessive enthusiasm for any particular knowledge claim, form of evidence, or method) and intellectual courage (a willingness to resist fear of the consequences of pursuing inquiry wherever it leads, including personal costs relating to life, livelihood, or reputation) (Montmarquet, 1993: 23). Like objectivity these other epistemic virtues relate to distinctive sorts of threat to the rational pursuit of inquiry, and the need to resist them.

Of course, it must be remembered that my reconceptualisation of objectivity here is premised on a view of academic research as having no other immediate goal than the pursuit of knowledge; an assumption that is certainly not accepted by all social researchers today. For example, standpoint theory is often associated with the idea that research is inevitably committed to political goals and is properly directed towards social change. I do not have the space here to argue against this position, but I have done so elsewhere (see Hammersley, 1995, 2000).

CONCLUSION

As with a number of other terms, today the word 'objectivity' is often avoided, treated with derision, or at least handled with great caution by social scientists. While part of the explanation for this is uncertainty about the meaning of the term, evidenced by its complex semantic history, the main cause, I have suggested, is the considerable influence, and subsequent collapse, of what we might call objectivism. This portrays scientific inquiry as needing to eliminate, or minimise, the effect on the research process of subjective beliefs and practices, in other words, of what is psychological, private, or implicit in character. Suppression of these beliefs and practices is taken to be necessary, from an objectivist point of view, because they are regarded as the main, if not the only, source of error. On this basis, it is required that inquiry follow explicit procedures that *anyone* could use, so that no reliance is placed upon the subjective features of the investigator, and so that the results can be checked by others using the same procedures.

Ideas approximating to objectivism were very influential within social science during the second quarter of the twentieth century, but came under sharp attack later. They are now rejected by many social scientists, and this has sometimes led to a jettisoning of the concept of objectivity itself, as well as to attempts fundamentally to reconstruct it. At the same time, the influence of objectivism has never been entirely extinguished.

In this chapter I have examined objectivism and the main reactions against it, and tried to clarify some important functional distinctions that objectivism conflates, so as to allow a more satisfactory view of the concept of objectivity. This is necessary, I suggested, because some of what this term refers to is essential to any defensible form of inquiry. I have argued that we should think of objectivity as an epistemic virtue that is designed to counter one particular source of potential error: that derive from preferences and preconceptions associated with commitments that are external to the task of knowledge production – in other words, those that relate to the various goals any researcher has as a person, citizen, etc. Objectivism was wrong to treat the preconceptions deriving from external roles as simply a source of error, and therefore as needing to be suppressed or eliminated: they can stimulate, and even be essential resources in reaching, true answers to factual questions. However, they *can* also be a source of error, and objectivity as an epistemic virtue is concerned with minimising the danger that they will lead us astray in assessing the likely validity of knowledge claims. It involves a deliberate and sustained attempt to counter any tendency for such external commitments, and the preconceptions and preferences associated with them, to interfere with the rational pursuit of inquiry (Rescher, 1997).

Of course, it remains to be seen whether this argument will be found persuasive by other social scientists, in a climate that tends to polarise objectivism and subjectivism, scepticism and dogmatism, despite various attempts to find some middle way (e.g., Williams, 2005, 2006a, b). Without a viable conception of objectivity it seems unlikely that social science can flourish or even survive; and yet the prospects for it being given proper recognition are not good, in a world where many intellectuals and academics betray their calling in favour of political, ethical and aesthetic engagements, oppositional or compliant; and where 'truth' is a word that is either suppressed or clothed in scare quotes (Benson and Stangroom, 2007; Blackburn, 2006), lest it be taken to imply that there is something beyond rhetoric (Hammersley, 2008). In much the same way, claims to objectivity have either been denounced as special pleading or only allowed to stand once they have been re-specified as claims on behalf of oppressed or marginalised groups. What this makes clear is that recognition of the essential role that objectivity needs to play depends upon more fundamental changes in attitude on the part of social scientists; ones that, at present, still seem a long way off.

NOTES

1 In short, they usually operate as 'scare quotes'. Note that my putting quotation marks around 'objectivity' in this chapter does not conform to this usage – instead, it signals when I am *mentioning* not *using* the word.

2 Anscombe (1965: 158–9) had pointed this out earlier. Collier (2003: 133) links it to a shift from ontology to epistemology within Western philosophy. See Dear (1992: 620–21) for a detailed explication of the original

meanings of these terms and how 'objectivity' came to mean disinterestedness. See also Zagorin (2001). Accounts of the current range of meanings given to the term include Megill (1994) and Janack (2002).

3 See also Farrell's (1996) illuminating account of changing conceptions of subjectivity in the history of philosophy, and the theological background to this.

4 This too has been employed in diverse ways, but it has not been debased to the same extent as 'positivism'. Indeed, Ratner (2002) defines it in a positive manner, different from my usage here, tracing it back to Dilthey.

5 This idea can be traced back at least to the writings of Francis Bacon. See Gaukroger (2001: 127).

6 For some background to this, see Hammersley (2008).

7 There are many different interpretations of the term 'reflexivity', see Lynch (2000).

8 For discussion of standpoint theory and the notion of marginality, see Pels (2004). See also Pohlhaus (2002).

9 This is what Pels (2004) calls 'the spokesperson problem'.

10 Though, arguably, even they cannot avoid reliance upon them (Porpora, 2004).

11 As part of this, we will not only have to distinguish objectivity from other epistemic virtues but also to sort out its terminological relations with near synonyms like 'detachment' and 'neutrality', see Montefiore (1975).

12 I have identified the type of error associated with objectivity elsewhere as one form of culpable, systematic error that can be termed 'motivated bias'. See Hammersley and Gomm (2000). It is worth noting that there are preconceptions and preferences that can lead us astray that are generated by the research process even though they are not intrinsic to it. There include a researcher's public and/or private attachment to the truth of some knowledge claim or to the value of some method or source of data, the desire to find an interesting pattern or some clear answer to the research question, and so on. One aspect of this – bias deriving from theoretical commitments – was the preoccupation of seventeenth century natural philosophers, see Dasron (1994). Perhaps objectivity should be regarded as concerned with these kinds of threat to validity too.

13 Of course, there may well be disagreement about *which* considerations should, and should not, be taken into account in any role or decision.

14 There is a considerable literature on epistemic virtues, and on virtue epistemology more generally. See Kvanvig (1992); Montmarquet (1993); Zagzebski (1996); Axtell (2000); Brady and Pritchard (2003); DePaul and Zagzebski (2003). Another line of approach is to draw on Merton's discussion of the scientific ethos, and the literature dealing with this, see Merton (1973: part 3); Stehr (1978); Mulkay (1980); Hollinger (1983). Relations with near synonyms. like 'detachment' and 'neutrality', see Montefiore (1975).

15 There is a considerable literature on epistemic virtues, and on virtue epistemology more generally. See Kvanvig (1992); Montmarquet (1993); Zagzebski (1996); Axtell (2000); Brady and Pritchard (2003); DePaul and Zagzebski (2003). Another line of approach is to draw on Merton's discussion of the scientific ethos, and the literature dealing with this, see Merton (1973: part 3); Stehr (1978); Mulkay (1980); Hollinger (1983).

REFERENCES

Anscombe, E. (1965) 'The intentionality of sensation'. In R. Butler, (ed.) *Analytical Philosophy*, Second Series. Oxford: Blackwell.

Axtell, G. (ed.) (2000) *Knowledge, Belief, and Character: Readings in Virtue Epistemology*. Lanham, MA: Rowman and Littlefield.

Bar On, B.-A. (1993) 'Marginality and epistemic privilege'. In L. Alcoff and E. Potter (eds) *Feminist Epistemologies*. New York: Routledge.

Benson, O. and Stangroom, J. (2007) *Why Truth Matters*. London: Continuum.

Blackburn, S. (2006) *Truth: A Guide for the Perplexed*. London: Penguin.

Brady, M. and Pritchard, D. (eds) (2003) *Moral and Epistemic Virtues*. Malden, MA: Blackwell.

Bruun, H.H. (1972) *Science, Values and Politics in Max Weber's Methodology*. Copenhagen: Munksgaard. Second edition. Aldershot: Ashgate, 2007.

Collier, A. (2003) *In Defence of Objectivity: On Realism, Existentialism and Politics*. London: Routledge.

Daston, L. (1994) 'Baconian facts, academic civility, and the prehistory of objectivity'. In A. Megill (ed.) *Rethinking objectivity*. Durham, NC: Duke University Press.

Daston, L. and Galison, P. (2007) *Objectivity*. New York: Zone Books.

Dear, P. (1992) 'From truth to disinterestedness in the seventeenth century'. *Social Studies of Science*, 22(4): 619–31.

DePaul, M. and Zagzebski, L. (eds) (2003) *Intellectual Virtue: Perspectives from Ethics and Epistemology.* Oxford: Oxford University Press.

Eisenhart, M. (1998) 'On the subject of interpretive reviews'. *Review of Educational Research*, 68(4): 391–9.

Eisner, E. (1992) 'Objectivity in educational research'. *Curriculum Inquiry*, 22(1): 9–15. (Reprinted in M. Hammersley (ed.) (1993) *Educational Research: Current Issues.* London: Paul Chapman.)

Ellis, C. and Bochner, A.P. (2000) 'Autoethnography, personal narrative, reflexivity: researcher as subject'. In N.K. Denzin and Y.S. Lincoln (eds) *Handbook of Qualitative Research*, Second edition. Thousand Oaks, CA: Sage.

Erlandson, D.A., Harris, E.L., Skipper, B.L., and Allen, S.D. (1993) *Doing Naturalistic Inquiry: A Guide to Methods.* Newbury Park, CA: Sage.

Farrell, F.B. (1996) *Subjectivity, Realism and Postmodernism.* Cambridge: Cambridge University Press.

Gaukroger, S. (2001) *Francis Bacon and the Transformation of Early-modern Philosophy.* Cambridge: Cambridge University Press.

Gouldner, A. (1973) *For Sociology.* Harmondsworth: Penguin.

Haack, S. (1998) *Manifesto of a Passionate Moderate.* Chicago: University of Chicago Press.

Hammersley, M. (1995) *The Politics of Social Research.* London: Sage.

Hammersley, M. (1997) *Reading Ethnographic Research*, Second edition. London: Longman.

Hammersley, M. (2000) *Taking Sides in Social Research: Essays on Partisanship and Bias.* London: Routledge.

Hammersley, M. (2002) *Educational Research, Policymaking and Practice.* London: Paul Chapman.

Hammersley, M. (2003) 'A Guide to Natural Histories of Research'. Available at (accessed 6.04.09): http://www.tlrp.org/rcbn/capacity/Activities/Themes/Expertise/guide.pdf

Hammersley, M. (2004) 'Action research: a contradiction in terms?' *Oxford Review of Education*, 30(2): 165–81.

Hammersley, M. (2008) *Questioning Qualitative Inquiry.* London: Sage.

Hammersley, M. and Gomm, R. (2000) 'Bias in social research', chapter 6. In M. Hammersley *Taking Sides in Social Research: Essays on Partisanship and Bias.* London: Routledge.

Harding, S. (1991) *Whose Science? Whose Knowledge? Thinking from Women's Lives.* Ithaca, NY: Cornell University Press.

Harding, S. (1992) 'After the neutrality ideal: science, politics, and "strong objectivity"'. *Social Research*, 59(3): 568–87.

Harding, S. (1993) 'Rethinking standpoint epistemology: "What is strong objectivity?"' In L. Alcoff and E. Potter (eds) *Feminist Epistemologies.* New York: Routledge.

Harding, S. (1995) '"Strong objectivity": a response to the new objectivity question'. *Synthese*, 104: 331–49.

Harding, S. (ed.) (2004) *The Feminist Standpoint Theory Reader.* London: Routledge.

Hawkesworth, M.E. (1994) 'From objectivity to objectification: feminist objections'. In A. Megill (ed.) *Rethinking Objectivity.* Durham, NC: Duke University Press.

Hollinger, D.A. (1983) 'In defence of democracy and Robert K. Merton's formulation of the scientific ethos'. In R.A. Jones and H. Kuklick (eds) *Knowledge and Society: Studies in the Sociology of Culture Past and Present*, vol. 4. Greenwich, CT: JAI Press.

Janack, M. (2002) 'Dilemmas of objectivity'. *Social Epistemology*, 16(3): 267–81.

Keat, R. and Urry, J. (1975) *Social Theory as Science.* London: Routledge and Kegan Paul.

Kvanvig, J.L. (1992) *The Intellectual Virtues and the Life of the Mind: On the Place of the Virtues in Epistemology.* Savage, MD: Rowman and Littlefield.

Lather, P. (2007) *Getting Lost: Feminist Efforts Toward a Double(d) Science.* Albany, NY: State University of New York Press.

Lincoln, Y.S. and Guba, E.G. (1985) *Naturalistic Inquiry.* Beverley Hills, CA: Sage.

Lukács, G. (1971) *History and Class Consciousness: Studies in Marxist Dialectics.* Cambridge, MA: MIT Press.

Lynch, M. (2000) 'Against reflexivity as an academic virtue and source of privileged knowledge'. *Theory, Culture and Society*, 17(3): 26–54.

Megill, A. (ed.) (1994) *Rethinking Objectivity*. Durham, NC: Duke University Press.

Merton, R.K. (1973) *The Sociology of Science: Theoretical and Methodological Investigations*. Chicago: University of Chicago Press.

Montefiore, A. (1975) Part 1, in A. Montefiore, (ed.) *Neutrality and Impartiality: The University and Political Commitment*. Cambridge: Cambridge University Press.

Montmarquet, J.A. (1993) *Epistemic Virtue and Doxastic Responsibility*. Lanham, MA: Rowman and Littlefield.

Mulkay, M. (1980) 'Interpretation and the use of rules: the case of the norms of science'. In T.F. Gieryn (ed.) *Science and Social Structure: A Festschrift for Robert K. Merton*. New York: Transactions of the New York Academy of Sciences, Series II, Vol. 39, April 24.

Myrdal, G. (1969) *Objectivity in Social Research*. New York: Pantheon.

Newell, R.W. (1986) *Objectivity, Empiricism and Truth*. London: Routledge and Kegan Paul.

Pels, D. (2004) 'Strange standpoints, or how to define the situation for situated knowledge'. In S.G. Harding (ed.) *The Feminist Standpoint Reader: Intellectual and Political Controversies*. New York: Routledge.

Pohlhaus, G. (2002) 'Knowing communities: An investigation of Harding's standpoint epistemology'. *Social Epistemology*, 16(3): 283–93.

Polanyi, M. (1958) *Personal Knowledge*. Chicago: University of Chicago Press.

Porpora, D. (2004) 'Objectivity and phallogocentrism'. In M.S. Archer and W. Outhwaite (eds) *Defending Objectivity: Essays in Honour of Andrew Collier*. London: Routledge.

Radford, M. (2007) 'Prediction, control and the challenge to complexity'. Oxford Review of Education. Available at: http://dx.doi.org/10.1080/03054980701772636

Ratner, C. (2002) 'Subjectivity and objectivity in qualitative methodology'. *Forum Qualitative Sozialforschung/Forum: Qualitative Social Research* [On-line Journal], 3, 3. Available at: http://www.qualitative-research.net/fqs/fqs-eng.htm

Rescher, N. (1997) *Objectivity: The Obligations of Impersonal Reason*. Notre Dame, IN: University of Notre Dame Press.

Schwandt, T.A. and Halpern, E.S. (1988) *Linking Auditing and Metaevaluation: Enhancing Quality in Applied Research*. Newbury Park, CA: Sage.

Stehr, N. (1978) 'The ethos of science revisited: social and cognitive norms'. In J. Gaston (ed.) *Sociology of Science*. San Francisco CA: Jossey Bass.

Williams, B. (2002) *Truth and Truthfulness: An Essay in Genealogy*. Princeton: Princeton University Press.

Williams, M. (2005) 'Situated objectivity'. *Journal for the Theory of Social Behaviour*, 35(1): 99–120.

Williams, M. (2006a) 'Situated objectivity and objects in sociology'. Paper given at the American Sociological Association annual conference, Montreal. Available at (accessed 6.04.09): http://www.allacademic.com//meta/p_mla_apa_research_citation/1/0/3/0/2/pages103025/p103025-1.php

Williams, M. (2006b) 'Can scientists be objective?' *Social Epistemology*, 20(2): 163–80.

Zagorin, P. (2001) 'Francis Bacon's concept of objectivity and the idols of the mind'. *British Journal of the History of Science*, 34: 379–93.

Zagzebski, L.T. (1996) *Virtues of the Mind: An Inquiry into the Nature of Virtue and the Ethical Foundations of Knowledge*. Cambridge: Cambridge University Press.

2

Setting Up Sociological Research

Geoff Payne

It is not a novel thing to say that research needs to be a reflective process, but it would be something of an innovation if we were to take the social context of research activity more seriously. Despite, or perhaps indeed because of, our impressive technical developments in recent years, we are too busy doing research to bother over-much about the conditions of production of sociological knowledge. Our collective research quality could benefit from reviewing the process through which people end up as researchers, and how 'junior' researchers become involved in carrying out projects often with little awareness of what really goes on in data capture, what informants are doing when we research them, or how the data captured and analysed with our sophisticated techniques actually relate to theoretical questions. In discussing the way research in general is situated in sociology, rather than a particular technique, this chapter is less a resolution than a prolegomenon to such a review.

Of course, this begs the initial question that sociology, even less than sociological research, is not a unitary discipline. The chapter suggests several ways of conceptualising the discipline that also impinge on how we do research. Starting with illustrations from unpublished works – after all, why should we only look at our best products? – which show authors with considerable abilities who have not grasped the basic relationship between evidence and theory, sections on 'sociology as publications' and 'sociology as taught' demonstrate the ways that research techniques have become isolated from sociological thinking. Taking the example of the interviewee as an active, knowing and disobligingly complex social being, the latter part of the chapter suggests that we over-estimate the quality of the data we capture, and our capacity to make sense of it, instead placing excessive faith in our technical expertise and the shared conventions of our sociological schoolings. In particular, our assumptions about what our informants tell us, and what may be missing from our data, need re-consideration.

The following sections therefore treat research not as a separate act but as located in a longer process of training, professionalisation and continuing practice. This will allow us to question some taken-for-granted assumptions about how we carry out our research. The common theme connecting the discussion is what actually takes place within research projects, rather than what we like to present to the outside world, and to ourselves, as happening. Researchers of a more qualitative, and feminist, disposition would probably object to the implication that we lack reflexivity and self-awareness, and in part they would be justified. However, a life-time of social research has left me sceptical about the capacity of many colleagues (if one may generalise for the moment) to confront their own short comings – and I do not exclude myself from this concern.

FOUR UNFAIR ILLUSTRATIONS

This can be illustrated by examples of unpublished sociological work; those papers submitted to journals but not accepted. There appears to have been no systematic research into the content of empirical research in such papers. Even assuming that a proportion of the submission 'traffic' consists of works re-circulating in search of a home, the rejection rate of the major journals suggests that for every published article there are at least two more which are not part of the visible published record. That is a considerable quantity of sociological activity: the fact that it is unsuccessful is inadequate grounds for ignoring it. Indeed, one might even argue that its greater volume makes it more significant than the minority of work which is published.

Articles rejected for publication, or work-in-progress papers at small, specialist conferences of like-minded colleagues, are admittedly by definition minor, unsuccessful, or 'unacceptable' by the mainstream canons of the discipline. On the other hand, these papers have been produced by sociologists who believe that their work is suitable for publication on the basis of many months of hard labour. The deficiency of the end-product is not so much a problem of individual failings, but a question of what social processes have generated deficient work. What was lacking in the training and management of these (generally less-experienced) researchers? Why were they allowed to engage in poor research and produce deficient work, and not discouraged from attempting to get it published?

One is constrained in discussing this opaque body of sociological production both by the anonymity of authorship rules of submission and the conventions of confidentiality of reviewing and editorial board membership, and yet it is here that we best see the soft underbelly of the profession. Several recent articles (from among about three dozen seen in the last year) are described here as anecdotal illustration (and not as a proper sample). Because they were anonymised and not subsequently accepted for publication, I obviously cannot give bibliographic references for them: if this lack of chapter and verse troubles the reader, I can only suggest that the examples are regarded as fictional inventions, because their function is heuristic rather than strictly evidential. As their purpose is general illustration, rather than any criticism of the individual authors, it is perhaps better that they remain unidentified. The following accounts contain deliberate minor distortions intended to sustain anonymity. The minor breach of the ethics of confidentiality will I hope be compensated by adhering strictly to the principle of anonymity.

Example A is a study of that old chestnut, the relationship between education and occupational outcome. The authors explored the extent to which educational attainment explains occupational outcomes (a classic question in social mobility analysis) drawing on a large national American survey data-set collected for other purposes, and deploying MVA techniques. Despite some neat and indeed quite impressive innovation in the statistical analysis, the results could be anticipated well in advance because the topic has already been so well-researched. Predictably, it was found that, as in all the other cases, education and occupation are associated but not to the extent that common sense might suggest. Nevertheless, the fact that the topic is an old chestnut presumably justifies its selection as a topic, and the authors explained their work clearly and structured their argument in a cogent fashion. Why then was I unhappy with the explicit finding claimed by the research team? Because in fact their research design turned out to not sustain this conclusion.

In the first place, the experience of education was operationalised as 'number of years of completed full-time education'. There was no discussion of alternative indicators such as part-time schooling, vocational training undertaken as part of employment, differences in school or college environment, or subject specialisation. There was almost no discussion of qualification level achieved, and no comment on the convenient fact that number of years of completed full-time education is a quantitative measurement. The reason for the simplistic definition of education was given in a single sentence: the large and highly-regarded data-set being deployed in the secondary analysis did not contain sufficient information for a more elaborated conception of what 'education' means.

But worse was to follow. The researchers – who can by no means be described as lacking ability, given the sophistication of their analytical techniques – explain briefly that because women's experience of employment differs from that of men, and that it is not easy to assign women to categories of occupational class, no females were included in the analysis. Similarly, as people of colour and immigrants are subject to specific discriminations in the markets for both education and employment, they too needed to be excluded. The claimed finding, that education is moderately associated with occupation, is therefore nothing of the kind. What was actually established was that there is a moderate association between number of years of full-time education and occupational achievement among the American-born white males who comprise at best 40% of the adult population, which is a very different thing from what was explicitly envisaged at the outset. What makes this actual finding sociologically interesting is not that the moderate statistical association which applies to only a sub-set of the population, but rather, first, why it apparently does not apply to females and people of colour, and second, what market ramifications does the situation of these other groups have on the occupational achievement of white males? Even if markets are gendered and racialised, it makes little sense to study one part of the market in isolation from the rest.

This may seem an extreme case but it is not totally atypical. Much of mainstream social mobility research in the last quarter of the twentieth century dealt only with survey data on males. The major European CASMIN project is a classic example. Certainly most of my own early work in this field is open to this stricture. Thus, the illustration is part of a wider failure to recognise the limitations of one's data: even in the case of the specific experiences of distinctive minority groups, these must always be seen in the context of the majority group experience (e.g. Iganski et al., 2001).

A second example is a work-in-progress paper on voluntary association membership. This began with an excellent discussion of the literature, leading to a clever re-casting of the issues in terms of social capital in post-modern society, which was truly impressive. However, the data consisted of the number of voluntary association memberships at time $t = 1$, and the number of voluntary associations joined or left between $t = 1$ and $t = 2$. In other words, the design treated all voluntary associations (e.g. trade union, church, residents group, sports club, learned body, gym, parents support group and political party), all levels of membership (passive member; active participant, committee member or officer) and all geographical areas (neighbourhood, region, nation, or global) as identical. As in the first example above, the justification offered for this confounding of activities was that the data-set being used in the secondary analysis did not have any further evidence to offer. In other words, the research question, despite its impressive elaboration, could never be answered with the information available. Why was the research worker being allowed to waste their time (and public funds) on a project which manifestly could never be successful?

Both of these examples come from the quantitative tradition, but equivalent cases can be found in qualitative research. Example C claimed to show that the capitalist class had imposed new conditions of exploitation on labour by demanding that workers maintain high levels of physical fitness and a healthy appearance while at work. The data consisted of a small number of semi-structured interviews with the staff and gym users at two gyms located in a Financial Services district. Informants (mainly gym staff) were quoted as agreeing that more people these days were concerned about how they looked when at work, and that they felt physical fitness was important for career progression. These self-interested replies of the gym staff were taken at face value. No interviews were obtained with any members of the capitalist class or their service class managers. There was no specification of which 'workers' were being subjected to this new form of exploitation, or how many were suffering it, at what stages of their careers, or at what sites. No time frame for the new trend was indicated. No interview quotations referred directly to the core research hypothesis. To adapt a recent British advertising slogan, the research in question did not do 'what it says on the tin'.

In example D, the researcher's explicit aim was to explore how gender determined conditions of employment and academic output in universities. The article consisted of a thoughtful and insightful discussion of the content of extensive interviews completed with six married female academics, although one case was given most attention. The six women, all employed by one high status university, reported how difficult and drawn-out had been the process of obtaining tenured posts. They felt that their careers had been held back by this experience. This was taken to show how gender discrimination works in higher education, an area where universalistic criteria of performance are supposed to apply.

As an explication of some females' experience of academic life, this research may be acceptable. However, as an account of gender it is obviously deficient. The high status university that was the research site is distinctive in having very few tenured posts: first, men as well as women experience difficulty and delays in moving from temporary funded posts onto faculty (even if the degree of difficulty is not the same). Second, as the university is within easy commuting distance of at least half a dozen other high status institutions, let alone an even larger number of less prestigious universities, what was really interesting was the neglected question of why the six women made the choice to restrict their ambitions to the one campus, and therefore whether their 'difficulties' were less imposed upon them than to some extent self-inflicted. Third, the choice of that university as a research site was not discussed (it happened to be the one at which the researcher was a woman on 'soft money'). Its lack of typicality may have shone light on the specific issue of tenured and non-tenured employment, but that was not how the paper was framed. Instead it claimed to be about gender inequalities in higher education, which is not at all the same thing.

We are not talking here about articles submitted to journals that are then rejected for the conventional reasons that they are badly written, about obscure topics, show a lack of knowledge of the field, offer no evidence or contain computation errors, or do not sufficiently advance sociological knowledge. The point about these four examples is that their methods are fundamentally flawed. The data discussed in them do not relate to the research questions at their hearts. Nor have these been the only cases recently encountered, which suggests that this problem extends beyond the illustrations given here.

METHODS AS TAUGHT

All four of these examples show an incapacity to connect sociological questions with appropriate selection of data and awareness of what data really are. This basic methodological problem can be found to varying degrees across a range of sociological research, where issues have not been thought through, or there has been an over-reliance on the principle of *faute de mieux*. This has its roots in the way students come to think about sociology, and particularly in how we see the choice of informants and their answers. It is this set of problems that we need to address.

Such a swinging critique of actual research practice may be accused of over-generalisation. Making statements about what is taking place in sociology is no easy task: exceptions to every attempted rule abound. On what basis can one characterise the research practices of an entire discipline? In earlier discussions of sociological research methods in the UK, my co-researchers and I made several attempts to capture the discipline's contemporary geist, first examining undergraduate programme documentation, arguing that 'we are what we teach'. This approach sees sociology, and the way it researches, as its public face; in that most sociology students will not become professional sociologists but carry away an image of the discipline into their subsequent lives as members of the public. It also treats undergraduate education as the first phase of a professional socialisation process, in which undergraduate experience of research (or its lack) largely determines choices of topic and method in graduate school, while this in turn locates young sociologists on specific career tracks in which their methodological preferences are effectively pre-set for life.

In our 1980s exploration of the teaching of research the choice of data was essentially serendipitous. Our content analysis of undergraduate programme documentation in Britain was part of a wider project (Eggins, 1988) initiated by the Council for National Academic Awards (CNAA). The coverage was governed by the CNAA's remit as custodian of academic standards in the UK's institutions of higher education which subsequently became the country's 'new' or 'post-1992' universities (Payne et al., 1988, 1989). There was nothing special about the year in which the research was carried out, nor which years were included in the study: we simply used the documentation available for current courses. We did not debate questions of sampling, taking all available data for a time period that was externally determined. Our 'sample' was therefore time-specific and institutionally-constrained, rather than a response to any supposed methodological crisis within the discipline or dependent on the logic of some concern purely internal to British sociology.

This phase of research found research methods to be a core element in all institutions, covering both qualitative and quantitative approaches, but with an emphasis on the former. The most common teaching pattern was one (or two) free-standing module(s) in the second year of the degree programme. Qualitative methods were taught by sociologists who made other contributions to the programme, whereas quantitative methods were more often taught by statisticians from outside of the sociology department. Only a minority of programmes involved the students in hands-on researching (final year dissertations were then uncommon), and there was no evidence of research methods being taught as part of other modules. We coined the phrase 'the ghetto-isation of methods' to describe the way that doing research, and how sociological 'knowledge' has been generated, was not integrated into the mainstream programmes.

In a later phase of this work, we asked students and lecturers directly about their perceptions of what was being taught, rather than relying on module documents (Williams et al., 2004, 2008). Although this exposed us to low response rates among undergraduates it gave a more direct and informative access to what happens in class. Among our findings were that qualitative and quantitative methods continue to be covered in most programmes, with teaching now repatriated to sociology departments. Dissertations have become standard for Honours degrees. Research methods otherwise still tend to sit in isolation, and the depth of knowledge of statistical techniques is questionable. Most students perceive sociology as a humanities discipline, and prefer writing essays to analysing sociological data.

Although there are national differences, these patterns are not unique to the UK: the Netherlands is an example of paying greater attention to the development of quantitative skills (Parker, 2011). In the US, the American Mathematics Association has promoted the adoption of minimum quantitative skills for undergraduates, an approach endorsed by the National Science Foundation which funded the ASA-supported Integrating Data Analysis project (Gillman, 2006; Howery and Rodriquez, 2006). The full impact of these initiatives is yet to be seen, with many American students still gaining little experience of doing research. Parker's transnational survey indicates that the key issue is increasingly seen as the extent to which data analysis and hands-on research can be embedded across the curriculum so that undergraduate research practice is systematically encouraged, rather than leaving this to graduate school (Healey, 2008). What matters is not the specific research method used, but rather the practice of researching *per se*.

Two conclusions follow from this work. First, in most countries it is thought proper to introduce undergraduates to research methods, so that research would appear to be part of the sociological canon. However, apart from the dissertation, students are still not called upon to use their methods knowledge, and their learning of methods is separated from the rest of 'sociology'. Right from the start there is a gap between methods as technique and methods as sociological reasoning. Second, the level of skills acquired is low. For example, students probably know what a probability sample is but could not design and set up such a sample: their experience of working with the strict logic of probability is insignificant. Even after graduate school, young sociologists will have practised only a limited range of skills, and acquired only a 'black box' comprehension of others (typically, quantitative techniques that can be learned in a formal way). What they are less likely to have acquired is a rounded understanding of how data collection and data analysis need to be embedded in sociological reasoning.

Our commentaries on the content of undergraduate education, and the methods used in recent research, not least by 'junior researchers', in which we treat sociology 'as what we publish' (Payne et al., 2004) have been taken in some quarters as an implicit antagonism towards qualitative methods (May, 2005). However, our intention has always been to promote the positive value of quantitative research without denigrating other approaches, and to insist on the need for skills in a range of methods – in short, for methodological pluralism. This stance of measured neutrality allows us to criticise shortcomings in both qualitative and quantitative practice. Not least it fosters a degree of circumspection when it comes to the interpretation and presentation of one's research findings.

The way in which students are introduced to a discipline says a lot about how its practitioners perceive it. The isolation of research methods from the remainder of sociological thinking and analysis makes it harder for young sociologists early in their careers fully to comprehend data collection and research design. This is excaberated by teaching organised around the convenient but spurious dichotomy between qualitative and quantitative styles of research. Although both modes of research have deficiencies in how they see sampling and interviewing, they could each learn a great deal from the other.

OBLIGING AND DISOBLIGING INFORMANTS

I recently found myself living in an area selected by the UK's Office of National Statistics for testing new surveys. In rapid succession I was interviewed at length about health provision; employment; and twice on household consumption in terms of both diet and expenditure. By coincidence, I had also signed up as a panel member of an internet survey company so that I could volunteer my attitudinal prejudices, and curiosity stirred, I had begun to reply to every market research questionnaire disguised as prize draws that came my way (as yet without pecuniary success!). I even started to agree to be interviewed on the street by market research interviewers in search of quotas. In this way, after many years of carrying out social research as an investigator, I encountered social research extensively for the first time from the perspective of informant.

Up to this point in my career, I had followed the British Market Research Society Guidelines not to participate in data collection as a respondent. Following the Society's logic, as a 'knowing person' I was not a typical informant – but then on the other hand, the population includes such knowing people, and despite what we may or may not contribute, we are part of the universe from which samples are drawn. The experience of my new participation suggests that the trouble lies less in what we may do to the research findings (where we are likely to be a tiny minority of possible outliers), or as commercial rivals who might gain from seeing potentially advantageous new ways of data collection, but rather in what the experience may do to us as researchers.

Readers may like to ask themselves how often they have been the subject of research in, say, the last three years? If my informal (non-representative sample) soundings of colleagues are anything to go by, your answer is likely to be 'not (or hardly) at all'. None of my acquaintances has been interviewed more than once, and almost all had not experienced being interviewed, within that time-frame. However, to be interviewed once, or from time to time at long intervals, as I guess most sociologists have been, is not enough. Such single events may make one aware of specific technical shortcomings and the substantive nature of the project in question, but they are insufficiently intense to generate a deeper awareness of what 'doing being interviewed' is like, or to provide a platform on which to build a revision of what we mean by 'interviewee'.

As practitioners, our dominant experiences of data collection have been as student, research assistant, investigator, writer, teacher and critic. We therefore conceive of data collection as an active process of doing unto others, not as done to ourselves. Our primary conceptualisation is not as 'respondent', 'subject', 'interviewee', 'informant' or 'participant', but as researcher. This stipulation also extends to retrospective reflexive accounts of how research was actually carried out. In short, sociological research can be defined as an activity that social scientists practice on other people, even in 'collaborative' projects.

This assertion is a prelude neither to a naïve insistence that first-hand experience of 'being on the receiving end' is a pre-requisite for carrying out research, nor a polemic in favour of partnership or co-designed research. My point is that seeing social research from the other side of the questionnaire, laptop, or tape recorder can be a chastening experience: at least it has been for me. The challenge was not so much the discovery that other researchers' techniques, notably in question phrasing, questionnaire design and interviewing skills, leave great room for improvement – that was simply confirmation of something of which I, like many colleagues, have long been aware. Indeed, for academics and especially teachers of research methods, other researchers' inadequacies are our stock-in-trade. Rather, my experience made me realise that the way many professionals conceptualise the interviewee is inadequate. If I could be a thinking social agent during interview, why should I attribute to other informants a lesser state of consciousness? The logical conclusion of this insight is that social researchers should be much more cautious and humble about what they claim to have found in their collection of data.

Of course, there is no single model of 'the interviewee' in sociology. Conceptions range from the highly personalised to the faceless statistical unit, and from the downtrodden co-victim to the obdurate and misguided refuser. Unlike much of research in social psychology (conveniently practiced on a captive audience of psychology undergraduates, particularly in America), few sociologists take the view that subjects are always essentially co-operatively re-active. My reading of standard textbooks, the specialist literature (much of it written as guidance for inexperienced researchers) and more general accounts of findings based on empirical study, suggests that we unconsciously operate with one or more of the following models of the respondent, depending on the conditions of what is being researched:

- The refusenik
- The negative deviant

- The elite member
- The passive
- The simple-minded and potentially confused
- The co-operatively re-active
- The keen to please or excessively deferential
- The potential victim/ethically protectable
- The co-participant (feminist)
- The excessively garrulous.

I have deliberately omitted the special method of reflexive auto-ethnography, where the 'interviewer' and 'interviewee' is the same person, which I accept represents a limiting case. I anticipate that my outline typology is not an exhaustive list, but the identification of additional types does not invalidate its underlying principle, but rather strengthens my point. If informants can play these different roles – and change from one style to another during the course of data collection – this must surely raise doubts about probability sampling which treats respondents as inter-changeable uniform units, and how informants can bias the readings that qualitative researchers take from the interview encounter.

My interest here lies mainly in the first two categories of the typology, because the other categories are better represented in the literature. 'Refuseniks' are those people who decline to be interviewed. There is an extensive literature about ways of reducing the number of refusals in survey research, as well as statistical techniques for adjusting results to compensate for low response rates. Both of these tend to treat refuseniks as if they are either a uniform category, or sit on a monotonic continuum between acceptance and refusal. By definition we have little knowledge of them, although of course if we have some alternative parameters it is possible to identify their socio-economic position, gender, age, etc. through comparisons which by subtraction show their collective characteristics. The development of post coding geo-demographics and similar ecological descriptors offers an even more precise way of typifying those who we cannot successfully interview.

However, the key word here is 'typifying'. The underlying assumption is that refuseniks resemble those who we *do* interview, except for the single quirk of their refusal. If we can know some of their face sheet social features, we assume we can interpolate values for them from the sub-sample which they most resemble.

Alternatively, provided that our achieved sample is not seriously deficient in some social category, we need not worry unduly. But this begs the question of why some people refuse interviews. What if the refuseniks do not differ in most obvious respects (class, gender, age, etc.) but only in some other respects, one of which is their propensity to refuse? The propensity to refuse may be an indicator of a different set of social dispositions. Refusal may simply be a matter of non-co-operation due to inconvenience, an unwillingness to modify the refusenik's plans for spending their next hour. But does this indicate a personality type, or an actor whose embedding in their social routine is distinctive from other people? It is not implausible to suggest that refusal may be associated with one or more of attitude sets reflecting anti-authoritarianism; individualism and conservatism; anti-intellectualism; Asberger's Syndrome; mild paranoia; or even anti-social attitudes or socio-pathological tendencies.

In case this seems excessive, consider the second category of 'negative deviant', a category in which I would place myself – or rather, a category that I find myself in despite having started interviews in a 'co-operatively re-active' frame of mind. The longer the interview, the less co-operative I become. The poorer the question design, the more irritated and obstructive I become. To date, I have never terminated an interview, but my patience is not limitless. For example, where a series of questions ask me to make fine discriminations (or even express degrees of agreement/disagreement with Likert-like statements) or to engage in acts of careful recollection or calculation, I progressively find myself *unable to be bothered to be accurate*. I see no reason why similar reactions should not be experienced by other respondents. If that is so, the data we often collect is likely to be unreliable.

Nor do I find that this shift in response mode occurs only in survey research. Although my experience of being on the receiving end of qualitative research is more limited, I would argue that the same underlying process also operates. One's personal relationship with, say, a participant observer shifts over time: it may grow into stronger rapport and therefore 'openness', or decay into antagonism. When it comes to semi-structured interviews, the scope for destructive replies is even greater than with structured questionnaires.

A particular case in point is what informants 'volunteer' during interview. The conventional assumption seems to be that with good interviewing, informants will talk comprehensively about topics; and in providing answers, will depict their sense of issues. If the informant has any ideas or feelings about an issue, they will become expressed and conversely, the expression of responses means that the researcher can tell what issues matter to the informant. In other words, the *salience* of an issue can be evaluated by the informants replies (see for example Savage et al.'s (2001) explanation of class identity). However, it may be that where there are intense feelings or strong but controversial opinions are held, informants adopt precisely the opposite tack by remaining completely silent. It all depends on what image of the informant we bring to the table. There seems to be no simple way of knowing whether silence may also be an indicator of salience.

The model of the informant that I am sketching is of a knowing being, whose orientation cannot be tied down to some standardised social identity which is accessed via core sociological variables. This informant is knowing in both, the sense of being able to react to the interview, and to change their orientation during interview; a social person who not only reacts to the researcher in a dynamic way during the specific setting of the data capture process, but whose social persona is complex and multi-faceted in a way that cannot easily be reduced to a simple social type. Because people share certain social characteristics, such as class, gender, ethnicity and age does not entitle us to *assume* a consistent similarity of experience, values, attitudes or responses among them. Our task as researchers is to *discover* to what extent such patterns exist, but informants are under no obligation to assist us. Statistical techniques intended to compensate for gaps in our data due to informant non-co-operation, but which actually involve extrapolation or replacement based on the data from other informants which we do have, are both tautological and open to the charge of reliance on an 'over-socialized conception of man'.[1]

OBLIGING AND DISOBLIGING SAMPLES

Until recently, the problem of selecting who we study has not received much attention outside of survey research, or at least so one might believe from reading most published accounts. In the quantitative tradition, the mechanics of sampling are conventionally made a matter of record: in pre-analysis working papers (increasingly available on the internet); in methodological appendices to monographs; and in end-of-project reports to stake-holders. Journal articles may give cursory technical details, but they normally provide links through bibliographic referencing that allow readers to follow up any sampling questions.

Some big surveys have established such a reputation that they can be invoked almost as brand names, thus removing any need for further discussion because the product's qualities (and even any limitations) are universally acknowledged: many sources available from Statistics Canada, the ONS and the ESDS in the UK, and ICPSR in the US provide examples. In the UK, a growing trend towards cost-effective secondary analysis of large data-sets, particularly of omnibus or repeated surveys, is allowing junior researchers to dispense with the impedimenta of primary data collection, although this often still embroils them in statistical issues of weighting or problems of data definition. While there is no shortage of statistical literature on how to compensate for sampling defects, this typically shows little sensitivity to the initial character of the data capture. Because there is an expectation that sampling needs to be explained, researchers are required to give the matter some consideration, albeit only in a highly technical way.

This framework provides considerable comfort for the researcher, but it is not without its own constraints once one moves beyond synchronic analysis. The UK National Child Development Study (NCDS) offers a case in point. Probably the most widely-deployed data-set in educational, health and social inequality trend research, the prominence of the NCDS primarily depends on the absence of alternative, comprehensive and large data-sets for people born in the late 1950s. However, by its seventh re-survey sweep in 2004, attrition and non-response had reduced its original sample of 17,634 to 9,175, i.e. 52% (and if one were interested in comparing data from all seven sweeps, only 33.8% of the original sample can be directly used). While much of this 'missingness', to use a term from Carpenter and Plewis (this volume, Chapter 23) is not a total loss of cases, but rather partial loss of items or single sweeps, it remains reasonable to speculate that the survivors, in their adult status, differ sociologically from those who have disappeared from view, *even if on certain specified variables (with or without compensatory re-weighting) they do not.* How else are we to explain their non-compliance?

In distinguishing between the impact of various causes of missingness in the NCDS (e.g. for the case or item levels) Carpenter and Plewis show how in certain circumstances, such as 'Missing at Random', less biased estimates can be recovered from surviving data. However, their ingenious methods of tackling data which are 'Missing Not at Random' remains based on the assumption that there are no substantial differences between survivors and the missing. If we posit that some individuals have a lower propensity to co-operate with social surveys – especially repeated longitudinal studies – than others (due, say, to their social location, identity, or personality), the question remains whether they differ in the other social characteristics represented by the variables in the survey. If so, the recovery of estimates from the survivors is 'the most difficult situation to adjust for', as Carpenter and Plewis acknowledge in their introduction to this topic.

Attrition is of course a problem for all longitudinal studies, as is the need to rely on original research techniques that become out of date. Those re-using the NCDS have remained silent about the awkward matter that professionally-trained survey interviewers were not used to collect NCDS data until the 1981 sweep. Prior to this, data were collected by and from Health Visitors and school personnel who, with all due respect, can hardly be described as sociologically literate. Almost all secondary analyses of the NCDS have ignored this limitation, presumably on the grounds that there is no alternative data-set. Even if those collecting the data had been better trained in the collection of sociological data, the basic research tools of the 1950s were still primitive. A quarter of a century later, Hope and Goldthorpe (1974) were still attempting to establish the first coherent, explicit and all-inclusive method of scoring social class in the UK. It is little wonder that during the early 1990s, in examining nearly 80 multivariate analysis assignments using unweighted NCDS data (presented as part of the University of Ulster's excellent Social Research Masters degree requirements, and reviewed in my role as External Examiner), I found almost no statistically significant associations between the NCDS variables. The quantitative tradition may be better placed than other methods when it comes to information about sampling, but that does not mean that its record is beyond reproach, especially when it comes to *faute de mieux* justifications.

Nonetheless, at least there is a framework for discussing the sampling. In qualitative research the question has hardly been raised outside of the extended case study method in ethnography, so that the conventional discourse provides less scope for exploring it. It is no defence to argue that qualitative methods do not involve generalisation (Denzin, 1983; Lincoln and Guba, 1985). As an earlier close inspection of a series of journal articles showed (Payne and Williams, 2005), sociologists who base their interpretations on data collected from small numbers of informants (say, less than 50 individuals) do make explicit generalising claims that their findings have society-wide application and implications (Fahrenberg (2003) makes a similar point for interpretative methodologies in psychology and other social sciences).

This presents an almost intractable difficulty. It is no solution to train the users of such methods to eschew generalising statements (although that might not in itself be a bad thing). Such a policy would merely obscure the underlying fact that we need to know the logical status of the small-scale study. If the point of selecting a research site and its human occupants is *not* to generalise in respect to other similar cases, does the choice matter? On the one hand, if each study is self-contained and free-standing, its relationship with previous and subsequent research is problematic. In this view, sociology should be as non-cumulative as the field of literature where one short story is no guide to the plot or characters of another. If, as the constructivists would have us believe, all social phenomena are unique because they are context and time specific, what is the purpose of even exploring similarities of subjective, individual perspectives when our own explorations are themselves unique? But on the other hand, if each study is unique, then as readers we still need to know why the site and its informants were selected because this is an essential part of the unique events being catalogued.

Nor is it easy to connect the small-scale to larger populations by using principles from probability theory. This requires no elaborate statistical reasoning because any attempt falls at the first hurdle: there is usually minimal information about the supposed population, typically manifested in the absence of a sampling frame, a point conceded by Mayring (2007; para. 16) despite his optimism about probabilistic approaches. Indeed, where the research is concerned with small, unusual categories of persons, as in the case of hard-to-access minorities, the actual number of such people is open to dispute. If the topic involves studying what happens within an organisation, we seldom have a complete list of similar organisations, and even here it is necessary to specify the geographical unit – locality, state, region or nation – containing the sites. However, even if this were not so, the populations tend to be small, and so the sample size has to be large relative to the population size.

Thus, if we think of a type of organisation or a hard-to-access category of persons, conventional standards of sampling are going to present a logistical challenge. Sampling conventions (Krejcie and Morgan, 1970) dictate that an adequate sample of a population consisting of 10 or less organisations requires a sample that is a census. If there are 100 organisations or cases, we need to sample 80 of them, or if the hard-to-access set numbers 1000, we need to access well over a quarter of them. There are very few instances of qualitative work that covers either 10 organisations or in excess of 200 in-depth interviews. In cases which do come readily to mind like the life-work of Michael Burawoy (e.g. 1991), or Savage et al.'s (2001) study of class consciousness in Manchester, the relationship between sample and population is not entirely clear. To express it the other way round, if we have the resources for, say, 40 in-depth interviews, the generalising power under probability is to a population no bigger than 50.

If qualitative research cannot draw on probability theory, how should field sites be selected? Under present conventions, there is little rigour in sampling. Where this involves access to an organisation or an established group, the 'selection' is normally done on the basis of a previous contact. Supervisors of postgraduate students act as patrons, activating their social networks to sponsor their protégées to gate-keepers. Researchers' prior work experience or contacts provide another pragmatic route to access, but usually with little consideration of the theoretical implications of researching a specific site. A similar pragmatism applies in contacting hard-to-reach informants, where snow-balling is seldom seriously questioned in terms of how non-typical the resulting sample is likely to be. We are rarely told in detail about the participants in focus groups.

This does not matter if we assume that the sample of persons makes no difference to the information collected, but this is hardly a strong position to adopt. The findings of studies are very commonly used to generalise – or what in qualitative discourse is more often referred to as 'developing theories' – as Payne and Williams (2005) have shown. Who we choose for our sample determines our findings:

> Questions of generalisation are tied to those of *sampling* because the sample is the bearer of those characteristics that it is wished to infer to a wider population. (Williams, 2000: 216, original emphasis)

To give one illustration, if a study site has been chosen 'because of the willingness of local authority access officers to take part in the research' (Edwards and Imrie, 2003: 245), it is not unreasonable to ask whether the same results would have been found had access somehow been possible to sites where access officers were *unwilling* to co-operate? Is willingness to co-operate a social characteristic associated with others like support for evidence-based practice, openness to new ideas, and confidence in the high quality of one's organisation?

Most qualitative research falls into this category described by Mason (1996: 92–93), as being based on small selections of units which are acknowledged to be part of wider universes but not chosen primarily to represent them directly. There are far too few cases where the case selection – especially of the single case study – is explicitly justified by the need for very detailed scrutiny. It would be much better to reflect on generalization *ex ante*, which means to select the single case, or the site, following prior considerations. Looking for a typical case, a representative case, a frequent occurring case or a theoretically interesting case would be a good strategy (Mayring, 2007: 6). That means that it would be good to formulate a case definition as part of the research design rather than burying what turns out to be a 'pragmatic solution' in a brief discussion of methods. A sample need not be typical of the wider population, but its a typicality needs to be confronted, justified in advance, and subsequently integrated into any attempt to 'generate theory'.

SOME CONCLUDING REMARKS

Doing empirical research is central to the being and identity of most sociologists. That does not mean that we are as good at it as we like to think, or that we follow through the implications of our focus on research. I have illustrated several ways in which we can and sometimes do fall short: by using data which are not fit for purpose (particularly with respect to the current fashion for secondary analysis of large data-sets); by not exercising our responsibilities as teachers and supervisors of research; by making excessive claims from limited studies; by over-estimating informants willingness to co-operate and under-estimating the significance of non-response, because we have under-theorised the interview encounter and over-theorised the atypical case. This is a case for methodological innovation less as specific new techniques, and more as basic thinking about interviewing and sampling.

As one example of where this might lead, (I have tried in my exposition to indicate the limits of my own *illustrations* and sampled evidence when I have been making broad generalisations) is something that sociologists should be learning this kind of caution while they are undergraduates. The best long-term investment in producing good research is to reform the undergraduate curriculum, placing research practice not only at its heart but in every corner of its corpus. The issue is not which methods should be taught, but that the research itself should occupy its proper place. Such an innovation would not only improve our technical performance, but also provide a framework in which future generations of sociologists could start reflecting about the research act, in fundamental ways.

It seems to me that there is currently a need for a little more humility among researchers. While we need endlessly beat ourselves up about the limitations of our efforts, much of our writing tends too far in the opposite direction. Faced with perceived threats from rival methodological stances, we not only make excessive claims for our own findings, but become needlessly drawn into denigrating the work of others based in those different methodological camps. Much of this dialogue of the deaf fails to see the simple point that we can describe the social at different *levels of detail.* The broad view of national patterns offers one perspective, gaining society-wide knowledge and generality at the expense of detail. The interpretation of small-scale interactions provides us with accounts of fine social detail and process, but cannot at the same time characterise the wider picture. Temperamentally, we may prefer one level of analysis to the other, or become interested in topics best-suited for this or that method of research, but that should not become routinised in our discipline's culture as exclusionary or hegemonic practice.

Core elements such as sampling and interviewing, which are fundamental to a range of research styles, raise problems throughout sociology that extend beyond the narrow confines of our own preferred approaches. Unless we continue to refine our tools and perspectives by drawing on our *collective* expertises, we stand to lose our claims to provide valuable and uniquely sociological knowledge.

Indeed, when we take seriously the rise of geodemographic systems, transactional databases, and the extension of State-controlled inter-connected personal records (in the name of national security and administrative efficiency), the need to be more aware of what we know and how we know it becomes more acute. How else are we to acquire the sophisticated descriptions required to challenge the results of the 'rules of thumb' (Savage and Burrows, 2007: 887) routinely applied by the managers of commercial databases or the security services? This is a task which can only be achieved by greater co-operation within the discipline. There are many rooms in sociology's mansion, and we can still learn a lot from talking with the guys next-door.

NOTES

1 Readers who share my moderately obsessive disposition might care to check on the frequent mis-referencing of Wrong's original article: I estimate about 80% of Google hits (January 2009) write 'oversocialized' as two words or hyphenated; mis-spell socialized with an s not a z; refer to the concept, not the conception; or even more remarkably attribute the bibliographic source to the AJS instead of the ASR).

REFERENCES

Burawoy, M. (1991) 'The extended case study method'. In M. Burawoy (ed.) *Ethnography Unbound.* Berkley: University of California Press.

Denzin, N. (1983) 'Interpretive interactionism'. In G. Morgan (ed.) *Beyond Method: Strategies for Social Research.* Beverly Hills: Sage.

Edwards, C. and Imrie, R. (2003) 'Disability and bodies as bearers of value'. *Sociology*, 37(2): 239–56.

Eggins, H. (ed.) (1988) *Review of Sociology Courses and Teaching.* London: CNAA.

Fahrenberg, J. (2003) 'Interpretation in psychology and social science – New approach or a neglected tradition?' *Forum Qualitative Sozialforschung / Forum: Qualitative Social Research*, 4(2), Art. 45. http://www.qualitative-research.net/fqs-texte/2-03/2-03fahrenberg-d.htm (Accessed 22.12.2008).

Gillman, R. (2006) *Current Practices in Quantitative Literacy.* Washington, D.C.: Mathematics Association of America.

Healey, M. (2008) *Linking Research and Teaching: A Selected Bibliography.* University of Gloucestershire. http://www.glos.ac.uk/shareddata/dms/5B8F006BBCD42A039BA6832547DBAC47.pdf (accessed 16.7.2008).

Hope, K. and Goldthorpe, J. (1974) *The Social Grading of Occupations.* Oxford: Oxford University Press.

Howery, C. and Rodriguez, H.(2006) 'Integrating Data Analysis (IDA): Working with Sociology Departments to address the quantitative literacy gap'. *Teaching Sociology*, 16: 23–38.

Iganski, P., Payne, G., and Payne, J. (2001) 'Social Inclusion? the changing position of Britain's Minority Ethnic Groups'. *International Journal of Sociology and Social Policy*, 21(4–6): 184–211.

Krejcie, R. and Morgan, D. (1970) 'Determining sample size for research activities'. *Educational and Psychological Measurement*, 30: 607–10.

Lincoln, Y. and Guba, E. (1985) *Naturalistic Inquiry.* Beverly Hills, CA: Sage.

Mason, J. (1996) *Qualitative Researching.* Thousand Oaks, CA: Sage.

May, C. (2005) 'Methodological pluralism, British sociology and the evidenced-based state'. *Sociology*, 39(3): 519–28.

Mayring, P. (2007) 'On generalization in qualitatively oriented research'. *Forum Qualitative Sozialforschung/Forum: Qualitative Social Research*, 8(3): Art. 26. http://nbn-resolving.de/urn:nbn:de:0114-fqs0703262. (accessed 22.12.2008).

Parker, J. (2011) 'Best practices in quantitative methods teaching: comparing social science curricula across countries '. In G. Payne and M. Williams (eds) *Teaching Quantitative Methods.* London: Sage (in press).

Payne, G. and Williams, M. (2005) 'Generalisation in quantitative research'. *Sociology*, 39(2): 295–314.

Payne, G., Lyon, S., and Anderson, R. (1988) 'The teaching of social research methods'. In H. Eggins (ed.) *Review of Sociology Courses and Teaching.* London: CNAA.

Payne, G., Lyon, S., and Anderson, R. (1989) 'Research methods in the public sector curriculum'. *Sociology*, 23(2).

Payne, G., Williams, M., and Chamberlain, S. (2004) 'Methodological pluralism in British sociology'. *Sociology*, 38(1): 153–63.

Savage, M., Bagnall, G., and Longhurst, B. (2001) 'Ordinary, ambivalent and defensive: class identities in the north-west of England'. *Sociology,* 35(4): 875–92.

Savage, M. and Burrows, R. (2007) 'The coming crisis of empirical sociolgy'. *Sociology,* 41(5): 885–99.

Williams, M. (2000) 'Interpretivism and generalisation'. *Sociology*, 34(2): 209–24.

Williams, M., Hodgkinson, L., and Payne, G. (2004) 'A crisis of number?' *Radical Statistics*, 85: 40–54.

Williams, M., Payne, G., Hodgkinson, L., and Poade, D. (2008) 'Does British sociology count? Sociology students' attitudes toward quantitative methods'. *Sociology*, 42(5): 1003–21.

3

Feminist Methodology

Gayle Letherby

INTRODUCTION

As many feminist researchers have argued and Sandra Harding (1987: 3) succinctly puts, 'it is not by looking at research methods that one will be able to identify the distinctive features of the best feminist research' (see also, e.g. Roberts, (1981) 1990; Stanley, 1990; Reinharz, 1992; Maynard and Purvis, 1994; Stanley and Wise, 1993; Millen, 1997; Ribbens and Edwards, 1998; Ramazanoglu with Holland, 2002; Letherby, 2002, 2003a; Hesse-Biber, 2007a). So, there is no such thing as a feminist method, rather what is distinctive about feminist research is a sensitivity to the significance of gender within society and a critical approach to the research process. Thus, rather than focusing on the methods (tools for gathering evidence/collecting data), feminists are concerned with the methodological reflection of the researcher(s). Methodology, concerned as it is with the 'getting of knowledge', is key to understanding the relationship between knowledge and power (Stanley and Wise, 2008: 222) and is thus an essential part of the feminist project:

> Within feminism, the term 'feminist methodology' is also used to describe an ideal approach to doing research – one which is respectful of respondents and acknowledges the subjective involvement of the researcher. This leads us to a question which Cook and Fonow (1990: 71) ask: 'is feminist methodology that which feminists *do* or that which we *aim for*'? (Letherby, 2003a: 5)

> Feminist methodology is at the heart of the feminist project of changing the world because it is the focal point for bringing together theory, practical research methods, and the production of new knowledge. (Stanley and Wise, 2008: 221)

Not surprisingly, feminist methodological debate, alongside developments within feminist politics and women's movements, has been central to the feminist critique of the social sciences since the late 1970s (Okley, 1992; Wise and Stanley, 2003; Delamont, 2003). In this chapter I summarise and reflect on this debate, highlighting some of my own feminist methodological concerns.

FEMINIST METHODOLOGY AND THE ACADEMY

It was not until the second half of the twentieth century that women began to enter the academy in any great numbers. Historically, the focus of academic endeavour was men and male experience. Yet, as Dorothy Smith (1988: 19–20) notes, not all men were represented and therefore in the physical and social sciences, the arts and humanities:

> . . . the perspectives, concerns, and interests of only one sex and one class are represented as general. Only one sex, and class are directly and actively involved in producing, debating and developing its ideas, creating its art, in forming its medical and psychological conceptions, in framing its laws, its political principles, its educational values and objectives.

Additionally, and equally problematic, was the unquestioned adoption of the so-called 'scientific' method as the best way to study both the natural and the social world. The view here is that the 'expert neutral knower' (the researcher) can be separated from what is known that different researchers exposed to the same data can replicate results and that it is possible to generalize from research to wider social and physical populations. From this perspective, reality (the truth) is 'out there' and the researcher can investigate and discover the 'truth' independent of observer effects (Stanley and Wise, 1993; Letherby, 2003a). Furthermore, those that aim for this 'scientific' approach to social science argue that the research process is linear and orderly – 'hygenic' in fact (see Stanley and Wise, 1993; Kelly et al., 1994). This approach is generally known as positivism and associated with quantitative methods [but it is important to remember that not all quantitative researchers are aiming for positivism/a 'scientific' approach, see Oakley (1999) for further discussion].

Early critics of a 'scientific' social science were themselves male and although they were critical of the claims to objectivity, value-freedom and the search for the 'truth' their research still tended to focus on male experience and the sexist aspects of the approach were not challenged (Morley, 1996; Letherby, 2003a). From the 1970s feminist researchers began to criticize both male-dominated knowledge production and the methodological claims made by researchers who argued that their work was objective and value-free:

> Masculine ideologies are the creation of masculine subjectivity; they are neither objective nor value free nor inclusively 'human'. Feminism implies that we recognize fully the inadequacy

> for us, the distortion, of male-centred ideologies and that we proceed to think and act out of that recognition. (Rich, 1986: 207 cited by Stanley and Wise, 1993: 59)

The feminist critique of the historical male-centred approach to research can be summarised as follows:

- the selection of sexist and elitist research topics;
- biased research including the use of male-only respondents;
- claims to false objectivity;
- inaccurate interpretation and over-generalization of findings – including the application of theory to women from research on men;
- exploitative relationships between researcher and researched and within research teams.

Yet, as Caroline Ramazanoglu with Janet Holland (2002: 165) argues, feminist approaches retain three elements of the 'scientific method':

- the possibility of being able to differentiate between better-grounded and worse-grounded stories of gendered social existence;[1]
- a general commitment to reasoned argument (despite the problematic history of rationality);[2]
- the need to justify knowledge claims.

One significant difference between traditional and feminist approaches is the insistence that research should mean something to those being studied and should lead to change. Thus, '[f]eminist research is . . . not research about women but research for women to be used in transforming their sexist society' (Cook and Fonow, 1990: 80). In addition, feminist researchers are concerned to:

- give continuous and reflexive attention to the significance of gender as an aspect of all social life and within research, and consider further the significance of other differences between women and (some argue) the relevance of men's lives to a feminist understanding of the world;
- provide a challenge to the norm of 'objectivity' that assumes knowledge can be collected in a pure, uncontaminated way;
- value the personal and the private as worthy of study;
- develop non-exploitative relationships within research;
- value reflexivity and emotion as a source of insight as well as an essential part of the research process.

As this chapter demonstrates, feminist work has had an impact both on how social science researchers think about methodology and on the academy more generally:

> . . . there are more women students, researchers, teachers and managers in further and higher education than ever before and as Evans (1995) argues, education is no longer about DWMs (dead white males) and 'feminists can claim to have developed one of the now great critical traditions within the Western academy, that of suggesting that the universalistic assumptions of knowledge in our society are false, and partial, because they are drawn from the experience of only one sex' (Evans, 1997: 122). Feminists and others working outside of western assumptions have been influential in these changes. (Letherby, 2003a)

Taking my own discipline – Sociology – as an example Liz Stanley (2005: 4.1) insists on the 'transformative impact of a combination of feminism, gender and women's studies, in a world-wide context and also in the UK, on the domain ideas and working practices of Sociology and most other disciplines . . .'. Furthermore, writing with Sue Wise, she suggests that recognition of this impact coupled with the growth of other perspectives and approaches within the discipline means that it is no longer relevant to speak of feminist thought as other to the mainstream:

> . . . . Given the proliferation of sub-areas, specialisms and national differences, the idea that there is 'a mainstream' becomes difficult to sustain, for it is more a matter of centres and peripheries in each of these areas of activity, with their own key texts, dominant ideas, gurus, preferred ways of working, journals, book series and so forth. Consequently any claim that feminist Sociology is 'other' makes little sense to us – it all depends on which national Sociology, the specific feminist Sociology or sociologist, where people are organisationally located, and what sub-area of specialism is being referred to.
>
> Here for instance (and again with regard to UK Sociology in particular), ideas about the work/leisure relationship and domestic divisions of labour, or concerning reflexivity and the grounded nature of sociological modes of inquiry, have gained wide currency but are not seen as particularly feminist in character. However, those of us with 30 year involvement in the discipline can note that the emphasis given them in feminist teaching, debate and publications have played an important role in ensuring their wider sociological currency. (Wise and Stanley, 2003: 2.5–2.6)

Despite this, others still contend that despite the influences of feminism, sociological theory remains heavily dominated by male thinkers and writers (Delamont, 2003; Abbott et al., 2005) and some feminist academics, including feminist sociologists, continue to argue for the need to challenge the mainstream/malestream.

ENDURING MYTHS

Just as feminism is surrounded by myths so is feminist methodology. Here I consider the (arguably) two most persistent ones: that feminists favour qualitative methods and that feminists are not interested in men and men's experiences.

Despite much evidence to the contrary, many critics of and researchers new to feminist research approaches believe that feminists not only prefer to use qualitative methods but above all celebrate the in-depth qualitative interview as the most valuable method. So where has this misconception come from? Many feminists HAVE argued that the in-depth interview that takes a life-history approach is a good way of achieving an 'equal' relationship between interviewer and interviewee. By letting individuals tell 'their story' this method allows the researched an active part in the research process and project as well as making the researcher more vulnerable and therefore diluting the power imbalance in favour of the researcher (Oakley, 1981; Graham, 1984; Stanley and Wise, 1993). In addition, qualitative methods focus on the 'experiential' and allow people to 'speak for themselves' (Stanley and Wise, 1993). So, the argument goes, there is methodological value in a method which encourages the production of research for women rather than research about or of women (Oakley, 1981; Bowles and Klein, 1983). However, there are potential problems with this not least because all women do not share the same experience and are divided by other variables such as ethnicity, class, sexuality and so on and this is likely to affect the research process and researcher/respondent matching is impossible to achieve (Ramazanoglu, 1989). Further, as Janet Finch (1984) argues the very fact that women are 'happy to talk' may be an indication of their powerlessness and researchers need to be very careful that information freely given cannot be used against those who gave it. Many others agree with this and add that some objectification of the researched is inevitable as the researcher has the ultimate control over the material (e.g. Ramazanoglu, 1989; Ribbens, 1989; Stacey, 1991; Cotterill, 1992; Letherby, 2003a).

In a paper focusing on gendered research philosophies and practices, Ann Oakley (1998: 708) argues that the 'critique of the quantitative' overlaps with the 'critique of mainstream/malestream' and thus '[t]o be a feminist social scientist one must have a certain allegiance to the qualitative paradigm'. This has resulted, she adds, in a 'paradigm war' with male researchers being associated with quantitative methods of data collection and women researchers with qualitative methods (especially the in-depth interview). Oakley (1998: 709) argues that there is a danger that quantitative and qualitative approaches are represented as 'mutually exclusive ideal types'. But Oakley was not the first to point this out, nor was she the first feminist to make use of other methods (for discussion and examples see Reinharz, 1992; Kelly et al., 1994; Stanley and Wise, 1993; Letherby and Zdrodowski, 1995; Letherby, 2003a; Minor-Robino et al., 2007). Furthermore, Jennifer Platt's (2007) recent analysis of British authorship in Sociology journals suggests that although women have always employed qualitative methods in a majority of their empirical articles, so have men. It is also important to remember that although historically, feminists were particularly critical of the survey method, it was its epistemological appropriation by those who attempted a 'scientific', 'value-free' approach and the tendency of researchers to concentrate on male concerns that was the issue here (Oakely, 1981; Stanley and Wise, 1993; Graham, 1984). Indeed, as noted earlier, much of the work challenging traditional philosophical approaches was equally gender blinkered.

Cautioning against choosing favourite methods without proper consideration of the research aims and objectives Liz Kelly and colleagues (1994) argue that by using only small-scale studies the researcher can be misled into believing that s/he has some knowledge that has not actually been collected. They argue that appropriate methods should be chosen to suit research programmes rather than research programmes being chosen to 'fit' favourite techniques. In addition, Oakley (2004: 191) suggests: 'The most important criteria for choosing a particular research method is not its relationship to academic arguments about methods, but its fit with the question being asked in the research'. Kelly et al. (1994: 35–6) add:

> Rather than assert the primary of any method, we are not working with a flexible position: our choice of method(s) depends on the topic and scale of the study in question. Whenever possible we would combine and compare methods, in order to discover the limitations and possibilities of each.

This is necessary, they argue, to ensure access to all of women's experiences.

In consideration of the myth that feminist researchers are only interested in researching women and women's experiences, it is important to acknowledge that the first concern of early second wave feminist research was to make women's lives visible. In 1987, Sandra Harding noted that whilst studying women was not new studying them from the perspective of their own experiences, so that they could understand themselves and their position within the social world had 'virtually no history at all' (p. 8). Yet, if we accept that man is not the norm and woman the deviation and if we want to fully understand the life experience and chances of all men and women we need to consider the social construction of both femininity and masculinity and focus our research on women and men's experience. Thus, 'taking gender seriously' means bringing men back in (Morgan, 1981; Laws, 1990). Within this, as Ellen Annandale and Judith Clark (1996: 33) note, we should remain

> . . . congnizant of the possibility that 'patriarchal discourse need not be seen as homogeneous and uniformly oppressive' . . . for women or uniformly liberating and unproblematic for men, and that women do not need to be portrayed as inevitable victims and men as victors.

Thus, men can be victims, women can be powerful, men and women often share experiences of powerless and an understanding of the differences between women in terms of power and privilege is a vital part of the feminist project. Given this (and I appreciate the contradiction here), it is surprising that the recently published 758-page *Handbook of Feminist Research* (Hesse-Biber, 2007a) makes little reference to feminist research with men.

EPISTEMOLOGICAL CONCERNS

Having considered the position of feminism within the academy and some myths surrounding the feminist research process, in this section of the chapter I consider some of the debate surrounding feminist epistemological approaches and the relationship between this and feminist methodology. Feminist researchers argue that we need to consider how the researcher as author is positioned in relation to the research process, and to ignore the personal involvement of the researcher within research is to downgrade the personal (Stanley, 1990; Stanley and Wise, 1993; Letherby, 2003a). Thus, feminists are concerned with who has the right to know, the nature and value of knowledge and feminist knowledge within this, the relationship between the method, how it is used and the 'knowledge' produced. Thus, feminists are concerned with the relationship between the process and the product of feminist research and how epistemology becomes translated into practice (Letherby, 2003a, 2004).

There is critique of the 'romance with epistemology' which Kelly et al. (1994: 32) argue:

> seems more concerned with attempting to convince the predominantly male academy that a privilege status should be accorded to 'women's ways of knowing' than with enabling us

> to better discover and understand what is happening in women's lives, and how we might change it.

But for me (at least), 'knowing' and 'doing' are intertwined (see Letherby, 2003a, 2004) and the power of feminist methodology is its constant critical and self-critical engagement on the knowing/doing relationship.

An early critique of traditional male-centred 'scientific' epistemology was feminist empiricism (FE). FE leaves intact much of the traditional 'scientific' understandings of the principles of adequate inquiry but feminist empiricists seek to use 'traditional' methods and approaches more 'appropriately', challenging the way that methods are used rather than challenging the methods themselves. For example Magrit Eichler (1988) insists on non-sexist research and the elimination of sexism in titles; sexism in language; sexist concepts; sexism in research designs; sexism in methods and sexism in policy evaluation. FE then challenges the 'value-freedom' of traditional approaches but does not challenge the goals of such an approach (Stanley and Wise, 1993; Letherby, 2003a; Abbott et al., 2005).

Feminist standpoint epistemology (FSE), like feminist empiricism, begins from the view that 'masculine' science is bad science because it excluded women's experience. Feminist standpoint epistemologists advocate the development of a 'successor science' to existing dominant social science paradigms. They argue that the 'personal is political' and drawing on Marxist ideas suggest that women are an oppressed class and as such have the ability not only to understand their own experiences of oppression but also to see their oppressors' viewpoint. The view here is that research based on women's experience provides a more valid basis for knowledge because 'it gives access to a wider conception of truth via the insight into the oppressor' (Millen, 1997: 7.2). It is not just that the oppressed see more – their own experience and that of the privileged – but also that their knowledge emerges through the struggle against oppression: in this instance the struggle against men. Advocates of FSE argue that objectivity *is* possible but that the critical scrutiny of all aspects of the research process is necessary to achieve objectivity. This presents a challenge to traditional notions of objectivity which Harding (1993) argues are weak because the researchers' own values, assumptions and so on are hidden.[3] For Harding feminist objectivity acknowledges that '*knowledge and truth are partial, situated, subjective, power imbued, and relational.* [and] The denial of values, biases, and politics is seen as unrealistic and undesirable' (Hesse-Biber, 2007: 9 original emphasis).

There are some problems with taking a standpoint position. Focusing on the standpoint of one particular group can imply that their perspective is more real, more accurate and better than that of others. Also, if we accept a position which implies that there is only one (real, accurate, best) experience this can only be built upon the suppression of less powerful voices. The view that more oppressed or more disadvantaged groups have the greatest potential for knowledge also implies that the greater the oppression, the broader or more inclusive one's potential knowledge. This leads to an unproductive discussion about hierarchies of oppression, that is those who are more oppressed (if this is possible to measure) are potentially more knowledgeable. Even if we find the most oppressed group of all, how do we know that their way of seeing is the 'most true'? In addition, a specific problem with FSE is the focus (of some supporters) on biology and traditional values given to women and womanhood, which positively re-defines 'female' characteristics but in doing so reinforces feminine stereotypes (e.g. see Griffin, 1983; Ruddick, 1990 and for critique Wajcman, 1991; Letherby, 1994). Any standpoint position brings with it the danger of viewing a group of people as all the same and, as noted above, women are not a homogenous group.

Yet once we acknowledge the existence of several standpoints it becomes impossible to talk about 'independent truth' and 'objectivity' as a means of establishing superior or 'better knowledge' because there will always be alternative knowledge claims arising from contextually grounded knowledge of different standpoints (Letherby, 2003a).

Feminist postmodernism (FP) provides a radical critique of both traditional (masculine) approaches and FE and FSE. FP completely rejects the possibility of the objective collection of facts and from this perspective there are no universal theories and any attempt to establish a theory, a truth, is oppressive, whether from the perspective of male or female experience. Thus, FP (like other forms of postmodernism) rejects any claim to knowledge which makes an explicit appeal to the creation of a THEORY/a TRUTH. Feminist postmodernism then takes issue with the whole notion of a standpoint (Millen, 1997). For postmodernists there is not one truth but many truths, none of which is privileged (Flax, 1987; Ramazanoglu with Holland, 2002; Abbott et al., 2005). The emphasis on difference and the empowerment/emancipation of the other connects well with the concerns of feminists (e.g. Maynard, 1994; Letherby, 2003a; Hesse-Biber, et al., 2004) but there are problems here too; for if all explanations are equal feminist readings of female oppression are no more valid than any other perspective on women's experience (e.g. Jackson, 1992; Hesse-Biber et al., 1999).

PROCESS AND PRODUCT

There have been attempts to bring together the strengths of FSE and FP together and feminists argue that we should acknowledge that there are material conditions that women share and yet recognise the importance of difference and the significance of each of the multiple identities that individuals occupy (e.g. Di Stephano, 1990; Stanley and Wise, 1993; Letherby, 2003a; Naples, 2003). By doing this we acknowledge that gender is a 'difference that makes a difference' even if it is not the only difference, or even the defining feature of a persons' life (Di Stephano, 1990: 78).

Stanley and Wise's (1993, 2006) feminist fractured foundationalism (FFF) is a methodological approach which 'recognises both that there is a materially grounded social world that is real in its consequences (foundationalism), and insists that differently-situated groups develop often different views of the realities involved (fractured)' (Stanley and Wise 2006: 1.6). This position does not dispute the existence of truth and a material reality but acknowledges that judgements about them are always relative to the context in which such knowledge is produced. Further, this is an approach which aims for a transparent feminist research process and also challenges the view that researchers (in relation to their respondents) hold a position of 'epistemic privilege' (Stanley and Wise, 2006: 1.4).

In my own writings I have also tried to work towards a position that challenges traditional claims to objectivity and recognizes both the personhood of the researcher and the complexity of the researcher/respondent relationship and yet allows for useful things to be said. Given the association of objectivity with masculinity and 'masculine knowledge', many feminists reject the pursuit of objectivity and instead argue that 'bias' is inevitable. I agree and argue '. . . it is better to understand the complexities within research rather than to pretend that they can be controlled, and biased sources can themselves result in useful data' (Letherby, 2003a: 71). However, and ironically, 'this acknowledgement of subjectivity by feminists and the associated 'super-sensitivity' to the relevance of the personhood of the researcher could feasibly lead to the conclusion that our work is more objective, in that our work, if not value-free, is value-explicit' (Letherby, 2003a: 71). Yet, given that the word objectivity has so many connotations with the traditional, authorized approach I first referred to this acknowledgement of the inevitability of bias and the usefulness of reflection on it as 'theorized subjectivity' (Letherby, 2003a, b).[2]

In a critique of my position, Wise and Stanley (2003: 1.37) argue that 'theorised subjectivity' helps resist slipping back into conventional malestream notions of objectivity, which position the academic researcher/theorizer as different in kind from those she does research 'on' but retains, indeed is even predicated upon, an 'objectivity/subjectivity binary'. But for me 'theorized subjectivity' is different from 'strong objectivity' which:

> . . . combines the goal of conventional objectivity – to conduct research completely free of social influence and or personal beliefs – with the reality that no one can achieve this goal . . . and recognizes that objectivity can only operate within the limitations of the scientists' personal beliefs and experiences. (Hesse-Biber et al., 2004: 13, see also Harding, 1993)

'Theorized subjectivity' relies on a recognition that, while there is a 'reality' 'out there', the political complexities of subjectivities, and their inevitable involvement in the research/theorizing process make a definitive/final statement impracticable. Rather what is practicable, desirable and necessary is the theorization of the subjective (which includes the researcher's motivation and practice and the respondent's expectations and behaviour) and its significance to knowledge production (Letherby, 2003b). My starting point thus recognizes the values (both positive and negative) of the subjective.

Whilst I agree with Stanley and Wise (1993, 2006) that as researchers we are not intellectually superior to our respondents I do think it is important that we acknowledge our intellectual privileges and the implications of these. I agree that we all 'observe, categorize, analyse, reach conclusions' and thus that 'people theorize their own experience . . . and so researchers of the social are faced with an already "first order" theorized material social reality' (Stanley, 1990: 208). So I believe that respondents as well as researchers are reflexive, theorising individuals. Reflexivity – both descriptive (the description of one's reflection) and analytical (involving comparison and evaluation) – are essential parts of the research process and both researchers and respondents engage in it. But as researchers we are in a privileged position, not only in terms of access to multiple accounts, but also in terms of discipline training which enables us to engage in 'second order theorizing' which involves 'interpretation', not just 'description' of respondents' as well as the researchers' analytical processes (Letherby, 2002).

Furthermore, I, like other (feminist) researchers, do make strong knowledge claims and argue that my research is 'broader', 'fuller' than what has gone before. So, I am arguing that my research is in some ways 'superior', and stands as a successor to what has gone before:

> At many places in my writing I have presented several sides of an argument but accept that I evaluated these in terms of MY feminist and sociological standpoints. So I have the final say. I am not only claiming a privilege here but also a 'superiority': a right to be regarded as a knower in a way that respondents do not have. This may involve some misrepresentation of their words but a final decision is necessary if (feminist) research is to say anything at all, have any effect at all, and not be concerned solely with issues of representation rather than 'reality' itself (Kelly et al., 1994). (Letherby, 2003a: 4.4)

In my own work then I start from an epistemological position that rejects a simplistic foundationalist/standpoint position. I do believe that I am in a position to generate the 'true story' of any experience I research but I do believe that 'my story' can stand in opposition to and as a criticism of 'other stories' (both feminist and non-feminist, academic and lay). Thus, 'doing feminist methodology' highlights for me the problems in taking an epistemological position. I find myself arguing for an epistemological position somewhere between 'epistemic privilege' and postmodernism/relativism. I do not claim to have ever found 'the answer' but by starting to ask different questions of a different/under-researched groups I believe that my research highlights complexities of differences of experience that have previously not been considered. I do not claim that my work is by definition superior to other knowledge claims and indeed I accept that it should be subject to critical enquiry (Stanley and Wise, 1993). Thus, I agree with Millen who reflecting on her own research, writes:

> Whilst I do not believe that there is some sort of final, complete reality, and I am aware that my own subjectivity as a female feminist scientist has affected the outcome of my research. I do believe in a compromise between a completely subjective, unique and creative account of experience and a partly reproducible, objective and contextualised understanding in which my subjectivity has been critiqued. As Lorraine Gelsthorpe (1992: 214) remarks, 'a rejection of the notion of "objectivity" and a focus on experience in method does not mean a rejection of the need to be critical, rigorous and accurate'. (original emphasis). (Millen 1997: 8.5)

In terms of feminist 'claims to know', Louise Morley (1996: 140) notes that at one time, 'grounded theory was seen as highly compatible with feminism' because of its concern 'to locate theory in participants' worlds' and because 'it aided the process of breaking out of the confines of andocentric theory'. However, many feminists now reject grounded theory as 'no feminist study can be politically neutral, completely inductive or solely based on grounded theory, as all work is theoretically grounded' (Ibid. see also Stanley and Wise, 1990; Letherby, 2003a). Thus, the personhood of the researcher is relevant to theoretical analysis just as it is to research design and fieldwork and as Holland and Ramazanoglu argue, there is 'no technique of analysis or methodological logic that can neutralize the social nature of interpretation' (cited by Morley, 1996: 142). What is distinctive about feminist research is that it admits this. So for feminist methodologists 'conscious subjectivity' replaces the 'value-free objective' of traditional research (Duelli Klein cited by Wilkinson, 1986: 14; see also Morley, 1996; Letherby, 2002; and my position on 'theorized subjectivity' as outlined above).

Reflecting on the status of knowledge and issues of involvement Barbara Katz-Rothman (1996: 51) goes so far as to suggest that there has been a fundamental shift in methodological thinking where an 'ethic of involvement has replaced an ethic of objectivity'. From this perspective, writing from personal experience rather than from a position of 'detached objectivity' is likely to give the writer 'credentials'. She adds:

> In the circles I travel in now, if you see an article by a colleague on breast cancer you write to see how she is, wonder when she was diagnosed. If you see an article on Alzheimer's you assume someone's got a parent or in-law to help. I can track my colleagues' progression through the life cycle, through crises and passages, by article and book titles. (Katz-Rothman, 1996: 51).

I would suggest that this is going too far. Connections are made between respondents and researchers within the research process and experience is sometimes the motivation for research. But, it is not always possible or desirable to research issues close to us (Wilkinson and Kitzinger, 1996). Furthermore, identification should not be seen as a prerequisite to 'good' research and it is inaccurate to assume that *all* the research is grounded in the autobiography of researchers. In addition, researchers do not always identify with respondents and vice versa even when they share an experience and/or identity (Letherby and Zdrodowski, 1995). Thus, researchers do not have to draw on their own life experiences to do *good* work but our life experiences/identity are present at some level in all that we do and that it is important to acknowledge this (Cotterill and Letherby, 1993; Finc, 1994; Lctherby, 2003a; Katz Rothman, 2007). With this in mind I feel more comfortable with Katz Rothman's later reflections on the production of 'accountable' knowledge (see also Stanley, 1999; Letherby, 2003a):

> Whether the stories we use are our own, or those of our informants, or those we cull from tables of statistically organized data, we remain story-tellers, narrators, making sense of the world as best we can . . . . We owe something . . . to our readers and to the larger community to which we offer our work. Among the many things we owe them, is an honesty about

> ourselves: who we are as characters in our own stories and as actors in our own research. (Katz-Rothman, 2007: unpaginated)

Power then is a recognized part of the feminist methodological process, present through choice of topic, through fieldwork relationships to representation of findings. Yet, it is important not to over-passify respondents by always defining them as vulnerable for the power dynamics in the respondent/researcher relationship is often dynamic (Cotterill, 1992; Letherby, 2002, 2003a). Several writers – feminists and others – have also argued that emotion is an integral part of the research process (e.g. Ramsay, 1996; Young and Lee, 1996; Hesse-Biber, 2007b; Sampson et al., 2008). Traditionally women researchers across the social sciences have been portrayed as 'more accessible and less threatening than men' which coupled with their 'superior' communicative abilities has thought to make the interactions of fieldwork generally easier (Warren, 1988: 45). This supports more general stereotypical expectations of women as primarily responsible for 'working with emotions' (e.g. see Hochschild, (1983) 2003; James, 1989; Ramsay, 1996) and belittles the emotional work that women and men researchers do. Clearly, displays of emotion can be difficult and even dangerous for both the researcher and the researched and female and male researchers have written about this (e.g. see Peter Collins, 1988; Karen Ramsay, 1996). Helen Sampson and colleagues (2008) suggest though that emotional risk is gendered:

> The feminist agenda has arguably shifted the paradigm for qualitative research and women and feminists are not exclusively affected by this, just as the paradigm is not only influenced by feminist researchers. However, whilst there are male researchers who conduct research with concern for participant and researcher relationships, the evidence of the inquiry suggests that it is female researchers who suffer greater exposure to emotional risk as the result of their attachment to feminist methods. Male researchers' preoccupations appear to be more related to physical risk and their concerns revolve around physical violence and fear of such violence, of putting their 'bodies on the line' when doing research. (Sampson et al., 2008: 929)

Reflecting on the place of emotion in the research process Stanley and Wise (2006: 3.4) distinguish between the necessary 'analytical dimensions of emotion' and 'wallowing or describing emotion for the sake of moral credentialism'. But emotion *is* integral to (feminist) methodological processes not least because emotion is part of life and emotional expression within the research process is often data in itself (e.g. Hochschild, (1983) 2003; Young and Lee, 1996; Lee-Treweek and Linkoale, 2000; Gray, 2008).

SEARCHING FOR THE TRUTH OR WORKING FOR CHANGE?

> Reviewing debates in the methodological literature about competing definitions of 'political' . . . it becomes apparent that definitions vary tremendously in terms of how all encompassing they are. Narrow definitions tend to focus on 'explicit political ideologies and organized coercive institutional power of the modern nation state' (Hughes, 2000: 235) while others are much broader and note that all human interactions are micro-political processes. (Hammersley, 1995; Noaks and Wincup, 2004: 20)

Having established that the feminist research process is itself an emotional, political endeavour I return now to the political significance of the feminist research product for, as noted above, feminists are concerned to undertake research *for* rather than research *about* women. Martyn Hammersley and Roger Gomm (1997) argue that taking a political approach to research results in bias and leads to faulty knowledge. Thus, they argue that research should be motivated by the wish to produce the 'truth' and that 'knowledge production' must be systematically fore fronted in the collection, analysis and presentation of evidence. Not surprisingly, because of their open political commitment feminists are accused of not producing valid and authoritative knowledge. In answer to this I return to my view that subjectivity is inevitable within the research process and that reflection on the significance of this subjectivity adds to the accountability of our products. There are links here to the work of Karl Mannheim who argues that all knowledge is 'socially rooted' and . . . [t]he proper theme of [the sociology of knowledge] is to observe how and in what form intellectual life at a given historical moment is related to the existing social and political forces (Mannheim, 1968: 60, footnote).

The debate about whether or not research and researchers should have political aims extends beyond the feminist community[3] but specifically here for many feminists, feminist research *is* feminist theory in action. Thus, once again the values of feminist researchers are explicit which makes methodological transparency even more important (and I would suggest more likely) so that both our process and our resulting product are clear and thus open to critical scrutiny by others (Stanley, 1984; Stanley and Wise, 1993; Letherby, 2003a; Hesse-Biber, 2007a). A further complication here is that:

> Feminism is not a unitary category which encapsulates a consistent set of ideas within an identifiable framework. It is not a neat and coherent phenomenon which can be measured in quantitative terms (Griffin, 1989). So, as Griffin notes, the concept of feminism is under continual negotiation and there is not one feminism but many. So, for most women, the identification of oneself as feminist is not straightforward and involves social, political and personal decisions and choices. (Letherby, 2003a: 136)

Which means that researchers necessary to be sensitive to 'the conundrum of how not to undercut, discredit or write-off women's consciousness as different from our own' (Stanley, 1984: 201). In addition, as Ramazanoglu with Holland (2002) note, the development of and debates surrounding feminist methodology have taken place during a period of increasing inequality for many worldwide. With this in mind they suggest that: '[f]eminism remains inherently contradictory because gender is only part of people's lives. In order to transform unjust gender relations, more than gender must change' (p. 68). Reflecting on the relationship between politics and practice they add:

> The interrelations of gender with other power relations leave the inequalities and injustices of everyday life barely changed for the most disadvantaged. But for those who have the resources to do so, thinking about how and why feminists can justify their claims to knowledge has significant political and ethical implications. The inseparability of epistemology, ethics and politics encourages feminists to imagine how human relationships could be different, and how a better social world could work. (Ramazanoglu with Holland, 2002: 169)

FINAL THOUGHTS

As this chapter has highlighted, the discussions surrounding feminist methodology are part of a broader debate focusing on the relationship between knowing and doing/product and process within the social sciences. The feminist critique of the mainstream has in turn led to critique of the feminist approach and debate amongst feminists themselves. Researching and writing in a different and challenging way has attracted criticism. Taking 'gender (and other differences) seriously' and exploring associated new topics and new approaches sometimes leads to different forms of re/presentation and writing which too sometimes attracts criticism (e.g. Stanley and Wise, 1993; Temple, 1997; Letherby, 2003a). In 1995 Morley wrote:

> Academic feminism can serve to both articulate and challenge dominant ideologies. But there is always the threat of dismissal of this knowledge and its relegation to the status of maverick research, on the basis that emotions and personal involvement subvert knowledge. (p. 119)

Whilst some would argue that feminism no longer stands outside of the mainstream (see above) feminist methodologists who acknowledge the political aspects of the research process and who undertake their work with the hope of political impact are involved in methodological debates in particular and specific ways. Feminist researchers have of course been influenced by others [see Holland and Stanley (2007) for a consideration of the significance of Alvin Gouldner's ideas on reflexive Sociology, including reflexivity in the research process]. In turn feminist methodological practice has influenced the mainstream, not least in relation to the place and significance of politics, power and emotion with research and with reference to the relationship between the research process and the research product. But sometimes debts are forgotten and at times feminism's influence may be even denied, but this has always been the case. Arguably, one big influence of the feminist approach on the mainstream is the willingness to give honest accounts of the research experience. In 2003 I wrote:

> It is important to provide accounts of the fieldwork involved in empirical research because as many researchers (including feminists) have shown, there is often divergence between how research has actually been done and what is reported in research accounts and in textbooks. The result is that methodological accounts often do not prepare researchers for the problems and satisfactions they are likely to encounter . . . So, our experiences of research should be written up for others to consider, reflect on, agree with and reject. (Letherby, 2003: 159–60)

I still believe that we need to tell our stories, whether feminist or not.

NOTES

1 The standpoint approach is not the preserve of those concerned with researching women's experience. For example, some researchers working in the areas of disability, ethnicity and race and childhood argue for a standpoint

approach. When searching for an epistemology based on the experience of African American women, the values and ideas that African writers identify as being characteristically 'black' are often very similar to those claimed by white feminist scholars as being characteristically female. This suggests that the material conditions of oppression can vary dramatically and yet generate some uniformity in the epistemologies of subordinate groups (Hill-Collins, 1989). Similarly, researchers working in the area of childhood have argued that as both women and children are subject to patriarchy, those in power regard both groups as social problems and both groups find it hard to have their points of view heard and respected (Mayall, 2002).

2 I think that it is interesting to compare my argument for 'theorized subjectivity' (Letherby, 2003a, b) to Malcolm Williams' (2005) argument for 'situated objectivity'. Williams (2005: 108) argues for the existence of a value continuum and continues:

> To be objective in science commits us to values of law. Objectivity, then, is not an homogeneous value and its context will determine its relationship to other values (and therefore what it is in context). This is a key point, because when we talk about objectivity in science we are talking about something different to objectivity in other spheres. But, if my argument about the value continuum is right, then the meaning of objectivity in any discipline will relate to its internal use *and* its use in the relationship of that discipline to the rest of the social world (original emphasis).

Thus, 'theorized subjectivity' and 'situated objectivity' are both 'value-explicit' positions.

3 See, for example, the recent debate on 'public sociology' (Burawoy, 2005; Scott, 2005) and the debate on the future of Sociology in *Sociological Research Online*, Volumes 10 and 11 (Holmwood, 2007); some pieces in the special issue of *Sociology* on 'Sociology and its public face(s)', Volume 41, No. 5; and Holland and Stanley (2008).

REFERENCES

Abbott, P., Wallace, C., and Tyler, M. (2005) *An Introduction to Sociology: Feminist Perspectives*, 3rd edn. London: Routledge.

Annandale, E., and Clark, J. (1996) 'What is Gender? Feminist theory and the sociology of human reproduction'. *Sociology of Health and Illness*, 18(1): 17–44.

Bowles, G. and Klein, R.D. (eds) (1983) *Theories of Women's Studies*. London: Routledge and Kegan Paul.

Burawoy, M. (2005) 'For public sociology'. *American Sociological Review*, 70: 4–28.

Collins, P. (1998) 'Negotiated selves: reflections on 'unstructured' interviewing'. *Sociological Research Online*, 3(3): www.socresonline.org.uk/socresonline/3/3/2.html

Cook, J. and Fonow, M.M. (1990) 'Knowledge and women's interests: issues of epistemology and methodology in feminist sociological research'. In J. McCarl Nielsen (ed.) *Feminist Research Methods: Exemplary Readings in the Social Sciences*. Boulder, CO: Westview.

Cotterill, P. (1992) 'Interviewing women: issues of friendship, vulnerability and power'. *Women's Studies International Forum*, 15(5/6): 593–606.

Cotterill, P. and Letherby, G. (1993) 'Weaving stories: personal auto/biographies in feminist research'. *Sociology*, 27(1): 67–79.

Delamont, S. (2003) *Feminist Sociology*. London: Sage.

Di-Stephano, C. (1990) 'Dilemmas of difference: feminism, modernity and postmodernism'. In L. Nicholson (ed.) *Feminism/Postmodernism*. London: Routledge.

Eichler, M. (1988) *Non-Sexist Research Methods*. London: Allen and Unwin.

Evans, M. (1995) *An Introduction to Second Wave Feminism*. London: Sage.

Evans, M. (1997) *Introducing Contemporary Feminist Thought*. Cambridge: Polity Press.

Finch, J. (1984) 'It's great to have someone to talk to: the ethics and politics of interviewing women'. In C. Bell and H. Roberts (eds) *Social Researching: Politics, Problems, Practice*. London: Routledge and Kegan Paul.

Fine, M. (1994) 'Dis-tance and other stances: negotiations of power inside feminist research'. In A. Gitlin (ed.) *Power and Method: Political Activism and Educational Research*. London: Routledge.

Flax, Jane (1987) 'Postmodernism and gender relation in feminist theory'. *Signs: Journal of Women in Culture and Society*, 12: 334–51.

Gelsthorpe, L. (1992) 'Response to Martyn Hammersley's paper on "Feminist Methodology"'. *Sociology,* 26: 213–18.

Graham, H. (1984) *Women, Health and the Family.* Brighton: Wheatsheaf.

Gray, Breda (2008) 'Putting emotion and reflexivity to work in researching migration'. *Sociology,* 42(5): 935–52.

Griffin, S. (1983) 'Introduction'. In J. Caldecott and K. Leland (eds) *Reclaim the Earth.* London: The Women's Press.

Hammersley, M. and Gomm, R. (1997) 'Bias in social research'. *Sociological Research Online,* 2(1): www.socresonling.org.uk/socresonline/2/4/7

Harding, S. (1987) *Feminism and Methodology.* Milton Keynes: Open University Press.

Harding, S. (1993) 'Rethinking standpoint epistemology: what is strong objectivity?' In L. Alcoff and E. Porter (eds) *Feminist Epistemologies.* New York: Routledge.

Hesse-Biber, S.N. (ed.) (2007a) *Handbook of Feminist Research: Theory and Praxis.* California: Sage.

Hesse-Beber, S.N. (2007b) 'Feminist research: exploring the interconnections of epistemology, methodology and method'. In S. Hesse-Biber (ed.) *Handbook of Feminist Research.* California: Sage.

Hesse-Biber, S.N. and Gilmartin, C. and Lydenberg, R. (eds) (1999) *Feminist Approaches to Theory and Methodology: An Interdisciplinary Reader.* New York: Oxford University Press.

Hesse-Biber, S.N. Leavy, P., and Yaiser, M.L. (2004) 'Feminist approaches to research as a *process*: Reconceptualizing epistemology, methodology, and method'. In S.N. Hess-Biber and M.L. Yaiser (eds) *Feminist Perspectives on Social Research.* New York: Oxford University Press.

Hill-Collins, P. (1989) 'Black feminist thought'. *Signs: Journal of Women in Culture and Society,* 14(4): 745–73.

Hochschild, A.R. ((1983) 2003) *The Managed Heart: Commercialization of Human Feeling, 20th Anniversary edn.* Berkeley: University of California Press.

Hollands, R. and Stanley, L. (2007) 'Rethinking "current crisis" arguments: Gouldner and the legacy of critical sociology'. *Sociological Research Online,* 14(1): http://www.socresonline.org.uk/14/1/1.html.

Hollands, R. and Stanley, L. (2008) 'Rethinking "current crisis" arguments: Gouldner and the legacy of critical sociology'. *Sociological Research Online,* 14(1): www.socresonline.org.uk/14/1/1

Holmwood, J. (2007) 'Sociology as public discourse and professional practice: a critique of Michael Burawoy.' *Sociological Theory,* 25(1): 46–66

Jackson, S. (1992) 'The amazing deconstructing woman'. *Trouble and Strife,* 25: 25–31.

James, N. (1989) 'Emotional Labour: skills and work in the social regulation of feelings'. *Sociological Review,* 37(1): 5–52.

Katz-Rothman, B. (1996) 'Bearing witness: representing women's experiences of prenatal diagnosis'. In S. Wilkinson and C. Kitzinger (eds) *Representing the Other: A Feminism and Psychology Reader.* London: Sage.

Katz-Rothman, B. (2007) 'Writing ourselves in sociology'. *Methodological Innovations Online,* 2(1): www.methodolgicalinnovationsonline.org.

Kelly, L., Burton, S., and Regan, L. (1994) 'Researching women's lives or studying women's oppression? Reflections on what constitutes feminist research'. In M. Maynard and J. Purvis (eds) *Researching Women's Lives From a Feminist Perspective.* London: Taylor and Francis.

Laws, S. (1990) *Issues of Blood: The Politics of Menstruation.* Basingstoke: Macmillan.

Lee-Treweek, G. and Linkogle, S. (eds) (2000) *Danger in the Field: Risk and Ethics in Social Research.* London: Routledge.

Letherby, G. (1994) 'Mother or not, mother or what?: problems of definition and identity'. *Women's Studies International Forum,* 17(5): 525–32.

Letherby, G. (2002) 'Claims and disclaimers: knowledge, reflexivity and representation in feminist research'. *Sociological Research Online,* 6(4): www.socresonline.org.uk/6/4

Letherby, G. (2003a) *Feminist Research in Theory and Practice.* Buckingham: Open University Press.

Letherby, G (2003b) 'Reflections on where we are and where we want to be: Response to 'looking back and looking forward: some recent feminist sociology reviewed'. *Sociological Research Online,* 8(4): www.socresonline.org.uk/8/4

Letherby, G. (2004) 'Quoting and counting: an autobiographical response to Oakley'. *Sociology,* 38(1): 175–89.

Letherby, G. and Zdrokowski, D. (1995) 'Dear researcher: the use of correspondence as a method within feminist qualitative research'. *Gender and Society,* 9(5).

Mannheim, K. ((1936) 1968) *Ideology and Utopia: An Introduction to the Sociology of Knowledge* (with a Preface by Louis Wirth). London: Routledge and Kegan Paul.

Mayall, B. (2002) *Towards a Sociology of Childhood: Thinking from Children's Lives.* Buckingham: Open University Press.

Maynard, M. (1994) 'Race, gender and the concept of "difference" in feminist thought'. In H. Ashfar and M. Maynard (eds) *The Dynamics of 'Race' and Gender: Some Feminist Interventions.* London: Taylor and Francis.

Maynard, M. and Purvis, J. (eds) (1994) *Researching Women's Lives from a Feminist Perspective.* London: Taylor and Francis.

Millen, D. (1997) 'Some methodological and epistemological issues raised by doing feminist research on non-feminist women'. *Sociological Research Online,* 2(3): www.socresonline.org.uk/socresonline/2/3/3.html

Miner-Rubino, Jayaratner, K.E., and Konik, T.J. (2007) 'Using survey research as quantitative method for feminist social change'. In S.N. Hesse-Biber (ed.) *Handbook of Feminist Research.* California: Sage.

Morgan, D. (1981) 'Men, masculinity and the process of sociological inquiry'. In H. Roberts (ed.) *Doing Feminist Research.* London: Routledge and Kegan Paul.

Morley, L. (1995) 'Measuring the muse: feminism, creativity and career development in higher education'. In L. Morley and V. Walsh (eds) *Feminist Academics: Creative Agents for Change.* London: Taylor and Francis.

Morley, L. (1996) 'Interrogating patriarchy: the challenges of feminist research'. In L. Morley and V. Walsh (eds) *Breaking Boundaries: Women in Higher Education.* London: Taylor and Francis.

Naples, N.A. (2003) *Feminism and Method: Ethnography, Discourse Analysis and Activist Research.* New York: Routledge.

Noakes, L. and Wincup, E. (2004) *Criminological Research: Understanding Qualitative Methods.* London: Sage.

Oakley, A. (1981) 'Interviewing women: a contradiction in terms?'. In H. Roberts (ed.) *Doing Feminist Research.* London: Routledge.

Oakley, A. (1998) 'Gender, methodology and people's ways of knowing: some problems with feminism and the paradigm debate in social science'. *Sociology,* 32(3): 707–32.

Oakley, A. (1999a) 'Gender, methodology and people's ways of knowing: some problems with feminism and the paradigm debate in social science'. *Sociology,* 32(4): 707–32.

Oakley, A. (1999b) 'People's ways of knowing: gender and methodology'. In S. Hood, B. Mayall and S. Oliver (eds) *Critical Issues in Social Research.* Buckingham: Open University.

Oakley, A. (2004) 'Response to quoting and counting: an autobiographical response to Oakley'. *Sociology,* 38(1): 191–2.

Okley, J. (1992) 'Anthropology and autobiography: participatory experience and embodied knowledge'. In J. Okley and H. Callaway (eds) *Anthropology and Autobiography.* London: Routledge.

Platt, J. (2007) 'The Women's Movement and British Journal Articles 1950–2004', *Sociology,* 41(5): 961–75.

Ramazanoglu, C. (1989) 'On feminist methodology: male reason versus female empowerment'. *Sociology,* 26(2): 201–12.

Ramazanoglu, C. with Holland, J. (2002) *Feminist Methodology: Challenges and Choices.* London: Sage.

Ramsay, K. (1996) 'Emotional labour and qualitative research: How I learned not to laugh or cry in the field'. In E.S. Lyon and J. Busfield (eds) *Methodological Imaginations.* Basingstoke and London: Macmillan Press.

Reinharz, S. (1992) *Feminist Methods in Social Research.* Oxford: Oxford University Press.

Ribbens, J. (1989) 'Interviewing women: an unnatural situation'. *Women's Studies International Forum*, 12(16): 579–92.
Ribbens, Jane and Edwards, Rosalind (eds) (1998) *Feminist Dilemmas in Qualitative Research.* London: Sage.
Roberts, Helen (ed.) ((1981) 1990) *Doing Feminist Research.* London: Routledge and Kegan Paul.
Ruddick, S. (1990) *Maternal Thinking.* London: The Women's Press.
Sampson, H., Bloor, M., and Fincham, B. (2008) 'A price worth paying?: considering the "cost" of reflexive research methods and the influence of feminist ways of "doing"'. *Sociology,* 42(5): 919–34.
Scott, J. (2005) 'Sociology and its others: reflections on disciplinary specialisation and fragmentation'. *Sociological Research Online,* 10(1): www.socresonline.org.uk/10/1/scott.html
Smith, D. (1988) *The Everyday World as Problematic: a Feminist Sociology.* Milton Keynes: Open University Press.
Stacey, J. (1991) 'Can there be a feminist ethnography?'. In S. Gluck and D. Patai (eds) *Women's Words, Women's Words, Women's Words: The Feminist Practice of Oral History.* New York: Routledge.
Stanley, L. (1984) 'How the social science research process discriminates against women?'. In S. Acker and D. Warren Piper (eds) *Is Higher Education Fair to Women?* London: Routledge.
Stanley, L. (ed.) (1990) *Feminist Praxis: Research, Theory and Epistemology in Feminist Sociology.* London: Routledge.
Stanley, L. (1999) 'Children of our time: politics, ethics and feminist research processes'. Paper presented at 'Feminism and Educational Research Methodologies' conference. Institute of Education, Manchester Metropolitan University (June).
Stanley, L. (2005) 'A child of its time: hybrid perspectives on othering in sociology'. *Sociological Research Online,* 10(3): www.socresonline.org.uk/10/3
Stanley, L. and Wise, S. (1990) 'Method, methodology and epistemology in feminist research processes'. In L. Stanley (ed.) *Feminist Praxis: Research, Theory and Epistemology.* London: Routledge.
Stanley, L. and Wise, S. (1993) *Breaking Out Again: Feminist Ontology and Epistemology.* London: Routledge and Kegan Paul.
Stanley, L. and Wise, S. (2006) 'Putting it into practice: using feminist fractured foundationalism in researching children in the concentration camps of the South African War'. *Sociological Research Online*, 11(1): www.socresonline.org.uk/11/1/stanley
Stanley, L. and Wise, S. (2008) 'Feminist methodology matters!'. In D. Richardson and V. Robinson (eds) *Introducing Gender and Women's Studies* , 3rd edn. Houndsmills: Palgrave Macmillan.
Temple, B. (1997) '"Collegiate accountability" and bias: the solution to the problem?', *Sociological Research Online*, 2(4): www.socresonline.org.uk/socresonline/2/4/8
Wajcman, J. (1991) *Feminism Confronts Technology.* Cambridge: Polity.
Warren, C. (1988) *Gender Issues in Field Research.* Newbury Park, CA: Sage.
Wilkinson, S. (1986) *Feminist Social Psychology: Developing Theory and Practice.* Milton Keynes: Open University Press.
Wilkinson, S. and Kitzinger, C. (eds) (1996) *Representing the Other: A Feminism and Psychology Reader.* London: Sage.
Williams, M. (2005) 'Situated objectivity'. *Journal for the Theory of Social Behaviour,* 35(1): 99–120.
Wise, S. and Stanley, L. (2003) 'Review article: looking back and looking forward: some recent feminist sociology reviewed'. *Sociological Research Online*, 8(3): www.socresonline.org.uk/8/3
Young, E.H. and Lee, R. (1996) 'Fieldworker feelings as data: "emotion work" and "feeling rules" in the first person accounts of sociological fieldwork'. In V. James and J. Gabe (eds) *Health and the Sociology of the Emotions.* Oxford: Blackwell. pp. 97–114.

4

What is an Effect? Coming at Causality Backwards

David Byrne

> There is more to the world than patterns of events . . . (Andrew Sayer *Realism and Social Science*, Sage, 2000: 14)

Debates about causality have generally focused on the character of the causal side of the binary pair: Cause and Effect. Arguments here have been both ontological – in relation to the actual nature of causes themselves, and epistemological – in relation to how causes may be known. In crude summary the contemporary state of the debate might be characterized by saying that there is an ontological argument between positivists and critical realists with critical realists asserting the complex, contingent and generative character of cause, and an epistemological debate between critical realists and post-modernists with the latter reducing the social world to merely knowledge of it (Carter and New, 2004: 3). This chapter is firmly set in the critical realist camp and endorses both the understanding of causation as complex and generative and our ability to make knowledge claims about the world as it is. However, the argument draws on Complexity Theory (Byrne, 1998; Cilliers, 1998) as well as scientific realism and asserts that our understanding will be advanced if we think about the nature of effects in the social world.

The chapter will work through an account of the central premises of both complexity theory and scientific realism as these can be synthesized into 'complex realism'. It will develop an account of the nature of effects in terms of the character of the trajectory of complex systems and will work back from that account to a discussion of causality in complex systems in relation to the idea of control parameters. The argument will then be developed through two examples. The first of these will outline how we might describe complex social systems and their trajectories through social indicators measured across time. We can then observe effects, in the case of the example of the Leicester Urban Area, the effect of the transformation of an industrial urban system into a post-industrial urban system. This permits us to start to reason retroductively about the causes of such transformations, about the effects understood in terms of radical shifts in the trajectories of the system. The second example will use a study of school outcomes in the North East of England to show how we can deploy systematic comparison in an exploratory fashion in order to identify causes of difference. This approach gels very well with the important principle of path dependency for social systems – in other words our understanding is that the range of future possibilities for such systems is a function of their past history.

It is important to emphasize that our account of causality is based on a retroductive approach. We observe what has happened and attempt to generate an account of why it has happened. So we necessarily start from the effect – from what is, and go backwards to the best explanation which seems to fit the facts, the essence of abductive reason with abduction and retroduction understood as essentially synonyms.

The central premise of social complexity is simple. The interesting objects in the social world at whatever level – micro, meso, macro – are themselves complex systems. There are numerous definitions of complex systems and it is useful to reproduce both an early version and a canonical more recent version before turning to a specification in the language of mathematical dynamics. Let us begin with Weaver who distinguished a set of problems which could neither be described in the simple deterministic terms of Newtonian mechanics nor addressed by probabilistic techniques in the form of frequentist statistical methods which describe the aggregate behaviour of multiple simple entities. It was not just a matter of multiple variate components:

> . . . much more important than the mere number of variables is the fact that these variables are all interrelated . . . these problems, as contrasted with the disorganised situations with which statisticians can cope, *show the essential feature of organisation.* We will therefore refer to this group of problems as those of *organised complexity.* (Weaver, 1958 (italics in original))

Rosen extends this account by specific reference to causality. He defines a complex system precisely in terms of the necessarily complex character of generative causality for such systems:

> . . . a simple system is one to which a notion of state can be assigned once and for all, or more generally, one in which Aristotelian causal categories can be independently segregated from one another. Any system for which such a description cannot be provided I will call complex. Thus, in a complex system, the causal categories become intertwined in such a way that no dualistic language of state plus dynamic laws can completely describe it. Complex systems must then process mathematical images different from, and irreducible to, the generalized dynamic systems which have been considered universal. (Rosen, 1987: 324)

It is rather important to distinguish complex systems from other systems which have the potential for non-linear change. Mathematical dynamics employs the concept of state space – If a system can be described in terms of n variables, then its state space is n dimensional and we can describe its condition at any single point in time in terms of coordinates in that n dimensional space where the coordinates are the values of the n variables at that single point in time. If we have measurements of the values of the variables through time, then we have an $n + 1$ dimensional space, with the extra variable being time and we can observe the path the system takes through its phase space. This path may take the form of an *attractor*. If the behaviour of the system was truly random, then as we measured its condition at repeated time points (note such measurements are inherently discrete rather than continuous) then it could be anywhere in the state space at any time point. If, however, we find that its trajectory is confined to a limited part of the state space, then we describe the path of that trajectory as an attractor. Mathematical dynamics distinguishes between conservative systems which essentially do not have the potential to transform the 'volume' (general shape) of their attractor and dissipative systems in which the form of the attractor may change. Another way of putting this is to distinguish among equilibric systems which do not change their position in the state space, close to equilibric systems which move back towards their original position if disturbed, and far from equilibric systems in which radical transformation of the attractor space of the individual system is possible.

All complex systems are non-linear in potential behaviour – that is to say, changes in state can be radical and not proportionate to changes in the factors generating transformation – but not all non-linear systems are complex systems. It is important to distinguish between chaotic systems, in which very small changes in the values of system significant variates – control parameters[1] in dynamics terminology – can generate radical changes in the attractor state of the system and do so repeatedly, and complex systems which are substantially more robust but do have the potential for radical change.

In general, mathematical dynamics deals with the trajectories of single systems but it is useful for us to consider multiple systems – in the language of the physical sciences, ensembles of systems – and to consider that we might extend the idea of attractor to represent a domain in state space occupied by a set of systems with other attractors representing other domains. Position in a given attractor can then be regarded as representing membership of a category, that is, as a specification of kind. In this sense we can see change for a single system as involving movement to a new attractor set which implies that there has been a change in the kind of thing the system is.

Let me present a list of the characteristics of complex systems understood in this way:

1 Complex systems are inherently emergent. They cannot be understood by a process of analysis alone. Neither are they simply holistic. Understanding must address parts, the whole, interactions among parts and interactions of parts with the whole.

2 Complex systems are not chaotic. Therefore, they do not change radically and frequently in consequence of small changes in key determinant parameters.
3 Complex systems are robust. Most of the time they continue to maintain the same general form with ongoing constant small changes within that form. In complexity terminology, most of the time their state space coordinates are located in a torus attractor. However, robustness is not the same as stasis, even with stasis understood as allowing change within an attractor. Robustness also resides in the capacity for radical change with continued existence.
4 Significant change in complex systems is qualitative and radical, not incremental. In complexity terminology it takes the form of phase shifts. Change in complex systems can be thought of as a process of metamorphosis – the system changes radically whilst continuing to exist. In terms of state space it moves to a new attractor.
5 Complex systems are nested and intersecting. All systems are contained within and intersect with other systems. Boundaries are fuzzy and plastic. Moreover, the nested character of a set of systems is not hierarchically deterministic. Systems nested within have a recursive deterministic relationship with the systems within which they are nested. Potentially every level has implications for every other level.
6 In consequence of the above, complex systems display a high degree of *autonomy*. This does not mean that they can become anything, but it does mean that what they can and do become is in large part a function of the system, its own components and systems nested within it. It is, however, important to recognize that the context – surrounding environment of the system – has implications for the range of potential new states available to any system.
7 The range of potential future states for a system which undergoes phase shift transformation is greater than one, but nonetheless limited. There are alternative futures but not an infinity of possibilities. Future state is path dependant but not path 'determined' in the usual sense of determination as exact specification.

It seems useful to introduce a term: 'effectality' – a neo-logism coined to try to express the view that in dealing with complex systems we really need to think as much about 'what is an effect?' as we do about the nature of causality itself. The central proposition around which the argument of this piece is founded is that for complex systems, effects are to be understood in terms of the location of those systems within their possible state space. We might consider effects to then fall into four kinds. The first is the kind of 'specifying original position' – in other words, what kind of thing is the complex system – another way of saying what is its position in the possible state space – when it first comes into existence. The second is the kind of 'staying the same' – in terms of the language of attractors describing a system which stays within the boundaries of a torus attractor. Aspects may change somewhat over time but the system remains essentially what it was. The third kind of effect is the kind of 'undergoing phase shift' – which at least metaphorically implies that the system while remaining coherent changes its fundamental character. Crooke et al. note that Parsons made exactly this kind of distinction between close to equilibric and far from equilibric systems in terms of the causal processes which he considered drove social change.

> Parsons makes a distinction between what might be called developmental processes and what might be called phase-shift processes. The former consist in a continuous and incremental elaboration and separation of sub-systems, which does not alter the general overall pattern of society. By contrast, phase-shift processes are fundamental differential leaps or evolutionary breakthroughs, typically caused outside the social realm (e.g. in the realms of culture or personality) which reorient the social pattern. (Crooke et al., 1992: 5)

The biological process of metamorphosis provides us with a good heterologous analogy (see Khalil, 1996) for phase shifts in social systems, not least because there is a direction to metamorphosis, although social systems may revert to their earlier form. The final kind of effect is 'terminating' – the system ceases to exist in any form which can be regarded as continuing its inherent integrity. Thus what matters about complex systems is how they come into existence, whether they stay much the same – occupy a torus attractor to use the language of mathematical dynamics – or change to some new state which is radically different, whilst maintaining their integrity as a system – or cease to exist. Understood in this way the nature of an effect for an existing system is rough stability – the essential character of social systems in the Parsonian framework, or radical and qualitative change which may involve termination of the system although it usually does not do so. Effects for existing systems are either about close to equilibric stability or non-linear transformation. We can also see both the creation of a new system and the termination of a system as non-linear transformations. In neither case – stability or transformation – are we dealing with the incremental linear change as this is understood in the causal descriptions which characterize Newtonian mechanics and which have served as a metaphor for change across the whole of the social sciences but particularly for that form of quantitative social science which draws on the General Linear Model.

Another way of thinking about this is to recognize that we can see the terms trajectory and history as synonyms when we are considering complex systems. Here we can profitably use Braudel's formulation of the idea of the *longue durée*. A system whose trajectory can be described by a torus attractor – conventionally represented in three dimensions by a doughnut or three dimensional ring – is essentially passing through a *longue durée*. That is to say whilst things change, the essential character of the system remains the same, as for the social organization of early modern rural France. Phase shifts mark the end of the *longue durée*. This approach which directs us away from understanding effects in terms of changes in single dependent variables measured at whatever level, the usual focus of linear causal modelling, requires us to devote careful attention to the means by which we might identify effects. That is to say how can we establish that something has stayed the same or changed its kind?

Identification of the special instances of coming into being or ceasing to be are relatively straightforward but establishing whether a change is one of kind or simply movement within the space state boundaries of present kind is more difficult. Here we are faced with establishing transitions which involve changes of kind.

A CHANGE OF KIND IN A SINGLE SYSTEM – INDUSTRIAL TO POST-INDUSTRIAL LEICESTER

Let me illustrate this with an example drawn from my current research project investigating the nature of post-industrial industrial cities. All sorts of relevant issues emerge in work of this kind. There is an issue of definition by boundary setting. As Cilliers notes:

> Boundaries [of complex systems] are simultaneously a function of the activity of the system itself, and a product of the strategy of description involved. In other words, we frame the system by describing it in a certain way (for a certain purpose) but we are constrained in where the frame can be drawn. The boundary of the system is therefore neither a function of our description, nor is it a purely natural thing. (2001: 141)

What are the boundaries of a city? Traditionally, statistical descriptions take administrative definitions but these, whilst reflecting realities of governance, are themselves constructs.[2] I have tried to work with available approximations of urban areas – in the case of my UK examples with definitions based on judgements in relation to development patterns and journey to work areas. So for Leicester I define the city as the City of Leicester plus all of an adjacent district and parts (wards) of two other districts. However, this definition itself is dynamic. Certainly at the time of the UK's first census in 1801 or even in 1901 or 1951 it would have been incorrect to include free standing agricultural, industrial and coal mining villages as part of the Leicester metropolitan area. Suburbanization and industrial change has made them now in important but not absolute senses – Leicester.[3]

Leicester provides a good example to illustrate the argument about change in complex systems. Let us agree with Jane Jacobs, a participant in the original Macy seminars – a key intellectual event in the development of complexity theory, that cities are complex systems:

> Cities happen to be problems in organized complexity, like the life sciences. They present 'situations in which half a dozen quantities are all varying simultaneously *and in subtly interconnected ways*' [original emphasis]. Cities, again like the life sciences, do not exhibit *one* [original emphasis] problem in organized complexity, which if understood explains all. They can be analysed into many such problems or segments, which, as in the case of the life sciences are also related with one another. The variables are many, but they are not helter-skelter; the are 'interrelated into an organic whole'. (Jacobs, 1961: 433)

If we look at the trajectory of Leicester over the last thousand years we find that a market town with a population of 2,000 at the time of the Domesday book was by the end of the eighteenth century a mix of market town and industrial centre[4] with a population of 17,000. The town grew with great rapidity through the nineteenth century on the basis of industrialization to achieve a population of 230,000 by 1914 and 290,000 by 1961 which was the peak of its industrial fortunes. That population was simply the population of the administrative unit called Leicester City. The population of the Leicester urban system was roughly double that of the core administrative unit.

Currently, as of the 2001 census, Leicester City has a population of 280,000, which is 47% of the total population of the Leicester Urban Area[5] which has a population of 579,000. For the urban area as a whole there are 260,000 employed workers of whom 46% are female and 35% worked in industrial sectors.[6] Economically active people comprised 62% of the urban area's adult[7] population.

Of the economically active, 65% were full time employees, 19% were part time employees, 11% were self-employed and 6% were unemployed. Of the urban area's population, 75% described themselves as 'White British', 15% as Indian or Indian British and no other ethnic identity exceeded 1% of the population. There were 230,000 households in the urban area. Of these, 70% were owner-occupied, 19% were social housing and the rest were other tenures. Twenty-seven per cent of households contained dependent children. Of the households containing dependent children, 63% contained two married parents, 13% contained two cohabiting parents and 24% were headed by a single parent. The above standard descriptive statistics for 2001 can be considered as constituting measurements at a single time point of ten variate traces[8] of the trajectory of the Leicester Urban Area as a complex urban system, viz.

1 Total population of the area.
2 Distribution of the population between urban core and suburban / exurban periphery.
3 Ethnic composition of the population.
4 Proportion of population aged 16–74 economically active.
5 Total employed population.
6 Distribution of the working population by sector of employment.
7 Distribution of the working population by kind of economic activity.
8 Distribution of the working population by gender.
9 Total households.
10 Tenure of households.

Some of the above variates are absolute measures, for example, total population, and some are relative proportions. We can treat all of them as representing the individual dimensions of the multi-dimensional state space of the Leicester Urban Area. Let us consider what the measurements were at another point in time – in 1971 when the present local authority boundaries were established. This is laid out in Table 4.1 together with some available data from 1911.[9] Boundaries and definitions change but since we are dealing with variate traces of a complex system and not with reified variables, then this does not matter. We have time-ordered descriptions of the system as a whole which are slightly differently constructed – and we have to be sure that the constructions, that is, the operationalizations are only slightly different – and on that basis we can see if things have changed in any radical way. The very obvious change on this time series is in the significance of industrial employment. In the industrial era, which certainly lasted until 1971, it ran at about 60% of all employment. By 2001 it was less than 60% of that level at 35% overall. Actually at this level the Leicester Urban Area is significantly less de-industrialized than most former industrial UK conurbations but it still has de-industrialized in terms of employment base from what had been one of the world's highest ever levels. Leicester traditionally was a centre for industries which employed women, an important factor in the city's historic prosperity since working class households were not dependent on one wage, so its workforce has not changed dramatically in terms of gender composition, in contrast with industrial city regions with a history of primarily male employment in heavy industry.

There are other significant changes. In 1911 less than 3% of Leicester and Leicestershire's population were born outside the UK (which then included the whole of Ireland). By 1961 the equivalent figure was still just over 3% but by 1971 this had risen to nearly 9% and although birthplace no longer is a significant descriptor for ethnic differentiation by 2001 we can see that 25% of the Leicester Urban Area's population self-identified as other than White British. This figure will have risen significantly since then with a large recent immigration of workers from EU accession states, principally Poland. Another change of significance is in household composition. In the East Midlands tenure changes were not so dramatic as in other post-industrial industrial city regions but the location of dwellings and population did shift with a definite movement towards suburban and ex-urban residence for families countered by an increase in single young people, especially third level students, living in the urban core.

Table 4.1 Leicester Urban Area – Characteristics over time

	2001	*1971*	*1911*
Total population	579,000	534,000	Would not be meaningful to identify an urban area at this date
Percentage of ethnic identity other than White British	24.7	8.8*	Less than 1**
Total of working age	420,000	392,000	School leaving age much lower so not valid comparison
Total economically active	261,000	261,000	235,000
Percentage of working age economically active	62.1	66.5	Very different conception of working age
Percentage of economically active female	46.6	38.2	35.1**
Percentage of economically active in industrial employment	34.5	58.7**	63.1**
Total households	230,000	177,000	Only figures for dwellings available
Percentage of owner occupied	70.0	57.1	At this point great majority of accommodation privately rented
Percentage of social tenants	18.7	23.7	See above

* Based on birthplace data.

** Figures for the whole of Leicestershire.

CHANGES OF KIND IN MULTIPLE SYSTEMS – EXPLORING ENSEMBLE OF TRAJECTORIES THROUGH CLASSIFICATION

The assertion that the Leicester city region has undergone a transformation from an industrial to a post-industrial form is based essentially on a single measure of the actual employment base of the working population which could be graphed over time and which shows a massive decline between 1971 and 1991 at which point it roughly stabilizes.[10] There really is no challenge to the notion that this city has de-industrialized but we cannot construct a general description of social change on the basis of a single case. Such single cases have ideographic value but we always want to have some basis for generalization. Here we can return to the idea of exploring the trajectories of ensembles of cases. Suppose we are interested in the trajectory of Western and Central European industrial city regions between 1961 and 2001. We might decide to include in this set all Western and Central European city regions with a population of over 500,000 and which are not capital cities. All the issues about boundaries and incompatibility of data sets arise, but the latter in particular do not matter much if we think of measures as traces rather than as operationalizations of 'real' variables. In 1961 these cities were industrial. Even European capital cities had very large industrial workforces but all non-capital cities of 500,000 plus were primarily industrial zones. Now many are not and at the same time the transition to post-industrial status has happened in different ways for different places. There are roughly 140 such industrial city regions in Western and Central Europe and we can classify them using standard numerical taxonomy approaches such as Cluster Analysis or by using a classificatory neural net approach.

Another element of change is in relation to the 'ethnic' composition of such cities. As it happens, despite frequent statements that Leicester is on course to become the UK's first majority ethnic city, this is not the case[11] and a combination of Polish and other accession state immigration and convergence of immigrant fertility to the UK norm means that this is not happening. Actually even if it did, it would not in Leicester's case represent a fundamental change of any significance since the adherence of most of Leicester's largest 'ethnic' group, Hindus of Gujarati origin, to UK social norms and cultural forms in public life means that they are not engaged in 'change of kind' cultural transformation. These remarks stem from a consideration of the differences between Leicester and Rotterdam, another European 'post-industrial' city with a very large 'ethnic' component in its population. Rotterdam's Dutch ex-colonials from Surinam and Indonesia do not represent a cultural challenge. Indeed most Surinamese supported Pym Fortyn's extraordinary 'culturalist' politics which began in that city and represented one of the most significant elements in European politics. It is the very large Muslim minorities, especially the Moroccan minority, in the city which are seen (perhaps wrongly, it has to be said although this will have consequences) as a challenge to the Dutch norm of live and let live. So we cannot simply see a measure of differential ethnicity as meaning the same thing in different places.

We have to contextualize precisely because that enables us to explore difference. It is by the identification of factors of difference – John Stuart Mills' original method of differences – that we get to start to construct a retroductive account of causality, although unlike Mills, we are not seeking single specific causes but rather complex interactions of factors.

The crucial thing is to construct typologies through classification at different time points. There is of course a lot of work involved in assembling even crudely approximate data sets but this can be done and we can construct our typologies AND map changes between them. The key thing here is that membership of a class in a typology should be regarded as a marker for an effect and we can map both changes, that is transition from industrial to post-industrial form, and look at the particular kind of post-industrial form. Here effects are constituted in terms both of stasis against change, and if change, then the particular kind of change.

This idea has general application when we have data for an ensemble of systems. For example, Wendy Dyer (in this volume) has used it to track trajectories of persons passing through a custody diversion process in Teesside in the UK. She recorded all stages for the cases in that system – what they were like on entry, what processes were applied to them by the custody diversion process in terms of assessment and provision, and their status in relation to re-offending at points in time afterwards. Here the effects were re-offending within a given time period with a further division of re-offending into violent crime and other crimes. Dyer was able to construct models of the multiple different combinations of initial status and treatment process which were associated with the different outcomes of offending or not re-offending. We can use this form of reasoning to describe patterns of effects whenever we have longitudinal data for ensembles of similar cases which enables us to construct such time-ordered trajectory mappings.

EXPLORING CAUSALITY WITH EFFECTS UNDERSTOOD IN THIS WAY

The implications of this proposal about the nature of effects is that we explore causality by working backwards from specific different effects – retroduction. In other words we should engage with processes of retroduction to explain what has happened and in terms of applied social science develop a retrodictive approach to guiding actions towards the achievement of desired outcomes. This is very much in accord with the general critical realist programme of explanation. We are dealing with effects understood as system states and understand these system states to be the product of complex AND multiple generative mechanisms. Charles Ragin's conception of configuration and his method of Qualitative Comparative Analysis (QCA) (Ragin, 2000) enable us to address causation in precisely this retroductive fashion. Fielding and Lee describe the procedure thus: 'Unlike the data matrix in quantitative research, where the analytic focus is on variables displayed in the columns of the table, it is the rows which are important here. What is being examined for each row is the configuration of causes associated with the presence or absence of an outcome for the case' (1998: 158). There is explicit recognition of 'causal complexity' (Coverdill et al., 1994: 57), that is of the possibility of multiple and/or different causal patterns associated with a given outcome. Essentially the procedure starts with a specification of different effects – understood in complexity terms as different states of similar systems in an ensemble of systems – and works out on the basis of descriptions of the characteristics of those system, sets of causal configurations which give rise to the outcomes observed. The simplest way of illustrating this is in relation to a binary effect – where an outcome either happens or does not as with re-offending in Dyer's study.

CONTROL PARAMETERS

The idea of control parameter is central to understanding of causality in complex systems. Essentially the idea is that the trajectories of complex systems do not depend on all aspects of those systems but on subsets of them. This may be a single aspect – for example the Black Death as an external disturbance transformed feudal Europe. The robust system of feudalism with embedded emergent capitalist cities was transformed by the resultant labour shortages and generalization of wage labour so that the capitalist form spread generally *despite* the fact that urban mortality was higher than rural mortality. However, it is much more likely to be combinations of internal aspects in interaction along with external factors. So the de-industrialization of Western and Central Europe's industrial city regions reflects the external factors of generalized massive increases in industrial productivity in capitalism and the ability of capital to move globally to cheaper labour bases. That said the actual and very different post-industrial trajectories of those systems depend on the interaction of internal aspects of the city regions with national characteristics particularly at the policy level and with global factors. This indicates that causality is not simply internal but depends on the interaction of systems at all levels with those within which they are nested.

The QCA method suggested above is illustrated by examples which utilize variate trace information which describes only the internal aspects of the systems themselves. However, we can easily see how it can be extended to include information about variate difference in relation to systems external to the systems for which we are exploring causality. The example of city regions illustrates this. We can easily incorporate national level variate traces which differ from nation state to nation state. What this amounts to is an explicit and systematic way of conducting comparative research in general.

At first sight the idea of control parameters, of aspects of complex systems which have a governing influence on the trajectories of the systems, may seem to contradict the anti-reductionist character of complexity theory as a whole. In this way of thinking the control parameter is not likely to be a single variate characteristic unless that characteristic is on its own both a sufficient and necessary cause.

We may well have single variate characteristics which are sufficient causes without being necessary but far more common is the situation where we have a whole set of complex configurations as sufficient but not necessary causes. We can see these complex configurations as control parameters, albeit in most cases, since they do not retrodictively describe the outcome for all cases with that set of characteristics, as probabilistic rather than deterministic control parameters. Even understood as probabilistic these methods are actually better at predicting outcomes than conventional linear methods such as logistic regression but the key point is that they are part of an iterative process of establishing causality. In other words we establish what we can and then proceed to look for other variates to enter into the causal story.

Configurations whether expressed as sets of variates or in textual description are models of control parameters. But they are models which are simultaneously incomplete and necessary. Cilliers addresses this issue through a discussion of models which whilst they can never be perfect representations of complex systems may still be useful to us:

> . . . models have to reduce the complexity of the phenomena being described, they have to leave something out. However, we have no way of predicting the importance of that which is not considered. In a non-linear world where we cannot track a clear causal chain, something that may appear to be unimportant now may turn out to be vitally important later. Or *vice versa* of course. Our models have to "frame" the problem in a certain way and this framing will inevitably introduce distortions . . . . This is not an argument against the construction of models. We have no choice but to make models if we want to understand the world. It is just an argument that models of complex systems will always be flawed in principle and that we have to acknowledge these limitations. (2001: 138)[12]

If we think of configurations, with that term covering both quantitative and qualitative representation of configurations, as models, then we can proceed further following Cilliers and understand that our models are attempts: '. . . to grasp the *structure* (original emphasis) of complex systems' (2001: 139). Here structure is *not* a static arrangement, a meaning which the common usage of the word can only too easily imply. It is the whole dynamic system in action with potential for radical change being part of the character of that system. Moreover, complex systems are structured in hierarchies not of strictly defined and separate subunits but, as Cilliers puts it, of messy (with the messiness being indispensable), interpenetrating and mutable (although robust) hierarchical orders of components (2001: 143). Of particular significance is that these hierarchies are context dependent. In general they are inherently mutable entities.

The implication of this for case based research, whether the ideographic investigation of the specific instance or comparative investigation of multiple instances, is that what we are trying to do is to identify, however incompletely, temporarily *and* locally, the nature of the structure of control parameters *and* the potential of those parameters for bringing about a given state of the system – a qualitative condition of the case. That is what we can do in terms of establishing causality on the basis of cases, and we can do so without falling into the trap of reification of variables outwith cases which has been the false road of quantitative social science for so long and has led to a wholly artificial and disabling separation of the quantitative and qualitative modes of social research.

DETERMINISM VS. PROBABILITY

Another point worth making before concluding is that these methods are best applied when we have, as we so often do have, information about all the cases of interest to us rather than about any probabilistic sample of cases. For example, for Western and Central European post-industrial industrial cities – we do have information about all cases in the form of data from Eurostat. There are missing values but all the cases are present. This is actually a very common situation and we should be careful not always to think in terms of establishing probabilistic causality on the basis of inferential statistics. Probabilistic causality is about predicting what will happen on the basis of information about a given set of cases across that set of cases as a whole. Comparative methods based on data about all cases, albeit all cases within a given range of time, enable us to move towards what might best be called 'incomplete deterministic' accounts of causation. When we establish a truth table characteristically several, often indeed most, of the configurations have 'contradictory' outcomes. In other words not all the cases with the set of attributes represented by the configuration, the row in the truth table, have the same outcome state. For example in a study looking at secondary schools in the North East of England (Byrne, forthcoming) of twelve schools which had the characteristics

> no sixth form – that is, only delivered the curriculum to age 16,
> high proportion of children from low income households indicated by eligibility for free school meals,
> high proportion of children with special needs,
> mixed gender entry,
> comprehensive entry,
> high absenteeism,
> not religious.

Only one belonged to a set of 'adequately achieving schools' established by cluster analysis of examination performance indicators. Examination of qualitative information about that school established that it had in place a fully developed system of staff led and senior pupil engaging mentoring from the point where children entered the school. The other eleven did not. That appeared to account for the difference in outcome.

Rihoux and Ragin pertinently remarked that:

> . . . policy researchers, especially those concerned with social as opposed to economic policy, are often more interested in different kinds of cases and their different fates than they are in the extent of the net causal effect of a variable across a large encompassing population of observations. After all, a common goal of social policy is to make decisive interventions, not to move average levels or rates up or down by some miniscule fraction. (2004: 18)[13]

This is absolutely correct and the example described above illustrates how we can use the comparative approach to determine what *might* make a difference and then try it out. Retroductively we can use the method, which moves in this sort of example for using QCA to explore a quantitative data set to then turning to qualitative materials to expand our causal understanding *in context*, to establish what has made a difference to the way things are now.

The final concluding point is that this kind of approach which defines effects in terms of system state and then works backward to try to establish by whatever means, (because narratives are just as valid an approach as for example QCA), to establish what caused that system state as opposed to other possible system states, is both deterministic and breaks down the wholly artificial divide between quantitative and qualitative ways of describing social causality. Sure, QCA uses numbers as attribute labels and attributes have to be constructed from either measures or qualitative descriptions, but this is simply a way of representing compound elements in causal process. We do not have reified variables and we should not have a privileging of measurement and its products. What we have are multi-mode and multi-form representations of real systems and their trajectories which can inform our search for causal accounts in the social world.

NOTES

1 Although the language of control parameters tends to still describe these as single 'variables' it is crucial to recognize that control parameters are often complex entities in the form of either sub-systems of the system itself or complex interactions of system sub-systems with elements external to the system.

2 So London has a population of seven million but is actually at the centre of a complex poly-centric conurbation with a population of some twenty million which extends into three English regions – London itself, the South East and the Eastern region.

3 Interestingly there is now a real question as to whether what certainly was a real spatial entity from the time of the Mercian kingdom of the sixth century A.D. through the mid twentieth century – the village based agricultural and industrial county of Leicestershire surrounding a major city, has any real existence beyond the non-trivial ones of being both an administrative entity and a source of local identity. It certainly is no longer in any meaningful sense a social system other than in relation to those two components and if, as current UK central government policy would like, its administrative function is transferred to sets of districts, then it would become simply a residual source of identity through sport.

4 Leicester's industrial development was based on light industrial innovation in the form of stocking making frames although it also had access to coal from the Leicester coalfield.

5 Leicester City plus the adjacent districts of Oadby and Wigston, Blaby and Charnwood.

6 Defined here as including manufacturing, mining, construction and transport/communications.

7 That is aged between 16 and 74.

8 See Byrne (2002) for an explanation of this term.

9 Local government in England was substantially revised in 1974. Some of the 1971 census data was recomputed for the new local authority boundaries but not employment data. However, Leicester and the other parts of the Leicester Urban Area were the most industrial parts of what has always been an industrial county so using figures for the whole county probably slightly underestimates the industrial employment levels in the Leicester Urban Area.

10 It must be emphasized that this is primarily a change in employment base. The decline in proportion of local GDP due to industry is much less than the decline in employment because one of the drivers is increased productivity in existing industry as well as the relocation of industrial production and capital usually referred to as the new international division of labour.

11 I am grateful to Ludi Simpson for advice on this.

12 For me the additional factor in our modelling is the potential for purposeful action to achieve a possible outcome. In other words models plus action may enable determination.

13 To which I will add that this applies with equal force to practitioners in all forms of medical and social intervention. There is enormous emphasis these days on evidence based practice but most of the evidence is based precisely on the frequentist statistical analysis of linear cause across 'large encompassing populations', which evidence *cannot* be applied to the single case with which the practitioner is at any one time engaged.

REFERENCES

Byrne, D. (1998) *Complexity Theory and the Social Sciences.* London: Routledge.

Byrne, D. (2002) *Interpreting Quantitative Data.* London: Sage.

Carter, R. and New, C. (eds) (2004) *Making Realism Work.* London: Routledge.

Cilliers, P. (1998) *Complexity and Postmodernism.* London: Routledge.

Cilliers, P. (2001) 'Boundaries, hierarchies and networks in complex systems'. *International Journal of Innovation Management*, 5(2) 135–47.

Coverdill, J.E., Finlay, W., and Martin, J.K. (1994) 'Labour management in the Southern textile industry: comparing qualitative, quantitative and qualitative comparative analysis'. *Sociological Methods and Research*, 23: 54–85.

Crooke, S., Pakulski, J., and Waters, M. (1992) *Postmodernization.* London: Sage.

Fielding, N.G. and Lee, R.M. (1998) *Computer Analysis and Qualitative Research.* London: Sage.

Jacobs, J. (1961) *The Death and Life of Great American Cities.* London: Jonathan Cape.

Khalil, E.L. (1996) 'Social theory and naturalism'. In E.L. Khalil and K. Boulding (1996) *Evolution, Order and Complexity.* London: Routledge, pp. 1–39.

Ragin, C. (2000) *Fuzzy Set Social Science.* Chicago: University of Chicago Press.

Rihoux, B. and Ragin, C. (2004) 'Qualitative comparative analysis (QCA): state of the art and prospects'. Paper presented at: APSA 2004 Annual Meeting, Panel 47-9, Chicago.

Rosen, R. (1987) 'Some epistemological issues in physics and biology'. In B.J. Hiley and F.D. Peat *Quantum Implications: Essays in Honour of David Bohm.* London: Routledge, pp. 314–27.

Sayer, A. (2000) *Realism and Social Science.* London: Sage.

Weaver, W. (1958) 'A quarter century in the natural sciences'. *The Rockefeller Foundation Annual Report.* New York: Rockerfeller Foundation.

PART 2

Design and Data Collection

Introduction

Malcolm Williams and W. Paul Vogt

The collection of chapters in this section is eclectic, but united in their focus on a desire to improve the inputs into our research through advances in design or in the collection of data. Arguably all social research leads us back to the perennial issues of reliability and validity. The first of these ultimately is about whether we can believe in the results of our research. Is it consistent and if we repeated it would we get the same results? (Payne and Payne, 2004: 196). The second of these (though it takes different forms) is whether our research is a reasonable likeness of the world we wish to represent. Both enter into analysis of data, but much more importantly we can think of them as quality control features of our inputs – our designs and our data collection. If these are unfit for purpose, then (as Payne reminded us in the previous section) our analyses, however sophisticated, cannot answer our research questions.

'Post paradigm' approaches to data and data production

In the Introduction we talked about two important characteristics of social research in recent decades: the 'paradigm wars' and their post war settlement, and technological and scientific advances. The innovatory approaches here can be seen as beneficiaries of one or both of these, none more so than that of Emma Uprichard, whose thinking has been influenced by, what might be termed, a 'post paradigm' approach to ethnography, but also by the insights of complexity theory – itself only made discoverable as a result of advances in fast computing. Social systems are complex ones par excellence, because the feedback loops are the result of the situated reflexive individual agent within multiple and dynamic social systems. Individuals (because they have agency) cannot just inform us about the past, but their narratives of future belief and action can inform the object of our study. In Uprichard's chapter, the methods are perhaps traditional, it is rather our thinking about design that produces the innovation in validity.

The next three chapters illustrate the difficulty faced by editors of a volume on methodological innovation. Each of these could have comfortably fitted the section on analysis, but though they are ostensibly about this, their innovation lies (as in Uprichard) in quite different ways of approaching research and although they are far from traditional, they remind us of the importance traditionally placed on the links between design, theorising and analysis.

Uprichard and Dyer's chapters can be located in emerging approach to research that one of us has characterised as 'contingent realism' (Williams, 2009). This approach is realist in the sense that it shares with critical realism (see, e.g. Carter and New, 2004) a commitment to the reality of social structure, but nevertheless emphasises the importance of the contingent nature of case trajectories in the creation of structures. Dyer's, as Uprichard's, is grounded in both realism and complexity theory, both of which have hitherto been long on theory and short on translating this into empirical research. Dyer's work is then as exceptional as it is original. She uses longitudinal data and clustering techniques to map the different psychiatric and criminal pathways experienced by mentally disordered offenders. The originality lies in the use of a case based approach, but one informed by complexity, specifically strange attractors, phase space and Poincaré Maps to inform decisions about ordering.

Ian Rees-Jones explores an approach that is, as yet, little known in the Anglophone world, but has its origins in the work of Pierre Bourdieu. Bourdieu, as Rees-Jones reminds us, was a methodological pluralist, whose only methodological rules was that it is 'forbidden to forbid'. Thus, Correspondence Analysis (CA), whilst it is described as summarising the associations between a set of categorical variables and displays these graphically, is actually more of an approach to research that challenges our preconceptions about variable based approaches. As with Dyer's case based cluster analysis, it does not depend on traditional methods of significance testing and has been consequently criticised as lacking rigour. But as we noted in the Introduction, the battery of statistical tools available to frequency or linear based analyses is the product of over a hundred years of statistical development. CA and its derivative Multiple Correspondence Analysis (MCA) (sometimes referred to as homogeneity analysis) start from quite different philosophical premises about how we should think about data. It uses map points to represent all variables in a sub-space with as few dimensions as possible. The method combines the advantages of multi-dimensional and non-linear methods and provides simple graphic overviews of complex systems. MCA, as Dyer's case based cluster approach and the following chapter by Ragin and Schneider, on Qualitative Comparative Analysis (QCA), do not readily fit our traditional quantitative or qualitative paradigms. Rees-Jones, very much in the spirit of this volume, discusses these criticisms, but nevertheless believes MCA would pay to be developed further.

Had this volume been published five years ago there is little doubt the QCA would have been a candidate entry for innovation. It is not yet mainstream, but has attracted many adherents and indeed some critics. The latter in the manner of the previous approaches, because QCA (and its development) similarly does not observe the rules of traditionally understood qualitative or quantitative research. In the chapter in this volume Charles Ragin and Andrew Schneider begin by considering the traditional division of labour between theory building and theory testing. Qualitative researchers concentrate on the case and build theory, whereas it is expected that quantitative research should specify the range of likely causal conditions, captured in the models to be tested, in advance. This, Ragin and Schneider argue, leads to methodological misunderstandings and reproach from both sides, the former finding necessary causal conditions at the level of the case and the latter denying their possibility because statistical significance amongst the specified causal variables cannot be established. Through the device of simple 2×2 cross-tabulations, Ragin and Schneider demonstrate the differences between analysing social phenomena in terms of set relations and analysing them in terms of relationships among variables. They demonstrate the utility of the case based approach for both theory building and theory testing.

The ingenuity of Mike Thelwall's work lies in a relatively straightforward exploitation of the resources available to us on the Web. The post paradigmatic character of the previous chapters in the part arises from oppositional relationships to the more traditional paradigms. In other words they bring on the new, by ringing out the old. Thelwall's starting point is the possibility of data arising from the time compression afforded by the technology of the Web. What is different is a recognition of a change in the ontological conditions of the production of social data. Thelwall asks us to contrast the time lag of several years in the publication of Anne Frank's diary, a historical record of the experience of the Holocaust, with the immediacy of Salam Pax's blog of the experience of the 2003 Iraq War. The 'blog', 'Facebook' and, 'Twitter' have changed the landscape of sociability and our traditional data collection methods have yet to catch up with these developments, but Thelwall shows us how we can use web trends and data to very quickly assess and indeed detect global attitudes, or indeed social differences across the globe. Thelwall's work might be seen as the beginning of the social science response to the challenges to traditional methods identified by Savage and Burrows, that were discussed in the Introduction.

Capturing Validity

The representation of the likeness of the world has been the contested territory in methodology throughout the history of social science. The previous chapters in this part are evidence for the emergence of a post paradigmatic social research, yet these adventurous new approaches should not lead us to ignore the methodological insights that stem from methods that have their provenance in the earlier paradigms. To extend the paradigm analogy further to its Kuhnian origins, Newtonian laws continue to hold as limiting cases within the successor Einsteinian paradigm and so it is that there remains much work to do in our more traditional methodological approaches.

Anthony Onwuegbuzie and his colleagues remind us of the continuing centrality of literature reviews and the growth of research syntheses. Indeed, they note the frequent inadequacies and difficulties researchers experience in an era when research 'production' is so prolific, what they term the 'information explosion'. This is an important and even growing problem for researchers and in this chapter some novel strategies are proposed. In particular, Onwuegbuzie et al. liken the literature review process to doing qualitative research and suggest four major sources for research syntheses (i.e. talk, observations, drawings/photographs/videos and documents) to present various data collection strategies.

The chapter by Tony Bryant and Kathy Charmaz clearly demonstrates that there is innovation even in a method as popular as Grounded Theory (GT). Its central tenet, the discovery of theory from data has been abused and misused and Bryant and Chalmers preface their exposition of current innovation by guiding us through its history, discussing the paradoxes that the original innovation in the work of Glaser and Straus produced. The work of Charmaz and Bryant has been the development of a constructivist form of Grounded Theory, which has led to a significantly firmer conceptual and philosophical basis and resulted in a flourishing of GT-oriented writing linking the method to pragmatism, action research, critical theory and other methodological approaches. As Bryant and Charmaz demonstrate, a method can innovate whilst retaining its central features.

Tim May (2001: Chapter 6) described the interview as a 'conversation', a perhaps obvious insight, but one we have sometimes lost sight of and especially, of course, in survey research, where a desire for standardisation and reliability often undermines the validity of our constructs. The chapters by Giampietro Gobo and Nastasi and Hitchcock take two quite different approaches to the validity issue.

Gobo's chapter begins with dilemma of improved validity in open-ended interview questions, but the loss of standardisation and the gain in the latter through the use of closed-ended response alternatives with the consequent loss of validity, occupied the methodological debate. Whilst standardisation underlies the success of survey methodology, it has also produced biases. Gobo's remedy to this dilemma is to innovate by re-discovering and adapting two classic approaches from the past: Likert's technique called 'fixed question/free answers', and Galtung's procedure named 'open question/closed answer'. Both procedures are guided by the same principle: let the interviewee answer freely in his/her own words and make the interview into a conversation.

In bringing the conversation back in, Gobo is not abandoning reliability. Rather reliability of measures are underwritten by their likeness to the world, which is also the theme of the chapter by Bonnie Nastasi and John Hitchcock. Social scientists and psychologists have long known that cultural factors can influence the meaning of any given psychological construct, even where a given construct might be universally or broadly recognised, associated behavioural manifestations of it are likely to differ from one culture to the next. Mixed methods approaches can allow us to make headway in overcoming these issues and Nastasi and Hitchcock show what might be achieved through illustrating their work in building an 'ethnographic survey' in Sri Lanka. The ethnographic survey is characterised by grounding every item in the qualitative data and results from related analyses. The surveys were then administered, factor analysed and the results were compared with qualitative findings to establish cross-method triangulation. Whilst the constructs identified were unique to the context, the methods themselves have a much wider utility.

Arguably those who inhabit particular social worlds know those worlds best and it perhaps follows from that the research on those worlds best reflects that knowledge if it is conducted by its inhabitants. What Ros Edwards and Claire Alexander term 'peer researchers', have the potential to provide insider knowledge (Merton, 1973: 129), which can be complemented by the outsider knowledge and skills of professional researchers. Edwards and Alexander provide a critical account of an increasingly popular approach to researching and evaluating areas such as service provision. Innovation in this approach lies less in method (though this is important) and more in the development of the social relations involved, such as 'matching' interviewer and interviewer, notions of representation and mediation and associated power issues between academics, peer/community researchers and the subject group or 'community'.

The final chapter in this part, from W. Paul Vogt and his colleagues is a clear demonstration that the search for reliability through Randomised Control Trials (RCTs) can lead to inadequacies in the validity of measurement. Their chapter is not a critique of RCTs, but rather a plea for methodological pluralism in research design, to fit the method to the question, rather than judging all methods by how closely they resemble the 'gold standard' of RCTs. Randomised assignment is often not possible in evaluation studies, key variables can't be manipulated and there is a lack of external validity. In their chapter they argue for the use of comparative case studies in programme evaluation. The description of their method, particularly the need to do in-depth work to identify the variables to be investigated, not only shows the limitations of RCTs, but also how the evidence they can reveal is more valid and more convincing.

REFERENCES

Carter, B. and New, C. (eds) (2004) *Making Realist Work: realist Social Theory and Empirical Research.* London: Routledge.

May, T. (2001) *Social Research*, 3rd edn. Buckingham: Open University Press.

Merton (1973) *The Sociology of Science: Theoretical and Empirical Investigations.* Chicago: University of Chicago Press.

Payne, G. and Payne, J. (2004) *Key Concepts in Social Research.* London: Sage.

Williams, M. (2009) 'Social objects, causality and contingent realism'. *Journal for the theory of Social Behavior,* 39: 11–18.

5

Narratives of the Future: Complexity, Time and Temporality

Emma Uprichard

INTRODUCTION

There is a long established tradition of using personal narratives in social science. Although narrative research encompasses a vast diversity of approaches, in general, there is a shared emphasis on the past and the notion of reconstituting the past through personal story-telling (Clandinin, 2000; Reissman, 1993, 2008). In contrast, the idea of narratives of the *future* is explored in some detail here. Indeed, from a complex systems perspective to the social world (see Byrne's chapter in this volume as well as Byrne, 1998; Cilliers, 1998; Cohen and Stuart, 1994; Waldrop, 1992) exploring narratives of the future, it is suggested, ought to be a fundamental and routine part of the complexity driven social scientist's methodological repertoire.

The discussion is not a defense of the 'narrative' *per se*, but rather a discussion about the ways in which time and temporality inform social objects of study. The 'social objects' considered here are similar to those delineated by Williams (2009), which are socially constructed but real in their consequences, ontologically contingent in the sense that prior to their existence they only exist probabilistically, and once in existence they have 'causal properties' with respect to effecting the existence of other social objects. Taking Williams' argument a little further, a key feature of these social objects is that time and temporality are also ontologically intrinsic to them. This general presupposition is already widely acknowledged with respect to the past; hence why narratives are so widely used in historical or retrospective studies. However, like narratives of the past, narratives of the future also inform social objects of study in important ways. Extending Williams' argument further still, the social objects are complex. This involves the explicit acknowledgement that the objects of study are dissipative, open, non-linear, multi-dimensional, social systems which are situated in time and space (see Byrne, 1998; Kiel and Elliott, 1997; Prigogine 1980; Prigogine and Stengers, 1984; Reed and Harvey, 1992).

The argument presented here is in many respects a very simple one. At its heart is the view that the future matters. It matters in everyday life and it matters to the lives of everybody; it is an intrinsic part of the time and temporality in which all things are necessarily situated. This is already a theme that is well argued by Adam and Groves (2007), but what is presented briefly here is an acknowledgement of future matters specifically in social research, since the way the future of a social object is perceived feeds back onto how it is constructed in the present. In turn, in order to study social objects in the present, narratives of the future that are associated with them are also important. Indeed, it will be suggested that from a complexity point of view, narratives of the future are fundamental.

To be clear, the use of the term 'narrative', as it used here, is spelt out in part by Lawler in the following:

> I am not using 'narrative' here to indicate a 'story' that simply 'carries' a set of 'facts'. Rather, I see narratives as *social products* produced by people within the context of specific social, historical and cultural locations. They are related to the experience that people have of their lives, but they are not transparent carriers of that experience. Rather, they are interpretive devices, through which people represent themselves, both to themselves and to others. Further, narratives do not originate with the individual: rather, they circulate culturally to provide a repertoire (though not an infinite one) from which people can produce their own stories. (Lawler, 2002: 242)

In addition, narratives are assumed to be interpretive devices that can also be used to produce stories about the social world, albeit from a particular standpoint. And it is this aspect that is especially important here because individual biographies *and* the ways in which these interact with macro-level social dynamics are considered to be an important part of how the social world works. Narratives enable the exploration of how some of these interactions manifest themselves at both micro and macro levels and help therefore in understanding trajectories of change more generally (Uprichard and Byrne, 2006). What is presented is a philosophical account of how narratives of the future inform the object of study as it is both being in present and becoming in the future, and a discussion about why their inclusion in social research for such purposes is especially important. As such, this discussion relates to particularly methodology rather than to method. That said, the method that is implied throughout is that of the semi-structured interview, whether that be an individual or group semi-structured interview. The specific position to this method is that intrinsic to Holstein and

Gubrium's (1995, 1997) notion of 'active interviewing', whereby the interviewer and the interviewee are considered to have co-produced the interview data in active collaboration with one another. They explain:

> Both parties to the interview are necessarily and ineluctably *active*. Meaning is not merely elicited by apt questioning, not simply transported through respondent replies; it is actively and communicatively assembled in the interview encounter. Respondents are not so much repositories of knowledge – treasuries of information awaiting excavation, so to speak – as they are constructors of knowledge in collaboration with interviewers. (Holstein and Gubrium, 1997: 106)

One of the main implications of this approach is there is an acknowledgement of issues of power, control, authority and expertise in the production of the data. Moreover, these issues are articulated through a collaborative exercise between the interviewer and the interviewees. From this perspective, data produced in the interview is seen as 'materials for analysis' (Roulsten et al., 2001: 769), which are co-constructed by the interviewer and interviewees interacting together during the interview.

This deliberately moves away from perceiving interview data as untarnished representations of the respondents' external realities. Instead, there is an inherent subjectivity in the production of all knowledge (Madill et al., 2000: 3). Interview material, however, comes in part from the research informants and is seen as potentially allowing the researcher glimpses of the structuring and generative mechanisms in which they are embedded. As Hammersley and Gomm explain, the approach adopted here is that:

> Reality, even 'inner reality', is not something that exists as a self-displaying manifold which is open to view if only we can get into the right position, or acquire the right spectacles, to see it. Rather, it is something that we have to make sense of through concepts. At the same time, these concepts do not create something out of nothing but capture the nature of some act of reality more or less adequately. So, what people say – in interviews and elsewhere – can help us to understand their dispositions, even thought they do not have complete, direct or definitive knowledge of these . . . Often they *will* be a source of bias, but it may still be possible to detect and discount this through methodological assessment. Nor does the fact that interview accounts are always constructions mean that they cannot be accurate representations. (Hammersley and Gomm, 2004: 96–7)

Thus, whilst interview data are not treated as literal descriptions of social reality, they are used as a resource to know about it (Atkinson and Silverman, 1997; Silverman, 1985, 1993).

Note that this argument applies to knowing the social world whatever the time frame under observation. The interview method does not dictate the temporal horizon intrinsic to any particular research design any more than a hammer dictates whether a nail or a piece of wood is actually hammered. The choice of which temporal horizons are examined remains the choice of the researcher. All that is suggested here is that asking individuals about their desired and projected futures ought to be part of the social scientist's methodological tool box (see also Uprichard and Byrne, 2006 on this issue).

As well as there being particular assumptions related to the method underpinning this discussion, the approach to time and temporality is quite specific also. Here, Barbara Adam's extensive work on time and social theory (see, e.g. Adam, 1995, 1998, 2004, 2007) is used as a backdrop to the discussion. That is, time and temporality are taken to be real *ontological* entities which shape the world, as seen in the 'ageing process', for example, but they are also shaped by social life as well (see Prigogine 1980, 1997; Prigogine and Stengers, 1984 on this issue). The 'past', 'present' and 'future' are considered to be particular 'timescapes' (see Adam, 1998) which, although ordered chronologically, do not sit independently of each other, nor of our experiences of them in everyday life. That said, it is George Herbert Mead's work on time and temporality that is more explicitly used than that of Barbara Adam, mainly because he offers an important access point to the temporal recursivity that runs through this particular discussion here, although this arguably features more or less strongly across Adam's work too.

It is worth noting what is *not* being argued here. In arguing that narratives can inform the future, it is *not* being argued that knowledge about the future in its entirety can ever be obtained; this is thought to be too ambitious a task. This is primarily because it is assumed that any social science methodology needs to account for the *complexity* of the social world (Byrne, 1998; Khalil and Boulding, 1996; Reed and Harvey, 1992, 1996). This position presumes that the social emerges from complex systems, which involve contingent, multiple non-linear interactions. Complex systems are, therefore, unpredictable insofar as it is impossible to determine the *exact* future of a system. What is possible, however, is a notion of possible futures. Much like a series of multiple choice options or those story-like descriptions of possible futures involve 'scenario thinking' (see Kahn and Wiener, 1972), where these scenarios are 'perhaps accompanied by a description of forthcoming events leading to that future' (Henshel, 1982: 60). As Staley (2002: 38) puts it, 'If a prediction is a definitive statement of what the future will be, then scenarios are heuristic statements that explore the plausibilities of what might be'.

The advantage of thinking about the future as a possible set of scenarios is that it provides a way of empirically considering future events specifically from the social actor's point of view. In addition, according to the National Intelligence Council (2004: 21), 'Scenarios offer a more dynamic view of possible futures and focus attention on the underlying interactions that may have particular policy significance. They are especially useful in thinking about the future during times of great uncertainty.' Importantly, however, '*scenarios are not meant as actual forecasts,* but they describe possible worlds upon whose threshold we may be entering, depending on how trends interweave and play out' (National Intelligence Council, 2004: 16, original emphasis). In turn, and following Cartwright, this involves a focus on what *can* happen instead of what *will* happen, since what *will* happen is usually unknowable or only knowable under specific *ceteris paribus* conditions of laws, which are only real theoretically rather than what happens ontologically (see Cartwright, 1999).

That said, even where linear laws of change have appeared to allow prediction of, say, states of motion of physical bodies, this too is also seen to be problematic (see Cartwright, 1999, 2000, 2004, 2006). As Cartwright sums up:

> . . . a good deal of our knowledge . . . is not of laws but of natures. These tell us what *can* happen, not what will happen, and the step from possibility to actuality is a hypothesis to be tested or a bet to be hedged, not a conclusion to be credited because of its scientific lineage. (Cartwright, 1999: 10)

The issue, therefore, is not so much about predicting the *exact* trajectory that a system will take, and indeed this is primarily how what is advocated here differs from classical notions of 'prediction'; classical notions of prediction tend to imply determinism. Yet from a complexity perspective, the arrow of time suggests that there is nothing determined (although there may be path dependencies) and there is always a necessary conflict between prediction and the uncertainty of the future (Prigogine, 1980, 1997; Prigogine and Stengers, 1984; Nicolis and Prigogine, 1989). Instead, what is put forward is an argument for the use of the interview as a way of constructing multiple possible futures of a system's trajectory through personal narratives, and more specifically, how those possible futures impact on how we conceptualise objects of study in the present. If the classical notion of prediction comes into this discussion at all, then it is with regards to concocting relatively accurate probabilistic short-term forecasts concerning the outcome of, say, a handful of possible (non-determined) futures.

Of course, what *can* happen, at least theoretically, might be an infinite list of possibilities. However, the possible futures that are the focus of this chapter are considered to be both knowable and more or less probable, even if they remain only hypothetical and ultimately end up being falsified as time unfolds. Just as our understanding of the present conditions our narratives about the past, so do our narratives of the present help us to contemplate the future, which in turn recursively impacts on how we consider the present. Thus, our narratives of the present are never independent of the narratives of the past or future. Conversely, our narratives of the future are also dependent on the narratives we construct about the past and present.

The concern is not whether these possible futures actually occur or are ultimately revealed to be more or less 'right' or 'wrong'. Changes or events that are thought to occur in the future may never actually materialise. What is important is the extent to which those future scenarios affect the way objects of study are conceptualised in the present. What actors think will happen may shed light on what is happening now; what is thought to be happening now impacts on the way it is explored methodologically. Note that this is the case even if what is thought to be happening now or in the future turns out to be incorrect later. The point is that narratives of the future offer important insights relating to the ontological dynamics involved in social objects of study, which subsequently effect how we go about methodologically studying a particular object of study. It is this 'temporal recursivity' *vis á vis* objects of study in the present, and the methodological implications that this temporal recursivity entails, that is explored here.

A PHILOSOPHY OF THE FUTURE

Although there may be important ontological differences between the past and the future insofar as with respect to the past, as Wordsworth puts it in *Ode to Immortality*, that 'Which having been must ever be', whereas with respect to the future, that which is being must yet become, they are nevertheless similar insofar as they are both contingently emergent through the irreversible dynamics of time. Therefore, when it comes to epistemological processes involved in knowing the social world, constructions of the future share a number of similarities with those about the past and present (see also Staley 2002 on this issue).

Following Bhaskar's (1979: 31) argument about the fact that 'it is because sticks and stones are solid that they can be picked up and thrown, not because they can be picked up and thrown that they are solid', it is arguably because of the real dynamics of the irreversibility of time (Prigogine, 1980) that they can be constructed and interpreted in similar ways, even if the fact that they can be handled in this sort of way may be a contingently necessary condition of our knowledge of their different temporal phenomenological experiences. To put it another way, although past and future are understood differently, they are nevertheless 'made of the same stuff'; just because we have more or less data or knowledge about them does not mean they are fundamentally different social objects. It is precisely because of the narrative element to the dynamics of time and temporality itself in both the physical and social worlds (Prigogine 1980), and therefore in the lives of individuals and our experiences of being in the world, that our narratives of the past and the future need to be considered together when it comes to knowing the dynamics of the present. This of course has methodological implications for social scientists in terms of how they conduct research.

By drawing on George Herbert Mead's (2002(1932)) *Philosophy of the Present* and applying some of his ideas about the past and its importance on the present to ideas about the future, it is suggested that the past and future have at least three things in common, specifically with respect to knowing the present. First, although it is possible to build up knowledge about both the present and the future, these constructions are always subject to change. Constructions of the past and future are always evolving, and importantly they can only ever be constituted in the present (Adam, 1990: 142). As Oakeshott (1995: 8, cited in Adam, 1990: 143) writes, 'Both future and past, then emerge only in a reading of present and a particular future or past is one eligible to be evoked from a particular present and is contingently related to the particular present from which it is evoked'. Similarly, Mead writes, 'the historian does not doubt that something has happened. He [*sic*] is in doubt as to what has happened'. Similarly, Bourdieu

(1990: 15) notes, 'The essential thing about historical realities is that one can always establish that things could have been otherwise, indeed *are* otherwise in other places and other conditions'. Hence, in contemplating the future, one is in no doubt that something will happen, or even that something could happen; what is in doubt is *what* will happen. Equally, the essential thing about future realities is that one can always establish that a thing could become otherwise, indeed *will* become otherwise in other places and other conditions.

To this extent, although researchers concerned about the past or the future may be dealing with different time frame, they each have to grapple with elements of uncertainty. The historian may build up a relatively convincing case about what happened (in much the same way as a detective needs to build up evidence to support the case), but there is no absolute certainty that any particular description of events is the one and only version of those events. Similarly, descriptions about the future can only be multiple rather than singular. This is not to say that all descriptions of the future are equally valid any more than all descriptions of the past are. Like the past, knowledge about the future, and in turn the validity of the narratives of the future, are always subject to change as new layers of knowledge – in the present – become available (see Reed and Harvey (1996) on the ontological nesting of irreducible layers of reality and the subsequent layering of knowledge). In other words, uncertainty is real in both retrospective and prospective studies because of this 'ontological nesting of irreducible layers'; we cannot get away from this.

Second, as has already been implied in the first point, constructions of the past and the future are each dependent on constructions of the present. For Mead, 'the past is such a construction that the reference that is found in it is not to events having a reality independent of the present which is the seat of reality, but rather to such an interpretation of the present in its conditioning passage as will enable intelligent conduct to proceed. It is of course evident that the materials out of which that past is constructed lie in the present' (p. 57). Similarly, what is suggested here is that constructions of the future are not independent of the present, but are instead an interpretation of the present (and the past) in its condition passage as it is perceivable. In other words, constructions of the future are dependent upon the constructions of the present and past. Mead explains this as follows:

> our pasts are always mental in the same manner in which the futures that lie in our imaginations ahead of us are mental. They differ, apart from their successive positions, in that the determining conditions of interpretation and conduct are embodied in the past as that is found in the present, but they are subject to the same test of validity to which our hypothetical futures are subject. And the novelty of every future demands a novel past. (Mead, 2002(1932): 59)

Indeed, Bergson's (1910) concepts of *temps* and *durée* are precisely about the way that the present is always constituted in emergence and that time as a whole – whether it be past, present or future time – are actively constantly created and recreated. Hence, even though the temporal order of the past and future differ, they share similarities insofar as they are each constructed based on the knowledge of the present, and since the present is always changing, so too must our constructions of the past and the future constantly shift according to this new 'updated' and 'emergent' knowledge of the present.

Mead argues that 'we orient ourselves not with reference to the past which was a present within which the emergent appeared, but in such a re-statement of the past as conditioning the future that we may control its reappearance' (p. 46). That is to say, the present is considered in relation to constructions of the present-to-future trajectories, just as the future is constructed with respect to constructions of the present-to-future trajectories. To this extent, narratives of the future are but re-constructed possibilities, relative to our re-interpretations of the past and the present as conditioning the parameters of the range of possible futures.

Third, although emergent phenomena are necessarily unforeseeable and therefore render knowing the future problematic, this problem is not uncommon to knowing the past. That is, in relation to the historian's predicament, Mead argues that even if the historian were to know all about the present, it would not be possible for him or her to determine what has happened in the past. Mead suggests that this is primarily because of the possibility of emergence:

> It is that there is and always will be a necessary relation of the past and the present but that the present in which the emergent appears accepts that which is novel as an essential part of the universe, and from that standpoint rewrites its past. (Mead, 2002(1932): 43)

Similarly, in relation to the researcher's predicament about the future, there is and always will be a necessary relation of the present and the future, but the possibility of emergent phenomena in the future renders it impossible to predict or even hypothetically consider the future in its entirety. Nevertheless, as Mead puts it, the 'irrevocable past and the occurring change are the two factors to which we tie up all our speculation in regard to the future' and which – importantly – ultimately act as a 'determining condition of what is taking place' (p. 45). The ways in which the future impacts on the present, then, are not just epistemological; they are ontological. Moreover, this temporal ontology involves an important dynamic that has effects at the level of the individual social agent.

NARRATIVES OF THE FUTURE AS STRUCTURING STRUCTURES

What Mead's 'philosophy of the present' offers, then, is a way of constructing a philosophy of possible futures which has ontological implications with respect to the present, that is the future acts as a 'determining condition' of the present. Popper (1959) too has suggested something similar, although he comes at it from the very different angle of single case probability for physical occurrences. In his 'world of propensities', he argues that the propensity of an event – that is its 'dispositional properties' – is ontological and relational, and always dynamic, even if the absolute probabilistic value (which varies from 0 to 1, where 0 implies logical impossibility, that is the event cannot ever occur, and 1 implies logical necessity of occurrence, i.e. the event has occurred) is unchanging. More precisely still, Popper suggests, albeit tentatively, the propensity of an event is dependent on how that event is perceived and understood; vice versa, how it is perceived and understood can change the event's propensity to occur. He writes:

> Now, in our real changing world, the situation and, with it, the possibilities, and thus propensities, change all the time. They certainly may change if we, or any other organisms, *prefer* one possibility to another; or if we *discover* a possibility where we have not seen one before. Our very understanding of the world changes the conditions of the changing world; and so do our wishes, our preferences, our motivations, our hopes, our phantasies, our hypotheses, our theories. (Popper, 1995: 17; original emphasis)

Now, there are problems involved in applying Popper's propensity work to the social world – see Williams (1999) for a good overview and alternative. However, the notion that every thing has its own propensity, which is relationally determined, yet always changing relative to the totality of its environment, is a powerful one in complex social science, primarily because of the importance given to exploring the nested ontology of a thing-in-the-world at the level of both cause and meaning. Conversely, what is interesting is that Popper's physical world of propensities is echoed in Bourdieu's theory of social change. And whilst not going into the details of his work here, Bourdieu (1984, 1990a, b) also recognised the importance of time and temporality on individual and collective 'structuring structures' and 'dispositions'. Indeed his theory of 'habitus' and 'field' is arguably a temporal argument about how change occurs:

> The habitus, a product of history, produces individual and collective practices – more history – in accordance with the schemes generated by history. It ensures the active presence of past experiences, which, deposited in each organism in the form of schemes of perception, thought and action, tend to guarantee the 'correctness' of practices and their constancy over time, more reliably than all formal rules and explicit norms. (Bourdieu, 1990b: 54)

Although Bourdieu refers most frequently to past events and the effects of history and how these feed into the present 'structuring structures', he also argues that the individual habitus 'adjusts itself to a probable future which it anticipates and helps to bring about because it reads it directly in the present of the presumed world'. In fact, he goes as far as suggesting that individual agents' disposition to 'cut their coats according to their cloth' renders individuals 'to become the accomplices of the processes that tend to make the probable a reality' (Bourdieu, 1990b, 64–5). For example, the desired futures that individuals might have for themselves, those around them and the world in which they live may vary according to, among other things, their habitus. This in turn impacts on the ways in which individuals choose (and think they can choose) to act in the world. Thus, what individuals do in the present, how they experience the present, feeds into what individuals think they can do in the future, which in turn feeds back into what is done in the present and how the present is experienced and lived out. It is worth repeating the gravity of Bourdieu is implying here: individuals become accomplices of the processes that *help to make the probable a reality*. Like Popper's 'world of propensities', then, Bourdieu's world of 'probable futures' is one which is weighted towards particular outcomes, which in fact tend not to be dissimilar to the way that similar events tended to unfold most frequently in the past.

Bourdieu's philosophy has indeed been criticised as being a deterministic theory of social reproduction that does not adequately account for the radical kinds of social changes witnessed in recent decades (see, e.g. Chiou, 1992; Jenkins, 1982). However, one might argue that, where the social is assumed to be complex, as it is here – that is dynamic, changing, non-linear, existing in a state far from equilibrium, is sensitive to initial conditions, etc. – that even when such a system reproduces itself, the outcome is *likely* to be very different at some point in time. Indeed, elsewhere Bourdieu himself points out that 'the same habitus can lead to very different practices and stances depending on the state of the field' (1990a: 116). Thus he may be overstating things by suggesting that the individual habitus adjusts itself such that individuals 'cut their coats according to their cloth', even if they may *tend* to do so. What is central to the construction of narratives about possible futures therefore is a notion that individuals may also – taking Bourdieu's analogy further – 'cut their coats – or trousers or dresses, etc. – in quite *un*foreseeable ways and according to completely different rules and a feel for a *new* game'.

Even where we acknowledge that there may be some element of a reproducing dynamic that is in part 'driven' by the way our orientation to the future feeds back into present day action(s) through the structuring structures, dispositions or propensities, etc., one possible future must always be the 'unknowable'; the 'unknowable future' is the 'constant' narrative, if you like. By this I mean that, if we think about narratives of the future as a list of multiple choice options, then one possible scenario needs to be 'none of the above'; there is an acknowledgement of the 'known unknown'. This is of course an important qualification to what was stated above about how the narratives of the future being discussed here are 'knowable'. But it is an important qualification because it not only explicitly accepts the limits of our knowledge about the future, but it also positions the possibility of emergent phenomena as central to narratives about the complex social world more generally. After all, future emergent phenomena are by definition unknowable, yet emergent phenomena are intrinsic to the complex social world. Therefore, there is a need to conceptualise the future such that the possibility of emergence is also acknowledged. The 'known unknown' possible future is simply a way of explicitly accounting for unknowable future emergence and plays an important 'hinge' to what is being argued here.

Nevertheless, even by conceptualizing narratives of the future as tentative, hypothetical and imaginary, and there is an acknowledgement that there is always a 'known unknown' possible future, as Mead points out, there is a rather convoluted, but important, temporal, iterative and recursive dynamic whereby actors, individually or collectively, may re-describe events, which were previously unforeseeable, in new ways that subsequently help to foresee the once unforeseeable possible futures, which are of course now past, yet help to re-describe the present. He explains this in the following passage:

> The difficulty that immediately presents itself is that the emergent has no sooner appeared than we set about rationalizing it, that is, we undertake to show that it, or at least the conditions that determine its appearance, can be found in the past that lay behind it. Thus the earlier pasts out of which it emerged as something which did not involve it are taken up into a more comprehensive past that does lead up to it. (Mead, 2002(1932): 46)

What hindsight allows the reflexive agent, then, is a way of re-interpreting the past such that events which were previously considered to be unforeseeable may be re-constructed such that the unfolding events are not only explicable, but are seen as the 'inevitable' or 'most probable'. This theme is also apparent in Taleb's (2007) emergent 'black swans', where a 'black swan event' is one involving the following:

> First it is an *outlier*, as it is outside the realm of regular expectations, because nothing in the past can convincingly point to its possibility. Second, it carries an extreme impact. Third, in spite of its outlier status, human nature makes us concoct explanations for its occurrence *after* the fact, making it explainable and predictable. (Taleb, 2007: xvii–xviii)

Of course, this acknowledgement does not change the fact that narratives of the future may impact on how the present is perceived or lived out; it simply accentuates the 'cumulative laying up of knowledge', which strips away layer after nested layer of reality (Harvey and Reed, 1996). Thus, even if we accept that individuals may be 'predisposed' to act in certain ways (Bourdieu, 1990) or that the outcome of events may be 'weighted' towards the 'changing propensities that influence future situations without determining them in a unique way' (Popper, 1990: 12), the ontological uncertainty *of* everyday life *in* every day life is both real and enduring, even though retrodictive knowledge may seem more certain than prospective knowledge. In other words, despite arguing for knowledge about narratives of the future and suggesting that these feed back into the ontological predispositions or propensities everyday life in the present in important ways, the indeterminacy of the complex dynamic world is still recognised (Prigogine and Stengers, 1984; Nicolis and Prigogine, 1989).

This being the case, where does that leave the empirical social scientist, who remains interested in knowing the social world in spite of its complexity of the epistemological limits it entails? What methodological approaches might be appropriate to a future sensitive approach to the social, which also acknowledges the complex ontology of social objects? After all, as Harvey and Reed (1996) argue, 'the ontology of the subject matter [ought to] dictate the range of methods employed, and not vice versa' (p. 321). But what might this involve where time and temporality – and for our purposes here, that of the future in particular – are considered key dimensions to such a methodological project? In the concluding section of this chapter, both a pessimistic and an optimistic answer are provided respectively.

CONCLUSION: METHODOLOGICAL IMPLICATIONS

The bad news is the methodological challenge of studying the complex social world has never been greater. Not only does the complexity turn in the social sciences raise serious methodological and epistemological challenges to empirical social researcher (see, e.g. Byrne, 1998; Kiel and Elliott, 1997), but the ubiquitous digitization of data has, for some, raised an 'empirical crisis' more generally (Savage and Burrows, 2007). Although software and technological developments also bring with them a range of innovative methods, there is still, as Harvey and Reed (1996) stress, a need to concoct research designs that are both methodologically and ontologically congruent with the specific object of study. Time and temporality are, in my view, key to developing such research designs. This requires an epistemological approach to time and temporality, where time acts as a 'marker of time' of things 'being' in the present, past and future; longitudinal data and longitudinal studies will certainly be part of that approach. In addition, it requires an ontological approach time as 'ageing' where things are seen as 'becoming' in the past, present and future. This 'two-pronged attack' on time and temporality is in part what Prigogine argues for in studying dissipative dynamic systems. The same needs to apply to complex social systems. Exploring narratives of the future is simply one way of addressing that challenge.

The good news – at least epistemologically, if not always methodologically! – is that studying the social world involves human beings. People come in all shapes and sizes, a wide, albeit limited, range of ages and cohorts; they come from all kinds of social and cultural backgrounds, from all areas of the globe. Unlike the biological taxonomist's predicament, the sociologist's research sample is relatively accessible, widespread and relatively easy to find. Indeed, the increased digitization of data, particularly in the guise and rise of Web 2.0 applications, such as Facebook, YouTube and Twitter etc., in which millions of people voluntarily donate masses of private and personal data without the sociologist even asking them to do so have made some previously 'hard to reach' populations or 'sensitive data' very easy to come by.

Yet it is not simply that research participants or social data are increasingly accessible that ought to provide the social scientist with some hope about tackling the methodological challenge of studying the complex social world, although this is certainly part of the good news. What is more interesting and more significant, particularly with regards to learning about narratives of the future and the way that they shape the present, is the more mundane fact that people are *part* of the social world. Indeed, this is both a logical and ontological necessity of being and becoming in the world as it too is being and becoming (Heidegger, 1962). But people are of course more than a part of the complex social world, they are an embedded part of it. As Peat writes:

> We can no longer adopt the privileged position of assuming that we lie outside a system as impartial observers who can objectify the world and discover its underlying mechanisms.

> Rather we are all part and parcel of the complex patterns in which we live and our thoughts, beliefs and perceptions have a profound effect on the world around us. (Peat, 2007: 928)

Thus, whilst each individual is subject to a particular standpoint, this remains an embedded and temporal standpoint. This relates directly to Emirbayer and Mische's (1998) notion of agency, which is based precisely on an *embedded* agent, who is embedded in the social in important ways, including temporally. Agency, they argue (1998: 63), is 'a temporally embedded process of social engagement, informed by the past (in its habitual aspect), but also oriented toward the future (as a capacity to imagine alternative possibilities) and toward the present (as a capacity to contextualise past habits and future projects within the contingencies of the moment)'. As noted briefly above, Bourdieu's dialectical habitus-field model also assumes that agency contributes to the structures and systems from which the social emerges:

> at every stage within the limits of the structural constraints which affect their acts of construction both from without, through determinants connected with their position in the objective structures, and from within, through the mental structures – the categories of professional understanding – which organize their perception and appreciation of the social world'. (Bourdieu, 1988: xiv)

Rudd (2009) too argues that the individual is a reflexive temporal agent who acts for reasons. It is the task of critical social scientists, therefore, to explore, interpret and re-describe those reasons, and attempt to explore the ways in which they may or may not matter in explaining the dynamics of the social being and becoming in the present and future.

The importance of the individual agent in producing, interpreting and experiencing the social world is by no means 'news'. But what makes it 'good news' is that, in order to know about the social world, social researchers not only need to approach people as 'informants' in their studies, they can do so. Moreover, the researcher can communicate with the selected informants, observe and interpret them, etc. The entire social sciences are based on this very premise and the reason behind all methodological enterprises in which research participants are involved. Bateson's (1984) description of the survey method, for example, assumes the possibility that people can acquire, and convey to others, knowledge of that part of the social world that they encounter, either at first or second hand, in the course of ordinary living. He argues that 'the survey method assumes not just that people *can* know the world but that they *do* know it'. That is, if we ask someone about his or her world, then we can expect that, under normal conditions, that person will 'tell it as it is'.

This begs the question, although research 'informants' are normally approached to learn more about the past and present, why not also ask them about what they think the future may hold? Indeed, why not ask how they themselves perceive the future to impact on the present? Their reasons behind their answers? Their concerns about the implications on their ability to act in the world? And so on; the conversation can of course go as deep or as broad as may be necessary (within practical and ethical limits of course). After all, implicit in the social scientist's approach to obtaining narratives of the past is the assumption that individuals *can* talk about the past, so it is rather curious that when it comes to asking individuals about the future, there might be a perception that individuals are somehow unable to talk about the future. This perception is simply unfounded. There is no intrinsic reason why researchers cannot ask individuals about their desired and projected futures, any more than it is impossible to obtain data of a highly sensitive nature. The extent to which a researcher can elicit narratives of the future from an individual or groups of individuals depends on the interviewing skill of that researcher, not on the temporal horizon of the narratives obtained during the interview.

Likewise, what one does exactly with the narratives of the future once they are obtained depends on the research aims and design of the study. For example, it is possible, just as it is with ordinary interviews, to record and transcribe the interviews, and then to use a chosen qualitative analytical approach, such as Grounded Theory, to help interpret and make sense of the data. Thus, whilst one might transform qualitative narrative material into quantitative variables and to input this information into a quantitative model, which in some cases, depending on the aims of the project, might also be deemed appropriate, this is not considered to be the first and foremost objective of the narratives. Despite the temptation that some researchers may have to move from qualitative narratives of the future to quantitative predictive models, the view proposed here is that there is great value in qualitative material in and of itself, if only because being in the world is a temporal experience. The irreversible arrow of time is part of the physical and social world in which we are necessarily embedded. History matters. But so does the future. Hence, as stated from the outset, the argument presented is in its essence a very simple one. The future matters and it matters in all kinds of ways, not least in the way that our constructions of the future feed back into the ways individuals experience and act in the present.

What is fortunate is that there is in social science a readily available and 'tried and tested' methodological device – that is the interview – through which to explore the ways in which the future matters in everyday life as well. For a long time social scientists have been asking individuals to describe various aspects of their lives. However, there is no methodological reason why they cannot begin to ask individuals to describe their desired and projected futures. After all, the future is but one of many aspects of individual's life. Given its relative importance to everyday life it is a wonder that it has been such an overlooked topic of investigation.

Obtaining narratives of the future derived from interviews that seek to deliberately elicit individual's desired and projected futures, is then, simply one of many possible methodological approaches that explicitly reflects the social and temporal ontology of the complex social world. Another is of course the very likely 'known unknown' possibility that other suitable temporal methodological approaches may crop up in the future, which may also impact in more or less important ways on how the present or the future is constructed and experienced. And so the methodological challenge of studying the complex social world goes on and will no doubt continue to go on, even if it is unclear for now how exactly it will do so.

ACKNOWLEDGEMENTS

I would like to thank Andrew Webster for his comments on an earlier version of chapter which was presented as part of the Department of Sociology's SATSU lunchtime 'brown bag' seminars, which ultimately resulted in this focus on narratives in this particular way. Additional thanks are due to Malcolm Williams for the phrase 'narratives of the future', as well as his patience and insightful comments raised in this chapter.

REFERENCES

Adam, B. (1990) *Time and Social Theory*. Cambridge: Polity Press.
Adam, B. (1995) *Timewatch: The Social Analysis of Time*. Cambridge: Polity Press.
Adam, B. (1998) *Timescapes of Modernity. The Environment and Invisible Hazards*. London: Routledge.
Adam, B. (2004) *Time*. Cambridge: Polity Press.
Adam, B. and Groves, C. (2007) *Future Matters: Action, Knowledge, Ethics*. Leiden: Brill.
Atkinson, P. and Silverman, D. (1997) 'Kundera's immortality: The interview society and the invention of the self'. *Qualitative Inquiry*, 3(3): 304–25.
Bateson, N. (1984) *Data Construction in Social Surveys*. London: Allen and Unwin.
Bergson, H. (1910) *Time and Free Will*. London: Sonneschein & Co.
Bourdieu, P. (1984) *Distinction: A Social Critique of the Judgement of Taste*. London: Routledge & Kegan Paul.
Bourdieu, P. (1988) *Homo Academicus*. Stanford, CA: Stanford University Press.
Bourdieu, P. (1990) *The Logic of Practice*. Stanford, CA: Stanford University Press.
Bourdieu, P. (1990a) *In Other Words: Essays Towards a Reflexive Sociology*. Stanford, CA: Stanford University Press.
Bourdieu, P. (1990b) *The Logic of Practice*. Stanford, CA: Stanford University Press.
Byrne, D. (1998) *Complexity Theory and the Social Sciences: An Introduction*. London: Routledge.
Cartwright, N. (1999) *The Dappled World: A Study of the Boundaries of Science*. Cambridge: Cambridge University Press.
Cartwright, N. (2000) 'An empiricist defence of singular causes'. *Philosophy*, 46: 47–58.
Cartwright, N. (2004) 'Causation: One word, many things'. *Philosophy of Science*, 71(5): 805–19.
Cartwright, N. (2006) 'Where is the theory in our "theories" of causality?' *Journal of Philosophy*, 103(2): 55–66.
Chiou, T.-J. (1992) 'Bourdieu's dialectic logics of reproduction theory'. *Bulletin of Social Education*, 21: 233–81.
Cilliers, P. (1998) *Complexity and Postmodernism*. London: Routledge.
Clandinin, J. (2000) *Narrative Inquiry: Experience and Story in Qualitative Research*. San Francisco: Josey-Bass.
Cohen, J. and Stewart, I. (1994) *The Collapse of Chaos*. Harmondsworth: Penguin.

Emirbayer, M. and Mische, A. (1998) 'What is agency?'. *American Journal of Sociology*, 103(4): 962–1023.
Hammersley, M. and Gomm, R. (2004) 'Recent radical criticism of the interview in qualitative research'. *Developments in Sociology*, 20(9): 91–101.
Harvey, D.L. and Reed, M. (1996) 'Social Science as the Study of Complex Systems'. In L.D. Kiel and E. Elliot (eds.) *Chaos Theory in the Social Sciences: Foundations and Applications.* Ann Arbor: University of Michigan Press.
Heidegger, M. (1962) *Being and Time*, translated by John Macquarrie and Edward Robinson. London: SCM Press.
Henshel, R. (1982) 'Sociology and social forecasting'. *Annual Review of Sociology*, 8(8): 57–79.
Holstein, J. and Gubrium, J. (1995) *The Active Interview.* Thousand Oaks, CA: Sage.
Holstein, J. and Gubrium, J. (1997) 'Active interviewing'. In A. Bryman and R. Burgess (eds) *Qualitative Interviewing*, Volume II. London: Sage. pp. 105–21.
Jenkins, R. (1982) 'Pierre Bourdieu and the reproduction of determinism'. *Sociology*, 16(2): 270–81.
Kahn, H. and Wiener, A.J. (1972) 'The use of scenarios'. In A. Toffler (ed.) *The Futurists.* New York: Random House. pp. 160–63.
Keil, D. and Elliott, E. (eds) (1997) *Chaos Theory in the Social Sciences.* Ann Arbor: Michigan University Press.
Khalil, E. and Boulding, E. (1996) *Evolution, Complexity and Order.* London: Routledge.
Lawler, S. (2002) 'Narrative in social research'. In T. May (ed.) *Qualitative Research in Action.* London: Sage. pp. 242–58.
Madill, A., Jordan A., and Shirley C. (2000) 'Objectivity and reliability in qualitative analysis: Realist, contextualist and radical constructionist epistemologies'. *British Journal of Psychology*, 91(1): 1–20.
Mead, G.H. (1932/2002) *The Philosophy of the Present.* (First published in 1932 by Chicago University Press). New York: Prometheus Books.
National Intelligence Council (2004) *Mapping the Global Future. Report of the National Intelligence Council's 2020 Project.* Pittsburgh, PA: US Government Printing Office.
Nicolis, G. and Prigogine, I. (1989) *Exploring Complexity: An Introduction.* New York: Freeman.
Peat, D. (2007) 'From certainty to uncertainty: Thought, theory and action in a postmodern world'. *Futures*, 39(8): 920–9.
Popper, K. (1959) 'The Propensity Interpretation of Probability'. *British Journal for the Philosophy of Science*, 10: 25–42.
Popper, K. (1990) *A World of Propensities.* Bristol: Thoemmes.
Prigogine, I. (1980) *From Being to Becoming: Time and Complexity in the Physical Sciences.* San Francisco: W.H. Freeman.
Prigogine, I. (1997) *The End of Certainty: Time, Chaos, and the New Laws of Nature.* 1st Free Press. London: Free Press.
Prigogine, I. and Stengers, I. (1984) *Order Out of Chaos.* New York: Bantam.
Reed, M. and Harvey, D. (1992) 'The new science and the old: Complexity and realism in the social sciences'. *Journal for the Theory of Social Behaviour,* (pp. 356–79).
Reed, M. and Harvey, D. (1996) 'Social science as the study of complex systems'. In L. Keil and E. Elliott (eds) *Chaos Theory in the Social Sciences.* Ann Arbor: University of Michigan Press. pp. 295–324.
Reissman, C. (1993) *Narrative Analysis.* London: Sage.
Reissman, C. (2008) *Narrative Methods for the Human Sciences.* London: Sage.
Roulsten, K., Baker, C. and Liljesrom, A. (2001) 'Analyzing the researcher's work in generating data: The case of complaints'. *Qualitative Inquiry*, 7(6): 745–22.
Rudd, A. (2009) 'In defense of narrative'. *European Journal of Philosophy*, 17(1): 60–75.
Savage, M. and Burrows, R. (2007) 'The coming crisis of empirical sociology'. *Sociology*, 41(5): 885–99.
Silverman, D. (1985) *Qualitative Methodology and Sociology.* Aldershot: Gower.
Silverman, D. (1993) *Interpreting Qualitative Data: Methods for Analysing Talk, Text and Interaction.* London: Sage.
Staley, D. (2002) 'A history of the future'. *History and Theory*, 41(4): 72–89.

Taleb, N.N. (2007) *The Black Swan: The Impact of the Highly Improbable*. London: Allen Lane.

Uprichard, E. and Byrne, D. (2006) 'Representing complex places: a narrative approach'. *Environment and Planning A,* 38(4): 665–76.

Waldrop, M. (1992) *Complexity: The Emerging Science at the Edge of Order and Chaos.* New York: Simon and Schuster.

Williams, M. (1999) 'Single case probabilities and the social world: The application of Popper's propensity interpretation'. *Journal for the Theory of Social Behavior*, 29(2): 187–201.

Williams, M. (2009) 'Social objects, causality and contingent realism'. *Journal for the Theory of Social Behaviour*, 39(1): 1–18.

6

Mapping Pathways

Wendy Dyer

INTRODUCTION

Approaches to the evaluation of services which 'process' people (e.g. health and social services, and the criminal justice system) have tended to focus on discrete periods (e.g. referral, important decision points such as 'decision to assess', court sentence, re-offence, etc.). In other words, they have concentrated on the variable rather than the case (Byrne, 1998; Byrne and Ragin, 2009). While such approaches can provide important overall descriptions and make interesting discoveries, they are also open to fundamental criticism – they ignore difference at an individual case level. People referred to such services are not the same: they will have, for example, different backgrounds and different health and social care needs, consequently services will 'process' them in different ways, which will lead to different outcomes.

This chapter describes how this methodological challenge lead to the development and application of an approach which used a framework based on Complexity Theory, longitudinal data and clustering techniques to map the different psychiatric and criminal pathways experienced by mentally disordered offenders (MDOs) processed by a Custody Diversion Team (CDT) in the United Kingdom. This chapter is not intended to provide an explanation of Complexity Theory (there are many excellent books available which give more detailed description than could be replicated here), instead it concentrates on the practical application of a theory which has been much discussed but rarely applied. It begins with a brief description of the policy and practise which gave rise to the methodological problem.

A POLICY OF CUSTODY DIVERSION

CDTs were introduced in the UK at the beginning of the 1990s because of concerns about the crimes committed by mentally disordered people and the prevalence of psychiatric disorder in the prison population. The two central arguments stated:

1 The policy of community care was failing those who needed it most – for example, on 17 December 1992, Christopher Clunis, a 31-year-old London-born Afro-Caribbean stabbed to death Jonathan Zito. In the following enquiry it transpired that Clunis had been shunted between authorities and services in the absence of adequate follow-up procedures. A known paranoid schizophrenic patient, Clunis had avoided taking his medication and had become increasingly disturbed, manifesting violent behaviour. For many reasons including the avoidance of stigmatising a person from an ethnic minority and the lack of resources, the system failed to support either Clunis himself or his family. His condition deteriorated and he murdered a complete stranger. Huge public outcry and media amplification of the threat of violence followed cases like this (Ritchie et al., 1994);
2 Following de-institutionalisation, or the large scale closure of psychiatric hospitals, minor nuisance behaviour committed by people who previously had or who would have been hospitalised were now being criminalised. While numbers varied depending on who was being studied, how and by whom, a ball park figure was provided by Gunn and his colleagues who reported that male sentenced prisoners were more than twice as likely to have a mental disorder when compared with the general population (Gunn et al., 1991a, b).

So CDTs were introduced with the aim of identifying MDOs and diverting them from the criminal justice system and prison to care and treatment by the health and social services.

> Mentally disordered offenders, should, wherever appropriate, receive care and treatment from health and social services rather than in custodial care. (Department of Health and Home Office, 1991: Community Group para. 2.1)

CDTs were then generally accepted as a positive step, avoiding the stigma attached to a prison sentence and the development of a long criminal career by ensuring people received the care and treatment they required (NACRO, 1993).

THE NORTH EAST CUSTODY DIVERSION TEAM

The North East Custody Diversion Team (NE CDT) at the focus of the study represented a big multi-agency investment by the areas health, probation and social services. It included Psychiatrist, Psychologist, Community Psychiatric Nurses, Social Worker and Probation Officer. The team aimed to identify MDOs as early as possible within the criminal justice process, assess them, identify health and social care needs and divert them to appropriate services in order to meet needs. However, it quickly became apparent that the majority of people identified by the NE CDT were not ill enough and had committed fairly serious offences so that diversion away from the criminal justice system was neither possible nor appropriate. Instead, the NE CDT would support these MDOs through the criminal justice process, providing, for example, reports to court with details of the assessment and diagnosis, needs identified and possible court disposals recommended. The important point was that not everyone referred to the NE CDT was the same: they had different backgrounds, had committed different offences, had different needs, and the NE CDT processed them in different ways which lead to different outcomes.

PROBLEM TO DATE

This point had been picked up by Jill Peay (1994) who pointed out that 'mentally disordered offenders . . . are not a single, easily identifiable [or unified] group' (op. cit.: 1121); instead there are many different types of people with different psychiatric and criminal histories. CDTs may 'process' different people in different ways. Therefore, there may be not only one type of outcome but many variations in outcomes for different people who have been processed in different ways. What worked for some might not work for others.

However research to date had treated them as a single group, focusing on discrete periods in the process such as referral and outcome (e.g. Riordan et al., 2000; James, 2000; McGilloway and Donnelly, 2004), in other words focusing on the variable rather than the case.

The challenge was how to move beyond this focus in order to understand the different careers or pathways experienced by those referred to such services. As Watson (1993) argued, what was needed was an attempt to understand the complex ways in which some individuals become channelled through particular institutional and extra-institutional careers. Similarly, Rubington and Weinberg (2008) refer to the process of 'social typing', a Symbolic Interactionist Approach to understanding deviance which emphasises the importance of social phenomena – who types whom, on what grounds, in what way, before or after what acts and with what effects (op. cit.: 3).

DATA SOURCE

In terms of the data available to the research, the NE CDT maintained a database of information about each individual referral and re-referral to the service. The Microsoft Access database is relational as shown by the 'one to many' relationships in Figure 6.1. Data is archived instead of overwritten and lost.

Data were supplied to the project in this original form and so the first task was to export it into the software packages chosen to manipulate, manage and explore the information – in this case Microsoft Excel for data manipulation and SPSS for analysis.

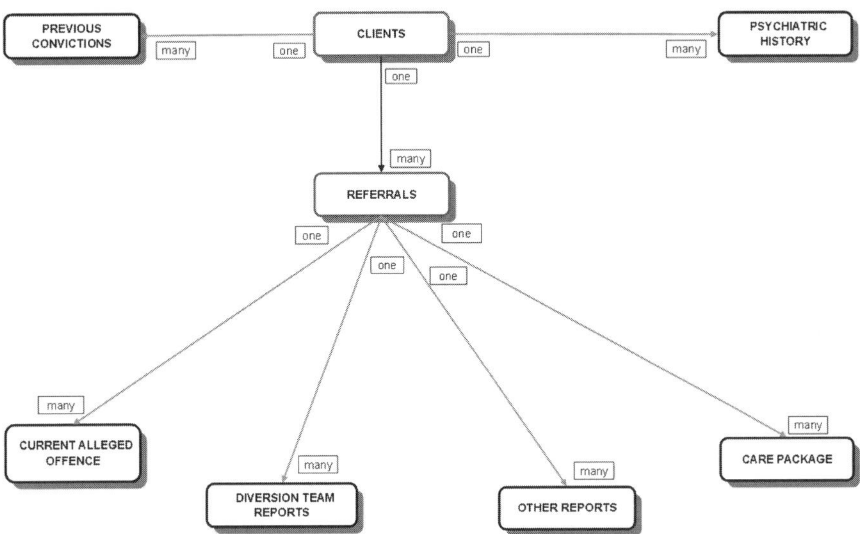

Figure 6.1 NE CDT database schematic

This data manipulation stage was important because the dataset contained 1011 clients, who had been referred to the service 1300 times, with each referral described by a minimum of 140 variables. The aim was to structure this large and complex dataset in such a way that it would provide a framework for the analysis that was to follow. A spreadsheet was constructed from the relational database with each case occupying one row only.

COMPLEXITY THEORY

Complexity Theory provided the context necessary to begin to see a way in which to order and then explore this very large dataset. It is difficult to define exactly what 'it' (Complexity Theory) is, as by its very nature it is complex. As Waldrop (1992) argues:

> complexity … is so wide-ranging that nobody knows quite how to define it, or even where its boundaries lie. But then, that's the whole point. (p. 9)

That said, the understanding of Complexity Theory which initially drove this methodological development seemed clear – complex systems sit between simple order on the one hand and complete randomness on the other (sometimes referred to as 'the edge of chaos'). Again, as Waldrop argues:

> The edge of chaos is the constantly shifting battle zone between stagnation and anarchy, the one place where a complex system can be spontaneous, adaptive and alive. (p. 12)

The NE CDT processed different people in different ways so that the MDO pathways produced were neither simple nor random. Depending on decisions taken by the team, pathways could bifurcate or follow one of many different trajectories. The decisions taken by the team, and therefore the pathways produced, were not infinite so we might expect to identify patterns within and even between trajectories.

The concepts discussed by Complexity Theory, in particular strange attractors, phase space and Poincaré Maps, provided the context necessary to begin to see a way in which to order and then explore the NE CDT dataset:

Strange attractors are time-ordered patterns towards which other nearby trajectories converge

Why a 'strange attractor' rather than a 'simple attractor'? An example of a simple attractor is often given as a swinging pendulum which passes through a range of values within limits in an exact and ordered way.

Strange attractors are also states towards which a dynamic, time-ordered system settles:

> nature constrained, disorder channelled into a pattern with a common underlying theme, stability. (Gleick, 1997: 152)

They are attractors which mean that nearby trajectories converge on them; they are sensitive to initial conditions; and they exist in multi-dimensional space (phase space) but have only finite dimensions.

However, unlike simple attractors, with strange attractors or higher order attractors there is indeterminacy within boundaries but also more than one set of boundaries. Changes or interactions between control parameters determine which of the bounded sets the system will move through.

It could be conceived that a smaller number of MDO career patterns might be identified ($n < 1011$, where n = career patterns and 1011 the number of MDOs referred to the NE CDT) which act like strange attractors with other trajectories converging on them, representing common or shared patterns of experience. It could also be conceived that depending on initial conditions (i.e. the psychiatric and criminal history of the individual referred, current index offence and decisions made by the NE CDT) the individual will be processed either within the boundary determined by the criminal justice system or the boundary determined by the mental health services. In other words, there are two domains and an individual referred to the NE CDT may experience a 'phase shift' towards one or the other depending on initial conditions.

Phase space is the space of the possible and provides the axis within which the strange attractor can be mapped

The strange attractor lives in multi-dimensional phase space and phase space gives a way of turning numbers into pictures (a phase space portrait), abstracting every bit of essential information from a system of moving parts and making a flexible road map to all its possibilities.

> The geometry of dynamical systems takes place in a mental space, known as phase space. It's very different from ordinary physical space. Phase space contains not just what happens but what might happen under different circumstances. It's the space of the possible. (Cohen and Stewart,1994: 200)

In multi-dimensional phase space the complete state of knowledge about a dynamical system, a single instant in time, collapses to a point. That point is the dynamical system – at that instant. At the next instant, though, the system will have changed ever so slightly and so the point will move. The history of the system can be charted by the moving point, tracing its orbit through phase space with the passage of time. Every piece of a dynamical system that can move independently is another variable, another degree of freedom. Every degree of freedom requires another dimension in phase space, to make sure that a single point contains enough information to determine the state of the system uniquely: one-dimension where only a single number is required to stand for temperature or population, and that number defined the position of a point on a one-dimensional line; two-dimensions where one variable is on the horizontal axis and the other on the vertical – if the system is a swinging, frictionless pendulum, one variable is position and the other velocity, and they change continuously, making a line of points that traces a loop, repeating itself forever.

So, the state space is all the possible states in which a system might exist in theoretical terms. Or as Byrne (1998) puts it 'We can think of this in system terms as defining the state of the system in terms of a set of *n* co-ordinates in *n* dimensional space when we have *n* parameters' (p. 24). In other words, what information is required at the point of referral to the NE CDT (the parameters of the referral stage), form the axes of a multi-dimensional plane within which the state of the referral can be plotted. In practice 58 variables were used to 'nail down' the state of the system at the referral stage (i.e. 58 dimensions in phase space), including: referral reason, referring agency, current contact with health/ social services, current psychiatric diagnosis, psychiatric medication compliance, current index offence, status in criminal justice system, probability of self harm or harm to others, etc.

Poincaré Maps are slices we take from the strange attractor at important points along the axis so we can see what is happening at one point, and then again what is happening at the next point, and so on

To convert these multi-dimensional skeins into flat pictures the technique is to make a return map or a Poincaré Map, in effect taking a slice or Poincaré section from the tangled heart of the attractor, removing a two-dimensional section just as a pathologist prepares a section of tissue for a microscopic slide. The Poincaré section removes a dimension from an attractor and turns a continuous line into a collection of points, implicitly assuming that much of the essential movement can be preserved. The process corresponds to sampling the state of a system ever so often, instead of continuously. When to sample – where to take the slice from

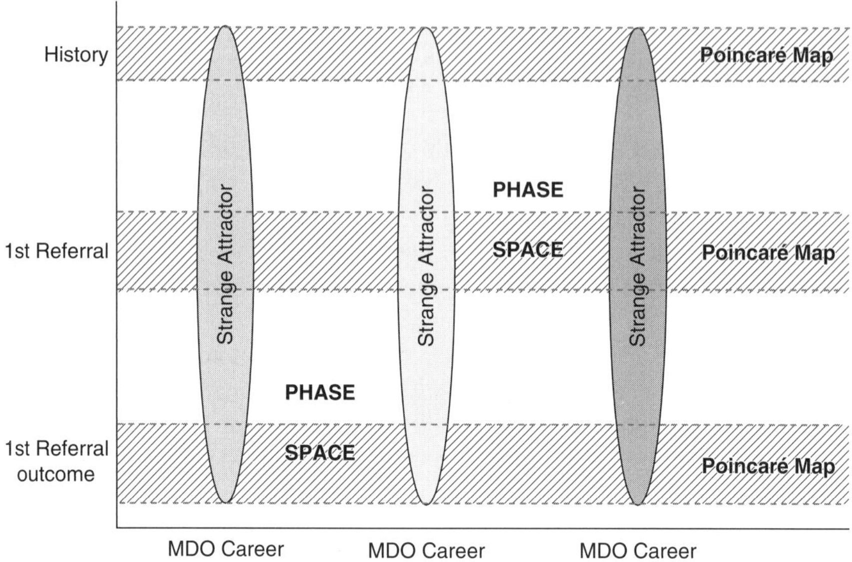

Figure 6.2 Complexity Theory and the search for MDO attractors

a strange attractor – is the question that gives a researcher some flexibility (Gleick, 1997). The most informative interval might correspond to some physical feature of the dynamical system, or to a regular time interval, freezing successive states in the flash of an imaginary strobe light.

For a more detailed discussion of these concepts refer to Gleick's (1997) chapter entitled 'Strange Attractors', pp. 121–53 and Byrne in this volume.

It could be conceived that the search for MDO psychiatric/criminal career patterns or trajectories was a search for strange attractors (see Figure 6.2).

TIME-ORDERED DATASETS

A total of three datasets were constructed for this project. Table 6.1 gives examples of the types of variable available to construct these datasets. 'History' variables described psychiatric history and previous convictions in some detail. 'First Referral' variables include reason for referral, current contact with services, current offence and what the NE CDT did with them. 'First Referral Outcome' include needs identified, deficit in meeting needs, outcome from the CJS and if people were subsequently re-referred.

Each dataset represented a slice through time. Joining together these time-ordered sections would allow the project to model the time evolution of this dynamical system.

Table 6.1 Examples of variables used to construct the datasets

History	*First referral*	*First referral outcome*
First episode type	Referral reason	Most severe
Elapsed time first episode (months)	Referral method	Least severe
First diagnosis	Referring agency	Least severe final outcome from the CJS
Age at first episode (years)	CDT primary worker	Most severe final outcome from the CJS
Most recent episode type	Case duration	Needs identified
Elapsed time last episode (months)	Intensity of support	Actioned by
Most recent diagnosis	Diagnoses	Provider
Age at latest episode (years)	Current medication	Agency
Diagnostic uncertainty	Taking medication	Service provided
Voluntary admissions	Probability of self harm	Disparity between assessed need and service provided
Compulsory admissions	Probability of harm to others	Service deficit
First/serious offence type	Location of assessment	Client re-referred to the CDT following discharge
Elapsed time first pre-con (months)	Current CJS status	
First/serious sentence	History of harm	
Age at first offence (years)	CDT primary assessor	
Most recent/serious offence type	CDT secondary assessor	
Elapsed time last pre-con (months)	Remand status	
Most recent/ serious sentence	Current to GP	
Age at most recent offence (years)	Current to probation officer	
Most serious offence	Current to CPN	
Most serious sentence	Current to solicitor	
Count of each offence type	Current to social worker	
Prison sentence (n)	Current to psychiatrist	
Hospital order (n)	Current to psychology	
First incident	Count of each offence type	
Elapsed time	Most severe current offence	
Co-careers	Least severe current offence	
History of harm	CDT report author	
	Other report	

The three datasets also represented key periods or multifurcation points in the careers of these individuals referred to the NE CDT. 'Multifurcation' means that these datasets represent points in a trajectory where one of two or more things may happen. For example, from the History dataset to First Referral individuals may be assessed and diagnosed as mentally disordered by the CDT or not; from First Referral Output individuals may be re-referred or not (see Figure 6.3).

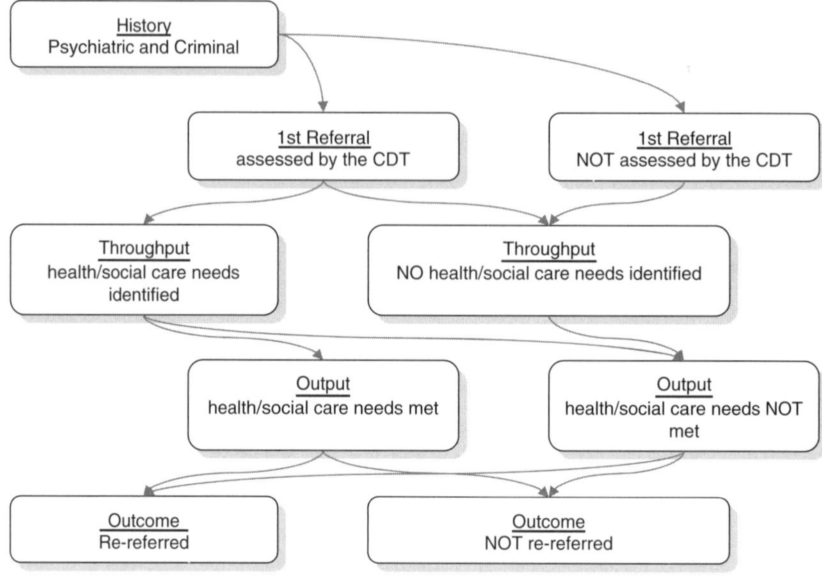

Figure 6.3 Examples of possible pathways

CREATING A 'HOLOGRAM'

Trying to map even the most simple pathways or trajectories can blow the mind in terms of the complexity involved – this project had 1011 cases each described by 140 variables. The project had developed very smoothly up until this point; however, now it felt like things were 'drowning in data'! It was clear what needed to be done but not how to do it. One of the ideas during this stage of the research was to try and create a 'hologram'. The plan was to print each of the 1011 careers or pathways on to acetates, pile them on top of each other and look down through them in order to identify patterns or strange attractors, which certain cases were more likely to converge towards/experience.

However, the University's department secretary was unhappy about ordering a couple of thousand overheads, and as a colleague pointed out, with that many acetates all piled on top of each other, the effect would become opaque. So it was back to the drawing board.

CLUSTER ANALYSIS

The solution came in the form of an epiphany. What the project was trying to do in the search for patterns or strange attractors was to identify a smaller number of pathways or careers towards which the experiences of people converged. Cluster analysis offered the solution. Rather than recourse to reductionism or limiting linear analysis, cluster analysis offered the chance to use as many variables as considered relevant to uncover groups or types within each of the three datasets. Data would be simplified with minimal loss of information as cluster analysis groups together those things that are most similar.

> By applying clustering techniques, information regarding '*N*' cases can be reduced to information concerning a smaller number of '*g*' groups. Construction of a taxonomy simplifies the observations with a minimal loss of information. (Lorr, 1983: 4)

and

> . . . in many fields the research worker is faced with a great bulk of observations which are quite intractable unless classified into manageable groups, which in some sense can be treated as units. Clustering techniques can be used to perform this data reduction, reducing the information on the whole set of say *N* individuals to information about say *g* groups (where hopefully *g* is very much smaller than *N*). (Everitt, 1974: 4)

Also important in applying cluster analysis to the three time-ordered datasets it would be possible to identify career patterns by tracing movements between groups from one set of clusters to the next.

CLUSTER OUTPUT – AGGLOMERATION SCHEDULE

There are a number of different clustering techniques – for example, some begin with all cases as separate entities and combine the two most similar, and the two most similar, until all cases are combined into one cluster; others begin with the dataset as one cluster and continues to subdivide into finer subsets. In this instance, the agglomerative hierarchical techniques (which joins the two most similar together) was selected because criteria have been developed for determining the level in the hierarchy at which there is an optimum number of clusters present – otherwise known as the stopping rule. 'Mojena's Rule' for example (developed by Mojena, 1977) uses the distribution of the clustering criterion to determine when a significant change from one stage to the next implies a partition that should not have been undertaken.

The agglomerative hierarchical methods are the most popular of the clustering techniques. Although the number of algorithms available is considerable, nearly all are variations of three approaches: linkage methods, centroid methods and minimum-variance methods. The basic procedure is however the same. The process begins with the computation of a distance or similarity matrix between all possible pairs of entities. For example, a very common similarity coefficient is the product moment correlation coefficient and perhaps the most common distance measure is Euclidean distance. Once the indices are available the matrix is searched for the closest (or most similar) pair *i* and *j*. Then *i* and *j* are merged to form cluster *k* and the matrix entry values are modified to reflect the change. The matrix is searched again for the closest pair and the two are merged into a new cluster. The process is followed until all entities are in one cluster. Sneath and Sokal (1973) used the acronym SAHN to characterise the procedure: sequential, agglomerative, hierarchical and non-overlapping.

The particular agglomerative hierarchical cluster technique selected for this project was the Minimum-Variance method (otherwise known as Ward's method after Ward (1963) who proposed this general hierarchical clustering programme). The procedure is based on the premise that the most accurate information is available when each entity constitutes a group. Consequently, as the number of clusters is systematically reduced from k, k - 1, k - 2, ..., 1, the grouping of increasingly dissimilar entities yields less precise information. At each stage in the procedure the goal is to form a group such that the sum of squared within-group deviations about the group mean of each profile variable is minimised for all profile variables at the same time. The value of the objective function is expressed as the sum of the within-group sum of squares (called the error sum of squares, ESS). Each reduction in groups is achieved by considering all possible pairings and selecting the pairing for which the objective-function value is smallest. Each cluster previously formed is treated as one unit. When the complete hierarchical solution has been obtained, the ESS values may be compared to ascertain the relative homogeneity of the groups formed. A sharp increase in the ESS indicates that much of the accuracy has been lost by reducing the number of groups (the basis of 'Mojena's Rule').

Table 6.2 shows the initial output from a cluster analysis run in SPSS. The most important column is the one in the middle, highlighted in dark grey. It is the sum of the squared deviations about the mean of each variable calculated for each cluster (the ESS described above). The aim of the method selected is to minimise the within cluster deviation around the mean because if the same or similar things are grouped together there should be little variation.

What tends to happen is that the variation will increase gradually and then there will be a sudden increase, indicating that things have been forced to group together which are not similar (i.e. according to 'Mojena's Rule' clustering should stop at this point). Because the figures tend to be large it is easier to calculate the difference, shown by the light grey, subtracting one stage from the next.

STOPPING RULE

The clearest way to identify the sudden jump in variance is to plot it as a graph. Chart 6.1 demonstrates the optimum number of clusters based on the Table 6.2 output is four.

The chart provides an easily accessible visual representation of the coefficient differentials, which can then be examined for extreme directional changes (if there were two or more possible breaks each cluster number would be explored in turn and a judgement made concerning which provides the optimal grouping. Such decisions form a part of much research).

In order to identify which case belonged to which cluster it was a simple task of re-running the cluster analysis, specifying the number of clusters to be saved, i.e. in this case four. SPSS inserts a new column at the end of the dataset

Table 6.2 Initial output from SPSS cluster analysis

Cluster Combined			Coefficients	Stage Cluster First Appears		Next stage	
stage	Cluster 1	Cluster 2		Cluster 1	Cluster 2		
1	976	1009	0	0	0	20	
2	1005	1006	0	0	0	3	
3	28	1005	0	0	2	12	
↓	↓	↓	↓	↓	↓	↓	Difference in coefficient values – 223.8382 – 218.4109 = 5.427277 i.e. (stage 411) – (stage 410)
408	24	185	207.9484	394	354	424	↓
409	16	369	212.9984	364	371	424	
410	21	50	218.4109	360	399	423	
411	66	110	223.8382	382	393	422	5.427277
412	220	232	229.31	346	389	425	5.471863
413	64	144	234.8577	252	402	429	5.547623
414	8	18	240.488	395	367	430	5.63031
415	37	318	246.3797	400	358	426	5.891769
416	146	296	252.6655	361	377	423	6.285721
417	43	268	259.1308	390	404	433	6.465363
418	54	328	266.0058	397	392	421	6.875
419	71	506	272.9501	398	386	427	6.944244
420	31	49	280.2911	381	406	434	7.341034
421	6	54	287.9061	383	418	435	7.61499

Table 6.2 (*Continued*)

422	13	66	296.4888	403	411	432	8.582703
423	21	146	305.1715	410	416	428	8.682739
424	16	24	314.6067	409	408	429	9.435181
425	131	220	325.1424	407	412	428	10.53571
426	37	89	337.1067	415	239	431	11.96429
427	28	71	349.35	333	419	440	12.24326
428	21	131	361.7119	423	425	439	12.36191
429	16	64	375.5803	424	413	438	13.86838
430	8	12	389.7621	414	391	433	14.18182
431	37	88	404.7371	426	388	434	14.97501
432	13	72	420.9609	422	405	436	16.22385
433	8	43	437.7602	430	417	435	16.79926
434	31	37	456.8019	420	431	437	19.04169
435	6	8	478.61	421	433	438	21.80807
436	13	33	507.1273	432	278	437	28.5174
437	13	31	537.3878	436	434	440	30.26041
438	6	16	572.0668	435	429	439	34.67908
439	6	21	624.9693	438	428	441	52.90247
440	13	28	705.9538	437	427	441	80.9845
441	6	13	842.3281	439	440	0	136.3743

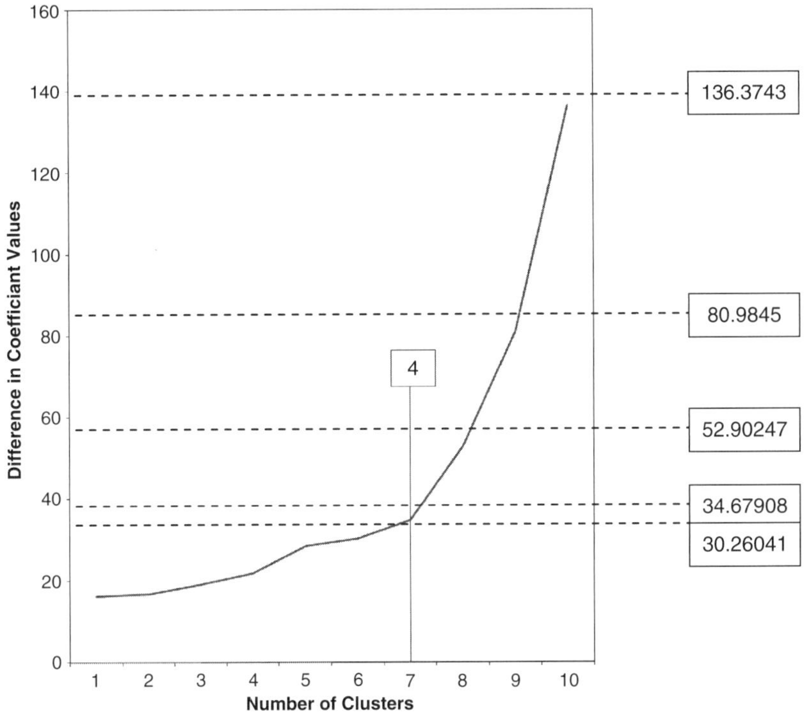

Chart 6.1 A demonstration of Mojena's Rule

identifying cluster membership. So, using the same agglomerative hierarchical cluster technique, the Minimum-Variance method or Ward's method, cluster analysis was performed on each of the three datasets (History, First Referral and First Referral Outcome) which represented slices through the MDO career pathway at subsequent points in time. The next step was to trace movement from one cluster at one career period to another cluster at the next period. This involved the creation of one final dataset which included all cases and which cluster they belonged to at each career period.

It was possible then to simply cluster these cluster memberships in order to identify overall career patterns. The result was the identification of five MDO careers.

MDO CAREER TYPOLOGY

Figure 6.4 provides an overview of the five types of psychiatric/criminal careers experienced by MDOs referred to the NE CDT (more detailed findings are discussed elsewhere, see Dyer, 2006).

Careers 1 and 5 were experienced by MDOs – people who previously had or who would have been in receipt of care and treatment by the health and social services. The people experiencing Career 5 had psychiatric history prior to

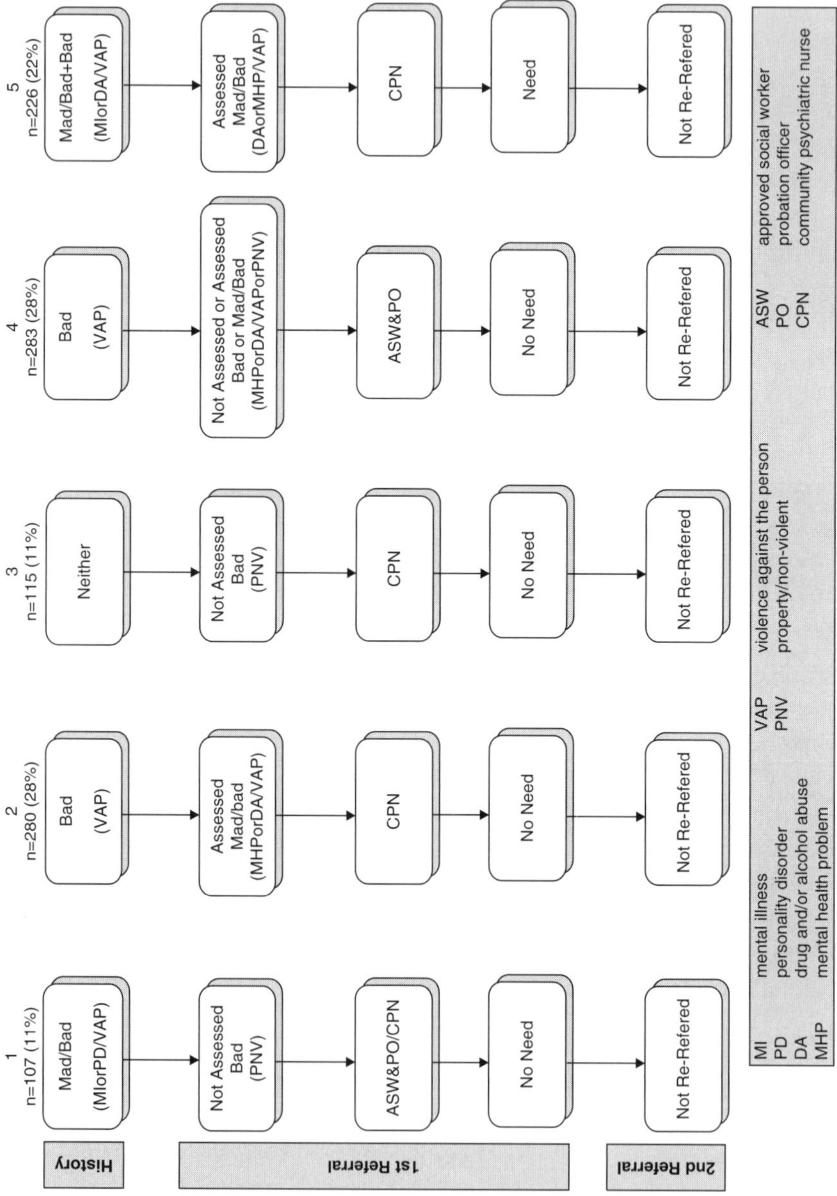

Figure 6.4 Career typology of individuals referred to the NE CDT (n = 1011)

referral to the NE CDT as well as the beginnings of a criminal career. Significantly, when assessed by the CDT Nurses, they had health and social needs identified. The NE CDT then referred this group of people to other agencies in order that needs were met. Consequently, no-one experiencing this career was re-referred to the NE CDT, meaning they either did not go on to re-offend or they did not become part of a mental health/criminal justice revolving door. Career 1 had no health or social care needs identified. Whilst they compared with Career 5, having both a psychiatric history and previous convictions prior to referral to the NE CDT, they were not selected for assessment which could have led to the identification of need. Consequently, everyone experiencing this career went on to be re-referred again to the NE CDT, meaning they either re-offended or became part of a mental health revolving door.

Careers 2 and 4 had two groups of people who were career criminals. Prior to referral to the NE CDT they had no previous psychiatric history but plenty of previous convictions, mostly for violent offences and they were referred to the NE CDT having been accused of further violent offences. The diagnoses given by the NE CDT Community Psychiatric Nurses, Social Worker and Probation Officer on assessment were vague, mental health problems or drug/alcohol misuse. The fact that no health or social care needs were identified emphasise the inappropriateness of their referral. Whilst no-one was re-referred to the NE CDT, meaning they did not become part of a mental health revolving door, this did not mean that they did not go on to re-offend, they probably did being more like career criminals than MDOs.

Career 3 were referred to the NE CDT for the provision of information only. Minimal data was recorded describing the people involved or any actions taken by the NE CDT. This group of people were not re-referred to the CDT.

DISCUSSION

The search for an alternative methodology was informed by an early interest in the concept of 'deviant careers' – an idea which implied:

- time – a career unfolds over time as part of a life course,
- change – a career consists of key periods when an act or decision causes a change of direction down one of a number of alternative paths.

Cause and effect – but not simple cause, it had always seemed clear that what impacted upon people's lives causing them to unfold or develop in a particular way was complex rather than singular or linear (Williams and Dyer, 2009). Whilst it was never an intention to join others and indulge in a superficial and ignorant dismissal of the quantitative possibilities of sociology, it did seem that what was going on in social statistics at the time was reductionist, positivist and linear and therefore unable to deal with complex or non-linear factors or transformations (Byrne, 1998). What was needed was a 're-think' about the tools that had been developed for the analysis of data about the real world in complex terms.

Complexity Theory provided the framework within which to situate this understanding of what the world is like and to reformulate the tools through which we could know it. It enabled the project to:

- describe the system, i.e. institutional careers of those referred to the NE CDT, as a whole rather than in terms of its parts. In other words, it was not enough to analyse the individual variables describing those referred and subsequent diversion team activity. Instead what was needed was an exploration of all of the information available which described context and action, in order to identify emergent patterns;
- plot the way the system or careers changed – systems were temporal and dynamic. Careers existed in time and they changed through time;
- concentrate on the identification of changes of kind – in phase shifts in which the systems or careers underwent radical transformations. Referral to the NE CDT indicated a multifurcation point in the careers of those referred. Depending on the interaction of causal factors, these people would be directed down one of a number of alternative career paths each leading to a different type of outcome.

While Complexity Theory provided the framework, cluster analysis provided the tools used to uncover career pathways. The central principle of numerical taxonomy is simple: to establish classifications which minimise within-group variation among cases in the categories and to maximise between group variation (i.e. to put together things that are more like each other). The application of cluster analysis in this instance was case centred and case driven, which meant that it could be used to identify groups of MDOs who shared similar characteristics. The construction of three time-ordered datasets (History, First Referral and First Referral Outcome); the initial application of cluster analysis to each of these separate datasets; and finally the overall cluster analysis of the dataset detailing each case's three cluster membership, meant that cluster analysis could be used to identify common or shared patterns of experience.

Among other things, the approach developed offers an alternative way of evaluating services which 'process' people (as described at the beginning of this chapter). It hopefully goes some way to avoiding one of the major criticisms of other methods which ignore the differences between subjects (MDOs are not a single group of people and what might work for one may not for another). Services which process people may process different people in different ways. This methodological approach identifies the common pathways experienced by different groups of people, and the positive or negative outcomes which follow. For example this project was able to make a number of recommendations for service improvement. The two careers identified which were the most important and relevant to the service provided by the NE CDT were Careers 1 and 5. Career 5 involved people who had both a psychiatric and criminal history, were referred to the team, assessed, had their health and social care needs identified and met, and were not re-referred to the diversion team again. This career was akin to an 'ideal type' – a model of what it was hoped a typical referral would look like. In comparison, Career 1 referrals, who also had a psychiatric and criminal history, were not assessed by the NE CDT and as a consequence had no health and social care needs identified and were all re-referred to the team again at a later date.

This 'revolving door' outcome was not one which could be considered positive or beneficial. Indeed in the case of these people, the NE CDT could be charged with maintaining them as 'mentally disordered offenders'. To avoid this outcome a simple recommendation was that that everyone referred with a psychiatric and criminal history was assessed by the team and their needs identified and met, regardless of the nature of their offending or the existence of current care packages.

With a little imagination it is possible to see how this cluster based methodology could be useful across a number of subjects which have access to time-ordered case-based data, and where the onus is on exploring different pathways to similar outcomes.

Finally, I would like to mention the application and development of this cluster based methodology used in a follow-up study which concentrated specifically on the outcomes of custody diversion for violent offenders (Carpenter and Dyer, 2007). This study used three main methods (logistic regression, cluster analysis and qualitative comparative analysis) for analysing the large dataset which was collated from the probation service, the mental health trust and the team itself. Each of these methods demonstrated potential for predicting the outcomes of the NE CDTs interventions:[1]

1 Regression analysis revealed that the presence of some key variables, notably previous convictions and psychiatric history, greatly increased the odds of an MDO being reconvicted, admitted to psychiatric hospital or receiving mental health care.
2 Cluster analysis produced a series of distinct, clinically recognisable careers. These gave an holistic picture of individuals and how they were processed by the NE CDT. The outcomes of each career was markedly different, something which was not evident through regression analysis. Recognition by clinicians that an individual MDO was following a particular career could potentially lead to more targeted intervention.
3 Qualitative comparative analysis (QCA) is a development of Ragin's (2000) approach to the systematisation of comparative method through the use of Boolean logic in relation to truth tables, which specify the multiple configurations which can lead to particular outcomes. This approach offers another way of modelling complex and multiple causation in the trajectories of cases.

   In terms of the NE CDT study, QCA proved to be the most technically challenging. However the output of QCA (Truth Tables) could potentially offer practitioners guidance in risk based decision making (by examining the actual configuration for any given case against the actual truth table, a risk loading could be assigned to that case), and therefore deserves further exploration.

In contrast with regression analysis which attempts to create a model which fits the data, the cluster based method and QCA allowed for the identification of multiple causal configurations which can generate a given outcome. This fits the reality of complex open systems where the same outcome can be generated in a variety of fashions.

NOTE

1 While only brief details are provided here, full description and discussion will be provided in a forthcoming article to be published in the journal Methodological Innovations Online.

REFERENCES

Byrne, D. (1998) *Complexity Theory and the Social Sciences.* London: Routledge.

Byrne, D. and Ragin C. (2009) (eds) *The Sage Handbook of Case Based Methods.* London: Sage.

Carpenter, J. and Dyer, W. (2007) *Outcomes of Custody Diversion for Violent Offenders.* Department of Health, National Forensic Mental Health R&D Programme.

Cohen, J. and Stewart, I. (1994) *The Collapse of Chaos.* New York: Penguin Books.

Department of Health and Home Office (1991) *Review of Health and Social Services for Mentally Disordered Offenders and Others Requiring Similar Services – Report of the Community Advisory Group.* London: HMSO.

Dyer, W. (2006) 'The psychiatric and criminal careers of mentally disordered offenders referred to a custody diversion team in the United Kingdom'. *International Journal of Forensic Mental Health,* 5(1): 15–28.

Everitt, B. (1974) *Cluster Analysis.* London: Heinemann Educational Books Ltd.

Gleick, J. (1997) *Chaos: The Amazing Science of the Unpredictable.* London: Minerva.

Gunn, J., Maden, A., and Swinton, M. (1991a) 'Treatment needs of prisoners with psychiatric disorders'. *British Medical Journal*, 303: 338–41.

Gunn, J., Maden, T., and Swinton, M. (1991b) 'How many prisoners should be in hospital?' Home Office Research and Statistics Department, *Research Bulletin No. 31*, 9–15.

James, D. (2000) 'Police station diversion schemes: role and efficacy in central London'. *Journal of Forensic Psychiatry*, 11: 532–55.

Lorr, M. (1983) *Cluster Analysis for Social Scientists: Techniques for Analysing and Simplifying Complex Blocks of Data.* London: Josey-Bass Publishers.

McGilloway, S. and Donnelly, M. (2004) 'Mental illness in the UK criminal justice system. A police liaison scheme for Mentally Disordered Offenders in Belfast'. *Journal of Mental Health*, 13: 263–75.

Mojena, R. (1977) 'Hierarchical grouping methods and stopping rules: An evaluation'. *Computer Journal*, 20: 359–63.

NACRO Mental Health Advisory Committee (1993) *Diverting Mentally Disturbed Offenders from Prosecution.* London: NACRO.

Peay, J. (1994) 'Mentally disordered offenders'. In M. Maguire, R. Morgan, and R. Reiner (eds) *The Oxford Handbook of Criminology*, pp. 1119–60. Oxford: Clarendon Press.

Ragin, Charles C. (2000) *Fuzzy-set Social Science.* Chicago: University of Chicago Press.

Riordan, S., Wix, S., Kenny-Herbert, J., and Humphreys, M. (2000) 'Diversion at the point of arrest: mentally disordered people and contact with the police'. *Journal of Forensic Psychiatry*, 11(3): 683–90.

Ritchie, J., Dick, D., and Lingham, L. (1994) *Report of the Inquiry into the Care and Treatment of Christopher Clunis.* London: HMSO.

Rubington, E.S. and Weinberg, M.S. (2008) *Deviance: The Interactionist Perspective*, 10th Edition. Boston: Allyn & Bacon.

Sneath, P.H.A. and Sokal, R.R. (1973) *Numerical Taxonomy.* San Francisco: W.H. Freeman.

Waldrop, M.M. (1992) *Complexity: The Emerging Science at the Edge of Order and Chaos.* Harmondsworth: Penguin Books.

Ward, J.H.J. (1963) 'Hierarchical grouping to optimize an objective function'. *Journal of the American Statistical Association*, 58: 236–44.

Watson, W. (1993) 'Future directions for research'. In W. Watson and A. Grounds (eds) *The Mentally Disordered Offender in an Era of Community Care*, pp. 191–200. Cambridge: Cambridge University Press.

Williams, M. and Dyer, W. (2009) 'Single-case probabilities'. In: D. Byrne and C. Ragin (eds) *The Sage Handbook of Case Based Methods.* London: Sage.

7

Correspondence Analysis: A Case for Methodological Pluralism?

Ian Rees-Jones

INTRODUCTION

In the wake of Bourdieu's (1984) pioneering work on stratification and forms of distinction and taste, there has been an increasing interest in and use of correspondence analysis in social research. Despite what one might describe as an Anglo-Saxon lag in the take up of these methods, in recent years they have been applied to studies of cultural preferences and tastes among social groups (Savage et al., 2005), health and health inequality (Greenacre, 2002; Gatrell et al., 2004), lifestyles (Batista-Foguet et al., 2000) and taste (Blasius and Friedrichs, 2008). Essentially Correspondence Analysis (CA) summarises the associations between a set of categorical variables and displays these graphically (Phillips, 1995; Le Roux and Rouanet, 2004). Multiple Correspondence Analysis (MCA) (sometimes referred to as homogeneity analysis) maps points representing all variables into a sub-space with as few dimensions as possible. The method combines the advantages of multidimensional and non-linear methods and provides simple graphic overviews of complex systems (Hans et al., 2000). This chapter considers the foundations of MCA and in particular the claims made by some working in the field that it is a relational procedure that sets it aside from other forms of data analysis. By contrasting this position with a more sceptical approach to the primary theoretical status of the technique and drawing on a worked example of the application of the method, the chapter will discuss the strengths that MCA has in relation to the analysis of categorical data. The chapter will conclude with an argument that MCA should be developed and exploited in the context of a pluralist approach to method.

THEORY

Multiple Correspondence Analysis formed a cornerstone of Bourdieu's approach to the study of social relations. It informed his work on class distinction and lifestyles (Bourdieu, 1984) as well as later work on the construction of the housing market in France (Bourdieu, 2005). Although committed to what he referred to as methodological polytheism Bourdieu set out his preference for correspondence analysis in a now oft-quoted statement:

> similarly, if I make extensive use of correspondence analysis, in preference to multivariate regression for instance, it is because correspondence analysis is a relational technique of data analysis whose philosophy corresponds exactly to what, in my view, the reality of the social world is. It is a technique which 'thinks' in terms of relations, as I try to do precisely with the notion of field. (Bourdieu and Wacquant, 1996: 96)

In recent years Bourdieu's work has received renewed attention and this offers some insight into the methodological and theoretical basis to MCA. Bourdieu conceived the habitus as the concept for integrating individual and structural levels of analysis within the social space of lifestyles. But as Bennet (2007) argues, Bourdieu's stress on the *unity* of the habitus is problematic. By unity Bourdieu referred to the sets of choices of persons, goods and practices uniting all those who are the product of similar socio-economic conditions. While Bourdieu was never fully consistent in his writing on the unity of habitus, sometimes emphasising it and at other times appearing more probabilistic, in his account, Bennet suggests that he was too fixed in his approach and that those who occupy contradictory economic and cultural positions find a destabilised habitus. By focusing on those aspects of taste and lifestyles that distinguish class groups, Bourdieu may have over-dramatised differences that are often of minor significance in the activities of any one class. Deviations are largely seen to prove the rule so, for example, middle class 'slumming' in cultural choices might be interpreted as ironic while similar working class tastes are seen to be unknowing and fixed. As we shall see one of the criticisms of MCA is that the analysis tends to reinforce such assumptions. Citing Lahire (2003) Bennet suggests that a more pluralistic account of the conditions (both historical and present) that structure individual tastes, dispositions and practices is possible. In this sense greater emphasis is placed on the potential for individuals to reject or amend the influences of the conditions that formed the habitus of earlier periods over their lifecourse.

Some criticisms of the method have implied that it has a 'polarising logic' (Ranciere, 2004). While MCA may provide an analysis of objective relations it cannot provide an analysis of the interaction within a social field and 'objective relations do not operate on the basis of mere homology between fields' (de Nooy, 2003: 325). But Bennet goes further to argue that conceiving of the Habitus as a structured and structuring structure is no more than a rhetorical device that impedes ethnographic and historical research. Bourdieu's conclusion in distinction of a unified class habitus is:

> partly a reflection of the ways in which multiple correspondence analysis converts cultural data into binary opposites which do not allow fine graded distinctions to be taken into account and which, if not guarded against, exaggerate differences at the expense of shared tastes. (Bennett, 2007: 214)

SUMMARY OF THE METHOD

Correspondence analysis has antecedents in Pearson's work on the chi-squared statistic (Pearson, 1906) and Fisher's work on contingency tables (Fisher, 1940). It is now used in a diversity of disciplines including biology, environmental science, linguistic and social sciences. A detailed history of the technique can be found in de Leeuw (1983) who tracks MCA back to the work of Guttman (1953) and Burt (1950). The method was more fully developed in France by Jean-Paul Benzécri (1973) and it is sometimes referred to as homogeneity analysis. Michailidis and de Leeuw (1998) in their review of the main techniques of homogeneity analysis suggest that the many ways of approaching the analysis of categorical data may explain why the analysis appears to have been reinvented many times.

Beh (2004) states that correspondence analysis allows graphical representation of the row and column categories in a contingency table. Simple CA is its application to a two-way contingency table while MCA is the analysis of the pattern of relationships of several categorical variables. Similar in many ways to principal components analysis, MCA involves undertaking a standard correspondence analysis on an indicator matrix. It is used to analyse observations coded as binary variables. For example, in the category 'Gender', Male might be coded (0, 1) and Female might be coded (1, 0). The analysis can accommodate ordinal and ratio variables by re-coding so, for example, a score on a scale of −5 to +5 can be recoded as <0, 0, >0. In such a scheme a score of 3 would be coded (0, 0, 1).

Greenacre (2002) gives a summary of the main aspects of MCA using an analysis of the Spanish National Health Survey as an exemplar. The advantages of CA/MCA are that it allows relationships between categorical variables that would otherwise be too complex to view in a contingency table to be viewed graphically. CA aims to produce a map of cross-tabulations where each row and column is represented as a point or a *profile*. The profiles of a row are the set of percentage responses for each category in that row adding up to 100%. The profiles define the point in multidimensional space. Each profile is made up of a certain number of cases and the *masses* weight each row profile according to the number of cases. *Distances* between profiles are calculated as the weighted

Euclidian distance or chi-squared distance. *Inertia* is a geometric measure of the dispersion of the profiles in multidimensional space. The higher the inertia the more spread out the categories are from the origin. The inertia is decomposed along the principal dimensions or axes allowing the construction of a 'map'. Reduction of dimensionality refers to the selection of the principal dimensions in a low dimensional space (usually two or three dimensions). This presents a number of methodological problems that have led to different forms of analysis being developed including; detrended CA, canonical CA and joint CA (Greenacre 1984, 1993, 2006). Greenacre (2002) uses eigenvalues and the squared correlations to identify important points on the map. Inertia is the variance of the solutions and the eigenvalue is the percentage of explained inertia or the percentage of inertia explained by a factor/dimension. However, the emphasis on different forms of output to aid interpretation of data differs according to various schools of thought. For example, Le Roux and Rouanet (2004) emphasise interpretation based on analysis of both the clouds (maps) of variables and clouds (maps) of individuals.

In summary, the primary goal of CA/MCA is to transform a contingency table into a graphical display. The percentage of variance explained by each dimension is usually adjusted. In interpreting the visual outputs from MCA the aim should be to identify those categories that cluster together. However, maps are only representations of general patterns so the significance of the distances between categories should not be overstated. The method is exploratory and descriptive and one consistent criticism is the lack of hypothesis testing involved. This has led some to view the method as 'theory less'. But it is important to note that the underlying basis for CA and MCA is geometric rather than statistical and this criticism may be based on an overly restricted view of theory as hypothesis testing.

MULTIPLE CORRESPONDENCE ANALYSIS OF WELSH HEALTH SURVEY DATA

To enable discussion of the method, data for the Welsh Health Survey 2004/2005 are used as a simple illustration of MCA. The survey was based on a representative sample of adults aged 16 and over living in private households in Wales. The household response rate for the survey was 73% with 16,000 adults and 4,100 children participating in the survey. The survey involved a short household interview and a self-completion questionnaire which was later collected by the interviewer. Along with socio-demographic data the adult questionnaire covered topics such as health service use, health status, illness and health behaviours (smoking, alcohol, fruit and vegetables, exercise, height and weight). For the purposes of this simple illustrative analysis a sub-sample of working age adults (20–59) was examined focusing on gender, socio-economic status (based on eight categories of the NS-SEC), smoking, consumption of fruit and vegetables alcohol and exercise. This allows us to construct a health lifestyle space for Welsh

Table 7.1 Variables used in the analysis

Sex	*Smoking*
1 Male	1 I smoke daily
2 Female	2 I smoke occasionally but not every day
	3 I used to smoke daily but do not smoke at all now
	4 I used to smoke occasionally but do not smoke at all now
	5 I have never smoked
FruitVeg	*Exercise*
(Daily number of portions)	0 Exercise
0 None	1 No exercise
1 <5	
2 ≥5	
Alcohol	*NS-SEC*
1 Never	1 Higher managerial and professional
2 Special occasions	2 Lower managerial and professional
3 < Once a week	3 Intermediate
4 Weekends	4 Small employers and own account workers
5 Weekends/week days	5 Lower supervisory and technical
6 Most days	6 Semi-routine
7 Everyday	7 Routine
	8 Never worked and long term unemployed

adults using MCA. In this case the data were transformed using SPSS 12.0 and MCA was undertaken using XLSTAT version 2007.7.

Table 7.1 shows the variables utilised in the analysis. Five active variables were employed in the analysis and these included, along with gender, four indicators of key health lifestyles: smoking, alcohol, exercise and consumption of fruit and vegetables. Five categories of smoking were used, seven categories of alcohol consumption, three categories of fruit and vegetable consumption and two categories of exercise. A measure of socio-economic occupation (the NS-SEC) was used as a supplementary variable in the analysis incorporating an eightfold categorisation. To allow the maps produced by the analysis to be read more easily the variable categories are numbered and their details shown in the table. For example, 'smoking-1' on the map refers to the response 'I smoke daily' while 'smoking-5' refers to 'I have never smoked'.

Figure 7.1 shows the health lifestyle space for men and women. The figure shows the position of lifestyles in the first two dimensions from the MCA output. When interpreting the map those categories that are close to one another can be said to be similar so that they can be considered to be more likely to have been mentioned by the same respondents. For example, women, never smoked and drinking less than once a week cluster closely together. In addition to this it is important to examine the extent to which categories contribute to the dimensions or axes. In this case the first dimension (the horizontal axes) accounted for 44.66% of adjusted inertia (explained variance) while the second dimension (vertical axis) accounted for 23.82% of adjusted inertia (explained variance).

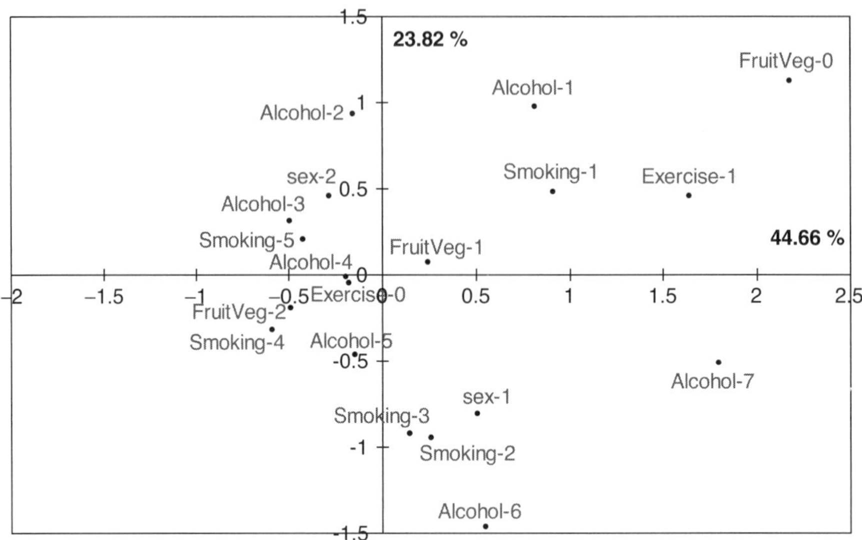

Figure 7.1 Health lifestyle space of Welsh adults

By examining the contributions of individual variables to each dimension it is possible to discern that the first dimension is determined by a contrast between smoking daily, lack of exercise and no fruit and veg in the top right quadrant and never having smoked and more than five portions of fruit and veg a day in the left side of the map. The second (vertical) dimension appears to be largely determined by gender and alcohol consumption with women and low alcohol consumption clustering in the top half of the map and men and high alcohol consumption clustering towards the bottom half of the map. It would appear therefore that in terms of the health lifestyle space of Welsh adults there are distinct patterns. The horizontal axis might be said to reflect health maintenance with the positive part of the axes characterised by low levels of health maintenance and the negative part reflecting relatively high levels of health maintenance. The vertical axes might be said to reflect a gendered space in relation to a specific form of lifestyle activity namely alcohol consumption where the negative side is dominated by men and high levels of alcohol intake. Women therefore are relatively close to low levels of alcohol consumption but it is interesting to note that women are also closer than men in relation to the health maintenance variables.

Having set out a simple MCA analysis using a limited set of lifestyle variables it is also possible to project socio-demographic characteristics of the sample into the social space. In this case we utilise the eightfold classification NS-SEC as a supplementary variable. Figure 7.2 shows the same MCA with the supplementary variable included. As we can see, there is no change to the adjusted inertia, the dimensions or the contribution of variables to the dimensions. The process is very much akin to projecting the supplementary variable on to the social space.

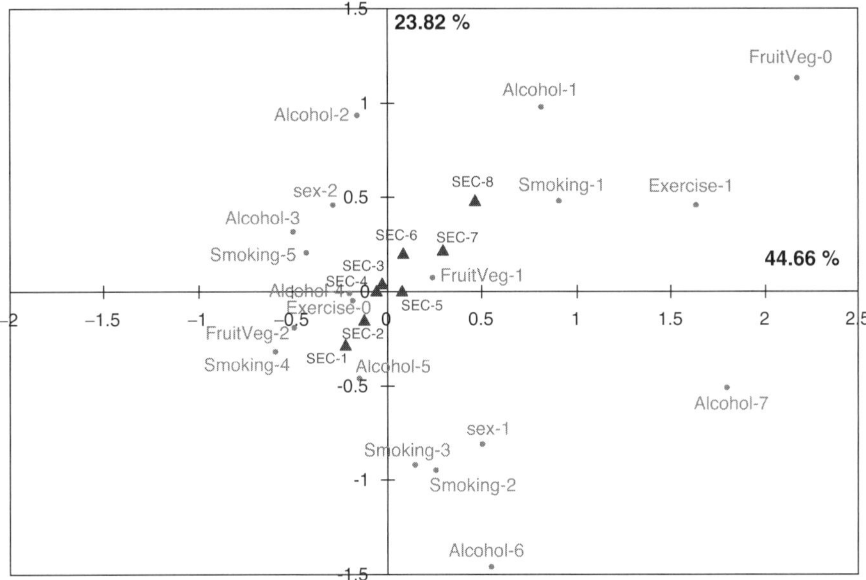

Figure 7.2 Health lifestyle space of Welsh adults, with NS-SEC as a supplementary variable

The figure shows, as we might expect, a clear gradient moving down at a 45 degree angle from the top right quadrant where long-term unemployed, routine and semi-routine occupations cluster with low levels of health maintenance down towards the bottom left where higher managerial and professional groups cluster with the higher health maintenance variables. It is interesting to note however, that alcohol consumption does not follow this gradient with higher social groups being relatively closer to medium to high levels of alcohol consumption reflecting that alcohol consumption cuts across class distinctions and has a complex patterning. In a separate analysis for men and women (not shown here) the NS-SEC classification showed a more distinct patterning for men and tended to cluster around the origin for women.

DISCUSSION

As we have previously noted MCA is explorative and descriptive. To some extent this has hindered its adoption within Anglo-Saxon social science as it does not immediately conform to standard approaches based on statistical tests of significance that could provide generalisation to a larger population. However, MCA can lend itself to a view of generalisation as '*moderatum*' in the form of categorical hypotheses (Williams, 2000; Payne and Williams, 2005) and Le Roux and Rouanet (2004: 234) discuss a numerical measure of the *importance* of the deviation between the coordinates of two modalities on an axis (>1 being large and <0.5 being small). Further, the chi-squared distance is defined by Greenacre (2002: 0171) as a Mahalanobis distance (used in cluster analysis) though it differs from Euclidian distance in taking account of the correlations of the data set.

Breiger (2000) argues that CA has been criticised as being unable to move beyond description and being prone to data fishing and suggests that these criticisms have meant that advantages of CA, as understood by French, Dutch and Japanese researchers, have not travelled well in Anglo-Saxon academia (see also Goodman (1996) for similar criticisms). A further criticism is that by focusing on distances between points the analysis may give too much credence to insignificant phenomena where differences are large. MCA, however, may have particular strengths in relation to identifying patterns of response where there is incomplete or missing data. A relatively unexplored area is its use in the analysis of trend or longitudinal data so that temporal changes might be shown on a symmetric map as points corresponding to successive time points linked to show patterns in profiles over time.

Beh refers to the theoretical similarities and philosophical differences between CA and log-linear models (Beh, 2001, 2004). While Moser (1989) argues that MCA can supplement log-linear models by helping to identify and interpret models. In this way combining log-linear statistical modelling with graphic analysis may 'result in more complete and parsimonious summaries of contingency table data' (Moser, 1989: 189). Again schools of thought differ. For example, Rouanet et al. (2000) argue that MCA should be supplemented by other methods. However, other techniques such as regression should be integrated into the geometric representation rather then juxtaposed with it. Attempts have been made to combine MCA with other forms of analysis. For example, Gatrell et al. (2004), in their analysis of health inequalities, undertook a preliminary multivariate logistic regression to identify categories for inclusion in their MCA. This led to criticism from Veenstra (2007) who suggested that their analysis was inconsistent with Bourdieu's approach because of their method of identifying categories and because of the lack of attention to cultural tastes and practices in their data. As a consequence, Veenstra argues their analysis does not present a *true* representation of social space that displays class boundaries. It should be noted however, that Gatrell et al. argue there is no such thing as *the* social space because the subsequent MCA construction of social space is dependent on the selection of categorical variables. This is a small illustration of a continual tension within the literature relating to the selection of variables for inclusion in an MCA. It should be noted that Veenstra's own analysis of Canadian data found that distinctive cultural tastes were a strong feature of higher class grouping while poor health lifestyles (smoking and heavy drinking) were more distinctive of lower social class groupings. While these findings chime with the analysis presented above of Welsh Health data no doubt the analysis presented here might be subject to similar criticisms of being based on the limited categories of the survey data.

Wuggenig (2007) argues that Bourdieu rejected mainstream approaches precisely because he saw in CA a method that was in tune with his relational conceptions of social reality. Wuggenig also argues that Bourdieu's aversion to mainstream log-linear models is based partly on an aversion to variable centred approaches which 'tend to dissimulate the system of relations that constitutes the principle of the force and form specific to the effects recorded in particular correlation or regression coefficients' (Wuggenig, 2007: 309). However, Chan and Goldthorpe (2007), in response to Wuggenig's comments, criticise Bourdieu's (1984) reliance on MCA by highlighting problems with the original data that relate to poor sampling, lack of transparency and poor questionnaire design. Most crucially they argue that it is unwise to suggest that any theoretical position can only be empirically tested using one technique. Indeed, to argue that CA/MCA are techniques that have a particular affinity with relational sociology, and affinity that is absent from 'mainstream' log-linear modelling is 'nothing more than mystification' (p. 320). There is no reason to believe that MCA (despite its strengths as a descriptive tool) is in any way unique in relation to other forms of variable analysis. For example, Lamont et al. (1996) use multiple regression to look at the extent to which the drawing of and support for cultural and moral boundary setting is related to structural (SEC, gender, race), geographical and educational factors as well as participation in cultural, religious lifestyles clusters. They conclude that both moral and cultural boundaries are best explained by structural factors and the cultural repertoires that are in turn influenced by geographic location and participation in lifestyle cluster. Race and education were highly significant predictors of cultural boundaries while income, education, geography, race and gender were significant predictors of moral boundaries. Their analysis suggests that it is not *essential* to undertake MCA to gain insights into the relationship between lifestyles and social space. Chan and Goldthorpe (2007) also suggest that while MCA displays the *gross* effects of stratification variables on patterns of lifestyle it can tell us very little about their *net* effects (for example whether education or class are of equal or less importance in determining lifestyles). Accordingly, they suggest that MCA may hide nuanced differentiations within class and lifestyle groupings thus perhaps leading to incorrect interpretations and in Bourdieu's case an assumption of class homology that other forms of analysis with the same data (for example latent class analysis, regression) might refute.

CONCLUSION

It is axiomatic that different methods allow us to pursue different ways of examining the same phenomena. Bourdieu believed that sociologists need to mobilise a range of methods of observation and measurement in order to better understand the inter-relationships between structure and agency, between material and cultural worlds and between lifestyle, class and social space. In this sense CA/MCA has important strengths and, when used in conjunction with other methods, provides a very useful, if underused, means of analysing social relations. We should not forget that when referring to his own laissez-faire approach to using MCA, Bourdieu emphasised his own commitment to methodological pluralism and a long standing resistance to what he saw as the methodology police: ‘In such matters, I would be tempted to say that only one rule applies: it is forbidden to forbid’ (Bourdieu and Wacquant, 1996: 227).

REFERENCES

Batista-Foguet, J.M., Mendoza, R., Perez-Perdigon, M., and Rius, R. (2000) Life-styles of Spanish school-aged children: Their evolution over time. Use of Multiple Correspondence Analysis to determine overall trends over time in a sequential, cross-sectional study. In A. Ferligoj and A, MrVar (eds) *New Approaches in Applied Statistics*. Metodoloski zvezki: FDV.

Beh, E.J. (2001) Partitioning Pearson’s chi-squared statistic for singly ordered two-way contingency tables, *The Australian and New Zealand Journal of Statistics*, 43: 327–33.

Beh, E.J. (2004) Simple correspondence analysis: A bibliographic review, *International Statistical Review*, 72(2): 257–84.

Bennet, T. (2007) Habitus Clivé: Aesthetics and politics in the work of Pierre Bourdieu. *New Literary History*, 38: 201–28.

Benzécri, J.P. (1973) *L’Analyse des donnees: I and II, La Taxinomie*. Dunod: Paris.

Blasius, J. and Friedrichs, J. (2008) Lifestyles in distressed neighbourhoods: A test of Bourdieu’s ‘taste of necessity’ hypothesis. *Poetics*, 36: 24–44.

Bourdieu, P. (1984) *Distinction: A Social Critique of the Judgement of Taste*. London: Routledge.

Bourdieu, P. (2005) *The Social Structures of the Economy*. Cambridge: Polity.

Bourdieu, P. and Wacquant, L. (1996) *An Invitation to Reflexive Sociology*. Cambridge: Polity.

Breiger, R.L. (2000) A tool kit for practice theory. *Poetics*, 27: 91–115.

Burt, C. (1950) The factorial analysis of qualitative data. *J. Statist. Psychology*, 3: 166–85.

Chan, T.W. and Goldthorpe, J.H. (2007) Data, methods and interpretation in analyses of cultural consumption: A reply to Peterson and Wuggenig. *Poetics*, 35: 317–29.

De Leeuw, J. (1983) On the prehistory of correspondence analysis. *Statistica Neerlandica*, 37: 161–4.

de Nooy (2003) Fields and networks: Correspondence analysis and social network analysis in the framework of field theory. *Poetics*, 31: 305–27.

Fisher, R.A. (1949) The precision of discriminant functions. *Annals of Eugenics*, 10: 422–9.

Gatrell, A., Popay, J., and Thomas, C. (2004) Mapping the determinants of health inequalities in social space: can Bourdieu help us? *Health and Place*, 10: 245–57.

Goodman, L.A. (1996) A single general method for the analysis of cross-classified data: Reconciliation and synthesis of some methods of Pearson, Yule, and Fisher, and also some methods of correspondence analysis and association analysis. *Journal of the American Statistical Association*, 91: 408–28.

Greenacre, M. (1993) *Correspondence Analysis in Practice*. London: Academic Press.

Greenacre, M. (2002) Correspondence analysis of the Spanish National Health Survey. *Gac Sanit*, 16(2): 16–70.

Greenacre, M. (2006) From simple to multiple correspondence analysis. In M. Greenacre and J. Blasius (eds) *Correspondence Analysis and Related Methods*. Boca Raton: Chapman & Hall, CRC, pp. 41–76.

Greenacre, M.J. (1984) *Theory and Application of Correspondence Analysis*. London: Academic Press.

Guttman, L. (1953) A note on Sir Cyril Burt’s Factorial Analysis of qualitative data. *The British Journal of Statistical Psychology*, 6: 1–4.

Hans, D., Ojasoo, T., and Dore, J. (2000) Deaths from breast cancer: Tackling multidimensionality and non-linearity by correspondence analysis. *Journal of Steroid Biochemistry and Molecular Biology*, 74: 195–202.

Lahire, B. (2003) From the habitus to an individual heritage of dispositions. Towards a sociology at the level of the individual. *Poetics*, 31: 329–55.

Lamont, M., Schmalzbauer, J., Walker, M., and Weber, D. (1996) Cultural and moral boundaries in the United States: Structural position geographic location and lifestyle explanations. *Poetics*, 224: 31–56.

Le Roux, B. and Rouanet, H. (2004) *Geometric Data Analysis, from Correspondence Analysis to Structured Data Analysis*. London: Kluwer Academic Publishers.

Michailidis, G. and de Leeuw, J. (1998) The Gifi System of Descriptive Multivariate Analysis. *Statistical Science*, 13(4): 307–36.

Moser, E.B. (1989) Exploring contingency tables with correspondence analysis, *CABIOS*, 5(3): 183–9.

Payne, G. and Williams, M. (2005) Generalisation in qualitative research. *Sociology*, 39(2): 295–314

Pearson, K. (1906) On certain points connected with scale order in the case of the correlation of two characters which for some arrangement give a linear regression line. *Biometrika*, 5: 176–8.

Phillips, D. (1995) Correspondence analysis. *Social Research Update*, 7, Winter 1995, Department of Sociology, University of Surrey.

Ranciere, J. (2004) *The Philosopher and His Poor*. Durham, NC: Duke University Press.

Rouanet, H., Ackerman, W., and Le Roux, B. (2000) The geometric analysis of questionnaires. The Lesson of Bourdieu's La Distinction. *Bulletin de Méthodologie Sociologique*, 65: 5–15.

Savage, M., Gayo-Cal, Warde, A., and Tampubolon, G. (2005) Cultural capital in the UK: A preliminary report using correspondence analysis. *CRESC Working Paper Series*, 4, CRESC University of Manchester.

Veenstra, G. (2007) Social space, social class and Bourdieu: Health inequalities in British Columbia, Canada. *Health and Place*, 13: 14–31.

Williams, M (2000) Interpretivism and generalisation. *Sociology*, 34(2): 209–24.

Wuggenig, U. (2007) Comments on Chan and Goldthorpe: Pitfalls in testing Bourdieu's homology assumptions using mainstream social science methodology. Social stratification and cultural consumption: The visual arts in England. *Poetics*, 35: 306–16.

8

Case-Oriented Theory Building and Theory Testing

Charles C. Ragin and
Garrett Andrew Schneider

THE CONVENTIONAL VIEW: DIVIDED LABOR

For most social scientists, theory testing is synonymous with variable-oriented research (Amenta, 1991; Geddes, 1990; Odell, 2001). After all, hypotheses in the social sciences are most often formulated in terms of relationships between variables. These variables and the hypotheses they constitute are often seen as relatively 'caseless' in the sense that they are derived from general theory, and are not grounded, *per se*, in specific cases (Ragin, 2000). Indeed, according to some (e.g. Przeworski and Teune, 1982), a sign of good social research is that it is purged of case names and case identities. The purpose of theory testing, in this view, is to evaluate the implications of general models against relevant empirical evidence, usually involving as many cases as possible (Pahre, 2005). The use of many cases, typically a sample drawn from what is believed to be a very large population, reinforces the goal of making the research more about variables and their relationships and less about cases, *per se*.

While it is not uncommon to assess a general theory using a single case, many social scientists view this practice as an empty rhetorical exercise. After all, what's one case? Those who are more favorably inclined toward case-oriented research tend to see this use of theory as an exercise in theory building, for it is unusual for an empirical case to conform well to any given theory. In fact, many case-oriented researchers study the cases they study precisely because these cases challenge existing theory and offer opportunities to revise or refine it (Bradshaw and Wallace, 1991; Orum et al., 1991). For these reasons, it is commonplace to associate qualitative, case-oriented research with the task of theory building, and quantitative, variable-oriented research with the task of theory testing (Gerring, 2007; Gross, 2008; Reuschemeyer, 2003). After all, researchers working in the analytic tradition of qualitative inquiry examine cases in an in-depth manner and try to learn from them, giving induction an important role in both the production of social scientific knowledge and the representation of social phenomena (e.g. Glaser and Strauss, 1967). In a similar vein, it is often argued that the models that quantitative researchers test should be as well specified as possible in advance of their testing; otherwise, the results of their assessment may be distorted (Western, 1996). This seemingly natural division of labor between these two camps is reinforced by an alleged status system that portrays qualitative researchers as fieldworkers and quantitative researchers as ivory tower scientists, far removed from the social phenomena they study.

PROBLEMS WITH THE CONVENTIONAL VIEW

While convenient, this view of the division of social scientific labor masks an analytic chasm that separates much qualitative and quantitative research. This chasm exists because qualitative research is largely concerned with the analysis of asymmetric set relations, while quantitative research is largely concerned with the analysis of symmetric relationships among variables (Ragin, 2000, 2008).[1] This important contrast is largely overlooked by those who portray qualitative analysis as a primitive form of quantitative analysis (e.g. King et al., 1994). As we show in this chapter, there are striking differences between analyzing social phenomena in terms of asymmetric set relations and analyzing social phenomena in terms of symmetric relationships among variables.

Consider, for illustration, the following scenario. A researcher using qualitative methods studies several cases in depth – a small number of firms that are very successful in investing in and retaining their most valuable employees. The researcher documents causally relevant conditions shared by these cases and then constructs a general, composite argument about how these firms accomplish retention. Suppose this argument details four specific causal conditions (which we label for convenience X_1 to X_4) based on the shared commonalities. A second researcher reads the report of this study and decides to test it with a large sample using quantitative methods. This researcher collects information on a random sample of firms and finds that as independent variables X_1 to X_4 do not distinguish more successful from less successful firms, using various measures of retention. In short, the second researcher shows that there is no statistically significant difference in the retention rates for firms with and without these four aspects, considering these aspects one at a time or in a multivariate equation estimating their net effects.

What went wrong? Usually, the researcher using quantitative methods will claim that the qualitative researcher's 'sample' was 'too small' and 'unrepresentative' (e.g. Geddes, 1990). Thus, the identification of X_1 to X_4 took advantage of specific aspects of the selected cases. The quantitative researcher might speculate further that the qualitative researcher chose these firms because they were consistent with his or her preconceptions or prejudices, thereby committing one of the cardinal sins of empirical social science. The qualitative researcher might counterattack by arguing that causally relevant commonalities identified through in-depth study are very difficult to represent as 'variables,' and that the quantitative researcher's crude attempt to operationalize them fell far short (e.g. George and Bennett, 2004). Indeed, the qualitative researcher might argue that it would take in-depth knowledge of each of the many firms included in the quantitative study to capture these causal conditions appropriately and contextually. After all, there are many different ways to implement a given strategy (e.g. X_1), and such actions can be identified only when each case is studied as a whole, and not parsed into generic variables.

These criticisms and counter-criticisms are quite common. However, the incongruity between these two hypothetical studies can be resolved without resorting to reproach. The qualitative researcher in this example selected on instances of the outcome (successful retention) and identified four causally relevant conditions shared by the cases in question. In essence, this researcher worked backwards from the outcome to causes and thus identified potential *necessary* conditions for the outcome (Ragin, 2000). Are these conditions truly necessary? In part, this is an empirical question. To gain confidence, the researcher should examine more instances of the outcome (i.e. conduct more case studies of firms with successful retention), to see if the new cases agree in displaying these four causally relevant conditions or their causal equivalents (Ragin, 2000). But it is also a question about existing knowledge. Is the argument that these four conditions are necessary consistent with existing theoretical and substantive knowledge? Do they make sense as necessary conditions? Do they ring true as necessary conditions for the actors involved? If the researcher's findings are consistent with existing substantive and theoretical knowledge, then the argument that these four conditions are necessary is reinforced.

How should the quantitative researcher respond to the argument that these four factors are necessary conditions? At a more abstract level, the specification of necessary conditions is relevant primarily to the identification of cases which are 'candidates' for an outcome. Cases cannot be considered suitable candidates for an outcome if they do not meet the necessary conditions. Furthermore, many cases may meet the necessary conditions for an outcome and still not exhibit the outcome because they lack additional conditions which, when combined with the necessary conditions, establish sufficiency for the outcome. In fact, the cases displaying the outcome in a large *N*, variable-oriented study may be only a relatively small minority of those that satisfy the necessary conditions. Thus, while there are clear gains to theory from being able to specify necessary conditions (see Goertz and Starr, 2003; especially Goertz, 2003), as in the hypothetical qualitative study just described, the identification of causally relevant commonalities shared by instances of an outcome does not establish the conditions that are sufficient for an outcome. Thus, the quantitative researcher's finding that these four conditions do not distinguish low retention firms from high retention firms in a variable-oriented study of a large sample of firms does not directly challenge the qualitative researcher's implicit argument that these conditions (or their causal equivalents) are necessary.

The variable-oriented analysis of these four conditions across a large sample of firms is much more directly relevant to their sufficiency. To test the argument that these four conditions are *jointly sufficient* for the outcome, the quantitative researcher would have to show that cases that combine these four causal conditions are the ones that are most likely to exhibit the outcome. In other words, the variable-oriented researcher could evaluate their joint sufficiency by examining the correspondence between the combination of the four causes, on the one hand, and the outcome, on the other, across a large sample of firms. Because the focus is on the combination of the four conditions and not their net effects, the conventional quantitative researcher would be saddled with examining a four-way interaction. Still, this analysis would be an evaluation of their joint sufficiency, not of their necessity, and the results of this analysis would not bear in a direct manner on the implicit claim of necessity made by the qualitative researcher.

This example illustrates the problems that may arise when the results of qualitative research are subjected to standard statistical analysis using a large *N*. They also illustrate the analytic chasm separating qualitative research, with its focus on set relations and its attention to necessity and sufficiency as set relations, and quantitative research, with its focus on testing hypotheses about relationships between variables and their net effects (Ragin, 2000, 2008). Until these fundamental analytic differences between qualitative, case-oriented research and quantitative, variable-oriented research are recognized and well understood, researchers working in different methodological traditions will continue to misunderstand and misrepresent each other's work. The hypothetical scenario just sketched illustrates how the presumably natural division of labor between case-oriented work (focused on theory building) and variable-oriented (focused on theory testing) can break down, due to a fundamental analytic mismatch.

In this chapter we reject the conventional, 'division-of-labor' view of social scientific work and argue that theory building and theory testing is commonplace in both variable-oriented and case-oriented work. However, there are fundamental differences between variable-oriented and case-oriented research in the *nature* of both theory building and theory testing, and these differences follow from the focus of case-oriented researchers on asymmetric set-theoretic relations, in contrast to the focus of conventional variable-oriented researchers on symmetric relationships among variables. We argue that from the perspective of case-oriented research, conventional variable-oriented research conflates two very different types of assessment.

THE VARIABLE-ORIENTED APPROACH

Variable-oriented theory testing

The template for variable-oriented theory testing is well known and relatively well established. For convenience, a simplified summary of its main features is shown in Table 8.1. As presented, conventional theory testing moves from the selection of a dependent variable or a key independent/dependent variable relationship to the identification of relevant theories and competing independent variables. Different variables are associated with different theories and subjected to a multivariate analysis in which the researcher assesses the net effect of each independent variable. In the course of these assessments, researchers discard independent variables that seem least robust, least important, or only weakly justified by theoretical or substantive knowledge. In the end, the researcher apportions explained variation in the dependent variable among the independent variables that remain and, if feasible, makes causal inferences about the independent impact of key variables based on their estimated effects.

One important feature of variable-oriented theory testing is that it starts with fully specified or even over-specified models (usually based on inclusive lists of relevant causal conditions) and then seeks to simplify them, focusing on the key causal variables. In effect, variable-oriented theory testing is a process of separating the wheat from the chaff, so that a relatively lean representation of the evidence remains in the end. Variables that lack robust net effects may be discarded altogether, perhaps meriting only brief mention in the summary of the results.

Variable-oriented theory building

By contrast, variable-oriented theory building can be seen as the *reverse* of theory testing. That is, rather than winnowing the relevant independent variables, as in

Table 8.1 Variable-oriented theory testing

1. Select or define a dependent variable or a key independent/dependent variable relationship.
2. Read relevant theory and study existing research. Based on this knowledge, develop a list of relevant independent variables. Associate the different independent variables and their expected effects with different theoretical perspectives.
3. Add to the list of independent variables any control variables that may be relevant to the target data set.
4. Specify measures or indicators of the dependent and independent variables. Cases must vary meaningfully on each variable.
5. Locate or assemble a relevant data set.
6. Conduct multivariate analyses of the effects of the independent variables on the dependent variable.
7. Identify the most important independent variables, eliminating those that seem least influential (weak effects on dependent variable) or marginal (weakly justified by theoretical or substantive knowledge).
8. Construct different specifications of the model until a cogent and robust set of results is achieved. Make causal inferences, if possible.

theory testing, novel variables may be introduced. These new variables may have important but overlooked net effects on the dependent variable, or they may partition the set of relevant cases into distinct subpopulations. They may be drawn from new or overlooked theories, newly acquired substantive knowledge (which is often case-based), or perhaps identified using mundane research procedures such as the examination of residuals in multiple regression analysis. While there are many forms of theory building, some for example simply focusing on the rearrangement of the variables in a given causal model, the important point here is that theory building often involves an elaboration of new ideas about how to best model or represent a given social phenomenon using variables. These elaborations typically involve adding complexity to existing models, which in turn frequently entails the introduction of new variables.

The addition of a new variable to a given set of independent variables usually involves a straightforward analysis of its unique contribution to explained variation in the dependent variable. For example, if a new variable can account for why some cases have higher or lower predicted values on the dependent variable than expected (based on an existing model), then it is a good candidate for inclusion in the model. The new variable also presents the researcher with an opportunity for theory building, assuming the new variable is not conceptually redundant with those already in the model. For illustration, consider Table 8.2, which shows a 'before and after' distribution of cases consistent with an increment to explained variation in a dependent variable. For convenience, the illustration uses dichotomies. In the 'before' panel there is a single independent variable (X_1); in the 'after' panel there are two (X_2 is added to the analysis). The addition of X_2 improves prediction; cases that lack both causal conditions have the lowest probability of the outcome, while cases that exhibit both causal conditions have the highest probability of the outcome. In this example, the addition of X_2 explains why some of the cases lacking X_1 in the 'before' panel exhibit the outcome (they also had X_2, a cause of the outcome) and why some cases with a presence of X_1 in the 'before' panel failed to display the outcome (they lacked X_2).

Table 8.2 Adding causal variables in variable-oriented research

A. Before X_2

	X_1 absent	*X_1 present*
Outcome present	9 (41%)	12 (63%)
Outcome absent	13 (59%)	7 (37%)

B. After X_2

	Neither X_1 nor X_2 present	*Only one of the two (X_1 or X_2) present*	*Both X_1 and X_2 present*
Outcome present	5 (33%)	8 (53%)	8 (73%)
Outcome absent	10 (67%)	7 (47%)	3 (27%)

This way of evaluating new variables, assessing their separate increments to explained variation, assumes that both X_1 and X_2 independently increase the probability of the outcome.

Of course, readers of this volume are familiar with the basic principles just sketched. This brief illustration is offered to provide a backdrop for the presentation of case-oriented theory testing and building offered in the next section.

THE LOGIC OF THE CASE-ORIENTED APPROACH

Case-oriented theory testing

Many good theories are based on exemplary or otherwise 'telling' cases, not on abstract notions about how variables *per se* ought to behave (see, e.g. Feagin et al., 1991; Pahre, 2005). Thus, the starting point of case-oriented theory testing is often a single, well-studied case or a small number of comparable cases.

Generally, when researchers study cases in an in-depth manner, they focus on a qualitative outcome of some sort, a change that occurred over a specific period of time, signaling some sort of shift or transformation relevant to the case as a whole (e.g. Clemens, 1997; MacKenzie, 2006; Heilleiner, 1994). Accounts and explanations of these qualitative changes typically invoke convergent causal conditions – a specific *combination* of causally relevant conditions that prompted the change. In many respects, these combinations can be seen as *causal recipes* (Ragin, 2008) because all the relevant ingredients for change must be in place for it to occur. Specifying a causal recipe entails not only listing the relevant ingredients, but also identifying the processes and mechanisms involved in the production of the outcome (Steel, 2004; Bennett, 2008; Bennett and George, 2004). Even as lists of combined conditions, causal recipes are pregnant with implications about processes and mechanisms (see, e.g. Boswell and Brown, 1999).

Of course, not all case studies have the derivation of causal recipes as their primary goal. Many seek simply to account for the specificity of a given case, which is no small task in itself (Eckstein, 1975; Bradshaw and Wallace, 1991). Still, depending on the goals of the study, the specification of a causal recipe for a chosen case may be considered a hypothesis relevant to other cases. In this way, the endpoint of a case study may be a testable hypothesis about other cases, especially when this endpoint is a more or less 'portable' causal recipe linked to a general outcome – a qualitative change experienced by other cases as well. The case is viewed not just as an empirical event but also as a token of a type of empirical phenomenon which is analyzed in order to develop a general hypothesis that explains events of that type.

Consider, for example, the case of 'Three Strikes and You're Out' in California, a mandatory minimum sentencing law enacted in 1993 under which 87,500 people have been incarcerated at an estimated cost of $10.5 billion (Brown and

Jolivette, 2005; Ehlers et al., 2004). Through analysis of newspaper articles, first-hand testimonials, public opinion surveys, and economic, political, demographic, and crime statistics, researchers have concluded that California enacted such a punitive change to its penal code because of (1) interest group mobilization, (2) widespread public fear of social disorder, (3) a highly visible and sensationalized crime, and (4) electoral competition among politicians (Schneider, 2008). This explanation of punitive change to the penal code cites a specific *combination* of conditions which have the character of a recipe: all four conditions were met simultaneously in the case of California, and together they explain the dramatic policy change and consequent expansion of California's penal system.

Using the analysis of California as a springboard, a researcher could move in either of two theory-testing directions. The first possible direction would be to find other instances of punitive change to state-level penal codes and examine the extent to which they agree in displaying the same recipe, the same combination of four causal ingredients found in California: Do all (or virtually all) instances of punitive policy change display these four antecedent conditions? This strategy employs the common qualitative research strategy of 'selecting on the dependent variable', an approach that is almost universally, but mistakenly, condemned by quantitative researchers (see, e.g. King et al., 1994; Geddes, 1990; for a defense, see Dion, 1998; Ragin, 2000, 2008). The second direction would be to try to find other instances of California's recipe and examine whether these states also experienced punitive changes to their penal codes. In essence, the researcher would select cases on the basis of their scores on the independent variable. In this example, however, the 'independent variable' is a causal recipe with its four main conditions all satisfied. The goal of the second strategy would be to assess the sufficiency of the recipe: Does it invariably (or at least with substantial consistency) lead to punitive policy change?

Both of these strategies are set-theoretic in nature and conform to the two general set-theoretic approaches described in Ragin and Rihoux (2004) and Ragin (2008). The first is an examination of whether instances of the outcome (punitive change to the penal code) constitute a subset of instances of a combination of causal conditions (i.e. California's recipe). The researcher examines other states that introduced major changes to their penal codes, making them overwhelmingly more punitive, to see if the same combination of four ingredients existed in these other states. This demonstration would establish that the four causal conditions in question are consistent with necessity. The second is an examination of whether instances of a specific combination of causal conditions (again, California's recipe) constitute a subset of instances of an outcome (punitive change to the penal code). The researcher would identify states that experienced the same coincidence of these four conditions, to see if they instituted substantial punitive changes to state penal codes as a consequence. This demonstration would establish that the combination of causal conditions is consistent with sufficiency. Of course, both strategies could be used, and if both subset relations are confirmed, then the two sets (the set of cases with California's causal recipe and the set of cases with punitive changes to the penal code) would coincide. While it might appear that the two strategies together constitute a correlational analysis, it is important to recognize that correlations are strong when there are many 'null-null' instances – cases that lack both the causal recipe and the outcome. Neither of the two research strategies just described depends on or uses such cases in any direct way. It is also important to understand that from a case-oriented viewpoint, these two tasks – the assessment of sufficiency and the assessment of necessity – are distinct and should not be conflated, as they are in a conventional variable-oriented analysis based on correlations.

Table 8.3 summarizes case-oriented theory testing. It is important to understand that different ideas about the causal recipe in question motivate different research strategies, especially with regard to case selection. If the researcher suspects that the conditions identified in the recipe are necessary-but-not-sufficient, then the next analytic step is to examine other instances of the outcome. Specifically, the researcher seeks to certify that instances of the outcome reside in cell 2 of Table 8.3, with no cases in cell 1. Cases in cell 4 do not challenge the argument of necessity.[2] By contrast, if the researcher suspects that the recipe is sufficient-but-not-necessary, then the next analytic step is to examine other instances of the causal combination. Specifically, the researcher seeks to certify that instances of the causal combination reside in cell 2 of Table 8.3, with no cases in cell 4. Cases in cell 1 do not challenge the argument of sufficiency.[3]

Of course, it is common for a hypothesis based on one case to be disconfirmed in other cases, just as it is common for variable-oriented researchers to find that the fully specified models they start with (when testing theory) are in fact misspecified. For example, suppose that the 'true' recipe for punitive change to the penal code has five ingredients, not four, indicating that the researcher overlooked an important ingredient in the case of California. The results of the sufficiency analysis of the four-condition recipe would reveal cases in cell 4, which in turn would challenge the argument of sufficiency. The cell 4 cases would have only four of five causal conditions in the 'true' recipe and thus would not exhibit the outcome. Alternatively, suppose the recipe based on California's experience is needlessly complex and should have only three causal ingredients, not four. The results of a necessity analysis of the four-condition recipe would

Table 8.3 Case-oriented theory testing: necessity versus sufficiency

	Causal recipe absent	*Causal recipe present*
Outcome present	Cell 1: cases in this cell challenge the argument of necessity but are not relevant to the assessment of sufficiency.	Cell 2: cases in this cell can confirm necessity or sufficiency, depending on the researcher's goals.
Outcome absent	Cell 3: cases in this cell are not directly relevant to the assessment of either necessity or sufficiency.	Cell 4: cases in this cell challenge the argument of sufficiency but are not relevant to the assessment of necessity.

uncover cases in cell 1, indicating that not all four conditions are necessary for the outcome.

The key point is that in case-oriented theory testing, the standard 2 × 2 table of outcome cross-tabulated against cause (which in case-oriented research is usually a causal recipe, not a single independent variable) is disaggregated and dissected because the different cells of this table have different interpretations and different analytic uses. This approach thus contrasts sharply with conventional variable-oriented research, where the usual endpoint of the analysis of a 2 × 2 table (or its correlational equivalent) is a summary measure of association describing the whole table. It is also important to emphasize that these summary statistics reward researchers for having as many cases as possible in cell 3 (the null–null cell). By contrast, cell 3 plays no direct role in the case-oriented assessment of either sufficiency or necessity.

Case-oriented theory building

More striking than the contrast between variable-oriented and case-oriented theory testing is the contrast between the two with respect to theory building. The key consideration here is the same as the one just sketched for case-oriented theory testing; that is, it is very important to distinguish between situations where the focus is on sufficiency (cases with the causal condition or recipe constitute a subset of the cases with the outcome) from those where the focus is on necessity (cases with the outcome constitute a subset of the cases with the causal condition or recipe).

For example, consider the case-oriented researcher who initially believes that X_1 is *sufficient* for the outcome. Thus, instances of X_1 should constitute a subset of instances of the outcome, which is another way of stating that cases that have X_1 should all exhibit the outcome. Assume the evidence is mixed and that some cases of X_1 fail to exhibit the expected outcome. To resolve the contradiction, the researcher compares cases with and without the outcome (i.e. cases in cells 2 and 4 of Table 8.3) and tries to identify what was overlooked. The researcher concludes that X_1 must be combined with X_2 for the outcome to occur because the cases that combine these two conditions consistently exhibit the outcome, while X_1 cases that lack X_2 fail to exhibit the outcome. Thus, this foray into theory building results in a recipe for the outcome that is more elaborate and less inclusive than the initial recipe.

The 'sufficiency-centered' strategy is summarized in Table 8.4. As in Table 8.2, there is a 'before X_2' panel and an 'after X_2' panel. Observe that in this investigation, the objective is to establish that the causal condition or recipe is a subset of the outcome. In effect, the goal is to empty 'cell 4' of cases. This can be accomplished by reformulating the causal argument from 'X_1' to 'X_1 combined with X_2,' which in effect shifts some cases from the second column (in the before panel) to the first column (in the after panel). If the researcher effectively empties cell 4 of cases by making the causal argument more detailed and thus *less* inclusive, then

Table 8.4 Case-oriented theory building: sufficiency-centered

A. Before X_2

	X_1 *absent*	X_1 *present*
Outcome present	Cell 1: 16 (40%)	Cell 2: 14 (70%)
Outcome absent	Cell 3: 24 (60%)	Cell 4: 6 (30%)

B. After X_2

	X_1 *or* X_2 *(or both) absent*	*Both* X_1 *and* X_2 *present*
Outcome present	Cell 1: 19 (39%)	Cell 2: 11 (100%)
Outcome absent	Cell 3: 30 (61%)	Cell 4: 0 (0%)

an explicit, set-theoretic connection between cause and effect can be established. The resulting causal argument is made more restrictive through the use of logical *and* (set intersection). Generally, this use of logical *and* entails moving to a more combinatorial and nuanced conceptualization of causation.

The shift from the 'before' to the 'after' panel in Table 8.4 moves cases not only from cell 4 to cell 3 (thus emptying cell 4 of cases) but also moves cases from cell 2 to cell 1. Elaborating a causal argument in a combinatorial manner, as demonstrated in the table, therefore, may also reduce its 'coverage', which means that fewer instances of the outcome are explained. However, the cases that move from cell 2 to cell 1 do not challenge the sufficiency of the causal argument specified in the 'after' panel; they are simply not explained by the causal combination in question. From a purely statistical viewpoint (i.e. focusing on the distribution of cases across all four cells), the explanatory gain that accrues in the shift from the 'before' to the 'after' panel of Table 8.4 may be trivial or even negative. However, from a set-theoretic viewpoint, the difference is decisive, especially given the goal of theory building, because one of perhaps several recipes for the outcome has been clarified and refined.[4]

The distinctiveness of the case-oriented approach to theory building is even more apparent when attention is directed to theory building focused on the assessment of *necessary conditions*. Consider the case-oriented researcher who speculates initially that X_1 may be a necessary condition for an outcome. Thus, instances of the outcome should constitute a subset of instances of the cause, which is another way of stating that instances of the outcome should share X_1 as an antecedent condition. Assume the evidence is mixed and that some cases of the outcome lack X_1 as an antecedent condition. Such cases reside in cell 2 and thus challenge the argument of necessity (see Table 8.3). To resolve the contradiction, the researcher compares instances of the outcome with and without X_1 (i.e. the cases in cells 1 and 2 of Table 8.3). The key task at this point, assuming that theoretical and substantive knowledge supports the idea that X_1 may be a necessary condition, is to see if there is some other condition that is causally equivalent to X_1 which is found in the cases of the outcome that lack X_1 (i.e. the cases in cell 1). That is, is there a causal condition shared by the cell 1 cases that is *substitutable* for X_1 as a necessary condition? When two conditions are substitutable as necessary conditions, if either is present, then the antecedent condition in question is satisfied.[5] Assume in this example that the researcher studies cases in cell 1, identifies X_2 as a substitutable necessary condition and concludes that X_1 and X_2 are causally equivalent as necessary conditions with respect to the outcome in question. The causal argument is then reformulated to state that the presence of either 'X_1 *or* X_2' is a necessary condition for the outcome. This exercise in case-oriented theory building results in a recipe for the outcome that is *more inclusive* than the initial recipe because more cases display X_1 *or* X_2 than only X_1.

The 'necessity-centered' strategy is summarized in Table 8.5. As in Tables 8.2 and 8.4, there is a 'before X_2' panel and an 'after X_2' panel. Observe that in this investigation, the objective is to establish that the outcome is a subset of a causal condition or recipe. In effect, the goal is to empty cell 1 of cases. This can be accomplished by reformulating the causal argument from 'X_1' to 'X_1 *or* X_2,' which in effect shifts some cases from the first column (before panel) to the second column (after panel). If the researcher effectively empties cell 1 of cases by making the causal argument more inclusive, then an explicit, set-theoretic connection between cause and effect can be established. The resulting causal argument is made more inclusive through the use of logical *or* (set union). This use of logical *or* entails the adoption of a substitutable conception of necessary conditions, which in turn broadens the conceptualization of the necessary condition. In other words, this analytic step involves moving up the 'ladder of abstraction'

Table 8.5 Case-oriented theory building: necessity-centered

A. Before X_2		
	X_1 absent	*X_1 present*
Outcome present	Cell 1: 5 (33%)	Cell 2: 25 (62.5%)
Outcome absent	Cell 3: 15 (67%)	Cell 4: 15 (37.5%)
B. After X_2		
	Both X_1 and X_2 absent	*Either X_1 or X_2 present*
Outcome present	Cell 1: 0 (0%)	Cell 2: 30 (62.5%)
Outcome absent	Cell 3: 12 (100%)	Cell 4: 18 (37.5%)

(Sartori, 1970) to a more general conceptualization of the causal condition. Note the contrast with case-oriented, sufficiency-centered theory building, illustrated in Table 8.4, where joining X_1 and X_2 via logical *and* (set intersection) entails a narrowing of the empirical focus via a less inclusive causal formulation.

The shift from the 'before' to the 'after' panel in Table 8.5 moves cases not only from cell 1 to cell 2 (thus emptying cell 1 of cases) but also moves cases from cell 3 to cell 4. Elaborating a causal argument in a substitutable manner, as demonstrated in the table, therefore, can increase the number of cases with the causal condition that *lack* the outcome (cell 4 cases). However, the cases that move from cell 3 to cell 4 do not challenge the necessity of the causal argument specified in the 'after' panel. The cases in cell 4 are simply those that meet the necessary condition but lack additional, unspecified causal conditions that would establish sufficiency. From a purely statistical viewpoint (i.e. focusing on the distribution of cases across all four cells), the gain that accrues in the shift from the 'before' to the 'after' panel of Table 8.5 may be trivial or even negative. However, from a set-theoretic viewpoint, the difference is decisive, especially given the goal of theory building.[6]

Summary

The major contrasts between case-oriented and variable-oriented theory building are clear. Conventional variable-oriented theory building:

1 gives a major role to cases in the 'null–null' cell (cases that display neither the cause nor the outcome), treating them as important theory-confirming cases;
2 typically focuses on identifying causal variables that independently increase the probability of the outcome, net of the effects of other causal conditions; and
3 is based on an assessment of the distribution of cases across all cells, which usually involves the calculation of a summary statistic assessing the impact of the added variable on the fit of the model as a whole.

Case-oriented theory building, by contrast:

1 has little interest in cases residing in the 'null–null' cell;
2 has relatively little use for summary statistics describing whole tables;
3 focuses on causal variables that empty *either* cell 1 *or* cell 4 of cases, treating these as analytically distinct tasks, with the first focused on establishing necessity and the second on establishing sufficiency;
4 may culminate in tabular patterns that from the viewpoint of variable-oriented research represent little or no gain in the fit of the model as a whole. From a set-theoretic viewpoint, however, the gain may be decisive.

CONCLUSION

The contrasts between variable-oriented and case-oriented research in both arenas, theory testing and theory building, are striking. The case-oriented approach, in effect, deconstructs a key variable-oriented analytic device, the cross-case correlation, into its two main components. Using the most elemental form of this device, the 2 × 2 table, this chapter demonstrates that conventional variable-oriented analysis conflates two very different research strategies. The first strategy – investigating causal conditions that constitute supersets of the outcome – focuses on the first row of this 2 × 2 table, while the second strategy – investigating causal conditions that constitute subsets of the outcome – focuses on the second column (see Table 8.3). When testing theory, these different conceptualizations of the connection between the cause and outcome dictate different case selection strategies. To examine whether it is true that the causal condition or recipe is a superset of the outcome, the researcher selects on instances of the outcome. To assess whether it is true that the causal condition or recipe is a subset of the outcome, the researcher selects on instances of the causal condition or recipe. Of course, these two case selection strategies can be used jointly, as long as researchers respect their separate and distinct goals. That is, from a case-oriented perspective the two strategies should not be combined into a single assessment, yielding a single summary statistic. Of course, such summary statistics constitute the foundation of almost all conventional forms of variable-oriented analysis.

This interest in separable dimensions of the cross-case correlation carries over into case-oriented theory building. Again, the key concern is whether the researcher is interested in establishing the causal condition (or recipe) as a *superset* or as a *subset* of the outcome. As illustrated in Tables 8.4 and 8.5, different ideas about the nature of the connection between cause and outcome motivate different theory building strategies. If the researcher believes that the causal condition or recipe is a *subset* of the outcome (i.e. one of perhaps several sufficient-but-not-necessary causal conditions or recipes), then theory building may involve a restriction of a recipe's empirical scope, which in turn entails specifying the causal recipe more narrowly using logical *and* (i.e. combining causal conditions via set intersection). If the researcher believes that the causal condition is a *superset* of the outcome (e.g. a necessary-but-not-sufficient condition), then theory building may involve an expanded conceptualization of the causal condition, making it more empirically inclusive via logical *or* (i.e. specifying substitutable necessary conditions).

The demonstrations offered in this chapter focus on the most elementary form of variable-oriented analysis, the 2 × 2 table. It is important to point out that these same issues arise in more sophisticated forms of cross-case analysis. For example, as shown in Ragin (2000, 2008), the correlation coefficient, which is conventionally used to assess the relationship between two continuous variables, also conflates the two case-oriented analytic strategies described in this chapter. Using fuzzy sets, it is possible to assess set-theoretic relations between case aspects that vary by level or degree, and thus to disentangle the two assessments central to case-oriented theory testing and building (Ragin, 2006). These fuzzy set-theoretic procedures exactly parallel those shown in this chapter using crisp sets and 2 × 2 tables. Using fuzzy sets, researchers can test whether a given causal recipe, based on a single well-studied case, holds across other cases either as a subset or as a superset of the outcome. They also can assess whether the use of logical *and* to combine causal conditions improves the consistency of the cross-case evidence with the subset relation signaling sufficiency, and they can assess whether the use of logical *or* to specify substitutable conditions improves the consistency of the cross-case evidence with the subset relation signaling necessity.

The analytic models presented in this chapter are, of course, very simple, involving at most two causal conditions. More complex analyses involving multiple causal conditions and complex causal recipes are possible using Qualitative Comparative Analysis (QCA; Ragin et al., 2007). With QCA, it is possible to assess all possible configurations of conditions and thereby to assess complex patterns of both necessity and sufficiency, all within a set-theoretic framework. In short, because it is set-theoretic in nature, QCA honors the analytic distinctions central to case-oriented theory testing and building.

NOTES

1 Our emphasis throughout this chapter is on qualitative research that compares empirical cases, regardless of how 'cases'are defined (Ragin and Becker, 1992). We do not address qualitative research that is more exclusively concerned with the interpretation of a single case in relative isolation from other empirical cases.

2 Of course, cell 4 cases are still indirectly relevant to the investigation, especially if researchers are interested in exploring the possibility that they have overlooked a necessary condition. Contrasts between cases in cell 4 and cell 2, for example, may reveal overlooked commonalities among the cell 2 cases, not found in the cell 4 cases. However, this exploration of evidence is better understood as a form of theory building, not as theory testing.

3 Cell 1 cases are still indirectly relevant to the investigation, especially if researchers are interested in exploring the possibility that they have included too many conditions in the causal recipe that is being tested. Contrasts between cases in cell 1 and cell 2, for example, may reveal that some cases in cell 1 display a specific subset of the ingredients specified in the recipe and also exhibit the outcome. This exploration of evidence is better understood as a form of theory building, however, not as theory testing.

4 There are other qualitative strategies that accomplish this same objective – emptying cell 4 of cases – that do not involve extending the causal argument in a combinatorial manner using logical *and*. One strategy is to evaluate cell 4 cases to determine if they are truly relevant to the investigation – do they meet the researcher's scope condition? If they do not, they can be excluded from the analysis, thereby emptying cell 4 of cases. Another is to examine the cell 4 cases to see if they display outcomes that are equivalent in some way to the outcome displayed by the cell 2 cases. If so, then the researcher might reformulate the definition of the outcome, in a more inclusive manner, so that the cell 4 cases are included as instances and thus transferred to cell 2. Of course, this reformulation of the outcome might also shift cases from cell 3 to cell 1. However, from the viewpoint of sufficiency analysis, such transfers are largely neutral.

5 A simple example: a steady income *or* the ownership of valuable assets might be considered substitutable necessary conditions for getting a loan from a bank.

6 There are other qualitative strategies that accomplish this same objective – emptying cell 1 of cases – that do not involve elaborating the causal argument via substitutable causes and logical *or*. One strategy is to evaluate cell 1 cases to determine if they are truly relevant to the investigation – do they meet the researcher's scope condition? If they do not, they can be excluded from the analysis, thereby emptying cell 1 of cases. Another is to examine the cell 1 cases to see if they display outcomes that are different in some way from the outcome displayed by the cell 2 cases. If so, then the researcher might narrow the definition of the outcome, making it less inclusive, so that the cell 1 cases are excluded as instances and thus transferred to cell 3, following the respecification of the outcome. Of course, this respecification might also shift cases from cell 2 to cell 4. However, from the viewpoint of necessity analysis, such transfers are largely neutral.

REFERENCES

Amenta, Edwin. (1991) 'Making the Most of a Case Study: Theories of the Welfare State and the American Experience'. *International Journal of Comparative Sociology* 32: 172–94.

Bennett, Andrew. (2008) 'Process Tracing: A Bayesian Perspective'. Pp. 702–21 in *The Oxford Handbook of Political Methodology,* edited by Henry E. Brady and David Collier. Oxford: Oxford University Press.

Bennett, Andrew and Alexander George. (2004) *Case Studies and Theory Development in the Social Sciences.* Boston: MIT Press.

Boswell, Terry and Cliff Brown. (1999) 'The Scope of General Theory: Methods for Linking Deductive and Inductive Comparative History'. *Sociological Methods and Research* 28(2): 154–85.

Bradshaw, York and Michael Wallace. (1991) 'Informing Generality and Explaining Uniqueness: The Place of Case Studies in Comparative Research.' *International Journal of Comparative Sociology* 32: 154–71.

Brown, Brian and Greg Jolivette. (2005) *Three Strikes: The Impact After More than a Decade.* Sacramento: Legislative Analysts' Office.

Clemens, Elizabeth S. (1997) *The Peoples' Lobby: Organizational Innovation and the Rise of Interest Group Politics in the United States, 1890–1925.* Chicago: University of Chicago Press.

Dion, Douglas. (1998) 'Evidence and Inference in the Comparative Case Study.' *Comparative Politics* 30: 127–45.

Eckstein, Harry. (1975) 'Case Study and Theory in Political Science'. Pp. 79–137 in *Handbook of Political Science,* Volume 7, edited by Fred I. Greenstein and Nelson W. Polsby. Reading, MA: Addison-Wesley.

Ehlers, Scott, Vincent Schiraldi, and Jason Zeidenberg. (2004) *Still Striking Out: Ten Years of California's Three Strikes.* Washington D.C.: Justice Policy Institute.

Feagin, Joe R., Anthony M. Orum and Gideon Sjoberg. (1991) *A Case for the Case Study.* Chapel Hill, NC: University of North Carolina Press.

Geddes, Barbara. (1990) 'How the Cases You Choose Affect the Answers You Get: Selection Bias in Comparative Politics'. Pp. 131–50 in *Political Analysis,* edited by James A. Stimson. Ann Arbor: University of Michigan Press.

George, Alexander L. and Andrew Bennett. (2004) *Case Studies and Theory Development in the Social Sciences.* Cambridge: The MIT Press.

Gerring, John. (2007) *Case Study Research: Principles and Practices.* Cambridge: Cambridge University Press.

Glaser, Barney G. and Anselm L Strauss. (1967) *Discovery of Grounded Theory: Strategies for Qualitative Research.* Chicago: Aldine Publishing Co.

Goertz, Gary. (2003) 'The Substantive Importance of Necessary Condition Hypothewes'. Pp. 65–94 in *Necessary Conditions: Theory, Methodology, and Applications,* edited by Gary Goertz and Harvey Starr. Lanham, MD: Rowman & Littlefield.

Goertz, Gary and Harvey Starr. (2003) *Necessary Conditions: Theory, Methodology, and Applications.* Lanham, MD: Rowman & Littlefield.

Gross, Neil. (2008) *Richard Rorty: The Making of an American Philosopher.* Chicago: University of Chicago Press.

Helleiner, Eric. (1994) *States and the Reemergence of Global Finance: From Bretton Woods to the 1990s.* Ithaca: Cornell University Press.

King, Gary, Robert O. Keohane, and Sidney Verba. (1994) *Designing Social Inquiry: Scientific Inference in Qualitative Research.* Princeton: Princeton University Press.

MacKenzie, Donald. (2006) *An Engine, Not a Camera: How Financial Models Shape Markets.* Cambridge: MIT Press.

Odell, John S. (2001) 'Case Study Methods in International Political Economy'. *International Studies Perspectives* 2: 161–76.

Orum, Anthony M., Joe R. Feagin, and Gideon Sjoberg. (1991) 'The Nature of the Case Study'. Pp. 1–26 in *A Case for the Case Study*, edited by Joe R. Feagin, Anthony M. Orum, and Gideon Sjoberg. Chapell Hill: University of North Carolina Press.

Pahre, Robert. (2005) 'Formal Theory and Case-Study Methods in EU Studies'. *European Union Politics* 6: 113–46.

Przeworski, Adam and Henry Teune. (1982) *Logic of Comparative Social Inquiry*. New York: Kreiger Publishing.

Ragin, Charles C. (2000) *Fuzzy-Set Social Science*. Chicago: University of Chicago Press.

Ragin, Charles G. (2006) 'Set Relations in Social Research: Evaluating Their Consistency and Coverage'. *Political Analysis* 14(3): 291–310.

Ragin, Charles C. (2008) *Redesigning Social Inquiry: Fuzzy Sets and Beyond*. Chicago: University of Chicago Press.

Ragin, Charles C. and Howard S. Becker (eds). (1992) *What Is a Case? Exploring the Foundations of Social Inquiry*. New York: Cambridge University Press.

Ragin, Charles C. and Benoit Rihoux. (2004) 'Qualitative Comparative Analysis (QCA): State of the Art and Prospects'. *Qualitative Methods* 2: 3–13.

Ragin, Charles C., Kriss Drass, and Sean Davey. (2007) Fuzzy-Set/Qualitative Comparative Analysis 2.0. Tucson. Arizon: Department of Sociology, University of Arizona.

Reuschemeyer, Dietrich. (2003) 'Can One or a Few Cases Yield Theoretical Gains?' Pp. 305–36 in *Comparative Historical Analysis in the Social Sciences*, edited by James Mahoney and Dietrich Rueschemeyer. Cambridge: Cambridge University Press.

Sartori, Giovanni. (1970) 'Concept Misformation in Comparative Politics'. *American Political Science Review* 64(4): 1033–41.

Schneider, Garrett Andrew. (2008) 'Interest Organizations, Policy Change, and the Prison Boom: Towards a Social Movements Perspective on Incarceration Growth'. Unpublished manuscript.

Steel, Daniel. (2004) 'Social Mechanisms and Causal Inference'. *Philosophy of the Social Sciences* 34: 55–78.

Western, Bruce. (1996) 'Vague Theory and Model Uncertainty in Macrosociology'. *Sociological Methodology* 26: 165–92.

9

Investigating Human Communication and Language from Traces Left on the Web

Mike Thelwall

INTRODUCTION

The social computing/web 2.0 revolution of blogs, Wikipedia, social network sites (SNSs) and web forums heralds an era in which an increasingly wide section of the world's population is creating content for the web (e.g. O'Reilly, 2006; Sunstein, 2007). Although this content could be relatively formal, such as part of a Wikipedia article, much of it is more casual in style, such as blog postings, comments on a BBC news stories or comments on others' blog postings. At the most informal end of the spectrum is communication in SNSs like MySpace, instant messaging, and contributions to chatrooms, web bulletin boards or forums. This is likely to be informal in the sense of ignoring standard written structures, spelling and grammar (Danet et al., 1997; Thelwall, 2009b; Baron, 2003; Crystal, 2006).

An almost accidental consequence of web 2.0 is that the web has become an enormous repository of the informal language, thoughts and opinions of a mass of the population. The scale and accessibility of this resource is unique in human history. Two examples serve to set this in context: The diary of Anne Frank is an enormously significant document and was only published to a wide audience after her death. Today's Anne Frank might be just one of hundreds or thousands keeping her diary as a blog and having an ongoing following. Recent politically significant examples include Salam Pax, who blogged from inside Iraq during the Iraq war (Thompson, 2003). On a larger scale, from 1936 a UK social research organisation attempted to monitor the public mood through 'mass-observations', including interviews and reported overheard conversations to generate a pooled corpus from which the public mood could be gauged (Mass-Observation-Archive, 1991). This was a way of checking newspaper pronouncements of the public mood. Today this labour-intensive exercise would be redundant because the public mood can be diagnosed by sampling blogs, forums and SNSs. In fact, the reincarnation of the Mass-Observation Organisation recently launched an initiative for UK citizens to record details of their life on a particular day in blog form (BBC, 2006).

Market research companies have also exploited web 2.0 by monitoring customer feedback or brand perceptions in specialist forums or general blogs. For the latter case, companies like Nielsen (www.nielsen.com) monitor millions of blogs and for any given client, perhaps only one in 50,000 blog postings is in any way relevant and so the task is like looking for a needle in a haystack. Nevertheless, with modern computer technology it may take less than a second to find the needle.

This chapter describes methods for finding needles in the web haystack for a variety of social science goals. In other words, these are methods to identify web trends and data relevant to particular social science research topics. This is relevant not only for those who research the web and web use but also for those researching human behaviour, language or opinion topics that may be represented or discussed somewhere on the web. As a methods chapter, the primary goal is to introduce new techniques, most of which are simple and fast. These techniques are illustrated with findings about political opinions, swearing and web pages about computing pioneer Alan Turing in blogs, SNSs and the whole web. Variants of these methods have been used in information science, medical informatics, communication science, social psychology, corpus linguistics, politics and sociology. This chapter is organised by increasing order of complexity, starting with methods that require a few hours to learn, yet are powerful and widely useful.

BLOG AND SEARCH ANALYSIS: GLOBAL MIND READING?

Several groups of researchers have attempted to take advantage of blogs, forums or Twitter to identify or track public opinions or expressions or the public mood. Whilst these have tended to use complex methods, simple alternatives are introduced below. The project www.wefeelfine.org uses a computer program that continually monitors blogs from a variety of sources and every time it finds the phrase 'I feel' or 'I am feeling' it adds the whole sentence to a 'word cloud' animation. The result is a continuously evolving web animation that samples emotions expressed in blogs. A more quantitative approach counts, amongst other things, the proportion of positive and negative words using www.wefeelfine.org data as well as song titles and lyrics (Dodds and Danforth, in press). This monitors fluctuations in the global 'mood' over time as reflected in songs and blogs. For example, it found that Barack Obama's election was apparently the happiest time in 2008 and Michael Jackson's death was the saddest in the first half of 2009.

Simple methods to extract public opinion data from blogs

Analysing public expressions from the web on a large scale can also be used to gain insights into public opinion for a particular topic or issue of interest (Thelwall, 2007; Smith, 2007). This is easy to achieve using a number of free online tools such as blog search engines. For example, suppose that somebody was researching public reactions to Michael Jackson's death and how this changed day-by-day in the first week. This would be almost impossible to do without the web because the researcher would need to be prepared from the outset to interview people to get a large enough daily sample to draw conclusions about trends and it would not be appropriate to interview people a long time afterwards because of hindsight bias (Fischhoff and Beyth, 1975).

This kind of study is relatively simple to do with the web, exploiting the fact that many people record their feelings in blogs and blog postings are time-stamped and relatively permanent and hence are an excellent source of evidence. The simplest way to access this evidence is to use a blog search engine such as Google Blog Search with the query 'Michael Jackson', restricting the date as appropriate. For example, a search for posts containing 'Michael Jackson' and written on 26 June 2009 returned a list of matching blog postings, estimating that there were a total of 50,563 from this date. This could be used to extract a sample for a content analysis, perhaps comparing the results with those from subsequent days to identify trends.

A considerable advantage of blog searching is that it gives free and easy access to a large volume of data. Its disadvantage is that the sample is uncontrolled: bloggers are not representative of the whole population; they tend to be in richer nations, have access to the Internet and seem to be well educated, with a disproportionate number of students (Herring et al., 2007). Moreover, it is often difficult to find out specific information about individuals, such as their age and nationality. Nevertheless, sampling in this way is cheap and convenient compared to most alternatives and is a useful method as long as conclusions are drawn carefully from the results, taking into account sampling issues.

Detecting trends and events from blogs

In addition to the public opinion sampling approach discussed above, blogs can also be used to detect trends and events within topics or broad issues. The simplest way to do this is via the graphing tool of the blog search engine BlogPulse.

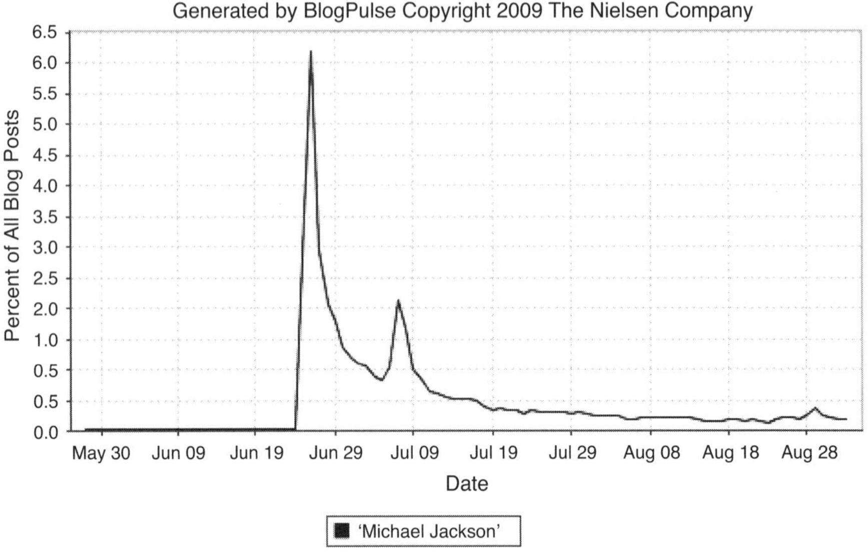

Figure 9.1 A BlogPulse graph of the proportion of blog posts mentioning 'Michael Jackson' over a 6 month period in 2009

This plots the number of blog posts matching a query on each day for the past six months, illustrating any trends. Figure 9.1 shows the percentage of blog posts mentioning Michael Jackson after his death and it is clear that the event was widely blogged about for weeks, but then apparently became a much less common topic without completely subsiding even after several months. The first spike in Figure 9.1 is triggered by news of the death of Michael Jackson and the second by a memorial service.

The same technique can be used to detect rather than to investigate events. For this, a query for a broad issue or topic must be constructed and then spikes in the graph may point to relevant events. For example, Figure 9.2 is for blogs mentioning 'Obama' and each spike suggests an event when his actions were widely blogged about. Reading posts from the spike date would reveal the cause of the event. The graph also reveals that he has been continually in the news for this half year. Note that the periodic fluctuations every seven days are caused by politics being discussed less on Sundays. Although the graph has many spikes, it is still easy to identify the tallest spike, which presumably represent the most-discussed events. The tallest spike is on June 4 and reading blog posts from this date (clicking on the BlogPulse graph produces a list) reveals discussion of Obama's visit to the Middle East. This process can be fully automated with the use of specialist software. One project used this approach to automatically detect public fears about science by automatically monitoring a large number of blog posts on a daily basis (Thelwall and Prabowo, 2007).

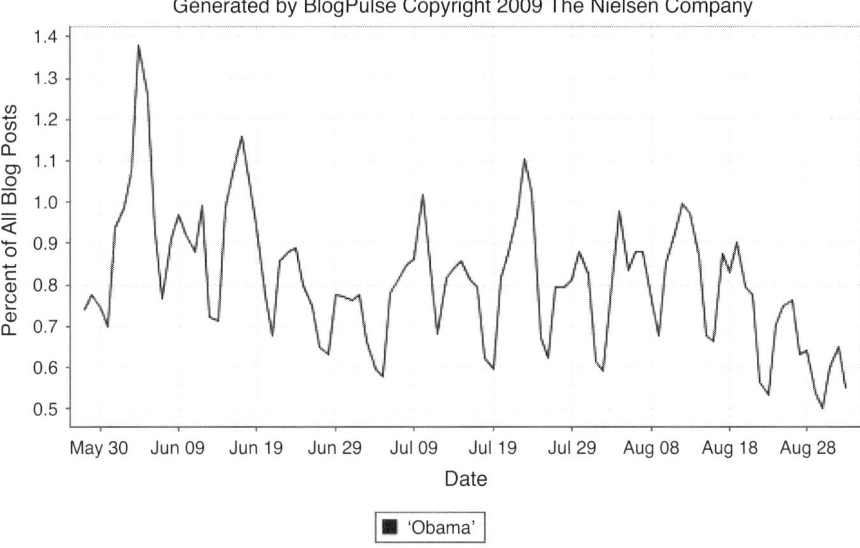

Figure 9.2 A BlogPulse graph of the proportion of blog posts mentioning 'Obama' over a 6 month period in 2009

Finally, blog search graphs can also be used to detect overall trends in interest in a topic, by checking whether the line plotted slopes upwards or downwards. Figure 9.3 shows an apparent decrease in interest in global warming over a period of three months.

Limitations with blogs as evidence

There are several limitations with the use of blog search engines. The main limitation, as discussed above, is that the sample of bloggers chosen is uncontrolled and is in some ways unrepresentative of the world's population. Hence the evidence from a blog search graph is rarely likely to be conclusive but should be triangulated with other methods, or used for initial exploratory research. A second important point is that the results are dependent upon good choices of queries for inferences about the underlying topic interest. For example, a graph for 'genetically modified food' might show a decrease but this might be due to bloggers switching to the phrase 'GM food' rather than becoming less interested. This risk can be minimised by experimenting with different queries.

The problem that bloggers are not fully representative of the general population or that topics blogged about may not fully reflect public interests can be partly mitigated through triangulation with a different data source: Google searches. A significant proportion of web users search with Google and so its searchers are likely to be more representative than bloggers of the general population. The free Google Trends web site (www.google.com/trends) can be used to exploit this.

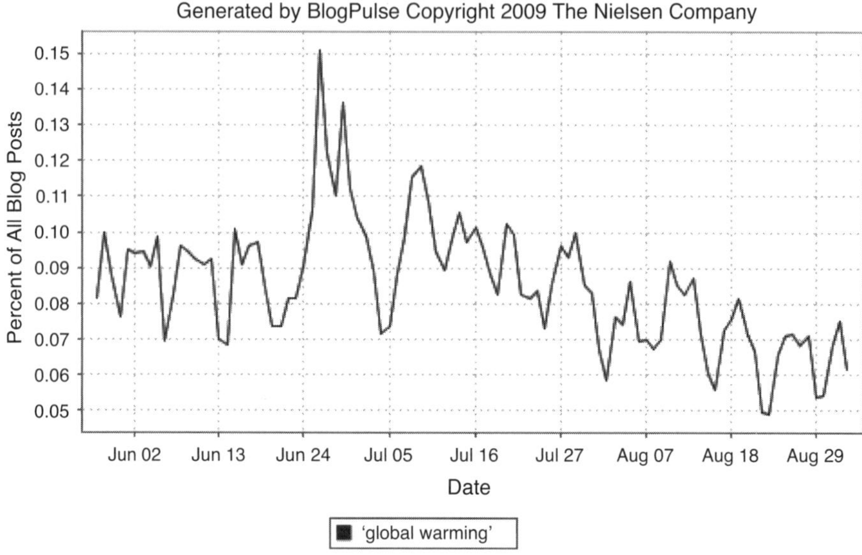

Figure 9.3 A BlogPulse graph of the proportion of blog posts mentioning 'global warming' over a 3 month period in 2009

It generates graphs similar to blogpulse.com except that the graphs illustrate searches submitted to Google rather than words in blog posts. They are useful for triangulation in the sense that if the Google Trends graph for a query has the same shape as a BlogPulse graph then any events or trends identified are unlikely to be restricted to bloggers. For instance, compare the relevant portion of Figure 9.4 to Figure 9.3. The disadvantage of the Google Trends graphs is that there is no context to diagnose why the search terms were used. For example, a small spike on a Michael Jackson graph might relate to a concert, a news story or someone else with the same name. In contrast, the blog search graphs can be checked for content by reading the underlying blog posts. Hence, blog graphs should normally be used as the primary source with Google Trends graphs used for (data) triangulation.

Another limitation is that the graph methods only work well for events that are fairly widely blogged about. Less popular issues are likely to generate erratic graphs from which patterns cannot be diagnosed. In practice this means that the methods work best for issues that receive national media coverage.

In addition to blog search engines and Google Trends there are a few similar services, such as forum, bulletin board and chatroom search engines. Together these form a collection of easy-to-use free online tools through which researchers can access a huge quantity of predominantly informal comments and information left online by a substantial section of web users. As the above examples illustrate, this is particularly useful for evidence of public opinion or interest

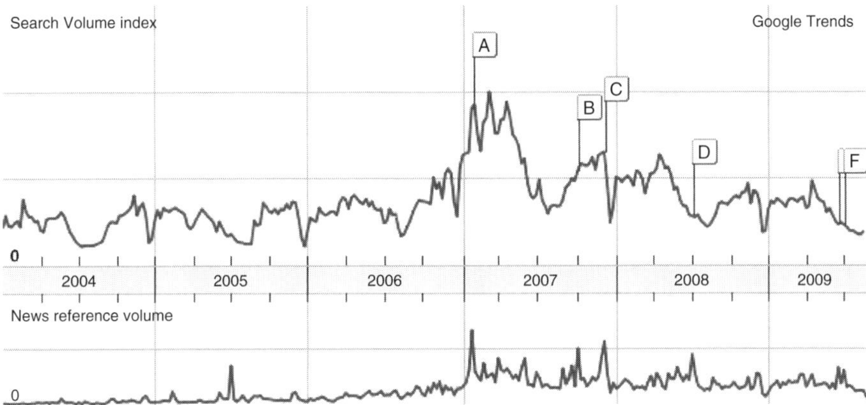

Figure 9.4 A Google Trends graph of the trends in 'global warming' searches from 2004 to 2009 (top) compared to news volume for the same period (bottom). Reproduced with permission.

and one powerful feature is that the data can be gathered retrospectively, normally up to about six months after an event.

SOCIAL NETWORK SITES

The Social Network Sites (SNSs), such as Facebook and MySpace, are web sites that allow people to join, set up a personal profile page, and publicly connect to other members as 'Friends' (Boyd, 2006). In 2009, Facebook and MySpace were in the top ten most visited web sites in the world, a testament to the importance of the genre. SNSs seem to be popular because they allow friends and acquaintances to connect to each other and either extensively communicate or just stay in touch (Thelwall and Wilkinson, in press; Boyd, 2006). This seems to provide a new way for an old and important human function of maintaining a personal network (Tufekci, 2008; Donath, 2007). The communication in SNSs can take the form of private messages, like e-mail or instant messaging, or public broadcasts, such as posting or commenting on pictures or a blog, or leaving public comments on another's profile.

For researchers, SNSs are not only a fascinating new phenomenon but also a potential new window into the lives, networks and communications of ordinary web users. Unlike blogs, information about SNS members is normally easily available, with age, gender and location often included as standard on members' profile pages, along with a photograph. In some SNSs, like Facebook, most or all information is only accessible to registered Friends and is therefore not useful for research. In contrast, in MySpace and Bebo members can opt for a public profile that anyone can access. This makes these two sites particularly valuable for researchers. In particular, it is possible to retrieve three types of data to study: friendship networks via the public lists of Friends on each profile page; self-reported personal information such as religion, favourite music and reason for using the site; and public communications between Friends.

Examples of SNS research

Several studies have already exploited publicly available SNS information on a large scale. These have typically used computer programs to download sufficient data from the sites, but alternative techniques are discussed below. One investigation cross-referenced personal information with personal networks to study homophily, the tendency for Friends to be similar. It found a significant homophily in almost everything investigated except gender – both males and females had a majority of female Friends (Thelwall, 2009a). Another study analysed homophily in personal taste expressions in MySpace, finding that Friends seemed to deliberately express their musical and other tastes differently from each other (Liu, 2007).

One particularly interesting aspect of SNSs is the informal language used in communication between Friends. Whilst new language styles for forms of electronic communication such as text messages have long been recognised, they are normally private and difficult to investigate without controlled experiments or specific groups of volunteers (Palfreyman and Al Khalil, 2007; Lee, 2007). In contrast, comments exchanged between Friends in MySpace are often public and are hence accessible for research on a huge scale. A study of swearing patterns took advantage of this. Swearing is normally self-censored from written text but this is not the case in MySpace, with a majority of members apparently hosting some swearing on their profile (Thelwall, 2008). The study counted occurrences of strong, medium and mild swearing in a sample of 9,376 public member profiles, finding that strong swearing (predominantly variations of the word 'fuck') was more prevalent in male than female profiles in the US but there was no gender difference in the UK. This study also characterised swearing contexts and is apparently the largest published study of swearing in any context. This latter point illustrates how convenience of access to information in SNSs can greatly aid some types of research. Another study of language in MySpace examined all words used, finding that some non-standard terms were amongst the most frequent, including haha and lol (Thelwall, 2009b) and another suggested that SNS Friends tend to live moderately close together (Escher, 2007).

The above discussed studies illustrate the potential for large scale analyses with SNSs. This is aided by the ability to randomly sample members via their numerical IDs, aiding the extent to which the results can be generalised. Nevertheless, more holistic research into SNS users and uses has tended to take a different approach, using interviews or questionnaires rather than analysing profile contents (Boyd, 2008). This approach, whilst giving the best insights into

SNSs overall, tends to be based upon small and non-random samples and hence can be complemented by studies of the kind discussed above.

Simple methods to access large-scale SNS data

There is a simple way to harness SNSs in research without employing specialist software for data collection and despite the lack of a convenient search tool like blogpulse.com for blogs. The simple alternative is to use a site-specific search in Google or another search engine. The site-specific search is the addition to a query of the command 'site', followed by the domain name of the relevant part of the SNS. To illustrate this, all personal profiles in MySpace have URLs that start with http://profile.myspace.com/. The domain name of this URL is profile.myspace.com. Thus to search for information in MySpace profiles, the command site:profile.myspace.com can be added to any query. For instance, if the goal was to identify or count the number of times the expression 'silly cow' was used then the query

'silly cow' site:profile.myspace.com

would achieve this. Viewing a sample of the results could be used to ascertain, for example, whether there was a gender bias in users of the phrase. Similarly, the search

'Michael Jackson' site:profile.myspace.com

would give a list of MySpace profiles and the search

'Michael Jackson' site:www.bebo.com/Profile.jsp

would give a list of English Bebo profiles containing this phrase and visiting a sample could address issues such as gender profile of the fan base. A useful technique for this data (and for blogs) is content analysis (Neuendorf, 2002): drawing up a list of common contexts or other relevant categories and then using human coders to classify a sample according to the devised scheme (see also Bar-Ilan, 2004). This is particularly useful for exploratory research that does not have a specific hypothesis to test. Note also that the above method generates what linguists might call a list of concordances: words or phrases displayed in natural (for MySpace) use contexts.

The site Twitter qualifies as an SNS although it emphasises posting short messages to friendship networks. It has some dedicated search engines, such as Twitter Search (search.twitter.com), although these did not have large archives at the time of writing and so were useful only to access recent Twitter posts. Should this change then these specialist search engines would form a useful addition to the techniques discussed here for blogs and SNSs.

In summary, SNSs like Bebo and MySpace allow researchers to access information about their users and uses either via specialist data collection software or via advanced search engine queries. This gives an opportunity to study aspects of SNS use as well as any phenomenon, like language, that is discussed or reflected in SNSs.

HYPERLINK NETWORKS

Hyperlinks in web pages are normally designed to help visitors to navigate to relevant web pages, often within the same site but sometimes on other sites. It has long been known by Google and others that hyperlinks tend to connect similar pages and tend to point to useful or important pages (Kleinberg, 1999; Brin and Page, 1998). Hyperlinks are therefore not only included in web search engine ranking algorithms (Arasu et al., 2001) but can also be used to illustrate the connectivity of the web. Examples of the latter include networks of the 'whole' web (Broder et al., 2000), web sites of groups of universities (Ortega et al., 2008; Ortega and Aguillo, 2008), web sites of research networks (Heimeriks et al., 2003) and groups of IT company web sites (Vaughan, 2005). Such diagrams need software to produce, but there are several free programs that can help. This section describes one application and then discusses software for network diagrams.

Alan Turing case study

Alan Turing was a mathematician and computing pioneer who contributed to code breaking in the Second World War and who committed suicide after persecution by the British government for his sexuality. In September 2009 he received a formal apology from the UK prime minister (http://www.number10.gov.uk/Page20571). A small link analysis was conducted by identifying popular web pages or web sites about him and plotting the links between them.

Figure 9.5 is a direct link diagram: each node represents one of the web pages or web sites about Alan Turing and arrows represent hyperlinks between these sites (as identified and drawn by LexiURL Searcher, see below). These web pages are surprisingly well interlinked. The Wikipedia page is less central in the network than his biographer's site and a fan site.

Figure 9.6 is a co-inlink (Björneborn and Ingwersen, 2004) diagram for the same collection of sites. Lines between sites have thicknesses proportional to the total number of web pages that simultaneously link to both sites/pages. Whilst Figure 9.5 shows the internal organisation of the high profile Turing pages, Figure 9.6 gives a perspective on how the rest of the web views these pages. The four central pages are the Wikipedia article, the fan site, the biographer's site and an entry in the Stanford Encyclopaedia of Philosophy. This last page is interesting because Turing seems to be rarely thought of as a philosopher as the page itself recognises, 'Alan Turing (1912–1954) never described himself as a philosopher, but his 1950 paper "Computing Machinery and Intelligence" is one of the most frequently

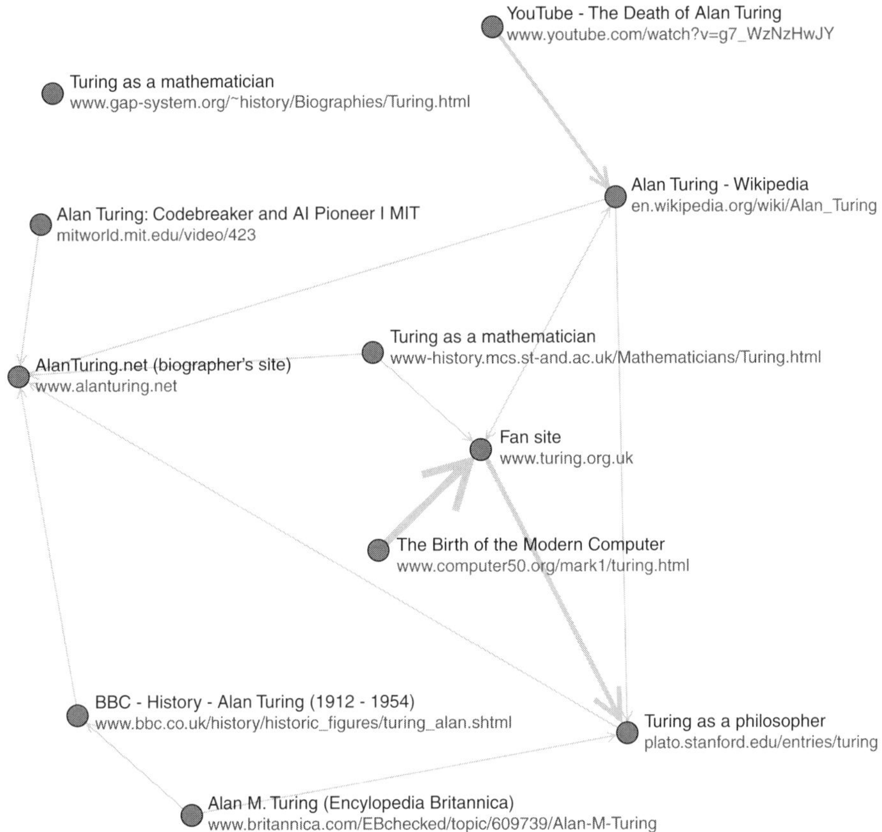

Figure 9.5 A network diagram of the links between 11 popular pages or sites about Alan Turing

cited in modern philosophical literature' (http://plato.stanford.edu/entries/turing/, accessed 11 September 2009). The academic pages that focus on his mathematics or computing are relatively peripheral in this diagram.

Link analysis tools

Four tools that can be used to generate network diagrams are TouchGraph, LexiURL Searcher, IssueCrawler and SocSciBot. The first two work by sending relevant queries to search engines, then synthesising and plotting the results. The last two fetch pages from the web directly instead of using search engines.

TouchGraph Google Browser is the easiest to use but is probably the least useful for research (http://www.touchgraph.com/TGGoogleBrowser.html). It can be fed a single URL and then automatically generates an almost instant colourful and interactive network centred upon that URL, using Google's 'related sites' information. This diagram tends not to be very useful for research because it

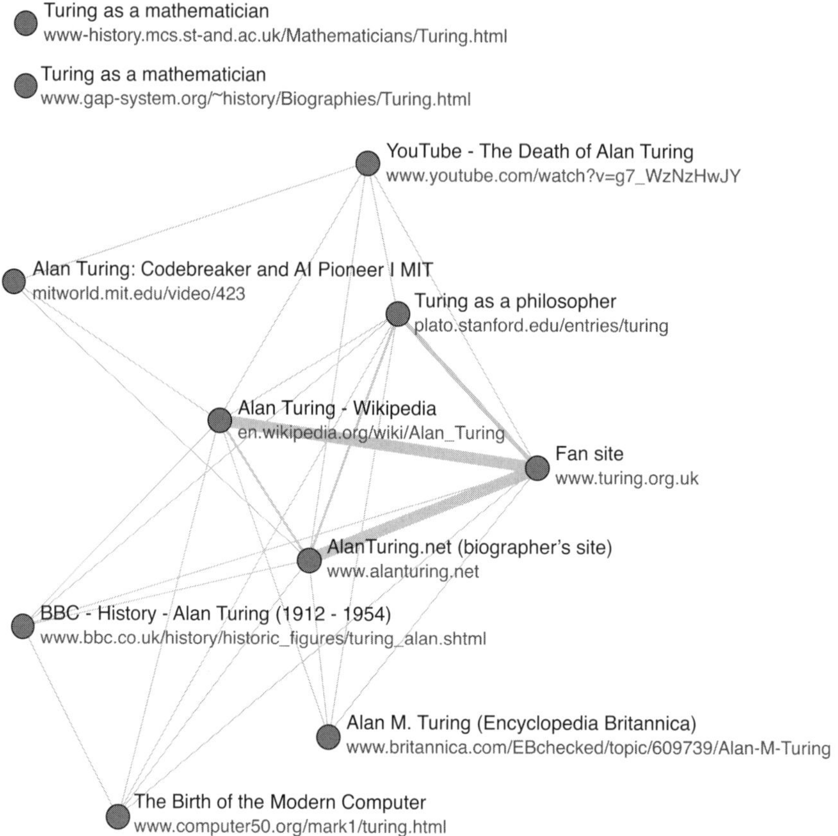

Figure 9.6 A network diagram of the co-inlinks between 11 popular pages or sites about Alan Turing

cannot be built from collections of web sites; it is not clear how the diagram is produced – since it depends upon Google's related sites feature – and it is quite small. Nevertheless it is interactive and easy to use and so may have value as an exploratory tool. TouchGraph can also create graphs for keywords rather than URLs.

IssueCrawler (Rogers, 2002, 2005) is designed to draw network diagrams of collections of web sites relevant to given issues. It is free online – after registration, commands must be submitted and then the network is produced after a short delay. Below is a succinct description of what it can do.

> The IssueCrawler is web network location and visualisation software. It consists of crawlers, analysis engines and visualisation modules. It is server-side software that crawls specified sites and captures the outlinks from the specified sites. Sites may be crawled and analyzed in three ways: co-link, snowball and inter-actor. Co-link analysis crawls the seed URLs and retains the pages that receive at least two links from the seeds. Snowball analysis crawls sites and retains pages receiving at least one link from the seeds. Inter-actor analysis crawls the

seed URLs and retains inter-linking between the seeds. The Issue Crawler visualises the results in circle, cluster and geographical maps. (http://www.govcom.org/Issuecrawler_instructions.htm#1.3, 11 September, 2009)

LexiURL Searcher is a general purpose program for processing search engine data and one of its features is drawing network diagrams. It must be downloaded in order to run and only runs on Windows machines. Once downloaded, LexiURL Searcher can be fed with a list of web sites or URLs in order to draw a network diagram either of the links between the sites/URLs or of the co-inlinks between them, as in Figure 9.6. Like IssueCrawler, it is not instant and may take an hour for a network of 50 sites.

SocSciBot is similar to LexiURL Searcher in that it must be downloaded before being used and only runs on Windows. It also takes some time to gather data to produce a network diagram of links within a collection of web sites. It is most useful for a collection of small web sites.

CONCLUSIONS

The methods described in this chapter illustrate how it is possible to extract patterns from traces of human behaviour on the web. In all cases data is used in a way that the creator would be unaware of and did not intend. This is one of the advantages of the passive data gathering approach: it does not take up the time of the people whose work is surveyed and they cannot change their reaction in response to the study purpose or in response to being studied. Nevertheless, some different issues are generated.

An ethical problem arises if the creators of the analysed content are considered to be study participants because informed consent would then be needed. This is not an issue, however, because individuals are not participating, only documents created by them and visible in public on the web. Permission is not needed to research these public documents (Thelwall and Ackland, 2008). In terms of sample bias, as discussed above, this is normally impossible to avoid, not least because people without access to the internet are unlikely to create content that can be studied. In all cases this limitation must be considered when analysing and reporting the results. If possible triangulation with other sources should also be used. Another significant issue is that web information may be inaccurate; either deliberately or accidentally misleading for the purpose of the study. For example, a blogger or social network site member may assume an incorrect age or gender (Hinduja and Patchin, 2008). Finally, the creation of web content is normally voluntary and possibly subject to a range of unknown influences. For example, a blogger may be upset about many things but only blog about the one they consider to be most popular or interesting. Another person might write a comment about an issue that they don't care much about as a way to spend some idle time.

Despite the limitations, the web can be a valuable source of public opinion and other data about language and commonly discussed topics. There is a range of free and simple-to-use tools to access this information, such as blogpulse.com and LexiURL Searcher, although some techniques are more complex or require more specialist software. Social scientists are encouraged to try them for their own area of expertise to see what insights the web can yield. Especially recommended are quick exploratory pilot studies and studies that triangulate web data with other data sources, interviews or other research methods.

REFERENCES

Arasu, A., Cho, J., Garcia-Molina, H., Paepcke, A., and Raghavan, S. (2001) Searching the web. *ACM Transactions on Internet Technology,* 1: 2–43.

Bar-Ilan, J. (2004) Blogarians – A new breed of librarians. *Proceedings of the American Society for Information Science & Technology.*

Baron, N.S. (2003) Language of the Internet. In A. Farghali (ed.) *The Stanford Handbook for Language Engineers.* Stanford: CSLI Publications.

BBC (2006) Blog records Britons' daily lives. *BBC,* Retrieved 23 October, 2006 from: http://news.bbc.co.uk/1/hi/technology/6048392.stm.

Björneborn, L. and Ingwersen, P. (2004) Toward a basic framework for webometrics. *Journal of the American Society for Information Science and Technology,* 55: 1216–27.

Boyd, D. (2006) Friends, Friendsters, and MySpace Top 8: Writing community into being on social network sites. *First Monday,* 11, Retrieved 29 April, 2009 from: http://firstmonday.org/htbin/cgiwrap/bin/ojs/index.php/fm/article/view/1418/1336.

Boyd, D. (2008) Taken out of context: American teen sociality in networked publics. *Information Management and Systems.* Berkeley: University of California.

Brin, S. and Page, L. (1998) The anatomy of a large scale hypertextual Web search engine. *Computer Networks and ISDN Systems,* 30: 107–17.

Broder, A., Kumar, R., Maghoul, F., Raghavan, P., Rajagopalan, S., Stata, R., Tomkins, A., and Wiener, J. (2000) Graph structure in the web. *Journal of Computer Networks,* 33: 309–20.

Crystal, D. (2006) *Language and the Internet,* Cambridge: Cambridge University Press.

Danet, B., Ruedenberg, L., and Rosenbaum-Tamari, Y. (1997) 'Hmmm.Where's That Smoke Coming From?' Writing, Play and Performance on Internet Relay Chat. *Journal of Computer-mediated Communication,* 2, Retrieved 3 March, 2008 from: http://jcmc.indiana.edu/vol2/issue4/danet.html.

Dodds, P.S. and Danforth, C.M. (in press) Measuring the happiness of large-scale written expression: Songs, blogs, and presidents. *Journal of Happiness Studies.*

Donath, J. (2007) Signals in social supernets. *Journal of Computer-Mediated Communication,* 13, Retrieved 17 June, 2008 from: http://jcmc.indiana.edu/vol13/issue1/donath.html.

Escher, T. (2007) The geography of (online) social networks. *Web 2.0, York University,* Retrieved 18 September, 2007 from: http://people.oii.ox.ac.uk/escher/wp-content/uploads/2007/09/Escher_York_presentation.pdf.

Fischhoff, B., and Beyth, R. (1975) 'I knew it would happen': Remembered probabilities of once-future things. *Organizational Behavior and Human Performance,* 13: 1–16.

Heimeriks, G., Hörlesberger, M., and Van den Besselaar, P. (2003) Mapping communication and collaboration in heterogeneous research networks. *Scientometrics,* 58: 391–413.

Herring, S.C., Scheidt, L.A., Kouper, I., and Wright, E. (2007) A longitudinal content analysis of weblogs: 2003–4. In M. Tremayne (ed.) *Blogging, Citizenship, and the Future of Media.* London: Routledge.

Hinduja, S. and Patchin, J.W. (2008) Personal information of adolescents on the Internet: A quantitative content analysis of MySpace. *Journal of Adolescence,* 31: 125–46.

Kleinberg, J.M. (1999) Authoritative sources in a hyperlinked environment. *Journal of the ACM,* 46: 604–32.

Lee, C.K.M. (2007) Text-making practices beyond the classroom context: Private instant messaging in Hong Kong. *Computers and Composition,* 24: 285–301.
Liu, H. (2007) Social network profiles as taste performances. *Journal of Computer-Mediated Communication,* 13, Retrieved 5 June, 2008 from: http://jcmc.indiana.edu/vol13/issue1/liu.html.
Mass-Observation-Archive (1991) Mass-Observation Archive diaries: An introduction.
Neuendorf, K. (2002) *The Content Analysis Guidebook.* London: Sage.
O'reilly, T. (2006) Levels of the game: The hierarchy of Web 2.0 applications. Retrieved 4 June, 2007 from: http://radar.oreilly.com/archives/2006/07/levels_of_the_game.html.
Ortega, J.L., Aguillo, I., Cothey, V., and Scharnhorst, A. (2008) Maps of the academic web in the European Higher Education Area: An exploration of visual web indicators. *Scientometrics,* 74: 295–308.
Ortega, J.L. and Aguillo, I.F. (2008) Visualization of the Nordic academic web: Link analysis using social network tools. *Information Processing & Management,* 44: 1624–33.
Palfreyman, D. and al Khalil, M. (2007) 'A funky language for teenzz to use': Representing Gulf Arabic in instant messaging. In B. Danet and S.C. Herring (eds) *The Multilingual Internet: Language, Culture, and Communication Online.* Oxford: Oxford University Press.
Rogers, R. (2002) Operating issue networks on the Web. *Science as Culture,* 11: 191–214.
Rogers, R. (2005) *Information Politics on the Web.* Cambridge, MA: MIT Press.
Smith, A.G. (2007) Issues in 'blogmetrics' – case studies using BlogPulse to observe trends in weblogs. *Proceedings of ISSI 2007,* pp. 726–30.
Sunstein, C.R. (2007) *Republic.com 2.0.* Princeton: Princeton University Press.
Thelwall, M. (2007) Blog searching: The first general-purpose source of retrospective public opinion in the social sciences? *Online Information Review,* 31: 277–89.
Thelwall, M. (2008) Fk yea I swear: Cursing and gender in a corpus of MySpace pages. *Corpora,* 3: 83–107.
Thelwall, M. (2009a) Homophily in MySpace. *Journal of the American Society for Information Science and Technology,* 60: 219–31.
Thelwall, M. (2009b) MySpace comments. *Online Information Review,* 33: 58–76.
Thelwall, M. and Ackland, R. (2008) The ethics of large-scale Web data analysis (webmetrics). *NCRM Research Methods Festival 2008,* Retrieved 11 September, 2009 from: http://www.ncrm.ac.uk/RMF2008/festival/programme/eres/pres1/Webmetrics_ethics.ppt.
Thelwall, M. and Prabowo, R. (2007) Identifying and characterising public science-related concerns from RSS feeds. *Journal of the American Society for Information Science & Technology,* 58: 379–90.
Thelwall, M. and Wilkinson, D. (in press) Public dialogs in social network sites: What is their purpose? *Journal of the American Society for Information Science & Technology.*
Thompson, G. (2003) Weblogs, warblogs, the public sphere, and bubbles. *Transformations,* 7, Retrieved 27 June, 2006 from: http://transformations.cqu.edu.au/journal/issue_07/article_02.shtml.
Tufekci, Z. (2008) Grooming, gossip, Facebook and MySpace: What can we learn about these sites from those who won't assimilate? *Information, Communication & Society,* 11: 544–64.
Vaughan, L. (2005) Exploring website features for business information. *Scientometrics,* 61: 467–77.

10

Innovative Qualitative Data Collection Techniques for Conducting Literature Reviews/Research Syntheses

Anthony J. Onwuegbuzie,
Nancy L. Leech and
Kathleen M. T. Collins

Those who don't know history are destined to repeat it.

Edmund Burke (1729–1797)

Edmund Burke was an Anglo-Irish philosopher who is credited as being the philosophical founder of modern political conservatism. His famous quotation above is just as true today – if not more – as it was in the eighteenth century. Moreover, his statement is not only applicable to the field of politics; it also is extremely relevant to the field of research. If, for instance, a medical researcher conducts an experimental study to investigate the efficacy of a drug that numerous researchers previously have found to cause serious side-effects, his/her study can have dire consequences on the participants. As another example, if a researcher representing the social and behavioral sciences utilized an instrument that has been found repeatedly to possess poor psychometric properties, then the score validity of the findings would be extremely questionable. Simply put, with very few exceptions (e.g. grounded theory research (Glaser and Strauss, 1967), wherein some proponents argue against an initial literature review before data collection; for an excellent discussion, see McGhee et al., 2007), conducting research without adequate knowledge of previous, relevant methodology and empirical findings represents poor practice.

Undoubtedly, the most effective way to become familiar with previous research methodology and findings in a given area of research is by conducting an extensive and rigorous review of the related literature. Due to the importance of knowing what methods have been implemented in the past and what findings have emerged, the literature review represents the most important step of the research process in empirical research studies – for qualitative research, quantitative research, and mixed research studies alike (Boote and Beile, 2005; Combs et al., 2010; Onwuegbuzie et al., 2010a). As declared by Boote and Beile (2005):

> A substantive, thorough, sophisticated literature review is a precondition for doing substantive, thorough, sophisticated research. 'Good' research is good because it advances our collective understanding. To advance our collective understanding, a researcher or scholar needs to understand what has been done before, the strengths and weaknesses of existing studies, and what they might mean. A researcher cannot perform significant research without first understanding the literature in the field. Not understanding the prior research clearly puts a researcher at a disadvantage. (p. 3)

Similarly, Garrard (2009) concluded that 'Given the vast number of scientific publications produced over the past several decades, information retrieval and analysis in the form of a critical review of the literature have become more crucial than ever' (p. 4).

Unfortunately, a significant proportion of authors experience difficulty conducting and writing the literature review. Interestingly, Alton-Lee (1998), who examined reviewers' comments for 58 manuscripts submitted to *Teaching and Teacher Education* over a one-year period (i.e. 142 reviews), documented the following criticisms associated with the literature review of the manuscripts: inadequate literature reviews (50.0%), theoretical flaws (53.4%), parochial focus (39.7%), failure to link findings to the extant literature (34.4%), and failure to contribute to international literature (36.2%). Further, Onwuegbuzie and Daniel (2005), who examined 52 manuscripts submitted over a two-year period to the journal *Research in the Schools*, reported that 40% of the submitted manuscripts contained inadequate literature reviews. Moreover, authors who wrote inadequate literature reviews were more than six times more likely to have their articles rejected for publication than were authors who wrote adequate literature reviews.

Yet, despite evidence to the contrary (Alton-Lee, 1998; Boote and Beile, 2005; Onwuegbuzie and Daniel, 2005), many research textbook authors understate the complexity of the literature review process. For example, in a section of the textbook entitled '*The Purpose of the Literature Search*', Gravetter and Forzano (2008) stated that 'The research process begins with an introduction that summarizes past research (from your literature search) and provides a logical justification for your study' (pp. 48–9). However, the literature review process is much more complex than merely summarizing the extant literature. This and the many other simplistic and misleading definitions in research methodology textbooks led Boote and Beile (2005) to declare that 'graduate students could be forgiven for thinking that writing a literature review is no more complicated than writing a high school term paper' (p. 5). As concluded by Onwuegbuzie et al. (2010a), 'is it any wonder then that the literature review does not hold a high status in the research process – as reflected by the lack of formal training that doctoral students receive on how to conduct literature reviews?' (p. 172).

In preparation for writing this chapter, we examined the curriculum of graduate-level school psychology programs across the United States. Specifically, we examined the website of every National Association of School Psychologists (NASP)-approved graduate-level school psychology program (n = 183), using the list provided by NASP. All the school psychology programs were NASP-approved between 1987 (i.e. Temple University, George Mason University) and 2010 (i.e. Azusa Pacific University, Fairfield University, Chicago School of Professional Psychology, Capella University, Georgian Court). Surprisingly, of the 175 approved graduate-level school psychology programs for which a full list of courses was accessible, only four programs (2.3%) offered a literature review course as either a required course or as an elective. An examination of counseling programs yielded similarly low numbers of required literature review courses. These findings support our contention that the literature review process is not considered sufficiently complex or important to justify courses that provide students with formal and systematic instruction on conducting literature reviews.

Our inspection of the standards developed by professional organizations in the fields of social psychology, counseling, and other social and behavioral science fields did not yield any literature-review-based standards. NASP (2000) has adopted and promotes 'an integrated set of comprehensive standards for preparation, credentialing, and professional practice in school psychology' (p. 5). This 62-page document contains (a) guidelines for the provision of school psychological services, (b) principles for professional ethics, (c) standards for the credentialing of school psychologists, and (d) standards for training and field placement programs in school psychology. The section entitled 'Professional Practices – General Principles' and subsection 'Research, Publications, and Presentation' (i.e. IV.F.) provides standards pertaining to designing and implementing research in schools; working in agencies without review committees; maintaining legal procedures when conducting research; publishing reports of their research; dealing with information presented through various impersonal media; upholding copyright laws; avoiding plagiarism; fabricating and falsifying data; making research data available for evidence when appropriate; correcting errors after the publication or presentation of research and other information; maintaining authorship integrity; publishing data or other information that make original contributions to the professional literature; and reviewing manuscripts, proposals; and other materials for consideration for publication and presentation. These standards appear to cover every major stage of the research process, from research planning to research initiation, to dissemination of research findings, which is laudable. However, there is not a single mention of literature reviews.

Similarly, although the American Counseling Association's (2005) 24-page 'Code of Ethics' provides standards pertaining to research responsibilities, rights of research participants, relationships with research participants (when research involves intensive or extended interactions), reporting results, and publication, standards for conducting literature reviews are missing. Nor are there any literature review-based standards in the American Educational Research Association's (AERA's) 15-page 'Standards for Reporting on Empirical Social Science Research in AERA Publications' (AERA, 2006) or AERA's (2000) 12-page 'Ethical Standards'. Thus, even professional organizations that oversee and regulate representing numerous applied social and behavioral science fields do not appear to deem it important to set standards for conducting and writing literature reviews. Yet, surely, there could be dire consequences for representatives of the helping professions (e.g. educators, counselors, psychologists) if they relied on techniques that were not extracted from rigorous literature reviews? So, why do poor literature reviewing practices not represent an ethical issue that justifies professional organizations adopting and promoting unique standards for literature reviews?

Interestingly, Leech and Goodwin (2008), who investigated the qualitative, quantitative, and mixed methods course requirements of 100 schools of education across the United States, reported that the mean number of required methods courses was 4.48, with some schools of education requiring as many as 11 methods courses. So, clearly, program directors recognize the importance of research methods courses; yet, they do not appear to place the same value in literature review courses. The findings of Leech and Goodwin (2008), coupled with our findings regarding the scant number of required literature review courses that prevail, support Cooper's (1985) contention – made a quarter of a century ago – that 'Students in education . . . can take five or six statistics or methods courses without ever directly addressing the problems and procedures of literature review' (p. 33); yet, as we will demonstrate later, conducting a literature review represents a methodology in its own right and thus deserves a place within programs of graduate studies, alongside other research methodologies such as statistics, measurement, and qualitative research.

We believe that taking at least one literature review course that is focused specifically on *how* to conduct a review of the literature will help to provide students with a foundation in literature reviewing, and also optimally promote a culture of rigorous literature review integrated throughout the program, as a whole. In any case, as exemplified by our search of curriculum in two fields, school psychology and counseling, we have seen little evidence of stand alone literature review courses being offered, thereby leading us to suspect the degree that literature reviewing is integrated throughout programs.

Further, this situation is exacerbated because, as documented by Onwuegbuzie and Leech (2005), most research methodology textbooks contain only one chapter discussing the literature review process, further perpetuating the perception that literature reviews are not a central component of the research process. Even more disturbingly, some textbook authors devote only a few pages to this very important topic. For example, Best and Kahn (2006) allocate only three pages (pp. 39–41) to the review of the literature.

On a more positive note, recently a few authors have attempted to fill this void in the literature by writing chapters and books that provide step-by-step guides to conducting rigorous literature reviews (Combs et al., 2010; Dellinger and Leech, 2007; Fink, 2009; Garrard, 2009; Hart, 2005; Leech et al., 2010; Machi and McEvoy, 2009; Onwuegbuzie et al., 2010a; Ridley, 2008). Even more encouragingly, some of these authors provide a much more accurate definition and explanation of the literature review that acknowledges its complexity. In particular, Machi and McEvoy (2009) provide the following definition:

> A literature review is a written document that presents a logically argued case founded on a comprehensive understanding of the current state of knowledge about a topic of study. This case establishes a convincing thesis to answer the study's question. (p. 4)

Most recently, Onwuegbuzie et al. (2010a) define the literature review as 'an interpretation of a selection of published and/or unpublished documents available from various sources on a specific topic that optimally involves summarization, analysis, evaluation, and synthesis of the documents' (p. 173).

Notwithstanding, these latest definitions of literature reviews are still inadequate and potentially misleading because they suggest that literature review sources only stem from materials that already exist either in printed or digital forms. Indeed, virtually all authors who provide a definition of literature reviews explicitly give this impression. For example, Gay et al. (2009) specify that literature review sources 'can include articles, abstracts, reviews, monographs, dissertations, books, other research reports, and electronic media effort' (p. 80). Onwuegbuzie et al. (2010a) provide an even more comprehensive list of documents: 'Sources considered appropriate for conducting literature reviews include the following: research articles, opinion articles, essays, article reviews, monographs, dissertations, books, Internet websites, video, interview transcripts, encyclopedias, company reports, trade catalogues, government documents, congressional/parliamentary bills, popular magazines, and advertisements' (p. 173). Although this information is accurate, we believe it falls short because, as asserted by Onwuegbuzie et al. (2010c), literature reviews can stem from other sources. Specifically, using the framework of Leech and Onwuegbuzie (2008), Onwuegbuzie et al. (2010c) conceptualized that knowledge which informs literature reviews can be extracted from one of the following four major sources: talk, observations, drawings/photographs/videos, and documents. In fact, because *literature* (i.e. documents) represents only one of these four sources, Onwuegbuzie et al. (2010c) recommend that 'the terms *literature review* and *review of the literature* be replaced with the term *research synthesis*' (p. 23).

With this in mind, the purpose of this chapter is to provide a four-dimensional framework for extracting information relevant to any research topic. In particular, we identify innovative qualitative data collection techniques for maximizing one's ability to obtain pertinent knowledge through analysis of the literature. We contend that our framework represents a first step in an attempt to help reviewers collect information that facilitate an optimally comprehensive and rigorous literature review, or what is more aptly called a research synthesis.

FRAMEWORK FOR QUALITATIVE DATA COLLECTION TECHNIQUES IN THE LITERATURE REVIEW/RESEARCH SYNTHESIS PROCESS

The literature review/research synthesis process as a methodology

A methodology can be defined as a broad approach to scientific inquiry, with general preferences for certain types of designs, sampling logic, analytical strategies, and the like. In other words, a methodology identifies appropriate research objectives, research purposes, and research questions; broad research designs and procedures; appropriate sampling designs and logic; criteria of quality (e.g. validity/legitimation) for methodology and inferences; and standards for reporting (Greene, 2006). According to Greene (2006), methodology represents how the researcher is situated in the inquiry. Methodology also involves identifying logics of justification for each research strategy, with a strong methodology supported by all the individual elements being connected in a coherent manner. Each individual component must fit and work in unison with the other components in order to facilitate justifiable data collection, data analysis, and data interpretation for a given study. Thus, as noted by Greene (2006), methodology guides the researcher's lens such that

> what is important to see . . . is observed, recorded, and understood or explained in defensible ways . . . [and] . . . offers a kind of geographic information system (GIS) positioning of the inquirer in the inquiry context and also offers navigational tools that substantially direct the inquirer's journey in that context. (p. 93)

The literature review/research synthesis represents a methodology because it represents a broad approach to scientific research that encompasses a set of research objectives, research purposes, and research questions, as well as methods and procedures, criteria of quality, and standards for reporting. Each individual component of the literature review (e.g. selecting a topic, searching the literature, developing the argument, surveying the literature, critiquing the literature, and writing the review; see, e.g. Machi and McEvoy, 2009) must be compatible for the process to be optimal. Further, the literature review/research synthesis methodology is affected by the reviewers' philosophical assumptions and stances. For example, a certain philosophical belief system (e.g. post-positivism) might lead a reviewer to value the use of quantitative research synthesis (i.e. meta-analysis; Glass, 1976), whereas another philosophical belief system (e.g. constructivism) might lead a reviewer to value the use of qualitative research synthesis (e.g. meta-synthesis, meta-summary; cf. Sandelowski and Barroso, 2003).

The literature review/research synthesis process as a method

In the context of research, the term *method* represents the researcher's selection of the specific strategies and procedures implemented for research design, sampling design, data collection, data analysis, and the like. The literature review/research synthesis represents a method. Indeed, conducting a literature review/research synthesis is tantamount to conducting a study. Thus, all studies that contain a review of the literature actually represent two studies – a study of the previous knowledge (i.e. review of the literature/research synthesis) and the actual study conducted by the researcher(s). Thus, rather than seeing the literature review/research synthesis as a step that must be undertaken as quickly as possible so that the researcher can 'get on with the research of interest', the researcher should view the literature review/research synthesis as representing a *study within a study*. In the following section, we illustrate that the steps conducive toward conducting a rigorous and comprehensive literature review/research synthesis are analogous to the steps aligned to conducting a rigorous qualitative research study.

The literature review/research synthesis process as a qualitative research method

The literature review/research synthesis process resembles the qualitative research process in many ways. In particular, the collection of knowledge that informs a literature review/research synthesis very much resembles the data collection process in qualitative research. For example, a reviewer can utilize a grounded theory approach to the collection of knowledge, in which (a) information gathering and analysis of the information are interactive; (b) from the time the information collection begins, the analysis of the information takes place, from which further information collection ensues and so forth; (c) theoretical sampling occurs, wherein decisions about which information to collect, code, analyze, and interpret are directed by the emerging grounded theory; and (d) data saturation, informational redundancy, and/or theoretical saturation (Flick, 1998; Lincoln and Guba, 1985; Morse, 1995; Strauss and Corbin, 1990) occurs when no new or relevant information seems to emerge pertaining to a category, and additional collection and analysis of information no longer contributes to the understanding of the phenomenon that necessitated the literature review/research synthesis. Further, in the tradition of Glaserian grounded theory (i.e. Glaser and Strauss, 1967), the literature review/research synthesis process can undergo the following three stages: open coding, axial coding, and selective coding. Open coding, which is 'like working on a puzzle' (Strauss and Corbin, 1990: 223), involves the reviewer coding the information by chunking the information into smaller segments and attaching a descriptor, or a code, for each segment. The goal of the open coding phase is to develop theoretical sensitivity to new interpretations of the information in order to avoid the reviewer forcing information into existing categories. Axial coding, the next stage, is when the reviewer clusters the codes into similar categories and makes connections among the numerous categories. Selective coding, the final stage, involves seeking to identify those categories that relate closely to the central category. That is, selective coding is the 'process of integrating and refining the theory' (Strauss and Corbin, 1998: 143) such that the reviewer can 'create theory out of data' (Strauss and Corbin, 1998: 56). In the context of the literature review/research synthesis process, a theory represents a proposed explanation of the underlying phenomenon that emerges after all the relevant information has been collected, analyzed, evaluated, interpreted, and synthesized.

Alternatively, a reviewer can utilize constructivist grounded theory techniques for conducting a literature review/research synthesis. With this approach, the assumption is that both the literature review/research synthesis process and the information are socially constructed through actions; however, these actions are constrained by social and historical conditions (Bryant, 2002, 2003, this volume; Bryant and Charmaz, 2007, this volume; Charmaz, 2000, 2005, 2006). Further, although the reviewer uses many of the key elements of Glaserian grounded theory as presented previously, he/she believes that the reviewer plays an active and crucial role in the review process, especially in the ensuing interaction between the reviewer and the information 'from which codes and categories, and eventually a grounded theory should result' (Charmaz and Bryant, 2008: 376). The constructivist grounded theory reviewer 'favors theoretical understanding over explanatory generalizations' and 'seek[s] abstract understanding of empirical phenomena as situated knowledge' (Charmaz and Bryant, 2008: 376).

According to Onwuegbuzie et al. (2010c), there are three major goals of literature reviews: (a) the synthesis as an end in itself (i.e. independent work), (b) the synthesis for planning primary research, and (c) the synthesis for improving a study or understanding results from a current study. When the synthesis serves as an end in itself, it can be conducted to inform practice or to provide comprehensive understanding about a topic. The synthesis process tends to be much longer for the latter than the former (i.e. to inform practice), which tends to be solution-based. Syntheses falling under the first goal can be represented by an integrative review (i.e. synthesizing existing literature on a topic with the goal of understanding trends in that body of knowledge), theoretical review (i.e. exploring how theory frames and drives research), historical review (i.e. synthesis that situate literature in historical contexts), or methodological review (i.e. synthesis of research designs, methods, and procedures used to study a particular topic or phenomenon; or a synthesis of the efficacy of a specific research design, method, and/or procedure). When the goal of the synthesis is to plan and to design primary research, the synthesis typically is more refined, focusing on literature that helps to provide a theoretical framework and/or conceptual framework – depending on whether the primary study represents quantitative, qualitative, or mixed research – or guide the research questions and/or other research design. When the goal is to synthesize the extant literature in order to improve a study or to understand results better, the synthesis process tends to be similar to the first goal (i.e. an integrative review, a theoretical review, or a methodological review). The difference is that the reviews of the literature as a process occurs throughout the study or after the results have been identified. Thus, the goal of the synthesis determines its scope and, as such, can represent an initial and/or an on-going decision that the reviewer should make (Onwuegbuzie et al., 2010c, 178–80).

Because multiple goals prevail for conducting a literature review/research synthesis, a reviewer can utilize case study techniques. Moreover, if each source of information is viewed as a case, then, using Stake's (2005) typology, the literature review/research synthesis can represent an intrinsic case study (i.e. review designed to understand each particular case), an instrumental case study (i.e. review designed to examine a particular case primarily to provide insight into an issue or phenomenon, or to redraw a generalization), and a multiple case study (i.e. an instrumental case study extended to several cases). In a literature review/research synthesis that took the form of an intrinsic case study, the aim of reviewers is not to conduct a comprehensive literature review but to select sources of information to highlight (e.g. illustrative case, deviant case). The review is not undertaken primarily because the selected cases represent other cases but because in all its particularity, each case itself is of interest. In contrast, in a literature review/research synthesis that took the form of an instrumental case study, the aim of reviewers is to provide insight into a phenomenon or to obtain a generalization. Each selected source is of secondary interest. Finally, in a literature review/research synthesis that took the form of a collective case study (i.e. multiple case study), the aim of reviewers is to examine multiple cases in an attempt to examine a phenomenon. Simply put, it is an instrumental case study extended to several cases. Cases in the collection of sources may be similar or different – with both redundancy and variety being essential for representation. Cases are selected because the reviewer believes that understanding them would 'lead to better understanding, and perhaps better theorizing, about a still larger collection of cases' (Stake, 2005: 446).

Grounded theory and case study research represent just two sets of qualitative research methods that can be mapped onto the literature review/research synthesis process. And, the fact that qualitative research methods lend themselves to the literature review/research synthesis process means that a variety of innovative qualitative research strategies associated with qualitative data collection and data analysis can be used – many of which have not been utilized previously – to enhance literature reviews/research syntheses. It is to these data collection strategies that we now turn.

Data collection strategies in the literature review/research synthesis process

Leech and Onwuegbuzie (2008) present a typology wherein qualitative data can be represented by one of four major sources, namely, talk, observations, drawings/photographs/videos, and documents. We illustrate in the sections below that these four source types serve as relevant literature review sources. As noted previously, we believe that literature review sources should be expanded beyond pre-existing print and digital information, thereby expanding opportunities for literature reviewers to analyze literature review sources in multiple ways.

Talk

One of the biggest problems with relying solely on print and digital information as sources of literature reviews/research syntheses pertains to the time lag occurring between the emergence of information (e.g. study findings are explicated in a manuscript) and when the study findings are available to the public (e.g. when the manuscript is published). Special issues published in journals and book chapters are particularly susceptible to lengthy time lags inasmuch as the time between when the first set of authors and the last set of authors submit their works to journal/book editors could be longer than 2 years, potentially outdating some of the information provided in some of the works in the set. Similarly, backlogs in journals could delay publication of in press manuscripts by more than 3 years, as we have experienced on a few occasions (e.g. Onwuegbuzie and Leech, in press). Thus, even if the reviewer has access to the work as soon as it is published, at least some of the information might be dated. Further, even for works that are published in a timely manner, it is possible that some of the researcher's interpretations and/or conclusions explicated within the article might change over the passage of time. Unfortunately, the researcher's change of perspective does not appear anywhere in the work that is examined by the literature reviewer. As such, passage of time is the (literature) reviewer's nemesis!

An effective way of overcoming the issue of time lag – but one that is rarely used – is by the reviewer interviewing or talking directly with authors who have or are conducting research in the reviewer's area of interest. In particular, although reviewers could contact anyone of interest, they likely would find most fruitful to contact the prolific authors/researchers in the area of interest. These authors/researchers would be identified once the reviewer has reached saturation, as evaluated by his/her review of the literature up to that point. Reviewers have several means for validating whether they have identified the most prolific authors/researchers. Perhaps the most informal approach would be to examine the reference list of selected articles to determine how often these targeted authors/researchers have been cited. A more rigorous approach would be to use scholarly databases, such as Google Scholar (i.e. http://scholar.google.com/), and conduct a citation analysis of articles published in the topic area by the targeted authors/researchers. These search engines not only specify the number of times each article has been cited but provide the full citation information of each source that cites the author. An extremely innovative way of identifying the most prolific authors/researchers in an area is to use computer-assisted qualitative data analysis software such as NVivo 8 (QSR International Pty Ltd., 2008) and QDA Miner 3.2 (Provalis Research, 2009). For example, Frels et al. (in press) used the qualitative software QDA Miner (Provalis Research, 2009) and WordStat (Provalis Research, 2009) to conduct a content analysis and word count analysis to determine the number of publications associated with every author (primary and secondary) publishing in the *Research in the Schools* journal over the last 15 years.

Individual interviews

Once (prolific) authors/researchers have been identified, then they can be contacted for interview (i.e. 'talk'). If the reviewer works/resides in close proximity to the author, then the reviewer might attempt to conduct a face-to-face interview with the author. The advantage of conducting a face-to-face interview is that the reviewer can obtain non-verbal data that include proxemic (i.e. use of interpersonal space to communicate attitudes), chronemic (i.e. use of pacing of speech and length of silence in conversation), kinesic (i.e. body movements or postures), and paralinguistic (i.e. all variations in volume, pitch, and quality of voice) orientations (cf. Gorden, 1980). Reviewers then can incorporate these non-verbal data into their analyses of the interviews, thereby providing a context that can play into the reviewer's interpretations of the authors' words and insights (Fontana and Frey, 2005).

Most of the time, it would not be feasible for the reviewer to conduct a face-to-face interview of the author because they live in different regions of the country or even in different countries. Thus, reviewers would have to use other means of interaction. Fortunately, reviewers have many tools at their disposal. Indeed, the tremendous developments in computer-mediated communication (CMC) and Web 2.0 have greatly facilitated what some researchers refer to as *virtual interviewing*, which involves the use of some form of Internet connection, either synchronously or asynchronously, to interview one or more persons at a time. The advantages of virtual interviewing of prolific researchers compared to face-to-face interviewing include the following: a reduction in the challenges associated with time, location, and space; reduced cost of interviewing (e.g. travel); increased ability to contact authors/researchers who are difficult to reach (e.g. authors/researchers with limited mobility; authors/researchers who are extremely busy); increased participation of authors/researchers who routinely conduct research using CMC and Web 2.0 tools; and increased participation of authors/researchers who are very comfortable in virtual environments (Biddix, 2008; Onwuegbuzie et al., 2010d).

Depending on the author's preference, the reviewer could interview the author either asynchronously (e.g. email, websites) or synchronously (e.g. chatrooms, instant messaging, Second Life, and Short Message Service (SMS) via mobile telephones). Regardless of the form of interviewing used, reviewers should attempt to utilize the best practices associated with the genre of interviewing (see, e.g. Ellis and Berger, 2002; Fontana and Frey, 2005; Gubrium and Holstein, 2002; Holstein and Gubrium, 1995, 2004; James and Busher, 2009; Lobe, 2008; Salmons, 2009). In particular, we suggest that the reviewer uses member checking techniques (Lincoln and Guba, 1985) – conducted either asynchronously or synchronously, and either face-to-face or online – in order to maximize descriptive validity, interpretive validity, and theoretical validity (cf. Maxwell, 2005) of any interpretations that stem from the interview data.

Debriefing the reviewer

We recommend that reviewers who interview authors/researchers should be subjected to a debriefing interview, as conceptualized by Onwuegbuzie et al. (2008d). According to Onwuegbuzie et al. (2008), the process of debriefing involves the researcher – in this case the reviewer – being interviewed by another person who understands the underlying research topic. This interviewer would ask the reviewer questions that help him/her identify any latent biases, assess his/her hunches or intuitive feelings that emerge during or after the reviewer's interview of a prolific author, and increase the reviewer's understanding of the information extracted from the prolific authors/researchers. Providing responses to the debriefing interview questions also helps the reviewer leave an audit trail.

Onwuegbuzie et al. (2008) provide a typology of interviewing questions that the debriefer could ask the reviewers regarding his/her bias. These questions are based on the following eight concepts: (a) the researcher's experience with interviewing, (b) the researcher's understanding of the participant(s), (c) the researcher's depth of knowledge of non-verbal communication, (d) how the researcher interprets the findings from the interviews, (e) thoughts regarding how the study affected the researcher, (f) concerns regarding the impact of the study on the participants, (g) ethical or political issues that might have come up at any stage of the research, and (h) the researcher's identification of problems that stemmed from the interviews (Onwuegbuzie et al., 2008).

These authors also conceptualize questions that reviewers can be asked, which are based on Guba and Lincoln's (1989) five constructivist-based principles of *authenticity criteria*: fairness (i.e. 'the extent to which different constructions and their underlying value structures are solicited and honored within the evaluation process'; Guba and Lincoln, 1989: 246–7), ontological authenticity (i.e. the degree that the interviewees' levels of awareness have been impacted by participating in the interviews), educative authenticity (i.e. the degree that the interviewees are aware of but not necessarily in agreement with the constructions and values of other stakeholders (e.g. other prolific authors/researchers, consumers of their work), catalytic authenticity (i.e. the degree that the interviewees' awareness of their new constructions or thoughts regarding other stakeholders' positions that emerge from the interviews evolves into decisions and actions (e.g. revising their own positions; producing follow-up work in the area), and tactical authenticity (i.e. the degree that, as a result of their participation in the interviews, the interviewees are empowered to act).

Interviewing multiple authors

Alternatively, reviewers might be interested in interviewing one or more authors/researchers at the same time. For example, two or more co-authors/co-researchers might be interviewed simultaneously. Or multiple authors/researchers who do not represent co-authors/co-researchers but who have a mutual respect for each other might be interviewed simultaneously. In such cases, reviewers can conduct focus group interviews, either face-to-face or virtually, using some of the most recent innovations (cf. Morgan, 2008; Nicholas et al., 2010; Onwuegbuzie et al., 2009, 2010b; Palmer et al., 2010; Stancanelli, 2010; Vicsek, 2010).

Delphi-based interview procedures

Another way that the reviewer can collect data from multiple authors/researchers is by using a variation of the Delphi method, which is a technique for collecting data from a diverse group of people (usually experts) for the purpose of reaching a consensus about a given topic (Brewer, 2007). For example, in an attempt to obtain an inclusive definition of the concept of mixed methods research, and as part of their literature review, Johnson et al. (2007) asked 31 leading mixed methods research methodologists to share their *current* definitions of mixed methods research. As reviewers, Johnson et al. (2007) could have used the definitions provided by many of these methodologists in their published works. However, because the mixed methods research field is evolving, even many of the published definitions that were less than one-year old were considered to be in dire need of updating by their authors, indicating the time-lag limitations that we discussed previously. Using constant comparison analysis (Glaser and Strauss, 1967) to analyze the 19 definitions received from the selected mixed methodologists, Johnson et al. (2007) extract themes, which they then used to conceptualize an inclusive definition (i.e. consensus) of mixed methods research that has become popularized. Thus, collecting data beyond the published literature ended up being very fruitful for these reviewers.

Example of talk data that inform literature reviews/research syntheses

Frels' (2010) dissertation provides another example of the efficacy of the reviewer going beyond the extant print and digital literature by collecting information from *talk*. Frels (2010) conducted a qualitative inquiry wherein she (a) explored selected mentors' perceptions of experiences of the dyadic mentoring relationship in school-based mentors; (b) examined the perceptions of selected school-based mentors regarding roles, expectations, purposes, and approaches of mentoring; and (c) studied the actual experiences of selected school-based mentors with the dyadic relationship. As part of her literature review/research synthesis, she contacted via email correspondence three prolific authors/researchers with expertise in the area of mentoring. Each of these authors/researchers shared insights and disclosed valuable information related to her research topic. In addition, Frels (2010) consulted via Skype one prolific author/researcher/methodologist for insights with respect to evaluating the literature that she had selected. Subsequently, she integrated each researcher's expertise with her personal knowledge base and her understanding of the collected literature.

As can be seen, going beyond the traditional literature review by collecting *talk* information (i.e. information obtained via direct communication with authors/researchers in the area of interest) has several advantages. In particular, by interviewing authors/researchers – whether face-to-face or online, asynchronously or synchronously, individually or in groups, or verbally or in writing – reviewers give authors/researchers the opportunity to provide information that verifies, modifies, refutes, or updates, their findings, interpretations, and/or concepts/ideas located in their extant work. They can also inform the reviewers of their latest unpublished works, ongoing works, and/or future works, as well as those of other co-authors/co-researchers or authors/researchers with whose work they are familiar. Further, they can provide an up-to-date critique of the extant literature. Finally, authors/researchers can assist reviewers in selecting the most valid methods (e.g. most appropriate instruments) to use for their ensuing studies by providing an informed critique of the methodology and methods used in previous works. This last point is very important because not using the extant literature to make methodological decisions can have dire consequences. For example, Gibson and Dembo (1984) contended that their Teacher Efficacy Scale (TES) was based on Bandura's (1977) theory of self-efficacy. However, Dellinger (2005) documented that that this contention had been refuted repeatedly in the literature. Dellinger (2005) described how Gibson and Dembo (1984) developed their scale based on only two RAND items that lacked content-related validity (i.e. poor sampling validity and item validity), with numerous researchers demonstrating that the TES has poor psychometric properties (e.g. Coladarci and Fink, 1995; Guskey and Passaro, 1994; Henson, 2003; Tschannen-Moran et al., 1998; Witcher et al., 2006). In particular, several researchers have questioned the dimensionality of the TES (cf. Coladarci and Fink, 1995; Guskey and Passaro, 1994; Tschannen-Moran et al., 1998).

Despite the poor measurement validity associated with the TES, as well as its inadequate foundational validity (i.e. reflecting 'researchers' prior understanding of a construct and/or phenomenon under study'; Dellinger and Leech, 2007: 323) and historical validity (i.e. reflecting the 'type of validity evidence that accrues through utilization and cited relevance in the extant literature'; Dellinger, 2005: 44), many researchers still use the TES. Dellinger (2005) reported that of the 79 dissertation studies that were published between 2001 and 2003 in the area of teacher efficacy or teacher self-efficacy, approximately one half of them involved the use of the TES or a modified version of the TES. In fact, as of the time of writing, Google Scholar revealed 893 articles in which this scale was used either to collect efficacy data (the overwhelming majority of articles) or to assess/discuss the psychometric properties of the TES, still validating Henson et al.'s (2001) conclusion that it is 'the most frequently used instrument in the area' (p. 404) – despite its questionable score validity. And, if an instrument lacks score validity, then findings stemming from use of this instrument are not trustworthy. As surmised by Henson (2002):

> In sum, the TES suffered from numerous psychometric infirmities, but it found its way into, and became entrenched in, the research literature nonetheless. Because of the exciting possibilities and compelling early results of teacher efficacy research, the TES was quickly adopted. It was, after all, published in a leading journal and was developed through recognized and respected methodologies. Unfortunately, the theoretical and psychometric weaknesses were overlooked, and researchers of teacher efficacy prematurely foreclosed on the instrument's developmental identity. (p. 144)

The issues with the TES instrument provide just one example of how not undertaking a comprehensive and rigorous review of the literature can lead to poor methodological decisions on the part of the reviewer/researcher. Indeed, it is likely that if a reviewer had interviewed a prolific author in the area of teacher self-efficacy, he/she would have been made aware of the psychometric problems associated with the TES. Thus, collecting *talk* data as part of a literature review can help to transform a study.

Observations

A reviewer also can go beyond the traditional literature review by collecting *observations*. For example, a reviewer who is conducting a review of violence in the US public schools could obtain more contextual information by actually going to the site where extreme violence has taken place, such as in Columbine, Colorado. Once there, they could observe aspects of the school (e.g. size, location, security measures) that can be integrated with the extant literature. Also, the reviewer can collect some *talk* data, for instance, by interviewing witnesses to the tragic event.

An alternative technique for collecting and integrating observation information into the literature review/research synthesis is by mapping information from selected works to examine trends. Once the region is identified (either from information contained in the work or directly from the author(s) via *talk* (e.g. email, text, twitter, interview, focus group), the author can collect information about each region (i.e. observations) and then integrate this information into the literature review. For instance, a reviewer could map regions of the country or the world from where participants have been selected in an attempt to avoid overgeneralizing findings during a synthesis. For instance, Combs et al. (2009) conducted a review of the related literature on the effect of school configurations on student achievement. When these authors mapped from where the participants in the selected studies were located, they observed that a disproportionate number of studies had been conducted in northeastern United States and relatively few studies had been conducted in the southwest, which provided an additional rationale for conducting their study in the southwest United States.

Geographic information system

An even more innovative way of collecting and integrating observation data into the literature review/research synthesis is via the use of a geographic information system (GIS). A GIS allows users to collect and analyze a structured database comprising geographical elements that are spatially oriented to Earth (Goodchild et al., 2007; Institute, 2009). These data can be represented via maps, charts, models, and other visual forms. Thus, information from the extant literature can be integrated with GIS to enhance the reviewers' understanding of the underlying phenomenon by providing spatial and geographical contexts that facilitate the identification of patterns, trends, and relationships. Consequently, reviewers could use GIS, or other graphing applications, to map specific information (e.g. location of participants) across a region, country, continent, or world, and then link these data to qualitative-based sociological data (e.g. poverty, education, health, religion). For instance, after mapping the location of participants, Combs et al. (2009) could have linked the outcome data documented in the selected studies to qualitative-based sociological data. As an extension of this technique, interpretations from meta-analyses, meta-syntheses, and meta-summaries could be enhanced by mapping the meta-information. In any case, our recommendation is that, where appropriate and where possible, reviewers 'review and synthesize' spatially.

Photographs, videos, and drawings/paintings

Photographs, videos, and drawings/paintings provide another fruitful avenue for enhancing literature reviews/research syntheses. Traditionally, literature reviews/research syntheses involve a collection of text from the extant literature. At best, tables and figures contained in some sources are included. However, photographs are underutilized, despite the adage, 'a picture is worth a thousand words'. Similarly, literature reviews/research syntheses typically are devoid of drawings and paintings. Thus, we encourage reviewers to include photographs, drawings, and/or paintings as part of their literature reviews/research syntheses. As part of their interviews with prolific authors/researchers, reviewers could ask them to provide any available visual materials that are not contained in the extant literature.

Conveniently, CMC and Web 2.0 applications can be used to provide visual presentations that can be incorporated into literature reviews/research syntheses. For example, Youtube (*c.* 2005; a videosharing tool that allows anyone to upload, view, and share video clips), Panoramio (*c.* 2005; a photosharing tool), Flickr (*c.* 2004; a tool to access both videos and photographs), iMovie (*c.* 1999; a video editing software application), and iTunes (*c.* 2001; used for playing and organizing digital music and video files) can be used to capture visual information that can inform literature reviews by taking a snapshot of frames of interest and including them in the literature review/research synthesis write-up (i.e. obtaining the relevant permission to do so when needed). We hope that, in the future, editors of online journals will encourage authors of literature reviews/ research syntheses to include relevant links to video (and audio).

Documents

The use of documents, representing the fourth and final source for informing published literature reviews/research syntheses, has by far the longest history – at last 345 years – when, in 1665, Henry Oldenburg, Corresponding Secretary of the Royal Society, launched, at his own expense, the first academic journal in the English language, called the *Philosophical Transactions of the Royal Society.* Unfortunately, despite its long history, for the most part, reviewers have not taken full advantage of the advances in CMC and Web 2.0, especially those that have been launched within the last six years, such as the following: Facebook, MySpace, Bebo, Friendster, Orkut, and Second Life. For instance, Facebook (*c.* 2004), a social networking tool with more than 80 million users worldwide that allows people to socialize and to exchange information in numerous forms, can contain information that can be incorporated into literature reviews/research syntheses. In any case, we hope that, in the near future, reviewers utilize CMC and Web 2.0 to their greatest extent.

SUMMARY AND CONCLUSION

There is little doubt that we live in times of abundant information, or *information explosion*. Yet, when conducting literature reviews, much of this information is underutilized. Thus, the purpose of this chapter was to provide a framework for extracting more information relevant to any research topic. In particular, we identified innovative qualitative data collection techniques for maximizing the obtaining of pertinent knowledge. We contend that our framework represents a first step in an attempt to help reviewers collect information that facilitates an optimally comprehensive and rigorous literature review, or what is more aptly called a research synthesis. Specifically, we used Onwuegbuzie et al.'s (2010c) conceptualization of four major sources for research syntheses (i.e. talk, observations, drawings/photographs/videos, and documents) to present various data collection strategies that go far beyond the sources that are overwhelmingly used in traditional literature reviews – namely, materials that already exist either in printed or digital forms. Thus, whereas traditional literature are one-dimensional, our framework transforms the research synthesis process as being one that is multi-dimensional, interactive, emergent, iterative, and dynamic.

We contend that our framework enhances both representation and legitimation in the research synthesis process. Representation refers to the ability to extract relevant and up-to-date knowledge that informs the research synthesis process. By expanding the sources of information, reviewers would obtain richer interpretations and increased *verstehen* (i.e. understanding). In contrast, legitimation refers to the validity of interpretations stemming from the research synthesis. Taking a multi-dimensional approach to research syntheses puts the reviewer in a better position to assess knowledge saturation and theoretical saturation. Also, information in the extant literature can be verified directly, for example, by conducting interviews, focus groups, or observations.

We believe that our four-dimensional data collection framework could assist experienced and novice researchers alike in recognizing that the literature review/research synthesis process represents a study in its own right. Indeed, because the hallmark of our four-dimensional framework is the collection of *new* information, utilizing this framework in the conduct of a literature review/research synthesis likely has ethical implications. Therefore, we suggest that when reviewers seek to collect additional information from talk and observations in particular, they apply for approval to do so via their institution's institutional review board (IRB). This request for approval to collect literature review/research synthesis information involving human participants (e.g. interviewing prolific authors) could be combined with the request for approval for the actual study within the same IRB application. Although this addition to the IRB application would require additional work on the part of the reviewer, we believe it is well worth the effort – as illustrated by the works of Frels (2010) and Johnson et al. (2007).

As documented earlier, it is disturbing how few graduate students are exposed to literature review courses. Further, bearing in mind that qualitative research methods lend themselves to the literature review/research synthesis process – as was demonstrated earlier – it is disturbing that for some programs, courses in qualitative research methods typically are not required. For example, of the 175 approved graduate-level school psychology programs for which a full list of courses was accessible, only 15 programs (8.6%) require that students complete a qualitative course before they can graduate. It is also disturbing that, to date, no qualitative research textbook contains discussion of the important role that qualitative research can play in the literature review/research synthesis process. For example, in the latest edition of the *Handbook of Qualitative Research* (Denzin and Lincoln, 2005b) – one of the leading textbooks used in qualitative research courses in the United States – of the 44 chapters contained, no chapter contains a discussion of the literature review/research synthesis process. Indeed, the term 'literature' does not even appear in the subject index, neither do the terms 'review' or 'synthesis'. Thus, the time is rife for reversing this trend. As documented in the *Handbook of Qualitative Research* and in numerous other qualitative works, qualitative researchers have an array of innovative data collection strategies at their disposal. Thus, it has intuitive appeal to transfer some, if not many, of these strategies to the research synthesis process.

In order to ensure that good research synthesis practices are instilled in beginning reviewers, we recommend that they receive some form of mentorship. Unfortunately, this does not currently seem to be the case. Indeed, too many doctoral students are expected to conduct and write their literature reviews with very little guidance. Thus, we recommend that dissertation/thesis advisors/supervisors, instructors, and mentors consider using the meta-framework developed by Combs et al. (2010), which they called the *interactive literature review process* (ILRP). Utilizing the principles of Vygotsky's (1978) theory of social development, Kuhlthau's (2004) Information Search Process model, and Onwuegbuzie et al.'s (2008) framework for debriefing the researcher, the ILRP contains nine stages through which student researchers progress during the literature review/research synthesis process: (a) Stage 1: Exploring belief systems; (b) Stage 2: Initiating a review of salient literature (particularly regarding qualitative research designs); (c) Stage 3: Selecting a topic; (d) Stage 4: Exploring literature for themes; (e) Stage 5: Formulating a focus and selecting themes; (f) Stage 6: Analyzing, interpreting, and integrating other steps of the model with literature (e.g. belief systems); (g) Stage 7: Closing the literature search at a point of saturation; (h) Stage 8: Writing a review of literature; and (i) Stage 9: Evaluating this process (Combs et al., 2010). A central component of the ILRP is the series of interactive consultations – both verbally and orally – that are facilitated by the advisor, and which occurs during each of the nine phases of the process.

In advancing our concept, we are providing an alternative epistemological model of the literature interview in an attempt to help reviewers conduct more comprehensive and rigorous research syntheses and, thus, in turn, address both the crisis of representation (i.e. 'uncertainty within the human sciences about adequate means of describing social reality'; Schwandt, 2007: 48; see also Denzin and Lincoln, 2005a) and the crisis of legitimation (i.e. 'set of issues that arise from questioning the *authority* (claim that a text is an accurate, valid, true, and complete account of the experience) of the interpretive *text* characteristics' (italics in original); Schwandt, 2007: 46; see also Denzin and Lincoln, 2005a) to a greater extent than has been the case heretofore. We realize that our four-dimensional framework of conducting research syntheses adds a layer of complication to the research syntheses process; however, we believe that this increase in complexity is offset by the fact that our framework encourages reviewers to go beyond the collection of information that represent only printed or digital forms. Furthermore, we believe that our framework helps to transform the research synthesis process by enabling the reviewer to become a more active and proactive agent in the search for knowledge. The research synthesis process is not seen as a static process that occurs at one point in time, namely, before the underlying study is conducted; rather, the research synthesis process is viewed as a meaning-making process that takes place before, during, and after the study. Thus, through our four-dimensional framework, a new form of deconstructionism occurs wherein the traditional way of conducting literature reviews is scrutinized, the reviewer's biases and assumptions are exposed, and innovative ways of collecting knowledge are utilized.

We recognize that our expanded view of literature reviews brings to the fore its own set of methodological and analytical guidelines, principles, and stances, as well as its own set of methodological challenges. Notwithstanding, we hope that this chapter motivates reviewers to start *thinking outside the box* when conducting their literature reviews/research syntheses. For, if we continue with our current research synthesis practice – as was the case for the TES that researchers continue to use despite strong evidence of it having serious psychometric issues – those who do not know research techniques that are problematic are destined to repeat their use of them.

REFERENCES

Alton-Lee, A. (1998) A troubleshooter's checklist for prospective authors derived from reviewers' critical feedback. *Teaching and Teacher Education,* 14: 887–90.

American Counseling Association. (2005) *ACA Code of Ethics.* Alexandria, VA: Author. Retrieved 4 June, 2010, from http://www.txca.org/Images/tca/Documents/ACA%20Code%20of%20Ethics.pdf

American Educational Research Association. (2000) *Ethical Standards of the American Educational Research Association.* Retrieved 4 June, 2010, from http://www.aera.net/uploadedFiles/About_AERA/Ethical_Standards/EthicalStandards.pdf

American Educational Research Association (2006) Standards for reporting on empirical social science research in AERA publications. *Educational Researcher,* 35(6): 33–40.

Bandura, A. (1977) Self-efficacy: Toward a unifying theory of behavioral change. *Psychological Review,* 84: 191–215.

Best, J.W. and Kahn, J.V. (2006) *Research in Education*, 10th edn., Boston, MA: Pearson Education.

Biddix, J.P. (2008) Multitasking CMC to study connected organizations. In S. Kelsey and K. St.-Amant (eds) *Handbook of Research on Computer Mediated Communication*, Vol. 1, pp. 309–24. Hershey, NY: Information Science Reference.

Boote, D.N. and Beile, P. (2005) Scholars before researchers: On the centrality of the dissertation literature review in research preparation. *Educational Researcher,* 34(6): 3–15.

Brewer, E.W. (2007) Delphi technique. In N. J. Salkind (ed.) *Encyclopedia of Measurement and Statistics,* pp. 240–6. Thousand Oaks, CA: Sage.

Bryant, A. (2002) Re-grounding grounded theory. *Journal of Informational Technology Theory and Applications,* 4(1): 25–42.

Bryant, A. (2003) A constructivist response to Glaser. *FQS: Forum for Qualitative Social Research,* 4(1). Retrieved 4 June, 2010, from http://www.qualitative-research.net/fqs-texte/1-03/1-03bryan-e.htm. *Theory and Applications,* 4(1): 25–42.

Bryant, A. and Charmaz, K. (2007) Grounded theory in historical perspective: An epistemological account. In A. Bryant and K. Charmaz (eds) *The Sage Handbook of Grounded Theory,* pp. 31–57. London: Sage.

Charmaz, K. (2000) Constructivist and objectivist grounded theory. In N.K. Denzin and Y.S. Lincoln (eds) *Handbook of Qualitative Research*, 2nd edn., pp. 509–35. Thousand Oaks, CA: Sage.

Charmaz, K. (2005) Grounded theory in the 21st century. A qualitative method for advancing social justice. In N.K. Denzin and Y.S. Lincoln (eds) *Handbook of Qualitative Research*, 3rd edn. pp. 507–35. Thousand Oaks, CA: Sage.

Charmaz, K. (2006) *Constructing Grounded Theory: A Practical Guide Through Qualitative Analysis.* London: Sage.

Charmaz, K. and Bryant, A. (2008) Grounded theory. In L.M. Given (ed.) *The Sage Encyclopedia of Qualitative Research Methods*, pp. 374–7. Thousand Oaks, CA: Sage

Coladarci, T., and Fink, D.R. (1995, April) *Correlations Among Measures of Teacher Efficacy: Are they Measuring the Same Thing?* Paper presented at the annual meeting of the American Educational Research Association, San Francisco, CA.

Combs, J.P., Clark, D., Moore, G., Edmonson, S.L., Onwuegbuzie, A.J., and Slate, J.R. (2009, March) *Elementary Schools' Grade Spans and Academic Achievement.* Paper presented at the annual meeting of the American Educational Research Association, San Diego, CA.

Combs, J.P., Bustamante, R.M., and Onwuegbuzie, A.J. (2010) An interactive model for facilitating development of literature reviews. *International Journal of Multiple Research Approaches*, 4.

Cooper, H.M. (1985, March–April) *A Taxonomy of Literature Reviews.* Paper presented at the annual meeting of the American Educational Research Association, Chicago, IL. (ERIC Document Reproduction Services No. ED254541)

Dellinger, A. (2005) Validity and the review of the literature. *Research in the Schools,* 12(2): 41–54.

Dellinger, A. and Leech, N.L. (2007) A validity framework: A unified approach to evaluating validity of empirical research. *Journal of Mixed Methods Research*, 1: 309–32.

Denzin, N.K. and Lincoln, Y.S. (2005a) Introduction: The discipline and practice of qualitative research. In N.K. Denzin and Y.S. Lincoln (eds) *Sage Handbook of Qualitative Research,* 3rd edn, pp. 1–32. Thousand Oaks, CA: Sage.

Denzin, N.K. and Lincoln, Y.S. (eds) (2005b) *The Sage Handbook of Qualitative Research,* 3rd edn. Thousand Oaks, CA: Sage.

Ellis, C. and Berger, L. (2002) Their story/my story/our story: Including the researcher's experience in interview research. In J. Gubrium and J. Holstein (eds) *Handbook of Interview Research: Context and Method*, pp. 849–76. Thousand Oaks, CA: Sage.

Fink, A. (2009) *Conducting Research Literature Reviews: From the Internet to Paper.* Thousand Oaks, CA: Sage.

Flick, U. (1998) *An Introduction to Qualitative Research: Theory, Method and Applications.* London: Sage.

Fontana, A. and Frey, J.H. (2005) The interview: From neutral stance to political involvement. In N.K. Denzin and Y.S. Lincoln (eds) *The Sage Handbook of Qualitative Research,* 2nd edn, pp. 695–727. Thousand Oaks, CA: Sage.

Frels, R.K. (2010) The experiences and perceptions of selected mentors: An exploratory study of the dyadic relationship in school-based mentoring. Unpublished doctoral dissertation, Sam Houston State University, Huntsville, TX.

Frels, R.K., Owuegbuzie, A.J., and Slate, J.R. (in press) *Research in the Schools: The Flagship Journal of the Mid-South Educational Research Association.* In the *Heritage Volume.* Nashville, TN: Midsouth Educational Research Association.

Garrard, J. (2009) *Health Sciences Literature Review Made Easy: The Matrix Method.* Sudbury, MA: Jones and Bartlett.

Gay, L.R., Mills, G.E., and Airasian, P. (2009) *Educational Research: Competencies for Analysis and Applications,* 10th edn. Upper Saddle River, NJ: Pearson Education.

Gibson, S. and Dembo, M. (1984) Teacher efficacy: Construct validation. *Journal of Educational Psychology*, 76: 569–82.

Glaser, B.G. and Strauss, A.L. (1967) *The Discovery of Grounded Theory: Strategies for Qualitative Research.* Chicago: Aldine.

Glass, G. (1976) Primary, secondary, and meta-analysis of research. *Educational Researcher,* 5(10): 3–8.

Goodchild, M.F., Fu, P., and Rich (2007, June) Sharing geographic information: An assessment of the geo-spatial one-step. *Annals of the Association of American Geographers,* 97: 250–66.

Gorden, R.L. (1980) *Interviewing: Strategy, Techniques, and Tactics.* Homewood, IL: Dorsey.

Gravetter, F.J., and Forzano, L.B. (2008) *Research Methods for the Behavioral Sciences.* Belmont, CA: Wadsworth.

Greene, J.C. (2006) Toward a methodology of mixed methods social inquiry. *Research in the Schools,* 13(1): 93–8.

Guba, E.G. and Lincoln, Y.S. (1989) *Fourth Generation Evaluation.* Newbury Park, CA: Sage.

Gubrium, J.F., and Holstein, J.A. (2002) *Handbook of Interview Research: Context and Method.* Thousand Oaks, CA: Sage.

Guskey, T.R. and Passaro, P.D. (1994) Teacher efficacy: A study of construct dimensions. *American Educational Research Journal,* 31: 627–43.

Hart, C. (2005) *Doing a Literature Review: Releasing the Social Science Research Imagination.* London: Sage.

Henson, R.K. (2002) From adolescent angst to adulthood: Substantive implications and measurement dilemmas in the development of teacher efficacy research. *Educational Psychologist,* 37: 137–50.

Henson, R.K. (2003) Relationships between preservice teachers' self-efficacy, task analysis, and classroom management beliefs. *Research in the Schools,* 10(1): 53–62.

Henson, R.K., Kogan, L.R., and Vache-Haase, T. (2001) A reliability generalization study of the Teacher Efficacy Scale and related instruments. *Educational and Psychological Measurement,* 61: 404–20.

Holstein, J.A. and Gubrium, J.F. (1995) *The Active Interview.* Thousand Oaks, CA: Sage.

Holstein, J.A. and Gubrium, J.F. (2004) *The Active Interview.* In D. Silverman (ed.) *Qualitative Research: Theory, Method, and Practice,* pp. 140–61. Thousand Oaks, CA: Sage.

Institute, E.S.R. (2009) *Environmental Systems Research Institute.* Retrieved 9 June, 2010, from http://www.gis.com/whatisgis/index.html

James, N. and Busher, H. (2009) *Online Interviewing.* Thousand Oaks, CA: Sage.

Johnson, R.B., Onwuegbuzie, A.J., and Turner, L.A. (2007) Toward a definition of mixed methods research. *Journal of Mixed Methods Research,* 1: 112–33.

Kuhlthau, C.C. (2004) *Seeking Meaning: A Process Approach to Library and Information Services,* 2nd edn. Westport, CT: Libraries Unlimited.

Leech, N.L., Dellinger, A., Brannagan, K.B., and Tanaka, H. (2010) Evaluating mixed research studies: A mixed methods approach. *Journal of Mixed Methods Research,* 4: 17–31.

Leech, N.L. and Goodwin, L.D. (2008) Building a methodological foundation: Doctoral-level methods courses in colleges of education. *Research in the Schools,* 15(1): 1–8.

Leech, N.L. and Onwuegbuzie, A.J. (2008) Qualitative data analysis: A compendium of techniques for school psychology research and beyond. *School Psychology Quarterly,* 23: 587–604.

Lincoln, Y.S. and Guba, E.G. (1985) *Naturalistic Inquiry.* Beverly Hills, CA: Sage.

Lobe, B. (2008) *Integration of Online Research Methods.* Ljubljana, Slovenia: Faculty of Social Sciences, University of Ljubljana.

Machi, L.A., and McEvoy, B.T. (2009) *The Literature Review: Six Steps to Success.* Thousand Oaks, CA: Corwin Press.

Maxwell, J.A. (2005) *Qualitative Research Design: An Interactive Approach,* 2nd edn. Newbury Park, CA: Sage.

McGhee, G., Marland, G.R., and Atkinson, J.M. (2007) Grounded theory research: Literature reviewing and reflexivity. *Journal of Advanced Nursing,* 60: 334–42.

Morgan, D.L. (2008) Focus groups. In L.M. Given (ed.) *The Sage Encyclopedia of Qualitative Methods,* Vol. 1, pp. 352–4. Thousand Oaks, CA: Sage.

Morse, J.M. (1995) The significance of saturation. *Qualitative Health Research,* 5: 147–9.

National Association of School Psychologists (2000) *Professional Conduct Manual: Principles for Professional Ethics, Guidelines for the Provision of School Psychological Services.* Bethesda, MD: Author. Retrieved 4 June, 2010, http://www.nasponline.org/standards/professionalcond.pdf

Nicholas, D.B., Lach, L., King, G., Scott, M., Boydell, K., Sawatzky, B.J., Reisman, J., Schippel, E., and Young, N.L. (2010) Contrasting Internet and face-to-face focus groups for children with chronic health conditions: Outcomes and participant experiences. *International Journal of Qualitative Methods,* 9: 105–21.

Onwuegbuzie, A.J., Collins, K.M.T., Leech, N.L., Dellinger, A.B., and Jiao, Q.G. (2010) A meta-framework for conducting mixed research syntheses for stress and coping researchers and beyond. In: G.S. Gates, W.H. Gmelch, and M. Wolverton (Series eds.) and K.M.T. Collins, A.J. Onwuegbuzie, and Q.G. Jiao (eds), *Toward a Broader Understanding of Stress and Coping: Mixed methods approaches,* pp. 169–211. The Research on Stress and Coping in Education Series (Vol. 5). Charlotte, NC: Information Age Publishing.

Onwuegbuzie, A.J., and Daniel, L.G. (2005) Editorial: Evidence-based guidelines for publishing articles in *Research in the Schools* and beyond. *Research in the Schools,* 12(2): 1–11.

Onwuegbuzie, A.J., Dickinson, W.B., Leech, N.L., and Zoran, A.G. (2009) Toward more rigor in focus group research: A new framework for collecting and analyzing focus group data. *International Journal of Qualitative Methods,* 8: 1–21.

Onwuegbuzie, A.J., Dickinson, W.B., Leech, N.L., and Zoran, A.G. (2010) Toward more rigor in focus group research in stress and coping and beyond: A new mixed research framework for collecting and analyzing focus group data. In: G.S. Gates, W.H. Gmelch, and M. Wolverton (Series eds.) and K.M.T. Collins, A.J. Onwuegbuzie, and Q. G. Jiao (eds), *Toward a Broader Understanding of Stress and Coping: Mixed methods approaches,* pp. 243–85. The Research on Stress and Coping in Education Series (Vol. 5). Charlotte, NC: Information Age Publishing.

Onwuegbuzie, A.J. and Leech, N.L. (2005) A typology of errors and myths perpetuated in educational research textbooks. *Current Issues in Education* [On-line], 8(7). Retrieved June 3, 2010, from http://cie.asu.edu/volume8/number7/index.html

Onwuegbuzie, A.J. and Leech, N.L. (in press) Generalization practices in qualitative research: A mixed methods case study. *Quality & Quantity: International Journal of Methodology.*

Onwuegbuzie, A.J., Leech, N.L., Bustamante, R.M., Collins, K.M.T., and Combs, J.P. (2010c, February) *Qualitative analysis techniques for the review of the literature.* Paper presented at the annual meeting of the Southwest Educational Research Association, New Orleans, LA.

Onwuegbuzie, A.J., Leech, N.L., and Collins, K.M.T. (2008) Interviewing the interpretive researcher: A method for addressing the crises of representation, legitimation, and praxis. *International Journal of Qualitative Methods,* 7: 1–17.

Onwuegbuzie, A.J., Leech, N.L., and Collins, K.M.T. (2010d) Innovative data collection strategies in qualitative research. *The Qualitative Report,* 15: 696–726. Retrieved 8 June, 2010, from http://www.nova.edu/ssss/QR/QR15-3/onwuegbuzie.pdf

Palmer, P., Larkin, M., de Visser, R., and Fadden, G. (2010) Developing an interpretative phenomenological approach to focus group data .*Qualitative Research in Psychology,* 7: 99–121.

Provalis Research (2009) QDA Miner 3.2 [Computer software]: *The Mixed Method Solution For Qualitative Analysis.* Montreal, Quebec, Canada: Author. Retrieved 14 January, 2010, from http://www.provalisresearch.com/QDAMiner/QDAMinerDesc.html

QSR International Pty Ltd. (2008) *NVIVO: Version 8. Reference Guide.* Doncaster Victoria, Australia: Author.

Ridley, D. (2008) *The Literature Review: A Step-by-Step Guide for Students.* Thousand Oaks, CA: Sage.

Salmons, J. (2009) *Online Interviews in Real Time.* Thousand Oaks, CA: Sage.

Sandelowski, M. and Barroso, J. (2003) Creating metasummaries of qualitative findings. *Nursing Research,* 52: 226–33.

Schwandt, T. A. (2007) *Sage Dictionary of Qualitative Inquiry,* 3rd edn. Thousand Oaks, CA: Sage.

Stake, R.E. (2005) Qualitative case studies. In N.K. Denzin and Y.S. Lincoln (eds) *The Sage Handbook of Qualitative Research,* 3rd edn. pp. 443–66. Thousand Oaks, CA: Sage.

Stancanelli, J. (2010) Conducting an online focus group. *The Qualitative Report,* 15: 761–5. Retrieved 8 June, 2010, from http://www.nova.edu/ssss/QR/QR15-3/ofg2.pdf

Strauss, A. and Corbin, J. (1990) *Basics of Qualitative Research: Grounded Theory Procedures and Techniques.* Newbury Park, CA: Sage.

Strauss, A. and Corbin, J. (1998) *Basics of Qualitative Research: Techniques and Procedures for Developing Grounded Theory.* Thousand Oaks, CA: Sage.

Tschannen-Moran, M., Woolfolk Hoy, A., and Hoy, W.K. (1998) Teacher efficacy: Its meaning and measure. *Review of Educational Research,* 68: 202–48.

Vicsek, L. (2010) Issues in the analysis of focus groups: Generalisability, quantifiability, treatment of context and quotations. *The Qualitative Report,* 15: 122–41. Retrieved 8 June, 2010, from http://www.nova.edu/ssss/QR/QR15-1/vicsek.pdf

Vygotsky, L.S. (1978) *Mind in Society.* Cambridge, MA: Harvard University Press.

Witcher, L.A., Onwuegbuzie, A.J., Collins, K.M.T., Witcher, A.E., James, T.L., and Minor, L.C. (2006) Preservice teachers' efficacy and their beliefs about education. *Academic Exchange Extra.* Retrieved 11 June, 2010, from http://www.unco.edu/AE-Extra/2006/10/index.html

11

Grounded Theory

Antony Bryant and Kathy Charmaz

A *method*, I think, is like a shark. You know, it has to constantly move forward or it dies.[1]

INTRODUCTION

The Grounded Theory Method (GTM) is far and away the most widely claimed qualitative method by those researching on projects centred on human subjects. Its founding statements date from the mid-1960s, although its sharp rise in popularity and visibility date from the 1980s which also saw a profound and somewhat acrimonious division between the two founding fathers – Barney Glaser and Anselm Strauss. The energies expended on this discord might have undermined the method as a whole, but at least since the late 1990s the method has progressed to a considerable extent – both in terms of the extent of its use and its methodological development and enhancement. Most significant has been the development of a *constructivist* form of the method – associated particularly with the work of Kathy Charmaz and Antony Bryant.

Constructivist grounded theory has led to a significantly firmer conceptual and philosophical basis, resulting in a flourishing of GTM-oriented writing linking the method to pragmatism, action research, critical theory and other methodological approaches; also to an improved understanding of the breadth of GTM writing encompassing significant groups working across Europe, Asia and Central and South America as well as in the English-speaking tradition in general. This chapter explains and evaluates these developments within the context of concerns regarding methodological innovation, seeking to resolve the paradox that a method has to retain some central features while simultaneously allowing and even encouraging innovation and change – that is, avoiding becoming a *dead shark*.

THE EMERGENCE OF THE GROUNDED THEORY METHOD

The Grounded Theory Method was first developed by Glaser and Strauss – together with Jeanne Quint – in the 1960s. At the time it was not only highly innovative, but a direct challenge to the prevailing orthodoxies, methodologies and research protocols of American social science research.

What made *The Discovery of Grounded Theory* (Glaser and Strauss, 1967) innovative in 1967? Glaser and Strauss argued that the researcher could and even should dispense with the formulation of a preliminary hypothesis.[2] Instead, the research exercise should begin with the researcher seeking to gain some familiarity with the research domain, which would then lead to the 'discovery' of key characteristics or features forming the basis upon which an explanatory framework could be built. This would then facilitate development of innovative theoretical insights, grounded theories, as opposed to the incremental theoretical tinkering that characterized post-graduate research in the social sciences of the time. These two facets remain key strengths and attractions of the method, although GTM itself has undergone significant clarification, innovation and re-invention in the four decades since its inception, as we demonstrate in this chapter.

Glaser and Strauss had themselves individually undergone the standard US postgraduate experience, but in distinctively different strands of US sociological orthodoxy. Glaser came from the Columbia school of sociology which was noted for its quantitative approach developed by Paul Lazarsfeld and colleagues (see, e.g. Lazarsfeld and Rosenberg, 1955), although Lazarsfeld is also associated with pioneering work in qualitative methods and collaboration with Kurt Lewin (1999), a key figure in the development of action research. Strauss adhered to the Chicago school, associated with 'symbolic interactionism', and the work of John Dewey, (1922/1950, 1925/1952), George Herbert Mead (1934), Robert E. Park (1952), Herbert Blumer (1969) and others working within an interpretive orientation.[3]

The collaboration between Glaser and Strauss originated in part from each having suffered a parental bereavement. The Appendix to *Awareness of Dying* (1965b) stresses their experiences as an important factor. Strauss had experienced the illness and death of his mother in the early 1960s; Glaser had similarly suffered the loss of his father at around the same period. They worked on a study of what happened to dying patients in a variety of hospital settings ranging from the emergency room to terminal cancer wards. Glaser and Strauss, together with Jeanne Quint, published a number of papers which first introduced the embryonic method, including 'Discovery of Substantive Theory: A Basic Strategy for Qualitative Analysis' (Glaser and Strauss, 1965a) and 'The Constant Comparative Method of Qualitative Analysis' (Glaser, 1965).

By the time *The Discovery of Grounded Theory* was published in 1967, the approach had been renamed *Grounded Theory*, with the category of *substantive theory* being contrasted with that of *formal theory*.[4] The process of *constant comparison*, however, was very much central to the method. Moreover there were two further notable characteristics of the method. First, the method originated from insights gained from researchers' personal experiences and biographies; a departure from the orthodoxy of the dispassionate researcher.[5] Second, the method was practice-oriented from the outset. Two of the three founding texts (*Awareness of Dying* and *Time for Dying* (Glaser and Strauss, 1968)) had clear practical ramifications that Quint (1967) specifically developed. As a professional nurse, Quint went on from this early work to make significant contributions to the development of nursing practice, particularly strategies for palliative and hospital care. Quint's work partly explains why GTM engaged and sustained the interests of people working in care and associated medical and support areas, often combining professional employment with their research activities.

GTM: AN UNEASY ORTHODOXY

The most readily apparent innovation in this early work was the way in which the grounded theorist gathered and analyzed data simultaneously. The researcher repeated the process in an iterative fashion, as opposed to the standard approach of completing the data collection prior to its analysis. Moreover, rather than developing hypotheses for testing or coding against a predetermined set of categories, Glaser and Strauss worked through interviews, observations and other forms of engagement with the research problem, using their findings as the basis from which they developed initial codes and categories[6] which they then used to guide ensuing stages of data gathering: Hence the phrase 'the constant comparative method'. Glaser and Strauss created a method by which researchers could attain new theoretical insights in a *grounded* manner. This contrasted with the orthodoxy of derivation of hypotheses from existing *grand theories*, with the hypotheses then being tested against gathered data as a form of *verification* of the theories themselves.

From the outset, many qualitative researchers in the US and their students read and praised *Discovery*. Actual use of the method, however, developed slowly, and not all those who responded to the book actually used the method that Glaser and Strauss aimed to set forth. The *Discovery* book received an enthusiastic welcome from sociologists whose motivation for qualitative studies involved more than research practice *per se*. First, by arguing that scholars must evaluate qualitative research by its own canons, the book provided a rationale that legitimized inductive qualitative inquiry. Second, it simultaneously answered earlier criticisms of qualitative research as unsystematic, impressionistic and anecdotal.

Qualitative researchers embraced the arguments advanced in *Discovery* but the methodological guidelines remained opaque. Initially a number of sociologists influenced by the Chicago school attended to the method itself, but the major source of grounded theory practice remained home-grown. University of California – San Francisco [UCSF] doctoral students in sociology and nursing emerged as the main practitioners of GTM. The nursing profession had moved to make the doctorate a prerequisite for teaching and conducting research, and thus created their own doctoral programs in the 1970s. Meanwhile the sociology program at UCSF narrowed its focus to concentrate on medical sociology. Not surprisingly grounded theory studies appeared in areas connected with health care, nursing and the like. By the late 1970s, however, interest in the method had grown sufficiently for Strauss, in particular, to be constantly in demand to lecture and teach on the topic, and for students and potential grounded theorists to clamour for a clear and straightforward guide to the method itself. Eventually, in 1987, Strauss produced a set of 'rules of thumb' for generating formal grounded theories, which as Kearney (2007) notes 'reflected the demands on Strauss in his later career to revisit the basics of grounded theory technique at every turn, as diverse and expanding audiences attempted to grasp and apply the principles of the method' (p. 112).

Strauss' 1987 book, *Qualitative Analysis for Social Scientists*, together with the 'user-friendly' *Basics of Qualitative Research* (1990) – co-authored with Juliet Corbin – may be seen, in part, as responses to the demand for an accessible GTM manual or prescription for developing grounded theories. Strauss and Corbin's book became the focus of Glaser's (1992) rancorous criticisms of Strauss, but as Timmermans and Tavory (2007) argue, Strauss and Corbin's book propelled GTM into its position as far and away the most widely claimed method in the social sciences. So whatever its shortcomings, and the nature of the dispute between Glaser and Strauss, *Basics* put GTM firmly on the methodological map across disciplines, and of the research outputs claiming use of GTM that appeared in its wake, most drew on *Basics* even while acknowledging *Discovery* as the founding text.

By the time of Strauss' death in 1996, two clear GTM positions had emerged – Glaser's and Strauss/Corbin's. Some of the research literature alluded to this, but many 1980s and 1990s research articles claimed use of the method as if an untroubled continuity linked *Discovery* and *Basics*. GTM appeared to be an example of the inventions of today becoming the conventions of tomorrow, but this status resided on a precarious foundation. Most researchers took little or no account of the rift between its two founders, and others viewed the method as such with suspicion for several reasons. Some saw GTM as a 'quick and dirty' method, and certain conventional methodologists disliked the method because of its inductive logic and lack of quantification. Still other quantitative researchers in the US accepted the method because they saw it as more rigorous and systematic than most qualitative methods.

The attractions of the method outweighed the detractions and sustained its development and growing use – or claims to use. The method became rooted in specific disciplines or domains, particularly the practice-led disciplines from which the method had emerged, nursing being the prime example. Furthermore widespread and growing use of the method developed in continental Europe – strongly influenced by Strauss – and also in parts of Asia and Africa.

Glaser published prolifically during the 1990s, partly in order to explain the key features of what he termed 'classic' GTM, contrasting it particularly with the view propounded in *Basics*. He also acted as the focus for a group of GTM practitioners, providing a growing body of work that exemplified his position. In contrast, a growing but disparate body of researchers in a wide range of disciplines used GTM, but predominantly drew their methodological operations first-and-foremost from *Basics*.

GTM had then become an uneasy orthodoxy by the 1990s. A growing band of adherents made it increasingly popular, but often misunderstood and misapplied the method. Given the differences between Glaser's position and those that derived from and built on *Basics*, a danger arose that the method might quickly disintegrate as the contending parties battled for the one true GTM, and as other perspectives, such as postmodernism and narrative analysis, had emerged that challenged the method.

PARADOX AS A SPUR TO INNOVATION[7]

GTM was certainly a radical and important innovation, and a sufficiently large number of researchers adopted the method for it to become an orthodoxy of sorts by the 1990s. Its initial development radiated out from UCSF, and owed a great deal to the subsequent activities and careers of the PhD students taught by Glaser and Strauss. Several of the very first groups became key figures in their respective areas of expertise, carrying the influence of the methodological grounding they received into their chosen disciplines (Charmaz, 1983; Stern, 1984/1994). Using GTM in their subsequent careers, both as teachers and researchers, caused several of them to refine and advance the method; providing core components for the basis from which it has flourished. This is not a particularly unusual way for novel ideas and approaches to find their way into the mainstream. What is notable, however, is that the early popularity of the method owed a great deal to the personal efforts of Glaser, Strauss and their first generation of students and colleagues, and far less to its actually being taught as part of the standard methods syllabus in universities and research centres. At that time, few doctoral programs in sociology in the US included qualitative research in their required methodology courses, much less covered a method that had several specific guidelines as well as general implications.[8]

For some time, Glaser collaborated with Strauss on major research projects but by the early 1980s he no longer worked at UCSF and never took up any fulltime academic position. Strauss had accepted his position at UCSF with the agreement that he could create a doctoral program in sociology. In the 1960s, UCSF had plans to start a new graduate school for social science and to expand its doctoral programs in this area. The small graduate program in sociology survived later budgetary cutbacks but plans for the school did not. Nonetheless, Strauss remained at UCSF and by the early 1980s, had replaced Glaser as the teacher of the grounded theory doctoral seminars. Unlike Glaser, Strauss maintained strong links with his discipline and research practice more generally through a network of fellow Chicago school sociologists, symbolic interactionists and researchers from diverse fields.

GTM did not implode or dissipate in the 1990s and beyond, instead it actually took on a new lease on life. Several reasons account for this revitalization, and they can best be considered as emanating from paradoxes within and around the method, the resolution or avoidance of which have led in many instances to innovations and enrichment of the method. In many respects some of these paradoxes were present from the start, but have only surfaced relatively recently; delayed in doing so, in part, by the divergence between Glaser and Strauss and the ensuing dispute about the nature and operation of the method itself.

Paradox 1 GTM evolved as a result of a mix of personal and professional experiences and backgrounds, but the initial statements of the method strip away these characteristics almost completely – undermining to an extent the innovations themselves, almost as if the authors wished to make GTM more palatable to the orthodox research community.

Strauss and Glaser developed their ideas in concert, building on their specific but common personal experiences of bereavement. Yet this impression of having had profound researcher engagement with death is almost entirely absent from their key GTM texts: Their research interests centered on the social organization of dying, rather than the dying process *per se*. Thus, they placed no explicit emphasis on the patient's experience that later came to be a hallmark of grounded theory studies in medical sociology. Strauss did some early data collection but a team of assistants conducted most of the field research for the projects.

Strauss' later writings, as well as some of those pre-dating GTM itself, indicate an awareness of the active role of the researcher and a readiness to incorporate this within the method itself and the research process in general. Soon after the appearance of *Discovery*, Strauss led a team of researchers on a five-year project that used and adapted the ideas of GTM in several ways that did not find their way into Strauss' later methodological works,[9] for example using transcribed group discussion in lieu of writing memos. Moreover, as Kearney (2007) notes, Strauss also encouraged and defended the role of personal experience in the research process.

> [T]he personal experiences of each project member enriched both the data collection and the analysis. We emphasize this particularly because of firmly held canons, widespread among social scientists, about the biased subjectivity of personal experience, which ought therefore to be carefully screened out of research like potential impurities from drinking water. (Strauss et al., 1985: 294)

Previously Glaser and Strauss had warned against the potential weaknesses of narrative research monographs, since these often 'use a great deal of data – quotes or field note selections', and are 'descriptively dense, but alas theoretically thin'. Strauss et al. echoed a similar concern, noting that: 'We think twice about loading a theoretically oriented monograph with too many chunks of descriptive material and are fairly deliberate about those that are included' (Strauss et al., 1985: 296 – also quoted in Kearney, 2007).

This paradox remains at the heart of the method, and is often poorly understood by both GTM practitioners and its critics. Some researchers claim to use GTM, but fail to do much more than simply offer 'rich descriptions' or what Charmaz terms 'grounded description', as opposed to 'conceptualization'. What many GTM researchers often fail to achieve is this leap beyond the 'data' to the conceptual and theoretical – something that we address below.

Apart from his constant calls for conceptualization, as opposed to re-description, Glaser has not specifically addressed the issue of the researcher's personal relationship to the research context; no doubt, because he assumes 'data' are obvious and unproblematic, rather than constructed. In his view, what these data mean emerges in the analytic process if the researcher does not force preconceptions on them. In effect, Glaser views data as having narrow, singular meanings. Students who have learned GTM via *Basics* would, similarly, have been led towards a narrow understanding of data because of the emphasis on being scientific, despite the points at which research begins. Yet many GTM researchers, including several who worked with Strauss himself as part of a research team, have stressed the importance of some personal engagement of the researcher with the research context. Several key innovations and enhancements to GTM flow from this position as will be seen in the concluding sections of this chapter.

Paradox 2 Although clearly presented as a challenge to the orthodox social research community, GTM actually sought to mimic some of the core aspects of traditional social research – neutrality of researcher, primacy of data, induction, positivism in one form or another.

Glaser and Strauss specifically targeted the US sociological establishment in their early work. They identified Talcott Parsons, Robert K. Merton and Paul Lazarsfeld as new members of the pantheon, but noted that although they had generated their own grand theories or, in Lazarsfeld's case, a methodology to gather 'facts', they 'lacked methods for generating theory from data or at any rate have not written about their methods. This pantheon 'played "theoretical capitalist" to the mass of "proletariat" testers' (Glaser and Strauss, 1967: 10).

Yet despite being presented as a challenge to orthodox social research practices, the basis and practice of GTM were justified largely in terms that echoed those of the dominant research community. Glaser particularly stresses the neutral, even passive, role of the researcher when collecting data, but views the analyst of these data as active. The early works of grounded theory as well as Glaser's current approach grant data primary significance. Glaser and Strauss (1967) and more recently Glaser (1998) ignore what researchers collected and how they collected these data. They characterized the central issue of 'grounding' in terms that could be seen as trying to outdo positivist, verificationist, quantitative research at its own game.[10] For instance, in *Theoretical Sensitivity* (1978), Glaser borrowed terms from quantitative research and imbued them with new, sometimes contrasting, meaning such as his coding strategies and theoretical sampling. Coding became open-ended and inductive rather than predetermined and deductive. Theoretical sampling consisted of an advanced strategy in which the researcher sampled to check the researcher's emergent categories, instead of sampling for initial selection of participants. Deduction took second place to induction, but the ultimate basis for knowledge claims still lay firmly with the phenomena – the data – themselves. As will be seen later, this paradox is symptomatic of a deeper issue that led to many of the key innovations in GTM from the early 1990s onward.

***Paradox* 3** The two founders of the method together represent two key traditions of social research, but presented early formulations of the method without explicit links to either tradition, or to any other methodological or epistemological canon.

The absence of explicit links is understandable in the early writings, given that the authors were keen to stress the novelty of their approach and the ways in which GTM differed from existing approaches. They envisioned GTM as remedying the weaknesses of those approaches. In the *Discovery* book, Glaser and Strauss assert that their approach is phenomenological, meaning that they take research and theorizing back to the studied phenomena, not that they adopted the frame of phenomenological research. For Strauss (Strauss and Corbin, 1994), such links stood as rhetorical claims rather than a methodological heritage. Quite possibly for him the links to the Chicago school needed no further explication beyond what they provided in examples and footnotes. Sociologists in the Chicago school tradition discerned continuities between it and GTM. For some Chicago school sociologists, grounded theory was not new; it simply named and stated strategies they had used all along (Lofland, 2007).

In the ensuing decades, however, some GTM writers, including Strauss himself, went to great lengths to position GTM against other orientations, methods and disciplines or sub-disciplines. Thus in his very last major work, *Continual Permutations of Action* (Strauss 1993), Strauss specifically traced his intellectual development from the Chicago school and pragmatism, through the collaboration with Glaser and the subsequent generation of GTM practitioners, to his later focus on action and social order. Charmaz (2000b) suggests that Strauss' version of grounded theory represents how he worked out the methodological implications of pragmatism and by extension, symbolic interactionism. Recent writers, such as Strübing (2007a, b), have pointed to the influence of pragmatism – including James, Dewey and Peirce – not only on Strauss himself, but on GTM as a whole.[11]

Glaser on the other hand has retained a staunchly consistent line that GTM stands alone, and he has not engaged with these epistemological issues. In part his stance probably results from his personal history. Had he pursued an academic career, Glaser would almost certainly have had to engage with these issues to some extent; those working closely with him have encountered these issues when submitting their work for peer review or other forms of accreditation. Confusion over the scope of GTM further complicates the situation. For many it is exclusively or primarily a qualitative method, but Glaser always stresses that researchers can use GTM with any form of data – qualitative or quantitative or both. This point is then elided with the argument that in similar fashion the method can be used with any epistemological position.[12] Glaser is indeed correct in the former claim – although the subtitle of *Discovery* is *Strategies for Qualitative Research* – but the latter one remains less defensible in such straightforward terms.[13]

Paradox 4 GTM followed two other challenges or innovations to social research practice: Thomas S. Kuhn's work (1962) which taken to its logical extension (Kuhn himself denied having a radical constructionist approach) challenged all forms of knowledge claim – but particularly those based on positivism, data and observation and the idea of using the physical sciences as the model for all forms of knowledge and research; and Harold Garfinkel's (1967) challenge to social researchers who sought to claim elevated status for their insights into social practices and contexts – yet the work of those within GTM indicates no attempt to engage or even acknowledge these developments.

This paradox relates to the previous paradox, and again the absence of these associations may derive from Glaser and Strauss's initial need to stress novelty and distinctiveness. This absence is also partially explained by our earlier point regarding Glaser and Strauss' concern to justify GTM in terms akin to the norms of the orthodox, quantitatively-oriented, research community. The division between Glaser and Strauss may then explain the extended silence; but as we will illustrate below, once an effort to engage with these developments is made, GTM is actually enhanced and significantly strengthened in its appeal, scope and justifiability.

Put in its simplest terms, GTM challenged the prevailing orthodoxy of a theoretical elite supported by apprentice-type researchers going about their business of seeking out verification and elucidation of extant theories; the discipline as a whole, however, advancing a form of expert knowledge that drew on social contexts, but did not specifically recognize social actors themselves as theoretically insightful to any meaningful degree. Kuhn's arguments severely challenged, if not undermined, the ways in which disciplines and knowledge in general 'advanced' over time; Garfinkel, on the other hand, contested the claims of the 'experts', arguing that the accounts of social actors themselves were on a par with those of the experts.[14]

The early development of GTM had some resonances with both Kuhn and Garfinkel – but also some key differences. One of Kuhn's prime targets was the idea that the development from the past to the present day is one of progress towards ever-improving knowledge, truth and insight. Kuhn challenged this view of accumulated knowledge with his characterization of scientific revolutions, normal science and knowledge paradigms. Glaser and Strauss, to an extent, followed a similar line in seeking to undermine the way in which researchers were expected to tread the theoretical paths on offer from the grand theories and grand theorists. GTM was a method that encouraged novelty and potentially revolutionary insights. But, on the other hand, Glaser and to a considerably lesser extent, Strauss, still adhered to some of the traditional methods of analyzing and evaluating research findings – induction, empiricism of sorts (see below) and other aspects of the positivist orientation which Kuhn's position challenged.

Garfinkel's focus on the role of the accounts of the social actors stressed that such accounts were not simply a topic for research, but were constitutive of the social context and a key resource for the sustaining of social order. Clear similarities arise here with Glaser and Strauss' early work, particularly *Time* and *Awareness*, which relied heavily on the accounts of those involved in the research context. But as we have already pointed out, GTM aimed for more than a form of re-description, instead its originators specifically aimed at moving away from or beyond narrative accounts to provide conceptualizations and eventually full-fledged theories. Again beginning a resolution of these issues was delayed until the early 1990s, at which point the development of a significantly innovative form of GTM began to be a realistic option. By the mid-1990s, the initial furore over the Glaser–Strauss split began to subside. Second and third generation GTM users were developing their own formulations of the method, often having themselves encountered some of the epistemological challenges that had developed since the 1960s.

Paradox 5 Glaser and Strauss offered GTM as an agenda for qualitative research steering away from extensive re-description and ethnographic narrative – instead holding out a promise of theoretical rigour, robustness and parsimony. Their actions came at a time when, particularly in the US, qualitative research had become the very poor relation of quantitative research methods (and this may still be the case). Yet Glaser (2008) stresses that GTM is not simply restricted to qualitative data, but can be used with any data.

As has been noted already, Glaser's position on the potential scope of grounded theory is valid. Critically however, Glaser and Strauss both saw the necessity of providing a rigorous basis for qualitative research – both in the process and the outcome. Although the method can indeed encompass all forms and types of data, its distinguishing features distance it from the prevailing research process and outcomes of statistically-oriented, hypothetico-deductive research. These features remain paramount for GTM, and in fact provide the continuity between the earliest forms of the method and those now presented as innovative.

Paradox 6 Although the three founding texts have been termed the best tutorial on GTM, they are far too nuanced and subtle to serve as introductions or primers for novice researchers or those keen to find out more about different research methods and approaches. Strauss eventually responded to doctoral students' clamouring for a grounded theory methods manual (Kearney, 2007) by writing two books on the topic. Neither book used the term GTM in the title, but both gained a wider audience for the method, although his co-authored book with

Juliet Corbin, *Basics of Qualitative Research* (1990) resulted in an irreconcilable split between the two originators' approaches.

Although the overwhelming majority of researchers claiming use of GTM refer to *Discovery* – and sometimes *Awareness* and *Time* – as the core GTM text, its use as a model or primer is contentious. In fact many researchers refer to *Discovery*, but their actual use of the method is specifically derived from *Basics*. One strength of *Basics* is that it does outline a series of procedures and stages in the development of a grounded theory – the subtitle of the book is *Techniques and Procedures for Developing Grounded Theory*. But this procedural approach also proved to be a weakness, since it can all too easily be treated as a recipe or formula for doing GTM, an approach that Corbin (Corbin and Strauss, 2008) now disavows. Although we disagree with the style and tone of Glaser's critique of Strauss and Corbin particularly in *Basics of Grounded Theory Analysis* (1992), his substantive criticisms can be seen as a justified response to this issue (see also, Atkinson et al., 2003; Melia, 1996; Wilson and Hutchinson, 1996).

Yet the problem of how a novice researcher actually learns how to use the method remains. Possibly reading *Discovery* and the Appendix to *Awareness* might provide an understanding of the method, but in our experience with students this is not the case. In our earlier work we noted that far too many writers on GTM rely on a brief explanation of some key grounded theory strategy such as coding or memo-making, followed by the claim that the technique or activity is 'simple' or 'straightforward'. On the other hand, often those same authors point out that actual use or achievement is often dependent on a particular researcher's skill or extensive experience.[15]

To his credit, Glaser has been responsible for gathering and publishing a growing number of examples of use of GTM,[16] added to which the literature on use and example of studies in a wide array of disciplines is also extensive and expanding. In some cases, however, published examples are superficial, ambiguous, confusing or convoluted. Some grounded theorists' reliance on neologisms or clumsy categories undermines their analyses – and respect for the method. In other cases, the substance of the research may be good, but the methodological justification is often weak or confusing. Many studies erroneously claim use of GTM – often being nothing more than some form of coding; some authors simply mention GTM in the section on methods, and then fail to offer any convincing evidence for its use in the actual research. Others outline particular use of the method – that is Glaser's or Strauss/Corbin's – but then fail to justify or substantiate this in methodological details or even in the analysis itself. In general, far too many papers merely rely on invoking what we have termed the GTM mantra (Bryant, 2002), and do no more than that.

This paradox is not unique to GTM, all research methods involve stages of learning and proficiency, otherwise they would hardly be classified as methods. The literature on GTM itself has, however, developed in many ways and now several introductory texts and primers are available for interested students and researchers. In addition, GTM has now been accepted, albeit sometimes grudgingly, as a valid research approach in many disciplines.

***Paradox** 7* Although the method gained enormously in popularity during the 1980s and 1990s, students and researchers still report significant barriers to research proposals and findings founded on the method.

GTM is now taught in many standard research methods programs – particularly those that focus on qualitative research. But students and researchers continue to report problems in preparing proposals seeking to use GTM. Two key reasons account for this problem. First, many disciplines and departments remain strongly positivist in their assumptions and predispositions with regard to both quantitative and qualitative research; in numerous cases the gate-keepers do not even recognize that they are positivist, but are simply unaware of any alternatives to their assumed approach. Moreover, although GTM in its initial formulation allows for a positivist or objectivist orientation, when proposed as the sole method gate-keepers occasionally exclude it as a valid option because GTM appears to offer no way of producing verified, reproducible, quantitative results.[17]

Second, GTM practitioners report that university and research body review boards expect a research proposal in the form of a research overview, a statement of hypotheses and a literature review. Although the first and third of these may in fact be included even in the early days of a GTM-oriented study, the second one cannot. The turn towards evidence-based research, that is, with randomized clinical trials, has increased reliance on sophisticated quantitative research. Until more qualitative researchers serve on regulatory bodies, expectations for proposals with preconceived hypothesis-testing research designs will continue to form a significant barrier given the current environment characterized by risk assessment, ethical clearance and other research regulations. Perhaps once a sufficient body of evidence accrues, in the form of substantive and formal grounded theories, the balance of argument might tilt further in favour of those seeking to use GTM, and qualitative methods in general; but in some cases these institutional issues still impact upon researchers' choice of method.

***Paradox* 8** When finally, in the 1990s, a more sophisticated concept of GTM was articulated, the full extent of the use of the method was revealed – including many in Europe, particularly in continental Europe. In many cases this revealed the background from which Strauss in particular developed, and this is proving critical for the furtherance of the method and a greater and more profound understanding of its specific insights and promise.

For many researchers, even those with some familiarity with GTM, the method has been largely demarcated between *Discovery*, Strauss and Corbin's *Basics* (1990, 1998) and Glaser's *Theoretical Sensitivity* (1978). Once the issue of the objectivist or positivist nature of GTM was brought to the fore, however, so too were several rich strands of GTM use, many of which had been nurtured in non-English speaking contexts. Strauss had taught in Germany, in 1976 at the University of Konstanz, and here he had drawn on his wider concerns with theories of action and interaction in addition to GTM. For the next twenty years,

Strauss remained in close contact with German colleagues who spread the influence of GTM and whose understanding of the method centred largely on *Basics* but against a background of Strauss' engagement with pragmatism – particularly Dewey, Mead and Peirce. Strauss continues to have a strong legacy among qualitative social scientists in Germany.[18]

Paradox 9 Given these paradoxes, why do researchers flock to use or claim to use, GTM?

The previous eight paradoxes demonstrate that those wishing to use GTM need to engage with many complexities and ambiguities: Some conceptual, some institutional and some inhere in qualitative research today. Given the possible alternatives, why do researchers flock to use the method? Some commentators, such as Titscher et al. (2000) have suggested that claiming use of GTM can be a methodological cop-out, since it appears to justify neglect of basic research protocols such as a problem statement, clear hypotheses, clear procedures and validations of findings. To a very limited extent this can be the case; but it is far more the case that researchers are attracted to the method because it continues to offer the possibilities of a research process that will yield genuine insights and conceptual innovation.

Others may counter our point, arguing that a general turning away from quantitative research has arisen amongst many new researchers, particularly in the realm of social research, and that it is in precisely these areas GTM stands as the qualitative method *par excellence*. Whatever the exact causes may be, GTM does stand out as the method of choice in social research. Since the 1990s it has developed in a manner that has helped clarify, if not resolve, some of the paradoxes already mentioned: In so doing those developing the method have had to contend with the generic paradox and challenge – how can the method be taken forward, while retaining its distinctive characteristics?

CONSTRUCTIVIST GTM

Partly because of its chequered and divergent history, through the 1970s and 1980s GTM, in both its dominant forms, remained virtually untouched by the extensive epistemological developments that had actually appeared at around the same time as *Discovery* itself. Ironically, this failure to engage with or acknowledge such developments actually made GTM more attractive to a research context based largely on positivist assumptions – albeit usually in the context of quantitative research methods (see, e.g. Rennie et al., 1988). This objectivist model of the world relied on a relatively uncomplicated concept of data: Similar in many regards to those who invoked 'classic' GTM together with its accompanying mantra: 'All is data'. Therefore it was not too surprising that some journals, disciplines, departments and research institutions granted GTM some degree of acceptability as a method – albeit a predominantly qualitative and therefore contested one.

Fortunately, several people working within the GTM community had already prepared the ground to move the method beyond what Loïc Wacquant termed 'epistemological fairytale'. These grounded theorists included several of the first generation of students taught by Strauss and Glaser at UCSF. Kathy Charmaz' chapter in the second edition of *The Handbook of Qualitative Research* (2000a), signalled one of the key moments in this development. She had based this chapter on writings dating from the early 1990s that pointed to new ways of thinking about and doing grounded theory.[19] Charmaz laid out an analysis of GTM that offered a measured account of the distinction between Glaser's position and that of Strauss and Corbin, but then went on to develop a critique of both camps, simultaneously offering a developmental path for the method as a whole.

For Charmaz the distinctive features of GTM challenged several key 1960s assumptions about research:

- the 'arbitrary divisions between theory and research';
- viewing qualitative studies as preparatory for more rigorous quantitative work;
- viewing qualitative research as illegitimate and devoid of rigour;
- viewing qualitative studies as impressionistic and unsystematic;
- the separation of data collection from its analysis;
- seeing the only possible outcome of qualitative research as 'descriptive case studies rather than theory development'.

In both its dominant forms at the time, however, GTM exhibited key conceptual weaknesses. At the heart of these lay the term 'data', the process of 'emergence' and the idea of 'discovery'. The import of these was neatly encapsulated in phrases such as 'theory emerges from the data' or '[t]he basic theme in our book is the discovery of theory from data systematically obtained from social research' (Glaser and Strauss, 1967: 2). Many GTM researchers invoked exactly these phrases, and some of them produced influential and useful research outcomes; but taken at face value such an epistemological stance is far too simplistic, and for some, indefensible.

In *Discovery* Glaser and Strauss invited their readers to use grounded theory strategies flexibly and as they saw fit. The key innovation in GTM in recent years has arisen precisely because researchers have taken Glaser and Strauss at their word, simultaneously taking into account the key theoretical and methodological developments of the past four decades. The result is what has been termed the *Constructivist* form of GTM.

Constructivist grounded theory has been the key innovation of the past decade. Constructivist GTM (1) recognizes and retains the strengths of the method itself, while engaging with the philosophical debates and developments of the past 40 years or so; (2) offers clear guidelines for examining how situations and people construct the studied phenomenon; and (3) moves the method further in to the interpretive tradition (see Bryant, 2002, 2003; Bryant and Charmaz, 2007; Charmaz 2000a, 2005, 2006, 2007, 2008a, 2008b, 2009; Clarke, 2003, 2005, 2006; Clarke and Friese, 2007; Mills et al., 2006). The constructivist form of

GTM draws on the original sources of the method, particularly those associated with Strauss and his early interest in pragmatism. With regard to 'data', the major shift can be described as a move from its being 'found' to its being 'made'. The research data is not discovered, extracted or uncovered, with the researcher taking on the role of mineral prospector mining for information; rather the 'data' is the outcome of the researcher's active relationship with the research context, including the other social actors and their respective accounts. Thus, the constructivist approach acknowledges that grounded theorists construct situated knowledge reflecting how their respective research relationships arise in specific situations. Similarly, constructivist grounded theorists attend closely to the historical moment, social structures and situations in which their research participants are embedded. Clarke (2003, 2005, 2006; Clarke and Friese, 2007) has demonstrated how postmodern attention to the positionality of the researcher and the researched shapes knowledge and reforms the ontological and epistemological foundations of classic grounded theory.

Glaser and Strauss argued that theory is *discovered*, arising and emerging from data which has an independent existence, distinct to and external from the scientific observer. For constructivists neither data nor theories are discovered. Rather, researchers as social actors *construct* grounded theories based on prior experience and current concerns and interactions with people, perspectives and research practices. This builds on the pragmatist underpinnings of grounded theory (Charmaz, 2009).

Constructivism, as the term implies, is founded on the argument that social reality is socially constructed, with social actors continually contributing to the maintenance of social order and social change. This orientation pulls together the insights of Kuhn and Garfinkel, amongst many others, and helps resolve some of the paradoxes mentioned earlier.[20]

For instance, Paradoxes 2–4 all stem from the endemic, but perhaps unwitting, positivism in the early GTM source books. Glaser's conceptualizations of the analytic process inspired much of the content of the original method and relied on a positivist epistemology. We can discern positivist assumptions in the ways in which Glaser and Strauss sought to stress the originality and unique nature of the method, and to distinguish it from any others. The advent of a constructivist form of the method resolves the paradox of an innovative and revolutionary qualitative method taking on the mantle of the traditional quantitative ones. GTM is not one type of method trying to masquerade as another. The core features listed by Charmaz can be retained, but within a more sophisticated epistemology; one that can be used in response to the challenges posed by developments in philosophy of science, theories of knowledge and ideas about the role of social actors.[21]

It then becomes evident that GTM enhances and complements some of the key developments of the sociological and philosophical canon. The early GTM texts, particularly *Awareness* and *Time* can be re-read as profound examples of conceptual analyses founded on a context in which all the actors play constitutive and constructing roles. This re-reading also includes the researchers themselves, although not in the way that Garfinkel might argue. GTM in its constructivist form recognizes that social contexts are socially constructed, but then demands conceptualization by the researcher that can be offered as a deeper and more extensive of the context itself. Turner understood this point as early as 1983.

> This approach to qualitative data [GTM – eds] promotes the development of theoretical accounts which conform closely to the situations being observed, *so that the theory is likely to be intelligible to and usable by those in the situations observed*, and is open to comment and correction by them . . . The approach also directs the researcher immediately to the creative core of the research process and *facilitates the direct application of both the intellect and the imagination* to the demanding process of interpreting qualitative research data. It is worth noting that the quality of the final product arising from this kind of work is *more directly dependent upon the quality of the research worker's understanding of the phenomena under observation* than is the case with many other approaches to research. (Turner, 1983: 334–5, stress added)

Once GTM is taken on this constructivist path the links between the method and some of its precursors become more readily apparent. Covan (2007) has argued that echoes of Durkheim (1895/1982) resonate in Glaser and Strauss' early work, since both they and Durkheim not only sought to explain their specific forms of sociological method, but also to stress their legitimacy in terms of generating knowledge of the social world. Moreover, they shared a belief that while lay interpretations of reality were a resource for theorizing, the sociologist must transcend these.

Some commentators have pointed to the work of sociologists, from the Chicago school in particular, whose work can be seen as embodying many of the features that GTM brings to the fore. Covan (2007) sees parallels between GTM and *The Sociological Imagination* in which Mills (1959) argued for the necessity of understanding social situations by encompassing three dimensions: individual biographies, history and social structure, and which 'is, of course, grounded in the creative process of generating theory in consideration of the same dimensions' (p. 30). In addition, Lempert (2007) argues that Mills' book exemplifies a formal theory with 'analytic power' and extensive application.[22] So here we have a methodological departure – constructivist GTM – actually strengthening the links between the method as a whole and the tradition from which it develops.

Paradoxes 1 and 6 are also dissipated to some extent with the emergence of this new form of GTM. Students have continually contended with the GTM admonitions about keeping an open mind, and not delving into the literature at an early stage of research. From a constructivist standpoint, we simply have no basis for treating the researcher as an empty vessel, let alone a passive one (Dey, 1999; Henwood and Pidgeon, 2003). Students can be shown that whatever view one has of the research process, an open mind is certainly a prerequisite, but an empty head is an impediment; whether this is put in terms of the principle of the null hypothesis, falsification, humility or some of the phrases particularly used by Glaser. Equally researchers will always bring something of themselves to the research context – the findings and the data are not extracted as part of a mining process, they develop from the relationship between the researcher and the focus of study. In a similar fashion, any researcher will have a certain familiarity with some aspects of the literature pertaining to the chosen field and focus. Furthermore, researchers do not usually work in isolation, and so there will always be preceding and developing dialogues between researchers, their colleagues, advisors and the like.

GTM in some of its early formulations specifically admonishes researchers about engaging with the literature, on the assumption that by doing so it will influence their ideas and potentially destroy or divert their innovative insights, channelling them into the received wisdom. Possibly this view has some basis, but ignoring earlier research is an unrealistic option. Researchers have to demonstrate some knowledge of the field in the early – preliminary – stages of the research process: In any case it again places the researcher in a position of passivity and near vacuousness.

What is at stake here is researcher confidence, particularly for the novice or inexperienced researcher, something that should be a core concern with any method, and which was certainly one of the motivating factors for Glaser and Strauss. Their encouragement to researchers to develop their own concepts and theories was important in freeing doctoral students, in particular, from the confines of verification of existing 'grand' theories. Those seeking to use GTM without a grasp of the extant literature, however, often found themselves inundated with 'data', and so could not judge whether their own insights were truly innovative or simply reiterations of current or even already outdated ideas (Lofland, 2007). Constructivism builds on the confidence-giving features so important to Glaser and Strauss, but takes into account the realities and necessities of engaging with the wider research community and its mores.[23]

The institutional barriers of Paradox 7 have to some extent weakened, although numerous researchers, particularly in the US, report that they have to contend with all sorts of obstruction and impediment if they propose a study built around any form of qualitative research, including GTM. The constructivist form assists in such circumstances by recognizing the significance of positioning a study in the literature and scrutinizing its methodological and ethical implications, although it has stripped away the aspects of GTM that align with positivist, quantitative methods and assumptions. As we will touch on in the concluding sections, the entire issue about institutional barriers is bound up with the far deeper and complex one of trying to get people to understand the nature of issues about truth, forms of valid knowledge and expertise. What the constructivist form of GTM accomplishes, however, is to show ways in which research can be undertaken within part of what might be termed the wider neo-pragmatist program which can reconcile certainty and control with flexibility and agility.

GTM AND PRAGMATISM

The emergence of constructivist GTM has to be seen against the cognitive upheavals that particularly characterized the past 40–50 years, and became widely debated in the 1980s in the social sciences as part of the postmodern disenchantment with Enlightenment values and the development of science. Both proponents and critics of postmodernism sometimes see this trend as resulting in a complete relativism such that all knowledge claims are merely matters of opinion to be accepted, tolerated or rejected as questions of personal taste. The re-interpretation of the roots of GTM helps counter the most extreme and uncomfortable aspects of this upheaval, and locates the method in the vanguard of neo-pragmatism particularly as presented in the work of Richard Rorty (1999, 2007).

Glaser and Strauss' use of terms such as 'fit', 'grab', 'saturation' and 'theoretical sensitivity' has often proved a troublesome feature of the method. Students ask repeatedly for some clear and concise criteria for developing and evaluating these aspects, and the failure to respond to such requests leaves the method open to criticism – such terminological ambiguities possibly being indicative of severe conceptual weakness in the method as a whole. Even experienced researchers find it hard to articulate anything more precise than some fairly impressionistic guidelines. If we move away from what the pragmatists term the metaphysics of the real, and instead adopt the pragmatist view that theories and concepts are best considered in terms of their usefulness rather than their truthfulness then these features of GTM appear in a far clearer light.

Rorty has been particularly important in indicating how the pragmatist position evades and avoids the standard dualisms such as objective versus subjective, discovery versus invention, nature versus convention, reality versus appearance or found versus made. For Rorty, the leading neo-pragmatist of recent years, the sole purpose of human enquiry is not truth, but 'to achieve agreement among human beings about what to do, to bring about consensus on the ends to be achieved and the means to be used to achieve those ends' (1999: xxv). Theories or concepts are then judged not in terms of correspondence to reality, but whether or not they are useful in serving particular purposes and contexts. In other words do they 'fit', do they 'work', do they have 'grab'? Furthermore, the assessment of such characteristics cannot simply be couched in terms of impersonal objectivity, neither can they appeal to some deeply felt personal essence; instead there must be some effort to achieve consensus or intersubjectivity, which is the only possible goal for such endeavours as far as Rorty is concerned. In this sense, Rorty brings the critique of objectivity developed in the 1960s explicitly into the pragmatist agenda. Glaser and Strauss' appeals for a firm grounding of concepts and theories, and the practice-orientation of the method as a whole can then be seen as affording precisely the kinds of strategies and objectives that fit Rorty's pragmatist agenda.

It is unlikely that anyone who clings to what Rorty and others have termed a metaphysics of presence or foundationalism will be swayed by the brief paragraphs above, and many others may well not be fully convinced: But that is not the issue at this juncture. What is crucial is that social scientists can regard the constructivist form of GTM as an important complement to current philosophical and epistemological debates. GTM can draw on the re-emergence of pragmatism; likewise the pragmatic orientation can find in GTM a proven tool for research and study. In significant ways, our perspective not only builds on Rorty, but returns to the legacy of Anselm Strauss' theoretical works (see, e.g. 1959/1969, 1993), rather than his methodological statements (Charmaz, 2009). Moreover, this pragmatist perspective enhances some of the features of the method that have, to date, proved troublesome and awkward. Adopting this perspective also indicates the way in which Paradox 5 can be resolved.

Paradox 9 remains; but it is a welcome one. In part some of the recent innovations in GTM can be seen to enhance its attraction to researchers particularly in and around practice-oriented and practice-led disciplines. Practitioners can now draw upon a more sophisticated epistemological and methodological basis for explaining and justifying use of the method, even if it proves to be less immediately palatable to quantitative orthodoxies. It remains to be seen if GTM can sustain its position as the method of choice amongst qualitative researchers, and to what extent the *constructivist* form is taken up and developed as part of these efforts. As independent (Bryant, 2002, 2003; Charmaz, 2000a, 2006) and joint (2007) propagators of this key innovation we would like to think that our version of grounded theory will have wide appeal. In addition, some of the operational and cultural issues around GTM have been clarified or resolved such as those discussed in connection with Paradoxes 6 and 7.

CONCLUSION

Constructivist grounded theory resolves the paradoxes in earlier versions of grounded theory that we outlined above. It necessitates taking a different view of the researcher, the empirical world and the research process from those implicit or inherent in classical grounded theory. As one of us has written earlier of GTM, 'The method does not stand outside the research process; it resides within it' (Charmaz, 2008a; p. 160). The method and research process inextricably intertwine because grounded theory is an emergent method that develops as the research process unfolds.

Similarly, the researcher is an integral part of the process. Constructivist grounded theory shatters the notion of the neutral researcher removed from world. In whatever ways we collect data, we select and shape them. We influence what we see and find, even if only in the most mundane ways such as attending to certain actions, objects and events, and not to others. The viewer is part of what is viewed. We act upon and within the empirical world; we do not simply turn our gaze towards it.

A major implication of our position means treating theorizing about the research process as a form of practical action *in* the world, not merely *about* the world.

It also means qualifying our theories for the conditions and contingencies that frame them, rather than treating our theories as abstract generalizations that subsume variation and difference. To test the usefulness of theories, researchers must understand the social and historical conditions of their production. Ultimately, theorizing is a form of interpretive engagement with the studied phenomenon. It is this interpretive engagement inherent in constructivist grounded theory that holds untapped potential for advancing knowledge in both practice fields and social scientific disciplines.

Constructivist grounded theory comes at a propitious time to move in these directions. GTM is now an established part of the methodological armoury in many disciplines, and many others evince a growing interest in the method. Furthermore, the method is now readily amenable to combination with other methods and approaches, such as action research, ethnography and critical theory. The qualitative revolution that Lincoln and Denzin (1994) identified, has intensified, and constructivist grounded theory has become a vital part of this more extensive and robust qualitative tradition. The constructivist innovation has resulted in a new appreciation of some key aspects of the method as a whole, and judging by the increasing demand for examples and clarifications of GTM, the shark is very much alive and well, still retaining the key characteristics that marked out the method as innovative and useful when it first appeared.

NOTES

1 The original quote is taken from *Annie Hall,* 'A relationship, I think, is like a shark. You know, it has to constantly move forward or it dies. I think what we have on our hands is a dead shark'. – Alvy Singer (Woody Allen) to Annie Hall (Diane Keaton)

2 This approach corresponded with the open-ended Chicago school style of conducting life-history and ethnographic research but it constituted an innovation for social scientists who were unfamiliar with these methods.

3 Dewey being the most important influence.

4 This distinction is core to GTM – see Kearney (2007) and Glaser (2007).

5 Although in many contexts it is acceptable for the researcher to start from a place of personal interest.

6 Readers who are not familiar with these aspects of GTM, and those who are interested to find out more, are advised to refer to Charmaz (2005, 2006).

7 This and the ensuing sections of the chapter are derived from our introduction and chapter in the *Handbook of Grounded Theory* (Bryant and Charmaz, 2007) – some of the arguments are offered in more detail therein.

8 North American universities have been slow in making qualitative methods a routine requirement in doctoral programs and even slower in ensuring that those who teach these courses have gained substantial expertise in using and developing qualitative methods.

9 The chapters by Kearney (2007) and Wiener (2007) in the *Handbook* offer further details.

10 This is not to imply that all quantitative research is positivist; or all positivist research is quantitative.

11 See below – section on GTM and Pragmatism.

12 For instance, Judith Holton's (2007) chapter in the *Handbook of Grounded Theory.*

13 As an aside, one area of contention for Glaser has centered on the relationship between GTM and symbolic interactionism [SI]. Some GTM specialists, notably Adele Clarke, have argued that GTM and SI are 'a theory-methods package', but this has been vigorously challenged by Glaser. Although we can certainly discern a close and useful relationship between the two, it is not the only theoretical alignment for grounded theory.

14 We introduce Kuhn and Garfinkel here as notable representatives of key issues that, although not unique to the 1960s and beyond, were important foci of the period – and indeed remain so.

15 Editors' introduction – Bryant and Charmaz, 2007.

16 See for instance http://www.groundedtheoryreview.com/

17 This is to reiterate the point made above in Note 8 – space does not permit a more nuanced discussion of the relationships in question here.

18 Fritz Schuetze (2009) states that the influence of Anselm Strauss in Germany exceeds that of Erving Goffman.

19 The entry in the first edition had been provided by Strauss and Corbin (1994).

20 It also invokes another key text that appeared around the same period, 1967 – Peter Berger and Thomas Luckmann, *The Social Construction of Reality* (1967) (see Bryant and Charmaz, 2007).

21 See below, the section on GTM and Pragmatism, where other issues are raised in this regard.

22 A certain irony arises in this association with Mills' work since Glaser and Strauss (1967) targeted it as a specific instance of the sort of approach they sought to criticize and displace.

23 For excellent examples see Casper (1998), Clarke (1998) and Star (1989).

REFERENCES

Atkinson, P., Coffey, A., and Delamont, S. (2003) *Key Themes in Qualitative Research: Continuities and Changes.* New York: Rowan and Littlefield.

Berger, Peter and Luckmann, Thomas (1967) *The Social Construction of Reality.* Garden City, NY: Doubleday Anchor Books.

Blumer, Herbert (1969) *Symbolic Interactionism.* Englewood Cliffs, NJ: Prentice-Hall.

Bryant, Antony (2002). Re-grounding grounded theory. *The Journal of Information Technology Theory and Application*, 4: 25–42.

Bryant, Antony (2003, January) A constructive/ist response to Glaser. *FQS: Forum for Qualitative Social Research*, 4(1), http://www.qualitative-research.net/index.php/fqs/article/view/757 [Accessed 03-Dec-2008].

Bryant, A. and Charmaz, K. (2007) Grounded theory in historical perspective: An epistemological account. In A. Bryant and K. Charmaz (eds) *The Sage Handbook of Grounded Theory,* pp. 31–57. London: Sage.

Casper, Monica (1998) *The Making of the Unborn Patient: A Social Anatomy of Fetal Surgery.* New Brunswick, NJ: Rutgers University Press.

Charmaz. Kathy (1983) The grounded theory method: An explication and interpretation. In R.M. Emerson (ed.) *Contemporary Field Research,* pp. 109–26. Boston: Little Brown.

Charmaz. Kathy (2000a) Constructivist and objectivist grounded theory. In N.K. Denzin and Y. Lincoln (eds) *Handbook of Qualitative Research,* 2nd edn pp. 509–35. Thousand Oaks, CA: Sage.

Charmaz, Kathy (2000b) Teachings of Anselm Strauss: Remembrances and Reflections. *Sociological Perspectives*, 43(4): S163–S174.

Charmaz, Kathy (2005) Grounded theory in the 21st century: A qualitative method for advancing social justice research. In N. Denzin and Y. Lincoln (eds) *Handbook of Qualitative Research*, 3rd edn. Thousand Oaks, CA: Sage.

Charmaz, Kathy (2006) *Constructing Grounded Theory: A Practical Guide Through Qualitative Analysis.* London: Sage.

Charmaz, Kathy (2007) Constructionism and grounded theory. In J.S. Holstein and J. Gubrium (eds) *Handbook of Constructionist Research*, pp. 397–412. New York: Guilford.

Charmaz, Kathy (2008a) Grounded theory as an emergent method. In S.N. Hesse-Biber and P. Leavy (eds) *Handbook of Emergent Methods*, pp. 155–70. New York: Guilford.

Charmaz, Kathy (2008b) Reconstructing grounded theory. In P. Alasuutari, L. Bickman, and J. Brannen (eds) *Handbook of Social Research*, pp. 461–78. London: Sage.

Charmaz, Kathy (forthcoming, 2009) The legacy of Anselm Strauss for constructivist grounded theory. In N.K. Denzin (ed.) *Studies in Symbolic Interaction.*

Clarke, Adele E. (1998) *Disciplining Reproduction: Modernity, American Life Sciences and the 'Problem of Sex'.* Berkeley, CA: University of California Press.

Clarke, Adele E. (2003) Situational Analyses: Grounded theory mapping after the postmodern turn. *Symbolic Interaction*, 26: 553–76.

Clarke, Adele E. (2005) *Situational Analysis: Grounded Theory after the Postmodern Turn.* Thousand Oaks, CA: Sage.

Clarke, Adele E. (2006) Feminisms, grounded theory, and situational analysis. In S. Hess-Biber and D. Leckenby (eds) *Handbook of Feminist Research Methods,* pp. 345–70. Thousand Oaks, CA: Sage.

Clarke, Adele E. and Friese, Carrie (2007) Grounded theorizing: Using situational analysis. In A. Bryant and K. Charmaz (eds) *The Sage Handbook of Grounded Theory,* pp. 363–97. London: Sage.

Corbin, Juliet and Strauss, Anselm (2008) *Basics of Qualitative Research: Techniques and Procedures for Developing Grounded Theory.* Los Angeles, CA: Sage.

Covan, E.K. (2007) The discovery of grounded theory in practice: The legacy of multiple mentors. In A. Bryant and K. Charmaz (eds) *The Sage Handbook of Grounded Theory,* pp.58–74. London: Sage.

Denzin, Norman K. and Yvonna S. Lincoln (1994) Preface. In N.K. Denzin and Y.S. Lincoln (eds) *Handbook of Qualitative Research*, pp. ix–xii. Thousand Oaks, CA.

Dewey, John (1922/1950) *Human Nature and Conduct.* New York: The Modern Library.

Dewey, John (1925/1952) *Experience and Nature.* New York: Dover Publications.

Dey, I. (1999) *Grounding Grounded Theory.* San Diego: Academic Press.

Durkheim, E. (1895/1982) *The Rules of the Sociological Method.* New York: Free Press.

Garfinkel, Harold (1967) *Studies in Ethnomethodology.* Englewood Cliffs, NJ: Prentice-Hall.

Glaser, Barney G. (1965) The constant comparative method of qualitative analysis. *Social Problems*, Vol. 12, No. 4, Spring, pp 436–45.

Glaser, Barney G. (1978) *Theoretical Sensitivity.* Mill Valley, CA: The Sociology Press.

Glaser, Barney G. (1992) *Basics of Grounded Theory Analysis: Emergence vs. Forcing.* Mill Valley, CA: The Sociology Press.

Glaser, Barney G. (1998) *Doing Grounded Theory: Issues and Discussions.* Mill Valley, CA: Sociology Press.

Glaser, Barney G. (2007) Doing formal theory. In A. Bryant and K. Charmaz (eds) *The Sage Handbook of Grounded Theory,* pp. 97–113. London: Sage.

Glaser, Barney G. (2008) *Doing Quantitative Grounded Theory.* Mill Valley, CA: Sociology Press.

Glaser, Barney G. and Strauss, A.L. (1965a) Discovery of substantive theory: A basic strategy for qualitative analysis. *American Behavioural Scientist*, 8: 5–13.

Glaser, Barney G. and Strauss, A.L. (1965b) *Awareness of Dying.* Chicago: Aldine.

Glaser, Barney G. and Strauss, Anselm L. (1967) *The Discovery of Grounded Theory.* Chicago: Aldine.

Glaser, Barney G. and Strauss, A.L. (1968) *Time for Dying.* Chicago: Aldine.

Glaser, Barney G. and Strauss, Anselm L. (1971) *Status Passage.* Chicago: Aldine-Atherton.

Henwood, Karen and Pidgeon, Nick (2003) Grounded theory in psychological research. In P.M. Camic, J.E. Rhodes, and L. Yardley (eds) *Qualitative Research in Psychology: Expanding Perspectives in Methodology and Design*, pp. 131–55. Washington, DC: American Psychological Association.

Holton, Judith A. (2007) The coding process and its challenges. In A. Bryant and K. Charmaz (eds) *The Sage Handbook of Grounded Theory*, pp. 265–90. London: Sage.

Kearney, Margaret H. (2007) From the sublime to the meticulous: The continuing evolution of grounded formal theory. In A. Bryant and K. Charmaz (eds) *The Sage Handbook of Grounded Theory,* pp. 127–50. London: Sage.

Kuhn, Thomas S. (1962) *The Structure of Scientific Revolutions.* Chicago: University of Chicago Press.

Lazarsfeld, Paul and Rosenberg, Morris (eds) (1955) *The Language of Social Research; A Reader in the Methodology of Social Research.* Glencoe, IL: Free Press.

Lempert, L.B. (2007) Asking questions of the data: Memo writing in the grounded theory tradition. In A. Bryant and K. Charmaz (eds) *The Sage Handbook of Grounded Theory*, pp. 245–64. London: Sage.

Lewin, Kurt (1999) *The Complete Social Scientist: A Kurt Lewin Reader.* Washington, DC: American Psychological Association.

Lofland, Lyn H. (2007) Panelist, 'Author Meets Critics on *Constructing Grounded Theory: A Practical Guide through Qualitative Analysis*,' Annual Meetings of the Pacific Sociological Association, Oakland, CA. March 30th.

Mead, George Herbert (1934) *Mind, Self and Society*. Chicago: University of Chicago Press.

Melia, K.M. (1996) Rediscovering Glaser. *Qualitative Health Research*, 6(3): 368–78.

Mills, C.W. (1959) *The Sociological Imagination*. Oxford: Oxford University Press.

Mills, J., Bonner, A., and Francis, K. (2006) The development of constructivist grounded theory. *International Journal of Qualitative Methods*, 5(1): 1–10.

Park, Robert E. (1952) *Human Communities: The City and Human Ecologies*. Glencoe, IL: Free Press.

Quint, J. (1967) *The Nurse and the Dying Patient*. New York: Macmillan.

Rennie, D., Phillips, J.R., and Quartaro, G.K. (1988) Grounded theory: A promising approach to conceptualisation in Psychology. *Canadian Psychology*, 29(2): 139–50.

Rorty, R. (1999) *Philosophy and Social Hope*. London: Penguin.

Rorty, R. (2007) *Philosophy as Cultural Politics: Philosophical Papers*, Volume 4. Cambridge: Cambridge University Press.

Schuetze, Fritz (Forthcoming, 2009) Anselm Strauss's legacy in Germany today. In N.K. Denzin (ed.) *Studies in Symbolic Interaction*.

Star, Susan Leigh (1989) *Regions of the Mind: Brain Research and the Quest for Scientific Certainty*. Stanford, CA: Stanford University Press.

Stern. Phyllis (1984/1994) The grounded theory method: Its uses and processes. In B.G. Glaser (ed) *More Grounded Theory: A Reader*, pp 116–26. Mill Valley, CA: Sociology Press

Strauss, Anselm L. (1959/1969) *Mirrors and Masks*. Mill Valley, CA: The Sociology Press

Strauss, Anselm (1987) *Qualitative Analysis for Social Scientists*. New York: Cambridge University Press.

Strauss, Anselm (1993) *Continual Permutations of Action*. New York: Aldine de Gruyter.

Strauss, Anselm and Corbin, J. (1990) *Basics of Qualitative Research: Grounded Theory Procedures and Techniques*. Newbury Park, CA: Sage.

Strauss, Anselm and Corbin, J. (1994) Grounded theory methodology: An overview. In N. Denzin and Y. Lincoln (eds) *Handbook of Qualitative Research*, 1st edn, pp. 273–85. Thousand Oaks, CA: Sage.

Strauss, Anselm and Corbin, Juliet (1998) *Basics of Qualitative Research: Grounded Theory Procedures and Techniques*, 2nd. edn. Thousand Oaks, CA: Sage.

Strauss, A., Fagerhaugh, S., Suczek, B., and Weiner, C. (1985) *The Social Organization of Medical Work*. Chicago: University of Chicago Press.

Strübing, Jörg (2007a) Glaser vs. Strauss? Zur methodologischen und methodischen Substanz einer Unterscheidung zweier Varianten von Grounded Theory. In Katja Mruck and Günter Mey (eds) *HSR-Supplemente: Grounded Theory – Anmerkungen zu einem prominenten Forschungsstil*. Köln: Zentrum für Historische Sozialforschung, pp. 157–73.

Strübing, J. (2007b) Research as pragmatic problem-solving: The pragmatist roots of empirically-grounded theorizing. In A. Bryant and K. Charmaz (eds) *The Sage Handbook of Grounded Theory*, pp. 493–512. London: Sage.

Timmermans, S and Tavory, I. (2007) Advancing ethnographic research through grounded theory practice. In A. Bryant and K. Charmaz (eds) *The Sage Handbook of Grounded Theory*, pp. 493–512. London: Sage.

Titscher, S., Meyer, M., Wodak, R., and Vetter, E. (2000) *Methods of Text and Discourse Analysis*. London: Sage.

Turner, B. (1983) The use of grounded theory for the qualitative analysis of organizational behaviour. *Journal of Management Studies*, 20(3): 333–48.

Wiener, Carolyn (2007) Making teams work in conducting grounded theory. In A. Bryant and K. Charmaz, pp. 293–310.

Wilson, Holly S. and Hutchinson, Sally A. (1996) Methodologic mistakes in grounded theory. *Nursing Research*, 45(2): 122–4.

12

Back to Likert: Towards the Conversational Survey

Giampietro Gobo

RESCUE THE SURVEY

For decades, the dilemma between open-ended and closed-ended response alternatives preoccupied the methodological debate (Schuman and Presser, 1979). But like all dilemmas it found no solution, for 'the closed questions did not capture the same dimensions of meaning that (are) revealed by the open question' (Groves et al., 1992: 60).

Over the years, the survey has resolved the dilemma by opting for the second alternative. In fact, questionnaires generally comprise few questions with open-ended response alternatives. This choice has been determined by various factors which, in certain respects, have been the survey's fortune, making it the methodology most widely used in the social sciences, and also giving it great currency in the academic and scientific world.

Nevertheless in the long run, this methodological choice has also depleted the survey's appeal. Indeed, numerous researchers have both criticised and abandoned the method. Whilst in the 1950s a brilliant future was predicted for the survey, in recent times (at least in the academic world) it has suffered a crisis of identity and entered slow but inexorable decline. The postmodern wave and the rise of qualitative methods since the 1990s have dimmed the image of the survey, both in academe and public opinion. This tendency seems to have affected the younger generation of social scientists as well. A study by Payne et al. (2004) on 244 full-scale papers published in four leading British general sociology journals

(*Sociology*, *British Journal of Sociology*, *Sociological Review* and *Sociological Research Online*) between 1999 and 2000 found that 41% of them were based on qualitative research methods and only 14% on quantitative ones. In addition, the qualitative studies had been conducted mainly by junior staff, which shows that qualitative research involves a generation issue.

The survey has also lost favour with public opinion, and it is often ridiculed or considered a highly superficial tool with which to interpret social phenomena. Although the survey is still the methodology most widely used in social and market research (for instance, the spread of customer satisfaction policy has inundated the users of numerous services, from hospitals to museums, with questionnaires), its progressive loss of prestige has been evident for some time.

The survey now finds itself at a crossroads: either it must reverse its decline by renewing itself (in its data-collection practices and in how it relates to respondents) or it is bound to suffer severe setbacks.

I believe that the survey still has enormous potential; it can be definitively emancipated from its positivist origins; and it can regain the image and the prestige that it enjoyed at its beginning, in what we call its 'golden age'.

THE OLD DILEMMA

It has been said, for decades that one of the central issues in the methodological debate was the dilemma between open-ended and closed-ended response alternatives.

The origins of the debate date back to before the Second World War. However, it culminated in the mid-1940s when conflict erupted between two opposing factions: the *Division of Polls* headed by Elmo C. Wilson and the *Division of Program Surveys* headed by Rensis Likert (1903–1981), both of which were research divisions of the *US Bureau of Intelligence*, then directed by Keith R. Kane (see Converse, 1987: 195–201). In the spring of 1942 Kane asked Paul F. Lazarsfeld (1901–1976), a methodologist of Austrian origin, to examine the controversy and to find a methodological solution for it. Lazarsfeld's famous article of 1944 (*The Controversy over Detailed Interviews – An Offer for Negotiation*) was a re-working of the report that he submitted to Kane in 1942.

Besides personal issues, the conflict between Wilson and Likert was provoked by the different research techniques employed in the two divisions. The interviewers used by Wilson's *Division of Polls*, for example, asked respondents to choose one of the fixed response alternatives – as still prescribed by research handbooks today.[1] Instead, the interviewers who worked for Likert were instructed first to transcribe the interviewee's comments and then (on conclusion of the interview) to choose the response alternative which they considered to be the closest match with the interviewee's comment. Hence in the former case it was the interviewee who directly chose the answer; in the latter it was instead the interviewer who chose the answer, doing so on the interviewee's behalf.

Although this last procedure was not proof against distortions (principal among which were misunderstandings of the interviewee's opinions), it nevertheless made it possible to avoid numerous other distortions that might arise during the interview, which according to Likert should as closely as possible resemble a conversation. This manner of administering questionnaires thus came to be baptized the 'fixed question/free answers' technique.

Likert was aware that if the interviewer was to perform these tasks correctly, s/he had to be adequately trained in both how to conduct the probes and how to understand the meanings of the interviewees' statements.

Accordingly, in 1942 Likert asked the psychologist Carl Rogers (1902–1987), known at the time for his use of non-directive techniques[2] in psychotherapy sessions, to train interviewers in how to communicate with their interviewees and how to understand their emotions and reactions. The members of Likert's staff (in particular Charles F. Cannell and Victor C. Raimy) learned from Rogers how to formulate interviewee-centred probes and how to use pauses and silences as communication devices.

The researchers at the *Division of Program Surveys* also paid close attention to the procedures for codifying the narrative materials collected by open-ended questions. But they soon discovered the long-drawn-out and laborious nature of these procedures. Obviously, the criterion adopted by Likert required more time and money than did the criterion used by Wilson.

THE OUTCOME

In the decades which followed, the debate extended to all the social sciences, and at times it grew heated. Still today, there are those who believe that fixed response alternatives have considerable advantages. One of them is their greater rapidity of administration, classification and interpretation, contrary to open-ended ones, which are easy to set but difficult to examine (Oppenheim 1966: 41). Moreover, a series of pre-determined answers can help the interviewee understand the meaning of the question (Selltiz and Jahoda, 1963: 262), thereby reducing the rate of answers irrelevant to the purposes of the research (Bailey, 1978: 105). They can prompt interviewees to recall events that they would otherwise not remember (Schwarz and Hippler, 1987). And they can be used to address sensitive topics like age, income, political preferences, etc., which would receive higher refusal rates if investigated with open-ended questions.

Other scholars object that open-ended answers are much more valid than fixed-response alternatives, which force interviewees to think in the same way as the researcher. Answers with pre-established categories suggest the answer to respondents who in fact have no opinion on the matter (Selltiz and Jahoda, 1963: 261; Converse, 1964, 1970; Noelle-Neumann, 1970: 193).

In an attempt to mediate between the opposing factions, Lazarsfeld (1944) pointed out that the appropriateness of open-ended or closed-ended response alternatives depended on a certain number of circumstantial factors (aim of the interview, the interviewee's knowledge of the topic, degree of structuring in his/her opinions and attitudes, willingness to talk about the topic, ability to communicate, and, of course, the researcher's knowledge of these circumstantial factors). However, it is doubtful whether the decision to choose one of the two types of questions is ever actually taken after careful consideration of these factors.

In the same article, Lazarsfeld examined the results of two surveys on the attitude of Californians towards Japanese residents in California after the bombing of Pearl Harbour. The survey conducted by Likert used open-ended questions; the one by Wilson used closed-ended ones. Lazarsfeld reported that the two studies obtained substantially identical results, although Likert's group had not fully exploited the richness of the materials collected. Lazarsfeld therefore advocated cooperation between the two groups: open-ended questions would be useful at the beginning of the research as a pre-test (that is, to construct the questions for the questionnaire and check their operation) and, at the end of the same survey, to re-interview a subsample in order to contextualize the percentages obtained, Wilson's group would instead conduct the survey properly.

Likert forcefully opposed Lazarsfeld's proposal. As a consequence of his opposition, in November 1942 the Office of War Information, for which both groups worked, discontinued the funding for Likert's group (which continued to work for the Department of Agriculture until 1946). On conclusion of the war, various authoritative researchers – for instance Merton et al. (1946), Campbell (1945, 1946), Cartwright, Stouffer – began to adopt Lazarsfeld's compromise procedure. But the practice of using open-ended questions before and after interviews conducted with closed-ended questions gradually fell into disuse because it was found to be too cumbersome.

We know very well how things turned out: Wilson's standardized model prevailed, and contemporary practices of questionnaire administration consisted of having the interviewee choose an answer from a range of fixed response alternatives. This technique is certainly easier, but it produces numerous biases well known in the literature. The principal ones are these:

1 *misunderstanding of the response alternatives* by the interviewees: the existence of equal intervals between scale points has been questioned and criticized by Jordan (1965), Galtung (1967), Marradi (1980–1981), and Pawson (1982) because often respondents do not perceive as equal the intervals among response alternatives or scale points. This cognitive phenomenon has also been demonstrated by Amisano and Rinaldi (1988) and Gobo (1997);
2 *the multiple word meanings of response alternatives* due the communicative functions of quantifiers: respondents interpret in different ways and attribute *different* meanings to the *same* response alternatives as, for example, 'always', 'very often', 'often', 'never' (Simpson, 1944; Hakel, 1968). This phenomenon undermines the unidimensionality of the scale, the basis of comparability among respondents' responses and, in a broad sense, the validity of research results (Goocher, 1965, 1969; Moser and Kalton, 1951; Pepper, 1981; Hörmann, 1983; Newstead and Pollard, 1984; Groves, 1987, 1989; Bradburn and Miles, 1989; Moxey, 1990; Schaeffer, 1991; Pitrone, 1995; Moxey and Sanford, 1992; Gobo, 1997, 2006);

3 *the invented opinions* (or lies) phenomenon: fixed formats lead respondents to select an answer-opinion even if they do not have any opinions (Hartley, 1946; Ferber, 1956; Selltiz and Jahoda, 1963; Converse, 1964, 1970; Noelle-Neumann, 1970; Schuman and Presser, 1981; Schuman and Presser, 1983; Schuman and Scott, 1987);
4 *the influence of the response alternatives* on formation of the judgement: response alternatives are far from being a passive instrument collecting respondent's behaviour, attitudes or opinions only, because response alternatives play an 'informative function', affecting both respondent's attitudes and recall processes (Schwarz and Hippler, 1987; Clark and Shober, 1992; Schwarz, 1999);
5 *social desirability* effects (Kahn and Cannell, 1957; Cronbach, 1950; Crowne and Marlowe, 1960; Dohrenwend, 1966; Oppenheim, 1966; Hochstim, 1967; Sudman, 1967; Phillips and Clancy, 1972; Sudman and Bradburn, 1973; Blair et al., 1977; Stefanowska, 1979; Bradburn et al., 1979; Schwartz, 2000);
6 the *yea-saying* and *response set* phenomena: fixed formats lead respondents to select always the same response alternatives (Lentz, 1938; Cronbach, 1946, 1950; Gage et al., 1957; Couch and Keniston, 1960; Oppenheim, 1966; Hamilton, 1968; McKennell, 1974; Oskamp, 1977; Fisher et al., 1968; Bailey, 1978; Moun, 1988).

These are not biases of marginal importance. Indeed, at times their effect can be devastating (see Gobo, 2006: 286–7, Table 2). And researchers sincerely concerned with the quality of their data must necessarily seek remedies and try solutions able to reduce these biases.

BACK TO LIKERT

As we know, Likert lost the contest and his procedure fell into disuse. Nevertheless, a few decades later, the Norwegian methodologist Johan Galtung (1967: 120) reprised Likert's ideas and devised a variant of his procedure which he called 'open question/closed answer'.[3] Although this was apparently the reverse of Likert's 'fixed question/free answers' technique, in fact both procedures were guided by the same principle: make the interview into a conversation, let the interviewee answer freely in his/her own words, and thus release him/her from the researcher's schemes. Galtung describes it thus:

> for interviews, a distinction can be made between closed questions and closed answers. In the former, the respondent is given, orally, the answer alternatives: 'Which candidate do you favor, Allende, Frei or Duràn?', which means that the response variable is spelt out for him as in the questionnaire. In the latter he is asked 'Which candidate do you favor?' The question is open, but *the interviewer may have closed the answers by a precoding in his schedule. This, however, is only known to him and not to the respondent*, and hence serves only administrative purposes like facilitation of coding. It does not structure the mind of the respondent. (Galtung, 1967: 120, emphasis added)

However, Galtung did not push his proposal, and he seemed unaware of its potential to revolutionize the survey by making it much more interviewee-centred. Perhaps the cultural and scientific climate of the time was not ready for a change of such magnitude, because the procedure envisaged by Galtung required the interviewer to 'close' the open-ended questions put to the interviewee by interpreting the latter's answers and comments. For traditionalists, this was a decidedly delicate and 'dangerous' operation. Nevertheless, it made Likert's technique more agile, less time-consuming, and economically less costly.

The procedure described by Galtung is instead of vital importance if we wish to exploit a questionnaire's potential to the full. In fact, a survey is valid if it uses a wholly exhaustive set of response alternatives: or in other words, if these alternatives cover all possible states relative to a variable; or the entire range of the answers which an interviewee can give to a question. Given that this is difficult to achieve, researchers have dealt with the difficulty by including the residual response alternative 'Other'. Their (wholly ideal-typical) representation of the interviewee's reasoning is as follows:

1 the interviewer asks a question
2 the interviewee thinks and forms an opinion or a judgment
3 s/he looks at (or listens to) the response alternatives
4 s/he fails to find one corresponding to his/her opinion
5 s/he chooses the residual response alternative 'Other', furnishing the interviewer with an opinion not comprised in the range of the closed answers.

However, the results of surveys show that the response alternative 'Other' is little used by interviewees; not because they are generally satisfied by the response alternatives available to them, but rather because they are cognitively lazy. Hence, if we want to use closed-ended questions, as is correct to do in a survey, we must construct questions with exhaustive response alternatives. But, since this is very difficult to do, the alternative is to give the interviewers the task of collecting interviewee opinions which do not fall within the range of answers.

Second, experimental research on surveys shows that interviewees follow, not this ideal-typical chain of reasoning, but an entirely different one:

1 the interviewer asks a question
2 the interviewee looks at (or listens to) the response alternatives available
3 s/he adapts his/her opinion to the response alternatives available, letting him/herself be influenced by them.

In other words, the response scales are not simple and passive 'measurement instruments' used by interviewees to report their behaviours (Schwarz and Hippler, 1987: 164), but active instruments which *construct* the opinions and behaviours of interviewees, who are induced by social desirability to seek the median behaviour in the response alternatives. This is why Galtung's procedure could remedy these two serious biases.

Beyond mixed methods

This procedure represents also a getting over the (important) issue of combining qualitative and quantitative methods – termed 'mixed methods' – which has recently come back into favour. This issue has led those approaches which succeed a separate use of different methodologies (survey, discursive interviews, focus groups, etc.) within the same research project. However, it appears to be costly and time-consuming.

Galtung's technique (which I rename 'conversational survey') is a valid alternative, given that many of the advantages of mixed methods are obtained using a single method. In other words, Galtung's technique combines both qualitative and quantitative approaches *in a single instrument*, in the wake of other techniques (now widely used) like the 'delphi method' (Dalkey and Helmer, 1963) or the 'mystery shopper' (Gobo, 2008: 318–9) which rely on this mixed approach.

An application

In the autumn of 2001 I directed a survey on a probability sample of 629 students enrolled at the Faculty of Political Science of the University of Milan, where I currently teach. The sampling frame consisted of 7,115 students. The survey was carried out by means of telephone interviews conducted by 98 students attending my course on Social Research Methods (an average of six interviews per student). I constructed the questionnaire in class together with the students, and they invented all the fixed response alternatives. Moreover, they tested the questionnaire four times before drawing up the definitive version. They were therefore well acquainted with both the questions and the response alternatives.

It was an exceptional experience because it is rare for the researchers (those who construct the questionnaire), the interviewers, and the interviewees to share the same cultural and communicative code, as happened in this case because all of them had the same status: that of being students of political science.

Following Galtung's procedure, numerous questions were phrased with an open format as if they were open-ended questions. As the interviewee answered, the interviewer tried (*during* the telephone interview) to locate his/her answer within the pre-set range, which only the interviewer knew. If the answer could be placed within this range, the interviewer made a brief note which s/he then expanded on conclusion of the interview, inserting it in the residual response alternative 'Other'.

There follow some examples of questions available to the interviewer (because the interviewee was ignorant of the fixed response alternatives). The instructions for the interviewer are in brackets:

3. How do you travel to university? (*Free answer: also indicate several means of transport*)

1. On foot	❑
2. By bicycle	❑

3. By scooter or motorbike	❑
4. By car	❑
5. By tram/bus/trolley bus	❑
6. By coach	❑
7. By underground	❑
8. By train	❑
9. Other	❑

6. Who advised you to choose the Faculty of Political Science? (*Free answer but report the main source of influence*)

1. No one, I chose it myself	❑
2. Parents	❑
3. Brothers/sisters	❑
4. Relatives	❑
5. Friends/classmates	❑
6. Teachers at high school	❑
7. Acquaintances	❑
8. Employers and work colleagues	❑
9. Graduates in Political Science	❑
10. Career counsellors	❑
11. The Faculty Guide	❑
12. Newspaper articles	❑
13. TV	❑
14. Aptitude test	❑
15. Other ⋮	❑
98. Doesn't know/Can't remember	❑

18. What are your main difficulties with the course content, i.e. what is taught? (*Free answer but mark only the two main difficulties*)

1. No problems	❑
2. Lacks the **basic knowledge** to understand the course content	❑
3. The lectures are **difficult**	❑
4. The lectures are **unclear**	❑
5. The lecturers explain **too quickly**	❑
6. **Mismatch** between the content of lectures and exams	❑
7. The **syllabuses** are too wide-ranging	❑
8. The **syllabuses** are out of date	❑
9. The **teaching aids** are inadequate (course hand-outs)	❑
10. The **teaching technologies** are inadequate (OHPs, video recorders, etc.)	❑
11. The **set texts** are difficult	❑
12. Other ⋮	❑
98. Doesn't know	❑

19. What, in order of importance, are your three main difficulties with your degree course as a whole? (*Free answer but write the number next to the item indicated by the interviewer*)

1. No difficulties	
2. Difficulties with the lecturers	
3. Difficulties with the other students on the course	
4. Study load (excessively demanding syllabuses)	
5. Lack of information	
6. Course topics (difficult)	

7. Finding a suitable study method	
8. The high level of self-organization and self-management required	
9. Library services	
10. Lack of places to study	
11. The splitting of the Faculty among several sites	
12. The high costs of attending university	
13. Shortage of computers	
14. The disorganization of the Faculty (belated information, overcrowding, etc.)	
15. Too many exam sessions	
16. Other : :	
98. Doesn't know	

25. According to you, in what sectors do Graduates in Political Science have the best chances of finding employment? (*Free answer but mark three sectors at most*)

1. Politics and political party organizations	❑
2. Employers' associations (industrial relations)	❑
3. Trade unions (industrial relations)	❑
4. Civil service	❑
5. Teaching	❑
6. Human resources management	❑
7. Journalism, publishing, information media	❑
8. Research institutes (public and private)	❑
9. Marketing and advertising	❑
10. Public relations	❑

11. Diplomatic corps, EC and international organizations	❑
12. Banking and insurance	❑
13. Financial consultancy (accountancy, etc.)	❑
14. Business	❑
15. Social services	❑
16. Other ⋮	❑
98. Doesn't know	❑

5. What were the main reasons for your decision to enrol at the Faculty of Political Science? (*Free answer but mark three reasons at most*)	
1. No entrance test	❑
2. Relatively easy degree course	❑
3. Attendance not compulsory	❑
4. Compatible with work. Possible to work and study at the same time	❑
5. Not accepted by faculty of first choice	❑
6. Subjects not excessively technical; it is a non-specialist degree course	❑
7. Close to home	❑
8. Wanted to go to university but did not know which degree course to select (choice by exclusion)	❑
9. Multidisciplinary programme	❑
10. To address politicial, social and cultural issues	❑
11. Because s/he liked it	❑
12. Because of the subjects taught	❑
13. The good reputation of the Faculty	❑
14. The prestige of certain lecturers	❑
15. Useful for job	❑
16. Because of employment prospects	❑
17. To find a culturally stimulating environment	❑

18. Because some of his/her friends had enrolled 19. Persuaded to do so by parents	❑ ❑
20. Other ⋮	❑
98. Doesn't know/Can't remember	❑

Question no. 5 on motives (which guided the choice of the Faculty of Political Science), like other questions, has a long list of item-motives; too long for the interviewer to handle straightforwardly. To help the interviewer, the motives were then divided into three areas[4] matching the researcher's classification:

1 instrumental motives (items 1–8)
2 vocational motives (items 9–17)
3 social influence (items 18–19).

The interviewers were thus helped in their task (and also because they knew the items well, having been involved in writing them). Then, if they were not immediately able to locate the interviewee's answer in the range of the pre-established items, they continued to talk to the interviewee until they understood which precoded item best matched his/her case. If there was still no matching item, they marked 'Other', noting down key words from the reply. They then wrote a more developed comment (2–3 lines) upon completion of the interview.

If the interview was conducted face-to-face, the interviewer was also able to ask the interviewee if s/he agreed with the response alternatives selected (on his/her behalf). If the interviewee disagreed, the meaning of his/her comments was re-negotiated in order to find (at this point with the interviewee) the most appropriate response alternatives.

CONVERSATIONALIZING QUESTIONS: BROADENING THE INTERVIEWER'S TASKS

As I have emphasized, application of Galtung's procedure requires changing the interviewer's contemporary role and broadening his/her tasks.

The role of interviewer has long been discussed in the survey literature. As Converse (1987: 95) reminds us, in the 1920s and 1930s some academic, and especially a good deal of the market research, literature 'placed the interviewer in some sort of middle ground of freedom and responsibility, with questions less standardized (...) There was concern that trying to standardize the interview more fully might interfere with the communication process'.

The interviewer was advised to act responsibly, with the freedom to 'conversationalize' questions without modifying their meaning. The directors of market research studies believed that the standardization of interviewer's behaviour was mandatory in laboratory experiments, but that it could not work in interview situations, where constant adaptation of the questionnaire to respondents and social situations was necessary. This kind of interviewer autonomy is still fairly commonplace in market research, though nobody would admit to it.

At the beginning of the 1950s, this (wise) practice was replaced, at least in academic research, by another one (standardization) affected by the behaviourist perspective (Hamilton, 1929; Rice, 1929), and it still affects contemporary survey methodology. According to this practice, the response alternatives must be selected by respondents only. However, respondents are often biased in *their* interpretation of the meanings of response alternatives, which are often quite different from the meanings attributed by researchers. Because the assumption of a natural correspondence between psychological and numerical intervals has not yet been proven (Pawson, 1982: 54), and formal languages are incompatible with natural ones (Pawson, 1982, 1983), it is necessary to let interviewers act as interpreters in order to make them responsible for selection *on behalf of* the respondent (Galtung, 1967: 120) and for (always imperfect) translations from the respondent's ordinary language to the formal or mathematical language underlying measurement scales. As Groves states 'interviewers should be trained in the concepts inherent in the questions and be allowed to probe, rephrase and adapt the questionnaire to individual respondent needs' (1989: 404).

From this perspective, interviewers and respondents should work together to 'jointly construct' the meaning of questions and answers (Mishler, 1986), because there is a conflict between interviews as conversation and interviews as data-collection, owing to the fact that surveys (in order to succeed) rely on conversational norms which suppress 'interactional resources that routinely mediate uncertainties of relevance and interpretation' (Suchman and Jordan, 1990: 241) in conversations.[5] As Schober and Conrad (1997) have shown, in a laboratory experiment with trained telephone interviewers using both standardized techniques and flexible interviewing, there is no substantial difference in response accuracy when the concepts in the questions are clearly mapped onto the fictional situations of respondents. In addition, and even more interesting, when the mapping was less clear, flexible interviewing increased accuracy by almost 60%.[6]

The conversational survey and its enemies . . . and supporters

However, opposition to this procedure is widespread in the literature, even if it seems to be based more on a methodological narrative than on data. Hyman et al. (1942), Feldman et al. (1951), Hauck and Steinkamp (1964) and Clausen (1968) re-appraised the alarmism about the effect of interviewer's attitudes, opinion and personality on respondent's answers and showed a bias 'of moderate magnitude' (about 10%) (Hyman et al., 1954: 244). As regards Hyman et al.'s theory that interviewer's 'attitude-structure expectations' (1942: 59), 'role expectations'

(1942: 62) and 'probability expectations' (1942: 64), Hagenaars and Heinen (1982: 125) write that Hyman's statements are based upon few data. Likewise, Sudman and Bradburn (1974: 138) believe that the biases introduced by questionnaire tasks, social desirability, forgetting and so on, are more dangerous than the interviewer's behaviour. Bradburn and Sudman (1979: 50, and 171–2) conclude that interviewer errors do not have significant effects on the quality of data. Dohrenwend and Richardson (1956) argue that most errors are caused by overly tight control and that interviewers must learn to be more responsive to respondents. Peneff (1988) has provided a very revealing insight into practice on the ground. Having observed interviewers involved in a large field survey, Peneff maintains that in reality survey interviewers adopt the qualitative interviewer's skills. They try to interest respondents by letting their own personalities show, they interact in a non-neutral way, and add personal comments to avoid misunderstanding or refusal. This should not be seen as cheating, but as adapting the interview process to the subject's definition of the situation. The interviewers studied by Peneff, who were regarded by the field survey director as his most successful interviewers, proved to be those who used these techniques the most (the survey director was appalled when Peneff told him this). Peneff uses this finding to argue that in practice the methods of qualitative sociology penetrate the survey interview.

Nevertheless, the dogma on standardization is still alive. In a survey conducted in a valley area of South Wales, Michael Brenner – following the method of Cannell et al. (1975) – documented that approximately 30% of questions were not correctly asked by interviewers, and that this bias had a negative effect on 13% of responses (1982: 155). However, this result is inconsistent with the data presented by Brenner later: 'when these questions were asked directively so that definite answers were suggested to the respondents' the percentage of answers considered adequate (by the author) increased to 20% (1982: 157). This finding means that the interviewer's directive style produces a remarkable increase in the response quality, larger than when the methodologically correct non-directive style of asking questions is used. The complementary results of Brenner's research indirectly document the thesis of this essay: it is not the interviewer's non-standardized behaviour itself that is responsible for response errors, but only *some* incorrect moves by the interviewer in modifying question meaning, fast reading of questions, not using the card required with the question and so on.

Dijkstra and van der Zouwen (1988) have replicated both Cannell et al.'s (1975) and Brenner's (1982) studies. In relation to interviewers, they found: a mean of 4% of *deviations from the questionnaire*; 8% of *irrelevant behaviours*; a mean of 10% of *hinting* from the questionnaire (p. 30) and if the interviewer has to probe further, the percentage of suggestive questions posed by the interviewer ranges from 15 to 23% (p. 31); and finally 16% of *choosing behaviours* (on behalf of respondents). Because an interviewer's error does not *necessarily* produce a response error, the crucial question is this: to what extent do the interviewer's errors really affect the data quality? In other words, as Schober and Conrad stress:

> since interviewers always influence responses, this raises the question of which kinds of influence are benign and which are not. We argue that the criterion should be how interviewer behaviours affect response accuracy – that is, how well responses correspond with the definition the survey author had in the mind (2002: 69).

In this regard, it is important to recall Beatty's statement:

> We are, after all, interested in reducing *total* error in surveys. If attacking the slightest interviewers deviation brings about modest reduction of interviewer error – but simultaneously causes a *great increase* in error from the respondent, who is unable to draw on the communicative resources of an informed, intelligent interviewer – then the strategy is self-defeating (1995: 154).

Comparing the performance of *bad* interviewers who committed many errors with the style of *good* interviewers who made only a few, Dijkstra and van der Zouwen (1988: 32) show that the size of bias introduced by bad interviewers is not so marked as to point to the interviewer's performance. Indeed, even a serious error such as 'choosing behaviour on the part of the interviewer appeared to have the least effect in the observed relations between respondent type and respondent answer'.

Directing too much attention to interviewer's effects is like, to use an old saying, 'not seeing the wood for the trees'. The wood is the long list of biases mainly imputable to the questionnaire (or to the researchers as its designers) and to respondents (see Gobo, 2006: 286–7, Table 2).

CONCLUSION

From the 1930s onwards, the use of open-ended questions was resisted on the grounds that the procedure was uneconomical: in particular, such questions took longer (and were therefore more costly) to administer, classify and interpret (Oppenheim, 1966: 41).

However, Galtung's technique has two considerable advantages. First, it obviates these drawbacks (i.e. it is not so uneconomical); second, it yields all the advantages of open-ended questions, particularly their greater fidelity compared with closed-ended questions (which force interviewees to think in the same way as the researcher and to use his/her cognitive categories), and the fact that such questions grasp more dimensions of meaning (Groves et al., 1992: 60).

Galtung's technique therefore collects more valid answers without increasing the costs of administering the questionnaire. In fact, the conversation time between INT (interviewee) and R (respondent) lost in giving the answer compensates for the time taken by the interviewer (or by the interviewee, if s/he is given cards) to read the list of the response alternatives.

Obviously, this procedure releases the interviewer from the obligation of standardizing his/her behaviour. But only this, because the standardization of meanings (as we shall see) is still an irremovable obligation which can be fulfilled by flexible interviewing. Yet the magnitude of the (alleged) 'dangerousness' of the interviewer is still wholly to be quantified, given that interviewer's errors seem of secondary importance and far smaller than researcher's and respondent's errors. As Bradburn states 'the characteristics of the task(s of the questionnaire) are the major source of response effects and are, in general, much larger than effects due to interviewer or respondent characteristics' (1983: 291).

In addition Schaeffer reminds us:

> criticisms of traditional standardized interviewing are particularly effective when taken together with research which suggests that the recall of events may be improved by procedures that do not fit neatly within the linear structure of standardized interview (Means et al., 1992), that a less formal style of standardized interviewing may be more motivating (e.g. Dijkstra, 1987), and that interviewers do not always implement standardization well (...) and a formal standardized interview may not be the best social environment for stimulating and motivating recall of complex topics. (1995: 83)

This consideration leads to the problem of how to improve data quality, and how Galtung's procedure can be implemented efficaciously. Rather than pursing the illusory goal of improving the wording only in order to reduce the need for interviewer probes (as suggested by Fowler and Mangione, 1990: 46) because 'total elimination of interviewer error is impossible' (Beatty, 1995: 155), we can achieve data quality by giving the interviewer a more active role, in order to bridge questionnaire and respondent, and to reduce the gap between researchers' and respondents' meanings. In David Riesman's (1958: 305) words: 'the task of the interviewer, as I see it, (is) to adapt the standard questionnaire to the unstandardized respondents'.

Several studies[7] have evidenced that standardizing the stimuli (i.e. questions, items, response alternatives and interviewer's behaviour) does not necessary imply standardization of their meanings, which should remain the main aim of every data collection. As Houtkoop-Seenstra concludes:

> having studied tape-recorded standardized survey interviews for some years now, I have become increasingly convinced that the quest for standardization is no longer tenable, at least if its purpose is to generate not only reliable, but also valid, research data (...) We should allow interviewers-as-spokesperson to discuss with respondents the intended meaning and purpose of questions, as well as the respondent's answers. This discussion may increase the validity of the research data, even though a more flexible way of interviewing may at times cause inappropriate interviewer behaviour, such as presenting the respondent with leading questions. (2000: 180, 182)

Clearly, the aim of reducing respondent errors by broadening the interviewer's tasks will lead to an increase in interviewer effects. However, the dilemma is deciding which kind of errors we prefer to minimize. In addition, the magnitude of interviewer's errors is far smaller than those of respondent's because (a) a trained interviewer knows the purpose and correct meaning of questions, items and response alternatives better than respondents, and (b) the meanings in the (relatively small) 'interviewers' community' are more consistent than in the mass of socially and culturally different respondents.

In other words, the questionnaire and interviewer's behaviour must be interviewee-centred and *really* tailored to respondents and their differences.

NOTES

1 Galtung points out a terminological imprecision which had been circulating for decades at the time and is still current today: 'the response variable is spelt out for the respondent, so that all he has to do is to choose the value that comes closest to his response. This is the "closed question", a misnomer since it is really a "closed answer"' (1967: 119).

2 Rogers originally called his approach 'non-directive therapy' but later replaced the term 'non-directive' with the term 'client-centred' and then later used the term 'person-centred'.

3 When devising this procedure, Galtung was probably inspired by Bales' famous study (1951) in which he described an observational grid (consisting of a limited number of actions very similar to the responses alternatives of a questionnaire) for use by researchers to conduct systematic observation of the interaction between students and teachers.

4 These three categories have also been used as recode in order to deal with the problem of statistical significance.

5 It would be beyond the scope of this essay to go into the serious interactional problems which a standardized behaviour poses. Interviewers who strictly follow the rules of standardized interviewing (as stated, e.g. in Brenner, 1985: 19; Survey Research Center of Berkeley, 1990; Bailey, 1978; Fowler, 1984; Fowler and Mangione, 1990) frequently present themselves to respondents as impolite, insensitive and unintelligent because they ask redundant questions. Houtkoop-Seenstra (2000: 183) proposes: 'we should give interviewers the freedom to draw inferences and then verify them with the respondents. If a respondent (in a previous comment) mentions 'my husband', the interviewer should not ask whether the respondent is 'single, married, a widow or living together' but should be allowed to verify that the respondent is married (...) in a leading manner'.

6 Houtkoop-Seenstra (2000: 182) suggests allowing interviewers to accept unformatted answers because respondents 'have a hard time remembering the list of response options for the duration of the interview. When interviewers respond to an unformatted answer by re-offering the response options, thus implicitly informing the respondent how s/he should answer the questions, the transcripts show that respondents follow this rule for only a short time. A few questions later we find them providing unformatted answers again'.

7 Nuckols (1953); Cicourel (1964: 108); Galtung (1967: 116); Bourdieu et al. (1968: 70); Gostkowski (1974: 19); Marradi (1984); Pitrone (1984: 35–6); Mishler (1986); Briggs (1984); Suchman and Jordan (1990); Houtkoop-Seenstra (2000: 180–4).

REFERENCES

Amisano, Ernesto and Rinaldi, Giuseppe (1988) Confronto tra forme diverse di 'chiusura' degli items Likert. In A. Marradi (ed.) *Costruire il dato.* Milano: Angeli, pp. 44–62.

Bailey, Kenneth D. (1978) *Methods in Social Research.* New York: Free Press.

Bales, Robert F. (1951) *Interaction Process Analysis. A Method for the Study of Small Groups.* Reading (MA): Addison-Wesley.

Beatty, Paul (1995) Understanding the standardized/non-standardized interviewing controversy. *Journal of Official Statistics,* 11(2): 147–60.

Blair, E., Sudman, S., Bradburn, N., and Stocking, C. (1977) How to ask questions about drinking and sex: Response effects in measuring consumer behavior. *Journal of Marketing Research,*14: 316–21.

Bourdieu, Pierre, Chamboredon, J.C., and Passeron, J.C. (1968) *Le métier de sociologue. Problèmes épistémologiques.* Paris: Mounton.

Bradburn, Norman M. (1983) Response effects. In P.H. Rossi, J.D. Wright, and A.B. Anderson (eds) *Handbook of Survey Research.* New York: Academic Press.

Bradburn, Norman M. and Miles, Carrie (1989) *Vague Quantifiers.* In E. Singer and S. Presser (eds) *Survey Research Methods.* Chicago: University Pres.

Bradburn, Norman M. and Sudman, Seymour, Blair Edward (1979) *Improving Interviewing Method and Questionnaire Design.* San Francisco: Jossey-Bass.

Brenner, Michael (1982) Response-effects of 'role-restricted' characteristics of the interviewer. In W. Dijkstra and J. van der Zouwen (eds) *Response Behavior in the Survey-interview.* London and New York: Academic Press.

Brenner, Michael (1985) In M. Brenner, J. Brown, and D. Canter (eds) *The Research Interview. Use and Approaches.* London: Academic Press.

Briggs, Charles L. (1984) Learning how to ask: Native metacommunicative competence and the incompetence of the fieldworkers. *Language and Society*, 13: 1–28.

Campbell, Angus (1945) Interviewing for food habit surveys. *First Session: The Problem of Food Acceptability*, Committee on Food Habits (mimeographed).

Campbell, Angus (1946) Polling, open interviewing, and the problem of interpretation. *Journal of Social Issues*, 2: 67–71.

Cannell, Charles F., Lawson, S.A., and Hauser, D.L. (1975) *A Technique for Evaluating Interviewer Performance.* Ann Arbor, MI: Institute for Social Research.

Cicourel, Aaron Victor (1964) *Method and Measurement in Sociology.* New York: The Free Press.

Clark, Herbert H. and Schober, Michael F. (1992) Asking questions and influencing answers. In J.M. Tanur (ed.) *Questions about Questions. Inquiries into the Cognitive Bases of Surveys.* New York: Russel Sage Foundation, pp. 15–48.

Clausen, A.R. (1968) Response validity: Vote report. *Public Opinion Quarterly*, 32: 588–606.

Converse Jean Marie (1987) *Survey Research in the United States: Roots and Emergence 1890–1960.* Berkeley: University of California Press.

Converse, Philip E. (1964) The nature of belief system in mass-publics. In David E. Apter (a cura di), *Ideology and Discontent.* Glencoe: Free Press. 202–61.

Converse, Philip E. (1970) Attitudes and non attitudes: continuation of a dialogue. In Edward R. Tufte (ed.) *The Quantitative Analysis of Social Problems.* Reading: Addison-Wesley.

Couch, A.S. and Keniston K. (1960) Yeasayers and naysayers: Agreeing response set as a personality variable. *Journal of Abnormal and Social Psychology*, 60: 151–74.

Cronbach, Lee Joseph (1946) Response sets and test validity. *Educational and Psychological Measurement*, 6: 475–94.

Cronbach, Lee Joseph (1950) Further evidence on response sets and test design. *Educational and Psychological Measurement*, 10: 192–203.

Crowne, D.P. and Marlowe, D. (1960). A new scale of social desirability independent of psychopathology. *Journal of Consulting Psychology*, 24: 349–54.

Dalkey, N.C. and Helmer, O. (1963) An experimental application of the Delphi Method to the use of experts. *Management Science*, 9(3): 458–67.

Dijkstra, Wil (1987) Interviewing style and respondent behavior: an experimental study of the survey interview. *Sociological Research Methods and Research*, 16: 309–34.

Dijkstra, Wil and van der Zouwen, Johannes (1988) Types of inadequate interviewer behaviour. In Willem E. Saris, and Irmtraud N. Gallhofer (eds) *Sociometric Research, volume 1: Data Collection and Scaling.* London: MacMillan Press.

Dohrenwend Bruce P. (1966) Social status and psychological disorder: An issue of substance and an issue of method. *American Sociological Review*, 31: 14–34.

Dohrenwend, Barbara S. and Richardson, S. (1956) Analysis of interviewer behaviour. *Human Organization*, 15(2): 29–32.

Feldman, Jacob J., Hyman, Herbert H., and Hart, Clyde W. (1951) A field study of interviewer effects on the quality of survey data. *Public Opinion Quarterly*, 15: 734–61.

Ferber, R. (1956) The effect of respondent ignorance on survey results. *Journal of the American Statistical Association*, 51(276): 576–86.

Fisher, S.T., Weiss, D.J., and Davis, R.V. (1968) A comparison of Likert and pair-comparison techniques in multivariate attitude scaling. *Educational and Psychological Measurement*, 28(1): 81–94.

Fowler, Floyd J. Jr. (1984) *Survey Research Methods*. Bevery Hills: Sage.

Fowler, Floyd J. Jr. and Mangione, Thomas W. (1990) *Standardized Survey Interviewing. Minimizing Interviewer-Related Error*. Newbury Park: Sage.

Gage, N.L., Leavitt, G.S., and Stone, G.C. (1957), The psychological meaning of acquiescent set for authoritarianism. *Journal of Abnormal and Social Psychology*, 55: 98–103.

Galtung, John (1967) *Theory and Method of Social Research*. Oslo: Universitets Forlaget.

Gobo, Giampietro (1997) *Le risposte e il loro contesto. Processi cognitivi e comunicativi nelle interviste standardizzate*. Milano: Angeli.

Gobo, Giampietro (2006) Set them free. Improving data quality by broadening interviewer's task. *International Journal of Social Research Methodology. Theory & Practice*, 9(4).

Gobo, Giampietro (2008) *Doing Ethnography*. London: Sage.

Goocher, B.E. (1965) Effect of attitude and experience on the selection of frequency adverbs. *Journal of Verbal Learning and Verbal Behaviour*, 4: 193–5.

Goocher, B.E. (1969) More about often. *American Psychologist*, 24: 608–9.

Gostkowski, Zygmunt (1974) Toward empirical humanization of mass survey. *Quality and Quantity*, 8(1): 11–26.

Groves, Robert M. (1987) Survey research without an unifying theory. *Public Opinion Quarterly*, 51(4): 156–72.

Groves, Robert M. (1989) *Survey Errors and Survey Costs*. New York: Wiley & Sons.

Groves, Robert M., Fultz, Nancy H., and Martin, Elisabeth (1992) Direct questioning about comprehension in a survey setting. In J.M. Tanur (ed.) *Questions about Questions. Inquiries into the Cognitive Bases of Surveys*. New York: Russel Sage Foundation, pp. 49–61.

Hagenaars, Jacques A. and Heinen, Ton G. (1982) Effects of role-independent interviewer characteristics on responses. In W. Dijkstra Wil and J. van der Zouwen (eds) *Response Behaviour in the Survey-interview*. London and New York: Academic Press.

Hakel, M.D. (1968) How often is often? *American Psychologist*, 23(7): 533–4.

Hamilton, D.L. (1968) Personality attributes associated with extreme response style. *Psychological Bulletin*, 69: 192–203.

Hamilton, G.V. (1929) *A Research in Marriage*. New York: Boni and Liveright.

Hartley, Eugene L. (1946) *Problems in Prejudices*. New York: Columbia University Press.

Hauck, M. and Steinkamp, S. (1964) *Survey Reliability and Interviewer Competence*, Bureau of Economic and Business Research. Urbana , IL: University of Illinois.

Hochstim, J.R. (1967) A critical comparison of three strategies of collecting data from households. *Journal of the American Statistical Association*. 62: 976–89.

Hörmann, H. (1983) The calculating listener or how many are einige, mehrere, and ein paar (some, several, and a few)? In R. Bauerle, C. Schwarze, and A. Von Stechow (eds) *Meaning, Use, and Interpretation of Language*. Berlln de Gruyter, pp. 221–34.

Houtkoop-Seenstra, Hanneke (2000) *Interaction and the Standardized Survey Interview. The Living Questionnaire*. Cambridge: Cambridge University Press.

Hyman, Herbert H., Cobb, William J., Feldman, Jacob F., Hart, Clyde W., and Stember, Charles H. (1942) *Interviewing in Social Research*. Chicago: University of Chicago Press.

Hyman, Herbert H., Cobb, William J., Feldman, Jacob F., Hart, Clyde W., and Stember, Charles H. (1954) *Interviewing in Social Research*. Chicago: University of Chicago Press (new edition).

Jordan, Nehemiah (1965) The 'asymmetry' of 'liking' and 'disliking': a phenomenon meriting further reflections and research. *Public Opinion Quarterly*, 29(2): 315–22.

Kahn, Robert L. and Cannell, Charles F. (1957) *The Dynamics of Interviewing*. New York: John Wiley & Sons.

Lazarsfeld, Paul F. (1944), The controversy over detailed interviews – An offer for negotiation. *Public Opinion Quarterly*, 8: 38–60.

Lentz, Theodore F. (1938) Acquiescence as a factor in the measurement of personality. *Psychological Bulletin*, 35: 659.

Marradi, Alberto (1980/81) Misurazione e scale: qualche riflessione e una proposta. *Quaderni di Sociologia*, 29(4): 595–639.

Marradi, Alberto (1984) *Concetti e metodo per la ricerca sociale*. Firenze: La Giuntina.

McKennell, Aubrey (1974) Surveying attitudes structures: A discussion of principles and procedures. *Quality and Quantity*, 7(2): 203–94.

Means, B., Swan, G.E., Jobe, J.B., and Esposito, J.L. (1992) An alternative approach to obtaining personal history data. In P. Biemer, R. Groves, L. Lyberg, N. Mathiowetz, and S. Sudman (eds) *Measurement Errors in Surveys*. New York: John Wiley.

Merton, R.K., Fiske, Marjorie, and Curtis, Alberta (1946) *Mass Persuasion. The Social Psychology of a War Bond Drive*. New York–London: Harper & Brothers Publishers.

Mishler, Elliot G. (1986) *Research Interviewing. Context and Narrative*. Cambridge, MA: Harvard University Press.

Moun, Terbiørn (1988) Yea-saying and mood of the day effects. *Social Indicators Resarch*, 20: 117–39.

Moser, Claus A. and Kalton, Graham (1951) *Survey Methods in Social Investigation*. London: Heinemann.

Moxey, Linda M. (1990) *Expectations and the Interpretation of Quantifiers*, manuscript.

Moxey, Linda M. and Sanford, Anthony J. (1992) Context effects and the communicative functions of quantifiers: Implications for their use in attitude research. In N. Schwarz and S. Sudman (eds) *Context Effects in Social and Psychological Research*. New York: Springer-Verlag, pp. 279–96.

Newstead, S.E. and Pollard, P. (1984) *Quantifiers and Context*. Department of Psychology, Plymouth Polytechnic. Plymouth: Technical report.

Noelle-Neumann, Elisabeth (1970) Wanted: Rules for wording structured questionnaires. *Public Opinion Quarterly*, XXXIV(2): 191–201.

Nuckols, R. (1953) A note on pre-testing public opinion questions. *Journal of Applied Psychology*, 37(2): 119–20.

Oppenheim, A.N. (1966) *Questionnaire Design and Attitude Measurement*. New York: Basic Books.

Oskamp, S. (1977) *Attitudes and Opinions*. Englewood Cliffs, NJ: Prentice-Hall.

Pawson, Ray (1982) Desperate measures. *British Journal of Sociology*, 33(1): 35–63.

Pawson, Ray (1983) Language and measurement. *British Journal of Sociology*, 34(4): 491–7.

Payne, Geoff, Williams, Malcolm, and Chamberlain, Suzanne (2004) Methodological pluralism in British sociology. *Sociology*, 38(1): 153–63.

Peneff, Jean (1988) The observer observed: French survey researchers at work. *Social Problems*, 35(5): 520–35.

Pepper, S. (1981) Problems in the quantification of frequency expressions. In D.W. Fiske (ed.) *Problems with Language Imprecision*. San Francisco: Jossey-Bass.

Phillips, D.L. and Clancy, K.J. (1972) Some effects of 'social desiderability' in survey studies. *American Journal of Sociology*, 77(5): 921–38.

Pitrone, Maria Concetta (1984) *Il sondaggio*. Milano: Angeli.

Pitrone, Maria Concetta (1995) La formulazione delle domande: alcuni problemi metodologici. *Sociologia e Ricerca Sociale*, 47/48: 45–76.

Rice, Stuart A. (1929) Contagious bias in the interview: a methodological note. *American Journal of Sociology*, 35: 420–3.

Riesman, David (1958) Some observations on the interviewing in the teacher apprehension study. In P.F. Lazarsfeld and T. Wagner Jr., *The Academic Mind*. Glencoe, IL: Free Press, pp. 266–370.

Schaeffer, Nora Cate (1991) Hardly ever or constantly. *Public Opinion Quarterly*, 55: 395–423.

Schaeffer, Nora Cate (1995) A Decade of Questions. *Journal of Official Statistics*, 11(1): 79–92.

Schober, Michael F. and Conrad, Frederick (1997) Does conversational interviewing reduce survey measurement errors? *Public Opinion Quarterly*, 61: 576–602.

Schober, Michael F. and Conrad, Frederick (2002) A collaborative view of standardized survey interviews. In Douglas W. Maynard, Hanneke Houtkoop-Streenstra, Johannes der Zouwen, and Nora Cate Shaeffer (eds) *Standardization and Tacit Knowledge*. New York: Wiley, pp. 67–94.

Schuman, Howard and Presser, Stanley (1979) The open and closed question. *American Sociological Review*, 64(5): 692–712.
Schuman, Howard and Presser, Stanley (1981) *Questions and Answers in Attitude Surveys: Experiments on Question Form, Wording, and Context.* New York: Academic Press.
Schuman, Howard and Presser, Stanley (1983) Public opinion and public ignorance: the fine line between attitudes and non attitudes. *American Journal of Sociology*, 88: 7–19.
Schuman, Howard and Scott, J. (1987) Problems in the use of survey questions to measure public opinion. *Science*, 236: 957–9.
Schwarz, Norbert (1999), Self reports: How the questions shape the answers. *American Psychologist*, 54(2): 93–105.
Schwartz, Norbert (2000) Social judgement and attitudes: warmer, more social, and less conscious. *European Journal of Social Psychology* 30: 146–76.
Schwarz, Norbert and Hippler, Hans-J. (1987) What response scales may tell your respondents: informative functions of response alternative. In H-J. Hippler, N. Schwarz, and S. Sudman (eds) *Social Information Processing and Survey Methodology.* New York: Springer-Verlag, pp. 163–77.
Selltiz, Claire e Jahoda Marie (eds) (1963) *Research Methods in Social Relations.* New York: Holt & Rinehart.
Simpson, R.H. (1944) The specific meanings of certain terms indicating different degrees of frequency. *Quarterly Journal of Speech*, 30: 328–30.
Stefanowska, M. (1979) Feeling of 'cultural inadequacy' and validity of respondent answer in survey on book reading. In Z. Gostkowski (ed.) *Investigations on Survey Methodology.* Warszawa.
Suchman, Lucy and Jordan, Brigitte (1990) Interactional troubles in face-to-face survey interviews. *Journal of the American Statistical Association*, 85(409): 232–53.
Sudman, Seymour (1967) *Reducing the Cost of Surveys.* Chicago: Aldine.
Sudman, Seymour and Bradburn, Norman M. (1973) Effects of time and memory factors on response in surveys. *Journal of the American Statistical Association*, 68: 805–15.
Sudman, Seymour and Bradburn, Norman M. (1974) *Response Effects in Surveys.* Chicago: Aldine.
Survey Research Center (Berkeley) (1990) *Interviewer's Basic Training Manual.* Berkeley: Mimeo.

13

Mixed Methods for Construct Validation

John H. Hitchcock and
Bonnie K. Nastasi

INTRODUCTION

The literature on culture and how it influences human behavior is deep, broad, and informed by a number of specialties within the social sciences (Cole, 1996). Hence, it is unrealistic to attempt to do justice to the issues within a single chapter. Instead, we take a narrow focus on why culture should be carefully considered during psychological assessment and the provision of intervention services. In doing so, we review some of our own efforts to capitalize on mixed methods approaches to address the challenge of addressing cultural factors when dealing with a cornerstone of social science: construct identification and subsequent validation. The overall approach described here mixes elements of qualitative and quantitative inquiry to yield findings that are probably hard, if not impossible, to obtain using mono- or even multi-method approaches. We are not suggesting that mixed methods designs are inherently superior to other approaches; that determination is a function of the research question at hand. But in the examples discussed below, the research questions all have in common the concern of how can we account for culture when identifying constructs that we believe are influenced by shared ideas, behavioral norms, and values within a target group. Before describing the methods used, we first introduce a series of foundational ideas to justify our reasons for addressing cultural factors. Following this section, we summarize a host of research findings from work carried out in

Sri Lanka, a context that demands attention to cultural differences between the study participants and a study team largely comprised of US-based researchers. We conclude with discussion of the applicability of underlying methods to other research efforts.

FOUNDATIONAL ISSUES: CONSTRUCTS AND CULTURE

The notion of a psychological construct is fundamental to just about any social science endeavor and related validation is discussed across a voluminous literature base. Although the term *construct* has been defined in many different ways, we believe Crocker and Algina's (1986) description is adequate: 'Psychological attributes are constructs. They are hypothetical concepts – products of informed scientific imagination of social scientists who attempt to develop theories for explaining human behavior. The existence of such constructs can never be absolutely confirmed. Thus the degree to which any psychological construct characterizes an individual can only be inferred from observations of his or her behavior' (p. 4). This quotation yields two key ideas for this chapter: (a) When dealing with a psychological outcome practically anything one endeavors to measure or change is not directly observable.[1] (b) Identifying, measuring, and validating constructs is a cornerstone to just about any endeavor within the social sciences that is in the business of measuring attributes that cannot be directly observed. If for example there is considerable disagreement as to what depression means then it is hard to recognize its symptoms, and thus treating depression would be a nonstarter.

Our work is predicated on the notion that explanation of human behavior should be able to account for culture. Practically, American health and mental health organizations explicitly recognize the importance of culture and cultural differences in matters of service provision, practice, and research (e.g. American Psychiatric Association, 1994; American Psychological Association, 1990, 2003; USDHHS, 1999, 2001; Ysseldyke et al., 2006). Perhaps a fundamental reason for this attention is an understanding that failure to account for cultural influence can easily lead to poor service provision. Some argue that members of a majority group, at least in the US, are often unaware of their own culture and its influence,[2] and it is reasonable to assume that most mental health interventionists are members of a majority culture (Sue et al., 1999). Meanwhile, cultural differences can be construed as indicators of poor psychological functioning or even pathology on the part of a patient (see e.g. Castillo, 1997; Gallo et al., 1995; Hetherington and Martin, 1986; Lewis-Fernandez and Kleinman, 1995; Lopez and Guarnaccia, 2000; Rogler, 1999; Snowden, 2001; Sussman et al., 1987; Vega and Lopez, 2001).

An example generated by Egeland et al. (1983) illustrates this point. These authors consider the presenting symptoms of bipolar disorder among the Old Order Amish, a distinct and relatively famous cultural group within the US.

When in the manic phase, a member of this culture might engage in such behaviors as using pay phones (or perhaps it would be cell phones nowadays), use machinery, treat farm animals harshly, and perhaps have more than one sexual partner. Most readers can at once appreciate that these behaviors are normative when considering most Americans, but would be unusual for a member of the Old Amish Order since this group has been depicted in several movies and make up part of the US tourist industry. It should not, then, be much of a stretch to ask clinicians to account for such behaviors and indeed think of them as possible symptoms of a disorder. But what if the Amish weren't so well known? Or more to the point, what about cultural groups that are not as familiar and/or if subtle behavioral nuances were present that might be of interest to those who measure and seek to change behavior?

Our previous work in Sri Lanka yields such an example. The suicide rate among Sri Lankan adolescent girls is distressingly high and research findings suggest that girls in the country may be experiencing psychological difficulties if they reject parental expectations, seek leisure activities instead of studying and engage in masculine behaviors (Hitchcock et al., 2006). Interestingly, these behaviors are often normative, if not encouraged in the US. But in Sri Lanka, such behavior may be cause for concern and the potential basis for intervention.[3] Our data (described in later sections) suggest that this is probably a function of culturally informed behavioral expectations and values, and cultural notions of stress, coping, and adjustment. The larger point for now is that the Amish and Sri Lankan examples demonstrate how a psychological construct can very much be embedded within and influenced by culture, and that failure to account for this can have serious consequences on any measurement or intervention efforts.

Methodological framework

Culture must be defined if one is to address it. Nastasi (1998) states culture is a 'shared language, ideas, beliefs, values, and behavioral norms' (p. 169). Others take a similar tack; the US Department of Health and Human Services (DHHS, 2001) states, 'culture is broadly defined as a common heritage or set of beliefs, norms, and values' (p. 9). These definitions bring about a need to consider what is specific to a culture. *Culture specificity* considers the competencies of the target culture, the language of the population, and the values of the members of the culture (Nastasi, 1998). Hence, culturally specific services 'embody an individual's real-life experiences within a given cultural context (e.g. neighborhood) and his or her understanding of those experiences. When addressing the needs of a group (e.g. within a classroom), cultural specificity implies the consideration of both shared (classroom, school) and unique (family, neighborhood) real-life experiences of individual members' (Nastasi, 2000: 547).

Readers familiar with Bronfenbrenner's work will appreciate the attention given to context and inherent systems noted in the definition. Ecological systems theory (EST; Bronfenbrenner, 1989) takes into account different systemic levels that influence development. EST posits there are micro-systems (i.e. highly proximal contexts such as families or classrooms), meso-systems (the interrelationship between units within the micro-systems, such as parents and teachers), exo-systems (e.g. extended family, broader social services), and macro-systems (e.g. cultural ideologies). Textbooks often depict these systems as a set of circles with the micro-system as a bull's eye and a macro-system as an outer most ring, and the graphic implies that different system levels have different ways of influencing behavior and development.

Our notion of cultural specificity is somewhat rooted in EST. The idea is that a given psychological construct is to some degree influenced or formed by one or more ecosystem levels, keeping in mind that the systems serve more as a heuristic than a concrete guideline for understanding context. Indeed, it is commonly accepted that levels take on different meaning and/or salience from one culture to the next. For example, what is typically thought of as extended family (i.e. the exo-system) in the majority culture of the US (e.g. great aunts) may be viewed quite differently in other cultures. Complicating matters is the fact that contextual levels interact within cultures to create the highly variable circumstances we all know from our own experiences. For example, a great aunt may be typically thought of as extended family for most US children; furthermore, the macro-system may contribute to the notion that an aunt is in the extended realm via legal definitions of what is and what is not immediate family. But of course a great aunt may still be part of any child's micro-system; one might just expect this to be somewhat rare in the US compared to societies where the elderly tend to have much more prominent positions in families and 'extended' family tend to live under the same roof. The point here is that EST offers a guiding heuristic for understanding cultures, and it is important to recognize there are both macro-cultural elements and more micro-cultures that can be highly important contributors to an individual's behavior. The key is to understand these influences.

In his later work, Bronfenbrenner (1995, 1999) articulated research models that capture such complexity. He described the social address, process-context, person-process-context, and person-process-context-time models as ways to capture contextual and chronological aspects for understanding behavior and human development. A social address model is recognizable to most as it focuses on relatively straightforward comparisons based on, say, geography. This could be a simple comparison between, say, mathematic achievement levels between British and Japanese fifth graders (understanding such comparisons may still use complex and innovative designs). A process-context approach would include factors such as environmental mediators and moderators to understand such differences; the person-process-context model can address individual characteristics and how they interact with context; and a person-process-context-time model adds in a change or longitudinal element. All of these aspects are thought to continually interplay and this can be reflected in an explicit recognition that culture can make a dynamic (i.e. not fixed) contribution to how individuals perceive their world, and how they are perceived by others.

This segues to another foundational set of concepts that should be recognizable to most social scientists. The first is the idea that all of our assessment and resulting intervention work assumes that psychological constructs are moderated to some degree by culture. Messick (1995) helps justify this stance. In addition to reminding readers of the importance of construct validity – it is arguably *sine qua non*[4] in assessment work – it is intertwined with what is viewed to be socially valid. That is, there is a social element to construct validity in that others must agree that the psychological attributes we measure, but cannot directly observe, are real and worthwhile worrying about. Consider extreme test anxiety among children. Most educators view it to be a real phenomenon that can have a detrimental impact on academic performance and psychological functioning. We have found this to be the case in Sri Lanka as well and it is thus a socially valid construct to measure. But it is arguable that test anxiety is of little importance in societies that do not emphasize academic testing, and, in such societies, we would not get much traction by trying to define and measure it in related contexts. Our position then is that constructs should always be evaluated for the degree to which they are understood by a culture. In the extremes a construct may be unique to a culture or, on the other hand, could be universally recognized (we offer only the suggestion of this sort of continuum but not proof of it). It is probably the case that many constructs are recognized by most if not all cultures but their manifestations may vary widely.

In our work we have focused on Harter's (1990, 1999) description of *self-concept*. The construct has multiple meanings in the literature but here we are referring to the ideas and attitudes people have about themselves. This construct is important to psychologists because poor self-concept is thought to have undesirable manifestations in a number of affective and behavioral ways, whereas a high self-concept, particularly if well justified, is generally a marker for well-being. Harter argued there are separate domains of self-concept (e.g. academic, professional, family roles, physical ability) and some research suggests there are even finer delineations, such as self-concept in mathematics and reading achievement (Marsh and Shavelson, 1985). Self-concept is in part a social construction, particularly because the emotional valence placed on a skill is a function of whether one's self-concept is high in areas that are valued by others (Dai, 2002). For example, the authors of the current chapter work in a community of scholars that value strong research skills, so we tend to place greater values in our self-evaluation as researchers. Academic research skills may however have little value for someone in a sales profession. In this sense, one can see that self-concept, an important psychological construct, is moderated by one's culture.

This issue of perception raises a final foundational issue, and that is attending to how members of a culture view themselves, versus the perception of the researcher. Anthropologists are well acclimated to this idea, and refer to perceptions and information supplied by participants within a study as the *emic* perspective.

The *etic* perspective, meanwhile, refers to the views of the researcher and how emic data are conceptualized (Creswell, 2003). Why make this distinction? The answer is generally well ingrained for those trained in qualitative methods but we suspect this is not the case for many in the social and behavioral sciences. If one accepts the above assertion that culture can moderate psychological constructs, then one has to account for the etic perspective since it may not be congruent with how stakeholders view a given phenomenon. That is, researchers may inadvertently define a construct in ways that are incongruent with how the research participants might define it, or there may be a discrepancy in terms of understanding how behavioral manifestations might appear. Getting back to the above example with manic behavior exhibited by a member of the Old Order Amish community, failure to understand emic perceptions could lead to assumptions such as the use of pay phones (or cell phones) is normative (assuming of course the person performing an assessment is naïve about the relevant cultural nuances).

Such lack of congruence is not necessarily a problem, and indeed there may be times when a researcher might take umbrage with the perspectives among members in a target culture. But researchers should be able to explain why their perspective differs from members of a cultural group; failure to understand this may well lead to situations of considerable confusion and potential misrepresentation of the group in research findings. A summative point behind the research on cultural differences, service quality, and research interpretations is that there may be real value in appreciating the difference between etic and emic perspectives. Moreover, there may be value in integrating the emic and etic perspectives in order to advance theory that guides instrument and intervention development and service delivery. As it turns out, qualitative methodologies can be easily applied to help researchers sort out these distinctions. Although these approaches are often limited to small sample sizes because of their intensity and general nature of qualitative work, they can be mixed with quantitative designs if the researcher wishes to have a broader, normative view of constructs within a culture. This may be particularly helpful if the focus is aimed more at an exo-system level in Bronfenbrenner's EST terms. Moreover, the mixing of qualitative and quantitative methods can provide a systematic approach to integrating emic and etic views in construct and theory development and validation.

Demonstration

The research context

Much of the construct validation work for this project was conducted in Kandy, a city within the central province of Sri Lanka; the target population of the area was youth of age 12–19 and grade 7–12. Key issues that interested the principal investigator (second author of this chapter) were findings that Sri Lanka suffered from the second highest suicide rate in the world, and Sri Lankan social scientists pointed to low-self esteem, preoccupation with social norms, social stressors, and alcoholism as primary contributors. In addition, there was a dearth of mental health services (fewer than 20 psychiatrists in the country) and no related support could be found within the schools. However, because Sri Lanka maintained a British educational system since gaining independence in 1948, and thus maintained near universal K-12 education, there was an opportunity to develop school psychology services to address a host of mental health needs (Nastasi, 1998). Because Sri Lanka is obviously a different culture from the one US researchers were most familiar with, they needed to understand key cultural factors before developing assessment and intervention services. Understanding these differences highlighted the need for basic construct identification and validation. Although suicide rate was an initial reason the researchers were asked to help develop services, this proved to be a more distal focus compared to helping a broader population of students contend with an array of mental health concerns. This wider focus entailed the application of aforementioned self-concept theory, which already recognized the import of cultural variation but, along with Bronfenbrenner's work and some approaches to anthropology provided a basis for studying culturally specific stress and coping mechanisms. Indeed, the primary goal for the methods described below was to identify Sri Lankan adolescent conceptualization of stress, coping mechanisms, feelings of distress, and adjustment as a precursor for developing school-based interventions that might promote well-being.

Several of the methods described here, particularly the initial qualitative approaches, were conducted in the late 1990s although work is on-going. It is of course noteworthy that the findings described here were developed prior to the tsunami that occurred at the end of 2005, particularly since much of them focus on culturally-specific definitions of stress. Subsequent post-tsunami psychological programming required the addition of 'environmentally related' stressors (e.g. tsunami and other weather and climate related situations) to the model (Nastasi, Jayasena, Summerville, and Borja, in press). Furthermore, analysis of curriculum products from the post-tsunami program indicated both tsunami-specific stressors (loss of loved ones, loss of property, disruption to way of life) and developmentally and contextually relevant stressors (family or peer conflict, academic difficulties, school discipline practices).[5]

The application of mixed methods for construct identification and validation

How does one develop a culturally-specific theory for understanding stress, coping, and mental health when there are intense cultural differences that demand attention to the etic and emic perspectives, and then empirically evaluate whether the theory generalizes to a larger sample? The key is mixing ethnographic and factor analytic techniques through a series of phases that, in their entirety, constitute a mixed methods research program (Nastasi et al., 2007a). The two traditions are surprisingly complementary since construct development is a central concern to both. A common ethnographic goal is to gather data from multiple sources and generate a series of constructs that can capture and explain data (i.e. variation, trends, and common or emblematic occurrences). The whole process is in essence the development of a grounded theory (Brantlinger et al., 2005; Creswell, 2003). For this project, the process was carried out via a two-year ethnography that began in 1995. Data collection efforts included a series of stakeholder (i.e. parents, children, teachers, and school administrator) interviews and focus groups. Interviews were open-ended and exploratory, but guided by the aforementioned models of mental health, cultural context, and self-concept theory. In addition, participant observations of classroom processes were conducted, archival data (e.g. local newspaper stories dealing with stressful events, school records) were collected and analyzed, and efforts were made to identify the range of reports regarding matters of stress, mental health, and coping processes as well as data trends. Finally, analyses yielded ethnographically derived constructs and a broader grounded theory that, together, suggested Harter's self-concept framework applied (i.e. emotional valence about one's competencies could be predicted by the degree of congruence between a child's perceptions of skills and the degree to which these skills were valued by others). While this matches well with US-based findings on self-concept, the competencies and values were very much intertwined with Sri Lankan culture. In addition, findings indicated that stress was largely centered around school and family life, and coping mechanisms included culturally-specific adaptive and maladaptive behaviors (Nastasi et al., 2007b). Again, there were clear links to what one might expect in a US context. For example, coping strategies included emotion-focused approaches for dealing with negative effects and more direct problem-focused efforts to deal with sources of stress and support-seeking mechanisms. But there were culturally specific manifestations as well. For example, some emotion-focused approaches included the use of tantrums and pouting, which by themselves would not be unusual in many cultures. But from a US perspective, this was noteworthy since the sample was comprised of adolescents. Furthermore, praying was a prevalent strategy which is by no means a culturally-specific phenomenon but for many informants the religious outlets were Buddhist. The combination of common and unique mechanisms across cultures highlights the importance for sensitivity to the nuances of how support is sought and received, and has implications for developing interventions designed to promote effective coping skills.

Reports indicate that stress did, of course, lead to maladaptive behavior but examples were rooted in Sri Lankan culture. At an extreme end, when an adolescent committed suicide (or attempted it), it was considered commonplace for it to be a reaction to either poor test performance or a ruined love affair. A common method for suicidal behavior was ingesting an easily available and powerful insecticide. Extreme reactions to poor test performance was partially rooted in the fact that Sri Lanka kept elements of a British-based examination system from its days of being a colony. There are the Ordinary (O-level, at grade 10) and Advanced (A-level, grade 12) examinations which are almost exclusive determinates of not only college entry, but also the basis for selecting areas of study (i.e. one does not choose to be an engineer, doctor, or psychologist but has to score at a given test level). Further adding to the stressfulness of the exams is that fact that the success rate is low; only about 2% of students gain access to college while others tend to face bleak economic prospects. Furthermore, Sri Lankan culture is somewhat collectivist and family-based, where successes and failures of the individual reflect the family to a higher degree than most Americans experience. Such cultural differences are not necessarily difficult to understand or navigate, but do require attention during construct validation and of course would have implications for psychological intervention.

Another example of a cultural nuance (just one among many that could be cited) is that 'affairs' (i.e. 'love affairs', dating behavior) between students were actively discouraged, to the point that teachers assisted by prefects (student leaders who have disciplinary responsibilities) argued it was their job to search personal belongings for any evidence of such relationships (e.g. 'love letters') and to publicly punish students who engaged in them. The qualitative data suggested this state of affairs led to common but embarrassing situations for students that were likely to generate a number of behaviors that were viewed, both within the culture and by researchers, as maladaptive. Examples of such maladaptive behavior include rejecting school norms, using alcohol and illegal drugs, and again, in the extreme, suicide (as noted below maladaptive behaviors differed by gender).

The grounded theory was able to bring light to some of these mechanisms and identify constructs that focused on stress, coping, culturally valued competencies, and a breadth of behavioral reactions to scenarios that appeared to resonate with members of the target culture (i.e. students, parents, and educators). In sum, the ethnographic work yielded a systemic way of understanding what students perceived to be stressors, resources, successes and failures, likely reactions to them, and finally, maladaptive and adaptive behavior. But much of this was based on the series of participant observations, focus groups, individual interviews, and prolonged engagement in the country and the grounded theory was not built upon a large sample of students.[6] While there was reason to believe it would generalize to the larger population of Sri Lanka, it would be quite difficult to empirically check this using qualitative methods alone.

What served as a key link for this later step was the ethnographic survey (Schensul et al., 1999). Such surveys are based on ethnographic data, and can be developed to quantify findings based on qualitative work. But survey development also provides an opportunity to mix paradigms for the purposes of triangulating work for validation purposes. Analyses of qualitative data entail checking for credibility. This can be done via a number of methods, including member checks (i.e. debriefing with participants to see if findings appear to be accurate), asking researchers to specify their assumptions and the degree to which they remain reasonable, debriefing with researcher peers and collaborating with others to check for alternative perspectives, explicit searches for disconfirming evidence and developing auditing trails (see Brantlinger et al., 2005; Nastasi, 2006; Nastasi and Schensul, 2005). There are of course other procedures the qualitative methodologist might use, but all these can be easily intertwined with survey development. Piloting a survey can at once provide the standard advantages of calibrating items and procedures, and obtaining initial psychometric evidence for reliability, but also serve as a form of member checking. Peer debriefings and searches for disconfirming evidence can force the researcher to articulate assumptions and help generate an audit trail. In short, ethnographic surveys can be used for the standard reason any survey is developed, and that is, to gather data, which typically is quantified, from large groups of people. But the process of developing a survey provides rich opportunities to enhance understanding of qualitatively-derived data and theory, particularly using a mixed methods approach.

As specified in Hitchcock and colleagues (2005), an ethnographic survey was developed with all of these purposes in mind, but the primary purpose of the measure was to assess the perceptions of hundreds of Sri Lankan youth regarding culturally-valued competencies, stressors, and resources.[7] In this case, the 'survey' was intended to be used as a self-report measure (and in the case of teachers, an informant-report measure) consistent with standardized rating scales used in research and clinical practice. After piloting and back translating (i.e. translating items written in English to Sinhalese, and back to English), the measure was administered to 612 Sri Lankan adolescents (ages 12–19) representing the range of religious, economic, and other demographic groups located in the Central Province (students from all sectors of the province attend the schools in this central city). Hence, findings are probably quite representative of the region (and likely the country). The survey items were all grounded in ethnographic data and utilized a closed-ended three-point response option (i.e. a lot, some, not at all[8]). The particular subset of surveys were based on ethnographic findings that five constructs were thought to reflect adolescent and teacher views of competencies. These were labeled *good citizen* (behaviors that reflected competencies and behavioral expectations dealing with service to the society), *academic* (skills and efforts in the academic realm, not unlike previous findings dealing with academic self-concept construct), *friendship* (interpersonal competencies), *well-rounded personality* (dealing with non-academic skills and recreation), and *unsuitable behavior* (maladaptive behaviors that run counter to societal expectations).

After administration, the surveys were factor analyzed to determine if and to what degree quantitative factors (i.e. constructs) matched those derived from qualitative work. Exploratory factor analyses (utilizing a range of extraction methods with rotation techniques) were applied.[9] In theory, the effort should have yielded five constructs reflecting what was expected from the ethnography, but examination of scree plots and other techniques used to determine the number of factors involved (e.g. consideration of the number of items per factor, size of pattern coefficients/loadings) clearly suggested only three were to be found. As it turned out however, this was not particularly problematic as items based on the good citizen, friendship and academic constructs collapsed into a logically coherent factor we dubbed 'Socially Appropriate (Suitable) Behavior'. Meanwhile, Unsuitable Behavior items formed a factor that was entirely consistent with the ethnographic data. The reliability of the factors met standard approaches used in factor analysis. The sample size, number of items per factor, and pattern coefficient easily met the recommendations put forth by Gaudagnoli and Velicer (1988), and reliability coefficients on the scales ranged from 0.99 to 0.80. Of course, the item development was clearly reflective of their presumed constructs (Darlington, 2002; Kline, 1994).

The third factor we dubbed as 'Personal/Interpersonal Needs' represents some of the advantages of cross-method triangulation. This factor was based on activities that seem to be valued by adolescents (e.g. I participate in sports activities, I like to spend the day with friends), but not adults, and reflected often unmet needs according to focus group interviews with adolescents. The ethnographic data suggested that students were likely to comply with adult expectations but still wish for less parental pressure pertaining to academics, and more time to engage in social and recreational activities with peers. The quantitative data provided reason for renewed appreciation of such needs (and thus served as a way to identify and further investigate alternative perspectives). In addition, the re-emergence of Personal/Interpersonal domain as important to adolescents provided important insights for developing interventions. Indeed, reconsideration of some of the qualitative data suggests this construct is reasonable. In the end, cross-method triangulation appeared to have been achieved because the new factors were logical and consistent with the ethnographic data (if not perfectly so) and differences were not only explainable, but provided further insight into the data.

Readers may wonder why Confirmatory Factor Analysis (CFA) was not the primary quantitative methodology used. The answer can be gleaned from the fact that early examination of the data suggested the five qualitative constructs were not going to yield strong fit indices so it made sense to suspend expectations and adopt a more exploratory approach. Moreover, an exploratory approach could permit the emic view to assert itself in the data. Thus, although the items were all derived from the qualitative data, the initial categorization (coding) into five constructs was also directly influenced by researchers' etic view. In contrast to CFA, which is more likely guided by the etic perspective, exploratory factor analysis provided another opportunity to understand the emic view. Failure to replicate the exact factors in this case may in part be due to item sensitivity, but other issues also may have been at work. In addition, to re-analyze the qualitative data, researchers could also use member checking (returning to participants or representatives of the population of adolescents) to explore and resolve these discrepancies. Our subsequent intervention work provided further opportunity to understand the importance of personal and interpersonal domains for adolescents, thus reflecting a more iterative process of construct and theory development and validation (Nastasi et al., 2007b).

Extending the findings to account for gender

The culturally specific constructs were further evaluated to account for gender differences noted in the qualitative data (Hitchcock et al., 2006). An overriding theme in the ethnographic work suggested that: (a) behavioral expectations were higher for girls; (b) there were gender-specific perceptions of stress and competencies within the culture; and (c) Sri Lanka, like most countries, has fairly strong gender-based socialization processes (Sarkar, 2003). Furthermore, gender has implications for mental health (Romans, 1998) and accounting for gender differences is consistent with Bronfenbrenner's aforementioned person-process-context model of research.

To evaluate gender differences in these constructs, a mixed methods approach was again taken. Qualitative data suggested clear differences in unsuitable behaviors, where boys were more inclined to include violence and substance abuse as socially unacceptable (i.e. unsuitable), whereas girls hardly even included these elements in their descriptions. Instead, their focus was more on failure to comply with societal expectations surrounding responsibilities such as studying and providing domestic help. Girls also focused on engaging in relationships with boys, slandering, and failure to follow etiquette as unsuitable behaviors. Interestingly, a focus on pushing for independence was also construed as a form of Unsuitable Behavior among girls. For Personal/Interpersonal Needs, the qualitative data did not indicate strong gender differences in how the construct was defined, but girls reported in interviews that family expectations prevented them from engaging in recreational activities. For example, when mothers were unable to perform household duties (e.g. mothers commonly traveled out of the country to work), the daughters assumed responsibility for managing the household. Thus, although Personal/Interpersonal Needs resonated with both genders, different expectations about how boys and girls spent their time could influence opportunities for fulfilling these needs. In terms of Suitable Behavior, boys focused more on leadership roles and girls reported pressure to follow rules and engage in community services. In sum, there was reason to believe there were gender differences across the three constructs.

The surveys provided a basis for quantitatively evaluating these gender differences; two primary analyses were conducted. The first was to re-run factor structures for each gender, create related factor scores, and test for differences using Multivariate Analyses of Variance (MANOVA), with each overall factor score serving as a dependent variable. The analyses did not yield a significant gender difference on Unsuitable Behavior and Personal/Interpersonal Needs, but did show a statistically significant difference on Suitable Behavior. Checking for gender difference on Personal/Interpersonal Needs was worthwhile but the fact that none were found was not necessarily troubling. We were however surprised at not finding a gender-based difference on Unsuitable Behavior scores given the strong differences in the qualitative data. It was possible that the differences may not be a matter of magnitude so much as a fundamentally different perspective of how boys engage in Unsuitable Behavior relative to girls. Examination of the factor loadings for each group suggested there was indeed a different factor structure. Hence, we applied a technique rooted in structural equation modeling called a structure means analysis which tests for equivalence of factor loadings across groups (see Byrne, 1994). The strategy in essence constrains factor loadings to be equivalent; chi-square statistics are used to evaluate the presence of a difference. Chi squares showed the full three-factor model to be different across genders and isolated the Unsuitable Behavior factor as the culprit. The implication then is that the factor structure is gender specific. This is consistent with qualitative analyses, which show that girls described unsuitable behavior in fundamentally different ways than boys (e.g. not following etiquette and engaging in relationships as opposed to engaging in physical aggression, running away from home, or even carrying weapons).

The key finding here is that the qualitative data suggested that gender differences were important and this was supported by quantitative work. The substantive implication is that some attention might be paid to developing specialized interventions for boys and girls. And as we discuss later, a stress and coping curriculum yielded differential effects based on gender, providing further evidence of the importance of attending to gender in both assessment and intervention. Of course, gender differences are commonplace in psychological and educational research, but the critical issue here is that the combination of qualitative and quantitative methods helped to highlight and specify these differences from a cultural standpoint.

IDENTIFICATION OF ADDITIONAL CONSTRUCTS

The studies described thus far have gone a long way toward developing culturally specific psychological constructs pertaining to self-concept, as well as definitions of stress, coping, and associated behavior. This has positive implications for understanding Sri Lankan school culture, but there is another application as well. The work has provided a basis for developing an intervention technique which we believe to be culturally specific that can be evaluated via a randomized controlled trial (we omit details pertaining to the trial since this chapter focuses on construct validation).[10] We needed to properly assess intervention effects, and we needed to account for cultural factors in the outcome measure. Construct validity was achieved by combining ethnographic data with the analysis of survey data.

Qualitative data collected in the ethnography yielded constructs pertaining to stress, coping, social resources, emotional reactions, and adjustment difficulties related to stressful experiences, and provided the basis for the ethnographic survey.[11] Follow-up factor analyses were conducted to establish cross-method triangulation. Additionally, the survey was piloted and back-translated before going to scale. Going to scale in this case meant a sample needed for an 'efficacy' randomized controlled trial (RCT) mounted to test the impacts of an intervention tailored for Sri Lankan adolescents and not an effectiveness trial. An efficacy trial is one designed to test intervention impacts under optimal conditions. It can often be smaller in scale. By contrast, an effectiveness trial is designed to test intervention impacts in more real-world setting and often tends to be larger in terms of sample size. More importantly, since effectiveness trials involve real-world implementation, their results help make decisions about wider adoption of an intervention (see Flay, 1986; Society for Prevention Research, 2007). In this case, the intervention is not ready to go to scale in Sri Lanka as a school-based intervention, because it was conducted under highly controlled conditions (i.e. as an after-school program with small groups of students and with ongoing support and monitoring by a US–Sri Lankan research team). Another implication of the small trial is that the sample size on which the measure was based was relatively small (n = 121) and this limited us to the use of principal component extraction techniques. We are aware that these techniques are problematic, but our intent was to generate scale scores for use of outcome measures, and this application is one where use of principal components analyses has a role (Velicer and Jackson, 1990).

The measure utilized a question format in which a series of hypothetical stressful events were introduced to see how respondents would hypothetically react to them. This question format was related to the intervention, as the purpose of the intervention was to help students develop better coping skills and prepare them to respond to stressors common to their cultural experiences. Seven stressful events or situations were developed based on the ethnographic data; each event was envisaged as its own survey. Follow-up items were meant to assess respondent perceptions of feelings they might experience if faced with the event, resources (both personal and social/societal) they might access to deal with it, and the degree to which it might impact personal vulnerabilities and perhaps elicit problematic behaviors such as substance abuse. Again, students did not necessarily experience the events but were simply asked how they would react if faced with the situation, and it was crucial to develop scenarios that would resonate with their experiences. Because the intervention focused on helping students develop better coping strategies and attend to stressful feelings, the general hypothesis was that students in the intervention group would self-report fewer feelings of distress and better overall coping skills than students in the control group. If the data lead to this conclusion, our broader interpretation would be that students participating in the intervention could be expected to experience fewer adjustment difficulties.

The scenarios were meant to resonate with members of the target culture and thus were rooted in the ethnography. Sample scenarios include:

> *Scenario 2*. You have failed A/L (advanced-level) exams by a few points and are concerned about your future. You want to be an engineer. Your family cannot afford to send you to private school or to study abroad. You are not sure what you should do.

> *Scenario 4*. You have been having a secret love affair. You and your boy/girlfriend just broke up. You cannot talk to your family or your teacher about it. You have trouble sleeping. Your parents and teachers have asked you what is wrong but you cannot talk to them. You do not know what to do. Meanwhile one of the prefects (student leaders selected by teachers and administrators who participate in discipline of other students) who searched your school bag found a love letter and gave the letter to the class teacher. The class teacher called your parents. The parents and teacher forbid you to communicate with your lover.

> *Scenario 6*. Your mother has been working in the Middle East (as a domestic housekeeper) for about a year. She sends money home regularly for the family, but there is little direct

communication with the children. You are the eldest child and have been taking care of the four younger children. Your father has brought a step-mother from the village to live with you to help with household tasks. When you object to the step-mother living in the house, your father beats you severely. Because of the severe abuse, you are considering leaving home. Some of your friends have already left home and have formed a gang and invited you to become a member.

Scenario 7. It was the day before a big exam in school. You came home from school and, when you entered your home, your father is yelling at your mother. You father has been drinking arrack (local whiskey made from coconuts). He asks your mother for dinner. She says that dinner is not ready because she had to find money to buy rice. Your parents start arguing about money. When your mother serves dinner, the rice is overcooked. Your father starts yelling and throws the rice on the floor. Your mother says, "I'll cook more," and begins to cry. Your father tells you to clean up the mess he has made. Your mother says that you should study, not to clean up the mess that your father has made. Your father then starts beating your mother. (Nastasi et al., 2007a: 174)

As noted previously, ethnographic data indicated that students do experience extreme academic stress and are subject to embarrassing investigations of relationships. It was also commonplace for mothers to leave the household to earn money in another country and for fathers to engage in alcohol abuse, so scenarios like these should have been meaningful to respondents.

The results of the factor analysis were straightforward: three factors were identified for the first five scenarios (dealing primarily with stressors related to academic achievement and 'intimate' relationships), which we expected given previous work. Qualitative data (based on interviews) and member checks suggested that the follow-up items were reasonable queries given the scenarios (i.e. the questions about feelings, social resources, coping strategies, and adjustment problems were based on descriptions of such reactions in qualitative interviews).[12] One factor focused on adjustment difficulties and was consistent with the Unsuitable Behavior construct described above. It in essence focused on the degree to which respondents anticipated they would experience externalizing behavioral difficulties if faced with the particular stressful situation. Other factors included anticipated helpfulness of social support, feelings of distress, and problem-focused coping (attempts to resolve the stressful situation). Scale reliability estimates and the number of items per factor, along with the size of the factor loadings, indicated the scales had strong psychometric properties. The sixth and seventh scenarios (focused on family stressors) departed somewhat from our initial expectations and yielded findings that warranted additional investigation. Instead of three factors, five factors best represented the data for these scenarios: the same social support and feelings of distress constructs were noted and the problem-focused coping factor included items that dealt with caretaking. The new finding is the Unsuitable Behavior factor, which was observed in previous work, seemed to split into internalizing and externalizing versions of the construct. Items associated with suicidal thoughts loaded on the externalizing factor. At first glance this surprised us since it seemed to indicate suicide is viewed as a form of anti-social behavior and acting out, not necessarily a function of depression. This also occurred only on surveys dealing with complex family situations (no split in adjustment was found on other surveys even though each survey had the same response items). Although the quantitative work is exploratory, re-analysis of related qualitative data and member checks did support these findings; it may be that in some stressful events, suicide might be construed as a type of aggressive acting out. If such is the case, any intervention designed to help prevent suicidal behavior should be able to account for this nuance.

As stated previously, this last set of surveys were used in the context of an RCT (Nastasi et al., 2010). The findings suggest the intervention was successful; important null hypotheses were not retained and effect sizes based on the outcome measure were consistent with expectations. Furthermore, the findings suggested differential impact based on gender. Although this is more distal evidence, the fact that the measure operated as intended in the context of a trial suggests it resonated with students. The overall point that can be taken away from this discussion is that although mixed methods construct development is important for its own sake, the method can be extended for applied evaluation work. In this case the outcomes of a culturally-specific intervention were tested using culturally-specific measures.

CONCLUSION

In our approach to understanding culture, we view it *not* as a problem to be explained away, but an opportunity to add a rich dimension to research and practice. Addressing culture was of course an obvious concern to US-based researchers dealing with psychological constructs in Sri Lanka. The cultural differences between the two societies were not subtle. We do however contend that cultural differences can still be powerful factors within just about any society, including those in which researchers have experience but do not necessarily share the cultural perspective of all members. One might consider the 'professional culture' of the researcher to necessitate a cross-cultural perspective in reference to target study populations and the assumption that the researcher is not necessarily an accurate informant about the lay population (e.g. Kleinman et al., 1978). Indeed, the recent emphasis on evidence-based practice in social sciences and health professions necessitates examination of the cultural validity of existing assessment and intervention tools (e.g. Ingraham and Oka, 2006; Nastasi, 2006). The assumption that empirical evidence with a general population is sufficient for application to diverse groups within the population needs serious consideration, and may account for the oft-repeated concern about gaps between research and practice.

We believe the methods presented here provide a way to at least assess if researchers should be concerned with cultural nuances during intervention and psychological assessment, and more specifically to examine the cultural validity of evidence-based methods as well as their own 'cultural' biases that may be inherent in their professional perspective. Much of this is probably best done via qualitative methods. If qualitative data suggest that standard assessment approaches may be problematic (i.e. are not culturally valid), the ethnographic survey and subsequent steps involved with triangulating across qualitative and quantitative methods can provide helpful insights into how to account for cultural and other contextual matters. Similarly, the use of a mixed method approach to intervention development and evaluation could facilitate design or adaptation of evidence-based interventions to meet culture-specific needs of the target group.

One lesson from the work described in this chapter is that culture can potentially have a powerful impact on how psychological constructs are defined and manifest themselves via directly observable behavior. As noted above, this has been recognized as an issue by several major mental health organizations yet we are aware of few groups that have attempted to rigorously account for culture during assessment and intervention development. There are other emerging works in this regard (e.g. Pearce, 2002; Sue, 1998; Suzuki et al., 2001), but our review of the prevailing literature suggests many efforts range from ignoring cultural impacts to treating the matter as a vexing nuisance (see also Anastasi and Urbina, 1997; Reynolds et al., 1999; Rogler, 1999). We contend however that deliberate accounting for culture can be essential in some settings and researchers need methods for doing so. Clearly the content of the findings presented here are of limited interest outside of Sri Lanka but we hope the approach and philosophy behind it has wider appeal. As of this writing it appears that many fields have started to move past methodological paradigm wars toward embracing mixed methods, yet considerable work remains in terms of developing stronger designs (Tashakkori and Creswell, 2007). When it comes to developing measures, we hope to see continued applications of systematic qualitative inquiry that feature approaches for promoting data credibility as a means for item generation, and examining response behavior to cross-validate qualitative expectations (i.e. combining grounded theory with factor analytic work). This would lead to improving the overall approach while promoting the capacity of methodologists to regularly account for cultural and contextual nuances and to facilitate the development of evidence to support assessment and intervention that is culturally appropriate in a diverse global community.

NOTES

1 This is arguable if operating strictly within a behaviorist paradigm.

2 Cole (1996), among others, has used the metaphor, that is, if one could converse with fish, it would probably be to explain what water is since it is pervasive and all around their life. This is probably a bit extreme but it also may be hard to explain to members of a majority group that their behavior and cognitions may be influenced by culture.

3 For the purposes of this chapter, we suspend the broader questions around the merits of changing a culture and encouraging female conformity; our focus is on construct validation and not on the complex debate about cultural change. In addition, we use these examples to suggest that definitions of 'deviance' or 'maladjustment' are culturally constructed, and thus can vary widely across cultural groups and contexts.

4 *Sine qua non* means 'without which is not' and refers to that which is essential. Campbell and Stanley (1963) and Shadish et al. (2002) suggest internal validity is *sine qua non* in experimental design; we suggest that construct validity holds similar importance in assessment work.

5 Additional information can be obtained from the second author at Tulane University.

6 Although the sample included approximately 300 students across 18 schools, data were gathered via 33 group interviews and thus the individual perspectives of all the participants were not necessarily reflected.

7 Multiple ethnographic surveys were developed all with nuanced purposes. For now, we focus on one general version that is described in Hitchcock et al. (2005). Later in the chapter we will discuss another survey described in Nastasi et al. (2007a).

8 The decision to use three-point scale was based on prior research experience in Sri Lanka and the piloting of instruments which suggested that scales beyond three points were not meaningful within the culture.

9 These entail options such as principal axis extraction techniques, promax (oblique) rotation, etc. Given the size of the sample, number of items, and reliability of factors the results were not sensitive to the sundry choices.

10 Findings are presented in Nastasi et al. (2010).

11 The specific items and categories (e.g. feelings, coping strategies) were derived from the ethnographic data, and thus reflected experiences and language of the target population.

12 It is important to note here that the measures included items that reflected the experiences of both girls and boys thus permitting application across gender.

REFERENCES

American Psychiatric Association (1994). *Diagnostic and Statistical Manual of Mental Disorders,* 4th edn. Washington, DC: American Psychiatric Association.

American Psychological Association (1990). *Guidelines for Providers of Psychological Services to Ethnic, Linguistic, and Culturally Diverse Populations.* Washington, DC: Author.

American Psychological Association (2003). Guidelines on multicultural education, training, research, practice, and organizational change for psychologists. *American Psychologist,* 58: 377–402.

Anastasi, A. and Urbina, S. (1997). *Psychological Testing,* 7th edn. Upper Saddle River, NJ: Prentice Hall.

Brantlinger, E., Jiminez, R., Klingner, J., Pugach, M., and Richardson, V. (2005). Qualitative studies in special education. *Exceptional Children,* 71(2): 195–207.

Bronfenbrenner, U. (1989). Ecological systems theory. In R. Vasta (ed.) *Annals of Child Development: Vol 6. Six Theories of Child Development: Revised Formulations and Current Issues.* Greenwich, CT: JAI Press.

Bronfenbrenner, U. (1995). Developmental ecology through space and time: A future perspective. In P. Moen and G.H. Elder (eds) *Examining Lives in Context: Perspectives on the Ecology of Human Development,* pp. 619–47. Washington, DC: American Psychological Association.

Bronfenbrenner, U. (1999). Environments in developmental perspective: Theoretical and operational models. In S.L. Friedman and T.D. Wachs (eds) *Measuring Environment Across the Life Span: Emerging Methods and Concepts,* pp. 3–30. Washington, DC: American Psychological Association.

Byrne, B.M. (1994). *Structural Equation Modeling with EQS and EQS/Windows: Basic Concepts, Applications and Programming.* Thousand Oaks, CA: Sage.

Campbell, D.T. and Stanley, J.C. (1963). *Experimental and Quasi-experimental Designs for Research.* Chicago: RandMcNally.

Castillo, R.J. (1997). *Culture and Mental Illness: A Client-Centered Approach.* Pacific Grove, CA: Brooks-Cole.

Cole, M. (1996). *Cultural Psychology: A Once and Future Discipline.* Harvard University Press.

Creswell, J.W. (2003). *Research Design: Qualitative, Quantitative, and Mixed Methods Approaches.* Thousand Oaks, CA: Sage.

Crocker, L. and Algina, J. (1986). *Introduction to Classical and Modern Test Theory.* Belmont,CA: Wadsworth Group.

Dai, D.Y. (2002). The self in cultural context: Meaning and valence. In D.M. McInerney and S. Van Etten (eds) *Sociocultural Influences on Motivation and Learning,* Vol 2, pp. 3–22. Greenwich, CN: Information Age Publishing.

Darlington, R.B. (2002). *Factor analysis.* http://www.psych.cornell.edu/Darlington/factor.htm

Egeland, J.A., Hostetter, A.M., and Eshleman, S.K. (1983). Amish study III: The impact of cultural factors on diagnosis of bipolar illness. *American Journal of Psychiatry,* 140*:* 67–71.

Flay, B.R. (1986). Efficacy and effectiveness trials (and other phases of research) in the development of health promotion programs. *Preventive Medicine,* 15: 451–74.

Gallo, J.J., Marino, S., Ford, D., and Anthony, J.C. (1995). Filters on the pathway to mental health care, II. Sociodemographic factors. *Psychological Medicine,* 25: 1149–60.

Guadagnoli, E., and Velicer, W. (1988). Relation of sample size to the stability of component patterns. *Psychological Bulletin,* 103: 265–75.

Harter S. (1990). Issues in assessment of self-concept of children and adolescents. In A. LaGreca (ed.) *Through the Eyes of a Child,* pp. 292–325. Boston: Allyn and Bacon.

Harter, S. (1999). *The Construction of the Self: A Developmental Perspective.* New York: Guilford.

Hetherington, E.M. and Martin, B. (1986). Family factors and psychopathology in children. In H.C. Quay and J.S. Werry (eds) *Psychopathological Disorders of Childhood,* 3rd edn. pp. 332–90. New York: Wiley.

Hitchcock, J.H., Nastasi, B.K., Dai, D.C., Newman, J., Jayasena, A., Bernstein-Moore, R., Sarkar, S., and Varjas, K. (2005). Illustrating a mixed-method approach for identifying and validating culturally specific constructs. *Journal of School Psychology,* 43(3): 259–78.

Hitchcock, J.H., Sarkar, S., Nastasi, B.K., Burkholder, G.,Varjas, K., and Jayasena, A. (2006). Validating culture and gender-specific constructs: A mixed-method approach to advance assessment procedures in cross-cultural settings. *Journal of Applied School Psychology,* 22(2): 13–33.

Ingraham, C.L. and Oka, E. (2006). Multicultural issues in evidence-based interventions. *Journal of Applied School Psychology,* 22: 127–49.

Kleinman, A., Eisenberg, L., and Good, B. (1978). Culture, illness and care: Clinical lessons from anthropologic and cross-cultural research. *Annals of Internal Medicine,* 88: 251–8.

Kline, P. (1994). *An Easy Guide to Factor Analysis.* London: Routledge.

Lewis-Fernandez, R. and Kleinman, A. (1995). Cultural psychiatry: Theoretical, clinical and research issues. *Cultural Psychiatry,* 18: 433–45.

Lopez, S.R. and Guarnaccia, P.J. (2000). Cultural psychopathology: Uncovering the social world of mental illness. *Annual Review of Psychology,* 51: 571–98.

Marsh, H.W. and Shavelson, R.J. (1985). Self-concept: Its multifaceted, hierarchical structure. *Educational Psychologist,* 20: 107–23.

Messick, S. (1995). Validity of psychological assessment: Validation of inferences from persons' responses and performances as scientific inquiry into score meaning. *American Psychologist,* 50: 741–9.

Nastasi, B.K. (1998). A model for mental health programming in schools and communities. *School Psychology Review,* 27(2): 165–74.

Nastasi, B.K. (2000). School psychologists as health care providers in the 21st century: Conceptual framework, professional identity, and professional practice. *School Psychology Review,* 29: 540–54.

Nastasi, B.K. (2006). Special issue: Multicultural issues in school psychology: Introduction. *Journal of Applied School Psychology,* 22: 1–11.

Nastasi, B.K., Jayasena, A., Summerville, M., and Borja, A. (in press). Facilitating long-term recovery from natural disasters: Psychological programming for tsunami-affected schools of Sri Lanka. Accepted for publication in *School Psychology International.*

Nastasi, B.K. Schensul, S.L. (2005). Contributions of qualitative research to the validity of intervention research. *Journal of School Psychology,* 43(3): 177–95.

Nastasi, B.K., Moore, R.B., and Varjas, K.M. (2004). *School-Based Mental Health Services: Creating Comprehensive and Culturally Specific Programs.* Washington, DC: American Psychological Association.

Nastasi, B.K., Hitchcock, J.H., Burkholder, G., Varjas, K., Sarkar, S., and Jayasena, A. (2007a). Assessing adolescents' understanding of and reactions to stress in different cultures: Results of a mixed-methods approach. *School Psychology International,* 28(2): 163–78.

Nastasi, B.K., Hitchcock, J., Sarkar, S., Burkholder, G., Varjas, K., and Jayasena, A. (2007b). Mixed methods in intervention research: Theory to adaptation. *Journal of Mixed Methods Research*, 1(2): 164–82.

Nastasi, B.K., Hitchcock, J., Varjas, K., Jayasena, A., Sarkar, S., Moore, R.B., Burden, F., and Albrecht, L. (2010). School-based stress and coping program for adolescents in Sri Lanka: Mixed methods approach to testing effectiveness. In K.M.T. Collins, A.J. Onwuegbuzie, and Q.G. Jiao (eds) *Toward a Broader Understanding of Stress and Coping: Mixed Methods Approaches.* Charlotte, NC: Information Age Publishing, 5: 305–42.

Pearce, L.D. (2002). Integrating survey and ethnographic methods for systematic anomalous case analysis. *Sociological Methodology,* 32: 103–32.

Reynolds, C.R., Lowe, P.A., and Saenz, A.L. (1999). The problem of bias in psychological assessment. In C.R. Reynolds and T.B. Gutkin (eds) *The Handbook of School Psychology,* 3rd edn pp. 686–708. New York: John Wiley & Sons Inc.

Rogler, L.H. (1999). Methodological sources of cultural insensitivity in mental health research. *American Psychologist,* 54: 424–33.

Romans, S.E. (1998). Undertaking research with women. In S.E. Romans (ed.) *Folding Back the Shadows: A Perspective on Women's Mental Health*, pp. 23–34. Dunedin, NZ: University of Otago Press.

Sarkar, S. (2003). Gender as a cultural factor influencing mental health among the Adolescent students in India and Sri Lanka: A cross-cultural study. Unpublished Doctoral dissertation. University at Albany, State University of New York, Albany.

Schensul, S.L., Schensul, J.J., and LeCompte, M.D. (1999) *Essential Ethnographic Methods: Observations, Interviews, and Questionnaires. Ethnographer's Toolkit,* Book 2. Walnut Creek, CA: AltaMira.

Shadish, W.R., Cook, T.D., and Campbell, D.T. (2002). *Experimental and Quasi-Experimental Designs for General Causal Inference.* Boston: Houghton Mifflin.

Society for Prevention Research (2007). Standards of Evidence Criteria for Efficacy, Effectiveness and Dissemination. http://www.preventionresearch.org/StandardsofEvidencebook.pdf.

Snowden, L.R. (2001). Barriers to effective mental health services for African Americans. *Mental Health Services Research,* 3(4): 181–7.

Sue, S. (1998). In search of cultural competence in psychotherapy and counseling. *American Psychologist,* 53(4): 440–8.

Sue, D.W., Bingham, R.P., Porche–Burke, L., and Vasquez, M. (1999). The diversification of psychology: A multicultural revolution. *American Psychologist,* 54: 1061–9.

Sussman, L.K., Robvins, L.N., and Earls, F. (1987) Treatment seeking for depression by Black and White Americans. *Social Science Medicine,* 24: 187–96.

Suzuki, L.A., Ponterotto, J.G., and Meller, P.J. (eds) (2001). *Handbook of Multicultural Assessment.* San Francisco: Jossey-Bass.

Tashakkori, A. and Creswell, J.W. (2007). The new era of mixed methods. *Journal of Mixed Methods Research,* 1(1): 3–7.

U.S. Department of Health and Human Services (1999). *Mental Health: A Report of the Surgeon General.* Department of Health and Human Services, Substance Abuse and Mental Health Services Administration, Center for Mental Health Services, National Institutes of Health, National Institutes of Mental Health. Rockville, MD.

U.S. Department of Health and Human Services (2001). *Mental Health: Culture, Race and Ethnicity – A Supplement to Mental Health: A Report of the Surgeon General.* Department of Health and Human Services, Substance Abuse and Mental Health Services Administration, Center for Mental Health Services, National Institutes of Health, National Institutes of Mental Health. Rockville, MD.

Vega, W.A. and Lopez, S.R. (2001). Priority issues in Latino mental health services research. *Mental Health Services Research,* 3: 189–200.

Velicer, W.F. and Jackson, D.N. (1990). Component analysis versus common factor analysis: Some issues in selecting an appropriate procedure. *Multivariate Behavioral Research,* 25: 1–28.

Ysseldyke, J., Burns, M., Dawson, P., Kelley, B., Morrison, D., Ortiz, S., Rosenfield, S., and Telzrow, C. (2006). *School Psychology: A Blueprint for Training and Practice III.* Bethesda, MD: NASP.

14

Researching with Peer/ Community Researchers – Ambivalences and Tensions

Rosalind Edwards and
Claire Alexander

INTRODUCTION

In this chapter we present a critical consideration of the issues raised where academics conduct research with what are often referred to as peer/community researchers. By this we mean people who live within, and have everyday experiences as a member of, a particular geographical or social 'community', and who use their contacts and detailed lay knowledge in a mediating role, helping to gather and understand information from and about their peers for research purposes. Here, we are particularly concerned with peer/community researchers who work on research projects being undertaken by academics as lead researchers, although we also make some reference to literature on participative research generally, and further we are concerned with the practice from a lead researcher point of view.

It is slightly misleading to include a discussion of researching with peer or community researchers in a handbook addressing 'methodological innovations' without placing a caveat on assumptions about its recent pioneering nature. Many contemporary academic and career researchers regard themselves as charting new ground in involving members of the group they are studying in research, positing this 'with and for' participative approach as a radical alternative to the mainstream research paradigm where researchers are objective experts who do research 'on' subjects (e.g. Elliott et al., 2002; Fletcher, 2003; Kellett, 2005; Reason, 1994; Smith et al., 2002; Wadsworth, 1998)

Yet working with peer/community researchers, and a conception of this as part of an alternative and empowering research paradigm, has a long history. At the beginning of the twentieth century, for example, the influential thinker and town planner Patrick Geddes rejected universities as a base for research on urban locations and advocated the engagement of local people in studying their own communities, especially those who were excluded from public life, including children (Yeo, 2003). Geddes' ideas were an inspiration for what is known as the 'community self-survey movement' in both the United Kingdom and United States during the inter-war years (Bulmer, 1984), based on ideas about the creation and ownership of data as vested in local people, who were recruited as volunteers to conduct research (ideas that have echoes in the developmental and liberatory agenda exemplified by Paolo Friere).[1] The participative process of the community self-survey movement was seen as an empowering political community activity, as offering an educational experience to the volunteers, and – because local insiders were regarded as being able to reach people and information that outside academic experts could not – enabling access to better data.

This dual rationale of political empowerment and pragmatic data quality instrumentality has echoed down the years, although arguably it has nuances in the current context that mean that it takes on a somewhat different meaning. Indeed, social science research methods reflect the social conditions of a society at a point in time, shaped by its structural and cultural context (rather than methodological developments being a story of uni-directional progress) (Alasuutari et al., 2008). We begin this chapter with a review of those contemporary social conditions and their interaction with research methods, specifically in relation to some of the ambivalences attached to empowerment and instrumentalism in working with peer/community researchers. We also review the multidimensional political and practical tensions that weave themselves through notions of 'community' as well as positioning peer researchers as insiders and/or outsiders in relation both to the community or group under study and to the research and lead researchers. We then turn to explore and illustrate our critique of dominant notions of community and empowerment as part of working with peer researchers through three case studies of projects in which we have each been involved, in which we worked with peer/community researchers.

POLITICS OF EMPOWERMENT AND INSTRUMENTAL PRACTICALITIES

'User involvement' has become a constant refrain and often a requirement of research funders (Alasuutari et al., 2008). Conducting work that involves peer researchers has become increasingly popular, especially for studies with a service provision or evaluation focus, and particularly where the focus is on marginalised and disempowered groups such as minority ethnic populations, the disabled, children and young people. This 'democratisation' of the research process can be seen as part of what some commentators regard as a broader turn to democratisation in society. There are arguments that radical shifts are occurring, towards the linked, wider social processes of detraditionalisation, individualisation and globalisation (e.g. Bauman, 1987; Beck, 1992, 1999; Beck et al., 1994; Giddens, 1994, 1998). This has political implications for how researchers gain knowledge about people's social lives.

These sorts of arguments about the nature of contemporary society take some of the ideas about empowerment and development behind the community self-survey movement even further. In a democratised society, it is contended, top-down expertise and professional authority are subverted in favour of a more democratically inclusive and participatory quest for knowledge. Knowledge thereby is said to be demystified, with people gaining a greater awareness of contested opinions, access to a diversity of ways of understanding and information, and a sense of the importance of their own agency on the basis of this. In this view, we are moving towards a sort of 'self-critiquing' society in which everyone is engaged. Consequently, any claims to legitimacy on the basis of authoritative knowledge are subject to question. Such arguments about broad social shifts also have implications for social research methodology. As part of trends towards an egalitarian impulse, it is argued that the claims to knowledge and truth inherent in traditional research methodology, and its supposedly objective stance, embody relationships of power and privilege. In other words, in this view, traditional research practice is far from neutral. Feminist and minority/marginalised researchers in particular have been key in deconstructing and making transparent these relationships, and revealing knowledge production as a political process (e.g. Barnes, 1996; Gunaratnam, 2003; Smith, 1987; Stanley and Wise, 1993).

Researchers who take arguments about inclusivity and egalitarianism seriously can seek to dismantle the traditional research process and democratise it, equalising power relations between themselves and the subjects of their research (e.g. DeLyser, 2001; Fletcher, 2003; Harklau and Norwood, 2005; Kirby, 1999; Sixsmith et al., 2003; Stalker, 1998; Standing, 1998; Travers, 1997; and see contributions to Temple and Moran, 2006). A reciprocal manner of exchange and communication as equals during research interaction is promoted, with shared objectives and priorities blurring the boundaries between researcher and researched. There are also further arguments that there are, in fact, no claims to social scientific knowledge that are beyond contestation other than through personal experience and warrant. It is only the voices and involvement of those who are the subjects of research that can validate and provide faith in claims to knowledge (e.g. de Koning and Martin, 1996; Wahab, 2003).

Recognising research as a political process, though, can also lead to an opposing perspective on contemporary developments that place them as much more instrumentally-driven, even repressive, rather than empowering. In contrast to the posing of researching with peer/community researchers as a radical alternative (Finch, 1986), a more sceptical perspective argues that what is referred to as democratisation on the broad social level might more appropriately be seen as rationalisation; that generally, people's relationships are increasingly ruled by contracts and bureaucracy, and this is also the case for research (Evans, 2004). Bill Cooke and Uma Kothari believe that 'The (participatory) language of empowerment masks a concern for managerial effectiveness' (2001: 14). Indeed, shifts towards greater transparency and accountability in the research process are argued to have moved away from professional notions of internal excellence and specialist knowledge and judgement, towards bureaucratic accountability as auditability. The production of knowledge is said to have become increasingly like an assembly line process with its functional divisions of labour (Ritzer, 1998). Community researchers and other forms of user involvement are unhooked from the democratic impulse (a feature of the community self-survey movement) and become a functional, technical and instrumental aspect of research labour. The 'privileged access' through their own networks that is afforded to peer researchers is a tool for rapidly generating trust and accessing information from and about otherwise hard-to-reach research subjects that is of interest to those commissioning research (e.g. Bonner and Tolhurst, 2002; Boynton, 2002; Elliott et al., 2002; Griffiths et al., 1993; Kuebler and Hausser, 1997; Price and Hawkins, 2002; contributions to Temple and Moran, 2006; Wallman et al., 1980).

Indeed, when lead researchers argue for the importance of involving peer/community researchers, in tandem with political assertions that it is a more ethical, democratic and developmental practice, they also put forward pragmatic and instrumental notions of a rational practice that makes for better access and fuller or more accurate understanding (e.g. Harper and Carver, 1999; Kellett, 2005; Kirby, 1999; Petrie et al., 2006). For example, in discussing participatory research in general, Davydd Greenwood and colleagues assert 'Democracy in knowledge production gives the participants a stake in the quality of the results, increasing the reliability of information and the likelihood that results will be put into practice' (Greenwood et al., 1993: 177). There are two main problems with this view.

First, community involvement and 'better' data are not necessarily linked. There may be 'trade-offs' between research quality and empowerment in the mediating role of community researchers. For example, Barbara Beardwood and colleagues (2005) worked with peer researchers interviewing among the 'injured workers community'. They argue their collaborators helped to break down boundaries in an essentially wary population, but in interviews could find it difficult to refrain from centring their own experiences, as well as interrupting or leading the interviewee. Indeed, some decades ago, Emory Cowen and colleagues (1974) argued that academic researchers need to be willing to gamble with less precise and well controlled approaches, risking traditional standards of rigour, in order to gain the benefits of studying significant experiential issues with community researchers (see also Byrne-Armstrong, 2001). Eva Elliott and colleagues

(2002) conclude, for their research on drug users, that the trade-off between privileged access and quality of data was not always sufficient, however. We return to these sorts of posited off-settings below in discussing tensions around insider and outsider status.

Second, it is problematic to assume that research that involves community members (or any research) will necessarily bring about positive (or any sort) of social change. It is an unrealistic, and even cruelly misleading, burden to lay on peer researchers, that their contribution can redefine the relationship between their community and powerful organisations and institutional structures (Cooke and Kothari, 2001). Further, ideas about empowerment that reify it as an unalloyed good are underpinned by a simplistic conception of power that only serves to obscure its dynamics. Power is posed as something that a group or individual has either more of or less of, where those who have power can hand it over to (empower) those who have none. A more sophisticated consideration of power recognises that it is relational. Academic lead researchers cannot decide to transfer 'their' power to community researchers, who then 'have' that power and can use it wherever and whenever. Rather, groups and individuals are subject to differing power potentials in different social relationships and contexts (Cameron et al., 1992; Mauthner and Edwards, 2007). These relational differentiations also apply within groups, as we discuss with reference to the idea of community later on.

Indeed, there can be a fine line between involving and empowering community members as peer researchers and exploiting their labour and expertise. These political ambivalences are evident in pragmatic discussions about whether or not peer researchers should be paid for their involvement. For example, in relation to young people, Perpetua Kirby (1999) contends that payment can cut across the democratising process and become a form of instrumental control, while Gary Harper and Lisa Carver (1999) argue that, in order to be accorded full status and democratic say in the research, competitive wages should be paid to young people as peer researchers (see also Alderson, 2000; Smith et al., 2002). Where payment is opted for, it would seem that lead researchers often offer a fee per interview or honorarium, rather than a contract of employment (e.g. Clark et al., 2009; Elliott et al., 2002; Wallman et al., 1980). While the former practice may well be motivated by a desire to avoid jeopardising peer researchers' benefit status or involve them in taxable income complications, it may also be the case that – in the competitive world of research funding, despite research funding body assertions about user involvement – the greater expense of the pay and conditions associated with employment as a member of staff on a research project, on top of the time investment in training and support (see below), forces more of a budget-watching instrumental rather than well-remunerated empowering approach. It also is important to recognise that such pragmatic issues about whether and what type of employment contract have political implications in how they place peer researchers vis-à-vis their own communities and the lead researchers. We now turn to these issues of placement.

INSIDER/OUTSIDER POSITIONS AND POWER

The social processes associated with detraditionalisation, individualisation and globalisation that we have just discussed in relation to the empowering democratisation or instrumental rationalisation of research, are argued to have disembedded the nature of the social lives about which research knowledge is being gathered (Bauman, 1987; Beck, 1992, 1999; Beck et al., 1994; Giddens, 1994, 1998) 'Community' as a distinct body of people who are conscious of having something in common, leading to a sense of shared interests, identity and solidarity, has traditionally been thought of as integrally situated in local geographical context. While this understanding of where community is located continues, there are also arguments that these social relations are now more related to a variety of symbolic or imagined communities, personal communities of interest and attachment that are fluid rather than bounded (Anderson, 1991; Bauman, 1998; Cohen, 1985). In contrast to relatively straightforward equations of community and locality in the earlier community self-survey movement, wider social processes display a shift from community as locality to community as social characteristics/identity/shared lifestyle choice. This is why, in offering a definition of peer/community researchers at the start of this chapter, we referred to members of a particular geographical or social community.

In both the political empowerment and instrumental practicality rationales for working with peer/community researchers, being an 'outsider' in academic research terms and having a lack of formal research competence is regarded as offset by the valuable access to and familiarity with the local milieu that an 'insider' perspective can bring to bear. A number of trade-offs are posed in the insider/outsider research model (see Bonner and Tolhurst, 2002; Campbell, 2002; David, 2002; DeLyser, 2001; Langhout, 2006; Pitman, 2002; Price and Hawkins, 2002; Wadsworth, 1998), which we summarise here. The advantages of an insider position (which are thought to be embodied in peer researchers as mediators) are said to be that the researcher is part of and already knows the group, (sub)culture or location that is being studied. They have established relationships of acceptance, trust and empathy, and a feel for unspoken codes of behaviour and values, which can be built on for research purposes. Their 'local' knowledge is important in informing the construction of research knowledge. The downside of this position in the trade-off model is then said to be that peer researchers may tend to access people who they feel comfortable with. An insider perspective can mean that researchers equate their own experiences with those of their research subjects, and may essentialise their own community and culture vis-à-vis others. Further, the insider/outsider model of trade-offs also raises concerns about the way that wanting to present a positive, rather than potentially damaging, picture of their community can mean that peer researchers compromise their judgement, and thus compromise their mediating role. Over-familiarity is said to mean that they can take things for granted that an outside researcher would notice. Professional research codes of ethical practice, such as informed consent, privacy and confidentiality, may not sit easily with informal community norms, or may not be seen as consequential by the peer researcher.

Some of the ideas about academic research underlying the insider/outsider trade-off model, as being objective, unbiased and so on, have long been challenged, as described earlier in relation to ideas about democratisation, often from critical and feminist perspectives (e.g. Cohen et al., 2000; Denzin and Lincoln, 2000; Gray and Denicolo, 1998; Stanley and Wise, 1993). Rather than a distinction between objectivity (as impartial and unbiased) and subjectivity (as partial and involved), the two positions are seen as linked. Subjectivity is an inevitable aspect of objectivity and a combination of outsider and insider perspectives enable rigorous research through connecting knowledge and ideas about social life to grounded experience.

Lead researchers effectively attempt to bring insider/subjective and outsider/objective together when they seek to develop research skills in the peer/community researchers who they are working with through training and ongoing support and debriefing (e.g. Boynton, 2002; Clark et al., 2009). There are both political empowerment and pragmatic instrumental rationales for this practice. On the political side, training and debriefing is seen as a form of education and empowerment, giving peer researchers new skills and support in exercising them. Indeed, some lead researchers have negotiated accreditation for the training from their institutions to ensure that community researchers received a concrete benefit (e.g. Meyer et al., 2003). On the practical side, the process can be said to help lead researchers trust their community researchers to 'deliver' data of the type and standard required, and mitigates the sense of distance from the field that lead researchers can feel, just as much as it acts as a support mechanism for peer researchers (Elliott et al., 2002; see also Harper and Carver, 1999).

Support might also be needed beyond the end of the research, as community researchers 'exit' their role and lose their researcher identity, although there seems to be little acknowledgement in the literature of this and the fact that peer researches remain in their community after the research and have to deal with any consequences. Arguably, the very process of training and conducting research on their own community means that community researchers are differentially positioned from their peers. Ironically, those who are valued in the conduct of research because they are 'the same as' the subject research group, are separated and placed as different from those subjects through the process of researching them.

Indeed, rather than straightforward boundaries that are amenable to associated off-sets and trade-offs, insider/outsider positions are in fact complex and multidimensional. Shared 'structural'-or 'community'-based characteristics around age, race/ethnicity, gender, beliefs, behaviour, neighbourhood and so on do not mean that people have common identities and subjective realities, and researchers who have had a particular social experience do not necessarily empathise with their peers. Ideas of insider access to 'better' data on the basis of shared characteristics or shared lifestyles raise assumptions, first, about homogeneous social characteristics and group authenticity (as Twine, 2000, points out for race) and, second, about access to 'true' accounts that are unavailable directly to outsiders (as claimed for example by Alder and Sandor, 1990, for young people). This is in contrast to recognition that, while research subjects may give different sorts of account according to who they are talking to, one version is not necessarily 'better' or more illuminating than another (e.g. Rhodes, 1994; Dyck, 1997; Twine, 2000, on race/ethnicity; Elliott et al., 2002, on drug use).

For these reasons, Ken Moffatt and colleagues (2005) refer to 'experiential affinity' and 'parallel universes' as ways of understanding the mediating position of peer researchers. While useful, this formulation tends to place community members or peers as 'similar but different' in a pluralistic fashion, rather than acknowledging inequalities, hierarchies and the issue of power. As Roger Smith and colleagues note in relation to young people as peer researchers, 'Power relations between young people, perhaps based on gender or ethnic difference, may be as significant as power differentials between them as a group and statutory agencies' (2002: 194) (see also Mestheneos, 2006, on refugees as peer researchers; Cooke and Kothari, 2001, on participatory research). Communities and peer networks are not made up entirely of consensus and homogeneity, but also encompass relations of ambivalence, mistrust and conflict. The social hierarchies that exclude or marginalise some sections of a minority community are likely to be reflected in research with peer/community researchers who, even if they identify power imbalances, may feel unable to challenge them, or may have much invested in their continuance (David, 2002), or may themselves not be accepted by others in the community in their role as researcher and the shift from the personal to a professional relationship (Elliott et al., 2002). Indeed, safety and confidentiality are not just issues for lead researchers to consider in relation to research participants, but also apply to peer researchers (Boynton, 2002).

The existence of power relations that cannot be avoided also applies to relations between lead and peer researchers. Unacknowledged power differences can surface and disrupt the research process in research teams that encompass the subjects of research as co-researchers (Byrne-Armstrong, 2001; and see Clark et al., 2009). As Linda Mitteness and Judith Barker say:

> While ideologies of equality may be attractive, we have never seen instances where people of vastly different educational backgrounds, investments in the study, and research experience have been able to overcome issues of hierarchy and operate as equals throughout every portion of a research effort. We suggest that researchers need to get over the idea that a common ground is ever more than fleeting. Social hierarchies exist and are not mitigated by ideological stances to the contrary. (2004: 286)

Nonetheless, as with peer researchers' complex positioning as insiders and outsiders in relation to 'their' community, power relations between lead and peer researchers are multifaceted. They do not merely follow a straightforward hierarchical flow, but are changing and fluid. The balance of power, for example, can shift at different stages of the research process, in favour of lead researchers during recruitment and conceptualisation, and in favour of peer researchers during the data collection process given their greater 'insider' field knowledge (Mauthner and Edwards, 2007), as noted earlier in relation to training.

We now turn to explore and illustrate these sorts of shifts and the complexities of working with peer/community researchers through examples from three research projects in which either one or both of us have been involved. Threaded throughout these examples from practice are ambivalences and tensions around notions of 'community' and 'empowerment'.

EXAMPLES FROM PRACTICE

Our three examples of the practice of working with peer/community researchers concern: (i) lone mothers, (ii) people who need interpreters to access services and (iii) young parents. At the time that each of these pieces of research was conducted, and still the case, these were regarded as marginalised, 'socially excluded' groups, identified by politicians and the media as 'outsiders' from mainstream British society, and moreover as threats to social cohesion. The research on lone mothers was conducted in 1994/6, in the aftermath of the Conservative government's vilification of underclass single parents 'wedded to welfare' and the advent of New Labour's New Deal for Lone Parents. The research on people who need interpreters to access services took place in 2003/4, in the shadow of political blame for those who were not fully competent in the English language as creating their own social exclusion, and contributing to community fragmentation and discord. The research on young parents took place in 2006, in the context of teenage pregnancy being regarded as a pernicious social problem for the UK that required a specific ameliorative government strategy.

The overwhelming majority of the discussions about working with peer/community researchers that we have cited so far in this chapter proceed from and prioritise an empowerment perspective on the practice (with a few pieces taking quite a self-congratulatory tone). In some contrast, our primary motivation in working with peer researchers in each of the three projects was instrumental – to be able to access research participants who would otherwise be hard-to-reach or with whom we could not communicate. Empowerment of the community researclers was certainly a concern and we worked towards it in various ways, as we discuss below, but in truth it was secondary to pragmatic considerations.

CASE ONE – RESEARCHING WITH LONE MOTHER PEER RESEARCHERS

(carried out by Rosalind Edwards in collaboration with Simon Duncan: see Duncan and Edwards, 1999)

This research study looked at how lone mothers envisage the relationship between motherhood and paid work, which we eventually came to term their 'gendered moral rationalities'. It sought to depart from the prevalent mode of research on the topic, with its focus on lone mothers as a given taxonomic group living in the determining context of welfare regimes, to look at the variable social processes by which different groups of lone mothers actually make choices about taking up paid work or not. In other words, we wanted to move beyond treating lone mothers as a meaningfully delineated, essentially homogeneous social group in itself, whose behaviour was wrought by state policies. Rather, we saw lone mothers as social actors who developed their variable understandings of whether and how motherhood could be combined with paid work in negotiation with others in their local social circles, and we saw these understandings and networks as cross-cut by far more important social divisions of class, ethnicity and culture.

Part of our research design thus involved interviews with lone mothers, addressing their feelings and understandings about combining motherhood and paid work, relations with other people in their social networks, and their views about the local neighbourhood and labour market. We identified different thematic groups of lone mothers covering class, ethnicity and culture who we wanted to interview, and also a range of specific types of areas from which to draw these samples. Examples of the groups we selected include: African-Caribbean lone mothers living in inner city neighbourhoods, White working class lone mothers living on peripheral public housing estates, White middle class lone mothers living in suburban neighbourhoods, and White 'alternative' (counter-cultural, feminist) lone mothers living in gentrifying neighbourhoods.

Working with community researchers was not initiated by a requirement on the part of our research funder (the UK Economic and Social Research Council) or motivated by our own participatory political commitments. On a pragmatic level, previous experience had alerted us to the difficulties for White researchers (as was the case for us) in reaching Black lone mothers in particular (Edwards, 1996). Our solution to this access problem was to employ peer researchers, and we decided to extend the practice to most of the social groups we wanted to include in our research. We timetabled the interviews to take place over the Higher Education summer holidays, and largely recruited mature undergraduate students who were part of the groups and locations we had identified. These peer researchers thus already occupied a complex 'intermediate' position between community and academy, bringing yet another dimension to our previous point about insider/outsider positions being ambivalent and multidimensional.[2]

Once this instrumental course was decided, we then turned to the politics of the situation. In an effort to avoid any potential exploitation and ensure that the lone mothers/students benefited from working on the research, we employed them on a university research assistant contract over the summer, rather than offering a fee per interview. This gave the peer researchers access to staff facilities and services, paid their national insurance contributions, and – we hoped – looked more impressive on their CVs. Pragmatic and instrumental ideas (data quality) that then embraced a commitment to empowerment also underpinned the consultation with the peer researchers over the questions asked, the training we provided in interviewing, our wider research rationale and process, and the ongoing support we provided to them individually and also regularly getting together as a research team throughout the data gathering process. Unfortunately, in this early (for us) study with community researchers we did not think to conduct exit interviews with the lone mothers/students about the process of working on the research (as we did for peer researchers on later projects – see cases below). Further, at the end of their paid employment, and their return to their studies, we did not continue to involve the lone mothers. In part, we did not want them to work for no pay, but in greater part, we did not feel that our peer researchers had a sufficient grasp of the theoretical endeavour driving our project and of data analysis skills. This was a piece of research that was interested in the voices of its subjects, but not one in which we were committed to an empowerment that attempts to hand the research direction over to its subjects. We return to this relationship of power below.

One of the drawbacks of working with community researchers that is sometimes pointed to is that, as insiders, they tend to access and interview people they feel comfortable with. In our case, this was a bonus since we were interested in lone mothers' local social networks. We were attempting to capitalise on our lone mother peer researchers' established relations of acceptance and trust, by asking them to snowball within their own networks to interview lone mothers. Underlying this practice was an idea of community as both geographical and social; lone mothers as part of communities that are located in neighbourhoods and comprise networks of people with shared social characteristics and values. The process of snowballing illuminated the combined applicability and naivety of this conception. In most cases, the peer researchers did indeed know other lone mothers within their 'group' (such as the African-Caribbean inner city groups), and in some instances they were also part of networks that were based in relatively tightly defined areas (such as the White alternative gentrifying group). In these instances, there was no difficulty in gathering interviewees in a fast expanding snowball that soon reached our target of 10 lone mothers per group.

One particular group and location, however, highlights both the relevance of our idea that 'lone mothers' is not a category that represents a coherent social group reality, and our naivety in thinking that a local community existed that could be snowballed amongst. In the case of White middle class lone mothers living in an affluent suburb, it proved both difficult to reach them and hard to persuade those who were contacted to take part. Many did not want to associate themselves with such a 'stigmatised' group, and it was virtually impossible to snowball out to other lone mothers from those who were interviewed as they did not know or mix with other lone mothers locally. They wanted to keep their heads down and avoid being regarded by their married neighbours as part of the social threat to family and national life that lone motherhood was posed as representing at the time. We never reached our target of 10 interviewees for this particular group (though our analysis of ward census data showed that there were lone mothers living in the neighbourhood). As one of our interviewees in the area explained:

> I do find that there aren't any other single parents, that I've come across certainly, which is sometimes a bit frustrating ... I've been at school meetings where it has been said 'we don't want our children mixing with all those single parents (from the local public housing estate) because this is a nice area and we don't have those sorts of people'. And then I stick my hand up. And they're very apologetic, 'oh we don't mean you', because I'm a nice single parent, I'm the exception.

The idea of communities as networks of consensus and homogeneity, and of peer researchers as embedded in trusting 'insider' relationships within them that ensure rapid research access, had a hollow ring in these circumstances.

Issues of stigma, insider/outsider status, empowerment and trust are also raised in looking at the peer researchers mediating between their 'community' and the lead researchers. As noted earlier, peer researchers may have a lot invested in the image of their community presented. As part of their employment, we asked our peer researchers to transcribe the interviews that they carried out. This meant, as we have also noted, that, as lead researchers, we felt removed from the field, with debriefing sessions with the peer researchers just as much for our benefit in bringing a sense of closeness to the data as for support for the lone mothers. At one point, however, Ros felt she needed to do more to bring herself closer to the data in order to prepare herself for data analysis and decided to listen to some of the audiotapes in an effort to get a real sense of 'voice'. Listening to one tape she found that the peer researcher concerned, Hope, had not transcribed an illuminating discussion between herself and the interviewee that had occurred at the end of the interview, in which the interviewee said:

> Being Black does make a difference if you're a single parent. I think we're looked down on more ... being a single parent you're a burden anyway, and being Black is even worse. I think they expect more from us. I think that sometimes they think we're scrounging from them, more than a White single parent might have that pressure put on them ... Because they think it's the majority of us doing it.

When Ros checked back with Hope, it transpired that Hope had felt that the remarks were not necessarily relevant for the research, as well as a mix of embarrassment and betrayal at the thought of handing these words over to the 'them' being talked about in the form of a White academic. The complex pulls of insider/outsider positions in relation to both community and research for peer researchers are evident here, as is the fact that in the end the lead researcher had the power to override Hope's judgement about the relevance of the discussion. Indeed, the incident raised issues of trust about all the peer researchers – should all their audio recordings be checked against their transcripts?

Finally, this case study of researching lone mothers' gendered moral rationalities with peer researchers illustrates how misleading it can be to think that 'democratic knowledge production' is more likely to have an impact and be put to practical use. Whatever the level of involvement of community researchers in the project, its findings entered into a political context where successive governments were wedded to increasing lone mothers' uptake of paid work. No matter that the gendered moral rationality of some groups of lone mothers (in particular White working and middle classes) prioritised motherhood over paid work was given voice through the research; policymakers were not interested in responding.

CASE TWO – RESEARCHING PEOPLE WHO NEED INTERPRETERS WITH COMMUNITY RESEARCHERS

(carried out by Claire Alexander and Rosalind Edwards, in collaboration with Bogusia Temple: see Alexander, Edwards and Temple, 2004)

This research study explored the experiences of people who needed or had used interpreters in order to gain access to health, welfare, legal and other services in the UK. While a number of projects had previously focused on the role of the interpreter him/herself, or on the perspective of service providers, the main aim of this research was to consider views and experiences of users of interpreting services – those individuals or groups whose needs and wants have been previously overlooked or simply assumed. In a context in which the provision of interpreting services was under attack from the shift towards English language competence as a primary element in the granting of citizenship, on the one hand, and the 'professionalisation' of interpreting services, on the other, we wanted to place the need for, and use of, interpreters in the context of individual lives as a whole, and to restore some sense of agency and humanity to these debates. The project revealed two important aspects to the use of interpreters: first, the central role of trust in the relationship between the respondent and the interpreter, with distinctions drawn between what we saw as 'abstract' qualities centred on competence and professional knowledge, and 'personal' characteristics, rooted often in informal networks of family and friends and based on consideration of, and apparent commitment to, the respondent's needs, situation or preferences (Edwards et al., 2006). Second, the research explored the ways in which notions of minority ethnic 'community' were constructed (often with language as a key signifier), and how these boundaries were fractured and traversed by what we termed 'personal' communities (Alexander et al., 2007a, b).

The research was focused on five ethnic minority 'communities' based in London (Chinese, Kurdish) and Manchester (Polish, Gujrati Indian, Bangladeshi). The aim of this selection was to represent a variety of experiences of migration to, and settlement in, Britain, in terms of length of presence, levels of integration or marginalisation, legal status (as citizens, settlers or asylum seekers), degree of visibility in research or policy formation and the posing of new challenges. Within each group, we conducted 10 semi-structured interviews, with each group containing diverse experiences in terms of gender, family background, age and migration history. The sample was not, however, demographically representative but rather illustrative of the range and kinds of people who need and use interpreters. This varied significantly across/between groups with, for example the Gujerati Indian sample being predominantly older people, while the Kurdish group was comprised of mainly young men. The Polish group reflected both the needs of the older, established community and the younger, newly arrived Polish-Roma asylum seekers.[3]

Because of the focus of the project – people who need interpreters – the interviews were necessarily conducted by community researchers, who were fluent in the language of the relevant groups. The use of community researchers was driven in this case first and foremost by the practical exigencies of the research project. Apart from one lead researcher, Bogusia Temple, who has extensive experience in researching the Polish community and is a fluent Polish speaker, we recruited five researchers (two from the Chinese community and one each from the Bangladeshi, Gujerati and Kurdish communities), none of whom had previous experience of research of this kind. As well as language facility (in both the 'community language' and English), we selected our researchers on the basis of the potential access they had to communities that might be otherwise hard to reach. This was particularly important in the case of groups that are comparatively recent arrivals or are spatially dispersed (as with the Chinese and Kurdish communities), and, indeed, most of the peer researchers utilised some personal networks, as well as knowledge of their local community institutions, to access interviewees.

There were, of course, additional, less practical concerns, which were based around the politics of conducting research with hard to reach and vulnerable individuals and groups, particularly in the rather fraught context post the 2001 riots in the north of England[4] and the debates around language and citizenship. Given our desire to place the use of interpreters in a broader biographical context, it was felt that to conduct interviews ourselves through interpreters would be an unnecessarily disruptive and distancing gesture, and one which would present the research in a more formal and hierarchical format that would restrict the kinds of material we were hoping for. Conducting interviews in the interviewee's first language with someone from their 'community', we thought, might encourage confidence and a degree of trust that would enrich the material and mitigate some of the more hierarchical aspects of the research relationships. For this reason also we avoided recruiting our sample from organisations involved with providing interpreting services, and the ability to utilise our researchers' informal networks was an important resource in some (but not all) cases.

Well-resourced by the Joseph Rowntree Foundation, the project recruited five community researchers on university research assistant contracts for three months full-time or six months part-time, depending on the wishes/situation of the individual concerned, and they were given responsibility for selecting their sample,[5] conducting the interviews and transcribing them into English (though not with the analysis and writing up process). As with the previous study on lone mothers, we were keen to avoid exploitative working conditions and to give the peer researchers access to staff facilities and to relevant training, as well as the status that accrued from a formal connection to an institution of Higher Education (which also had practical benefits when seeking out potential interviewees through gatekeepers). They were all given training in conducting qualitative research at the beginning of the project and had ongoing supervisions with a designated lead researcher to monitor the progress of data collection. In addition, at the end of their contracts, we conducted exit interviews with each community researcher, enabling them to reflect on their experience of the study and their role within it, and allowing us to get an insight into the research process through their eyes.

What became apparent, particularly through these interviews, was the complex and often ambivalent position occupied by the 'community researcher' in relation to their imagined 'community'. This was partly around issues of access, which proved more difficult in some cases than we as lead researchers had initially imagined, but it speaks also to the construction of 'community' in 'community research', particularly around issues of ethnicity (Song and Parker, 1995). Mohib, our Bangladeshi researcher, noted that having a shared linguistic and cultural background gave him an advantage, particularly in negotiating the gender divide in the Bangladeshi community:

> When I found the sample I tried to treat them like sisters ... that really helps, as in all these things. How to approach people, and how to talk to them. The same with old people ... I know what language to use for the right people. Professional or like academic people won't know this.

However, our Kurdish researcher told us that while his commonalities with his interviewees was a benefit, 'The skills I bring to the research is my background, (because) I know about people's difficulties here because I faced them just like them', he still found that his early attempts at access through formal community centres were blocked by suspicious community leaders and a divided internal politics.[6] He, as with the other peer researchers, eventually drew upon informal networks of family and friends in making contacts, while others also used community networks built up from their other employment – in some cases in their role as interpreters. Anita, one of our Chinese speaking researchers, commented that making contacts through a community centre where she had worked as an interpreter was important in helping to establish trust, 'Because I'm introduced by their centre manager or by their worker so they trust their Chinese centre to know me ... they [are] a bit frightened to have an interview with a stranger'. Usha, our Gujerati speaking researcher also confirmed, 'if you don't know anyone, nowadays it is hard. They (community centres) don't allow any stranger to go and tape interviews'. Zhuang, our second Chinese speaking researcher, told us, 'the best way for Chinese is, ask your friends, so you have got someone who trusts them'. At the same time, several of the community researchers commented that this familiarity also raised some barriers – that personal trust had limits, particularly around issues of confidentiality in discussing highly private matters. Anita commented:

> People are not willing to tell you that much with the tape recorder. They talk to you freely without interview situation, you can talk to them as a friend ... but [if] you tell them you have to do the project or research ... they do not want to tell you too much.

Interestingly, issues of trust, or its lack, stood at the centre of the relationships between the community researchers and their interviewees. Indeed, this reflects the experience of 'professional' academic researchers and challenges the idea that utilising 'community' or 'peer' researchers necessarily ameliorates the research relationship in any straightforward way. It also shows that trust is more complex than arguments about 'matching' researchers (in terms of class, gender or ethnicity) might imply – a situation which reflected one of the key findings of the research itself. Our experience of this project suggests that the idea of 'community' in 'community research' needs more careful delineation if it is not to reinscribe essentialist ideas of individual and group identities and experiences (Alleyne, 2002; Alexander, 2004). Indeed, our peer researchers were keen to distinguish their position against that of their interviewees, particularly along the lines of class or professionalisation through their status as interpreters or researchers. Mohib commented to us that, 'The one thing I learned from this is that people don't understand ... Only two or three people understood the purpose of this research', while our Kurdish researcher spoke of the feelings of status he acquired through doing the research:

> It's difficult to mix with the people, educated respected people. You don't have a chance. You are all the time in the urban area and you have a chance to mix with street peoples. I find it more easy, as an educated man to mix with respected people who can respect you ... I find this only here in the South Bank University after I start to work.

Trust was also prominent in the relationship between the lead researchers (us and Bogusia) and the community researchers: indeed, the issues of distancing outlined in the lone mothers' project were rendered more starkly with this project because of the language and culture divide. This meant that we were unable to directly access the data collected and had to rely exclusively on the translation and interpretation of cultural and linguistic inflexions of the interviews. Similarly, we had to take at face value assurances about the logistics of conducting the research in the field, the range of interviewees selected and the rationale for this sampling. This meant that when we came to analyse the data, we were dealing with material that was already doubly mediated, at the time of collection and at the time of translation, before being translated again through our own analysis (Temple et al., 2006).

Here again, then, the use of peer/community researchers is not only a contested category, but one which was driven more by practical needs than political ones. While our community researchers were able to benefit from the research in terms of employment opportunities, additional training and, in some cases, status, their role in mediating or contributing to broader changes was recognised as minimal. Indeed, Zhuang commented:

> I think that for most of the interviewees they agreed to do interview with me simply because they think the interview does no harm to them … They are adults, they are all grown up; no-one can be so childish as to think that the interview could change the life of someone Chinese. Interview can change, but it takes a long, long time.

CASE THREE – RESEARCHING WITH YOUNG PARENT PEER RESEARCHERS

(*carried out by Claire Alexander and Rosalind Edwards, in collaboration with Simon Duncan: see Alexander, Duncan and Edwards, 2007*)

The final study we want to consider was a small piece of exploratory research on the experiences of teenage parents, which was funded by Upfront Teenage Pregnancy Team, part of Bradford City Council's Youth Service. The project was titled 'Listening to Young Mothers and Fathers' and was concerned with exploring the ways in which young parents understand and experience their roles as mothers and fathers and how this combines with employment, education and aspirations for the future. The research took as its point of departure the dominant attitudes towards teenage parents as being ignorant or feckless, and found that, in contrast to these stereotypes, young parents were responsible, ambitious and aspirational, were enmeshed in multiple networks of support and most often saw their role as being 'just a mother' or 'just a father', with all the problems and joys that any parenthood brings with it. The research also found that social policies directed towards young parents, particularly around housing, could serve to reinforce or ameliorate the experience of isolation, which had potentially serious repercussions for access to employment, education and childcare.

The project involved interviews with six young mothers and two young fathers all living in Bradford. All interviewees were aged between 18 and 21 years at the time of interview, and had one child born while they were aged between 16 and 19 years. The semi-structured interviews explored a range of themes covering the experience of motherhood/fatherhood, support networks, neighbourhood and community, education and employment, and were conducted by three peer researchers, all young women with children. Two of these, Amy and Kayleigh, were teenage mothers themselves, while the third interviewer, Yasmin, was slightly older, but had been a young mother when her first child was born. The former two peer researchers were both White young mothers living in outer areas of Bradford, while the latter was of Pakistani descent living in inner city Bradford. In contrast to the two projects described earlier, and due to the small size and limited resourcing of the project, the peer researchers were paid on an hourly rate (as well as travel and childcare expenses), and were responsible for finding interviewees (two mothers and one father each) and conducting the interviews.

Transcription of interviews was done within the University of Bradford. The peer researchevs were given a day of training by the research team and ongoing mentoring by Simon Duncan, as well as taking part in final exit interviews, and Simon was able to arrange for their work on the project to be accredited.

It is interesting to reflect that despite the comparatively poor conditions of employment, this project was designed with the strongest political commitment to the ideals of using peer/community researchers of any of the three cases discussed. This was in part underpinned by the expectations of the funders, a Council-sponsored organisation working with young parents and committed to the empowerment model of research. Working with peer researchers was thus less about practical issues of access or expertise, though we did want to see how effective peer research could be for a project of this kind, and more about the desire to pursue a participatory model of research, and to provide research experience (and wages) for the young women we employed. In Yasmin's case, there were additional practical reasons: the research team was keen to explore the dimension of ethnicity in the attitudes to, and experience of, young parenthood, and we hoped Yasmin would provide access to some young parents from Bradford's large Pakistani community. Although this was only partially successful – Yasmin was able to interview two young mothers, but due to the marriage patterns (and cultural silences) of the Pakistani community, was unable to find a young father – some important additional dimensions to the research were hinted at, particularly around the younger age of marriage, the status of young motherhood and the role of the extended family in parenting.

Given the very limited scope of the study, the three peer researchers, each relied initially on their own informal contacts, though these were only partially successful, again demonstrating the limits of trust on both sides. Amy, for example, told us that her own friends had ignored her requests for interview, while both Kayleigh and Yasmin had drawn on networks of friends and work contacts to find their interviewees, but had deliberately chosen to interview people they themselves did not know. All felt that their experience as young mothers added to the research and helped develop rapport with the interviewees, but it is interesting too that each preferred interviewing strangers. Yasmin commented that this made her feel more comfortable in her role as researcher, which might point to some of the contradictions in role and status that arise when one is interviewing known peers.

It is, of course, hard to draw many lessons from such a small study, but a number of issues arise from this particular project. The first is the seeming attractiveness of the community researcher/empowerment model to funders, and the ways in which this in turn may have unintended consequences for the kind and quality of material that is made available. Thus, although the peer researchers produced what we had asked of them, their lack of experience and confidence meant that the interview data was often very thin and that leads were not followed up as they would have been by a more experienced researcher. This was particularly obvious when trying to elicit sensitive information, around household income for example. Second, although the peer researchers themselves felt they had gained in confidence, knowledge and experience from the project, it is questionable what, if any, broader impact the research has made, even at the local level (and particularly given the recent slew of TV programmes aimed at demonising young mothers). Third, the researchers tended to look for, and therefore find, interviewees who were like themselves. While this was appropriate for a project of this size, it raises issues about how other groups would be accessed in a bigger project, and what silences and invisibilities are perpetuated through such forms of access. In other words, what constitutes 'community' or 'peer group' when using community/peer researchers? Fourth, the project raised interesting questions about the efficacy of training we undertook with these young women – although we had conducted similar training before with other researchers, their comparative youth and lack of academic background was not sufficiently taken into account. In the exit interviews, for example, Amy commented that the training was too general and did not prepare her for the actual experience of conducting an interview in a stranger's house talking about confidential issues, while Yasmin found the training helpful in conducting interviews but not in finding interviewees.

CONCLUSION

This chapter has been written from the point of view of academic researchers working with peer/community researchers. What is more, it is a critical review of issues arising out of largely pragmatic interest rather than political principles. Our aim has been to draw out some of the ambivalences attached to assumptions about empowerment in working with peer researchers, and tensions underlying unreflexive notions of a community from which peer researchers are drawn.

As our three case studies of work on lone mothers, people who need interpreters, and young parents, have illustrated, multidimensional issues of power and trust weave themselves through the process of working with peer/community researchers, and are evident both in relationships within the research team, between lead and community researchers, and within the field, between community researchers and the peers who are the topics of the research.

A focus on the relational dynamics of power reveals the ways that, within the research team, these shift and are played out over time. Peer researchers have control during the actual fieldwork process, with lead researchers reliant on them in this respect. Nonetheless, in the end, it is lead researchers who can both enable and over-ride on the basis of their differing power potential to peer researchers. Complexities of power are also evident in relations between community researchers and their peers, where community researchers may have some investment in distinguishing themselves from their peers and allying themselves with the research team, and other investments in protecting the image of community from the research gaze.

Interlinked with power relations and dynamics, trust is a recurring motif in our discussion of working with peer researchers. For us, it is a crucial but under-recognised feature of working with peer/community researchers. While it is sometimes mentioned as an issue in other's discussions of the topic, the practical dimensions and dilemmas are rarely drawn out. As insiders in their group, community researchers are thought to have established relationships of trust with the people they are researching, or even that only the involvement of subjects in research provides trustworthy knowledge. But communities are not entirely homogenous and consensual, and trust is contingent and variable. Relations of ambivalence and mistrust also exist and can place peer researchers in awkward or difficult positions in relation to members of their community, affect their desire or ability to access some research participants, and to discuss particular aspects of interviewees' lives. Similarly, in empowerment models, lead researchers are implicitly posed as trusting the peer researchers who they are working with simply on the basis that they are insiders. Yet relationships within a research team, between lead and community researchers, are also contingent and variable, shaped by concerns about data quality on the part of the former, and ambivalent positioning for the latter.

And a final recurring theme concerns the wider political context for research. As we noted early on in this chapter, user involvement has become a constant refrain for many research funders. This raises tensions and ambiguities around the relationship between politics and pragmatism in studies involving peer/community researchers. Research funders may want to commission research that is empowering, but may not fully consider what this can mean for the quality of research material collected. Funders' choices about empowerment inevitably mean practical choices for lead researchers around access and quality, and also inevitably place peer researchers in complex and shifting relationships with those they are mediating between. Furthermore, the legitimacy and warrant that community researchers are intended to bring to research may have limited reach. Any hopes for broad impact through working with peer/community researchers are often destined to be dashed. Relations of power within and between locational, lifestyle or personal communities and the institutional structures that shape their lives, are deeply rooted, and even small measures of social change are not guaranteed by conducting participatory empirical research, where the findings from such work go against the grain of current political interests.

Working with peer or community researchers can be a rewarding and illuminating endeavour. It is a process that we willingly undertook in all the three case studies we explored in this chapter, and are likely to do so again in other research in the future. As before, doing so will engage us in complex, practical decisions and dynamics of power and trust that need to be made explicit and addressed, rather than obscured or glossed over through assertions of political empowerment alone.

NOTES

1 Paulo Freire was an influential thinker about education as praxis – action that is informed by values and theory. In *Pedagogy of the Oppressed* (1972) in particular, he explored the possibilities of co-operative and respectful dialogue for liberatory practice. He critiqued educational forms that treat people as objects rather than subjects, and built a foundation for a pedagogy of the oppressed.

2 Our thanks to Malcolm Williams for bringing this point to our attention.

3 This group arrived in regular numbers from the mid-1990s, and preceded the current wave of post-accession Polish migrant workers. Asylum was claimed on the basis of ethnic discrimination and violence in the wake of the dismantling of the Soviet bloc. The group is mainly composed of young men, although there were some families included in the study.

4 In the spring and summer of 2001, rioting as a result of tensions between Asian and White youth, fuelled by the activities of far right groups (Amin, 2003).

5 Samplimh aimed at selecting a range of individuals who needed to use interpreters, to access a variety of experiences. Although not demographically 'representative' the aim was to reflect the varying profile and needs of the different communities – for example, the Gujerati interviewees who needed interpreters tended to be older, while the Kurdish and Polish Roma groups were younger and predominantly male. Where possible we aimed at gender balance and a range of ages, family backgrounds and migration histories, although this was sometimes affected by problems of access, particularly amongst newly arrived and dispersed communities (such as the Kurdish group). Sampling was discussed and reviewed on an ongoing basis in supervision meetings throughout the research.

6 For this reason, he preferred to remain anonymous in the production of the research report.

REFERENCES

Alasuutari, P., Bickman, L., and Brannen, J. (2008) 'Social research in changing social conditions'. In P. Alasuutari, L. Bickman, and J. Brannen (eds) *Handbook of Social Research Methods*. London: Sage.

Alder, C. and Sandor, D. (1990) 'Youth researching youth'. *Youth Studies*, November: 38–42.

Alderson, P. (2000) 'Children as researchers: the effects of participation rights on research methodology'. In P. Christiansen and A. James (eds) *Research With Children: Perspectives and Practices*. London: Falmer Press.

Alexander, C. (2004) 'Writing race: truth, fiction and ethnography in "The Asian Gang"'. In M. Bulmer and J. Solomos (eds) *Researching Race and Racism*. London: Routledge.

Alexander, C., Edwards, R., and Temple, B. (2004) *Access to Services With Interpreters: User Views*. York: Joseph Rowntree Foundation.

Alexander, C., Duncan, S., and Edwards, R. (2007a) *Listening to Young Mothers and Fathers: Research Findings on the Experiences of Teenage Mothers and Fathers in Bradford*. Report to Upfront Teenage Pregnancy Team, Bradford City Council Youth Service, Bradford: University of Bradford.

Alexander, C., Edwards, R., and Temple, B. (2007b) 'Contesting cultural communities: Language, ethnicity and citizenship'. *Journal of Ethnic and Migration Studies*, 33(5): 783–800.

Alleyne, B. (2002) 'An idea of community and its discontents'. *Ethnic and Racial Studies*, 25(4): 607–27.

Amin, A. (2003) 'Unruly strangers? The 2001 urban riots in Britain'. *International Journal of Urban and Regional Research*, 27(2): 460–3.

Anderson, B. (1991, 2nd edn) *Imagined Communities: Reflections on the Origin and Spread of Nationalism*. London: Verso.

Barnes, C. (1996) 'Disability and the myth of the independent researcher'. *Disability and Society*, 11(1): 107–12.

Bauman, Z. (1987) *Legislators and Interpreters*. Cambridge: Polity Press.

Bauman, Z. (1998) *Globalisation: The Human Consequences*. New York: Columbia University Press.

Beardwood, B.A., Kirsh, B., and Clark, N.J. (2005) 'Victims twice over: perceptions and experiences of injured workers'. *Qualitative Health Research*, 15(1): 30–48.

Beck, U. (1992) *Risk Society: Towards a New Modernity*. London: Sage.

Beck, U. (1999) *World Risk Society*. Cambridge: Polity Press.

Beck, U., Giddens, A., and Lash, S. (1994) *Reflexive Modernisation*. Cambridge: Polity Press.

Bonner, A. and Tolhurst, G. (2002) 'Insider-outsider perspectives of participant observation'. *Nurse Researcher*, 9(4): 7–19.

Boynton, P.M. (2002) 'Life on the streets: The experiences of community researchers in a study of prostitution'. *Journal of Community and Applied Social Psychology*, 12: 1–12.

Bulmer, M. (1984) *The Chicago School of Sociology: Institutionalisation, Diversity and the Rise of Sociological Research*. Chicago: University of Chicago Press.

Byrne-Armstrong, H. (2001) 'Whose show is it? The contradictions of collaboration'. In H. Byrne-Armstrong, J. Higgs, and D. Horsfall (eds) *Critical Moments in Qualitative Research*. Oxford: Butterworth-Heineman.

Cameron, D., Frazer, E., Harvey, P., Rampton, M.B.H., and Richardson, K. (1992) *Researching Language: Issues of Power and Method*. London: Routledge.

Campbell, J. (2002) 'A critical appraisal of participatory methods in development research'. *International Journal of Social Research Methodology*, 5(1): 19–29.

Clark, A. Holland, C. Katz, J. and Pearce, S. (2009) 'Learning to see: Lessons from a participatory observation research project in public spaces'. *International Journal of Social Research Methodology*, 12(4): 345–60.

Cohen, A.P. (1985) *The Symbolic Construction of Community*. London: Routledge.

Cohen, L., Mannion, L., and Morrison, K. (2000) *Research Methods in Education*. London: RoutledgeFalmer.

Cooke, B. and Kothari, U. (2001) 'The case for participation as tyranny'. In B. Cooke and U. Kothari (eds) *Participation: The New Tyranny?*. London: Zed Books.

Cowen, E.L., Lorion, R.P. and Dorr, D. (1974) 'Research in the community cauldron: A case history'. *Canadian Psychologist*, 15(4): 313–25.

David, M. (2002) 'Problems of participation: the limits of action research'. *International Journal of Social Research Methodology*, 5(1): 11–17.

De Koning, K. and Martin, M. (1996) 'Participatory research in health: setting the context'. In K. de Koning and M. Martin (eds) *Participatory Research in Health*, South Africa: National Progressive Primary Health Care Network.

DeLyser, D. (2001) 'Do you really live here? Thoughts on insider research'. *The Geographical Review*, 441–53.

Denzin, N.K. and Lincoln, Y.S. (eds) (2000, 2nd edn) *Handbook of Qualitative Research*. London: Sage.

Duncan, S. and Edwards, R. (1999) *Lone Mothers, Paid Work and Gendered Moral Rationalities*. Basingstoke: Macmillan.

Dyck, I. (1997) 'Dialogue with a difference: a tale of two studies'. In S. Roberts, H. Nast, and J.P. Jones (eds) *Thresholds in Feminist Geography*. Lanham: Rowman and Littlefield.

Edwards, R. (1996) 'White woman researcher – black women subjects'. *Feminism and Psychology*, 6(2): 169–75.

Edwards, R., Alexander, C., and Temple, B. (2006) 'Interpreting trust: Abstract and personal trust for people who need interpreters to access services'. Sociological Research Online, 11(1): www.socresonline.org.uk/11/1/edwards.html.

Elliott, E., Watson, A.J., and Harries, J. (2002) 'Harnessing expertise: involving peer interviewers in qualitative research with hard-to-reach populations'. *Health Expectations*, 5: 172–8.

Evans, M. (2004) *Killing Thinking: The Death of Universities*. London: Continuum.

Finch, J. (1986) *Research and Policy: The Qualitative Methods in Social and Educational Research*. Barcombe: The Falmer Press.

Fletcher, C. (2003) 'Community-based participatory research relationships with aboriginal communities in Canada: An overview of context and process'. *Pimatisiwin: A Journal of Aboriginal and Indigenous Community Health*, 1(1): 27–62.

Freire, P. (1972) *Pedagogy of the Oppressed*. Harmondsworth: Penguin.

Giddens, A. (1994) *Beyond Left and Right: The Future of Radical Politics*. Cambridge: Polity Press.

Giddens, A. (1998) *The Third Way: The Renewal of Social Democracy*. Cambridge: Polity Press.

Gray, D.E. and Denicolo, P. (1998) 'Research in special needs education: Objectivity or ideology?'. *British Journal of Special Education,* 25(3): 140–5.

Greenwood, D.J., Whyte, W.F. and Harkavy, I. (1993) 'Participatory action research as a process and as a goal', Special Issue on Action Research. *Human Relations*, 46(2): 177–89.

Griffiths, M., Gossop, M., Powis, B., and Strang, J. (1993) 'Reaching hidden populations of drug users by privileged access interviews: Methodological and practical issues'. *Addiction,* 88: 1617–26.

Gunaratnam, Y. (2003) *Researching 'Race' and Ethnicity: Methods, Knowledge and Power.* London: Sage.

Haarklau, L. and Norwood, R. (2005) 'Negotiating researcher roles in ethnographic program evaluation: a postmodern lens'. *Anthropology and Education Quarterly,* 36(2): 78–288.

Harper, G.W. and Carver, L.J. (1999) '"Out of the mainstream" youth as partners in collaborative research: Exploring the benefits and challenges'. *Health Education and Behaviour*, 26(2): 250–65.

Kellett, M. (2005) *Children as Active Researchers: A New Research Paradigm for the 21st Century?* NCRM Methods Review papers NCRM/003, ESRC National Centre for Research Methods.

Kirby, P. (1999) *Involving Young Researchers: How to Enable Young People to Design and Conduct Research.* York: Joseph Rowntree Foundation.

Kuebler, D. and Hauser, D. (1997) 'The Swiss hidden population study: Practical and methodological aspects of data collection by privileged access interviewers'. *Addiction*, 92(3): 325–34.

Langhout, R.D. (2006) 'Where am I? Locating myself and its implications for collaborative research'. *American Journal of Community Psychology*, 37: 267–74.

Mauthner, N. and Edwards, R. (2007) 'Feminism, the relational micro-politics of power and research management in higher education in Britain'. In V. Gillies and H. Lucey (eds) *Power, Knowledge and the Academy: The Institutional is Political.* Basingstoke: Palgrave Macmillan.

Mestheneos, E. (2006) 'Refugees as researchers: Experiences from the project "Bridges and fences: Paths to refugee integration in the EU"'. In B. Temple and R. Moran (eds) *Doing Research With Refugees: Issues and Guidelines.* Bristol: Policy Press.

Meyer, M.C., Torres, S., Cermeño, N., MacLean, L., and Monzón, R. (2003) 'Immigrant women implementing participatory research in health promotion'. *Western Journal of Nursing Research*, 25(7): 815–34.

Mitteness, L.S. and Barker, J.C. (2004) 'Collaborative and team research'. In C. Seale, G. Gobo, J.F. Gubrium, and D. Silverman (eds) *Qualitative Research Practice*. London: Sage.

Moffatt, K., George, U., Lee, B., and McGrath, S. (2005) 'Community practice researchers as reflective learners'. *British Journal of Social Work*, 35: 89–104.

Petrie, S., Fiorelli, L., and O'Donnell, K. (2006) '"If we help you what will change?" – participatory research with young people'. *Journal of Social Welfare and Family Law,* 28(1): 31–45.

Pitman, G.E. (2002) 'Outsider/insider: The politics of shifting identities in the research process'. *Feminism and Psychology*, 12: 282–8.

Price, N. and Hawkins, K. (2002) 'Researching sexual and reproductive behaviour: a peer ethnographic approach'. *Social Science and Medicine.* 55: 1325–36.

Reason, P. (1994) 'Three approaches to participatory inquiry'. In N.K. Denzin and Y.S. Lincoln (eds) *Handbook of Qualitative Research.* London: Sage.

Rhodes, P. (1994) 'Race-of-interviewer effect: A brief comment'. *Sociology*, 28: 547–58.

Ritzer, G. (1998) *The McDonaldisation Thesis*. London: Sage.

Sixsmith, J., Boneham, M., and Goldring, J.E. (2003) 'Accessing the community: Gaining insider perspectives from the outside'. *Qualitative Health Research*, 13(4): 578–89.

Smith, D.E. (1987) *The Everyday World as Problematic: A Feminist Sociology.* Boston: Northeastern University Press.

Smith, R., Monaghan, M., and Broad, B. (2002) 'Involving young people as co-researchers: Facing up to the methodological issues'. *Qualitative Social Work*, 1(2): 191–207.

Song, M. and Parker, D. (1995) 'Commonality, difference and the dynamics of disclosure'. *Sociology*, 29(2): 241–56.

Stalker, K. (1998) 'Some ethical and methodological issues in research with people with learning disabilities'. *Disability and Society*, 13(1): 5–19.

Standing, K. (1998) 'Writing the voices of the less powerful'. In J. Ribbens and R. Edwards (eds) *Feminist Dilemmas in Qualitative Research: Public Knowledge and Private Lives.* London: Sage.

Stanley, L. and Wise, S. (1993) *Breaking Out Again: Feminist Ontology and Epistemology.* London: Routledge.

Temple, B. and Moran, R. (2006) *Doing Research With Refugees: Issues and Guidelines.* Bristol: Policy Press.

Temple, B., Edwards, R., and Alexander, C. (2006) 'Grasping at context: cross language qualitative research as secondary qualitative data analysis'. *Forum: Qualitative Social Research*, 7(4), Article 10: www.qualitative-research.net/fqs.

Travers, K.D. (1997) 'Reducing health inequities through participatory research and community empowerment'. *Health Education and Behaviour*, 24(3): 344–56.

Twine. F.W. (2000) 'Racial ideologies and facial methodologies'. In F.W. Twine and J. Warren (eds) *Racing Research, Researching Race: Methodological Dilemmas in Critical Race Studies.* New York; New York University Press.

Wadsworth, Y. (1998) 'What is participatory action research?' *Action Research International*, Paper 2: http://www.scu.edu.au/schools/gcm/at/ari/p-ywadsworth98.html.

Wahab, S. (2003) 'Creating knowledge collaboratively with female sex workers: Insights from a qualitative, feminist and participatory study'. *Qualitative Inquiry*, 9(4): 625–42.

Wallman, S., Dhooge, Y., Goldman, A., and Kosmin, B.A. (1980) 'Ethnography by proxy: Strategies for research in the inner city'. *Ethnos*, 45(1/2).

Yeo, E.J. (2003) 'Social surveys in the eighteenth and nineteenth centuries'. In T.M. Porter and D. Ross (eds) *The Cambridge History of Science, Vol. 7: The Modern Social Sciences.* Cambridge: Cambridge University Press.

15

Innovations in Program Evaluation: Comparative Case Studies as an Alternative to RCTs

W. Paul Vogt, Dianne Gardner, Lynne Haeffele and Paul J. Baker

If one were to survey evaluation researchers about the best design for assessing program effectiveness, the majority would probably respond: randomized control trials (RCTs). RCTs are hardly a recent innovation, dating as they do to drug trials of the 1940s and even to Fisher's agricultural experiments of the 1920s. But the use of RCTs in evaluating programs has been greatly emphasized in recent years, even to the point of being virtually mandated for the evaluation of some government-sponsored programs. When RCTs are feasible they are indeed a powerful tool for detecting program outcomes. But often they are not feasible, or if feasible, not necessarily the best method for determining the effectiveness of programs. In this chapter we begin by discussing when RCTs are not possible or, if possible, not the most effective means of determining whether programs have achieved their goals. We then review new approaches to comparative case study research that give researchers a powerful set of tools for investigating some types of units of analysis that are of interest to social researchers – such as governments, economies, institutions, and programs – but that are not easily investigated with RCTs. We conclude with examples drawn from our research in educational program evaluation.

THE PROBLEM WITH GOLD STANDARD THINKING

When R.A. Fisher (1926) was pioneering experimental methods by comparing crop yields in the 1920s, he was constructing the metaphorical 'gold standard' in research methods, the randomized controlled trial (RCT).[1] And, at that time, the real gold standard, in monetary policy, was indeed in full swing. But, the monetary system's gold-bullion standard did not survive the Great Depression; it was abandoned by the UK in 1931. Following the Second World War, a gold-dollar standard was devised: international currencies were pegged to the US dollar, and the US guaranteed a fixed price for gold. This stop-gap gold standard unraveled in 1971. Like the bullion standard it was too inflexible to deal with financial shocks. Inflexibility is also the main negative result of pegging all other research methods to the RCT.

What do we have today instead of a gold-based standard in monetary systems? Basically currencies are in open market competition with one another. Users decide, on various criteria, what currencies are worth, mostly in terms of how they compare to other currencies. This open market system leads to fluctuations in currency values based on their comparative worth. That is a better model for the international monetary system, and it is a better model for how we ought to assess research designs – far superior to elevating one currency or one design to preferred status. In sum, we could use a bit of deregulation in our thinking about the comparative advantages of research designs. Ironically, the complete irrelevance of the gold standard in monetary policy has coincided with the salience 'gold standard' thinking in research methodology.

The problem with gold standard thinking arises mostly from attempting to rate other methods by their resemblance to RCTs. Doing so ignores the fact that all research questions can be approached in multiple ways, each of which has advantages and limitations. Choice of design should be driven by the research question, the context in which one is trying to answer it, and the objects of the research. It is not helpful to try to make research questions conform to a set of pre-existing criteria that assigns ranks to designs and methods apart from considerations of topics, contexts, and units of analysis.

This chapter is not meant as a critique of experiments in social research or even of using them in areas where they have previously been unusual. Indeed, in fields in which experiments are rare, research programs can be greatly enhanced by adding them (for examples from political science, see Druckman et al. (2006)). We only wish to question the inflexible application of RCTs to circumstances and research questions in which other designs are superior. The inflexibility we reject is pegging other methods to the RCTs and using RCTs as a common point of reference even when there is little advantage of doing so. The inflexibility of the RCT as gold standard has two main facets. First is the assumption that evidence gathered using RCTs will always be superior, regardless of the topic or setting, to evidence gathered in any other way. Second is the belief that research problems for which RCTs are impossible cannot be studied scientifically.

Evidence-based conclusions about real world problems require a range of research models broader than the RCT. The RCT is a wonderful design, but researchers do not benefit by making it a gold standard.

Our research in program evaluation has led us to question the presumption of the superiority of RCTs in five circumstances, some obvious, others perhaps less so: when random assignment is impossible, when manipulating variables is infeasible, when RCTs are not cost effective, when RCTs would distort the object of study, and when RCTs have limited external validity.[2] The limitations of RCTs are as follows.

When experimental methods are impossible because subjects cannot be randomly assigned

In educational research parents are unlikely to agree to the random assignment of their children to schools or programs. Similar limitations apply in the provision of health or other social service benefits; patients are often willing to participate only if they are guaranteed access to the new drug or procedure. Governments do not have or do not wish to exercise the power to compel potential subjects to be randomized. Ironically perhaps, governments often have the authority to compel *all* schools or social service providers to change, but compelling them to join the randomization pool an experiment is very rare. When RCTs are not possible, or would raise insuperable practical and ethical difficulties, it is much more useful to think about how to choose among methodological alternatives that are in fact possible. Ruing the fact that one research option is unavailable is not helpful.

When experimental methods are not feasible because key variables cannot be manipulated

Many variables of great interest in social research cannot be manipulated by investigators. Sex/gender, race/ethnicity, income levels, crime rates, and neighborhood characteristics are impossible for researchers to manipulate. While some simulations have been successful, such as résumés with altered names to indicate gender or ethnicity, direct manipulation is impossible. Of course, non-manipulable variables can frequently be studied as outcomes or covariates using well-established statistical techniques.

When, compared to other methods, RCTs are not cost effective

For complex, long-term social programs methods other than RCTs can yield a higher calibre of data, sometimes for fewer resources and less effort. It is simply erroneous to believe that no matter the kind of program or the context in which it operates, RCTs will inevitably produce the highest grade of evidence. Experimental methods are often inadequate to evaluate long-term multi-faceted programs because uncontrolled and unknown covariates can intervene. The problem is well known as the threat to validity called the history effect: variables not under the researcher's control emerge over the life of a program to confound interpretation. The standard RCT is too inflexibly structured to capture and control for such covariates. When studying the effects of fertilizer on wheat, Fisher had to wait until the end of the experiment, until harvest time, to measure outcomes. In long-term program evaluation it is neither necessary nor effective to refrain from analysis until the conclusion of the trial. Researchers can use many methods – from grounded theory interviews to Bayesian statistical analysis – to gather data and learn from them as the program unfolds (Chatterji, 2007; Palmer, 2002).

When an RCT would too greatly distort the object of study

One might think of this as a type of Heisenberg effect. For example, some education grants require partnerships between universities and schools. For obvious reasons, it would be very difficult to randomly assign meaningful partnerships. Other types of reform, such as whole-school reform, require enthusiastic volunteers; teachers and administrators have to vote to join the experimental condition. This obviously makes randomization impossible and introduces self-selection bias. But reasonable causal inferences are possible using techniques such as difference-in-difference regression (Bifulco, 2002).

When RCTs have limited external validity

There are many ways in which the external validity of a research program can be limited. For example, in drug trials of the cost effectiveness of Cox inhibitors, it was found that observational data from actual clinical practice was far superior as compared to data from RCTs (van Staa et al., 2009). As that study showed, external validity is an empirical question, not something to be settled by stipulation. Another area of limited external validity comes in programs funded by external grants that have eligibility and selection criteria that preclude random assignment. To be eligible a community or an institution such as a hospital or a university might have to provide matching funds. Thus, only communities with sufficient resources or institutions with enthusiastic managements might qualify. It would be hard to generalize from such groups of enthusiastic volunteers to a more general population of communities or institutions. Limitations on external validity are hardly confined to evaluation of social programs.

The most basic conclusion to which these limitations point is to challenge the very idea that there is or should be a single standard of excellence, a single set of criteria against which all other activities should be measured. The belief in one preferred method to accomplish complex human activities does not conform to most reasonable assumptions about the social world and human actions in it. The same is true for effective research designs. Were we all not so accustomed, through years of repetition, to believing claims about the superiority RCTs, it is unlikely that we would accept them so automatically today. While RCTs are superb when it comes to the internal validity of causal generalizations about variables that can be manipulated, they are often substantially less persuasive when it comes to external validity, especially in studies in which subjects cannot be randomly assigned and variables cannot be manipulated. Vast ranges of crucial human problems cannot feasibly be addressed by RCTs. For these problems – such as revolution, inequality, war, economic crises, and so on – it is irrelevant at best to compare the methods used to study them to RCTs. It is far too hypothetical to assert that *were we* able to study a problem with RCTs, this *would be* better than studying the problem using other methods. Surely it is more useful to direct attention to choosing among feasible methods and to improve upon them.

The goal of this part of the chapter has not been to question the value of RCTs in circumstances where they are appropriate. But, in the current climate of beliefs about the worth of methods in program evaluation, it has been necessary to clear a space, as it were, for the discussion of other methods. To clarify, we object not to RCTs or any other method, but to *gold standard thinking* about methods. We would object as strongly if we were researchers who suddenly start claiming that regression discontinuity designs or structural equation modeling or grounded theory or semi-structured interviews, or any of several other excellent methods was the gold standard by which all other methods had to be judged.

EXPERIMENTAL ALTERNATIVES TO RCTs

One good alternative to the RCT is the 'natural experiment'. The term natural experiment is often used loosely to apply to the study of any naturally occurring differences among groups. Making a distinction between a correlational study of existing variables and a natural experiment, strictly speaking, is difficult because the difference is mostly a matter of degree (Rutter, 2007). In what most people would term a natural experiment, the data are generated in a more-or-less natural process or by an event that can be interpreted as approximating an experimental intervention. The researcher 'finds' experimental conditions and collects the data generated by natural or social forces. For example, if the topic is the effects of different residential patterns, researchers cannot manipulate these so as to collect data. But a natural disaster, such as a hurricane, can provide an exogenous source of variation in residential patterns. The consequent residential changes can be studied as though they had been experimentally generated (Kirk, 2009). In a review of natural experiments in political science, Robinson and colleagues (2009) argue for their greater use, which means that researchers should devote more effort to searching for them. One source of somewhat 'natural' variation often used in political science has been legislative actions. And we have used these in a study of the effects of guaranteed tuition policies on student and university outcomes by comparing states that have and have not mandated this policy (Dean et al., 2009). Whether one calls this a comparative case study or a natural experiment is largely a matter of stipulation, as is the choice of methods used to analyze the data. Some advocates of the natural experiment have opined that the natural intervention needs to be clear enough that simple methods of analysis, such as *t*-tests of mean differences, can be used. Indeed, this is how some methodologists would define a natural experiment. But, this is to confuse the design used to collect the data with the methods used to analyze them. There is no reason beyond tradition to prefer rudimentary methods of analysis in either true or in natural experiments (Palmer, 2002). In our work, we have found that more advanced techniques, particularly difference-in-difference regression (Card and Krueger, 2000) to be more effective.

Another alternative to the pure RCT is to combine it with other methods. Some of the disadvantages of RCTs can be lessened by adding observational methods to the study protocol. RCTs are structured to focus on overall mean effects. In program evaluation, these can be less interesting than differential effects, which help identify what program elements could work in other settings and which with subgroups of the population. Discovering these differential effects often requires on-site observation (Plewis and Mason, 2005). In other terms, the typical experiment emphasizes the treatment and the outcome. This often leaves unresolved the causal processes of why and how a program worked. Causal processes or intervening variables are often crucial to being able to export findings learned in one context to others. Examples include Schneiderhan and Khan (2008) who used video observations of experimental processes and Sherman and Strang (2004) who incorporated ethnographic observations into an experimental program evaluation. Note that in both of these cases, the additional methods were brought in to supplement experimental work. In circumstances in which RCTs are not feasible (because of problems with randomization or manipulation of variables) such combinations would not be possible, of course.

Sometimes when experiments cannot be the chief design, they can be used as complements to other designs. The most common combination of that sort is the survey experiment in which a small-scale experiment is incorporated into a larger survey. Randomly selected survey respondents reply to different questions in order to learn how to improve the quality of survey questions, understand patterns of responses to survey questions, and clarify substantive issues studied with the survey. While survey and experimental research arose out of two different research traditions, it is remarkably easy to combine them by inserting an experiment into a survey. Substantial advantages can result for the program evaluator. Surveys are often built upon a random sample of a population, something quite rare in experiments. Some of the best studies for dealing with RCTs' external validity problems have come from survey experiments, and they have been helpful in reducing some vagaries of survey questions. (An excellent overview of survey experiments is Gaines et al., 2007; see also Krysan et al., 2009.)

While natural experiments, ethnographic supplements to experiments, or experimental supplements to surveys are all fine additions to the researcher's toolkit, they usually do not satisfy strong advocates of the use of RCTs in program evaluation.

One of the origins of the current emphasis on RCTs is that by nature they focus on causal outcomes. This is a welcome focus. There is a long tradition of studying *processes* of implementation more than or instead of the *results* of programs. That emphasis may have been intended, as some critics have claimed, as a way to avoid scrutiny. The call for the use of 'scientifically-based research in program evaluation', which has often been held synonymous with RCTs, has been seen as a way to counteract the overemphasis on processes rather than outcomes. The hope has been that scientifically-based research will lead to evidence-based practice. We share this hope, but we do not believe that RCTs exhaust the options for scientifically-based research. One strength of the RCT is that it aims to make causal inferences about program effects. We agree that programs need to have a theory of how they plan to bring about change and that this implies a causal theory, and that to test the theory of change one needs to study outcomes. But we do not think that RCTs are usually the best design for collecting data about the effectiveness of most programs. Instead, we contend that comparative case studies can be more effective in the majority of evaluation research projects. We turn now to a review of case study methods.

CASE STUDY RESEARCH

Case study investigations examine in depth one instance or a small group of related instances of a phenomenon. What distinguishes case study work is not a matter of design (all designs may be used to study cases) or of coding and measurement (all coding schemes may be employed). Rather case studies are defined by (1) *sampling*: a small number of instances and (2) *analytic purpose:* detailed analysis leading to one or more generalizations.

In case study analysis, as in all types of research, the choice of approach is largely determined by one's research question and one's analytic purposes. The analytic purpose is shaped by the researcher's assessment of the extant explanations or theories in the field. When there are few good theories that address one's research question, case study research can be undertaken to discover causal relations among variables in the case(s) so as to begin to *build a theory*. When explanations of outcomes are interesting but underdeveloped, case study research can be conducted with the aim of *refining the existing theories*. Finally, when the field and the theories in it are organized around a relatively small number of well-elaborated but competing explanations, one can undertake case study analysis with the aim of *testing one or more of these theories*. These three broad purposes – theory building, refining, and testing – often coincide fairly closely to the number of cases the researcher analyzes. To discover relations among variables in order to begin building a theory, one typically works with a few, perhaps only one, case. To specify or refine an existing theory, a middling number of cases, perhaps 4 to 15, could work well. Finally, to test a theory, a comparatively large number could be appropriate, as many as possible while still retaining in-depth knowledge of the particular cases – usually somewhere in the range of 10 to 40 cases. An individual researcher will rarely attempt this number, but teams increasingly do so.

Single-case analysis: Discovering, describing, and explaining causal links

What can researchers learn studying single cases? Quite a lot, many researchers seem to believe, because the single-case study is probably the most common of all case study types. One reason for its popularity is the requirement that the researchers know the cases in depth – and it is difficult to know more than one case really well. Single-case studies often do not seek to test a theory or hypothesis, or even to generate one. Rather they aim to *understand* a single case with the ultimate goal of understanding similar cases. Historians and anthropologists, in particular, often think more in terms of understanding cases than drawing generalizations from them.

Using a single case to test a theory is most likely to be definitive if the theory states that some causal condition is necessary. If a particular condition is thought to be necessary to produce a given outcome and the outcome occurred in a case that is missing the particular condition, then the case has tested, and disproven, the theory. Or if the theory claims that a causal condition is sufficient to produce a given outcome, and the case shows that it does not do so, this also disconfirms the theory.[3] In brief, in single-case tests of theory, disconfirming instances convey the most information. A single case that conforms to the theory may add something to the credibility of the theory, but typically not much. A single case can be instructive in a very rudimentary theory for which very little empirical work has been done or a theory about which a great deal of skepticism has been expressed. Then a single case can constitute a 'plausibility probe',[4] and a confirming instance could suggest that the theory is worth further inquiry.

Less is conveyed by a single case if the theory specifies a probabilistic link between the condition and the outcome. The main value of single-case research for theory testing – finding a disconfirming instance – is useful mostly for deterministic theories that postulate necessary and/or sufficient conditions. By contrast, if the theory states that the presence of X, or an increase in X, increases the probability of Y, then a single case, whatever the values of X and Y, tells the researcher next to nothing. Probabilistic theories can be tested only with relatively large probability samples.

More typically, one uses single-case research not to test a theory, but to build a theory. Single-case studies can help by discovering a new variable or by suggesting a hypothesis that could be tested with multiple-case research. Perhaps the most important type of theory building done with single-case research is examining and explaining the functioning of causal links or causal mechanisms – what are usually called mediating variables in variable-oriented research. For example, most of the causal mechanisms explaining the 'democratic peace theory' arose out of case study research. Briefly, and we are summarizing a huge literature here,[5] the theory (or observation) is that democratic nations hardly ever go to war *with one another*. Presuming that one accepts that this observation (theory) is accurate, the causal mechanisms linking democracy and peace become important. Perhaps peace between democracies persists because democracies tend to be prosperous and prosperous nations tend not to go to war with one another. Or perhaps decision making in democracies is fairly transparent and this facilitates successful bargaining among them. Those are two of several examples of causal mechanisms (intervening or mediating variables) postulated using single-case research and examined with multiple case study research.

The range of types of single-case studies is enormous. Here follow three cases of single-case studies that suggest the breadth of species variation in this genus. The first is from medical research, which is the home of origin for single-case research. A group of physicians discovered a new method of diagnosing a rare disease; the method of diagnosis and subsequent treatment were developed with a single patient. Previous problems with diagnosing the disease had led to overly aggressive treatments that caused unnecessary harm. Specifically, the team used a minimally invasive biopsy technique to make the diagnosis of a rare benign disease that historically was diagnosed with an invasive surgery (ureterectomy) for a presumed malignant condition. Improved diagnosis led to improved treatment of the disease, and those methods of diagnosis and treatment, the authors argue, should guide practice in subsequent cases (Abern et al., 2009). This degree of clarity about the implications of case study findings is rare in the social sciences.

A second example used intensive study of a single case to illustrate a methodological approach to the sociology of knowledge. In the early twentieth century, most members of the dominant group of sociologists in France rather abruptly abandoned the study of their own society (and other European societies) for the study of non-Western 'primitive' societies. To explain this dramatic shift Vogt (1976) proposed a method of analysis that combined necessary (but not sufficient) political, professional, and substantive conditions that led to the result. While the case was perhaps interesting in its own right, it was offered as a general way to examine the origins of changes in the development of academic disciplines.

Our third case of a single-case study comes from the sociology of health and social behavior, where there is a long-standing observation (aka, theory) that rich people tend to be healthier and live longer than poor people. To explain this fact one needs to specify mediating variables. A case study of cholesterol levels over time (1976–2004), and in relation to socio-economic status (SES), uncovered one link. In brief, in 1976, rich people tended to have higher levels of cholesterol than poor people. By 2004, the relation was reversed, and poor people tended to have higher levels. The change was brought about by the development of statins in the 1980. Statins were more available to higher-SES individuals (Chang and Lauderdale, 2009). Again, while the specific case was interesting, the goals of the case study were broader: to explain the relationship between SES and longevity by providing a mediating variable and also to illustrate a method for studying the diffusion of technological change in the health fields.

These three examples of single-case studies vary in many respects. The first involved a single patient with a rare disease who sought treatment at a university medical center. The second focused on a few dozen sociologists from the last century who were studied using historical techniques and data. The third employed a nationally representative sample of 36 thousand individuals to explicate the relationship between cholesterol levels and socio-economic status. These cases of single-case studies are strikingly different, but they also have much in common. While each is substantively intriguing, the researchers studying the cases aimed to make broader points, both about the population of other cases and about methods of studying them: the disease and how to diagnose and treat it; changes in knowledge and how to explain them; the relation between health and socio-economic status and how to investigate it. All three case studies were interested in causes – not only what happened but how and why it happened and what generalizations could be drawn from that causal knowledge to apply to future research and practice.

Small-N comparative case studies

When one works with more than one case, comparative approaches become possible, and there seems little point in working with multiple cases unless some sort of comparison is intended. Even in single-case studies, comparisons are imbedded in the case narrative. Indeed, it is probably impossible to think or even describe without implicit comparison. But the comparisons when working with multiple cases are explicit and often carefully planned. Explicit comparison allows a wider range of research questions to be addressed than does the single-case study. With small-*N* comparative studies the goal is sometimes theory testing, but is more often theory elaboration.

An older use of the term comparative studies harkens to the day when 'comparative' usually meant comparisons among countries. And this use is still very widespread, but there is no need to limit comparisons to nation states.[6] As we will see below, comparative case study techniques can be applied to many different sorts of units of analysis – including social and educational programs. Nonetheless the tradition of international comparisons is strong. As with single-case studies, so too with small-*N* comparative studies, the range of possibilities is enormous.

We begin our example cases with a two-case comparative study of the growth of a field of knowledge. Demography as a systematic discipline emerged in the nineteenth century. England and France were two of the main loci of this emergence. A two-case comparative study of the development of this discipline highlights the different paths demography took, which helps explain some of the features it retains today. The analytic strategy adopted by Schweber (2006) involved using published historical sources to focus on differences in the development of demography in the two national contexts. Of course, since the two cases were cases of the same thing, there were a good many similarities too. A different strategy for this topic could have been to focus on the largely simultaneous development of demography in the two nations and point to the broader intellectual, social, and economic factors contributing to its rise. But this would not have facilitated the fine-grained understanding of the aspects of demography that the author sought.

A second example of small-*N* comparative case studies also involves the nation-state as the unit of analysis. Israel, Taiwan, and Ireland, though small countries, have played disproportionately large roles in the development of innovations in the production of computer hardware and software in the late twentieth century. Breznitz (2007) uses a 3-by-2 comparison to conduct his analyses: three nations and two industries: hardware and software. In all three nations, government intervention to encourage economic growth was important in the software and hardware industries. Using extensive archival and interview research, the author focuses on differences in economic activity fostered by different government technology policies. While global and local market forces shaped the economic development of the software and hardware industries in these three nations, government decisions had an important, sometimes defining, impact. Different policies and different people implementing the policies had significant consequences. Breznitz's conclusion is that there is no general model for success – except a model that stresses government intervention to increase adaptability.

Our third example emphasizes similarities in what at first would seem widely disparate cases: deforestation in Ecuador's Amazon basin and suburban sprawl in New Jersey. Rudel (2009) considers these to be cases of how people transformed landscapes in the late twentieth century. The most common explanations have emphasized market forces such as how individuals calculate the value of land; these calculations are influenced by factors such as distance from central cities. While such calculations are important, so too are the social and political elements of land transformation. These have been omitted from most theoretical accounts of land use. Both deforestation and suburban sprawl were importantly fostered by government actions, such as incentives for individuals and for building infrastructure, especially roads. These government actions made it easier for local elites to profit from dividing large tracts of land into smaller units which they sold for increasingly intensive uses. By understanding two apparently very different cases as instances of the same more general phenomenon, the study improves our knowledge of each and shows how similar social and political forces can be enacted in very different cultural and economic settings. And these generalizations can be expanded to other cases – a good example is the transformation of millions of acres of grassland into a dustbowl in the US in the early twentieth century.

This brief look at examples of small-*N* multiple case studies makes it clear that they can deal with many topics, such as academic disciplines, government industrial policy, or environmental depredations. The methods have ranged from a historical comparison of the development of demography in France and England, to a comparative analysis of state intervention in computer industries in Israel, Taiwan, and Ireland, to extensive fieldwork on radical increases in population density in Ecuador and New Jersey.

As with most comparative case study research, the fact-to-generalization ratio is very high in all three of these studies. Enormous erudition taking years, sometimes decades, yields what some social scientists would think of as a strikingly disappointing number of general conclusions. These studies are characterized by great in-depth knowledge and attention to detail. But they are not narrow studies; they are breathtaking in their scope – multiple languages, extensive travel and fieldwork, and impressive familiarity with different social and political contexts are all in evidence. Comparative case study research is not for the faint of heart.

Note that our first two exemplars of small-*N* comparative case studies examined quite similar issues (the field of demography and the computer industry) in quite similar nations, but the analyses stressed differences. The study of Ecuador and New Jersey, on the other hand, stressed the similarities of phenomena that are not often thought of together: deforestation and suburban sprawl. Those two approaches illustrate John Stuart Mills' methods of similarity and difference. These are the building blocks on which most comparative studies have been erected. These two methods relate importantly to criteria for case selection: does one select similar cases and focus analysis on differences, or does one choose different cases and concentrate analytically on similarities? It takes theoretical justification to define cases as comparable. The same data from the same cases could be comparable for one research question but irrelevant for another.

Criteria for choosing cases – and for analyzing them[7]

Of the nine criteria or types of cases that follow the first three require that the researcher use two or more cases. The remaining criteria can be used either for single or multiple cases. The criteria are not mutually exclusive; indeed, combining the first two is often recommended as the soundest strategy (Caramani, 2009). When one selects cases opportunistically, as one often must do in ethnographic research, or when the cases are specified by an organization, as is often the case in program evaluation, these selection criteria can serve as guides to analytic strategies. The following criteria focus on choosing single cases or on selecting a small number of cases. Larger groups of cases are often selected as a population, such as all nations experiencing armed conflict, all instances of parliamentary democracy, or all projects in a program. We will consider larger populations of cases separately in a following section. The terms used to discuss approaches to case selection and analysis are often inconsistent and confusing. We use terms that are, we hope, simple and generic.[8]

Very similar cases – except for one outcome that is different

Two or more cases are seemingly similar, but they experienced different outcomes. For example, two factories are in the same industry, about the same size, and located in the same region of the same country. But one of them prospers and the other does not. One can explore reasons for the difference or test a theory of why such differences occur and see if they pertain in this case. If one is testing a theory about a causal or independent variable, one wants the dependent variable to be different; one also wants all the causal variables, *except one,* to be the same. Or, if as best one can tell, all the independent variables are the same, the task could be exploratory; one could look for a new causal variable to explain the difference in outcomes. This method for comparing cases is often called the 'most similar' method. The method and the label date back to the early nineteenth-century logical writings of John Stuart Mill. It is generally considered a strong method, stronger than its opposite, the 'least similar method', discussed as the next criterion.

Very different cases – except for one outcome that is the same

Two or more cases are very different but, surprisingly, they experience the same outcome. Again, this can be approached in an exploratory or confirmatory way. If all the causal variables are different, but the outcome is the same, one looks for an as yet undiscovered independent variable that can explain the similar outcome. In confirmatory work, one wants all the causal variables to be different, except one. An example might be if specific types of intergroup conflict occur in very different societies (modern industrial versus tribal, for example) one could rule out developmental and societal explanations for the differences and postulate other explanations.

These two methods – similar cases but different outcomes versus different cases but identical outcomes – are classics, and their logic is fundamental. But finding such cases – the same in all respects but one – is not easy. In practice, researchers make do with approximations of an ideal set of cases, ideal because it would make experimental reasoning about non-experimental data possible. Still, these ideal types of case study analysis have played an important role in the explanation of real-world data (versus laboratory-world data) throughout the history of the social sciences.

Diverse or contrasting cases

In this approach one selects two or more cases representing different aspects of the phenomena being studied; the differences are usually in predictors or independent variables. The outcome might be success, variously coded or measured. The predictors could be: public/private, large/small, and urban/suburban/rural. This results in a matrix of $2 \times 2 \times 3$, or 12 cases at minimum. The cases could be schools, hospitals, universities, or psychological clinics. The tricky problem here is that with just a few variables each with a few categories the number of cases needed to fill the matrix increases rapidly. It does not take many variables and categories to increase the number of cases to the level that intensive, in-depth analysis becomes impossible.

Typical or representative

A case may be chosen because it is typical or representative of some larger group of cases. A case can represent others in many ways, and the ways most important for one's project will depend on one's research question(s). 'Typicality' is one of those judgments where quantitative data are often relevant in making choices even when one plans to collect little quantitative data once the cases have been chosen. If the hospital is typical or representative, is it so in terms of its size, or its ownership (public or private), or its location (urban, suburban, rural), or its mission (teaching/research versus community health care)? When studying, for example, a large, private, urban, teaching hospital one should provide context. How is a 'large' hospital defined, perhaps by the number of beds, patients, and/or staff? How is the 'typical' number defined, perhaps by the mean or median? How many such hospitals are there – a few, dozens, hundreds? It can take remarkably little effort to gather such data, and a claim of typicality makes little sense apart from it.

Extreme or unusual

By contrast with the typical case criterion, one could want to study a site or case because it is unusual, because it is an extreme case of a phenomenon. If researchers are interested in the influence of new environmental regulations on economic development, they might want to look at a nation or state that had instituted the most stringent new regulations. If a regulation has an effect it should be identifiable and perhaps explicable where the regulation is strongest and its impact likely to be greatest. Or if one were looking into how a particular kind ethnic conflict comes about, one might well want to examine in detail, through observational or other methods, a case or cases of extreme conflict. In this case and in other analyses of extreme or unusual cases, observations and conclusions would not be used to generalize broadly about the sources of environmental regulations, ethnic conflict, and so on, but in a more exploratory way to identify possible origins of the phenomenon.

Deviant or unexpected

If everything you know from your review of the literature and theories about a particular sort of phenomenon leads you to expect something of a potential case, and that expectation proves wrong, this could be an important case to study. For example, in most states in the US it is possible to find schools, which by every predictor (poverty and crime rates, low social capital, and so on), 'ought to' perform poorly in tests of educational achievement, but the children perform well on the tests. Probing the source of such happy anomalies is a way to identify explanations for surprises. Analytically, it does not matter whether the surprise is happy or not – one could also study a site, group, or case characterized by a surprisingly high rate of unfavorable deviance, such as a high disease rate or high rate of business failure.

Influential or emblematic

The idea of an influential or emblematic case is based on the regression analysis concept of an 'influential observation'. An influential observation is one which, if dropped from the data set, would importantly change the conclusions. When it is a question of a case, rather than a datum in a data set, 'influential' usually refers to a case that epitomizes a theory: if the theory did not apply to the particular site or case, this would call the theory into question. For example, if a theory of the origins of fascism did not fit either the case of Nazi Germany or Fascist Italy, it wouldn't be much of a theory. On the other hand, if researchers' concentration on these two cases were so great that they were missing the origins of other types of fascism in other contexts, insisting that the theory fits the emblematic case might not be such a priority. One might instead try to identify a new subcategory of cases of the phenomenon studied.

Crucial or critical test case

Basically what one says in the crucial-case approach is: if it *is not* true here in these favorable conditions it will not be true anywhere. Or, conversely, if it *is* true here, even at this site or in this case where conditions make it highly unlikely, it could be true anywhere. This criterion is based on the notion of a crucial experiment. If the experiment succeeds in showing *X*, that more or less settles the issue. While many methodologists doubt that truly crucial experiments or cases are likely, it is surely true that some cases provide more important tests of a generalization than others. At a minimum, some cases provide tougher tests. If the test of a theory is too easy, it is likely to be of little interest.

Pathway or linking case

A case might provide important understanding of the causal paths or links between two associated phenomena. In variable-oriented research the link or path is called a mediating variable, and it is sometimes so labeled in case-oriented research as well. For example, it is widely believed that smaller classes lead to increased student learning. Assuming that this is true, it remains uncertain how or why this happens. Is it because teachers have more time to spend with each student, or because teachers are free to adopt methods that are impossible in larger groups, or because small classes improve teacher morale and they teach better as a consequence? It is common in research, even when the evidence for an association is very strong (stronger than the relation between class size and learning) that the pathways or causal mechanisms are often unexamined and unknown. One of the things in-depth study of a site or case can provide, often through "process tracing", is evidence about *how* things are related.

Of course, many other factors in addition to their potential analytic uses figure into a decision about which cases to select. Issues of resources and opportunities are often also crucial. Do you know the language well enough to read the documents or to understand what the observers are saying? Can you get access to the documents or sites? These issues are equally salient when selecting multiple cases.

Comparative analyses with an intermediate number of cases

With an intermediate number of cases (roughly 10 to 40), one typically selects a population or a group of cases, rather than choosing cases one at a time. However they are chosen, a comparatively large number of cases will mean that the researcher will necessarily have to trade some depth for breadth. The advantages and disadvantages of doing so are fairly obvious, tend to balance one another, and need not be elaborated on. Suffice it to say that for some research questions, a larger number of cases may be available and very helpful for making progress on research questions involving causality and theory testing.

In most case study research, even comparative case study research, methods have tended to be tailor-made with each researcher devising methods appropriate to the case or cases. Case study methods have been more an artisanal than standardized. They rarely constitute a formal system that can be exported to sets of problems other than those for which they were developed. Of course artisanal and tailor-made methods are often of the highest quality, but they frequently cannot easily be applied to new contexts. They are not likely to form the core around which a disciplinary consensus forms with teams of researchers attempting to advance the method. By contrast, Charles Ragin's qualitative comparative analysis (QCA) has reached a disciplinary consensus take-off point in a way that most other comparative case study methods have not. The method is characterized by a well-developed theoretical core as well as by algorithms and software. Of course, other excellent comparative methods exist, some of them by authors whose works are used in this chapter (George and Bennett, 2005; Gerring, 2007), but we focus here on Ragin's work because we have found it most applicable to our research problems, particularly because it is adaptable to studying an intermediate number of cases, which is especially useful for comparative program evaluation. QCA has been under systematic development for two decades. And it features a detailed and rigorous analysis system. We will only briefly review the general features of the method since these are discussed in Ragin and Schneider's chapter in this volume.

Qualitative comparative analysis (QCA) was first outlined by Ragin (1987), and it has since been used increasingly in sociology and political science. QCA is a method of inductive causal inference. It employs Boolean logic to study categorical attributes of cases (rather than statistics to study continuous variables). By doing so, it can combine some of the rigor of quantitative methods with in-depth, case-specific knowledge. It works most effectively with a small to medium number of cases, perhaps 20 to 50, and a handful of categorical variables (or "attributes" in the language of QCA), perhaps 3 to 10, although there are no set numbers. With more than an intermediate number of cases and variables QCA, like all methods of categorical data analysis, can become unwieldy. Then quantitative methods for categorical variables, such as logistic regression, may be more effective, although Ragin shows in a head-to-head comparison that QCA can be used to analyze problems and data typically thought of as treatable only by quantitative analysis techniques (Ragin, 2008).[9]

Still, the number of cases and variables is usually limited. Thus selecting appropriate ones is very important. To be effective, the choices have to be based on deep knowledge of the topic, of the cases, and of the variables or attributes. Often the case selection includes the entire 'population', such as all modern industrialized economies or all parliamentary democracies or all members of the

OECD or all states in the United States. In its original form only 'crisp' sets, composed of dichotomous variables, were analyzed in QCA. In a later development, methods for 'fuzzy' sets, composed of ordinal variables, were introduced. In fuzzy set QCA (fs/QCA) cases do not have only two values (yes/no, 1/0) but usually have 5 : 1 = completely in a set; 0 = completely out; 0.5 = wholly ambiguous; 0.8 = largely in; 0.2 = largely out. Assigning membership in sets to cases (in 'crisp set' analyses) or *degrees of* membership in sets (in 'fuzzy set' analyses) requires in-depth substantive knowledge of the cases and theoretical reasoning to make the attributions. The coding may comparatively become simple after the classification is complete, but both are arduous.

Crisp QCA uses sets that are Boolean or dichotomous, such as neighborhoods with high poverty and ethnic segregation. In earlier applications of QCA, such variables were coded with upper- and lower-case letters: POVERTY/poverty, SEGREGATION/segregation. In recent years most researchers have found 1 = yes and 0 = no more manageable, and this coding is required when moving to fsQCA. With such categorizations and codings, the researchers can use Boolean logic to discuss the causal relations among the sets/variables. Can the analyst find a causal link between poverty and segregation on the one hand and neighbourhoods having high asthma rates on the other? The key to undertaking such analyses with QCA is the 'truth table'. This is an array of the logically possible combinations of multiple variables. Ragin & Schneider discuss the logic behind these in Chapter 8 of this volume, and, in the next section, we provide a small example from our research.

For researchers thinking in terms of variable-oriented research, the big change in QCA is that rather than conducting analyses that end in changes in a dependent variable that are associated with degrees of change in an independent variable, in QCA one looks for necessary and sufficient conditions for the presence or absence of the outcome/dependent variable. Appreciating what this implies and how it influences the method of analysis requires an understanding of necessary and sufficient conditions and their roles in causal and explanatory generalization.

Necessary and sufficient conditions in causal generalization

Researchers differ on the role of generalization in case studies. Most would agree that one needs a general category of cases from which to select a case. But fewer think that after one studies the case, it is legitimate to generalize about the category. Advocates of QCA do not share this view, nor do we. Indeed, we would not bother to undertake our case study evaluations if there were no possibility of learning general lessons from them. Still, some case study researchers are strictly *ideographic* in the approach they advocate and view their work as descriptive of a singular or unique case from which little, if any, generalization is possible. Historians and anthropologists are probably most likely to make this claim (LaMont, 2009), often as a point of pride, but it is less common in other social sciences such as sociology, psychology, political science, and economics. By contrast to ideographic research, the so-called *nomothetic* approach seeks to establish universal principles or laws. This is if anything rarer, though not completely absent, among case study researchers in the social sciences.

In short, the majority of case study researchers are neither strictly ideographic nor nomothetic; they neither confine themselves exclusively to one case from which generalization is forbidden nor use case study results to formulate universal laws of social behavior. They mostly seek a middle ground between these two unattainable extremes. And that middle ground can produce something very important: In case studies we often see a strong and very fruitful tension between the particular and the general. Generalizations are tempered by specific case knowledge. Particular cases are examined in depth in order to say something about the generality of cases. The researcher's focus often alternates between these two, in a kind of dialogue between the specific and the general. For example, the financial crisis of 2008 had things in common with previous crises. Otherwise how would we know what it was? But, it was also unique in several respects, and these unique features need to be highlighted as well. But, those who study it are probably doing so not merely to satisfy their curiosity, but because they think the 2008 crisis might have something to tell us about crises in general, including, perhaps, future crises.

The middle ground between the particular and the general usually involves the *discovery* of causal relations and/or the in-depth *explication* of causal mechanisms. General discussions of causation identify three broad types of causal conditions: probabilistic, necessary, and sufficient. Because specifying probabilistic causal conditions requires large samples, they are of limited applicability for most case study research,[10] which is often referred to as 'small-*N*' research. By contrast, necessary and sufficient causal conditions are central to many methodological discussions among case study researchers. A probabilistic causal condition influences the *likelihood* of an outcome; a necessary condition is *required* for an outcome to occur, and a sufficient condition is *enough* by itself to bring about an outcome. For example, for it to snow tomorrow the air temperature must be 32°F (0°C) or colder. But a freezing temperature is not sufficient, not enough. Many cold days see no snowfall. Other conditions must necessarily be present, such as moisture in the air. Moisture is also not sufficient as many moist days are not snowy. Coldness and wetness are necessary but not sufficient.

Those distinctions seem simple enough, but there is a different way to conceive of necessary conditions – they can be seen as probabilities. If the temperature tomorrow is going to be above freezing point then the probability of snow is zero. If the temperature will be below freezing point, then the probability is higher, non-zero, but not 1.0 or 100%. The same reasoning applies to air moisture. Now, if the air is both cold *and* moist, the probability of snow is even higher – 100% if moist and freezing air are the only two necessary conditions and are together sufficient. It is hard to reconcile these two ways of understanding necessary conditions. Should necessary conditions be thought of as probabilists see them:

as truncated continuous variables where the value can either be zero or any positive number between zero and 1.0? Or should the necessary conditions be thought of as categorical – as either present or absent with no intermediate conditions? Suffice it to say that most case study researchers tend to think of necessary conditions categorically, not continuously and probabilistically. By contrast, large-*N* researchers usually think of causal conditions as increasing the likelihood of an outcome and may even deny the very existence of necessary conditions in the social world.

A sufficient condition is one which, by itself, can be enough to bring about an outcome. This might seem a tougher standard to meet. It is, but only if by sufficient one means *sufficient and exclusive*. Many sufficient conditions are not exclusive. A patient might die of cancer, a heart attack, an infection, an aneurism, or any of several other ailments. These will not always lead to death because people survive these conditions (they can be sufficient, but they are not necessary). That fact again gives the probabilist an entry – each of these sufficient conditions increases the probability of death but does not inevitably bring it about.

On the other hand, retrospectively, each of these ailments may be a sufficient *explanation* for a death. Thus, a condition that is sufficient to explain may not be sufficient to predict. Most case-study researchers are categorical data analysts who think that necessary and sufficient conditions can be identified, coded categorically, and used to analyze social life. When these researchers study necessary or sufficient conditions that are naturally continuous variables, such as temperature, those variables often have clear thresholds the attainment of which is necessary or sufficient for an outcome of interest.

Necessary conditions are easy to identify in the social world, but finding *important* necessary conditions is not so easy. For example, for two parties to come to a formal agreement, it is necessary that they have a language in common (if only through a translator) and that they have some means of communication (face-to-face, e-mail, telephone, etc.) While those two conditions are certainly necessary, one would not think much of a prediction or explanation that said: they were bound to agree; after all, both of them spoke English and had cell phones. So a common language and a means of communication are necessary, but trivial, conditions. They should probably be thought of as antecedent or background conditions. Or, to take a second example, researchers might be interested in the cause of a particular riot or of riots in general. If the researchers defined a riot as a violent civil disturbance involving three or more persons, one of the necessary conditions would be that three or more persons are gathered. But this is a trivial necessary condition in two ways: first, it is true simply because it is part of the definition; second, and more important, while it is true, the necessary condition explains or predicts nothing since the vast majority of meetings of three or more do not lead to riots.

Sufficient conditions are also easy to find, but finding an *exclusive* sufficient condition, or even one that greatly narrows the range of possible sufficient conditions, is hard. To continue with the same examples, a shared interest, a common enemy, or compatible strengths may be sufficient to explain a formal agreement between two parties. A riot can be caused by a religious conflict, an election dispute, an encounter of opposing football fans, a food shortage, a rumor, or any number of other conditions. When the list of sufficient conditions is long and varies greatly from case to case, the sufficient condition as an explanation for a case does not tell the researcher much. The challenge for case study investigators is to find necessary and/or sufficient conditions that are scientifically or theoretically interesting – conditions that help researchers to explain or predict by narrowing the range of the likely explanatory or predictor variables. We believe that this approach to understanding causes and making generalizations is very fruitful in our field of comparative program evaluation.

APPLICATIONS TO PROGRAM EVALUATION

Program evaluation is a branch of research that investigates the efficiency, effectiveness, and/or impact of organized interventions meant to bring about change. Like case study research, it is defined neither by research methods nor by coding (quantitative, qualitative, graphic) because it uses them all. Program evaluation employs all types of research methods in pursuit of the goal of gauging the outcomes of programs and projects. It takes place (almost by definition) in applied field settings in which the number of and threats from confounding variables can be formidable.

Evaluation research is distinguished from basic research by the goals of the research and the audiences for whom it is produced. The audiences for an evaluation research report are usually decision makers determining whether to expand, continue, revise, or terminate a program. Another audience is legislators and others hoping to scale up what has been learned from a social program to apply it to broader policy.

Research is rarely the main goal of the individuals implementing the program. Typically a program is created following what policy makers or legislators believe will help solve a problem. In the evaluation researcher's eyes, the problem the program addresses is the 'dependent variable', and the program's components are the 'independent variables'. Thus the key components of the research design have usually been decided before the evaluation researcher arrives on the scene. Usually, for most program implementers, evaluation is an afterthought or, sometimes, a dangerous intrusion into the work of the program. Program personnel are likely to believe that evaluations use resources that could better be devoted to doing the work of the program.

Some of the problems and strengths of evaluation research have to do with its origins in and its continuing links with government-sponsored programs. Evaluation research got its beginnings mostly as a consequence of government activism. Educational and social service programs receiving government funds commonly have had to undergo formal evaluations. As funding has expanded, so too has evaluation. In the last decade or so, the standards for program evaluation, especially for federally funded programs in the US, have been raised considerably. The turning point was the Government Performance and Results Act (GPRA) of 1993. In this legislation the Congress required federal agencies to evaluate their work. The idea was that evaluations would lead to improved programs and would help to justify continued funding. This law and its subsequent interpretations by government agencies have greatly increased the emphasis put on *outcomes* as the means to judge the effectiveness of programs. Similar pressures for accountability are evident in other nations as well (see Holt, 2007 for the UK; Luginbuhl et al., 2009 for Holland).

Many program evaluators, perhaps the majority, use case study methods, but there seems reluctance among many of them to use *comparative* techniques to do so. In our experience, many evaluators stress the difficulties of comparing, for instance, projects in the same program in cities, suburbs, and small towns, because this would be 'comparing apples and oranges.' Old sayings aside, for many purposes, it is quite natural to compare apples and oranges: both grow on trees, are good sources of vitamin C, important agricultural products, and so on. The fear must be that one will be treating apples and oranges as identical. But a comparativist's claim is simply that, for a specific research question, apples and oranges share attributes of interest for analytic purposes. The same is true of projects in cities, suburbs, and towns. Versions of the same project in different types of locality provide an ideal opportunity for comparative study – of the influence of locality on project outcomes. More generally, there are no limits on what cases can be compared, as long as the cases share common attributes (Caramani, 2009). While there is no point in studying cases with nothing in common, there is also no point in studying clones. Meaningful comparisons require both similarities and differences.

Making comparisons across cases in program evaluation is usually quite a lot easier than in the fields where the comparative method has been most fully developed: political science and historical sociology. There are several reasons: First, the cases are typically simpler and smaller, for example, schools trying projects versus nations experiencing revolutions. Second, projects are often similar *by design*; in grant supported programs, the basic lineaments of programs are fairly closely structured. Often several projects are funded by one broader program. Our efforts have mainly focused on comparative evaluation of cases (projects) and secondarily on the overall programs of which those projects were a part. Third, evaluators may have had some role of the design of projects that they later evaluate. All of these factors help comparative evaluation researchers identify attributes to be studied comparatively.

One interesting example of comparative case studies in the field of program evaluation is Stake's (2006) 'multiple case study analysis'. Like ours, his cases are projects that are part of a broader program, often with common funding, such as a social service or an educational program. Stake's methods are quite similar to ours in the techniques of data collection and the spirit with which the research is undertaken. The main difference is in the comparatively greater emphasis we place on explanatory and causal theories, and the concomitant effort to generalize beyond particular projects and programs to a broader set of cases.

When we test a theory it is generally the 'program theory' or the overall causal model of change around which the program is built – for example, intervention *X* will lead to output *Y*, which will foster outcome *Z*. Multiple program evaluation is a fruitful field for developing methodological ideas, because conditions are often quite favorable to successful comparative research. Multiple cases within a single program often aim, by design, to achieve the same outcomes, which may be measured in similar ways, as well as employ many of the same input variables. Those who fund programs often insist on these commonalities. While they require that all funded projects have the same basic goals, they rarely require that all projects attempt to achieve those goals in precisely the same ways. It is because the projects differ that we can learn something by studying them.

Still, in the conduct of the multi-project program evaluation we always see the tension between the individual project or case and the overall program – between the particular and the general. For example, in multi-site educational program evaluations in which we have been involved, the same general program theory was applied in quite different contexts – urban versus rural and elementary versus secondary schools. Of course, were there no such variance, there would be nothing to study or all the cases could be lumped into one super case. Variance is the portal to findings, such as that some parts of a program were easier to implement and/or were more effective in certain contexts than others. Each case is interesting, first in its own right, and second because it belongs to a general class of cases. From the standpoint of either usable evaluation knowledge or social science knowledge, it is the second, the general class of cases, which is more informative. In comparative case study program evaluation, the individual case study is instrumental in seeking broader knowledge.

Many program evaluators are understandably concerned with evaluating a single case and helping the project that has hired them to analyze its data and comply with the reporting requirements of the granting agency. This is important work, and comparative case study evaluations are almost necessarily parasitic on single-case work. By contrast, our work began with a comparative orientation. We were consultants not to an individual project but to the state agency, the Illinois Board of Higher Education (IBHE), that administered the general program, specifically the Illinois Teacher Quality (ITQ) grants. The funds were supplied by the national government but administered by the state. The state sponsors wanted more generally usable knowledge than they had obtained from evaluations in the past. Frequently in the past, the main yield from the individual project evaluations was an incommensurable pile of reports. The Board wanted to know what was common across cases, not only what was unique to particular cases, so that lessons could be learned that were applicable to subsequent grant activity. This is not to dispute that the ways the general conclusions might vary in specific contexts is crucial information. It indicates how a generalization might be applied. Still, in Stake's terms (2006: 44) while the analysis is built up empirically from a study of individual case studies, it is part of the 'highly reductive process of cross-case analysis' in which the researcher 'expects to lose much of the particularity of each case'. Or in Ragin's (1992) locution, 'casing' is a process in which the researcher creates objects of research; these objects are simplified; certain features of the empirical world are highlighted so that they can be studied as a group.

Our general orientation while working for the Illinois Board of Higher Education (IBHE) was to try to build the general out of the particular while remaining grounded in the latter. More specifically, our goals were to: (1) evaluate the state program to help improve it, (2) provide technical assistance to particular projects, and (3) conduct research on what makes programs more effective in general. These goals were intertwined. They were mutually supporting but also potentially conflicting. We were studying projects and the state-wide program of which they were a part, but we were also intervening as participant observers in the objects of our study. We were evaluating projects on how well they were achieving their goals and providing them with interim reports of our evaluations that were meant to help them achieve their goals. We were, in short, our own confounding variables.

We were consultants providing technical assistance to a state agency and to the projects it funded while simultaneously acting as social scientists doing comparative case study research. We think that each of these roles enriched the other, but some of us were more comfortable with this duality than others, and we realize that many researchers might find this blurring of roles inappropriate. Most comparative case study work in sociology and political science is retrospective and builds on historical or archival sources. Our cases were ongoing as we studied them. Indeed, they are still ongoing as of this writing.

Like many evaluation researchers we did not design what we studied. The broad outlines of the grant-supported projects were mandated by federal and state requirements. We did not select the projects for funding, and we probably would not have selected some of the projects that were funded. Rather than choosing projects on the basis of those that had highest probability of success or to insure that interested researchers had access to the variables most useful for comparative study, some projects were awarded funds to assure regional balance or to achieve other political and administrative goals. Some of the differences we found between comparative case study investigations in our more basic versus in our more applied research are listed in Table 15.1.

We take an approach program evaluation often called theory-based evaluation. We see every project, and the program that funds them, as operating under a 'theory of change'. This represents the beliefs of the project directors about how change occurs. Sometimes the theory of change is stated explicitly; sometimes it is implied. Either way, the project developers create a series of activities or interventions that they believe will bring about desired outcomes for participants. These activities should lead logically to specific products and effects

Table 15.1 Comparative case study research in basic and applied evaluation research

	Typical basic comparative research	*Typical applied program evaluation research*
Case selection	Selected by researchers for theoretical purposes; often defined by an outcome or dependent variable	Generally selected by granting agencies; often a group of projects funded from the same source
Variable selection	Selected by researchers to answer research questions	Determined jointly by funding agency and grantees
Time frame for research projects	Set by researchers; may extend over years or decades	Often set by funding agencies; often short turn around
Temporal design	Usually retrospective	May be retrospective but are often prospective as well
Data Collection	Multiple sources; often mainly archival or documentary research	Multiple sources; sometimes supplemented with (participant) observation

(Chen, 2005; Chen and Rossi, 1987; Weiss, 1997). If participants do not agree on their theory of change, project success becomes much more difficult (Hatch, 1998). If the theories of change do not adequately and reasonably connect intended results with project interventions, the opportunity to study change mechanisms through evaluation is lost (Weiss, 2000; Wholey, 2004). In the case of the ITQ grants we studied, we had an opportunity to test the viability of professional development partnerships, something that has been much discussed in the research on the subject (Desimone, 2009; Garet et al., 2001; Wayne et al., 2008).

When projects lack a theory of change that addresses why they are expected to work or what effects could be reasonably achieved, they tend to be fragmentary approaches that are not linked to change initiatives from the school, district, or state. In addition they frequently lack a comprehensive or systemic approach to accomplish some change in practice. This phenomenon is well-documented in the professional development literature (Desimone, 2009; Elmore, 2004; Hawley and Valli, 1999; Newmann et al., 2000). Without a comprehensive and coherent approach to what the project hopes to change and how, any evaluation 'logically' stops at providing evidence that actions were taken. It focuses on processes rather than outcomes. This failing in professional development practice and evaluation is also well-documented (Guskey, 2000; Killion, 1998).

We believe that project planning and implementation proceed most effectively when evaluation is considered from the beginning and not left to the end and treated as an add-on or a compliance gesture (Chen, 2005; Frechtling, 2007). Robust designs mean testable theories of change that imply the best evaluation approaches and methods. Design features, therefore, are a key test of the 'evaluability' of any project (Wholey, 2004). This is a basic tenet of theory-based program evaluation; the theory must be coherent and comprehensive enough that we would expect change as a result. A theory of change can be mapped as a logic model (Frechtling, 2007), which is a causal diagram applied to the components of a project as it leads to an outcome. It is essentially a picture of a theory of change.

Our work actually involved three levels of change theory. First there were the basic requirements of the federal and state granting agencies; they were quite specific as to what the outcomes were to be and how they were to be achieved. Second was our basic evaluation theory, which, in its simplest form, says that ongoing evaluation is a necessary component of successful projects. Hence, to assist projects we endeavored to help them with evaluation capacity building. Third, each project had its own theory of action, of how it planned to accomplish its goals. In this chapter, we focus on the theory of action laid out by the federal funding agency. This basic project model was required by the US Department of Education which funded the projects through state agencies. The general theory (or the 'logic model') of, the IBHE/ITQ program is sketched below.

1		2		3		4
Partnerships	→	Professional Development	→	Teacher Learning	→	Student Learning

The partnerships (1) are between school districts and universities and within universities between colleges of education and colleges of arts and sciences. The collaboration among partners leads to better professional development (2), which leads to increased teacher knowledge (3), which leads to growth in student learning (4). Each step or stage in this model requires that change occur and that it be documented and evaluated.

Our work involved intensive case study analyses of how each particular project implemented this general model. On the basis of reviewing the literature alluded to above and studying the cases, we postulated nine attributes of programs that could lead to the outcome of interest, which was improved student achievement, variously defined and measured. These nine attributes of successful programs became the causal or independent variables in the truth table given below.

Building a truth table

One difference between our research and that of most others employing QCA and truth tables is that our attributes (variables, conditions) are partly sequential. Each step in the four-step design is a necessary condition for the next. Thus, we might do better to conduct three QCA analyses: one each on (1) successful partnerships, (2) professional development, and (3) teacher learning before judging how each of these led or did not lead to improved student achievement. In the interests of simplicity, and because this sequencing presents us with methodological complications we do not know how to resolve,[11] we set aside that temporal element or causal chain for the purposes of this discussion.

Table 15.2 Truth table for comparative case analysis of 10 projects

Cases	*X1*	*X2*	*X3*	*X4*	*X5*	*X6*	*X7*	*X8*	*X9*	*Y*
1	0	1								0
2	1	1								1
3	0	0								0
4	1	1								1
5	0	0								0
6	0	1								1
7	0	0								0
8	0	0								0
9	0	1								0
10	1	1								1

Definitions of attributes in columns. Each is a question that may be answered Yes (= 1) or No (= 0).
X1: Improvement Orientation to Evaluation? X2: Realistic Theory of Change? X3: Partnership Stable?
X4: Partnership Roles Defined? X5: Clear Curricular Concept for PD? X6: Teacher Learning Reinforced?
X7: Causal Mechanism for Student Learning Defined? X8: Operational Definitions of Outcomes?
X9: Baseline and/or Comparison Group Data for Outcomes? Y: Improved Student Achievement?

Most of our variables are binary, or we have so described them here, and thus we use basic or crisp set QCA and do not use the fuzzy set variety (fsQCA). While many of the attributes or variables can be measured as continua or ranks, we treat them here in terms of thresholds: meet or not meet. We have stated and operationalized these attributes as a series of questions that can be used to code the variables. Each can be answered Yes (= 1) or No (= 0). Our theory is that for each of the nine project attributes, an answer of Yes/1 is a *potential* cause or condition (necessary or sufficient) of the outcome. The following coding scheme is used in Table 15.2.

Y: Improved Student Achievement? (The Outcome or Dependent Variable)
Do programs successfully improve student achievement? There are many ways to determine this, and most of them involve quantitative measurement, but it is also relatively easy, using several criteria, which might differ from project to project, to discuss student achievement as meeting (= 1) or not meeting (= 0) an acceptable threshold.

X1: Improvement Orientation to Evaluation?
Is the project's orientation to evaluation improvement or compliance? Is it using evaluation results for improvement or merely collecting data to comply with federal and state reporting requirements?

X2: Realistic Theory of Change?
Is the project evaluation linked to a realistic theory of change that can be used to assess when progress is being made? Are realistic causal mechanisms, based on a review of the research literature, part of the theory of change?

X3: Partnership Stable?
Is the partnership characterized by constancy of personnel in each partner institution, or is it staffed by temporary personnel who devote limited and part-time attention to the project?

X4: Partnership Roles Defined?
Are the roles, relationships, and responsibilities of each member of each partnership (university and district/school) identified very specifically? Are projects able to indicate precisely how they will work to achieve intended results with each partner? Have projects specified how partnership relationships operate at all levels, from leaders through practitioners?

X5: Clear Curricular Concept for Professional Development (PD)?
Is the professional development (PD) guided by a well-developed curricular concept, one that provides standards to judge whether progress in PD is being made and that includes methods for linking the instruction of teachers to methods of instruction leading to student learning?

X6: Teacher Learning Reinforced?
Is the teacher learning in professional development frequently reinforced and assessed in practice? Does the partnership foster the maintenance of teacher learning by the creation of viable networks of ongoing support among peers?

X7: Causal Mechanism for Student Learning Defined?
Does the project not only *assume* that teacher learning is likely to lead to student learning, or hope that it will, but also *specify* the mechanisms through which it will do so? Is the theory of change implied in the specified mechanisms based on a review of and analysis of relevant research?

X8: Operational Definitions of Outcomes?
Does the project have a specific plan for how it will gather data about student learning and how it will analyze the data thus collected? Does the plan include operational definitions of outcomes: how they will be identified, documented, and/or measured?

X9: Baseline and/or Comparison Group Data for Outcomes?
Has the project acquired baseline data or other comparison group data that will enable it to judge whether any changes in student learning are attributable to the project?

We used these nine attributes (independent variables) and one outcome (dependent variable) to construct the truth table shown in Table 15.2.

Because the projects are ongoing, the values inserted in Table 15.2 are only illustrative of the types of analysis that can be done. Looking at the table, we can see at a glance which cases/projects were successful (Column Y). Whether particular individual attributes are necessary or sufficient conditions can also be determined by eyeballing the truth table. The last column, Y, indicates that four cases – 2, 4, 6, and 10 – have positive outcomes: improved student achievement. Examining the first column, Attribute X1, improvement orientation, one can tell that while it may be helpful, it is not a necessary condition for a successful outcome, since one project (number 6) had improved student achievement without a positive value on X1. By contrast, X2, a realistic theory of change, was necessary since all successful projects had this attribute, but X2 was not a sufficient condition, since case numbers 1 and 9 had a realistic theory of change, but did not improve student learning.

This kind of analysis is a good beginning, but the chief goal in QCA is less to identify individual necessary and sufficient conditions, and more to gauge the influence of combinations or *configurations* of attributes, which is why the QCA method is also referred to as part of the class of 'configurational comparative methods' (Rihoux and Ragin, 2009). Finding necessary and/or sufficient *combinations* of attributes, particularly when these are not simple yes/no decisions, but are fuzzy set categories, can be very complicated indeed. Software for conducting these analyses (available at no charge from www.compasss.org) is all but necessary.

CONCLUSION

A truly fundamental question in this kind of analysis is: how does one determine the values to attribute to the cases? How did we know whether the project/case had an improvement orientation to evaluation, operated with a realistic causal theory of change, was a stable partnership with clearly defined roles, and so on? The short answer is we tried to develop in-depth knowledge of cases and pool our knowledge by sharing documents and engaging in elaborate discussions that amounted to seminars devoted to coding. Over nearly three years the researchers working on this set of projects drew upon multiple data sources. All public documents related to the grant funding processes formed the initial base. We built on this using site visits that included case specific interviews, focus groups, observations, and analysis of local grant documentation. Local documents included a variety of sources, from administrative documents, meeting agendas, professional development agenda, observation protocols for professional development and school sites, and in some cases, samples of student work. For each project one of the researchers was a primary case contact. In this study, inter-case comparisons were made to create 'individual project profiles that take into account the unique contextual variables of individual projects while providing an evaluation picture of the program overall' (Abell et al., 2007: 135).

The general methodological point is that the kinds of variables we identified as potentially important had to be investigated with in-depth case study methods. And the coding of those variables required deliberation. Even when the results of the coding looked like dummy variables (with crisp set QCA) or like Likert scales (with fuzzy set QCA), the process for arriving at the codes was very arduous and required as much time in theoretical work as we had already expended in fieldwork. Our work was and continues to be very much a team effort. The data collecting, coding, and analysis would not only have been impossible because of the large amount of work involved, but the quality of our analyses would have been much lower had any one of us tried to conduct the study as a solo researcher.

We did not begin our evaluation studies by formally incorporating sociological methods of comparative case analysis into the more applied research of program and project evaluation. Rather we worked as case study researchers in the past, so often, by devising methods tailored to our research problems. Over the course of our investigations we found that the framework provided by qualitative comparative analysis was of great help in doing program and project evaluation and enabled us to advance our thinking and devise new tools of conceptual analysis.

This chapter is an example of what is sometimes called 'translational research', that is taking research techniques developed in basic research and putting them into the language of more applied investigations. We 'translate' general research methods from historical sociology and political science into the language of the more applied methods used to conduct project and program evaluations. Our main innovation is to bring QCA into the realm of evaluation research where, to the best of our knowledge, it has been absent. But, we have also found the process of translation moves in both directions: 'back translation' has also been instructive. In addition to applying general social science methods to particular evaluation issues, we have also learned about comparative case study research methods in general by applying them to a specific set of problems.

The limitations of RCTs in the study of social and educational programs have long been known and discussed (e.g. Bracht and Glass, 1968), but they become more salient when examining a concrete case of multiple program evaluation such as the one discussed in this chapter. We could not have discovered the nine attributes leading to successful programs had the programs been evaluated using RCTs. Furthermore, now that we have discovered them, and essentially built a theory of the conditions for program success, that theory is not amenable to testing using RCTs – for the reasons discussed in our section on the limitations of RCTs, most importantly, the majority of the variables are not subject to researcher manipulation nor would it make sense to try to randomly assign projects to control and experimental groups based on many of them, such as a realistic theory of change, a stable partnership, a clear curricular concept. But, these attributes/variables are of considerable use as criteria for selecting new projects to be funded and as guidelines for directing technical assistance to the projects. We also intend to use them, and to refine them further, in additional comparative case study research, both retrospectively on an archive of cases we have developed in recent years and prospectively in work with future projects. Is there a role for the RCT approach in the kind of research we have been conducting on the comparative assessment of projects? Yes, but it is restricted to a few variables susceptible to experimental manipulation. That restriction means that RCTs are of limited relevance to understanding the causal conditions accounting for project success or failure.

NOTES

1 RCT can stand for randomized controlled trial, randomized clinical trial, and randomized controlled clinical trial. A variant is randomized *field* trials in which experiments are conducted in natural settings not laboratories.

2 An important distinction in experimental research is collecting data in a laboratory versus doing so in a natural setting. Because the latter (the field experiment) is by far the most common in program evaluation, we concentrate on it.

3 An often cited example is Lijphart (1975) who used the single case of the Netherlands to disconfirm a widely believed political and social psychological theory.

4 The term is from George and Bennett (2005).

5 For a brief review, see Slantchev et al. (2005).

6 An even older terminology used 'comparative' to mean: another nation. A single nation's political or educational system would be described and this would be comparative only in an implicit sense – often 'like us versus not like us'. Such articles abound in older back issues of excellent journals such as the *Comparative Education Review* and the *Journal of Comparative Politics.*

7 This section is based importantly on Gerring (2007: Chapter 5). We have also used suggestions drawn from Hobbs and Wright (2006), George and Bennett (2005), Ragin and Becker (1992), Miles and Huberman (1994), and Spradley (1980).

8 The best known examples of the confusing terms are: What Mill referred to as the 'method of difference' is called by Przeworski and Teune (1970) in a well-known text, the most *similar* design and what they call the *most different* design, Mill called the 'method of agreement'.

9 Researchers have offered refinements to Ragin's basic model and used it in areas beyond those in which it was developed. It is increasingly combined in various ways with traditional quantitative methods such as logic and other forms of regression analysis (for examples, Amenta et al., 2009; Grendstad, 2007).

10 Bayesian probability statistics may be used with small samples, but not many case study researchers have pursued this approach.

11 Caren and Panofsky (2005) and Schneider and Wagemann (2006) provide suggestions for ways to incorporate sequential elements into the basic QCA scheme.

REFERENCES

Abell, S.K., Lannin, J.K., Marra, R.M., Ehlert, M.W., Cole, J.S., Lee, M.H, Rogers, M.A.P., and Wang, C. (2007). 'Multi-site evaluation of science and mathematics teacher professional development programs: The project profile approach'. *Studies in Educational Evaluation*, 33: 135–58.

Abern, Michael R., Benson, Jonas S., and Hoeksema, Jerome (2009). 'Ureteral Mullerianosis'. *Journal of Endourology,* 23(12): 1933–5.

Amenta, Edwin, Neal Caren, et al. (2009). 'All the movements fit to print: Who, what, when, where, and why SMO families appeared in the *New York Times* in the twentieth century'. *American Sociological Review,* 74(4): 636–56.

Bifulco, Robert (2002). 'Addressing self-selection bias in quasi-experimental evaluations of whole-school reform'. *Evaluation Review,* 26: 545–72.

Bracht, Glenn H. and Glass, Gene V. (1968). 'The external validity of experiments'. *American Educational Research Journal,* 5: 437–74.

Breznitz, D. (2007). *Innovation and the State: Political Choice and Strategies for Growth in Israel, Taiwan, and Ireland.* New Haven, CN: Yale University Press.

Caramani, D. (2009). *Introduction to the Comparative Method with Boolean Algebra.* Thousand Oaks, CA: Sage.

Card, David and Krueger, Alan B. (2000). 'Minimum wages and employment: A case study of the fast-food industry in New Jersey and Pennsylvania'. *American Economic Review,* 90(5): 1397–420.

Caren, N. and Panofsky, A. (2005). 'TCQA: A technique for adding temporality to qualitative comparative analysis'. *Sociological Methods and Research,* 34: 147–72.

Chang, V.W. and Lauderdale, D.S. (2009). 'Fundamental cause theory, technological innovation, and health disparities: The case of cholesterol in the era of stains'. *Journal of Health and Social Behavior,* 50: 245–60.

Chatterji, Madhabi (2007). 'Grades of evidence: Variability in quality of findings in effectiveness studies of complex field interventions'. *American Journal of Evaluation,* 28(3): 239–55.

Chen, H.T. (2005). *Practical Program Evaluation: Assessing and Improving Planning, Implementation, and Effectiveness.* Thousand Oaks, CA: Sage.

Chen, H.T. and Rossi, P.H. (1987). 'The theory-driven approach to validity'. *Evaluation and Program Planning,* 10: 95–103.

Dean, Diane et al. (2009). Evaluating the effectiveness of guaranteed tuition on controlling college costs: A difference-in difference analysis. Paper Presented at the Annual Conference of the Association for the Study of Higher Education. November, 2009. Vancouver, British Columbia, Canada.

Desimone, L.M. (April, 2009). 'Improving impact: Studies of teachers' professional development: Toward better conceptualizations and measures'. *Educational Researcher,* 38(3): 181–99.

Druckman, James N., Green, Donald P., Kuklinski, James H., and Lupia, Arthur (2006). 'The growth and development of experimental research in political science'. *American Political Science Review,* 100(4): 627–35.

Elmore, R.F. (2004*). School Reform from the Inside Out: Policy, Practice, and Performance.* Cambridge, MA: Harvard Education Press.

Fisher, R.A. (1926). 'The arrangement of field experiments'. *Journal of the Ministry of Agriculture, Great Britain,* 33: 503–13.

Frechtling, J.A. (2007). *Logic Modeling Methods in Program Evaluation.* San Francisco: John Wiley & Sons.

Gaines, Brian J., Kuklinski, James H., and Quirk, Paul J. (2007). 'The logic of the survey experiment reexamined', *Political Analysis,* 15(1): 1–20.

Garet, M.S., Porter, A.C., Desimone, L., Birman, B.F., and Yoon, K.S. (Winter 2001). 'What makes professional development effective? Results from a national sample of teachers'. *American Education Research Journal,* 38(4): 915–45.

George, A.L. and Bennett, A. (2005). *Case Studies and Theory Development in the Social Sciences.* Cambridge, MA: MIT Press.

Gerring, J. (2007). *Case Study Research: Principles and Practices.* Cambridge: Cambridge University Press.

Grendstad, G. (2007). 'Causal complexity and party preference'. *European Journal of Political Research,* 46: 121–49.

Guskey, T.R. (2000). *Evaluating Professional Development.* Thousand Oaks, CA: Corwin Press.

Hatch, T. (1998). 'The differences in theory that matter in the practice of school improvement'. *American Education Research Journal,* 35(1): 3–31.

Hawley, W. and Valli, L. (1999). 'The essentials of effective professional development'. In G. Sykes and L. Darling-Hammond (eds) *Teaching as the Learning Profession: Handbook of Policy and Practice,* pp. 127–50. New York: Teachers College Press.

Hobbs, D. and Wright, R. (2006). *The Sage Handbook of Fieldwork.* London: Sage Publications.

Holt , D. Tim (2007). 'The official statistics Olympic challenge: Wider, deeper, quicker, better, cheaper', *The American Statistician,* 61(1): 1–8.

Killion, J. (1998). 'Scaling the elusive summit'. *Journal of Staff Development,* 19(4): 12–6.

Kirk, David S. (2009). 'A natural experiment on residential change and recidivism: Lessons from Hurricane Katrina', *American Sociological Review,* 74(3): 484–505.

Krysan, Maria, Couper, Mick P., Farley, Reynolds, and Forman, Tyrone A. (2009). 'Does race matter in neighborhood preferences? Results from a video experiment'. *American Journal of Sociology,* 115: 527–59.

LaMont, M. (2009). *How Professors Think: Inside the Curious World of Academic Judgment.* Cambridge, MA: Harvard University Press.

Lijphart, Arend (1975). 'The comparable cases strategy in comparative research', *Comparative Political Studies,* 8: 158–77.

Luginbuhl, R., Webbink, D., and de Wolf, I. (2009). 'Do inspections improve primary school performance?'. *Educational Evaluation and Policy Analysis,* 31(3): 221–37.

Miles, M.B. and Huberman, A.M. (1994). *Qualitative Data Analysis,* 2nd edn. Thousand Oaks, CA: Sage Publications.

Newmann, F.M., King, M.B., and Youngs, P. (2000). 'Professional development that addresses school capacity: Lessons from urban elementary schools'. *American Journal of Education,* 108(4): 259–300.

Palmer, C.R. (2002). 'Ethics, data-dependent designs, and the strategy of clinical trials: Time to start learning as we-go?'. *Statistical Methods in Medical Research,* 11: 381–402.

Plewis, Ian and Mason, Paul (2005). 'What works and why: combining quantitative and qualitative approaches in large-scale evaluations'. *International Journal of Social Research Methodology,* 8(3): 185–94.

Przeworski, A. and Teune, D. (1970). *The Logic of Comparative Social Inquiry.* New York: Wiley.

Ragin, Charles C. (1987). *Constructing Social Research.* Thousand Oaks, CA: Pine Force Press.

Ragin, Charles C. (1992). 'Casing and the process of social inquiry'. Pp. 217–26 in Ragin and Becker (1992).

Ragin, Charles C. (2008). *Redesigning Social Inquiry: Fuzzy Sets and Beyond.* Chicago: University of Chicago Press.

Ragin, Charles C. and Becker, Howard S. (1992). *What is a Case? Exploring the Foundations of Social Inquiry.* Cambridge: Cambridge University Press.

Rihoux, Benoît and Ragin, Charles C. (2009). *Configurational Comparative Methods: QCA and Related Techniques.* Thousand Oaks, CA: Sage Publications.

Robinson, Gregory et al. (2009). 'Observing the counterfactual? The search for political experiments in nature', *Political Analysis,* 17: 341–57.

Rudel, T.K. (2009). 'How do people transform landscapes? A sociological perspective on suburban sprawl and tropical deforestation'. *American Journal of Sociology,* 115: 129–54.

Rutter, Michael (2007). 'Proceeding from observed correlation to causal inference: The use of natural experiments'. *Perspectives on Psychological Science,* 2: 377–95.

Schneider, C.O. and Wagemann, C. (2006). 'Reducing complexity in qualitative comparative analysis (QCA): Remote and proximate factors and the consolidation of democracy'. *European Journal of Political Research,* 45: 751–86.

Schneiderhan, E. and Khan, S. (2008). 'Reasons and inclusion: The foundation of deliberation', *Sociological Theory,* 26(1): 1–24.

Schweber, L. (2006). *Disciplining Statistics: Demography and Vital Statistics in France and England, 1830–85.* Durham, NC: Duke University Press.

Sherman, L.W. and Strang, H. (2004). 'Experimental ethnography: the marriage of qualitative and quantitative research'. *Annals of AAPSS,* 595: 204–22.

Slantchev, B.L., Alexandrova, A., and Gartzke, E. (2005). 'Probabilistic causality, selection bias, and the logic of democratic peace'. *American Political Science Review,* 99(3): 459–62.

Spradley, J.P. (1980). *Participant Observation.* Fort Worth, TX: Harcourt Brace.

Stake, Robert E. (2006). *Multiple Case Study Analysis.* New York: Guilford Press.

Van Staa, Tjeerd-Pieter, Leufkens, Hubert G, Zhang, Bill, and Smeeth, Liam (2009). 'A comparison of cost effectiveness using data from randomized trials or actual clinical practice: Selective Cox-2 inhibitors as an example', *PLoS Medicine,* 6(12): 1–10.

Vogt, W. Paul (1976). 'The uses of studying primitives: a note on the Durkheimians, 1890–1940'. *History and Theory,* 40: 33–44.

Wayne, A.J., Yoon, K.S., Zhu, P., Cronen, S., and Garet, M.S. (2008). 'Experimenting with teacher professional development: Methods & motives'. *Educational Researcher,* 37(8): 469–79.

Weiss, C. (1997). 'Theory-based evaluation: Past, present and future'. *New Directions for Evaluation,* 76: 41–55.

Weiss, C.H. (2000). 'Which links in which theories shall we evaluate?' *New Directions for Evaluation,* 87: 35–45.

Wholey, J. (2004). 'Evaluability assessment'. In J.S. Wholey, H.P. Hatry, and K.E. Newcomer (eds) *Handbook of Practical Program Evaluation,* 2nd edn, pp. 33–62. San Francisco: Jossey-Bass.

PART 3

Integrating the Analysis of New Data Types

Introduction

Malcolm Williams and W. Paul Vogt

Many recent methodological innovations have come as a result of efforts to improve analysis of continuous quantitative data. In this section we consider innovations in analyzing data in different formats: research reports, mixed quantitative and qualitative data, sequences, including narrative sequences, and spatial data. Sometimes these new forms of analysis have involved translating one data type into another (usually qualitative into quantitative) and at other times inventing new ways of analysis and presentation.

Before the creation of meta-analysis in the 1970s (Glass, 1977) reviews of the research literature on a topic were mainly qualitative in nature. Even when reviewers were thorough and systematic, the conclusions tended to be impressionistic. Meta-analyses in psychology and social research, and the Cochrane reviews in medical research, almost immediately led to higher standards for research reviews and syntheses, even for conventional qualitative summaries, procedures were adopted to ensure that all the relevant sources were consulted so that they were not selected to promote a particular theory. The basic goal of meta-analysis was to make research reviews replicable, not impressionistic. Summarizing results quantitatively involved translating into comparable numbers findings that were often described in words: rejected null hypothesis, not statistically significant, and so on. Early quantitative summaries tended to be simple: standardized mean differences, Pearson *r* correlations, and odds ratios, were essentially the whole tool kit. The problem with these simple measures is that they are most appropriate to simple designs, such as a two-group experiment with a single outcome variable. Most social research is not like that. The norm is large numbers of variables in complex models. It has proven remarkably difficult to move beyond simple quantitative syntheses to summarize complex models.

Until recently we have lacked methods for analyzing 'multi-predictor models'. This is what Aloe and Becker provide in Chapter 16, specifically a way to represent data from multiple regression designs. Their method, explained and illustrated, is to use a semi-partial correlation of the predictor and the outcome variables. They explain how it can be used profitably in a wide range of studies. While there is still much work that needs to be done to synthesize results from studies with complex models, after decades of stasis the work of this chapter represents an important innovation.

Difficulties in analyzing quantitative data can be formidable. The difficulties grow exponentially when qualitative data are added to quantitative and analyzed to answer the same research question. The remaining five chapters in this section all show that the strain to innovate can be especially great when combining words and numbers or turning narratives into numbers and graphs or converting spatial relations into data that can be analyzed quantitatively.

Approaching a research problem from more than one methodological direction is often the only way to make progress on a topic. The increasing realization is that one of the fastest growing fields in recent years has been mixed-methods research. The term 'mixed methods' usually means combining methods for analyzing quantitative and qualitative data. Methods of mixing, combining, and integrating data that do not necessarily cross the quant-qaul divide include 'multi-method research' and our favorite, 'methodological pluralism.'

Much of the early work in mixed-methods research has been taxonomical because merely sorting out the number of possible mixtures is a formidable task. The choice problem in research methodology is greatly complicated when combining methods. Since there are many methods and many ways they can be combined, even the apparently simple task of merely systematically reviewing the options can be daunting. Just for the sake of argument, say that there are only five basic methods for collecting data: interviews, experiments, surveys, observations, and archival research. That would lead to 120 possible combinations and permutations of just those five ($5! = 120$). And things are much more complicated with methods for analyzing data since their number is much larger. Onwuegbuzie and colleagues (Chapter 17) provide an essential overview of the 'almost limitless number' of analytic options open to the researcher. The chapter constitutes an essential map for the researcher wanting to understand the terrain in the rapidly growing field of multi- and mixed-method research and what Onwuegbuzie et al. call 'crossover analyses'.

One of the most important but intractable kinds of phenomena in social research has been temporal or sequential data. Individuals' lives are characterized by temporal sequences and historical data are usually structured using time as a key variable. Texts summarizing historical data are often in narrative form and sequence analysis can be applied to the properties of narrative texts as well as to the life course events, such as work histories. The sequences in a work history seem simple enough: education, part-time employed, employed, unemployed, employed, part-time employed, and retired. But analyzing large numbers of sequences involves serious computational complexities. The most commonly discussed method of sequence analysis is 'optimal matching', (OM), best known perhaps in the works of Andrew Abbott (1995). Martin and Wiggins, in Chapter 18, provide an excellent introduction to optimal matching, its prospects and problems. It turns out that sequences, such as the work history sequences mentioned above, are remarkably diverse: finding a thousand different sequences in a large sample is not unusual. Optimal matching (OM), was first developed for the study of DNA and more recently adapted for investigations of social life. The basic idea of OM 'is to measure the dissimilarity between two sequences as a function of the number of steps it would take to transform one sequence into another'. The number of steps is the 'cost' of the match in OM jargon. Because time-ordered, sequential data are so common in social research, and because the problems of analyzing it are so intractable and have not been resolved, it is a field in which there continues to be much innovatory effort. Martin and Wiggins' chapter is a crucial overview.

To mix or combine methods of data analysis for quantitative and qualitative data usually involves translating one into the other or finding an Esperanto-like common language. Accurate translation is never easy especially when the translator wants to preserve the richness of the original. In Chapter 19 Franzosi outlines a method for quantifying the 'invariant linguistic properties of narratives', which he calls quantitative narrative analysis (QNA). Even though QNA uses numbers to code narratives, Franzosi sees his work as a form of combining or straddling quantity and quality. Other quantitative methods of analyzing texts, typically called 'content analysis', work mostly with word and phrase counts and lose much of the narrative structure. Franzosi (2010) builds on structural linguistics to discover methods to quantitatively code the properties of narratives. He is respectful of texts; he quantifies mostly because the amount of narrative material he is studying is too large to manage qualitatively. He sees QNA as linked with several other innovatory methods discussed in this volume: Ragin's qualitative comparative analysis (see Chapter 8 above), Griffiths' network analyses (see Chapter 18 and Franzosi's Figures 19.1 and 19.2), and Bison's approach to sequence analysis to be discussed next.

One of the great insights into the nature of narratives originating with early twentieth-century linguistics was that stories had an invariant structure and that there were patterns to the *sequences* or orderings of those structural elements. Bison, in Chapter 20, conducts sequence analysis by applying it to 'lexicographic indices' (LIs). His is a statistically rigorous method – one that he sees as sharply distinct from optimal matching – for comparing and identifying similarities and differences among narrative sequences. The results of the analyses are tables summarizing the numerical patterns, found by treating orders as distances, and network graphs depicting those same distance/order relations extracted from large numbers of textual narratives.

As we have seen in the discussion of the chapters on OM, QNA and LI, temporal sequences have been increasingly attracting the attention of social researchers of late. Even more recently, spatial relations among social actors have become important sites of methodological innovation, especially as new technology makes complex descriptions and analyses possible. Upon reflection, it seems obvious that social life takes place in space and time and that space and time – variables central to research in the physical sciences – have been understudied in the social sciences. Further, as we have seen in the chapters by Franzosi and Bison, temporal sequences can be fruitfully depicted spatially in graphs. Griffiths provides, in Chapter 21, an essential introduction to the components of this rapidly developing field. At minimum, spatial variables, such as neighbourhoods, provide a context in which social interactions are played out. But, as Griffiths suggests, geography may actually generate social processes, not simply provide a background for them. Studying spatial relations requires new statistical techniques as well as graphical ones. Ordinary regression analysis is inappropriate, because it assumes the independence of observations. But the whole point of spatial analyses is that observations are dependent on their spatial arrangement. Problems of autocorrelation that arise trying to use OLS regression for spatial analysis are very serious. In the kinds of study Griffiths advocates 'the value of the dependent variable is a function of the independent variables specified in the model *and* the value of the dependent variable at an earlier point in time (time series) or of neighboring areas (spatial regression)'. Modeling space and time simultaneously is exceptionally challenging. Griffiths' chapter makes it clear that this is an important area of research under rapid development and in which we can expect further innovation.

REFERENCES

Abbott, Andrew (1995). Sequence analysis. *Annual Review of Sociology*, 21: 93–113.

Franzosi, Roberto (2010). *Quantitative Narrative Analysis*. Los Angeles, CA: Sage Publications.

Glass, Gene V. (1977). Integrating findings: The meta-analysis of research. *Review of Research in Education*, 5: 351–79.

16

Advances in Combining Regression Results in Meta-Analysis

Ariel M. Aloe and Betsy Jane Becker

As primary researchers have used increasingly more sophisticated techniques for data analysis, meta-analysts have been challenged to develop statistical techniques suitable for computing and analyzing effect sizes from diverse multi-predictor models. Typically, the meta-analyst will need to synthesize data on relationships involving a predictor of interest and an outcome, taking into consideration the influence of other predictors in the model.

A new approach to representing data from multiple regression designs is presented in our chapter. Our index, that we denote as r_{sp}, is the semi-partial correlation of the predictor with the outcome of interest. This effect size can be computed when multiple predictor variables are included in each model, and represents a partial effect size in the correlation family.

In this chapter we first introduce the logic behind the use of r_{sp} to represent a focal predictor's relationship to an outcome. We make connections to Keef and Roberts' (2004) partial effect size for mean difference comparisons. Second, a broadly applicable method to compute the index is presented. We also give a variance of the estimator based on the delta method (e.g. Rao, 1973). Examples are included throughout the chapter, including a more extensive example of the computation and synthesis of the r_{sp} effect index for several published multiple regression studies. Finally, a set of recommendations for analysis of r_{sp} values is outlined.

Throughout this chapter we use examples drawn from an on-going synthesis of relationships between measures of teacher subject-matter knowledge in science and student science achievement (Aloe and Becker, 2008), as well as data concerning relationships between peer review rankings of the top 50 US schools of education and several predictors. This set of raw data includes the number of doctoral degrees granted (in 2004) by each school, the mean Graduate Record Examination (GRE) scores for entering doctoral students, and the percentage of students in each school who are doctoral candidates. (The schools-of-education data are available at http://isites.harvard.edu/icb/icb.do?keyword=k18618&page id=icb.page91322.)

THE LOGIC OF EFFECT SIZES

Meta-analysis techniques for the synthesis of univariate outcomes are well understood. However, in the last few decades the number of primary studies using multivariate techniques has increased notably, making simpler univariate approaches to meta-analysis more difficult to apply and justify. Consequently, researchers conducting quantitative reviews face the alternatives of omitting a large number of multivariate primary studies, or attempting to synthesize those multivariate studies and, in some cases, combining their results with ones obtained from univariate designs. However, when dealing with effects from multivariate designs such as multiple regression models, there is no universal approach on which meta-analysts agree. Thus new indices of effect magnitude, and methods of synthesizing them, are called for. In this chapter we argue for a new index – the semi-partial correlation.

Primary studies tend to report simpler components of multivariate results, such as canonical correlations or slopes, t statistics, and standard errors, and to omit more complex details such as full correlation matrices or variance–covariance matrices among slopes. When full covariance or correlation matrices are reported, it may be possible to apply Becker's (1992) techniques for synthesis. However, reporting these matrices is more the exception than the rule. Therefore, we need to find effect indices that can be computed based on other summary statistics that are likely to appear in study reports.

CORRELATIONS

Effect sizes should be scale-free indices which assess the magnitude of the relationship between an independent variable and a dependent variable. Our focus is on the use of effect sizes from the r family (e.g. the product moment correlation and point biserial correlation). The effect sizes represented by the r family can be interpreted as representing the strength of relationship between two (usually continuous) variables.

The product moment correlation r is one of the effects most typically used in meta-analysis. Let n be the number of observations of two variables X and Y which are continuous and bivariate normally distributed. The correlation formula can be written in many different ways; introductory statistics books often offer some formula algebraically equivalent to

$$r = \frac{S_{XY}}{S_X S_Y}, \tag{1}$$

where S_{XY} is the covariance between X and Y, and S_X and S_Y are the standard deviations for X and Y respectively.

The large sample variance of r (see, e.g. Olkin and Siotani, 1976) is var(r) = $(1-\rho_{XY}^2)^2/(n-1)$, and the expected value of r is ρ_{XY} in large samples (though r is a biased estimator in small samples). Furthermore, it is common to treat r as normally distributed in large samples, and we use this result below in deriving an asymptotic normal distribution for our proposed estimator. Typically, the variance of r is estimated by substituting r for ρ in var(r). This is important for meta-analysis because it enables the reviewer to compute an estimate of the uncertainty of each correlation in a review, using only the sample size and the sample value of r.

Example

For our example data for highly ranked schools of education, the dependent variable Y is a peer rating of school quality. In Table 16.1 we consider as predictors the average total GRE scores of graduate students in each school (X_1), and the number of doctoral degrees granted in 2004 by the school (X_2). Thus, r_{Y1} represents the correlation between the outcome Y (the peer ratings) and predictor X_1, r_{Y2} represents the correlation between Y and predictor X_2, and r_{12} represents the correlation between the two predictors (mean GRE score and number of doctoral degrees granted).

Specifically, using equation (1) the correlation values are $r_{Y1} = 0.657$, $r_{Y2} = 0.503$, and $r_{12} = 0.184$. Both predictors are significantly correlated with Y, but their intercorrelation does not differ significantly from 0. Table 16.1 also shows the variances of the two correlation values involving Y – they are var(r_{Y1}) = 0.0091 and var(r_{Y2}) = 0.0114.

ISSUES IN THE META-ANALYSIS OF REGRESSION RESULTS

Other Xs in the model

One of the major difficulties in the representation and synthesis of effects obtained from complex analyses such as regression models arises because of additional predictors (Xs) across studies (Becker and Wu, 2007). When a regression model is well specified, it provides an unbiased estimate of the slope of interest, which

Table 16.1 Values of r and r_{sp} and their variances for schools-of-education data

Index	*Focal predictor*	
	Mean GRE scores (X_1)	*Number of doctoral degrees (X_2)*
r	$r_{Y1} = 0.657$	$r_{Y2} = 0.503$
var(r)	$(1 - 0.567^2)^2/49 = 0.0091$	$(1 - 0.503^2)^2/49 = 0.0114$
$r_{sp} = \frac{t_f\sqrt{(1-r^2_{Y.12...p})}}{\sqrt{(n-p-1)}}$	$\frac{8.138\sqrt{(1-0.582)}}{\sqrt{(87-2-1)}} = 0.5740$	$\frac{5.512\sqrt{(1-0.582)}}{\sqrt{(87-2-1)}} = 0.3888$
$r_{sp} = \text{sgn}(t_f)\sqrt{r^2_Y - r^2_{Y(f)}}$	$\sqrt{0.582-0.503^2} = \sqrt{0.329} = 0.5739$	$\sqrt{0.582-0.657^2} = \sqrt{0.150} = 0.3872$
var(r_{sp})	0.0073	0.0084

in turn represents the relationship between its associated predictor and the outcome Y. However, in a multiple regression, each slope does not represent a simple bivariate X–Y relation. Because each slope is a partial regression slope, the interpretation of the slope of, say, X_p in a p predictor model is that it shows the effect of X_p on Y, controlling for (or 'holding constant') X_1 through X_{p-1}.

Having different Xs in the models that we find across studies can lead to apparent variation in the strength of relationship between the predictor of interest and the outcome (that is, variation in the observed slopes), particularly if the Xs are interrelated. Different primary studies frequently estimate different models, largely because researchers develop new models by adding or subtracting variables from existing ones. In practice, the presence of different predictors across models is almost always expected, given that researchers are always trying to improve upon previous research. As a result, when conducting a meta-analysis, it is common to find one's predictor of interest in models with a variety of other Xs.

How common is diversity in the predictors that appear in regression models examining a particular relationship? In Aloe and Becker's (2008) synthesis of teacher science knowledge that provides some of our examples, five studies reported regression analyses (but no correlation coefficients). As few as 3 and as many as 9 measures of teacher knowledge were included in the models that were analyzed, and some of those appear likely to be correlated with each other (though evidence of multicollinearity of the predictors was not discussed in any of the reports). The full models included between 7 and 27 predictors. Restricting the synthesis to only those studies reporting correlations would eliminate more sophisticated analyses, and more complex and presumably more realistic models of science achievement.

In another recent meta-analysis Aloe and Becker (2009) synthesized studies of the relationship between teachers' verbal ability and school outcomes. Fifteen effects were obtained from studies that reported multiple regression models. The 15 models from which those effects were drawn were all different. Although verbal ability and a few other predictors appeared in all of the models, some of the models contained 7 *X*s and others more than 20. Because none of the reports included a full correlation matrix among the variables examined, it is not clear how intercorrelated the other predictors were with teachers' verbal ability.

Multicollinearity

One particular concern in any multiple regression is the extent to which the predictors are interrelated, that is, the extent of multicollinearity (Becker and Wu, 2007). Ideally, all independent variables in such models will be highly correlated with the outcome but uncorrelated with each other. However, in reality this almost never happens because viable predictor variables in education and psychology are usually more or less correlated (Meehl, 1990). Even so, it is rare for primary-study authors to report on multicollinearity, or to give the correlations among predictors in their analyses. As we will see below, the extent to which a predictor of interest correlates with other predictors will affect our proposed partial effect-size index.

In our schools-of-education example the correlation between mean GRE score and number of doctoral degrees granted is not particularly high (0.18). A third predictor, the percentage of students who are doctoral candidates, shows a comparable correlation with GRE scores (0.17). However, it shows a somewhat higher correlation with number of doctoral graduates (0.33). When predictors are more highly intercorrelated, partial regression slopes and partial effect sizes may change a lot as additional predictors are included in the equation.

Scaling of X and Y

In addition to the fact that having different sets of predictors leads to different interpretations of slopes and to variation in the observed strength of relationship as indexed by the regression slope, one other issue must be considered in selecting an effect size for results from a multiple regression analysis. That is, both predictors and outcomes may be measured using different scales across studies. The scales are presumably meant to represent a common construct or latent variable, but if the measures themselves differ, the raw regression coefficients will not be commensurate. In some cases scales are comparable or can be translated to be comparable – such as when the variables represent money, time, or physical measures such as height or weight. But for many variables in education and the social sciences there are no 'natural' or true scales, thus making the raw regression slope a poor choice for an effect size. Any effect size used to represent regression results should be scale free or on a known scale. Our proposed index is scale free.

PARTIAL EFFECT SIZES

The d family

In spite of the fact that primary studies have become increasingly complex and multivariate, relatively little has been done to examine partial effect sizes in the context of meta-analysis. A key exception to this is the work of Keef and Roberts (2004). Keef and Roberts considered the case of treatment effects on continuous variables, and proposed the use of a partial standardized mean difference for this situation. Keef and Roberts called upon arguments made by Cooper and Hedges (1994a) and Becker and Schram (1994), stating that the synthesis of more complex models (and more complex study results) is likely to become increasingly important.

Keef and Roberts examined the case of the partial *d*-type (mean-difference) effect size, where a two-group comparison is examined by way of an analysis-of-covariance model. Specifically, their model was

$$Y_j = \alpha + \gamma D_j + \beta_2 X_{2j} + \ldots \beta_p X_{pj} + e_j,$$

where Y is an outcome score, D is a dummy variable representing a treatment or group effect, and X_2 through X_p are covariates. The errors e_j are assumed to have common variance σ_e^2 Keef and Roberts proposed using $g_{\text{adj}} = \hat{\gamma} / \hat{\sigma}_e$ as a partial index of treatment effects, since $\hat{\gamma}$ represents an adjusted mean difference (accounting for all covariates in the model) and $\hat{\sigma}_e^2$ is the residual variance – essentially the variance of the Y scores, partialling out the effects of all predictors.

It is not possible to predict whether a *d*-type partial effect size will be smaller or larger than the zero-order effect size without specific information about the data at hand. Because two possible adjustments are at play – the adjustment to the mean difference and also a reduction in the standard deviation – g_{adj} can be either smaller or larger than the unadjusted effect size. It can be larger than the typical standardized mean difference if the adjusted mean difference does not differ much from the unadjusted mean difference, but the standard deviation $\hat{\sigma}_e$ is much smaller than the unadjusted standard deviation S_Y. However, if the adjustment leads to a greatly reduced mean difference, but the residual standard deviation is not much smaller than the unadjusted standard deviation, g_{adj} could be smaller than a zero-order effect size.

A partial effect size for the r family

We propose a new index to be used to represent results of multiple regression analyses with continuous predictors. This index represents the partial association between the dependent variable (Y) and a predictor of interest (say X_f) controlling for the effects of other predictors in the model. In this case our model

$$Y_j = \beta_0 + \beta_1 X_{1j} + \beta_2 X_{2j} + \ldots \beta_f X_{fj} + \beta_p X_{pj} + e_j,$$

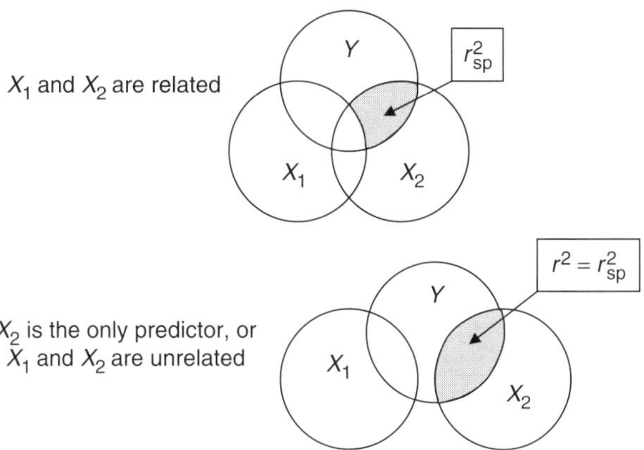

Figure 16.1 Schematic of r_{sp} for bivariate regression with focal predictor X_2

is similar to that of Keef and Roberts (2004), but our focal predictor is not a dummy variable – instead it is continuous. We will refer to the variable X_f as our focal predictor, and our index of effect will be the semi-partial correlation r_{sp} between X_f and Y.

The semi-partial correlation index is the correlation of Y with the part of X_f that is independent of all other Xs. The diagrams in Figure 16.1 show how r and r_{sp} may differ for the simple case with just two predictors. Here the focal predictor is X_2 (though similar diagrams could be created if the focal predictor were X_1). The shaded region in the upper part of the figure graphically represents r^2_{sp} for X_2. The part of X_2 that can be predicted from knowledge of X_1 is not contained in the shaded region. The zero-order correlation (squared) is represented by the shaded region in the lower part of Figure 16.1 – this diagram shows a second predictor totally unrelated to (i.e. not overlapping with) X_2, but if X_2 were the only predictor in the model, the same area would be shaded. Here, since X_1 and X_2 are unrelated, $r^2_{sp} = \mathrm{r}^2_{Y2}$ However, if X_1 and X_2 are correlated it is most typical that r_{sp} is smaller than the zero-order r value, as is seen when the two shaded regions in Figure 16.1 are compared. Below we show this result algebraically as well.

Pedhazur (1997) and others have pointed out that the squared semi-partial correlation can be expressed as the difference between two R^2 ('variance explained') values. Thus, if we define the focal X to be the fth predictor variable, we can write the formula for r_{sp} as

$$r_{sp} = \mathrm{sgn}(t_f)\sqrt{r_Y^2 - r_{Y(f)}^2}\,, \tag{2}$$

where r_Y^2 is the total variance accounted for by the model with p predictors and $r^2_{Y(f)}$ is the variance explained by the model with p - 1 predictors not including the focal predictor X_f. Figure 16.2 shows that when the focal predictor is X_f, r^2_{sp} is the total variance in Y explained by all predictors X_1 through X_p (the sum of all shaded areas) *minus* the variance explained by the p - 1 variables other than X_f.

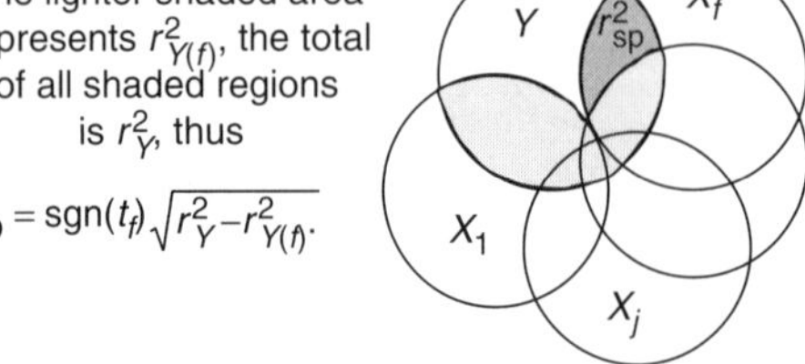

Many of the predictors are related, and the focal predictor is X_f.
r_{sp} represents the part of X_f that is related to Y but unrelated to any of the other Xs.
The lighter shaded area represents $r^2_{Y(f)}$, the total of all shaded regions is r^2_Y, thus
$r_{sp} = \text{sgn}(t_f)\sqrt{r^2_Y - r^2_{Y(f)}}$.
Y
r^2_{sp}
X_f
X_1
X_j

Figure 16.2 Schematic of r_{sp} for multiple regression with focal predictor X_f.

Unfortunately, it is rather unusual to find the second component of equation (2) – the R^2 for the reduced model excluding the focal predictor – in reports of regression model results. However, the semi-partial correlation can be obtained from other results that are typically reported for multiple regression models. It can be computed as

$$r_{sp} = \frac{t_f\sqrt{(1-r_Y^2)}}{\sqrt{(n-p-1)}}, \tag{3}$$

where t_f is the t test of the regression coefficient β_f for focal predictor X_f (i.e. the test of H_0: $\beta_f = 0$) in the multiple regression model, r_Y^2 is the total variance accounted for by the full model with p predictors, and n is the number of participants.

Example

Let us consider a two-predictor model for the peer ratings of schools of education, with mean GRE scores (X_1) and number of degrees granted (X_2) as predictors. The estimated model is $\hat{Y}_j = -22.57 + 0.61X_{1j} + 0.54X_{2j}$, with an overall explained variance of 58 percent (i.e., $r_Y^2 = 0.582$). Each slope has an associated t value, and these are $t_1 = 8.138$ and $t_2 = 5.512$, respectively. Both variables are significant predictors of the peer ratings.

We can compute two r_{sp} values, one for each predictor, and we use both equations (2) and (3) to obtain the r_{sp} values. Specifically, Table 16.1 shows the values of r and r_{sp} for the two predictors. The correlation values with peer ratings of quality are 0.66 and 0.50 for mean GRE scores and for number of doctoral degrees granted, respectively. The r_{sp} values are 0.57 and 0.39, and the values computed for the two formulas differ only in the third or fourth decimal place. These differences are likely due to rounding error in the calculations. Thus we can see that by partialling out the effect of the additional predictor from each of the variables, the unique contribution of each one is slightly smaller than its zero-order r.

LINEAR MODELS WITH TWO PREDICTORS

In this section we examine the general conditions under which one can obtain either r or r_{sp} from multiple regression results. We consider the simplest case, where only two predictors are in the model. However, the ideas presented here can be generalized to p-predictor models.

The general linear model with two predictors can be written as

$$Y_j = \beta_0 + \beta_1 X_{1j} + \beta_2 X_{2j} + e_j,$$

where Y_j is the value of the dependent variable (e.g. the peer rating in our example) for the jth case, X_{ij} is the value of the ith of $p = 2$ predictors for case j, β_0 is the intercept, β_i is the ith slope parameter, and e_j is the random error for the jth observation. The usual assumptions of constant error variance, normality and independence, apply. Suppose we are interested in the relationship between X_2 and Y. As above, we let r_{Y1}, r_{Y2}, and r_{12} be the sample correlations between Y and X_1, Y and X_2, and X_1 and X_2, respectively.

X_1 and X_2 are uncorrelated

When $r_{12} = 0$, the slope b_2 from the two-predictor model will be identical to the slope for the bivariate (one-predictor) regression model. That is, $b_2 = r_{Y2}\, S_Y / S_2$, where S_Y and S_2 are the standard deviations for Y and X_2, respectively. In such cases, we can compute the zero-order r directly from the t test of the regression slope for X_2.

To test the hypothesis that the slope for X_2 is zero in the population, a ratio of b_2 to its standard error (SE) is created and the result is compared to the t critical value with $n - p - 1$ degrees of freedom. The standard error of b_2 (e.g. Cohen et al., 2003) is

$$SE(b_2) = \frac{S_Y \sqrt{1 - r_Y^2}}{S_2 \sqrt{1 - r_{12}^2}\, \sqrt{n - p - 1}}, \tag{4}$$

where S_Y is the standard deviation of Y, S_2 is the standard deviation of X_2, and r_Y^2 is the squared multiple correlation for the full equation. With simple algebra it is possible to show that

$$t_2 = \frac{b_2}{SE(b_2)} = \frac{r_{Y2}(S_Y / S_2)}{\dfrac{S_Y \sqrt{1 - r_Y^2}}{S_2 \sqrt{1 - r_{12}^2}\, \sqrt{n - p - 1}}} = \frac{r_{Y2} \sqrt{1 - r_{12}^2}\, \sqrt{n - p - 1}}{\sqrt{1 - r_Y^2}}.$$

However, if $r_{12} = 0$ the numerator simplifies, and we can rewrite our equation as

$$t_2 = \frac{r_{Y2} \sqrt{n - p - 1}}{\sqrt{1 - r_Y^2}}. \tag{5}$$

Thus, we can compute the zero-order r via $r_{Y2} = t_2 \sqrt{1-r_Y^2} / \sqrt{n-p-1}$ if the t test for the slope of X_2 and the R^2 for the full equation are available. Similarly, if we substitute t_2 shown in equation (5) into the formula for r_{sp} given in equation (3), we can simplify that equation and find that $r_{sp} = r_{Y2}$ when $r_{12} = 0$.

X_1 and X_2 are correlated

In the situation where the predictor variables are correlated, that is, when $r_{12} \neq 0$, the t statistic for the test that the slope $\beta_2 = 0$ is

$$t_{2C} = \left(\frac{r_{Y2} - r_{Y1} r_{12}}{\sqrt{1-r_{12}^2}} \right) \frac{\sqrt{(n-p-1)}}{\sqrt{1-r_Y^2}}, \tag{6}$$

which holds because

$$b_2 = \left(\frac{r_{Y2} - r_{Y1} r_{12}}{(1-r_{12}^2)} \right) \frac{S_Y}{S_2} \quad \text{and} \quad SE(b_2) = \frac{S_Y \sqrt{1-r_Y^2}}{S_2 \sqrt{1-r_{12}^2}\sqrt{(n-p-1)}}.$$

We can solve for r_{Y2} and obtain

$$r_{Y2} = t_{2C} \frac{\sqrt{1-r_Y^2}\sqrt{1-r_{12}^2}}{\sqrt{(n-p-1)}} + r_{Y1} r_{12}.$$

However, this transformation of t_{2C} to r_{Y2} cannot be applied unless the values of r_{Y1} and r_{12} and the full-model R^2 are also available. Of course if all of these values are reported then r_{Y1} will also be reported, making the use of a transformation only possible if it is not needed!

Finally, we can substitute the slope t test t_{2C} from equation (6) into the formula for r_{sp} given in equation (3). This simple substitution leads to cancellations and yet another common form of the semi-partial correlation:

$$r_{sp} = \frac{t_{2C}\sqrt{1-r_Y^2}}{\sqrt{n-p-1}} = \left[\left(\frac{r_{Y2} - r_{Y1} r_{12}}{\sqrt{1-r_{12}^2}} \right) \frac{\sqrt{(n-p-1)}}{\sqrt{1-r_Y^2}} \right] \frac{\sqrt{1-r_Y^2}}{\sqrt{n-p-1}} = \left(\frac{r_{Y2} - r_{Y1} r_{12}}{\sqrt{1-r_{12}^2}} \right).$$

This formula also reveals that when all variables are positively intercorrelated, r_{sp} will often be lower than r_{Y2} because of the subtraction of the $r_{Y1} r_{12}$ term in the numerator. However, this may not hold true if a suppressor effect appears (e.g. $r_{12} < 0$, and r_{Y1} and r_{Y2} are both positive).

Transforming slope t tests to r using other approaches

In an effort to include the largest number of studies relevant to the topic of interest in meta-analysis, researchers have used other approaches to estimate r-family effect sizes from regression studies. Some interest has been shown in using the *t* test of the slope to represent the relationship between two variables in meta-analysis. For instance, Stanley and Jarrell (2005) encouraged the synthesis of *t* statistics from regression slopes. However they did not say how the *t* values should be analyzed, nor did they specify how to obtain a measure of effect size from a *t* value (if *t*s are not to be used directly). Similarly, Rosenthal and Rubin (2003) argued for the '*r*-equivalent' index, defined as

$$r\text{-equivalent} = \frac{t}{\sqrt{t^2 + df}} \tag{7}$$

where *t* is any *t* test (often obtained from a *p* value rather than reported directly), and *df* are the degrees of freedom of that test. McCartney and Rosenthal (2000) stated that it is possible to obtain a partial correlation from multiple regression analysis using equation (7) where $df = n - 2$ and *t* is a *t* test of a regression slope. However, Lipsey and Wilson (2001) stated that equation (7) is only appropriate when the *t* statistic is from a test of $\rho = 0$, that is, a test of a bivariate correlation. Rosenthal and Rubin suggest that equation (7) can be applied to *t*s from a variety of designs, but note that the behavior of *r*-equivalent values based on complex analyses is not well understood. Indeed, the literature contains no information regarding the behavior of this transformation for other kinds of *t* values. For instance, it is not completely clear under what conditions (if any) the *rp* obtained from equation (7) is a partial correlation, whether it would equal a zero-order *r* obtained using equation (1) (i.e. one computed directly from raw data), or whether it would ever equal the value of r_{sp}. This is a topic for further investigation.

THE VARIANCE OF r_{sp}

Nearly all effect-size indices used in meta-analysis have standard errors that can be computed from sufficient statistics, and that represent the uncertainty in the effect-size values. We next present the variance of the r_{sp} index.

Hedges and Olkin (1981) derived the asymptotic distribution of commonality and uniqueness values, through which it is possible to obtain the asymptotic variance of the difference in R^2 values $r_Y^2 - r_{Y(f)}^2$, which is the square of the r_{sp} index. The major difficulty in applying Hedges and Olkin's method is that a complex matrix is needed to compute the covariances among the elements. Fortunately, Alf and Graf (1999), motivated by Olkin and Finn (1995), developed simplified equations for the asymptotic variance of the difference between two squared multiple correlation coefficients, that is, for $r_Y^2 - r_{Y(f)}^2$. Consequently, the derivation of the variance of r_{sp} (which is the square root of $r_Y^2 - r_{Y(f)}^2$) can be achieved via a straightforward application of the delta method (e.g. Rao, 1973).

Let our function of interest r_{sp} be expressed as a function of the values $(r_Y, r_{Y(f)})$, as $r_{\text{sp}} = f(r_Y, r_{Y(f)}) = \sqrt{r_Y^2 - r_{Y(f)}^2}$. The vector $(r_Y, r_{Y(f)})$ has an asymptotically normal distribution with mean $(\rho_Y, \rho_{Y(f)})$ and variance

$$\Phi = \begin{bmatrix} \phi_{11} & \phi_{12} \\ \phi_{21} & \phi_{22} \end{bmatrix}$$

which is given below.

According to the delta method, the expected value of the function f would be the function applied to the expected value of $(r_Y, r_{Y(f)})$, which in large samples is $(\rho_Y, \rho_{Y(f)})$. So the expected value of $r_{\text{sp}}\sqrt{r_Y^2 - r_{Y(f)}^2}$ would be $\rho_{sp} = \sqrt{\rho_Y^2 - \rho_{Y(f)}^2}$. Second, the variance of the function of interest can be expressed as

$\text{var}_{\infty}(f(r_Y, r_{Y(f)})) = \mathbf{a}\Phi\mathbf{a}'$,

where the vector $\mathbf{a}$ contains the partial derivatives of the function f with respect to each of the correlations, and Φ is the 2×2 variance–covariance matrix for r_Y and $r_{Y(f)}$. From Olkin and Siotani (1976) and Olkin and Finn (1995)

$$\phi_{11} = \text{var}_{\infty}(r_Y) = (1 - \rho_Y^2)^2 / n,$$

$$\phi_{22} = \text{var}_{\infty}(r_{Y(f)}) = (1 - \rho_{Y(f)}^2)^2 / n,$$

and

$$\phi_{12} = \phi_{21} = \text{cov}_{\infty}(r_Y, r_{Y(f)}) = [0.5(2\rho_* - \rho_Y \rho_{Y(f)})(1 - \rho_Y^2 - \rho_{Y(f)}^2 - \rho_*^2) + \rho_*^3] / n$$

where $\rho_* = (\rho_{Y(f)} / \rho_Y)$, as derived by Alf and Graf (1999).

The two partial derivatives of f with respect to r_Y and $r_{Y(f)}$ evaluated at the values $(\rho_Y, \rho_{Y(f)})$ in the row vector $\mathbf{a}$ are

$$a_1 = \frac{\partial}{\partial r_Y}\left(\sqrt{r_Y^2 - r_{Y(f)}^2}\right)\bigg|_{\rho_Y, \rho_{Y(f)}} = \frac{1}{2}(\rho_Y^2 - \rho_{Y(f)}^2)^{-\frac{1}{2}}(2\rho_Y)$$
$$= \rho_Y / \sqrt{\rho_Y^2 - \rho_{Y(f)}^2},$$

and

$$a_2 = \frac{\partial}{\partial r_{Y(f)}}\left(\sqrt{r_Y^2 - r_{Y(f)}^2}\right)\bigg|_{\rho_Y^2, \rho_{Y(f)}^2} = \frac{1}{2}(\rho_Y^2 - \rho_{Y(f)}^2)^{-\frac{1}{2}}(-2\rho_{Y(f)})$$
$$= -\rho_{Y(f)} / \sqrt{\rho_Y^2 - \rho_{Y(f)}^2}.$$

Thus, we can write var(r_{sp}) = $\mathbf{a}\,\rho\,\mathbf{a}'$ as

$$\mathbf{a\Phi a'} = \begin{bmatrix} \frac{\rho_Y}{\sqrt{\rho_Y^2 - \rho_{Y(f)}^2}} & \frac{-\rho_{Y(f)}}{\sqrt{\rho_Y^2 - \rho_{Y(f)}^2}} \end{bmatrix} \begin{bmatrix} \phi_{11} & \phi_{12} \\ \phi_{21} & \phi_{22} \end{bmatrix} \begin{bmatrix} \rho_Y / \sqrt{\rho_Y^2 - \rho_{Y(f)}^2} \\ -\rho_{Y(f)} / \sqrt{\rho_Y^2 - \rho_{Y(f)}^2} \end{bmatrix}$$

Making the appropriate cancellations

$$\mathrm{var}(r_{sp}) = \frac{1}{\left(\rho_Y^2 - \rho_{Y(f)}^2\right)} \left[\rho_Y^2 \phi_{11} + \rho_{Y(f)}^2 \phi_{22} - 2\rho_Y \rho_{Y(f)} \phi_{12} \right].$$

Finally, substituting ϕ_{11}, ϕ_{22}, and ϕ_{12} we obtain

$$\begin{aligned} \mathrm{var}(r_{sp}) &= \frac{1}{n\left(\rho_Y^2 - \rho_{Y(f)}^2\right)} \Big[\rho_Y^2 (1-\rho_Y^2)^2 + \rho_{Y(f)}^2 (1-\rho_{Y(f)}^2)^2 \\ &\qquad -2\rho_Y \rho_{Y(f)} [0.5(2\rho_* - \rho_Y \rho_{Y(f)})(1-\rho_Y^2 - \rho_{Y(f)}^2 - \rho_*^2) + \rho_*^3] \Big] \\ &= \frac{\rho_Y^4 - 2\rho_Y^2 + \rho_{Y(f)}^2 + 1 - \rho_{Y(f)}^4}{n}. \end{aligned} \tag{8}$$

With this result, we can say that for large samples, r_{sp} has an asymptotically normal distribution with mean ρ_{sp} and variance var(r_{sp}) given in equation (8). Simulation studies by Aloe (2009) suggest that the bias in r_{sp} and its variance is quite low even for sample sizes as small as $n = 50$. For example, the largest bias value for r_{sp} for $n = 50$ shows that r_{sp} deviates from its true parameter value by, at most, just over 3 percent.

Typically, equation (8) would be calculated by substituting sample analogues for the population values. A seeming shortcoming of this estimator for the variance of r_{sp} is that some of the components needed to compute equation (8) are often not reported in primary studies. Specifically, while the R^2 for the full model (r_Y^2) is often presented, typically $r_{Y(f)}^2$ (which appears in equation (8) and is also used to estimate ρ_*) is often not reported. However, thanks to the relationship between the semi-partial correlation and the difference between multiple correlations we can compute the missing $r_{Y(f)}^2$ value. Beginning with equation (3), $r_{sp} = \mathrm{sgn}(t)\sqrt{r_Y^2 - r_{Y(f)}^2}$, we can solve for $r_{Y(f)}^2$. By so doing we obtain

$$r_{Y(f)}^2 = r_Y^2 - r_{sp}^2.$$

This may seem circular, but since r_{sp} is typically computed from equation (3), it is computed without explicit knowledge of $r_{Y(f)}^2$.

Values of var(r_{sp})

For our raw data example on peer ratings, we can calculate the variance of r_{sp} for each of the two predictors. The last row in Table 16.1 shows the values,

Table 16.2 Numerator of the variance of r_{sp} for selected values of r_Y^2 and $r_{Y(f)}^2$

r_Y^2	$r_{Y(f)}^2$	r_Y	$r_{Y(f)}$	r_*	r_{sp}	$n\ var(r_{sp})$
0.6	0.5	0.775	0.707	0.913	0.316	0.410
0.6	0.4	0.775	0.632	0.816	0.447	0.400
0.6	0.3	0.775	0.548	0.707	0.548	0.370
0.5	0.4	0.707	0.632	0.894	0.316	0.498
0.5	0.3	0.707	0.548	0.775	0.447	0.490
0.5	0.2	0.707	0.447	0.632	0.548	0.460
0.4	0.3	0.632	0.548	0.866	0.316	0.570
0.4	0.2	0.632	0.447	0.707	0.447	0.520
0.4	0.1	0.632	0.316	0.500	0.548	0.450

$\text{var}(r_{sp}) = 0.0073$ for the mean GRE scores and $\text{var}(r_{sp}) = 0.0084$ for the number of doctoral degrees granted. These values are slightly smaller than the variances of the bivariate correlations.

We also have computed the numerator of the variance of the r_{sp} index (i.e. $n\ \text{var}(r_{sp})$) for a variety of values of r_Y^2, $r_{Y(f)}^2$, and r_{sp}. These are shown in Table 16.2. Examining only the numerator of the variance of r_{sp} is also equivalent to setting n to 1 in equation (8). Columns 1 and 2 in Table 16.2 present three values of the total variance explained by the full model (r_Y^2) and five values of the variance explained with all the predictors except the predictor of interest ($r_{Y(f)}^2$). Their square roots, used to compute r_*, are in columns 3 and 4, and r_* is in column 5. The column 6 presents the r_{sp} values and column 7 presents the numerator of the variance of r_{sp} (or $n\ \text{var}(r_{sp})$) using equation (8).

According to Table 16.2, the larger the r_{sp} value becomes, the smaller the value of its variance. However, the value of the variance also depends on r_Y^2. Specifically, holding r_{sp} constant, $\text{var}(r_{sp})$ is smaller when the overall variance explained (r_Y^2) is larger. For instance, when $r_{sp} = 0.316$, the variance of r_{sp} is smallest for $r_Y^2 = 0.6$. This pattern also holds for the influence of $r_{Y(f)}^2$ on $\text{var}(r_{sp})$. This makes sense, because the variances of r_Y and $r_{Y(f)}$ decrease as r_Y and $r_{Y(f)}$ increase, and those variances are both components of $\text{var}(r_{sp})$.

ANALYZING r_{sp} VALUES

With the variance derived above, meta-analysis of the semi-partial correlations can proceed in a similar fashion to typical meta-analyses, as outlined for instance by Hedges and Olkin (1985) or in *The Handbook of Research Synthesis and Meta-analysis* (Cooper, Hedges and Valentine, 2009). Standard errors and confidence intervals can be computed for the individual r_{sp} values, and weighted analyses can be used to explore heterogeneity and to estimate central tendency and variation in the effects. We have several tentative recommendations about such analyses, but because r_{sp} is a new index, research on the behavior of r_{sp} in the meta-analysis context is not yet complete.

When we consider the fact that each semi-partial correlation may arise from a different regression model, it is conceivable that each r_{sp} in a meta-analysis may be estimating a different population parameter. This suggests that for overall analysis the random-effects model (Hedges and Vevea, 1998) is more appropriate than a fixed-effects approach. In addition this suggests that when analyzing a collection of r_{sp} values, the reviewer needs to include predictor variables that reflect differences in model complexity.

Examining study features

For further analysis of semi-partial correlations we suggest that the reviewer code and examine two sorts of features that are not examined when simple zero-order effects are the focus. First, we recommend that the meta-analyst code the number of predictors in each regression model. This information is needed to compute the semi-partial correlation r_{sp}, and should be easily obtained. It reflects the complexity of each model, and may represent the degree to which the individual r_{sp} values differ from the zero-order correlation, and from each other.

Second, we suggest coding indicator (or 'dummy') variables signifying the presence or absence of key covariates or control variables in each study's regression model. For instance, in our synthesis of the studies of teacher science knowledge and student achievement, a particularly important control variable is the student's prior achievement. If this is not controlled, the primary-study regression analyses cannot give a strong indication of the importance of the *current* teacher's level of science content knowledge for student achievement. This is because without controlling for inequalities in prior achievement levels, variation in current achievement levels may reflect contributions to the student's current level of performance made by any or all prior teachers. To the extent that the coded variables are important predictors of the outcome of interest, r_{sp} values from models that include those variables will be lower than zero-order *r*s, and may also be lower than other semi-partial correlations (from models without those control variables). The larger the number of valuable control variables that are included, the lower the semi-partial *r* may be for the focal predictor.

Because we do not have many effect-size values in our example data, we examine only three predictor variables in our illustration below. However in practice, one might expect to have a larger set of effects as well as a number of study characteristics to examine. Approaches like the weighted analogue to analysis of variance (e.g. Hedges, 1994), or weighted regression analysis (also called meta-regression, e.g. Thompson and Higgins, 2002) can be used. We use the regression approach for our example analyses below.

Combining rs and r_{sp}s

A last consideration for the analysis of r_{sp} values is whether to combine them with zero-order correlations. Technically, the semi-partial correlation is estimating a different parameter than the bivariate r. Thus, reviewers should use caution in combining effects computed using the r_{sp} formula with bivariate correlations, because r_{sp} values tend to be smaller than bivariate correlations. However, as was also noted above, it is likely that any collection of r_{sp} values *themselves* will represent a range of models, suggesting that one might view the bivariate r as the 'simplest' semi-partial r – one with nothing partialled out – justifying the decision to analyze all of the study outcomes together. It would then become an empirical question as to whether the values of r and r_{sp} indices differed from each other.

In cases where these two indices are analyzed together, variables representing the complexity of the models from which the r_{sp}s were drawn must be incorporated into analyses of the full set of effects. In such an analysis, for instance, the variable 'number of predictors' would be coded as '1' for outcomes that are bivariate rs, since the bivariate r represents a regression model with just one predictor. Similarly, dummy-variable indicators representing the presence of particular control variables would be coded as '0' for bivariate correlations.

Example

Data for this example are from five studies that explore the relationship of science teachers' content knowledge to students' science achievement using multiple regression analysis. These results are drawn from a more extensive synthesis (Aloe and Becker, 2008). The studies included in this example reported the elements needed to compute the partial effect size r_{sp} for multiple regression models for seven samples. Specifically, each study reported a t test of the slope for the predictor of interest (t), total sample size (n), the number of predictors in the model (p), and a measure of variance explained (r_Y^2). The r_{sp} value for each study is shown in Table 16.3, as are two dummy-variable predictors used below. For each study, the partial effect size for the r family, r_{sp}, was computed using equation (3). For instance, for Chaney (1995) the value of r_{sp} is computed as

$$r_{sp} = \frac{1.9\sqrt{(1-0.33)}}{\sqrt{(26435-27-1)}} = 0.0096.$$

In our meta-analysis example we first obtain the weighted average effect from the five studies that explore the relationship of teachers' science content knowledge to students' achievement. The variance of r_{sp} is needed, and it and the components needed to compute it are given in Table 16.4. The weights used are inverse variance weights; for the overall test of homogeneity the weight is $w = 1/\text{var}(r_{sp})$ and for other analyses a between-studies variance component is added to each variance to reflect unexplained variation in the r_{sp} values.

Table 16.3 Results of the studies of teacher science knowledge and student achievement

Study	t	n	p	r_Y^2	r_{sp}	*Prior achievement?*	*Life science?*
Chaney (1995)	1.9	26435	27	0.33	0.0096	0	0
Goldhaber and Brewer (1999)	1.3	2299	13	0.66	0.0159	1	0
Greenberg et al. (2002)	0.7	8130	16	0.31	0.0148	0	0
	2.1	8091	22	0.35	0.0188	0	0
Monk (1994)	–0.5	1513	12	0.43	–0.0097	0	1
	–2.2	900	15	0.50	–0.0523	0	1
Monk and King (1994)	–2.0	912	10	0.06	–0.0549	1	1

Table 16.4 Results of studies with variance values and weights

Study	n	r_{sp}	r_Y^2	$r_{y(f)}^2$	$var(r_{sp})$	w
Chaney (1995)	26435	0.0096	0.3300	0.3299	0.00003	39456.85
Goldhaber and Brewer (1999)	2299	0.0159	0.6600	0.6597	0.00015	6760.33
Greenberg et al. (2002)	8130	0.0148	0.3100	0.3098	0.00008	11923.91
	8091	0.0188	0.3500	0.3496	0.00008	12449.80
Monk (1994)	1513	–0.0097	0.4300	0.4299	0.00038	2654.44
	900	–0.0523	0.5000	0.4973	0.00056	1800.02
Monk and King (1994)	912	–0.0549	0.0600	0.0570	0.00103	972.86

We first show the confidence interval plot (also called the forest plot) for the effects representing the relationship of teacher science knowledge to student science achievement. Figure 16.3 shows that all of the effects are quite close to 0, though because the studies are quite large, two of the 95 percent confidence intervals do not contain 0. Also we can see that the last three effects have wider intervals. Those samples are somewhat smaller than the first four, though even all of the studies are large for the social sciences, the smallest sample size is 900.

The weighted mean effect size under the random-effects model was $\bar{r}_{sp} = 0.005$, with standard error $SE = 0.00867$ for the set of seven effects. We also compute the random-effects variance component. In the case of our data, the study results are heterogeneous ($Q = 13.58$, $df = 6$, $p = 0.035$). The simple method-of-moments estimator of the variance in true effects is computed as from the unweighted mean semi-partial correlation ($\bar{r}_{sp}$) and the mean var(r_{sp}), denoted $\bar{v}$, as $\hat{\sigma}_\rho^2 = [\sum (r_{sp} - \bar{r}_{sp})^2 / (k-1)] - \bar{v} = 0.0001$. This suggests that 95 percent of the distribution of population semi-partial correlations would lie between –0.0146

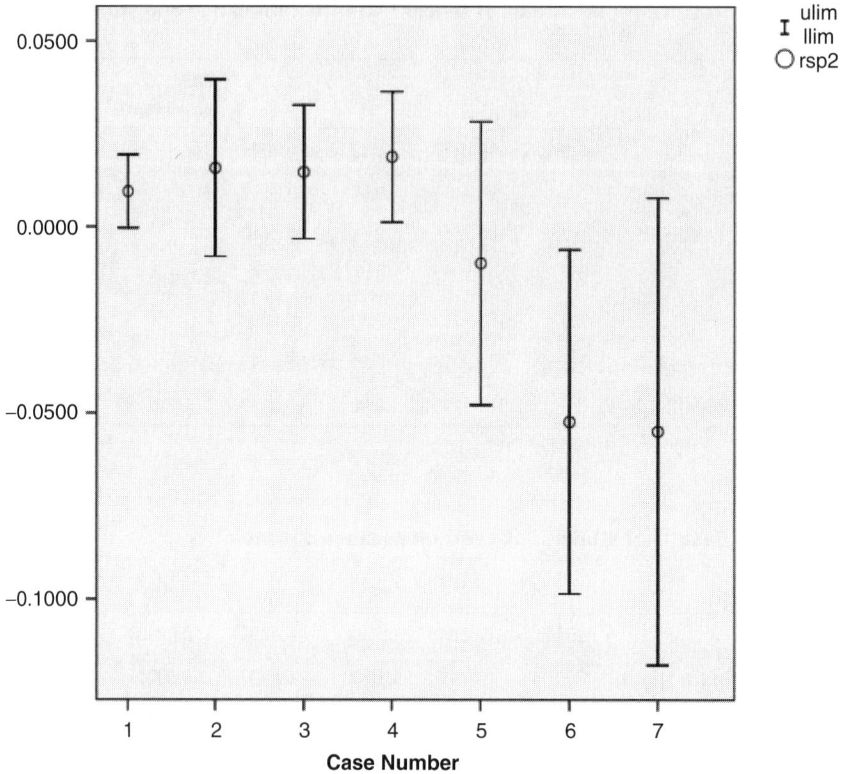

Figure 16.3 Ninety-five percent confidence intervals for r_{sp} values

and 0.0246 (assuming a normal distribution). This is quite a narrow range – relationships throughout this whole range would be considered trivial by any common rule of thumb. Also, the mean does not differ significantly from 0, and both positive and negative correlations are likely.

We next examine three different variables as possible predictors of the semi-partial correlation values. They are the number of *X*s in the regression model (*p* in Table 16.3 above) and two indicator variables. One indicator represents the presence of a measure of prior student achievement in the regression model, and the second concerns the subject matter of the teacher science-knowledge measure. Specifically the variable 'Life science?' indicates whether the measure of teacher knowledge tapped life-science content knowledge, versus general-science knowledge.

Table 16.5 summarizes the results for the overall model plus these three analyses. Both number of predictors in the model (*p*) and the use of prior achievement as a control variable showed no relationship to the outcome r_{sp}. However, there was a rather dramatic and significant relationship for the content of the teacher-knowledge measure as indicated by its slope of –0.04 ($z = -3.16$, $p < 0.01$). Specifically, studies that examine life-science content knowledge showed

Table 16.5 Analyses of four models predicting r_{sp}

Model	*Q_{Error} (df)*	*p value*	*Slope (SE)*
No predictors	13.58 (6)	0.035	–
Number of variables in the model (*p*)	12.90 (5)	0.024	0.0016 (0.0016)
Prior achievement controlled?	13.52 (5)	0.019	–0.0049 (0.0247)
Life science measure?	3.54 (5)	0.618	–0.0446 (0.0141)

Note: Q_{Error} is calculated using fixed-effect weights; slopes and *SE*s are calculated using mixed-model weights.

significantly lower semi-partial correlations than did the studies of general-science knowledge as a predictor of student achievement, by about 0.04. The means are $\bar{r}_{sp} = 0.0127$ for studies with general-science knowledge measures, and $\bar{r}_{sp} = -0.0319$ for studies of teacher life-science knowledge. This model explains all of the between-studies variation in r_{sp} values (as shown by the non-significant Q_{Error} value in Table 16.5) – thus in fact it simplifies to a fixed-effects model.

DISCUSSION

When estimating effect sizes from multiple regression models it may be of interest to partial out a variable or set of variables from the key predictors present in the model. For instance, a researcher may be interested in the proportion of variance in students' academic achievement explained by their teachers' content knowledge. This effect can be represented by the semi-partial correlation, r_{sp}. The r_{sp} can be seen as a partial effect in the *r* family. When the predictors in a multiple regression are completely uncorrelated, r_{sp} equals the bivariate correlation. On the other hand, when predictors are interrelated (as they typically are), r_{sp} represents the unique contribution to the outcome *Y* made by the focal predictor.

What is innovative about the index we offer here is that it will enable reviewers to include effects representing more complex, and presumably more sophisticated, studies into meta-analysis. While such studies continue to be in the minority in the meta-analysis we have conducted recently, we anticipate that future studies will become increasingly complex, and eventually most of the literature on any given topic will include such sophisticated analyses.

This chapter shows that we can compute r_{sp} and its variance with relatively minimal information that is typically presented in research reports. However, some reports do not give even the basic information required for use of this index. In particular when reports fail to present variance explained (R^2) values we cannot compute r_{sp}. Similarly r_{sp} cannot be computed if reports give only raw or standardized slopes with indicators of significance (such as asterisks) but no *t* test values. For these reasons, plus in general support of complete reporting of results in primary studies to facilitate later meta-analysis, we endorse the recommendations of the APA Publications and Communications Board Working Group on Journal Article Reporting Standards (2008). The Working Group recommends that authors report 'Direction, magnitude, degrees of freedom, and exact *p* level, even if no significant effect is reported' and also 'For multivariable analytic systems (e.g. multivariate analyses of variance, regression analyses, structural equation modeling analyses, and hierarchical linear modeling) also include the associated variance–covariance (or correlation) matrix or matrices' (2008: 843). Fully reporting the details of results will enable meta-analysts of the future to avoid making untestable assumptions and using *ad hoc* methods to compute (hopefully) comparable effect indices. A stronger case is made by Freese (2007), who argues for providing greater access to study results and associated data by capitalizing on the capacity to archive data on the internet. Such archiving would enable even more complete reporting of results, and facilitate better analyses by reviewers. In theory, we support this position. We suspect, however, that some researchers will be reluctant to allow such extensive access, as Freese himself noted. Many details of data ownership will need to be worked out before such archiving will be palatable to the majority of researchers.

In any case, our index can be easily applied without access to the complete data archives suggested by Freese. While further work is needed to investigate the behavior of r_{sp} and its variance, we believe this index will be a valuable contribution, furthering the meta-analysis of complex study results. In addition, further development may enable this index to be extended to other more complex models based on regression-like analyses such as hierarchical linear models.

ACKNOWLEDGMENTS

This research has been supported by grants from the National Science Foundation (NSF REC-0335656 and REC-0635592). Any opinions, findings, and conclusions or recommendations expressed in this material are those of the author(s) and do not necessarily reflect the views of the National Science Foundation.

REFERENCES

Asterisks (*) denote studies used in the meta-analysis example.

Alf, E.F. and Graf, R.G. (1999). Asymptotic confidence limits for the difference between two squared multiple correlations: A simplified approach. *Psychological Methods*, 4: 70–5.

Aloe, A.M. (2009). *A Partial Effect Size for the Synthesis of Multiple Regression Models.* Unpublished doctoral dissertation, Florida State University.

Aloe, A.M. and Becker, B.J. (2008). *Teacher Science Knowledge and Student Science Achievement.* Paper presented at the annual meeting of the American Educational Research Association, New York, NY.

Aloe, A.M. and Becker, B.J. (2009). Teacher verbal ability and school outcomes: Where is the evidence? *Educational Researcher*, 3(8): 612–24.

APA Publications and Communications Board Working Group on Journal Article Reporting Standards (2008). Reporting standards for research in psychology: Why do we need them? What might they be? *American Psychologist*, 63(9): 839–51.

Becker, B.J. (1992). Using results from replicated studies to estimate linear models. *Journal of Educational Statistics*, 17: 341–62.

Becker, B.J. and Schram, C.M. (1994). Examining explanatory models through research synthesis. In H.M. Cooper and L.V. Hedges (eds) *The Handbook of Research Synthesis*, pp. 357–81. New York: Russell Sage Foundation.

Becker, B.J. and Wu, M.J. (2007). The synthesis of regression slopes in meta-analysis. *Statistical Science*, 22(3): 414–29.

*Chaney, B. (1995). *Student Outcomes and the Professional Preparation of Eighth-grade Teachers in Science and Mathematics: NSF/NELS:88 Teacher Transcript Analysis*. Rockville, MD: Westat, Inc.

Cohen, J., Cohen, P., West, S.G., and Aiken, L.S. (2003). *Applied Multiple Regression/Correlation Analysis for the Behavioral Sciences*, 3rd edn. Mahwah, NJ: Erlbaum.

Cooper, H.M. and Hedges, L.V. (1994a). Potentials and limitations of research synthesis. In H.M. Cooper and L.V. Hedges (eds) *The Handbook of Research Synthesis*, pp. 521–9. New York: Russell Sage Foundation.

Cooper, H.M., Hedges, L.V., and Valentine, J. (eds) (2009). *The Handbook of Research Synthesis and Meta-analysis*. New York: Russell Sage Foundation.

Freese, J. (2007). Replication standards for quantitative social science: Why not sociology? *Sociological Methods Research*, 36: 153–72.

*Goldhaber, D.D. and Brewer, D.J. (1999). Teacher licensing and student achievement. In M. Kanstoroom and C.F.J. Finn (eds) *Better Teachers, Better Schools*, pp. 83–102. Washington, DC: Thomas B. Fordham Foundation.

*Greenberg, E., Skidmore, D., Rhodes, D., and Nesbitt, D. (2002). *Prepared to Teach: Teacher Preparation and Student Achievement in Mathematics and Science*. Washington, DC: American Institutes for Research.

Hedges, L.V. (1994). Fixed effects models. In H.M. Cooper and L.V. Hedges (eds) *The Handbook of Research Synthesis*, pp. 521–9. New York: Russell Sage Foundation.

Hedges, L.V. and Olkin, I. (1981). The asymptotic distribution of commonality components. *Psychometrika*, 46: 331–6.

Hedges, L.V. and Olkin, I. (1985). *Statistical Methods for Meta-analysis*. Orlando, FL: Academic Press.

Hedges, L.V. and Vevea, J.L. (1998). Fixed- and random-effects models in meta-analysis. *Psychological Methods*, 3(4): 486–504.

Keef, S.P. and Roberts, L.A. (2004). The meta-analysis of partial effect sizes. *British Journal of Mathematical and Statistical Psychology*, 57(1): 97–129.

Lipsey, M.W. and Wilson, D.B. (2001). *Practical Meta-analysis*. Thousand Oaks, CA: Sage Publications.

McCartney, K. and Rosenthal, R. (2000). Effect size, practical importance, and social policy for children. *Child Development*, 71: 173–80.

Meehl, P.E. (1990). Why summaries of research on psychological theories are often uninterpretable. *Psychological Reports*, 66: 195–244.

*Monk, D.H. (1994). Subject area preparation of secondary mathematics and science teachers and student achievement. *Economics of Education Review*, 13(2): 125–45.

*Monk, D.H. and King, J.A. (1994). Multilevel teacher resource effects on pupil performance in secondary mathematics and science: The case for teacher subject-matter preparation. In R.G. Ehrenberg (ed.), *Choices and Consequences: Contemporary Policy Issues in Education*, pp. 29–58. Ithaca, NY: ILR Press.

Olkin, I. and Finn, J.D. (1995). Correlations redux. *Psychological Bulletin*, 118: 155–64.

Olkin, I. and Siotani, M. (1976). Asymptotic distribution of functions of a correlation matrix. In S. Ikeda et al. (eds) *Essays in Probability and Statistics*, pp. 235–51. Tokyo, Japan: Shinko Tsusho Co. Ltd.

Pedhazur, E.J. (1997). *Multiple Regression in Behavioral Research: Explanation and Prediction,* 3rd edn. Orlando, FL: Holt, Rinehart, & Winston.

Rao, C.R. (1973). *Linear Statistical Inference and its Applications,* 2nd edn. New York, NY: Wiley.

Rosenthal, R. and Rubin, D.B. (2003). $r_{equivalent}$: A simple effect size indicator. *Psychological Methods*, 8: 492–6.

Stanley, T.D. and Jarrell, S.B. (2005). Meta-regression analysis: A quantitative method of literature surveys. *Journal of Economic Surveys*, 19: 299–308.

Thompson, S.G. and Higgins, J.P.T. (2002). How should meta-regression analyses be undertaken and interpreted? *Statistics in Medicine*, 21(11): 1559–73.

17

Toward a New Era for Conducting Mixed Analyses: The Role of Quantitative Dominant and Qualitative Dominant Crossover Mixed Analyses

Anthony J. Onwuegbuzie,
Nancy L. Leech and
Kathleen M. T. Collins

The analysis stage of the research process is central to both quantitative research and qualitative research because this stage represents the stage wherein the researcher first formally attempts to extract meaning from the collected data and hence begins to address the underlying research question(s). For both research approaches (i.e. quantitative research, qualitative research), the analysis stage typically is the most difficult because although numerous tools, such as analytical techniques and software packages, are available for both sets of researchers, it often takes many years to become a proficient quantitative analyst or qualitative analyst.

In Figure 17.1, we have identified 58 classes of established quantitative analysis techniques, some of which are discussed in this volume (see Griffiths, this volume; Kline, this volume; Pituch and Stapleton, this volume; Rees Jones, this volume). It should be noted that the number of classes would have far exceeded 58 if we had included all the established classes of non-parametric analyses.

Measurement Techniques	
Name of Analytical Technique	***Description***
Classical Test Theory	Analyzes the relationship among observed scores, true scores, and error in an attempt to predict outcomes of psychological and behavioral measurement
Item Response Theory (Latent Trait Theory, Strong True Score Theory, Modern Mental Test Theory)	Analyzes the probabilistic relationship between the response that a person provides (e.g. examinee) on a quantitative item(s) and item parameters (e.g. item difficulty, item discrimination, guessing parameter) and person parameters/latent traits (e.g. ability, personality trait)
Multilevel Item Response Theory	Estimates latent traits of the respondent at different levels and examines the relationships between predictor variables and latent traits at different levels
Exploratory Factor Analysis	Explores the underlying structure of correlations among observed variables in an attempt to reduce the dimensionality, wherein a small(er) number of factors significantly account for the correlations among the set of measured variables; utilizes estimates of common variance or reliability on the main diagonal of the correlation matrix that is factor analyzed
Principal Component Analysis	Explores the underlying structure of correlations among observed variables in an attempt to reduce the dimensionality, wherein a small(er) number of factors significantly account for the correlations among the set of measured variables; utilizes the total variance of each variable to assess the shared variation among the variables. That is, it uses 'ones' on the diagonal of the correlation matrix that is factor analyzed
Confirmatory Factor Analysis	Verifies the factor structure of a set of observed variables; it allows testing of the hypothesis that a relationship between observed variables and their underlying latent constructs exists
Multiple Factor Analysis (optimal scaling, dual scaling, homogeneity analysis, scalogram analysis)	Analyzes observations described by two or more sets of variables, and examines the common structures present in some or all of these sets
Hierarchical Factor Analysis	Differentiates higher-order factors from a set of correlated lower-order factors
Assessing One Variable/Participant at a Time	
Descriptive Analyses (i.e., measures of central tendency, variation/dispersion, position/relative standing, and distributional shape)	Summarize and describe a set of data one variable at a time in quantitative terms
Single-Subject Analysis	Analyzes observations from one or more individuals in which each individual serves as his/her own control (i.e. individual participant is the unit of analysis)
Assessing Differences through Variance Analysis	
Independent Samples *t* Test	Examines the difference between the means of two independent groups
Dependent Samples *t* Test (paired samples *t* test)	Examines the difference between the means of two groups, wherein the scores in one group is paired or dependent on the scores in the other group
Analysis of Variance (ANOVA)	Partitions the observed variance into components based on different sources of variation; one-way ANOVA examines the equality of several independent groups based on one dependent/outcome variable; factorial ANOVA examines the effects of two or more independent/explanatory/predictor variables and their interactions
Analysis of Covariance (ANCOVA)	Examines whether one or more factors (and their interactions) have an effect or are related to the outcome variable after removing the variance for which quantitative predictors (covariates) account
Multivariate Analysis of Variance (MANOVA)	Examines whether one or more factors have an effect or are related to two or more outcome variables

(*Figure continues on next page*)

Multivariate Analysis of Covariance (MANCOVA)	Examines whether one or more factors (and their interactions) have an effect or are related to two or more outcome variables after removing the variance for which quantitative predictors (covariates) account
Hierarchical Linear Modeling (HLM) (multilevel modeling, mixed effects modeling, covariance components modeling, random-coefficient regression modeling)	Analyzes variance in an outcome variable when data are in nested categories (i.e. students in a class, classes within a school, schools in one school district)
Multivariate Hierarchical Linear Modeling	Analyzes variance in multivariate dependent variables when the covariance structure of the independent variables is of interest
Repeated Measures Analysis of Variance (RMANOVA)	Involves an analysis of variance conducted on any design wherein the independent/predictor variable(s) have all been measured on the same participants under multiple conditions
Mixed Analysis of Variance (Mixed ANOVA)	Examines differences between two or more independent groups whereby repeated measures have been taken on all participants such that one factor represents a between-subjects variable and the other factor represents a within-subjects variable
Repeated Measures Analysis of Covariance (RMANCOVA)	Examines whether one or more factors (and their interactions) have an effect or are related to the outcome variables (i.e. repeated measures) after removing the variance for which quantitative predictors (covariates) account
Assessing Group Membership/Relationships	
Cluster Analysis	Assigns a set of observations, usually people, into groups or clusters wherein members of the group are maximally similar
Q Methodology	Involves finding relationships between participants across a sample of variables
Profile Analysis	Classifies empirically individual observations based on common characteristics or attributes measured by an observed variable(s)
Multivariate Profile Analysis	Classifies empirically individual observations based on common characteristics or attributes (i.e. multiple dependent variables) measured by observed variables (i.e. multiple independent variables)
Chi-Square Analysis	Involves any test statistic that has a chi-square distribution but generally analyzes the independence of two categorical variables via a contingency table
Chi-Square Automatic Interaction Detection (CHAID)	Examines the relationships between a categorical dependent measure (dichotomous, polytomous, ordinal) and a large set of selected predictor variables that may interact themselves; it involves a series of chi-square analyses (i.e. iterative, chi-square tests of independence) being conducted between the dependent and predictor variables
Multivariate Chi-Square Automatic Interaction Detection (MCHAID)	Examines the relationships between two or more categorical dependent measure (dichotomous, polytomous, ordinal) and a large set of selected predictor variables that may interact themselves; it involves a series of chi-square analyses (i.e. iterative, chi-square tests of independence) being conducted between the multiple dependent and predictor variables
Descriptive Discriminant Analysis	Explains group separation (i.e. categorical dependent/outcome variable) as a function of one or more continuous or binary independent variables
Predictive Discriminant Analysis	Predicts a group membership (i.e. categorical dependent/outcome variable) by one or more continuous or binary independent variables
Assessing Time and/or Space	
Time Series Analysis	Involves analyzing, using frequency-domain methods or time-domain methods, an ordered sequence of observations over time, taking into account the serial dependence of the observations for the purpose of modeling and forecasting

(*Figure continues on next page*)

Survival Analysis	Analyzes time-to-even data (i.e. failure time data)
Geostatistics	Analyzes spatiotemporal (i.e. existing in both space and time) datasets
Panel Data Analysis	Analyzes a particular participant or group of participants within multiple sites, periodically observed over a defined time frame (i.e. longitudinal analysis)
Correspondence Analysis	Converts data organized in a two-way table into graphical displays, with the categories of the two variables serving as points; this graphical display presents the relationship between the two categorical variables
Canonical Correspondence Analysis	Relates specific variables (e.g. types of species) to variables of interest (e.g. types of environments)
Fuzzy Correspondence Analysis	Similar to Correspondence Analysis, except uses 'fuzzy data' – data that are coded with multiple categories instead of the common '0' or '1'
Multiple Correspondence Analysis	Analyzes the pattern of relationships of several categorical dependent variables
Discriminant Correspondence Analysis	Categorizes observations in predefined groups using nominal variables
Proportional Hazard Model	Estimates the effects of different covariates influencing the times-to-failure of a system (i.e. hazard rate)
Explaining or Predicting Relationships Between Variables	
Linear Regression	Examines the linear correlations between one (simple regression) or more (multiple regression) binary or continuous explanatory variables and a single continuous dependent variable
Non-Linear Regression	Examines the non-linear correlations between one or more binary or continuous explanatory variables and a single continuous dependent variable
Probit Regression	Examines the non-linear correlations between one or more binary or continuous explanatory variables and a binomial response variable
Regression Discontinuity Analysis	Examines causal effects of interventions, wherein assignment to a treatment condition is determined, at least partly, by the value of an observed covariate that lies on either side of a fixed threshold
Logistic Regression (logit regression)	Examines the relationship between one (simple logistic regression model) or more (multiple logistic regression model) binary or continuous explanatory variables and a single categorical dependent variable
Multivariate Logistic Regression	Examines the relationship between one or more explanatory variables and two or more categorical dependent variable(s)
Descriptive Discriminant Analysis	Explains group separation (i.e. categorical dependent/outcome variable) as a function of one or more continuous or binary independent variables
Predictive Discriminant Analysis	Predicts a group membership (i.e. categorical dependent/outcome variable) by one or more continuous or binary independent variables
Log-Linear Analysis (multi-way frequency analysis)	Determines which of the sets of three or more variables (and/or interactions) best explains the observed frequencies with no variable serving as the dependent/outcome variable
Canonical Correlation Analysis	Examines the multivariate relationships between two or more binary or continuous predictor variables and two or more binary or continuous outcome variables
Path Analysis	Describes and quantifies the relationship of a dependent/outcome variable to a set of other variables, with each variable being hypothesized as having a direct effect or indirect effect (via other variables) on the dependent variable
Structural Equation Modeling (causal modeling, covariance structure analysis)	Involves building and testing statistical models; it encompasses aspects of confirmatory factor analysis, path analysis, and regression analysis
Multilevel Structural Equation Modeling	Used when the units of observation form a hierarchy of nested clusters and some variables of interest are measured by a set of items or fallible instruments
Multilevel Latent Class Modeling	Analyzes data with a multilevel structure such that model parameters are allowed to differ across groups, clusters, or level-2 units; the dependent variable is not directly observed but represents a latent variable with two or more observed indicators

(*Figure continues on next page*)

Correlation Coefficient	Measures the association between two variables
Multidimensional Scaling	Explores similarities or dissimilarities in data; it displays the structure of a set of objects from data that approximate the distances between pairs of the objects
Social Network Analysis	Involves the identification and mapping of relationships and flows among people, groups, institutions, web sites, and other information- and knowledge-producing units of different sizes; it provides both a visual and a mathematical analysis of complex human systems; the unit of analysis is not the individual, but an element consisting of a collection of two or more individuals and the linkages among them
Propensity Score Analysis	Replaces multiple covariates such that just one score is applied as a predictor rather than multiple individual covariates, thereby greatly simplifying the model; balances the treatment and control groups on the covariates when participants are grouped into strata or subclassified based on the propensity score; it adjusts for differences via study design (matching) or during estimation of treatment effect (stratification/regression)

Figure 17.1 Established classes of quantitative data analysis techniques and descriptions. (Note: For many of these analyses, non-parametric versions and Bayesian versions exist).

However, including all of the non-parametric analyses was beyond the scope of this chapter. In any case, the 58 classes of quantitative analyses that we present are more than sufficient to illustrate that quantitative analysts have numerous analytical techniques at their disposal.

We refer to the elements in Figure 17.1 as representing classes of *established quantitative analyses* instead of classes of established *statistical* analyses because our list includes classes of analytical techniques representing measurement theory. Although this list is not exhaustive, Figure 17.1 captures most of the major classes of parametric quantitative analytical techniques and a few non-parametric techniques (e.g. chi-square analysis). These quantitative analyses represent *classes* because each class contains multiple analysis techniques. For example, descriptive statistics can be subdivided into measures of central tendency, measures of variation/dispersion, measures of position/relative standing, and measures of distributional shape. Each of these categories, in turn, can be subdivided into several analysis types. For example, measures of central tendency include mean, median, and mode. Similarly, regression can be subdivided into techniques such as simple regression, multiple regression, hierarchical linear regression, all possible subsets linear regression, ridge regression, step-wise regression (although discredited; cf. Onwuegbuzie and Daniel, 2003; Thompson, 1995), commonality analysis, Cox proportional hazards regression, and Tobit regression. As another example, canonical correlation analysis includes traditional canonical correlation analysis, sparse canonical correlation analysis, and kernel canonical correlation analysis. Also, hierarchical linear modeling includes hierarchical generalized linear models, hierarchical models for latent variables, and hierarchical models for cross-classified random effects. These classes of quantitative analyses vary in complexity, with most of the parametric analyses varying in complexity as a function of the following four elements: number of independent variables involved, number of dependent variables involved, scales of measurement (i.e. nominal, ordinal, interval, ratio) of each of the independent variables involved, and scales of measurement of each of the dependent variables involved (Onwuegbuzie et al., in press a).

Alternatively conceptualized, the complexity of most of the parametric analyses varies according to its place in the general linear model (GLM) family because all parametric analyses (i.e. univariate and multivariate techniques), with the exception of predictive discriminant analyses, are subsumed by the GLM (Henson, 2000; Onwuegbuzie and Daniel, 2003; Thompson, 1998). For example, correlation analyses are a special type of regression analysis, which, in turn, is a special type of canonical correlation analysis, which, in turn, is a special type of path analysis, which, in turn, is a special case of structural equation modelling, and so forth. As such, although the less complex quantitative analyses (e.g. correlation coefficient) can be understood in a relatively short space of time, one or more term-/semester-long courses or intensive courses are needed to become proficient using the more complex GLM (and non-GLM) techniques (e.g. regression, structural equation modeling, hierarchical linear modeling). In any case, the array of available quantitative analyses makes the data analysis stage one of the most difficult stages – if not the most difficult stage – in the quantitative research process.

With respect to qualitative research, Leech and Onwuegbuzie (2008) identified 18 qualitative data analysis techniques (see Table 17.1), Miles and Huberman (1994) conceptualized 19 within-case analyses (see Table 17.2) and 18 cross-case analyses (see Table 17.3), yielding a total of 55 qualitative data analysis techniques. Tables 17.1–17.3 contain many of the most popularized qualitative data analysis techniques, although this list is by no means exhaustive. As is the case for quantitative analysis techniques, qualitative analyses vary in complexity, from less complex (e.g. word count) to the more complex (e.g. discourse analysis, qualitative comparative analysis) – with some of these analytical techniques necessitating whole term-/semester-long courses or intensive courses (e.g. discourse analysis). However, as noted by Leech and Onwuegbuzie (2007, 2008), many qualitative researchers are unaware of the numerous qualitative data analysis techniques, as presented in Tables 17.1–17.3, likely because most qualitative research textbooks – including the leading ones – devote relatively little attention to data analysis (e.g. only 2 of 44 chapters in the latest edition of the *Handbook of Qualitative Research*; Denzin and Lincoln, 2005b) and those books that do include data analysis tend to focus on one data analysis technique (e.g. discourse analysis; Phillips and Jorgensen, 2002) or, at best, only a few techniques (e.g. Grbich, 2007; Silverman, 2001). This lack of comprehensive treatment in data analysis in qualitative research textbooks likely makes it more challenging for researchers to become proficient in conducting an array of qualitative analysis techniques, thereby making the data analysis stage one of the most difficult stages – if not the most difficult stage – in the qualitative research process.

As difficult as the quantitative analysis stages and qualitative analysis stages are for researchers, it is even more complex for studies that necessitate *both*

Table 17.1 Most common qualitative analyses

Type of analysis	*Short description of analysis*
Constant comparison analysis	Systematically reducing data to codes, then developing themes from the codes.
Classical content analysis	Counting the number of codes.
Word count	Counting the total number of words used or the number of times a particular word is used.
Keywords-in-context	Identifying keywords and utilizing the surrounding words to understand the underlying meaning of the keyword.
Domain analysis	Utilizing the relationships between symbols and referents to identify domains.
Taxonomic analysis	Creating a system of classification that inventories the domains into a flowchart or diagram to help the researcher understand the relationships among the domains.
Componential analysis	Using matrices and/or tables to discover the differences among the subcomponents of domains.
Conversation analysis	Utilizing the behavior of speakers to describe people's methods for producing orderly social interaction.
Discourse analysis	Selecting representative or unique segments of language use, such as several lines of an interview transcript, and then examining the selected lines in detail for rhetorical organization, variability, accountability, and positioning.
Secondary data analysis	Analyzing non-naturalistic data or artifacts that were derived from previous studies.
Membership categorization analysis	Utilizing the role that interpretations play in making descriptions and the consequences of selecting a particular category (e.g. baby, sister, brother, mother, father = family).
Semiotics	Using talk and text as systems of signs under the assumption that no meaning can be attached to a single term.
Manifest content analysis	Describing observed (i.e. manifest) aspects of communication via objective, systematic, and empirical means (Berelson, 1952).
Latent content analysis	Uncovering underlying meaning of text.
Qualitative comparative analysis	Systematically analyzing similarities and differences across cases, typically being used as a theory-building approach, allowing the analyst to make connections among previously built categories, as well as to test and to develop the categories further.
Narrative analysis	Considering the potential of stories to give meaning to individual's lives, and treating data as stories, enabling researchers to take account of research participants' own evaluations.
Text mining	Analyzing naturally occurring text in order to discover and capture semantic information.
Micro-interlocutor analysis	Analyzing information stemming from one or more focus groups about which participant(s) responds to each question, the order that each participant responds, the characteristics of the response, the non-verbal communication used, and the like.

This table was adapted from Leech and Onwuegbuzie (2008).

Table 17.2 Miles and Huberman's (1994) within-case displays

Type of display	*Description*
Partially ordered:	
Poem	Composition in verse
Context chart	Networks that map in graphic form the interrelationships among groups and roles that underlie the context of individual behavior
Checklist matrix	Way of analyzing/displaying one major concept, variable, or domain that includes several unordered components
Time-ordered:	
Event listing	Matrix or flowchart that organizes a series of concrete events by chronological time periods and sorts them into multiple categories
Critical incident chart	Maps a few critical events
Event-state network	Maps general states that are not as time-limited as events, and might represent moderators or mediators that link specific events of interest
Activity record	Displays a specific recurring activity that is limited narrowly in time and space
Decision modeling flowchart	Maps thoughts, plans, and decisions made during a flow of activity that is bounded by specific conditions
Growth gradient	Network that maps events that are conceptualized as being linked to an underlying variable that changes over time
Time-ordered matrix	Maps when particular phenomena occurred
Role-ordered:	
Role-ordered matrix	Maps the participant's 'roles' by sorting data in rows and columns that have been collected from or about a set of data that reflect their views, beliefs, expectations, and/or behaviors
Role-by-time matrix	Maps the participant's 'roles', preserving chronological order
Conceptually Ordered:	
Conceptually clustered matrix	Text table with rows and columns arranged to cluster items that are related theoretically, thematically, or empirically
Thematic conceptual matrix	Reflects ordering of themes
Folk taxonomy	Typically representing a hierarchical tree diagram that displays how a person classifies important phenomena
Cognitive map	Displays the person's representation of concepts pertaining to a particular domain
Effects matrix	Displays data yielding one or more outcomes in a differentiated manner, focusing on the outcome/dependent variable
Case dynamics matrix	Displays a set of elements for change and traces the consequential processes and outcomes for the purpose of initial explanation
Causal network	Displays the most important independent and dependent variables and their interrelationships

Table 17.3 Miles and Huberman's (1994) cross-case displays

Type of display	*Description*
Partially ordered:	
Partially ordered meta-matrix	Displays descriptive data for each of several cases simultaneously
Case-ordered:	
Case-ordered descriptive meta-matrix	Contains descriptive data from all cases but the cases are ordered by the main variable of interest
Two-variable case-ordered matrix	Displays descriptive data from all cases but the cases are ordered by two main variables of interest that are represented by rows and columns
Contrast table	Displays a few exemplary cases wherein the variable occurs in low or high form, and contrast several attributes of the basic variable
Scatterplot	Plots all cases on two or more axes to determine how close from each other the cases are
Case-ordered effects matrix	Sorts cases by degrees of the major cause of interest, and shows the diverse effects for each case
Case-ordered predictor-outcome matrix	Arranges cases with respect to a main outcome variable, and provides data for each case on the main antecedent variables
Predictor-outcome consequences matrix	Links a chain of predictors to some intermediate outcome, and then illustrates the consequence of that outcome
Time-ordered:	
Time-ordered meta-matrix	Table in which columns are organized sequentially by time period and the rows are not necessarily ordered
Time-ordered scatterplot	Displays similar variables in cases over two or more time periods
Composite sequence analysis	Permits extraction of typical stories that several cases share, without eliminating meaningful sequences
Conceptually ordered:	
Content-analytic summary table	Allows the researcher to focus on the content of a meta-matrix without reference to the underlying case
Substructing	Permits the identification of underlying dimensions
Decision tree modeling	Displays decisions and actions that are made across several cases
Variable-by-variable matrix	Table that displays two major variables in its rows and columns ordered by intensity with the cell entries representing the cases
Causal models	Network of variables with causal connections among them in order to provide a testable set of propositions or hunches about the complete network of variables and their interrelationships
Causal networks	Comparative analysis of all cases using variables deemed to be the most influential in explaining the outcome or criterion
Antecedents matrix	Display that is ordered by the outcome variable, and displays all of the variables that appear to change the outcome variable

quantitative analysis and qualitative analysis – namely mixed methods research studies, or more aptly termed mixed research studies, which involve 'mix[ing] or combin[ing] quantitative and qualitative research techniques, methods, approaches, concepts or language into a single study' (Johnson and Onwuegbuzie, 2004: 17). In fact, a mixed research study might involve any one of the 58 classes of quantitative data analysis techniques and any one of the 55 qualitative data analysis techniques. Thus, if a researcher was to utilize only one quantitative analysis technique and one qualitative analysis technique within what can be termed as a *mixed analysis framework*, he/she would have at least 3,190 (i.e. 58 × 55) combinations of quantitative and qualitative analysis techniques from which to choose. This number of combination increases exponentially when classes of non-parametric quantitative analyses and classes of Bayesian analyses are included. Further, the number of combinations increases exponentially for mixed research studies in which at least two quantitative data analysis techniques and/or at least two qualitative data analysis techniques are used. Indeed, the myriad ways that quantitative and qualitative data analysis techniques can be combined provides credence to the assertions of Johnson and Onwuegbuzie (2004) that 'Ultimately, the possible number of ways that studies can involve mixing is very large because of the many potential classification dimensions' (p. 20). However, although this feature of mixed analysis suggests that mixed research 'truly opens up an exciting and almost unlimited potential for future research' (Johnson and Onwuegbuzie, p. 20), without guidance, the number of ways that mixed analyses can be undertaken is daunting and overwhelming for many – if not most – beginning researchers (e.g. doctoral students, emergent scholars) and even for experienced quantitative researchers and qualitative researchers who do not have much experience conducting mixed research techniques.

Clearly, more frameworks are needed to help researchers understand their options for data analysis techniques so that they can optimize their mixed analysis strategies. Consistent with our assertion, Greene (2008) concluded that the work undertaken by authors to provide guidance on conducting mixed analyses 'has not yet cohered into a widely accepted framework or set of ideas' (p. 14). Recently, in an attempt to develop an inclusive and integrated framework for conducting mixed analyses, Onwuegbuzie and Combs (in press) conducted a comprehensive review of the literature, identifying virtually every published methodological work (e.g. article, editorial, book chapter) in the area of mixed analyses. These mixed methodologists identified 13 criteria based on their interpretations of published mixed analysis typologies developed by various authors (e.g. Bazeley, 1999, 2003, 2006, 2009, in press; Caracelli and Greene, 1993; Chi, 1997; Creswell and Plano Clark, 2007; Datta, 2001; Greene, 2007, 2008; Greene et al., 1989; Happ et al., 2006; Li et al., 2000; Onwuegbuzie, 2003; Onwuegbuzie et al., in press b; Onwuegbuzie and Dickinson, 2008; Onwuegbuzie and Leech, 2004; Onwuegbuzie et al., 2007a, 2009b; Onwuegbuzie and Teddlie, 2003; Sandelowski, 2000, 2001; Tashakkori and Teddlie, 1998; Teddlie and Tashakkori, 2009; Teddlie et al., 2008; West and Tulloch, 2001). Onwuegbuzie and Combs' (in press) 13 criteria are delineated briefly below.

ONWUEGBUZIE AND COMBS' (IN PRESS) 13 CRITERIA FOR MIXED ANALYSES

The first criterion, identifying the *rationale/purpose for conducting the mixed analysis* is based on Greene et al.'s (1989) typology comprising the following five purposes for mixing: triangulation (findings from the quantitative data are compared to the qualitative results); complementarity (results of the analytical strand (e.g. quantitative) are interpreted to enhance, elaborate, illustrate, or clarify findings derived from the other strand (qualitative)); development (data are collected sequentially and the results of one analytical strand are used to inform data collected and analyzed in the other strand); initiation (contradictions or paradoxes that might reshape the research question are identified), and expansion (multiple analytical strands are implemented to expand the study's scope and focus).The *philosophy underpinning the mixed analysis* is the second criterion, and it reflects the viewpoint (Bazeley, 2009; Onwuegbuzie et al., 2009a) that there is not a one-to-one correspondence between the researcher's ontology/epistemology philosophical stance and the type of analysis selected for a particular study, thereby providing the opportunity for a researcher to utilize the most appropriate analysis (whether qualitative or quantitative) for addressing the research question (Bazeley, 2009).

The third criterion is the *number of data types that will be analyzed.* Onwuegbuzie and Combs (in press) note that contrary to the contention that both types of data (i.e. quantitative and qualitative data) must be collected to warrant a mixed analysis (Creswell and Plano Clark, 2007), collecting only one type of data (e.g. qualitative data) and transforming the type of data collected into the other type of data (e.g. qualitative data are quantitized; cf. Onwuegbuzie et al. (2007b) for an empirical example of this process) will permit the researcher to conduct a mixed analysis (Miles and Huberman, 1994; Onwuegbuzie and Teddlie, 2003; Tashakkori and Teddlie, 1998).

The *number of data analysis types* that will be used is the fourth criterion, whereby a mixed analysis encompasses one or more qualitative analysis types and one or more quantitative analysis types. The fifth criterion is the *time sequence of the mixed analysis*. The mixed analyses can occur concurrently or sequentially (Creswell and Plano Clark, 2007; Onwuegbuzie and Teddlie, 2003; Tashakkori and Teddlie, 1998; Teddlie and Tashakkori, 2009). A concurrent analysis involves conducting a mixed analysis such that the quantitative and qualitative analyses do not occur in any chronological order and thus are independent of one another. In contrast, a sequential analysis involves conducting one type of data analysis (e.g. quantitative data analysis), and utilizing the results to inform the subsequent analysis phase (e.g. qualitative data analysis); this sequence can occur in multiple phases. The sixth criterion is the *level of interaction between the quantitative and qualitative analyses*, which can be described as the point at which the two sets of analyses (i.e. the qualitative and quantitative analyses) interact (Onwuegbuzie and Combs, in press). The most common type appears to be parallel mixed analysis (Teddlie and Tashakkori, 2009). In this context, the researcher collects both forms of data and independently conducts both sets of analyses, utilizing techniques traditionally associated with the type of data collected (i.e. quantitative analysis of quantitative data; qualitative analysis of qualitative data). Parallel mixed analysis can elevate in complexity when multiple analytical strands are implemented within a study, thereby allowing the various strands to inform each other prior to the study's inference stage.

Onwuegbuzie and Combs' (in press) seventh criterion, *priority of analytical components*, refers to the emphasis given by the researcher to the analytical strands. The emphasis in this context reflects the researcher's decision to form a dominant emphasis (e.g. prioritize one type of analyses) or to place an approximately equal priority on both forms of analyses in terms of addressing the research question(s). The eighth criterion, the *number of analytical phases* reflects the various phases implemented in the mixed analyses process (Greene, 2007; Onwuegbuzie et al., in press b; Onwuegbuzie and Teddlie, 2003). For example, Onwuegbuzie and Teddlie (2003) identified the following seven steps informing the mixed analysis process: (a) data reduction, (b) data display, (c) data transformation, (d) data correlation, (e) data consolidation, (f) data comparison, and (g) data integration. *Linking to other design components* is the ninth criterion, and it reflects the views of Teddlie and Tashakkori (2009) and Creswell and Plano Clark (2007) who suggest that the type of data analysis conducted depends on the type of design utilized in the study. For example, researchers who hold this view would conduct a sequential mixed analysis whenever the mixed research design is sequential in nature (e.g. if the quantitative and qualitative data are collected sequentially, then the quantitative and qualitative analyses occur in the same order). The tenth criterion is the *phase(s) of the research process when all analysis decisions are made*, and these decisions can occur a priori, a posteriori, or iteratively within the study. When iteratively forming mixed analysis decisions, the researcher follows an emergent model of decision making, shaped by the type of data collected and the results of the various analyses. The *type of generalization*, the eleventh criterion, informs the mixed analysis design, such that it prompts the researcher to decide on making one or more of the following five types of generalizations identified by Onwuegbuzie et al. (2009) that stem from the research question(s) posed and the quality of data collected: (a) *external (statistical) generalizations* (i.e. making generalizations, predictions, or inferences on data yielded from a representative statistical (i.e. optimally random and large) sample to the *population* from which the sample was drawn (i.e. universalistic generalizability)); (b) *internal (statistical) generalizations* (i.e. making generalizations, predictions, or inferences on data obtained from one or more representative or elite study participants (e.g. key informants, sub-sample members) to the *sample* from which the participant(s) was selected (i.e. particularistic generalizability)); (c) *analytical generalizations* (i.e. 'the investigator is striving to generalize a particular set of (case study) results to some broader theory' (Yin, 2009: 43); and this set is 'applied to wider theory on the basis of how selected cases "fit" with general constructs' (Curtis et al., 2000: 1002)); *case-to-case transfer* (i.e. making generalizations or inferences from one case to another (similar) case; Miles and Huberman, 1994); and (e) *naturalistic generalization* (i.e. the readers make generalizations entirely, or at least in part, from their personal or vicarious experiences; Stake and Trumbull, 1982).

The twelfth criterion, analysis orientation, as conceptualized by Onwuegbuzie et al. (2009), comprises three types of analysis orientations: (a) case-oriented (i.e. analyses that focus primarily or exclusively on the selected case(s)), (b) variable-oriented (i.e. analyses that involve identifying relationships, which are often probabilistic in nature, among elements that serve as variables, and which lead to conceptual and theory-centered analyses), and (c) process/experience-oriented analyses (i.e. analyses that involve evaluating processes or experiences pertaining to one or more cases within a specific context over time). The former two orientations represent extensions of case-oriented and variable-oriented research (cf. Ragin, 1989a, 2008). Finally, the thirteenth criterion, *crossover nature of the analysis*, signifies that one form of data (e.g. qualitative) collected can be analyzed utilizing techniques traditionally associated with the alternative paradigm (e.g. quantitative) (Greene, 2007, 2008; Onwuegbuzie and Teddlie, 2003), thereby permitting a higher level of integration of quantitative and qualitative analyses (Onwuegbuzie and Combs, in press).

CROSSOVER NATURE OF MIXED ANALYSES

Of the 13 decision criteria, the most underdeveloped criterion is that pertaining to the crossover nature of mixed analyses. As noted by Onwuegbuzie and Combs (in press), this decision criterion represents an extension of Greene's (2007) 'broad analytic concept' (p. 153) of 'using aspects of the analytic framework of one methodological tradition in the analysis of data from another tradition' (p. 155). Interestingly, Teddlie and Tashakkori (2009) declared that 'We believe that this is one of the more fruitful areas for the further development of MM (mixed methods) analytical strategies' (p. 281).

Building on the works of Greene (2007, 2008) and Onwuegbuzie and Teddlie (2003), Onwuegbuzie and Combs (in press) introduced the concept of what they called *crossover mixed analyses*, whereby one or more analysis types associated with one tradition (e.g. quantitative analysis) are used to analyze data associated with a different tradition (e.g. qualitative data). According to these authors, the following nine crossover analysis types currently exist: (a) integrated data reduction (i.e. reducing the dimensionality of quantitative data/findings using qualitative techniques (e.g. thematic analysis of quantitative data) and/or qualitative data/findings using quantitative analysis (e.g. exploratory factor analysis of qualitative data); cf. Onwuegbuzie, 2003; Onwuegbuzie and Teddlie, 2003); (b) integrated data display (i.e. visually displaying both quantitative and qualitative findings within the same display; cf. Lee and Greene, 2007; Onwuegbuzie and Dickinson, 2008); (c) data transformation (i.e. converting quantitative data into data that can be analyzed qualitatively (i.e. qualitizing; Tashakkori and Teddlie, 1998) and/or qualitative data into numerical codes that can be analyzed statistically (i.e. quantitizing; Tashakkori and Teddlie, 1998)); (d) data correlation (i.e. correlating qualitative data with quantitized/quantitative data and/or quantitative data with qualitized/qualitative data; Onwuegbuzie and Teddlie, 2003); (e) data consolidation (i.e. merging or combining two or more data sets to create new or consolidated codes, data sets, or variables; cf. Louis, 1982; Onwuegbuzie and Teddlie, 2003); (f) data comparison (i.e. comparing qualitative and quantitative data/findings; cf. Onwuegbuzie and Teddlie, 2003); (g) data integration (i.e. integrating quantitative and qualitative data/findings either into a coherent whole or two separate sets of coherent wholes; cf. McConney et al., 2002; Onwuegbuzie and Teddlie, 2003); (h) warranted assertion analysis (i.e. examining all qualitative and quantitative data to produce meta-inferences; Smith, 1997); and (i) data importation (i.e. using follow-up results from quantitative analysis to inform the qualitative analysis, or vice versa; Greene, 2008; Li et al., 2000; Onwuegbuzie and Teddlie, 2003). As such, crossover mixed analyses can be used to (a) reduce, (b) display, (c) transform, (d) correlate, (e) consolidate, (f) compare, (g) integrate, (h) assert, or (i) import data, respectively.

Crossover mixed analyses are different from non-crossover mixed analyses. As noted by Onwuegbuzie and Combs (in press), non-crossover mixed analyses involve collection of both types of data (i.e. quantitative data and qualitative data) and the analysis of each data type using an analysis representing the same paradigmatic tradition (i.e. *within-paradigm analysis*; Onwuegbuzie et al., 2007a: 12)–that is, a quantitative analysis (cf. Figure 17.1) of quantitative data and a qualitative analysis (cf. Tables 17.1–17.3) of qualitative data. Consequently, mixed methodology researchers who exclusively conduct non-crossover mixed analyses uphold a conventional dichotomous distinction between quantitative analysis and qualitative analysis. This approach to mixed analysis is based on the assumptions that (a) quantitative and qualitative analyses are completely distinguishable from each other; (b) quantitative and qualitative analyses are different and thus should be conducted separately; (c) quantitative data require solely quantitative analyses; (d) qualitative data require solely qualitative analyses; (e) inferences pertaining to the quantitative data stem from the quantitative analysis; and (f) inferences pertaining to the qualitative data stem from the qualitative analysis. In fact, only after inferences from the quantitative analyses and inferences from the qualitative analyses have been made can meta-inferences (i.e. inferences from qualitative and quantitative findings being integrated into either a coherent whole or two distinct sets of coherent wholes; Tashakkori and Teddlie, 1998) be obtained.

Although such a within-paradigm analysis framework provides myriad combinations of mixed analyses, crossover mixed analyses represent an even higher degree of mixing because they involve *between-paradigm analysis*, which involves using an analysis procedure that is traditionally associated with one paradigm (e.g. qualitative analysis) to analyze data that are traditionally associated with the other paradigm (e.g. quantitative data). This crossover approach to mixed analysis is based on the assumptions that (a) quantitative and qualitative analyses are not necessary distinguishable from each other; (b) any differences between quantitative and qualitative analyses do not necessitate exclusive quantitative analysis of quantitative data and qualitative analysis of qualitative data; and (c) both quantitative analysis and qualitative analysis can address the same research questions. As such, crossover mixed analyses necessitate the mixing or combining of qualitative- and quantitative-based paradigmatic assumptions and stances. For instance, a mixed methodology researcher might use correspondence analysis (cf. Rees Jones, this volume) to examine how similar or dissimilar six participants who were interviewed in a qualitative phase of a mixed research study are with respect to the emergent themes (cf. Onwuegbuzie et al., in press b). In this example, as noted by Onwuegbuzie et al. (2009a), conducting such a crossover mixed analysis:

> involves either maintaining an analytical-philosophical stance that the human mind/perception and mathematical algorithms can be used sequentially to examine patterns in qualitative data or adopting an analytical-philosophical stance that transcends the stances underlying both paradigms (e.g. assuming that data saturation (i.e. qualitative information repeats itself such that no new or relevant information seem to emerge pertaining to a category, and the category development is well established and validated; Morse, 1995) and reliability (i.e. consistency or repeatability of participants' quantitative responses) represent parallel constructs). (p. 118)

FEATURES OF CROSSOVER MIXED ANALYSES

Crossover mixed analysis techniques involve three major elements that distinguish them from non-crossover mixed analysis techniques. First, each crossover mixed analysis necessitates some level of abductive logic or reasoning (cf. Morgan, 2007), which involves oscillating between inductive and deductive logic. Second, these crossover mixed analysis procedures also involve a form of intersubjectivity, which involves 'moving back and forth between various frames of reference' (Morgan, 2007: 71), as well as involving shared analysis and interpretations that result in shared meanings constructed by analysts in their interactions with each other. Third, these crossover mixed analyses involve the combining or merging of both insiders' (i.e. emic) views and the researcher-observer's (i.e. etic) views for analyzing data, and that the balance between the emic perspectives (i.e. stemming from the participants from whom data are collected) and etic perspectives (e.g. stemming from extant theories and model assumptions) is appropriate such that quality meta-inferences are yielded.

For instance, an analyst might conduct what Onwuegbuzie and Teddlie (2003) termed a sequential quantitative-qualitative analysis – specifically, a sequential follow-up interaction analysis – wherein once an interaction is observed from a quantitative analysis, such as an analysis of variance (cf. Figure 17.1), he/she would collect follow-up qualitative data (e.g. via individual interviews, focus group interviews, observations, photographs) on those participants who are most likely to increase understanding of how and why the interaction emerged (e.g. in a two-way interaction between gender and anxiety (high vs. low), an analyst would collect qualitative information on one or more of the following four subgroups: high-anxious males, high-anxious females, low-anxious males, low-anxious females). Any follow-up quantitative analysis of the interaction (e.g. examination of whether the interaction was ordinal or disordinal, *post-hoc* tests, statistical analysis of contrasts) would represent an etic-oriented analysis that is driven by statistical model assumptions (e.g. normality, equal variances), whereas the subsequent collection of qualitative data would lead to an emic-oriented analysis.

This utilization of abductive logic, intersubjectivity, and emic–etic perspectives makes the crossover mixed analysis process represent the highest form of combining quantitative and qualitative data analysis techniques. Figure 17.2 presents our three-dimensional model for categorizing and organizing mixed analyses. Specifically, as can be seen, the model includes three dimensions, each focused upon a given set of perspectives for analyzing quantitative and qualitative data, and each positioned at 90-degree angles to the other two. Dimension 1 (type of logic/reasoning) can be conceptualized as classifying the reasoning used during the crossover mixed analysis process, with inductive reasoning being located at one end of the continuum and deductive reasoning being located at the other end of the continuum. The mid-point of the continuum represents the place where inductive and deductive reasoning are most balanced – the point at which abductive reasoning is maximal. All other points of the continuum represent some level of abductive reasoning. In Dimension 2 (level of subjectivity), subjectivity lies at one end of the continuum and objectivity lies at the other end of the continuum. The mid-point of the continuum represents the place where subjectivity and objectivity most interact – the point at which intersubjectivity is maximal. All other points of the continuum represent some level of intersubjectivity. Finally, in Dimension 3 (lens), emic perspectives lie at one extreme of the continuum and etic perspectives lie at the other end, with the mid-point of the continuum representing the place where emic and etic viewpoints are maximally interactive. All other points of the continuum represent some combination of emic and etic viewpoints. Using the model, a given crossover mixed analysis can be positioned somewhere within the three-dimensional space as a way of indicating the multidimensional complexity or sophistication of crossover mixed analysis designs. For example, a mixed research study that was a pure replication of a previous mixed research study might necessitate deductive reasoning, or at least predominantly deductive reasoning, for all phases of the crossover mixed analysis process (i.e. Dimension 1); intersubjectivity (i.e. Dimension 2); and some combination of emic and etic perspectives (i.e. Dimension 3). However, the combination that yields the highest form of integrating (i.e. *greatest crossover*) is when the analysis process involves abductive logic, intersubjectivity, and both emic and etic perspectives.

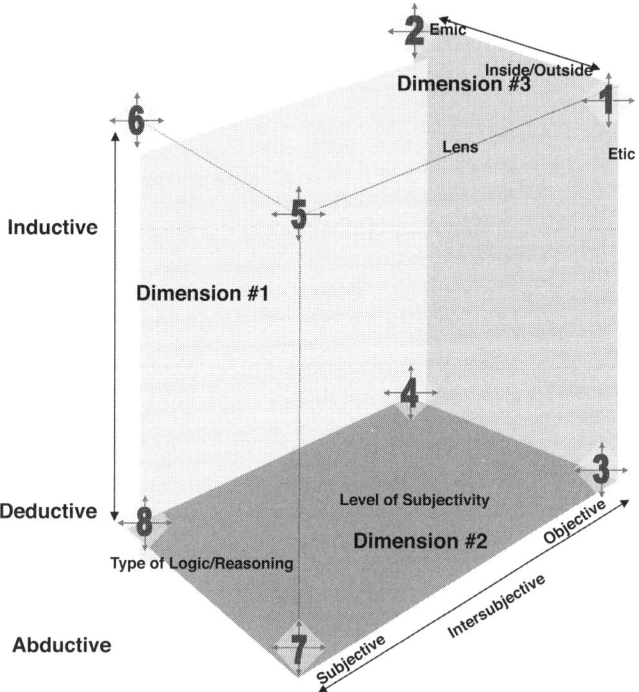

Figure 17.2 A three-dimensional model for categorizing and organizing crossover mixed analyses (Note: Directionality of the continua across each dimension is arbitrary. There is no intentionality of suggesting superiority of one continuum point or extreme over another. Rather, the appropriateness of the continuum point depends on the research goal, research objectives(s), mixing rationale and purpose, mixed research question(s), mixed sampling design, and mixed research design, as well as underlying philosophical assumptions and stances involved (e.g. dialectical pragmatist, postpositivist, constructivist, transformative-emancipatory). Encircled numbers represent eight possible combinations of the extreme points on the three dimensions of type of logic/reasoning, level of subjectivity, and lens.)

Another feature of a crossover mixed analysis is that the analyst has to make Gestalt switches (Kuhn, 1962) from a qualitative lens to a quantitative lens and vice versa, oscillating until maximal meaning has been extracted from the data. Further, crossover mixed analysis techniques do not only involve the analysis of quantitative and/or qualitative data but also a *creation* of quantitative and/or qualitative data that are subsequently analyzed using qualitative and/or quantitative analysis techniques, respectively. For example, an exploratory factor analysis of themes derived from the qualitative analyses would lead to the creation (i.e. extraction) of a higher level of abstraction termed (qualitative) meta-themes. A second-order factor analysis of the meta-themes would lead to the creation of meta-themes of even higher levels of abstraction.

Table 17.4 Teddlie and Tashakkori's (2009) partial list of analogous processes in quantitative and qualitative research

Analytical process	*Application to quantitative research*	*Application to qualitative research*
Data displays	Quantitative data displays (e.g. numeric contingency tables)	Qualitative displays or matrices (e.g. Miles and Huberman, 1994)
Effect sizes	Statistical indices, such as Cohen's (1988) *d* and Smith and Glass's (1977) delta	Qualitative effect size, such as manifest effect size (Onwuegbuzie, 2003)
Generation of themes	Exploratory factor analysis, quantitative data mining	Thematic analysis in general, including grounded theory, text mining
Maximizing between-group variations and minimizing within-group variations	Cluster analysis to identify a set of groups that both maximize between-group variations and minimize within-group variations	The categorizing component of the constant comparative method to maximize between-theme variations and minimize within-theme variations
Comparing analysis from one part of a sample with analysis from another part of the sample	In prediction studies, splitting the sample randomly in two, running exploratory regression analysis on the first subsample, then conducting confirmatory regression analysis on the second subsample	Archival storage of some of the qualitative data, using concept of referential adequacy, for later analysis, comparing original interpretations made on the basis of the first sample of data with new interpretations based on the second sample (e.g. Eisner, 1998; Lincoln and Guba, 1985)
Comparison of actual results with expected results	Pattern matching studies using quantitative data; in regression analysis, examining residual values, that compare expected versus predicted scores	Pattern matching studies using qualitative data – for example, the use of replication logic in multiple case designs that compare empirical results with predicted results based on previous cases (Yin, 2003); negative case analysis
Contrasting components of research design or elements to find differences	Focused contrast analysis to look for specific differences in particular parts of an analysis of variance design	Asking contrast questions (e.g. what is the difference between *X* and *Y*?) to determine the meaning of a phenomenon of interest (Spradley, 1979, 1980)

A mixed methodology researcher who conducts crossover mixed analyses is likely to focus more on the similarities between quantitative and qualitative analyses or on the differences in an attempt to fulfill one or more of Greene et al.'s (1989) purposes for mixing (e.g. triangulation, complementarity, development, initiation, expansion). Also, as noted by Teddlie and Tashakkori (2009), there are numerous analytical processes in quantitative and qualitative research that are analogous to each other. Some of these analogous processes are presented in Table 17.4. Additional analogous processes are presented in Table 17.5.

As noted by Onwuegbuzie et al. (2009), crossover mixed analyses are well suited for mixed methodology researchers that represent the following seven assumptions and stances: (a) pragmatism-of-the-middle philosophy (Johnson and

Table 17.5 Additional list of analogous processes in quantitative and qualitative research

Analytical process	*Application to quantitative research*	*Application to qualitative research*
Coding	Inductive coding, deductive coding, abductive coding, interpretive coding, open coding, axial coding, or selective coding of numeric data used an numeric codes	Inductive coding, deductive coding, abductive coding, interpretive coding, open coding, axial coding, or selective coding of textual/visual data
Assess consistency of findings	Computation and interpretation of score reliability coefficients; use of internal replication (e.g. bootstrap, jackknife, cross-validation)	Assessment of data saturation, informational redundancy, and/or theoretical saturation (i.e. no new or relevant information seems to emerge pertaining to a category, and the category development is well established and validated; Flick, 1998; Lincoln and Guba, 1985; Morse, 1995; Strauss and Corbin, 1990); triangulation of data: data triangulation (i.e. use of a variety of sources in a study), investigator triangulation (i.e. use of several different researchers), theory triangulation (i.e. use of multiple perspectives and theories to interpret the results of a study), and methodological triangulation (i.e. use of multiple methods to study a research problem)
Comparing findings across subgroups, groups, settings, or times	Obtaining external replication	Assessment of transferability by examining the degree to which qualitative findings can be generalized or transferred to other contexts or settings; assessment of naturalistic generalization wherein the readers make generalizations entirely, or at least in part, from their personal or vicarious experiences (Stake and Trumbull, 1982)
Analysis of one case at a time	Use of analyses such as single-subject analysis, time series analysis, or profile analysis to analyze data from one participant at a time	Use of within-case analyses (cf. Miles and Huberman, 1994)
Analysis of time	Analysis of patterns over time using techniques such as time series analysis, panel data analysis, survival analysis, and proportional hazard model analysis	Mapping of events that occur over time using analytic techniques such as event listing, critical incident chart, event-state network, activity record, decision modeling flowchart, growth gradient, time-ordered matrix, time-ordered meta-matrix, time-ordered scatterplot, and composite sequence analysis (cf. Miles and Huberman, 1994)
Analysis of non-observable data	Analysis of latent variables	Analysis of perceptions, beliefs, insights, cognition, intuition, and other sensory data

Onwuegbuzie, 2004), (b) pragmatism-of-the-right philosophy (Putnam, 2002; Rescher, 2000), (c) pragmatism-of-the-left philosophy (Maxcy, 2003; Rorty, 1991), (d) the dialectical stance (Greene, 2008; Greene and Caracelli, 1997; Maxwell and Loomis, 2003), (e) transformative-emancipatory stance (Mertens, 2003), (f) a paradigmatic stance (Patton, 2002; Reichardt and Cook, 1979), and

(g) communities of practice stance (Denscombe, 2008). However, crossover mixed analyses are most compatible with the assumptions and stances of the most recent mixed research philosophy, which was conceptualized by Johnson (2009), namely: dialectical pragmatism, which refers to an epistemology that requires the mixed methodology researcher to incorporate multiple epistemological perspectives.

QUANTITATIVE ANALYSIS CONTINUUM

Figure 17.3 presents what we refer to as the quantitative analysis continuum. As can be seen in this figure, on the left side of the continuum are descriptive statistics techniques that do not have any statistical modeling assumptions. The only assumptions associated with descriptive statistics are population assumptions (i.e. the data underlying the descriptive statistics are representative of the problem, topic, or class of objects being studied) and sampling assumptions (e.g. random sampling). Moving to the middle of the figure, the next class of analyses represents exploratory analyses such as exploratory factor analysis, cluster analysis, correspondence analysis, and multidimensional scaling. These analyses are exploratory in nature because they do not involve the direct testing of null hypotheses and thus do not yield *p*-values. In addition to the population assumptions and sampling assumptions (including sample size assumptions), exploratory analysis techniques have the assumption of no outliers in the data and minimal multicollinearity. The remaining classes of quantitative analyses on the continuum represent inferential analyses that, in addition to the population assumptions and sampling assumptions, each have statistical modeling assumptions that include the following: (a) distributional assumptions (i.e. assumptions about the probability distribution of these model errors), (b) structural assumptions (i.e. assumptions about the form of the statistical relationship between variables), and (c) cross-variation assumptions (i.e. assumptions involving the joint probability distributions of either the observations themselves or the random errors in a model such that observations or errors are statistically independent) (cf. McPherson, 2001). As such, the assumptions associated with inferential statistics are substantially greater than those associated with descriptive statistics. In the quantitative research continuum in Figure 17.3, it also can be seen that the inferential analyses increase in level of complexity, from analyses that involve one dependent variable and one or more independent variables at one level, to analyses that involve one dependent variable and one or more independent variables at two or more levels, to analyses that involve two or more dependent variables and one or more independent variables at one level, to analyses that involve two or more dependent variables and two or more independent variables at one level, to analyses that involve two or more dependent variables and two or more independent variables at two or more levels, to analyses that involve two or more dependent variables and two or more independent variables with some variables having a bidirectional relationship. Furthermore, the assumptions become increasingly

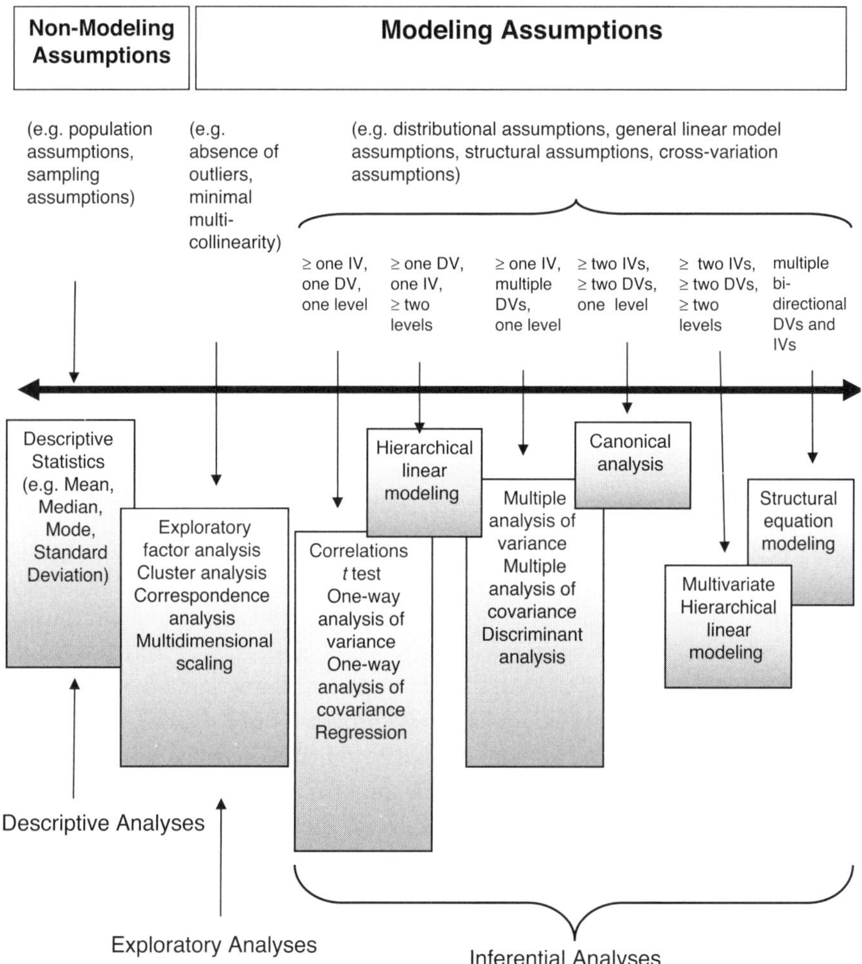

Figure 17.3 Quantitative analysis continuum

complex as the analyses are positioned on the right-hand side of the continuum. For example, in the parametric statistics case, one of the assumptions associated with the first set of analyses is (univariate) normality, whereas for the last three classes on the right, the parallel assumption is multivariate normality.

QUALITATIVE ANALYSIS CONTINUUM

Figure 17.4 presents what we refer to as the qualitative analysis continuum. As can be seen in this figure, on the left side of the continuum are qualitative analysis techniques that involve a strong use of quantitative analysis approaches such as word count (cf. Leech and Onwuegbuzie, 2007, 2008) and intrasample statistical analysis (Shaffer and Serlin, 2004). The word count analysis procedure is

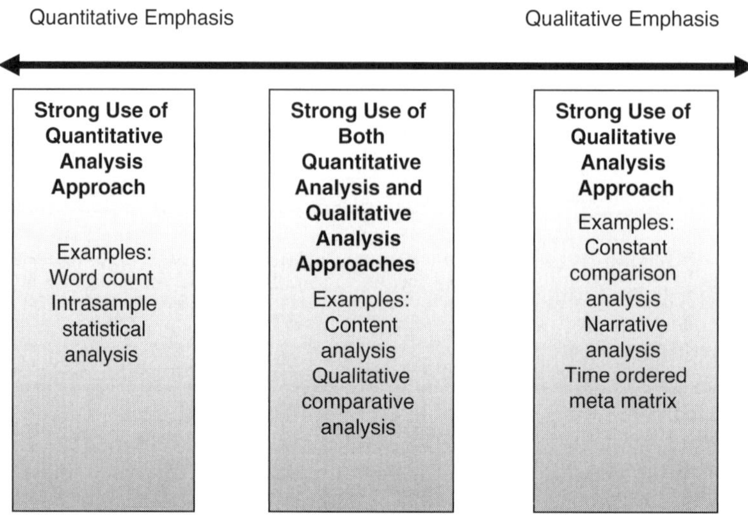

Figure 17.4 Qualitative analysis continuum

based on the belief that (a) all people have unique vocabulary and word usage patterns (i.e. 'linguistic fingerprints'; Pennebaker et al., 2003: 568) and (b) the more frequently a word is used, the more important the word is for that person (Carley, 1993). Miles and Huberman (1994) provided three reasons for counting words: (a) to identify patterns more easily, (b) to maintain analytic integrity, and (c) to verify a hypothesis. One of the main arguments made for using word count is that it provides qualitative researchers with more accurate and richer data and interpretations. Further, word count analysis allows qualitative researchers to specify the exact count rather than using terms such as 'many', 'most', 'frequently', 'several', 'always', and 'never', which are essentially quantitative (Sechrest and Sidani, 1995). Subsequently, utilization of word count analysis can lead the researcher to conduct an intrasample statistical analysis (ISSA) technique. An ISSA represents a technique:

> that combines methods and assumptions of qualitative and quantitative research within a single analytical process. … In so doing, ISSA provides a justification for coding qualitative observations and applying statistical analyses to draw conclusions about patterns of activity for data sets that do not readily lend themselves to analysis across individual participants. The results of such analyses do not 'generalize' in the traditional quantitative sense, but they do justify drawing statistically based conclusions about observations in a qualitative context. Conclusions drawn from ISSA are thus defensible both statistically and phenomenologically. … In so doing, ISSA analyses can provide additional justification for the qualitative work they support. (Shafer and Serlin, 2004: 14–15)

On the opposite end of the qualitative analysis continuum are qualitative analysis techniques that involve a strong use of qualitative analysis approaches such as constant comparison analysis, narrative analysis, and time-ordered meta-matrix. Although these procedures might include some form of quantitative analysis – for example, a conversation analysis might involve computation of the mean time between different speakers' utterances (i.e. timing of turn-taking; see, for example Bull and Aylett, 1998) or mean pitch of utterance (e.g. Levow, 2005) – it is typically not the main focus of the qualitative analysis procedure. Lying between these two extremes are qualitative analyses that utilize both quantitative and qualitative analysis assumptions and approaches such as classical content analysis and qualitative comparative analysis. In classical content analysis, the codes, which can be produced either inductively or deductively, are analyzed using quantitative procedures, qualitative procedures, or both (Leech and Onwuegbuzie, 2007, 2008). With respect to qualitative comparative analysis, the goal is 'to develop an original "synthetic strategy" as a middle way between the case-oriented, or qualitative, and the variable-oriented, or quantitative approaches' (Rihoux and Lobe, 2009: 473). Moreover, as noted by Ragin (1987), the goal of this analytic technique is to 'integrate the best features of the case-oriented approach with the best features of the variable-oriented approach' (p. 84). As will be seen in the following section, our conceptualization of the quantitative analysis continuum and qualitative analysis continuum is useful for developing the concept of crossover mixed analyses.

QUANTITATIVE DOMINANT AND QUALITATIVE DOMINANT CROSSOVER MIXED ANALYSES

One might assume due to the potential interactive and complex nature of crossover mixed analyses that only mixed methodology researchers can conduct such analyses. Yet, this is not necessarily the case. Indeed, as illustrated by Onwuegbuzie et al. (2009a):

> the ontological, epistemological, and methodological assumptions and stances representing all five paradigms (postpositivism, constructivism, critical theory, participatory, pragmatism) allow the conduct of both quantitative and qualitative analyses – at least to a small degree – with postpositivist and constructivist paradigms having the least potential to use analytical techniques that belong to a different paradigm, the critical theory and the participatory paradigms having excellent potential to use analytical techniques that belong to a different paradigm, and the pragmatist paradigm, almost by definition, having the greatest potential. (p. 130)

For example, the ontological, epistemological, and methodological assumptions and stances representing postpositivist researchers do not prevent them from using some qualitative analysis techniques, especially those that yield some frequency data such as word count and classical content analysis (cf. Leech and Onwuegbuzie, 2007, 2008) and those that are based on logical (deterministic) techniques such as qualitative comparative analysis (Ragin, 1987, 1989a, b, 1994, 2008). Similarly, ontological, epistemological, and methodological assumptions and stances representing constructivist researchers do not prevent them using both descriptive statistics and inferential statistics – even if the latter is to a small degree – 'not only to facilitate rich and detailed description but also can be used to assess and enhance trustworthiness, dependability, confirmability, transferability, and authenticity' (Onwuegbuzie et al., 2009a: 126). This assertion is evidenced by the fact that many computer-assisted qualitative data analysis software (CAQDAS) programs allow data to be imported to statistical software programs (e.g. Excel, SIMSTAT) for statistical analyses to be conducted. Interestingly, Denzin and Lincoln (2005a: 196) document that the training of constructivists includes both qualitative and quantitative techniques. Similarly, the ontological, epistemological, and axiological stances of critical theorist researchers do not prevent them from using, whenever needed, all forms of descriptive and inferential statistics.

As such, postpositivists, constructivists, critical theorists, and those representing many other research paradigms (e.g. participatory paradigm) potentially can conduct crossover mixed analyses, at least to a degree, and even more so when working with researchers who embrace other stances. Perhaps, the best way to illustrate this point is by conceptualizing that crossover mixed analyses can lie on a continuum with quantitative dominant crossover mixed analyses and qualitative dominant crossover mixed analyses at opposite ends of the continuum.

Quantitative dominant crossover analyses

Quantitative dominant crossover mixed analyses involve the analyst adopting a (quantitative) postpositivist stance, while, at the same time, believing that the inclusion of qualitative data and analysis can help address the research question(s) to a greater extent. At the lowest level of integration, quantitative dominant crossover mixed analyses would involve combining one or more sets of inferential analyses with qualitative analyses that generate some frequency data (e.g. word count, intrasample statistical analysis) – to reduce, display, transform, correlate, consolidate, compare, integrate, assert, or import data – because these data are closer to statistical data than those generated by other qualitative analyses. Indeed, more than 50 years ago, Barton and Lazarsfeld (1955) advocated the use of what they called *quasi-statistics*, which represent descriptive statistics that can be extracted from qualitative data. Interestingly, according to Howard Becker (1970: 81–82), a prominent symbolic interactionist, 'one of the greatest faults in most observational case studies has been their failure to make explicit the quasi-statistical basis of their conclusions.' Along this line of thinking, Maxwell (1996) stated that:

> Quasi-statistics not only allow you to test and support claims that are inherently quantitative, but also enable you to assess the *amount* of evidence in your data that bears on a particular conclusion or threat, such as how many discrepant instances exist and from how many different sources they were obtained. (p. 95) (emphasis in original)

At the highest level of integration, quantitative dominant crossover mixed analyses would involve combining one or more sets of inferential analyses with other types of qualitative analyses (see Tables 17.1–17.3) for the purpose of integrated data reduction, integrated data display, data transformation, data correlation, data consolidation, data comparison, data integration, warranted assertion analysis, and/or data importation. The utility of quantitative dominant crossover mixed analysis is that researchers have flexibility as to the extent to which their mixed analysis *crosses over*, and this form of analysis could be driven by their actual philosophical (i.e. postpositivist) assumptions and stances. For example, researchers embracing postpositivist research philosophies that are furthest removed from the belief systems of mixed methodologists (e.g. dialectical pragmatism, transformative-emancipatory) might only be comfortable combining inferential analyses with word count or ISSA as a means of conducting crossover analyses. In this context, such a postpositivist researcher might collect qualitative data (e.g. interview data, focus group interview data) and then analyze these data using word count to extract themes. The word count associated with each theme then could be correlated with quantitative data that have been collected (i.e. representing the dominant approach). In contrast, postpositivist researchers with a more qualitative orientation likely would be comfortable *crossing over* findings from a content analysis or qualitative comparative analysis with their findings from inferential analyses, whereas postpositivist researchers with the most qualitative orientations likely would be comfortable *crossing over* findings from strong qualitative analyses (e.g. constant comparison analysis, narrative analysis) with their findings from inferential analyses. In each case, however, the quantitative analysis would represent the dominant analysis, with the qualitative analysis being used in an attempt to fulfill one or more of Greene et al.'s (1989) five purposes for mixing.

Qualitative dominant crossover analyses

In contrast, qualitative dominant mixed analyses involve the analyst taking a (qualitative) constructivist, critical theorist, or participatory stance – or any other stance associated with the qualitative paradigm – with respect to the research process in general and the analysis process in particular, while, at the same time, believing that the addition of quantitative data and analysis can help them address the research question(s) to a greater extent. At the lowest level of integration, the crossover mixed analysis would involve combining one or more sets of qualitative analyses with descriptive statistics – to reduce, display, transform, correlate, consolidate, compare, integrate, assert, or import data – because descriptive statistics involve the least statistical assumptions. Thus, for instance, qualitative researchers with research philosophies such as constructivism, critical theory, or participatory, which are furthest removed from the belief systems of mixed methodology researchers might only be comfortable conducting a crossover analysis such as quantitizing their qualitative data (e.g. Sandelowski et al., 2009) by counting the number of participants who contribute to each emergent theme (e.g. via a constant comparison analysis) and converting this number to a percentage that yields an effect size measure (cf. Onwuegbuzie, 2003; Onwuegbuzie and Teddlie, 2003). This would be an example of data transformation.

At a higher level of integration, the crossover mixed analysis would involve combining one or more sets of qualitative analyses with exploratory analysis techniques.

Thus, for example, qualitative researchers with research philosophies that are somewhat nearer to the belief systems of mixed methodology researchers might be comfortable conducting a crossover analysis such as (exploratory) factor-analyzing the emergent themes (cf. Onwuegbuzie, 2003; Onwuegbuzie and Teddlie, 2003). This would be an example of integrated data reduction.

At the highest level of integration, the crossover mixed analysis would involve combining one or more sets of qualitative analyses with inferential statistics. Thus, for instance, qualitative researchers with research philosophies that are the nearest to the belief systems of mixed methodology researchers might be comfortable conducting a crossover analysis such as determining which characteristics of the participants best predict one or more of the emergent themes (cf. Onwuegbuzie et al., 2007b). This would be an example of integrated data correlation. In each case, however, the qualitative analysis would represent the dominant analysis, with the quantitative analysis being used in an attempt to fulfill one or more of Greene et al.'s (1989) five purposes for mixing.

EXAMPLES OF QUANTITATIVE DOMINANT AND QUALITATIVE DOMINANT CROSSOVER MIXED ANALYSES

It is often assumed that mixed analysis is conducted *only* in mixed research. However, the concept behind quantitative dominant crossover mixed analyses and qualitative dominant crossover mixed analyses is that they allow mixed analyses to be conducted within both quantitative and qualitative research studies without the researchers having to be mixed methodology researchers. It should be noted that some qualitative researchers have been conducting mixed analysis for many years, even though they did not declare it as such. For example, Becker et al. (1961/1977) provided more than 50 tables and graphs containing quantitative information in their qualitative works. These quantitative data complemented the narrative descriptions of their qualitative data – indicating that Becker et al. combined strong qualitative analyses with descriptive statistics. As another more recent example, Frels (2010) conducted a qualitative inquiry in which she (a) explored selected mentors' perceptions of experiences of the dyadic mentoring relationship in school-based mentors; (b) examined the perceptions of selected school-based mentors regarding roles, expectations, purposes, and approaches of mentoring; and (c) studied the actual experiences of selected school-based mentors with the dyadic relationship. In addition to collecting data via individual interviews and observations of mentoring sessions, Frels (2010) asked each of the 11 mentors to complete a quantitative instrument – namely, the 62-item Match Characteristics Questionnaire (MCQ; Harris and Nakkula, 2008), which measures match relationship quality (i.e. quality of matching between mentors and mentees) that included some of the following dimensions: (a) the degree to which adults feel close with youth; (b) the degree to which adults feel youth actively seek help with schoolwork; (c) the mentor's sense of fulfillment in the relationship;

(d) a combined score comprising the closeness, distance, and satisfaction subscales; and (e) the degree to which adults feel prepared to handle students' behavior. Frels (2010) used the MCQ subscale scores to conduct a series of crossover analyses (integrated data display, data transformation, data correlation, data comparison, data integration, warranted assertion analysis), which enabled her better to contextualize her qualitative findings. Indeed, we encourage qualitative researchers, whenever appropriate, to administer one or more quantitative instruments that tap the construct of interest or a correlate of that construct, so that a crossover mixed analysis can be used to increase *verstehen* (i.e. understanding).

Some quantitative researchers combine their quantitative analyses with some form of qualitative analysis (e.g. qualitative analyses with strong use of quantitative analysis). For example, some researchers collect qualitative data when developing instruments, such as by collecting evidence of content-related validity (e.g. by extracting information from a panel of experts). However, we argue that both quantitative and qualitative researchers can get even more out of their data by conducting crossover mixed analysis rather than non-crossover mixed analysis. For example, Onwuegbuzie et al. (2010) presented a meta-framework that they call an Instrument Development and Construct Validation (IDCV) process for optimizing the development of quantitative instruments. The IDCV contains 10 phases that detail how crossover mixed analyses can be used to develop and/or (score) cross-validate a quantitative instrument. These authors also presented a heuristic example which demonstrated that use of cross-over mixed analysis techniques led to the identification of two meta-themes, two themes, and three subthemes that were not identified solely from the quantitative analysis even though the initial instrument that was developed provided excellent psychometric properties (e.g. score reliability of the two factors were 0.97 and 0.89). Even though crossover mixed analyses represent the key feature of the IDCV, researchers do not have to be mixed methodology researchers to utilize this meta-framework. Indeed, the IDCV utilizes all nine cross-over mixed analysis types. Thus, quantitative researchers can decide on which of these nine crossover analysis types they will conduct depending on whether they are most comfortable using qualitative analyses that involve a strong use of quantitative analysis, qualitative analyses that involve a strong use of both quantitative analysis and qualitative analysis, or qualitative analyses that involve a strong use of qualitative analysis.

As can be seen, we believe that our conceptualization of quantitative dominant crossover mixed analyses and qualitative dominant crossover mixed analyses has appeal for not only mixed methodology researchers but also quantitative researchers and qualitative researchers.

CONCLUSIONS

Teddlie and Tashakkori (2009) stated astutely that 'In the future, we believe that MM (mixed methods) researchers will examine more closely the analytical frameworks used in either the QUAL or QUAN tradition and then develop analogous techniques for the other traditions' (p. 281). In our chapter, we have attempted to make this assertion a reality *now*, by illustrating how techniques developed for one tradition can be implemented to expand the interpretation of data associated with the other tradition. We encourage others to develop and delineate other examples so that it can no longer be stated that guidance on conducting mixed analyses 'has not yet cohered into a widely accepted framework or set of ideas' (Greene, 2008: 14). We will leave the last word to Jennifer Greene (2007: 163):

> So, the mixed methods analysis team should embark on their analytic journey in ways perhaps a bit more open, flexible, creative, and adventuresome than those of other inquirers – with routes more imagined than fixed, with guideposts drawn from the travels of others .... and with a commitment, if not fully to a mixed methods way of thinking, then more modestly to the importance of diverse ways of knowing and valuing.

REFERENCES

Barton, A. and Lazarsfeld, P.F. (1955). Some functions of qualitative data analysis in sociological research. *Sociologica*, 1: 321–61.

Bazeley, P. (1999). The *bricoleur* with a computer: Piecing together qualitative and quantitative data. *Qualitative Health Research*, 9: 279–87.

Bazeley, P. (2003). Computerized data analysis for mixed methods research. In A. Tashakkori and C. Teddlie (eds) *Handbook of Mixed Methods in Social and Behavioral Research*, pp. 385–422. Thousand Oaks, CA: Sage.

Bazeley, P. (2006). The contribution of computer software to integrating qualitative and quantitative data and analyses. *Research in the Schools*, 13(1): 64–74.

Bazeley, P. (2009). Mixed methods data analysis. In S. Andrew and E.J. Halcomb (eds) *Mixed Methods Research for Nursing and the Health Sciences*, pp. 84–118. Chichester: Wiley-Blackwell.

Bazeley, P. (in press). Computer assisted integration of mixed methods data sources and analyses. In A. Tashakkori and C. Teddlie (eds) *Handbook of Mixed Methods in Social and Behavioral Research*, 2nd edn, pp. 385–422. Thousand Oaks, CA: Sage.

Becker, H.S. (1970). *Sociological Work: Method and Substance.* New Brunswick, NJ: Transaction Books.

Becker, H.S., Geer, B., Hughes, E.C., and Strauss, A.L. (1977). *Boys in White: Student Culture in Medical School.* New Brunswick, NJ: Transaction Books. (Original work published by University of Chicago Press, 1961)

Berelson, B. (1952). *Content Analysis in Communicative Research.* New York: Free Press.

Bull, M. and Aylett, M. (1998, December). *An Analysis of the Timing of Turn-taking in a Corpus of Goal-Oriented Dialogue.* Paper presented at the Fifth International Conference on Spoken Language Processing, Melbourne, Australia.

Caracelli, V.W. and Greene, J.C. (1993). Data analysis strategies for mixed-method evaluation designs. *Educational Evaluation and Policy Analysis*, 15: 195–207.

Carley, K. (1993). Coding choices for textual analysis: A comparison of content analysis and map analysis. In P. Marsden (ed.) *Sociological Methodology*, pp. 75–126. Oxford: Blackwell.

Chi, M.T.H. (1997). Quantifying qualitative analyses of verbal data: A practical guide. *The Journal of the Learning Sciences*, 6: 271–315.

Cohen, J. (1988). *Statistical Power Analysis for the Behavioral Sciences*, 2nd edn. Hillsdale, NJ: Lawrence Erlbaum.

Creswell, J.W. and Plano Clark, V.L. (2007). *Designing and Conducting Mixed Methods Research.* Thousand Oaks, CA: Sage.

Curtis, S., Gesler, W., Smith, G., and Washburn, S. (2000). Approaches to sampling and case selection in qualitative research: Examples in the geography of health. *Social Science and Medicine*, 50: 1001–14.

Datta, L. (2001). The wheelbarrow, the mosaic, and the double helix: Challenges and strategies for successfully carrying out mixed methods evaluation. *Evaluation Journal of Australia*, 1(2): 33–40.

Denscombe, M. (2008). Communities of practice: A research paradigm for the mixed methods approach. *Journal of Mixed Methods Research*, 2: 270–83.

Denzin, N.K. and Lincoln, Y.S. (2005a). Paradigmatic controversies, contradictions, and emerging confluences. In N.K. Denzin and Y.S. Lincoln (eds) *Sage Handbook of Qualitative Research*, 2nd edn, pp. 191–216. Thousand Oaks, CA: Sage.

Denzin, N.K. and Lincoln, Y.S. (eds) (2005b). *The Sage Handbook of Qualitative Research*, 3rd edn. Thousand Oaks, CA: Sage.

Eisner, E.W. (1998). *The Enlightened Eye: Qualitative Inquiry and the Enhancement of Educational Practice*. Upper Saddle River, NJ: Merrill.

Flick, U. (1998). *An Introduction to Qualitative Research: Theory, Method and Applications*. London: Sage.

Frels, R K. (2010). *The Experiences and Perceptions of Selected Mentors: An Exploratory Study of the Dyadic Relationship in School-based Mentoring*. Unpublished doctoral dissertation, Sam Houston State University, Huntsville, TX.

Grbich, C. (2007). *Qualitative Data Analysis: An Introduction*. Thousand Oaks, CA: Sage.

Greene, J.C. (2007). *Mixed Methods in Social Inquiry*. San Francisco: Jossey-Bass.

Greene, J.C. (2008). Is mixed methods social inquiry a distinctive methodology? *Journal of Mixed Methods Research*, 2: 7–22.

Greene, J.C. and Caracelli, V.J. (1997). Defining and describing the paradigm issue in mixed-method evaluation. In J.C. Greene and V.J. Caracelli (eds) *Advances in Mixed-method Evaluation: The Challenges and Benefits of Integrating Diverse Paradigms* (New Directions for Evaluation, No. 74, pp. 5–17). San Francisco, CA: Jossey-Bass.

Greene, J.C., Caracelli, V.J., and Graham, W.F. (1989). Toward a conceptual framework for mixed-method evaluation designs. *Educational Evaluation and Policy Analysis*, 11: 255–74.

Happ, M.B., DeVito Dabbs, D.A., Tate, J., Hricik, A., and Erien, J. (2006). Exemplars of mixed methods data combination and analysis. *Nursing Research*, 55(2, Supplement 1): S43–S49.

Harris, J.T. and Nakkula, M.J. (2008). *Match Characteristic Questionnaire* (MCQ). Unpublished measure. Fairfax, VA: Applied Research Consulting.

Henson, R.K. (2000). Demystifying parametric analyses: Illustrating canonical correlation as the multivariate general linear model. *Multiple Linear Regression Viewpoints*, 26: 11–19.

Johnson, R.B. (2009). Comment on Howe: Toward a more inclusive 'Scientific Research in Education'. *Educational Researcher*, 38: 449–57.

Johnson, R.B. and Onwuegbuzie, A.J. (2004). Mixed methods research: A research paradigm whose time has come. *Educational Researcher*, 33(7): 14–26.

Kuhn, T.S. (1962). *The Structure of Scientific Revolutions*. Chicago, IL: University of Chicago Press.

Lee, Y-j. and Greene, J.C. (2007). The predictive validity of an ESL placement test: A mixed methods approach. *Journal of Mixed Methods Research*, 1: 366–89.

Leech, N.L. and Onwuegbuzie, A.J. (2007). An array of qualitative data analysis tools: A call for qualitative data analysis triangulation. *School Psychology Quarterly*, 22: 557–84.

Leech, N.L. and Onwuegbuzie, A.J. (2008). Qualitative data analysis: A compendium of techniques and a framework for selection for school psychology research and beyond. *School Psychology Quarterly*, 23: 587–604.

Levow, G.-A. (2005). *Turn-taking in Mandarin Dialogue: Interactions of Tone and Intonation*. Proceedings of the Fourth SIGHAN Workshop on Chinese Language Processing, pp. 72–8. Jeju Island, Korea: Asian Federation of Natural Language Processing.

Li, S., Marquart, J.M., and Zercher, C. (2000). Conceptual issues and analytical strategies in mixed-method studies of preschool inclusion. *Journal of Early Intervention*, 23: 116–32.

Lincoln, Y.S. and Guba, E.G. (1985). *Naturalistic Inquiry.* Beverly Hills, CA: Sage.

Louis, K.S. (1982). Sociologist as sleuth: Integrating methods in the RDU study. *American Behavioral Scientist*, 26(1): 101–20.

Maxcy, S.J. (2003). Pragmatic threads in mixed methods research in the social sciences: The search for multiple modes of inquiry and the end of the philosophy of formalism. In A. Tashakkori and C. Teddlie (eds) *Handbook of Mixed Methods in Social and Behavioral Research*, pp. 51–89. Thousand Oaks, CA: Sage.

Maxwell, J.A. (1996). *Qualitative Research Design.* Newbury Park, CA: Sage.

Maxwell, J.A. and Loomis, D.M. (2003). Mixed methods design: An alternative approach. In A. Tashakkori and C. Teddlie (eds) *Handbook of Mixed Methods in Social and Behavioral Research*, pp. 241–72. Thousand Oaks, CA: Sage.

McConney, A., Rudd, A., and Ayres, R. (2002). Getting to the bottom line: A method for synthesizing findings within mixed-method program evaluations. *American Journal of Evaluation*, 23: 121–40.

McPherson, G. (2001). *Applying and Interpreting Statistics: A Comprehensive Guide.* New York: Springer-Verlag.

Mertens, D. (2003). Mixed methods and the politics of human research: The transformative-emancipatory perspective. In A. Tashakkori and C. Teddlie (eds) *Handbook of Mixed Methods in Social and Behavioral Research*, pp. 135–64. Thousand Oaks, CA: Sage.

Miles, M.B. and Huberman, A.M. (1994). *Qualitative Data Analysis: An Expanded Sourcebook*, 2nd edn. Thousand Oaks, CA: Sage.

Morgan, D.L. (2007). Paradigms lost and pragmatism regained: Methodological implications of combining qualitative and quantitative methods. *Journal of Mixed Methods Research*, 1: 48–76.

Morse, J.M. (1995). The significance of saturation. *Qualitative Health Research*, 5: 147–9.

Onwuegbuzie, A.J. (2003). Effect sizes in qualitative research: A prolegomenon. *Quality & Quantity: International Journal of Methodology*, 37: 393–409.

Onwuegbuzie, A.J. and Combs, J.P. (in press). Emergent data analysis techniques in mixed methods research: A synthesis. In A. Tashakkori and C. Teddlie (eds) *Handbook of Mixed Methods in Social and Behavioral Sciences.* Thousand Oaks, CA: Sage.

Onwuegbuzie, A.J. and Daniel, L.G. (2003, February 12). Typology of analytical and interpretational errors in quantitative and qualitative educational research. *Current Issues in Education* [On-line], 6(2). Retrieved 30 May 2010, from http://cie.asu.edu/volume6/number2/index.html

Onwuegbuzie, A.J. and Dickinson, W.B. (2008). Mixed methods analysis and information visualization: Graphical display for effective communication of research results. *The Qualitative Report*, 13, 204–25. Retrieved 30 May 2010, from http://www.nova.edu/ssss/QR/QR13-2/onwuegbuzie.pdf

Onwuegbuzie, A.J. and Leech, N.L. (2004). Enhancing the interpretation of 'significant' findings: The role of mixed methods research. *The Qualitative Report,* 9: 770–92. Retrieved 30 May 2010, from http://www.nova.edu/ssss/QR/QR9-4/onwuegbuzie.pdf

Onwuegbuzie, A.J. and Teddlie, C. (2003). A framework for analyzing data in mixed methods research. In A. Tashakkori and C. Teddlie (eds) *Handbook of Mixed Methods in Social and Behavioral Research*, pp. 351–83. Thousand Oaks, CA: Sage.

Onwuegbuzie, A.J., Slate, J.R., Leech, N.L., and Collins, K.M.T. (2007a). Conducting mixed analyses: A general typology. *International Journal of Multiple Research Approaches*, 1: 4–17.

Onwuegbuzie, A.J., Witcher, A.E., Collins, K.M.T., Filer, J.D., Wiedmaier, C.D., and Moore, C.W. (2007b). Students' perceptions of characteristics of effective college teachers: A validity study of a teaching evaluation form using a mixed-methods analysis. *American Educational Research Journal*, 44: 113–60.

Onwuegbuzie, A.J., Johnson, R.B., and Collins, K.M.T. (2009a). A call for mixed analysis: A philosophical framework for combining qualitative and quantitative. *International Journal of Multiple Research Approaches*, 3: 114–39.

Onwuegbuzie, A.J., Slate, J.R., Leech, N.L., and Collins, K.M.T. (2009b). Mixed data analysis: Advanced integration techniques. *International Journal of Multiple Research Approaches*, 3: 13–33.

Onwuegbuzie, A.J., Bustamante, R.M., and Nelson, J.A. (2010). Mixed research as a tool for developing quantitative instruments. *Journal of Mixed Methods Research*, 4: 56–78.

Onwuegbuzie, A.J., Collins, K.M.T., and Leech, N.L. (in press). *Mixed Research: A Step-by-Step Guide.* New York: Taylor & Francis.

Onwuegbuzie, A.J., Collins, K.M.T., Leech, N.L., Dellinger, A.B., and Jiao, Q.G. (in press b). A meta-framework for conducting and writing rigorous, comprehensive, and insightful literature reviews for stress and coping research and beyond. In G.S. Gates, W.H. Gmelch, and M. Wolverton (series eds) and K.M.T. Collins, A.J. Onwuegbuzie, and Q.G. Jiao (eds) *Toward a Broader Understanding of Stress and Coping: Mixed Methods Approaches.* The Research on Stress and Coping in Education Series, Vol. 5. Charlotte, NC: Information Age Publishing.

Patton, M.Q. (2002). *Qualitative Research and Evaluation Methods.* Thousand Oaks, CA: Sage.

Pennebaker, J.W., Mehl, M.R., and Niederhoffer, K. (2003). Psychological aspects of natural language use: Our words, our selves. *Annual Review of Psychology*, 54: 547–77.

Phillips, L.J. and Jorgensen, M.W. (2002). *Discourse Analysis as Theory and Method.* Thousand Oaks, CA: Sage.

Putnam, H. (2002). *The Collapse of the Fact/Value Dichotomy and Other Essays.* Cambridge, MA: Harvard University Press.

Ragin, C.C. (1987). *The Comparative Method: Moving Beyond Qualitative and Quantitative Strategies.* Berkeley, CA: University of California Press.

Ragin, C.C. (1989a). *The Comparative Method: Moving Beyond Qualitative and Quantitative Strategies.* Berkeley, CA: University of California Press.

Ragin, C.C. (1989b). The logic of the comparative method and the algebra of logic. *Journal of Quantitative Anthropology*, 1: 373–98.

Ragin, C.C. (1994). Introduction to qualitative comparative analysis. In T. Janoski and A.M. Hicks (eds) *The Comparative Political Economy of the Welfare State: New Methodologies and Approaches*, pp. 299–319. New York: Cambridge University Press.

Ragin, C.C. (2008). *Redesigning Social Inquiry: Fuzzy Sets and Beyond.* Chicago, IL: University of Chicago Press.

Reichardt, C.S. and Cook, T.D. (1979). Beyond qualitative versus quantitative methods. In T.D. Cook and C.S. Reichardt (eds) *Qualitative and Quantitative Methods in Evaluation Research*, pp. 7–32. Thousand Oaks, CA: Sage.

Rescher, N. (2000). *Realistic Pragmatism: An Introduction to Pragmatic Philosophy.* Albany: State University of New York Press.

Rihoux, B. and Lobe, B. (2009). The case for QCA: Adding leverage for thick cross-case comparison. In D. Byrne and C.C. Ragin (eds) *Handbook of Case Based Methods*, pp. 472–95. Thousand Oaks, CA: Sage.

Rorty, R. (1991). *Objectivity, Relativism, and Truth: Philosophical Papers*, Vol. 1. Cambridge, London: Cambridge University Press.

Sandelowski, M. (2000). Combining qualitative and quantitative sampling, data collection, and analysis techniques in mixed-method studies. *Research in Nursing Health*, 23: 246–55.

Sandelowski, M. (2001). Real qualitative researchers don't count: The use of numbers in qualitative research. *Research in Nursing and Health*, 24: 230–40.

Sandelowski, M., Voils, C.I., and Knafl, G. (2009). On quantitizing. *Journal of Mixed Methods Research*, 3: 208–22.

Sechrest, L. and Sidana, S. (1995). Quantitative and qualitative methods: Is there an alternative? *Evaluation and Program Planning*, 18: 77–87.

Shaffer, D.W. and Serlin, R.C. (2004). What good are statistics that don't generalize. *Educational Researcher*, 33(9): 14–25.

Silverman, D. (2001). *Interpreting Qualitative Data: Methods for Analyzing Talk, Text, and Interaction*, 2nd edn. Thousand Oaks, CA: Sage.

Smith, M.L. (1997). Mixing and matching: Methods and models. In J.C. Greene and V.J. Caracelli (eds) *Advances in Mixed-method Evaluation: The Challenges and Benefits of Integrating Diverse Paradigms*, (New Directions for Evaluation No. 74, pp. 73–85). San Francisco, CA: Jossey-Bass.

Smith, M.L. and Glass, G.V. (1977). Meta-analysis of psychotherapy outcome studies. *American Psychologist*, 32: 752–60.

Spradley, J.P. (1979). *The Ethnographic Interview.* New York: Holt, Rinehart & Winston.

Spradley, J.P. (1980). *Participant Observation.* New York: Holt, Rinehart & Winston.

Stake, R.E. and Trumbull, D.J. (1982). Naturalistic generalizations. *Review Journal of Philosophy and Social Science*, 7: 3–12.

Strauss, A. and Corbin, J. (1990). *Basics of Qualitative Research: Grounded Theory Procedures and Techniques.* Newbury Park, CA: Sage.

Tashakkori, A. and Teddlie, C. (1998). *Mixed Methodology: Combining Qualitative and Quantitative Approaches.* Applied Social Research Methods Series, Vol. 46. Thousand Oaks, CA: Sage.

Teddlie, C. and Tashakkori, A. (2009). *Foundations of Mixed Methods Research: Integrating Quantitative and Qualitative Techniques in the Social and Behavioral Sciences.* Thousand Oaks, CA: Sage.

Teddlie, C., Tashakkori, A., and Johnson, R.B. (2008). Emergent techniques in the gathering and analysis of mixed methods data. In S.N. Hesse-Biber and P. Leavy (eds) *Handbook of Emergent Methods*, pp. 389–414. New York, NY: The Guilford Press.

Thompson, B. (1995). Stepwise regression and stepwise discriminant analysis need not apply here: A guidelines editorial. *Educational and Psychological Measurement*, 55: 525–34.

Thompson, B. (1998, April). *Five Methodological Errors in Educational Research: The Pantheon of Statistical Significance and Other Faux Pas.* Paper presented at the annual meeting of the American Educational Research Association, San Diego, CA.

West, E. and Tulloch, M. (2001, May). *Qualitising Quantitative Data: Should We Do It, and If So, How?* Paper presented at the annual meeting of the Association for Social Research, Wollongong, New South Wales, Australia.

Yin, R.K. (2003). *Case Study Research: Design and Methods*, 3rd edn. Thousand Oaks, CA: Sage.

Yin, R.K. (2009). *Case Study Research: Design and Methods*, 4th edn. Thousand Oaks, CA: Sage.

18

Optimal Matching Analysis

Peter Martin and Richard D. Wiggins

INTRODUCTION

In 1987, Rindfuss et al. published an oft-cited article entitled: 'Disorder in the life course. How common and does it matter?'. The authors criticized the assumption that life transitions usually occur in normative orders – that is, that most people progress through states of school, work, partnership, and parenthood in an orderly manner. According to this assumption, most people – variations by gender acknowledged – finished school before they started work, started work before they married, and married before they had children. Rindfuss and colleagues produced a convincing refutation of this view. They investigated the economic activities of Americans from the end of high school until eight years after. Every year, one dominant economic activity was recorded: Work; Education; Homemaker; Military; or Other. The yearly activities since the end of High School thus formed a sequence of eight elements. Assuming orderly life courses, we would predict that most people's lives follow one of a small number of normative sequences. For example, one might think that many men followed a pattern such as 'EEEEFFFF' (4 years of education followed by four years of full-time work). Many women might be expected to follow a pattern such as 'EEEEFFHH' (four years of education followed by two years of full-time work and two years as a homemaker). The assumption of orderliness implies that most people's lives would follow one of a small number of such predictable sequences. As Rindfuss et al. discovered, this was not the case. Rather, in a sample of 6,700 men, they found 1,100 different sequences. Women's lives were more diverse still: 7,000 women followed 1,800 different sequences.

It is for situations such as this, and because of the frequency of situations like this, that methods for the analysis of sequences are interesting for social scientists, and in particular for life course researchers (Elliott, 2005; Giele, 1998). Is there order among the disorder? How different are disorderly sequences from the normative, orderly ones? Can we reduce the large number of empirical sequences to a smaller number of classificatory categories? What kinds of people follow what kinds of sequences? Why? And with what consequences?

Optimal Matching (OM) is a form of sequence analysis that has been used to address research questions of this kind. Although it is primarily a descriptive technique, there is potential for its results to be used within causal analyses. In contrast to statistical models, OM does not make assumptions about the process that has generated the progression of elements that we call the sequence. Rather, OM takes the sequence as the unit of analysis. The basic idea is to measure the dissimilarity between two sequences as a function of the number of steps it would take to transform one sequence into the other. The first step of an OM analysis, which we might call 'Optimal Matching proper', is to calculate the dissimilarity of all possible sequence pairs in the sample. This results in a matrix of dissimilarities or distances. In the second step, this matrix is subjected to further analyses. Most commonly, cluster analysis is used to create a classification of sequences.

In 2000, Andrew Abbott and Angela Tsay's review of sociological studies using OM found 23 applications. Since then, the rate of publications has increased considerably, particularly in the research field of careers and the life course. OM has been described in social science textbooks (Aisenbrey, 2000; Elliott, 2005; MacIndoe and Abbott, 2004), and an OM algorithm has been implemented in STATA (Brzinsky-Fay et al., 2006). OM, then, is not a brand new method any longer, but is still sufficiently maverick that most authors feel obliged to introduce its technicalities in some detail in every publication (rather as if one were to explain the idea of minimizing squared errors every time one published an OLS regression analysis).

This chapter will introduce Optimal Matching and pay particular attention to (a) problematic aspects, including the thorny issue of validating the results; (b) crucial decisions to be made by the researcher; (c) innovative uses that have appeared in recent years; and (d) modifications of, and alternatives to, OM. The explication of the method and some of its technical intricacies will be the topic of the next, second, section of this chapter. The third section gives an overview over the various ways in which OM analysts have made use of 'ideal-typical' sequences for theory testing and sequence classification. In the fourth section, we consider criticisms of OM, some alternative methods of sequence analysis, as well as recent suggestions to modify the OM algorithm in order to make the distance calculation more meaningful from a sociological point of view. The short final section will inform about available software.

OPTIMAL MATCHING ANALYSIS – THE TECHNIQUE

Optimal Matching relies on an algorithm developed by Russian mathematician Vladimir Levenshtein (1966), and found its first scientific application in microbiology for the analysis of DNA and other molecular sequences. Among biologists, the OM technique was originally conceived of as mimicking real processes (such as gene mutation, splitting, transposition and so on), but it is now mostly used pragmatically as a pattern search technique. In social science, the types of sequences that have been analyzed by OM are quite diverse. Most applications involve what we would like to call status biographies: including employment careers, housing trajectories and partnership histories as well as mental patient's 'careers' of hospitalization and service use (to name just a few examples: Abbott and Hrycak, 1990; Martin et al., 2008; Pollock, 2007; Schoon et al., 2001; Stovel and Bolan, 2004; Stovel et al., 1996; Wiggins et al., 2007; Wuerker, 1996). Other types of sequences analyzed by OM include: the rhetorical structure of sociological journal articles (Abbott and Barman, 1997); the content of college textbooks (Levitt and Nass, 1989); the stepwise implementation of welfare policies (Abbott and DeViney, 1992); local yearly frequencies of lynching in the Southern United States (Stovel, 2001); the evolution of business networks (Stark and Vedres, 2006); and steps in English folk dances (Abbott and Forrest, 1986). Outside of social science, the patterns of birdsong and local dialects are among the topics studied with OM (see Sankoff and Kruskal, 1983 for examples). In the following, we shall describe the steps a researcher needs to take to perform an OM analysis.

DEFINING THE STATE SPACE

The first step is to define the space of states that a sequence is composed of. For example, the states of an employment biography may be different types of economic activity. For the purpose of illustration, we shall use a simple state space made up of five states:

- Full-time employed (F)
- Part-time employed (P)
- Unemployed (U)
- Education (E)
- Homemaking (H)

Figure 18.1 shows an example sequence, and also helps to illustrate basic terminology. In OM, the unit of analysis is the *sequence*, an ordered array of *elements*; each element records a single state. We use the term *section* to refer to any part of the sequence. A *spell* is a special kind of section consisting of a number of consecutive elements of the same state. Finally, a *transition* refers to a state change from one element to the next.

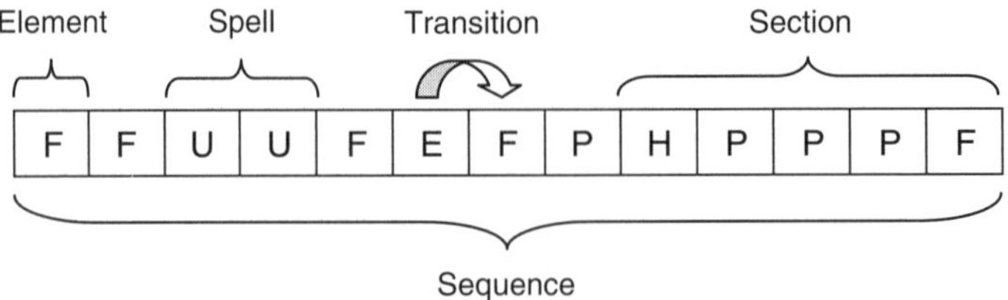

Figure 18.1 An example sequence with illustration of terminology

Often a state records quite simple information. However, in life course research some authors have used complex state spaces that combine different aspects of a person's biography: for example, Pollock (2007) used housing tenure, economic activity, partnership status and parenthood to create a four-dimensional state space.

MEASURING DISSIMILARITY: THE OM ALGORITHM AND OPERATION COST SPECIFICATIONS

The OM measures dissimilarity between two sequences by calculating a Levenshtein-distance, named after its inventor (Levenshtein, 1966). The idea of the Levenshtein-distance is to define dissimilarity between two sequences as a function of the minimum number of transformations it takes to turn one sequence into the other. There are three transformation operations: substitution, insertion, and deletion. To illustrate, consider the following two sequences, S_1 and S_2:

Element No.	1	2	3	4	5	6
S_1	E	E	E	F	F	F
S_2	E	E	E	P	P	F

It is possible to turn sequence S_1 into S_2 using two substitutions, namely by substituting a 'P' for an 'F' in the element positions 4 and 5. Note that the obverse is also possible: we could turn S_2 into S_1 by substituting two 'Fs' for two 'Ps'. In general, the dissimilarity between any two sequences S_1 and S_2 is equal to the dissimilarity between S_2 and S_1.

As an alternative to substitution, we could achieve the same transformation by deleting the two 'Fs' in positions 4 and 5 (which would result in the four-element sequence 'EEEF') and then inserting two 'Ps' between the last 'E' and the remaining 'F'. This transformation would require four operations: two insertions and two deletions.

Next, consider the following pair of sequences:

Element No.	1	2	3	4	5	6
S_3	U	F	U	F	U	F
S_4	F	U	F	U	F	U

These two sequences are structurally similar – both represent work biographies with frequent spells of unemployment – but they do not have a single common element of their six elements. Using only substitutions to turn S_3 into S_4, we would have to perform six operations. Using insertion and deletion, however, we only need two operations: for example, we can delete the first 'U' of S_3 and then insert a 'U' at the end, shifting S_3 one space to the left to align it with S_4. This example illustrates why OM is also called *optimal alignment:* one can think of the process of transforming one sequence into another as first aligning the two sequences to expose structural similarities and then performing insertions or deletions to make the ends match (as well as substituting any non-matching elements in the middle).

The principles of substitution, insertion and deletion are implemented in the Needleman–Wunsch algorithm (Needleman and Wunsch, 1970; Sankoff and Kruskal, 1983), which performs the complicated process of finding the 'cheapest' possible transformation between a pair of sequences (for an illustration of how this works, see Abbott and Forrest, 1986; for details on software see the final section at the end of this chapter).

SPECIFICATION OF SUBSTITUTION, INSERTION AND DELETION COSTS

Transformations can be weighted by assigning them different penalties, or costs. For example, we might regard the pair 'F' and 'P' as more similar to one another than the pair 'F' and 'U'. Thus, we might want to set the cost of substituting 'F' for 'P' (and vice versa) lower than the cost of substituting 'F' for 'U'. The researcher has to define a matrix that specifies the substitution costs for all pairwise combinations of states. Insertions and deletions, or 'indel' in OM jargon, are assigned a common indel cost (because an insertion in one sequence is equivalent to a deletion in the other).

Substitution cost specification is a sore point in the world of OM. It is neither obvious nor agreed among researchers which principles should guide it. What is more, the sensitivity of results to different cost specifications is not well understood. When sequence elements are quantities (such as, say, the number of lynchings in a locale in a given year (Stovel, 2001)), costs can be specified as a function of algebraic difference. For the more frequent case of categorical states, there are three approaches to substitution cost specification:

1 *Theoretically derived substitution cost matrices.* For example, Anyadike-Danes and McVicar (2003, 2005) base their matrix of substitution costs between different economic activity states on the principle of 'distance from the labour market'.

2 *Substitution costs derived from the probability of transition between states.* The 'easiness' of transition from state A to state B (and state B to state A) might be an indicator of the closeness of these states. Thus, some authors have assigned substitution costs inversely proportional to some function of the probabilities of cases in their sample to change between the two states concerned (Pollock, 2007; Stovel et al., 1996). This approach may seem objective, but it is not necessarily appropriate from a theoretical point of view. As mentioned above, the substitutions of the Needleman–Wunsch algorithm are *not* representations of transitions between states. Moreover, pragmatic considerations may speak against the transition probability approach. In one study this approach resulted in the lumping together of interesting subgroups, because the differences between these groups concerned 'easy-transition' states. The authors ended up departing from their initial 'pure' transition probability approach by modifying the substitution cost matrix according to pragmatic considerations (Stovel and Bolan, 2004).
3 *Unit substitution cost matrix.* As a third alternative, all substitutions may be assigned the same cost. This option might be chosen in the absence of reasons to assign differential costs. Martin et al. (2008) opted for a unit substitution costs matrix. They considered the ease-of-transition approach, but decided that it would end up overlooking an interesting subgroup of sequences: in their study of economic activity sequences, people who returned to education made a relatively 'easy' transition (from work to education and back again), but at an unusual time. A low substitution cost for their state pair 'Work-Education' might have led to the group of Returners to Education being lumped with larger groups of people in continuous employment.

The cost of *indels* has to be considered relative to substitution costs. In general, the higher the indel cost, the less often indels will be used by the algorithm, and the more weight is therefore given to the position of states within the sequence. When sequences represent a temporal order, we can say that the higher the indel cost, the more importance is given to *timing* in calculating sequence dissimilarity. Conversely, the lower the indel cost, the more importance is given to *similarity in sections*, even if those sections occur at different times. To illustrate, consider the following two sequences:

Element No.	1	2	3	4	5	6
S_5	F	F	F	H	P	P
S_6	F	H	P	P	P	P

Both sequences indicate a transition from Full-time work to Part-time work via an intermediate state, Homemaking. Note that we can turn S_5 into S_6 either by using *three substitutions*, or by using *four indels* (shifting S_6 two spaces to the right so that its section FHP aligns with the same section in S_5, and then inserting two 'F' before the beginning of S_6 and deleting the two 'P' at the end).

How should we set the indel cost? For the sake of simplicity, assume that we are working with a unit substitution cost matrix. Thus, three substitutions incur a cost of 3. If our aim was to emphasize the fact that S_5 and S_6 share a common subsequence, four indels would have to be cheaper than three substitutions. Consequently, the indel cost should be below 0.75. However, if we considered the differences in the timing of the section more important than their commonality of elements, the indel cost should be above 0.75.[1]

Note that two indels can always be used to perform the equivalent of a substitution. Therefore, if indels cost less than half a given substitution, then that substitution will never be used by the algorithm.[2] If indels cost less than half the lowest substitution, *only* indel will be used. Conversely, if the indels cost is very high relative to substitution costs, indel might be used rarely or not at all. It is useful to inspect the effects of varying the indel cost on sequence alignment.[3]

When sequences are of different length (in status biographies, this might be due to censoring), a number of insertions or deletions will be used, that is, at least equivalent to the number of elements by which the sequence lengths differ. If indel costs are high, this might lead to the assignment of relatively large distances to pairs of sequences of unequal length that are similar or even identical up to the point of censoring for the shorter sequence. To avoid such distortions, Stovel and Bolan (2004) specified two different indel costs: a higher one for pairs of sequences that have the same length, and a lower one for pairs of sequences that have different lengths. An alternative solution is to 'time-warp' sequences, for example standardize them to the same length (Abbott and Forrest, 1986; Abbott and Hrycak, 1990).

Another consideration, which has so far been ignored in the literature, is the insensitivity of indels to the state that is inserted or deleted. For example, consider three employment histories characterized by almost continuous full-time employment, interrupted merely by a short spell of either unemployment or education:

Element No.	1	2	3	4	5	6
S_7	F	U	F	F	F	F
S_8	F	F	F	U	F	F
S_9	F	F	F	F	E	F

If two indels are cheaper than two substitutions, these three sequences would be assigned the same distance from one another, even though S_7 and S_8 differ only in the *timing* of the intermediate state (unemployment), whereas both S_7 and S_8 differ from S_9 in the timing as well as the *type* of intermediate state (unemployment versus education). This is undesirable. Although in this simple example, the consequences in terms of misclassification of sequences may not be dire (as all three sequences represent largely stable employment careers), indel insensitivity may wreak more serious mischief in more complicated sequence comparisons. A solution for this problem might be to introduce a penalty for inserting a state that has not been deleted at a different place, and, analogously, for deleting a state that has not been inserted at a different place. As far as we are aware, this has never been tried. However, some of the alternatives to the Levenshtein distance that we shall discuss in the fourth section are sufficiently sensitive to recognize the greater similarity of the pair (S_7, S_8) relative to S_9.

CALCULATING AND ANALYZING THE DISTANCE MATRIX

In the classic application of OM, a comparison of all pairs of sequences results in an $n*n$ distance matrix containing $n(n-1)/2$ non-redundant elements. As the process of sequence alignment is symmetric, there is only one distance for each pair. Distances are commonly standardized by division through the length of the longer sequence, or by the maximum possible distance. Table 18.1 presents the matrix of distances between the nine example sequences used in this chapter, produced with the computer programme TDA (Rohwer and Pötter, 2005) using a unit substitution cost matrix and an indel cost of 0.7.

The distance matrix is usually subjected to cluster analysis (Everitt et al., 2001) to create an exploratory classification of sequences, although some authors have tried multidimentional scaling (Abbott and Forrest, 1986; Halpin and Chan, 1998). Figure 18.2 is a dendrogram representing the joining history in a simple agglomerative cluster analysis of the distance matrix presented in Table 18.1. A possible partition of the sample would result in the three clusters [S_1, S_2]; [S_5, S_6]; and [S_3, S_4, S_7, S_8, S_9]. Cluster membership may, of course, be used as a dependent or independent variable in multivariate analyses (e.g. McVicar and Anyadike-Danes, 2002).

EXTENDING THE REPERTOIRE: IDEAL TYPES

So far, we have described OM as a method producing an $n*n$ symmetric matrix of dyadic distances between every pair of cases. A different, or complementary, strategy is to compare observed sequences to one or several *reference sequences*. Dissimilarity measures between observed sequences and reference sequences can be used in a variety of fruitful ways, extending the use of OM to theory testing and to the improvement of classification. This section outlines a number of uses researchers have made of reference sequences in their work.

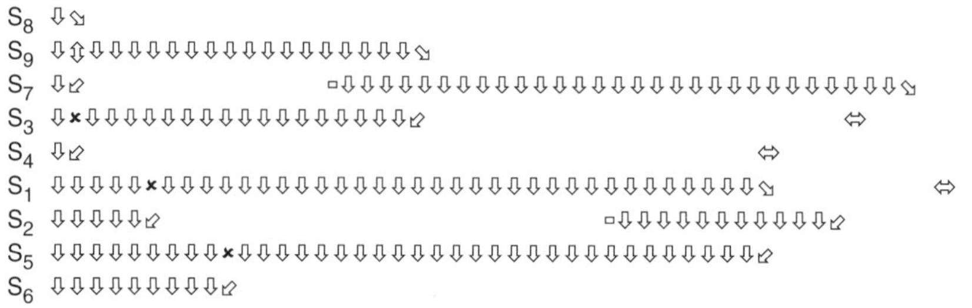

```
S8 ⇩⇘
S9 ⇩⇳⇩⇩⇩⇩⇩⇩⇩⇩⇩⇩⇩⇩⇩⇩⇩⇩⇩⇘
S7 ⇩⇙            □⇩⇩⇩⇩⇩⇩⇩⇩⇩⇩⇩⇩⇩⇩⇩⇩⇩⇩⇩⇩⇩⇩⇩⇩⇩⇩⇩⇩⇩⇘
S3 ⇩×⇩⇩⇩⇩⇩⇩⇩⇩⇩⇩⇩⇩⇩⇩⇩⇩⇩⇙                      ⇔
S4 ⇩⇙                                   ⇔
S1 ⇩⇩⇩⇩⇩×⇩⇩⇩⇩⇩⇩⇩⇩⇩⇩⇩⇩⇩⇩⇩⇩⇩⇩⇩⇩⇩⇩⇩⇩⇩⇩⇩⇩⇩⇩⇩⇘         ⇔
S2 ⇩⇩⇩⇩⇩⇙                       □⇩⇩⇩⇩⇩⇩⇩⇩⇩⇩⇩⇙
S5 ⇩⇩⇩⇩⇩⇩⇩⇩⇩×⇩⇩⇩⇩⇩⇩⇩⇩⇩⇩⇩⇩⇩⇩⇩⇩⇩⇩⇩⇩⇩⇩⇩⇩⇩⇩⇩⇙
S6 ⇩⇩⇩⇩⇩⇩⇩⇩⇩⇙
```

Figure 18.2 Dendrogram from cluster analysis of distance matrix
***Note*: Analysis of the distance matrix in Table 18.1 using the Ward method. The dendrogram illustrates the joining history produced by the agglomerative cluster algorithm**

Table 18.1 Matrix of distances created by OM from the nine example sequences

Sequences							S_1	S_2	S_3	S_4	S_5	S_6	S_7	S_8
E	E	E	F	F	F	S_1	0							
E	E	E	P	P	F	S_2	.33	0						
U	F	U	F	U	F	S_3	.63	.83	0					
F	U	F	U	F	U	S_4	.70	.90	.23	0				
F	F	F	H	P	P	S_5	.70	.73	.70	.63	0			
F	H	P	P	P	P	S_6	1.00	.67	.90	.83	.47	0		
F	U	F	F	F	F	S_7	.50	.83	.40	.33	.57	.83	0	
F	F	F	U	F	F	S_8	.57	.83	.40	.33	.50	.83	.23	0
F	F	F	F	E	F	S_9	.57	.80	.50	.57	.50	.83	.23	.23

Note: Unit substitution cost matrix; indel = 0.7. Raw distances were standardized through division by sequence length.

Methodologically, reference sequences have often been used as operationalizations of ideal-typical sequences. Ideal types are tools for representing messily multifarious reality through an informative simplification. Bauman (2007: 23–4) suggests that 'ideal types are not descriptions of social reality but the tools of its analysis and – hopefully – its comprehension. Their purpose is to force our picture of the society we inhabit to "make sense"; to achieve that purpose, they deliberately postulate more homogeneity, consistency and logic in the empirical social world than daily experience makes visible and allows us to grasp'. He goes on to recognise the 'messiness' or complexities of real data but suggests in accord with Weber (Weber, 1988/1904) that models are 'adequate at the level of meaning' and are 'indispensable for any understanding, and indeed for the very awareness of the similarities and differences, connections and discontinuities that hide behind the confusing variety of experience'.

To implement the logic of the ideal type in OM, we compute an $m*n$ matrix of dissimilarities between m reference sequences and n observed sequences. Such a matrix has served researchers in a wide field of applications and within different analytical strategies.

Using a normative reference sequence

Scherer (2001) used a single reference sequence (i.e. $m = 1$) representing continuous full-time work to derive a measure of dissimilarity between this 'standard' and the observed employment histories of British and West German young people after leaving full-time education or training. The dissimilarities were then treated as an interval level variable that facilitated comparisons by gender and country, and were used as the dependent variable in a regression analysis, which demonstrated that completed vocational training, rather than the level of education *per se*, was the strongest predictor of stable employment. On its own, the 'single reference sequence' method fails to make the most of OM, because it doesn't distinguish between qualitatively different deviations from the reference sequence (but Scherer's study employed this method as a complement to the standard OM procedure).

Operationalizing an ideal typology

Instead of using a single reference sequence, we may form a *set* of ideal-typical sequences to represent a theoretical classification. The study by Wiggins et al. (2007) illustrates this approach.[4] The authors constructed ideal types in an attempt to idealize typical life course passages into early old age, also described by other authors as the 'Third Age' (Gilleard and Higgs, 2002; Laslett, 1989; Young and Schuller, 1991). Individual histories were described along three separate trajectories for work, partnerships, and housing for people born in the 1930s in England and Wales and aged 65 to 75 years at the time of the original study (Berney and Blane, 1997). The empirical sequences for each trajectory were derived from a retrospective interview using time lines or life grids.

The ideal typology was developed prior to exploring how well each individual matched a particular idealization, and was based entirely upon the authors' own expectation of how the life course might unfold. These expectations were driven by their understanding of recent theories of the Third Age. Consider the housing trajectories defined by Wiggins et al. (2007) in their original article and reproduced here in Figure 18.3.

Each passage through life is represented by a horizontal block spanning the age years 16 to 70. This block is divided into six monthly intervals where the status of any individual is allowed to change. For housing it was decided to identify six states to combine a degree of urbanization with an indication of whether or not someone was living in a property they were buying or had bought. These six categories are theoretical constructs which can also be used to code actual recorded states. However, in the process of defining the idealized passages they are used to fill in the years from adulthood to early old age or becoming 'young-old'. Four pathways were constructed in this way.

Those passages assigned as a continuous experience of being in suburban owner occupancy were labelled as being 'Structurally Advantaged' and those assigned to being in a continuous state of renting in an urban area were labelled as being 'Structurally Disadvantaged'. The choice of these labels was influenced by Beck's work on first and second modernity (Beck, 2000); the authors wanted to contrast aspects of stable or stereotypical descriptions of the life course (first modernity) with passages which captured a degree of uncertainty arising from structural change (second modernity). Retirees in 'first modernity' were conceived to be in relatively stable occupations benefiting from post-war prosperity

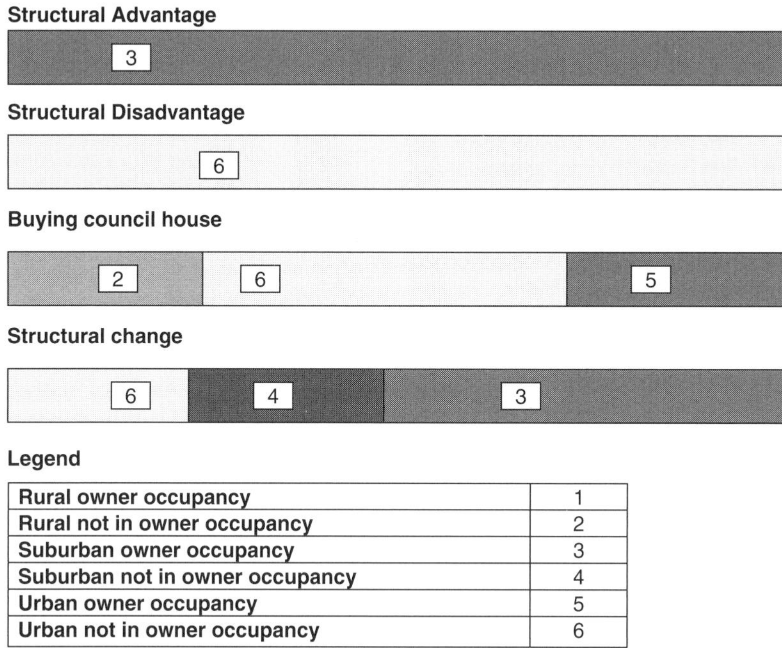

Figure 18.3 Four ideal-typical housing trajectories
***Note*: Reproduced from Wiggins et al (2008), with kind permission from Springer Netherlands.**

whereas those in 'second modernity' attempts to capture the move into retirement in a more unstable world. To better reflect the latter, two additional pathways were constructed: one to reflect a contextual change in council house provision where in the 1990s individuals living in council properties were given the 'right to buy'; the other to denote the relationship between residential and occupational mobility as well as the historical trend towards owning your own home. These pathways are respectively summarized as 'Buying a Council House' and 'Structural Change'. It happens then for this idealization that there are four possible approximations to life of the housing experience. In principle, there is no limit on the number of ideal types.

Applying OM, each individual history was then compared to the four ideal types, and an individual was assigned to the pathway that s/he is closest to. Anyone assigned to the 'Structurally Advantaged' pathway was considered as a being in the 'Third Age' for that set of passages. The contrasting labels 'Structural Advantage' and 'Structural Disadvantage' were also used in descriptions of labour market history and partnership. The analysis concluded by examining the relationship with third age ascription and quality of life as measured by a self-reported measure of subjective well-being (Wiggins et al., 2008). The relationship between Third Age status and quality of life was weak but indicative. Those who had recently bought their homes from the council reported similar levels of 'good' quality of life as those who were structurally advantaged. As over half of the sample fell into the category of being recent buyers from the council this was a fascinating finding. Interestingly, the result held equally for men and women. Whilst the predictive power of the assignment of individuals to ideal pathways could be questioned as a weakness in the original attempt to describe the Third Age it could also be the case that today's individual assessment of quality of life is more to do with their current situation than the past. The authors contend that the illustration demonstrates a template for addressing the theory of the Third Age in the context of life course experiences. Methods for testing the 'fit' of ideal type representations to the data are discussed in the next section.

Typological description

Ideal types may also be constructed to represent groups of sequences found via a cluster analysis. Here, the typology is not constructed prior to data exploration, but rather serves as a concise summary of an empirically derived classification. In such a strategy, the first step is to employ 'traditional' OM to derive an $n*n$ matrix and to cluster analyse this matrix. Each cluster found can then be represented by a typical sequence. This typical sequence may be defined as the observed sequence with the lowest within-cluster distance (Stovel, 2001), or may be determined via inspection of each cluster (Abbott and Hrycak, 1990; Stark and Vedres, 2006).

Typical sequences provide parsimonious descriptions of clusters, but they have further value in subsequent analyses. The analysis of Lloyds Bank employees' careers by Stovel et al. (1996) provides an interesting illustration of such a strategy. The authors developed 27 ideal typical career sequences from explorations on three selected cohorts of Lloyds Bank employees (employees starting in 1900–04, 1915–19, and 1930–34, respectively). Nine of these ideal-typical careers were considered to be traditional careers 'characterized by spatial immobility, promotions based on vacancies and the absence of spells in staff or senior clerical positions' (p. 387); the other 18 were considered to be modern careers 'characterized by significant spatial mobility, spells in staff positions, obtaining senior-clerical grades and promotions to management subsequent to a series of lateral and vertical moves' (p. 387). The full sample of Lloyds employees' sequences of job positions (careers starting between 1890 and 1939) was then divided into the 27 ideal types using OM. A simple analysis of the changing proportions of traditional versus modern careers by year of entry reveals a striking pattern of institutional change over time, and of the repercussions for individual employees (p. 389).

The stress measure

An ideal typology has other convenient advantages. Using ideal types, it is possible to assess the fit of the classification to the data using a simple stress measure akin to Kruskal's stress measures for multidimensional scaling (Kruskal and

Wish, 1978). In the context of OM, this measure was first suggested by Abbott and Hrycak (1990).

Stress is given by

$$STRESS = \sqrt{\frac{\sum_{i=1}^{n-1}\sum_{j>i}^{n}\left(d_{ij} - d_{i'j'}\right)^2}{\sum_{i=1}^{n-1}\sum_{j>i}^{n} d_{ij}^2}}$$

where d_{ij} is the distance between two sequences i and j; and $d_{i'j'}$ is the distance between the ideal-typical sequences i' and j' that represent i and j, respectively (cf. Martin et al., 2008).

Stress is a measure of badness-of-fit, a higher value indicating worse fit. Stress values fall between 0 and 1. When all sequences are identical to their ideal type (i.e. with no data reduction), stress is 0. When there is only one ideal type representing all sequences (i.e. with maximum data reduction), stress is 1. Stress may be interpreted as the proportion of the dissimilarities (summed over all sequence pairs) that is 'ignored' when using the ideal typology of sequences as a description of the sample.

As with measures of stress used in multidimensional scaling, there is no absolute criterion for good or bad stress. Stress will rise with the ratio of cases to ideal types, and might thus need to be weighed against parsimony. However, stress is particularly useful as a *relative* measure of fit. Stovel (2001) analyzed sequences representing the temporal succession of lynchings in 395 counties of the American Deep South between the years 1882 and 1930. A cluster analysis of the OM dissimilarity matrix yielded nine blocks of counties, which Stovel summarized using nine ideal-typical sequences. This typology was then compared to a theoretically derived classification of counties, where the grouping criterion was the proportion of African Americans living in each county at the time. Using the stress measure (as well as a statistical test of the difference of mean within- and between-group distances), Stovel shows that the OM-derived typology fits the data better than the theoretical one. She is thus able to make a strong case for conceptualizing the history of lynching as situated in unfolding time, rather than as being determined by a demographic condition measured at one point of time.

Ideal-typical sequences as aids in classification

So far, we have discussed the use of ideal types as a way of representing either theoretically or empirically derived typology of sequences. However, ideal-typical sequences may be used as an aid in constructing an empirical classification itself. This use of ideal types is motivated by concerns over the reliability of cluster analysis. Cluster analysis has a number of weaknesses: the common agglomerative clustering algorithms can have multiple solutions when the data contain ties (Morgan and Ray, 1995); and different cluster algorithms produce substantially different solutions (Everitt et al., 2001). Also, cluster enumeration is subjective to a certain extent. These problems are likely to be particularly relevant in many applications on OM derived $n*n$ matrices, because many sets of sequence data will not naturally fall into well-defined groups of similar sequences. Empirically, explorations of $n*n$ dissimilarity matrices with multidimensional scaling can often be expected to result in a continuous distribution of data points in space, rather than well-separated clusters. This was, indeed, the finding by Halpin and Chan (1998) on a sample of class careers, and by Halpin (2008a) on a sample of employment histories. In such cases, cluster analysis will impose arbitrary partitions between groups, and clusters will be unstable at the margins.

One analytical strategy to circumvent these problems is the use of a subset of the data as an exploration sample. Martin et al. (2008) explored a third of their sample of employment histories from two British birth cohorts using three different cluster algorithms. Turning each cluster solution into a set of ideal-typical sequences, they were able to compare the typologies suggested by each cluster algorithm by assessing the fit to the whole data set. They found that the Ward algorithm outperformed other cluster techniques. Moreover, due to the large number of ties in the distance matrix, the Ward algorithm produced multiple solutions, which differed in fit. In the end, the authors used the insight they had won through the close inspection of all tested cluster solutions to construct a typology that combined aspects of several of them. This researcher-constructed typology turned out to have a lower stress value than all Ward-derived cluster sets. Ultimately, the authors were interested in differences between the two cohorts. Having found the best-fitting typology, they were able to compare the two cohorts with greater confidence in the internal validity of the comparison than if they had settled for any one of the classifications suggested by straightforward cluster analysis.

Similarly, Stovel and Bolan (2004) were concerned with capturing the variability between different age groups in their sample of housing trajectories. If they had used cluster analysis on the whole sample, interesting small groups might well have been agglomerated with larger clusters and thus have escaped the analytic eye. To avoid this, the authors used cluster analysis for exploratory purposes only. They took eight subsamples derived from four different age groups. Each age group was represented by two subsamples, where one was a simple random sample, and the other a random sample of those sequences that contained at least one status change. The sequences in each of the eight samples were analyzed using OM-cum-cluster analysis. From inspection of the eight cluster solutions, each with 13–15 clusters, the authors constructed 25 ideal-typical sequences, which they then used to classify all sequences in their sample. They could thus compare their four age groups in terms of the probability of following each of the 25 types of trajectories. Again, using ideal type representations derived from cluster analytic exploration helped increase the confidence in the findings.

MODIFICATION OF THE OM ALGORITHM

Criticisms of OM

Methodologists have not always met OM with approval. Some critics have claimed that the social scientific use of OM contrasts unfavourably with its original uses in biology, because there deletions, insertions and substitutions represent hypotheses about actual chemical processes (such as mutations or 'copying mistakes' of DNA) that might, quite literally, have changed one sequence into another (Elzinga, 2003; Levine, 2000). Sociologically, the meaning of a substitution or indel is less clear, and certainly a substitution is not equivalent to an actual social event such as a transition (see the debate between Abbott, 2000; and Wu, 2000; cf. also Halpin, 2008b).

Moreover, a particular worry is connected to the arbitrariness of substitution and indel costs. As Abbott and Tsay (2000) and others (Anyadike-Danes and McVicar, 2003) have noted, often results of OM are robust to substantial variations in substitution and indel costs.[5] If one understands different cost regimes as different models about the social world, as some critics have done, this constitutes a lack of sensitivity: if different OM 'models' find essentially the same results, that seems to imply that OM models are not strictly falsifiable, and thus not proper models (Levine, 2000).

Among OM analysts, there have been two reactions to these critiques: firstly, authors have pointed out that it is a mistake to conceptualize the OM algorithm as a model of reality. Even in biology, not all theoretically salient chemical processes, such as transpositions of sections and element swaps, are represented in OM's operations (Abbott, 2000); moreover, cost regimes used in biology are not pure representations of theory, and indel costs in particular are usually derived pragmatically (Lesnard, 2006). In the case of social science, Abbott and others have stressed that OM is a pattern search technique and in itself makes no assumptions about the processes that have generated the sequences (Abbott, 2000; Lesnard, 2006). The intention of OM analysts is not to generate a model that would replace statistical techniques such as Event History Analysis, but rather to complement them in the toolbox of the longitudinal data analyst.

Sequence analysis, time and time-warping

It is a mistake, then, to evaluate OM with the yardstick of stochastic modelling. Nonetheless, OM analysts have questioned whether the straightforward substitution/insertion/deletion algorithm presented in the second part of this chapter is sociologically meaningful. Concerns have been raised mainly by researchers interested in temporal sequences, such as longitudinal life course data (Halpin, 2008a), or time use data (Lesnard, 2006). The general problem identified by these and other authors is how time is treated in the Levenshtein distance calculation. In the following, we shall discuss three alternatives to the

Levenshtein distance: Lesnard's Dynamic Hamming Distance; Halpin's OMv distance, and Elzinga's combinatorial method. While OMv may be regarded as a modification of the Levenshtein distance, the other two methods are not OM, but rather alternative methods of sequence analysis that we discuss here because they were explicitly suggested as improvements on the Levenshtein distance.[6]

Lesnard's dynamic hamming distance

As we said in the second section of this chapter, insertions and deletions have the effect of minimizing the influence the timing of states has on distance calculation. Lesnard (2006; see also Aisenbrey and Fasang, 2007) considers cases where all sequences are of the same length and have a common calendar (that is, the positions of the elements in each sequence refer to the same points in time, such as careers of a single birth cohort, or time use diaries referring to an equivalent 24-hour day). Here, insertions and deletions may arguably distort the sequence comparison by tearing apart the sequences' temporal structure. (It is not the same to be unemployed for two years between the ages of 16 and 18, say, as it is to be unemployed for two years in one's fifties.) Consequently, Lesnard argues against the use of indels for such data. Moreover, he invites us to consider whether substitution costs, also, should take account of time. Substitution costs matrices based on transition probabilities, as discussed in the second section of this chapter, do not take account of the possibility that transition rates vary by time. Aisenbrey and Fasang, analyzing the transition from work to retirement and referring to Lesnard, criticize that traditional OM implies that the substitution of the state 'pensioner' for the state 'employment' is treated the same, regardless of whether this substitution occurs at the age of 50 or 65 (Aisenbrey and Fasang, 2007). It is this sort of consideration that has lead Lesnard to propose a dynamic algorithm for the calculation of time-dependent substitution costs, called the Dynamic Hamming distance. The Dynamic Hamming distance results from a calculation that defines the cost of substituting element a for element b at time t as a function of the probabilities of making the transition from a to b, or b to a, from either $t-1$ to t, or from t to $t+1$. Following Lesnard (2006), the dissimilarity s between states a and b at time t is calculated as:

$$s_t(a,b) = 4 - \begin{bmatrix} p(X_t = a \mid X_{t-1} = b) + p(X_t = b \mid X_{t-1} = a) + \\ \qquad p(X_{t+1} = a \mid X_t = b) + p(X_{t+1} = b \mid X_t = a) \end{bmatrix}$$

The higher the probability of a transition between two states, the lower the cost of substitution of one for the other.

Halpin's OMv distance

Halpin (2008a) considered a different problematic implication in OMs tacit conceptualization of time. The OM algorithm doesn't recognize that, from a sociological point of view, adjacent states might be meaningfully related to one another. Specifically: 'from a sociological point of view, the deletion of a month from an 18-month spell is far less consequential than from a 2-month spell, but OM cannot recognize this' (Halpin, 2008a). Halpin therefore suggests adjusting the cost of operations according to the length of the spell, so that changing FFFFH to FFFHH will be less costly than changing FHPPP to HHPPP. In Halpin's algorithm, which he calls OMv, the normal substitution and indel costs apply, but are divided by the square root of the length of the longest spell affected by the operation. Thus, if substituting an H for the F in the sequence FFFFH, the substitution cost c(F, H) would be divided by $\sqrt{4} = 2$, as the length of the spell of element A was 4 in the original sequence. However, substituting an H for the F in FHPPP would not incur an adjustment, as $\sqrt{1} = 1$.

Halpin finds that his adjustments can make a substantial difference to the pattern of the resulting distances in artificial data sets where the variation between the number of spells per sequence is high. With real employment history data, however, distances calculated by OM and OMv correlate very highly with one another. When running cluster analyses on the two distance matrices produced by the two methods, clusters had roughly the same characteristics. In the 'simple OM' classification, however, clusters dominated by sequences with stable states (FFFFF) tended to be almost perfectly homogenous, while clusters dominated by sequences with one or more state changes were rather messier. In the modified OMv classification, some of the messiness was shifted to the stable-state clusters, so that the clusters made up of transition sequences became more homogenous. From a sociological point of view, there was no absolute criterion to decide whether OM or OMv constituted the better way of dividing the sample.

Elzinga's combinatorial method

Another alternative to the Levenshtein distance has been proposed by Elzinga (2003, 2005; cf. also Elzinga and Liefbroer, 2007). Dissatisfied with the inevitable arbitrariness of transformation costs, Elzinga has developed a method of distance calculation that is not concerned with sequence alignment, and uses neither substitutions nor indels. To understand Elzinga's method, we have to first introduce his concept of a 'subsequence'. A subsequence is any ordered array of elements that can be found within a sequence, regardless of whether the elements making up the subsequence are directly consecutive in the whole sequence or not. For example, the sequence EPF has seven subsequences: [E]; [P]; [F]; [EP]; [EF]; [PF]; [EPF].

To derive a distance for a given pair of sequences, Elzinga has developed a whole family of measures based on the comparison of subsequences. A full account of his ideas is beyond the scope of this chapter. In general, Elzinga's method defines the distance between a pair of sequences as a function of the number of subsequences they have in common, and the total number of subsequences in each sequence. In its simplest form, this distance can be expressed as:

$$d_{i,j} = 1 - \frac{\langle i, j \rangle}{\sqrt{\langle i \rangle \cdot \langle j \rangle}},$$

where $d_{i,j}$ is the distance between sequences *i* and *j*, $\langle i, j \rangle$ is the number of subsequences shared by *i* and *j*, and $\langle i \rangle$ is the number of subsequences *i* shares with itself. For example, if we wanted to compare the sequence EPF with the sequence EFU, we would find that they share three subsequences: [E]; [F]; [EF]. Their distance would thus be $d = 1 - 3/\sqrt{7^2} = 0.57$. Two identical sequences have a distance of 0, two sequences who don't share any subsequence have a distance of 1, and the distance of two sequences that share some but not all subsequences is some number between 0 and 1.

Elzinga's combinatorial method offers sequence analysts yet another way of handling time. Although it is possible to compute Elzinga's distance measure from sequence data with repeating elements (i.e. where spells are coded by several elements, as in our example sequences in the second section), this quickly becomes computation intensive with long sequences. Elzinga suggests encoding sequences in spells with a duration index. Thus, our example sequence S_2 (EEEPPF) would, in Elzinga's notation, appear as $E_3P_2F_1$. In the distance calculation, $E_3P_2F_1$ is considered to contain seven subsequences just like the simpler EPF (because both consist of three 'tokens'); and each subsequence match is weighted by the product of the summed duration indices (see Elzinga, 2005 for a detailed description).

Elzinga claims that his method requires much weaker assumptions than OM, and that it leads to intuitively and substantially more adequate dissimilarity matrices. There is certainly some indication that his distance measure may be superior to OM, at least in some cases. For example, recall that OM, problematically, measured our three example sequences S_7, S_8 and S_9 as equidistant from one another (see the second section). The results from Elzinga's method, in contrast, reflect the fact that S_7 and S_8 represent work careers interrupted by unemployment, whereas S_9 represents a career interrupted by a period of education: S_7 and S_8 are measured to be very close to each other ($d_{S_7,S_8} = 0.03$), but each is rather distant from S_9 ($d_{S_7,S_9} = 0.57$; $d_{S_8,S_9} = 0.56$).[7]

WHICH DISTANCE MEASURE FOR WHICH KIND OF DATA?

Researchers' efforts to modify or replace the OM algorithm in order to make sequence analysis more sociologically meaningful are commendable. However, it is unclear whether these modifications *per se* result in substantially superior results when applied to empirical data (however, see Elzinga, 2003).

Methodological studies on the effects of varying substitution and indel cost regimes, of different methods of time warping, and of alternatives to the Levensthein distance, are still rare. A number of researchers have conducted sensitivity analyses to ascertain the effects of certain variations for their particular data (e.g. Aisenbrey and Fasang, 2007; Anyadike-Danes and McVicar, 2003; Stark and Vedres, 2006). However, only simulation studies that systematically vary both algorithmic specifications and characteristics of sequence data would be capable of drawing more general conclusions about the advantages and disadvantages of the different ways to calculate inter-sequence distances. All attempts to do this are recent, and many are unpublished (Halpin, 2008a, b; Schröder, 2008). In the next few years, we expect to see increased efforts in this direction, as researchers try to develop a sound methodological base for sequence analysis.

Faced with the accusation that OM was inadequate as a model of social processes (Levine, 2000; Wu, 2000), Andrew Abbott replied, quite correctly in our view, that OM is not a statistical model, but a powerful pattern search technique (Abbott, 2000). The methodological debates around different distance calculation techniques should be understood as struggles to distinguish the merits of different heuristics, that is, as struggles to understand how theoretically meaningful patterns that exist in the data are best identified.

In one publication, however, a modification of the sequence data themselves, rather than of the distance computation, made a decisive difference to the data. As discussed above, Stovel (2001) analyzed sequences of lynchings in counties in the Deep South of the United States. Although the frequency of lynchings was, and is, morally appalling, and although their occurrence is historically highly relevant, for the data analyst lynchings are rare events and therefore present unique challenges. Stovel found that a straightforward count of lynchings per time period (for example, in the form 1 0 0 0 0 2 0 0 1 0 0 0) yielded a classification whose within-group distances were not significantly smaller than between group distances. Put simply, the data appeared to contain only noise, and no signal. However, the simple coding of states as the frequency of lynchings per time period assumes that lynchings are one-off events that have no social consequence beyond their occurrence. Stovel then represented the influence of past lynchings on the subsequent time periods through a decay function that allowed the social memory of lynchings to linger for three time periods after the event, while gradually declining. This new way of representing the sequences made a remarkable difference to the results, so that the cluster analysis yielded a significant 'signal' in the form of a typology of local lynching histories. This typology could be validated by testing theoretical assumptions about the relationship between the form of lynchings (ritualized or not, public or secretive) and the temporal structure of their occurrence. Methodologically, Stovel's study exemplifies that the use of sequence analysis is unlikely to follow a standard procedure, but each time has to be adapted to the data and the research problem at hand.

Quality of algorithm or quality of data?

In their 2000 review of OM applications, Abbott and Tsay (2000) expressed the opinion that sequence analysis will not attain recognition in the methodological canon until an application makes an incisive discovery in a research field that would not have been possible without OM. So far, this has not happened. Applications have yielded interesting and informative results, but no *eureka* insight capable of changing a research field. We rather suspect that if such an application is to come, it will not be attained by a refinement of the algorithm of distance calculation, but rather from the application on a particularly good set of data. To be direct, while classification of employment histories into ideal types such as 'continuous full time work', 'in and out of unemployment', 'return to education' and the like is surely informative, the data used in such a typical application are rather too general to yield penetrating insights into people's life courses. Of course, this is not the fault of the analyst: longitudinal surveys will not often yield data that are sufficiently specific to construct more than very general descriptions of lives, and of course one sometimes has to use suboptimal data rather than do no research at all. Nonetheless, we feel that the most notable and intriguingly complex findings using sequence analysis have not come from survey data, but rather from archives and historical records. The two studies by Katherine Stovel (and colleagues), discussed in various places in this chapter, come most readily to mind (Stovel, 2001; Stovel et al., 1996); and Abbott and Forrest's (1986) seminal article is still inspiring reading. Applications of sequence analysis will be interesting if the information carried by the sequences is relevant – this may not be the most arresting of insights, but is worth emphasizing as the focus of methodological research within the field appears to be shifting towards the (admittedly important) details of algorithm construction.

Software

Early users of OM relied on packages developed for biological applications (see Abbott and Tsay, 2000 for some examples), or on non-commercial programmes, often developed by the social scientists themselves (e.g. OPTIMIZE by Abbott and Prellwitz, 1997). Elzinga's programme CHESA (Elzinga, 2007) is capable of computing the Levenshtein (OM) distance as well as a whole family of measures derived from the author's combinatorial method. Until recently, the freeware TDA (Rohwer and Pötter, 2005) provided what was possibly the most accessible package. TDA can compute $n*n$ as well as $m*n$ matrices, and is able to handle very large data sets. However, TDA lacks options for easy graphical data exploration.

Most recently, the OM algorithm was implemented in the commercial data analysis programme STATA (Brzinsky-Fay et al., 2006), and in the TraMineR package for the freeware programme R (Gabadinho et al., 2008). Both STATA and TraMineR feature an extensive range of options for the exploration and graphical inspection of sequence data.

At the time of writing, the modification of, and alternatives to, the OM algorithm described earlier in this chapter are not implemented in a general statistics package, but with the current rapid development of sequence analysis in the social sciences, this might not be true anymore at the time of reading. It would be a sign of good health of sequence analysis if this little review was outdated soon. At the time of writing, OM is still the dominant method for measuring sequence dissimilarity in the social sciences, so much so that it is sometimes used synonymously with sequence analysis. As we hope to have indicated, this may soon cease to be the case, and OM may become just one method in a toolbox of measures that social scientists can use for making sense of sequence data holistically.

ACKNOWLEDGEMENTS

We would like to thank Anette Fasang, Brendan Halpin, Daniel Heussen, Laurent Lesnard and the editors for their generous and helpful comments on an earlier draft of this chapter, and Christian Erzberger for introducing each of us, at different times, to Optimal Matching. We are also grateful to Alison Evans for help with the literature search.

NOTES

1 MacIndoe and Abbott (2004: 349) have mistakenly claimed that setting the indel costs to a figure higher than half the highest substitution cost will mean that indel will never be used by the algorithm. This is not true, as our examples illustrate.

2 Therefore, the advice to set indel costs at around 1/10 of the highest substitution costs, although given with the authority of Andrew Abbott (MacIndoe and Abbott 2004: 349) and repeated by others (Brzinsky-Fay et al., 2006: 450), seems to defeat the purpose of specifying a detailed substitution cost matrix at all. If researchers want to use both indels and all kinds of substitutions, then an indel value slightly larger than half the highest substitution cost might be appropriate (cf. Halpin, 2008b: 8; Martin et al., 2008: 21). However, this must be decided on the merits of the specific data and the research question at hand.

3 The EXPLORE option of Abbott's OM programme OPTIMIZE (Abbott and Prellwitz 1997), which is available as freeware on the world wide web, is a useful tool in this respect, as it allows the visual inspection of the effects that different cost regimes have on sequence alignment.

4 Cf. also (Elzinga and Liefbroer, 2007), who also use ideal-typical representations of theoretical expectations. However, instead of the Levenshtein distance, they employ a distance measure based on a non-aligning technique suggested by Elzinga (2003, 2005: see also below, Section 4.2).

5 However, variations in cost regimes do appear to result in substantial differences where researchers are interested not only in finding the largest and relatively homogenous clusters in a sample, but also pay attention to smaller, generally fuzzier groups of sequences (Scherer, 2001; Stovel and Bolan, 2004). Researchers are left to decide on solutions on the basis of both theoretical and pragmatic considerations and their specific research interest.

6 Another alternative to the Levenshtein distance is the lexicographic index suggested by Ivano Bison (this volume).

7 The calculations were done using Elzinga's excellent CHESA programme, which is available online (Elzinga, 2007). To derive the distances, we selected the attribute 'Number of matching subsequences with duration vector' and computed normalized distances.

REFERENCES

Abbott, A. (2000). Reply to Levine and Wu. *Sociological Methods and Research*, 29(1): 65–76.

Abbott, A. and Barman, E. (1997). Sequence comparison via alignment and gibbs sampling: A formal analysis of the emergence of the modern sociological article. *Sociological Methodology*, 27: 47–87.

Abbott, A. and DeViney, S. (1992). The welfare state as transnational event. *Social Science History*, 16: 245–74.

Abbott, A. and Forrest, J. (1986). Optimal matching methods for historical sequences. *Journal of Interdisciplinary History*, 16: 471–94.

Abbott, A. and Hrycak, A. (1990). Measuring resemblance in sequence data: An optimal matching analysis of musicians' careers. *American Journal of Sociology*, 96(1): 144–85.

Abbott, A. and Prellwitz, G. (1997). OPTIMIZE (software): Prellwitz Computing Services. Available at: http://home.uchicago.edu/~aabbott/om.html#optimize [Access: 14/11/2008].

Abbott, A. and Tsay, A. (2000). Sequence analysis and optimal matching methods in sociology. *Sociological Methods and Research*, 29(1): 3–33.

Aisenbrey, S. (2000). *Optimal Matching Analyse. Anwendungen in den Sozialwissenschaften*. Opladen: Leske + Budrich.

Aisenbrey, S. and Fasang, A.E (2007). *Beyond Optimal Matching. The 'Second Wave' of Sequence Analysis*. New Haven: Working Paper 2007–02, Center for Research on Inequalities and the Life Course, Yale University.

Anyadike-Danes, M. and McVicar, D. (2003). *Parallel Lives: Birth, Childhood and Adolescent Influences on Career Paths*. Belfast: Northern Ireland Economic Research Centre.

Anyadike-Danes, M. and McVicar, D. (2005). You'll never walk alone: childhood influences and male career path clusters. *Labour Economics*, 12(4): 511–30.

Bauman, Z. (2007). *Consuming Life*. Cambridge: Polity.

Beck, U. (2000). *The Brave New World of Work*. Cambridge: Polity.

Berney, L. and Blane, D. (1997). Collecting retrospective data: accuracy recall after 50 years judged against historical records. *Social Science and Medicine*, 45: 1519–25.

Brzinsky-Fay, C., Kohler, U. and Luniak, M. (2006). Sequence analysis with Stata. *Stata Journal*, 6(4): 435–60.

Elliott, J. (2005). *Using Narrative in Social Research: Qualitative and Quantitative Approaches*. London: Sage.

Elzinga, C.H. (2003). Sequence similarity – a nonaligning technique. *Sociological Methods and Research*, 32(1): 3–29.

Elzinga, C.H. (2005). Combinatorial representations of token sequences. *Journal of Classification*, 22(1): 87–118.

Elzinga, C.H. (2007). *CHESA 2.1 User Manual*. Amsterdam: Vrije Universiteit. Available at: http://home.fsw.vu.nl/ch.elzinga/ [Access 14/11/2008].

Elzinga, C.H. and Liefbroer, A.C (2007). De-standardization of family life trajectories of young adults: A cross-national comparison using sequence analysis. *European Journal of Population*, 23: 225–50.

Everitt, B., Landau, S., and Leese, M. (2001). *Cluster Analysis*, 4th edn. London: Arnold.

Gabadinho, A., Ritschard, G., Studer, M., and Müller, N.S. (2008). *Mining Sequence Data in R with the TraMineR Package: A User's Guide*: University of Geneva [Online: http://mephisto.unige.ch/pub/TraMineR/Doc/TraMineR-Users-Guide.pdf].

Giele, J.Z. (1998). Innovation in the typical life course. In J.Z. Giele and G. Elder (eds) *Methods of Life Course Research: Qualitative and Quantitative Approaches* (pp. 231–63). Thousand Oaks, CA: Sage.

Gilleard, C. and Higgs, P. (2002). The third age: class, cohort or generation? *Ageing and Society*, 22: 369–82.

Halpin, B. (2008a). *Optimal Matching Analysis and Life Course Data: The Importance of Duration*. Limerick: University of Limerick. Available at: http://www.ul.ie/sociology/docstore/workingpapers/wp2008-01.pdf [Accessed 14/11/2008].

Halpin, B. (2008b). Understanding substitution costs: parameterising the optimal matching algorithm. *Paper presented at the 7th International Conference on Social Science Methodology, ISA RC33, 1–5 September 2008*. Naples, Italy.

Halpin, B. and Chan, T.W (1998). Class careers as sequences: An optimal matching analysis of work-life-histories. *European Sociological Review*, 14(2): 111–30.

Kruskal, J.B. and Wish, M. (1978). *Multidimensional Scaling*. London: Sage.

Laslett, P. (1989). *A Fresh Map of Life: the Emergence of the Third Age*. London: Weidenfield & Nicolson.

Lesnard, L. (2006). *Optimal Matching and Social Sciences. Document du travail du Centre de Recherche en Économie et Statistique 2006-01*. Paris: Institute Nationale de la Statistique et des Études Économiques.

Levenshtein, V.I. (1966). Binary codes capable of correcting deletions, insertions and reversals. *Soviet Physics Doklady*, 10: 707–10.

Levine, J.H. (2000). But what have you done for us lately? Commentary on Abbott and Tsay. *Sociological Methods and Research*, 29(1): 34–40.

Levitt, B. and Nass, C. (1989). The lid on the garbage can. *Administrative Science Quarterly*, 34: 190–207.

MacIndoe, H. and Abbott, A. (2004). Sequence analysis and optimal matching techniques for social science data. In M. Hardy and A. Bryman (eds) *Handbook of Data Analysis*. London: Sage.

Martin, P., Schoon, I., and Ross, A. (2008). Beyond transitions. Applying optimal matching analysis to life course research. *International Journal of Social Research Methodology*, 11(3): 179–99.

McVicar, D. and Anyadike-Danes, M. (2002). Predicting successful and unsuccessful transitions from school to work by using sequence methods. *Journal of the Royal Statistical Society Series A*, 165(2): 317–34.

Morgan, B.J.T. and Ray, A.P.G. (1995). Non-uniqueness and inversions in cluster analysis. *Applied Statistics*, 44(1): 117–34.

Needleman, S. and Wunsch, C. (1970). A general method applicable to the search for similarities in the amino acid sequence of two proteins. *Journal of Molecular Biology*, 48: 443–53.

Pollock, G. (2007). Holistic trajectories: a study of combined employment, housing and family careers using multiple sequence analysis. *Journal of the Royal Statistical Society Series A*, 170: 167–83.

Rindfuss, R.R., Swicegood, C.G., and Rosenfeld, R.A. (1987). Disorder in the life course: How common and does it matter? *American Sociological Review*, 52(December): 785–801.

Rohwer, G. and Pötter, U. (2005). *TDA User's Manual*. Bochum, Germany: Ruhr-Universität. Available at: http://www.stat.ruhr-uni-bochum.de/pub/tda/doc/tman63/tman-pdf.zip.

Sankoff, D. and Kruskal, J.B (eds) (1983). *Time Warps, String Edits, and Macromolecules*. Reading, MA: Addison Wesley.

Scherer, S. (2001). Early career patterns: A comparison of Great Britain and West Germany. *European Sociological Review*, 17(2): 119–44.

Schoon, I., McCulloch, A., Joshi, H., Wiggins, R.D., and Bynner, J. (2001). Transitions from school to work in a changing social context. *Young*, 9: 4–22.

Schröder, A. (2008). Substitution costs – Achilles' heel of optimal matching? *Paper presented at the 7th International Conference on Social Science Methodology, ISA RC33, 1–5 September 2008*. Naples, Italy.

Stark, D. and Vedres, B. (2006). The social times of network spaces: Network sequences and foreign investment in Hungary. *American Journal of Sociology*, 111(5): 1367–411.

Stovel, K. (2001). Local sequential patterns: The structure of lynching in the Deep South. *Social Forces*, 79: 843–80.

Stovel, K. and Bolan, M. (2004). Residential trajectories: using optimal alignment to reveal the structure of residential mobility. *Sociological Methods and Research*, 32(4): 559–98.

Stovel, K., Savage, M., and Bearman, P.S (1996). Ascription Into Achievement: Models of Career Systems at Lloyds Bank, 1890–1979. *American Journal of Sociology*, 102(2): 358–99.

Weber, M. (1988/1904). Die Objektivität sozialwissenschaftlicher und sozialpolitischer Erkenntnis. In J. Winkelmann (ed) *Max Weber: Gesammelte Aufsätze zur Wissenschaftslehre*. Tübingen: Mohr.

Wiggins, R.D., Erzberger, C., Hyde, M., Higgs, P., and Blane, D. (2007). Optimal matching analysis using ideal types to describe the lifecourse: An illustration of how histories of work, partnerships and housing relate to quality of life in early old age. *International Journal of Social Research Methodology*, 10(4): 259–78.

Wiggins, R.D., Netuveli, G., Hyde, M., Higgs, P., and Blane, D. (2008). The evaluation of a self-enumerated scale of quality of life (CASP-19) in the context of ageing: A combination of exploratory and confirmatory approaches. *Social Indicators Research*, 89(1): 61–77.

Wu, L.L. (2000). Some comments on 'Sequence analysis and optimal matching methods in sociology: Review and prospect'. *Sociological Methods and Research*, 29(1): 41–64.

Wuerker, A.K. (1996). The changing careers of patients with chronic mental illness. *Journal of Health Administration*, 23: 458–70.

Young, M. and Schuller, T. (1991). *Life After Work: The Arrival of the Ageless Society*. London: HarperCollins.

19

Quantitative Narrative Analysis

Roberto Franzosi

INTRODUCTION

In the *Chicago Record-Herald* of 23 May 1902, under the tile 'NEGRO TORTURED TO DEATH BY MOB OF 4,000', one reads (cited in Ginzburg, 1962: 45–6):

> LANSING, Tex., May 22 – Dudley Morgan, a negro accused of assailing Mrs. McKay, wife of a Section Foreman McKay, was burned to death at an iron stake here to-day. A crowd of 4,000 men, most of whom were armed, snatched him from the officers on the arrival of the train. Morgan was taken to a large field on the edge of town. An iron stake was driven into the ground and to this he was bound until he could only move his head. Heaps of inflammable material was then piled about him and he was given a few moments for prayer. It was 12:12 when all arrangements were completed. The crowd by this time numbered at least 5,000. The husband of the woman Morgan was accused of abusing applied the match and the pyre was soon ablaze. Then began the torture of the Negro. Burning pieces of pine were thrust into his eyes. Then burning timbers were held to his neck, and after his clothes were burned off to other parts of his body. He was tortured in a horrible manner. The crowd clamored continuously for a slow death. The Negro, writhing and groaning at the stake, begged piteously to be shot. Mrs. McKay was brought to the field in a carriage with four other women and an unsuccessful effort was made to get her near enough to see the mob's victim. The Negro's head finally dropped, and in thirty minutes only the trunk of the body remained. As the fire died down relic hunters started their search for souvenirs. Parts of the skull and body were carried away. The men who captured Morgan were then held above the heads of the mob while their pictures were taken. The last words of the doomed man other than the incoherent mutterings made in prayer were: "Tell my wife good-by."

This newspaper account gives us a description of a type of event called 'lynching' that dotted Jim Crow South in the United States. Between 1889 and

1931, according to NAACP figures (National Association for the Advancement of Colored People), 3,290 African-Americans, guilty or innocent of the crimes they were accused of, met their death through the summary justice of a lynching mob.

In the social sciences, events of this kind, have been typically studied as 'event counts' in econometric models where a 'dependent' variable Y_i measuring the number of events (e.g. lynchings) is regressed on a set of 'independent' variables $X_{1i}, X_{2i} \ldots X_{ki}$, each measuring different effects, and on an error term ε_i. The index i refers to time for time series models (e.g. month, quarter, year), space for cross-sectional models (e.g. country, state, county), or a combination of time and space for pooled time series-cross section models.

$$Y_i = \beta_0 + \beta_1 X_{1i} + \beta_2 X_{2i} + \cdots + \beta_k X_{ki} + \varepsilon_i \qquad (1)$$

From lynchings to strikes, race riots, cross-national political violence, and domestic crime rates, different sets of events have been studied with the help of variable-based, statistical models of the type of equation (1). What these models purport to explain is point-by-point variations in the level of Y as a function of a unitary change in each of the X variables. The signs of the estimated parameters β would indicate whether the effect of each variable X is positive or negative.

BUT WHERE ARE THE ACTORS?

No doubt, the application of statistical models of the type of equation (1) has produced a great deal of knowledge about human behavior in the social sciences. In the study of strikes, for instance, such models, estimated in a variety of institutional settings, leave little doubt that the temporal dynamics of strikes is affected, negatively, by the level of unemployment and, positively, by short-run labor-oriented parties in government (but negatively by long-run labor-oriented parties in government, as in Scandinavian countries) (for a survey of strike research, see Franzosi, 1989). My own work on post-Second World War Italian strikes has confirmed these findings and has also shown how Italy's dual bargaining structure, with national, industry-wide contracts and local, firm-based contracts, has produced distinctive, three-year cyclical patterns in strike indicators (Franzosi, 1994: 153–87).

Beck and Tolnay (1990: 531) used an equation such as equation (1) to estimate the relationship between the lynching of blacks in the Deep South between 1882 and 1930 and various conditions (e.g. size of black populations, percentage of blacks, black crime rate, deflated price of cotton, inflation in cotton prices, cotton bales produced). On the basis of their estimates of the parameters $\beta_0, \beta_1, \beta_2 \ldots \beta_k$ they conclude:

> Net of other factors, lynchings were more frequent in years when the "constant dollar" price of cotton was declining and inflationary pressure was increasing. Relative size of the black

> population was also positively related to lynching. We conclude that mob violence against southern blacks responded to economic conditions affecting the financial fortunes of southern whites – especially marginal white farmers. These effects were significantly more important in the decades before 1900, possibly because of the declining importance of agriculture, the "Jim Crow" disenfranchisement of blacks, and the increasing out-migration of blacks and whites from the Deep South.

And yet, for all these findings, there is more to strikes and lynchings than regression coefficients. Where are the actors? Where are the state, the employers, and, paradoxically, even the workers in an equation of strikes? Similarly, in regression models of lynchings, where is the Negro – the alleged perpetrator of a crime, sexual crime in particular, captured, tortured, emasculated, burned alive at the stake, his body parts carved out, pickled, and sold as souvenirs – the sheriffs, the mob, the prominent citizens who, confronting the mob, occasionally stood up against summary justice, the men, women, and children who danced at gala parties during and after the event, the photographs taken and sold by the thousands as postcards, like the one of a young man standing in a crowd under the charred corpse of Jesse Washington hanging from a utility pole sent back home with these words: 'This is the Barbecue we had last night[;] my picture is to the left with a cross over it[;] your son Joe' (picture No. 22 in the collection by James Allen and John Littlefield in www.withoutsanctuary.org). Indeed, where are the actors? Nowhere to be seen; forgotten, behind the coefficients of cotton price and percentage of blacks in a county.

Not everyone forgot the actors, of course. The historians certainly never forgot the actors and the event (Franzosi, 1996). And even social scientists have produced excellent monographs in the ethnographic/participant observation tradition where the actor, rather than the variable, plays the main character. Such is Raper's landmark sociological study of lynching (1933) or Fantasia's study of strikes (1988), to cite only two studies. Yet, is quantity *versus* quality, variables *versus* actors the only option? Is there a way to combine quantity and quality, variables and actors?

FROM EVENT COUNTS TO EVENT PROPERTIES

Ted Robert Gurr, an American political scientist who has dedicated a lifetime to the quantitative study of events, back in 1974 wrote that researchers 'repeatedly and mistakenly treat counts of conflict events as though they were conflict properties' (Gurr, 1974: 251). He recommended a shift in research focus from event counts to 'properties of conflict such as its duration, intensity, scale, and impact, either in single events or at the national level' (Gurr, 1974: 250). Gurr's ambitions, in retrospect, were rather limited (but the technology, or at least its knowledge in the social sciences, was simply not there yet for anything more ambitious). He stopped short of recommending a focus on actors, their actions in time and space, and their interactions. My goal in this chapter is to take Gurr's idea of conflict properties one step further to include actors and actions. I will illustrate a research technique that, by exploiting invariant linguistics properties of narrative, allows researchers to go 'from words to numbers', to combine narrative quality to statistical quantity: QNA (Quantitative Narrative Analysis).

Narrative and story grammars

The newspaper article of Dudley Morgan's lynching is a typical narrative text. This type of texts has been shown to have distinct, and perhaps invariant, structural properties, namely: (1) it is characterized by chronologically ordered sequences of events; (2) the number of steps in these sequences is limited and invariant within specific types of narrative; (3) the events are basically actors doing something pro or against other actors; (4) these events are typically expressed linguistically in terms of the simple surface structure Subject-Verb-Object, SVO (the canonical form of the language) (on narrative analysis, see Franzosi, 1998b, 2004).

Sequences (story versus plot)

The sequential nature of narrative is, no doubt, a distinguishing feature of narrative. For Labov (1972: 360–9), narrative is 'one method of recapitulating past experience by matching a verbal sequence of clauses to the sequence of events which (it is inferred) actually occurred', a definition that was to be repeated endlessly with minor variations: 'narrative ... [is] a succession of events' (Rimmon-Kenan, 1983: 2–3); 'The distinguishing feature of narrative is its linear organization of events' (Cohan and Shires, 1988: 52–3); 'A minimalist definition of narrative might be: A perceived sequence of non-randomly connected events' (Toolan, 1988: 7).

On the basis of a sequence of events, in the 1920s, the Russian formalists introduced the distinction between *story* vs. *plot* in narrative (*fabula* vs. *sjužet*) – distinction preserved by the French structuralists of the 1960s. For Tomashevski (1965: 67), 'plot (*sjužet*) is distinct from story (*fabula*). Both include the same events, but in the plot the events are arranged and connected according to the orderly sequence in which they were presented in the work'. The plot, in other words, refers to the way events are presented by the author to the reader. The story refers to a skeletal description of the fundamental events in their natural logical and chronological order (perhaps, with an equally skeletal listing of the roles of the characters in the story) (Bal, 1977: 4; Toolan, 1988: 9). It is the story – the chronological succession of events – that provides the essential building blocks of narrative. Without story there is no narrative (Rimmon-Kenan, 1983: 15). A story implies a change in situations where the unfolding of a specific sequence of events disrupts an initial state of equilibrium setting in motion an inversion of situation, a change of fortunes: from good to bad (tragedy, in the old Aristotelian poetics), from bad to good (comedy) (Tomashevski, 1965: 70; Prince, 1973: 28; Todorov, 1990: 30). In a sequence, some actions and events play a greater role than others in altering a narrative situation; they are sequential rather than consequential.[1]

The story of Dudley Morgan's lynching certainly presents this distinctive feature of a sequenced set of events, and where certain events are consequential, rather than sequential: Dudley Morgan's alleged assault of Mrs McKay (consequential action), *then* the authorities' arrest of the victim, *then* the mob's snatching of the victim from the authorities (consequential action), *then* the burning of the victim, *then* Mrs McKay's arrival to the field, *then* the relic hunters' taking of body parts as souvenirs, *then* the photo shoots, *then* … *then* … Of Dudley Morgan, we know 'the last words of the doomed man': 'tell my wife good-by'. Not all narratives of lynching tell us the victim's last words. Some do. Some tell us that the sheriffs resisted the mob's assault to the jail (sometimes, at the price of their lives). Some don't. Some lynchings end with the burning of the captive at the stake, like Dudley Morgan. Some don't – although most of them end with the hanging of the captive. It was Propp, in his seminal *Morphology of the Folktale* (1958[1928]), who argued that narrative (Russian folktales, in his case) is characterized by a finite set of 'functions' (31 of them, in fact, and where a function is a character performing a given action) and that these functions and their sequences are invariant across the wide variety of folktales – a stable form for a wide variety of contents. The question is: does the sequence of actions in lynching narratives possess fixed and predictable properties, like the Russian folktales (on these issues, see Griffin, 1993; see also Stovel, 2001)? More generally, do specific types of events (e.g. strikes, race riots) present distinct and invariant sequences of functions (actions)? Only a comparative analysis of event narratives would help us provide an answer to these questions.

Events and story grammars

If narrative is a sequence of events, what is an event? An event is a 'thing that happens', but not just any 'thing', but 'something that can be summed up by a verb or a name of action' (Rimmon-Kenan, 1983: 2). An event, then, is an action performed by human beings (or personified beings in narrative fiction). Actions, indeed, are the verbs found in the narrative of Dudley Morgan's lynching (e.g. assail, arrive, snatch, pile flammable material, torture, take photos). Linguistically, an event is typically expressed as the simple micro-level structure Subject-Verb-Object (SVO). The SVO structure is a general form of the language, and not just of narrative (indeed, 'the canonical form of the language'); but in narrative, both Subject and Object are typically social actors or organizations and the Verb is a verb of doing or saying (i.e. a social action). In narrative, the SVO structure has also been referred to as a 'story grammar'.[2]

A story grammar can be as simple as the basic three elements of the 'semantic triplet' SVO – the subject, the action, and the object of the action – or very complex, with the addition of a number of modifiers for each element of the SVO (such as type, number, organization, name and last name of the Subject and

Object and time, space, reason, outcome, instrument of Verb). Thus, the basic template of a story grammar broadly corresponds to the five Ws of journalism – Who, What, When, Where, Why – with the potential addition of several more elements.

Relationships between the various elements (or categories) of a story grammar can be expressed formally and rigorously with the help of 'rewrite rules'. Through a rewrite rule, we can express the simple SVO structure (or semantic triplet) in terms of its basic components:

<semantic triplet> → {<subject>} {<verb>} [{<object>}]

where the symbol → refers to a rewrite rule (or production), whereby an element to the left of the rule can be rewritten in terms of the elements to its right.[3] Each element of the triplet can then be further rewritten, down to its 'terminal' symbols (those found in the language itself):

<subject> → {<actor>} [{<characteristics>}]
<actor> → crowd | mob | posse | negro | sheriff | ...
<characteristics> → [{<type>}] [{<number>}] [{<organization>}] [{<space>}]
...
<verb> → <verbal expression> [{<circumstances>}]
<verbal expression> → bring | burn | shoot | kill | hang | ...
< circumstances > → [{<time>}] [{<space>}] [{<reason>}] [{<instrument>}] [{<outcome>}] ...
<object> → <subject>

An example

Using a story grammar of this kind, as a way of illustration, we can 'code' a few triplets from the Dudley Morgan's narrative.

Semantic triplet 1: (Subject: (Actor: *Dudley Morgan*) (Characteristics: (Race: *Negro*))) (Verb: (Verbal expression: *assail*) (Circumstances: (Type of action: *allegedly*))) (Object: (Actor: *Mrs McKay*))

Semantic triplet 2: (Subject: (Actor: *?*)) (Verb: (Verbal expression: *arrest*)) (Object: (Actor: *Dudley Morgan*))

Semantic triplet 3: (Subject: (Actor: *officers*)) (Verb: (Verbal expression: *take*) (Circumstances: (Space: (City: *Lansing*) (Direction: *to*)) (Instrument: *by train*)))

Semantic triplet 4: (Subject: (Actor: *crowd*) (Characteristics: (Number: *4,000*) (Subset: (Number: *mostly*) (Type: *armed*)))) (Verb: (Verbal expression: *snatch*)) (Object: (Actor: *Dudley Morgan*))

Semantic triplet 5: (Subject: (Actor: *crowd*)) (Verb: (Verbal expression: *take*) (Circumstances: (Space: (Location: *large field on the edge of town*) (Direction: *to*))))

...

The example shows that most narrative information found in the original newspaper article also appears in the coded output. Furthermore, coded output within the categories of a story grammar preserves much of the narrative flavor of the original text. But if this is quantitative narrative analysis, where are the numbers? To get to the numbers we need a further step: implement a story grammar in a relational database environment and then use SQL (Structured Query Language) to get frequency distributions of values within the various objects of the grammar (the numbers, at last).

COMPUTER APPLICATIONS OF A STORY GRAMMAR

The relational properties of a story grammar (with Subjects/actors related to Verbs/actions related to Objects/actors and where all these relationships are rigorously expressed through rewrite rules) lend themselves to the implementation of such complex linguistic schemes in a computer environment within RDBMS (Relational Database Management Systems). In many ways, without computer software there can be no application of a story grammar approach to narrative for a socio-historical project on a large scale. The sheer complexity and sophistication of such schemes as story grammars would limit their use to trivial, illustrative examples. For this reason, I have developed a specialized computer program for the analysis of narrative texts: PC-ACE[4] (Program for Computer-Assisted Coding of Events).[5] PC-ACE organizes information in a relational data format, with different text elements stored in different computer tables in the same database. PC-ACE does not do the hard work of automatically parsing text within the categories of a story grammar (Artificial Intelligence has yet to deliver on early promises of computer understanding of natural languages). All PC-ACE does (or any other currently available software of textual analysis, for that matter, except for basic word counts) is to provide a computerized tool that makes the task of sorting information within the categories of a story grammar easier and more reliable for a human coder.[6]

Using a complex story grammar and PC-ACE, over the last 30 years, I have been involved in three different socio-historical projects based on newspapers as sources of data:[7] industrial versus service-sector labor conflicts (some 14,000 newspaper articles coded yielding over 30,000 semantic triplets; Franzosi, 1997), the rise of Italian fascism between 1919 and 1922 (over 50,000 newspaper articles coded from three different newspapers and other historical sources, yielding some 300,000 semantic triplets; Franzosi, 1997, 1999), lynching events of African Americans in the US state of Georgia between 1875 and 1930.

DATA ANALYSIS

Despite the complexity of PC-ACE's relational database design (with tens of tables and specific information stored in specific tables, such as actors in an actor_table and actions in an action_table), the size of such datasets (with hundreds of thousands of objects coded), and the nature of the data (basically, words), the relational properties of the database make data queries (i.e. extracting information from the database) general via a simple query language: SQL (Structured Query Language). Through SQL, we can find answers to such questions as: What did sheriffs do? Were the victims of a lynching mob men or women, young or old? Were victims burned inside or outside a town? How did the black community react to lynching events? Similarly, on the rise of Italian fascism, we can approach such long-standing questions as: Did workers engage in violence during the 1919–1920 period of high working-class mobilization? Did fascist violence strike where workers had been most militant? What role did the landed elite or the police play in facilitating fascism? Which form did fascist violence take? Who/what were the targets of the violence?

SQL allows to extract information from a relational database and to convert words into frequency distributions (i.e. numbers) – numbers that can then be analyzed using standard multivariate statistical techniques (namely, factor analysis, Franzosi, 2004: 113–15, regression models, Franzosi, 2004: 115–17, or logistic models, Franzosi, 1994). However, the nature of the data collected via a computerized story grammar lends itself to novel approaches to the analysis of qualitative data, in particular, network analysis and Geographic Information Systems.[8]

Network analysis and its directed graphs provide an ideal tool to map the network of social actors involved in any event and their reciprocal roles, with a homologous relationship between story grammars (with subjects/actors related to objects/actors via a given action; 'mob burns negro') and network codes and relations (Franzosi, 1998a, 1999, 2004: 100–109; on network analysis, see Scott, 1992, and Wasserman and Faust, 1994). Figure 19.1 provides a picture of such a directed graph of some 387 actions of violence during lynching events in Georgia during the 1875–1930 period taken from various local and national newspapers. The graph clearly brings out the social relations of lynching violence: the negro (and his violence against women and/or white men), the mob and the crowd with their violence against negros, the police.

The availability of detailed temporal and spatial information on each event (and on individual actions within each event) that a grammar makes available can be used to map event/action distribution and diffusion through space (e.g. see the distribution of lynching events in Georgia by county in the map of Figure 19.2).

CONCLUSIONS

In this chapter, I have illustrated a technique (QNA) for the quantitative analysis of narrative data. With the help of three disciplines – linguistics/literary criticism, computer science, and statistics – I have set up a way to go 'from words to numbers'. QNA preserves much of the richness of information of events as expressed in the original textual, narrative form, while at the same time allowing the statistical analysis of the information.

Quantitative narrative analysis is based on invariant linguistic properties of the text itself. This is contrary to content analysis (see Franzosi, 2008), the traditional social science technique for analyzing quantitatively textual information, where coding schemes vary from project to project and are based on the investigator's specific substantive and theoretical interests. Furthermore, in QNA, the categories of the coding scheme (i.e. the story grammar) are rigorously interrelated through a set of rewrite rules. The downside of the approach is that it applies to narrative texts only – however broad this class of texts may be. Only narrative texts, in fact, possess the invariant linguistic properties highlighted in this chapter.

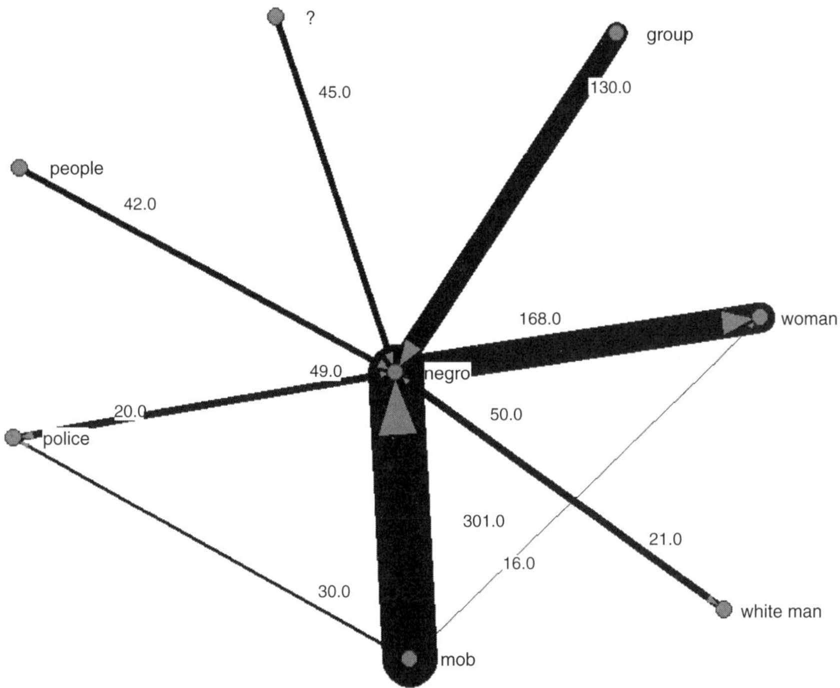

Figure 19.1 Network graph of lynching narratives (Georgia, 1875–1930)

Contrary to traditional, variable-based statistical approaches, the data made available by QNA – actors related to other actors via a set of actions in time and space – lend themselves to new types of statistical analyses focused on actors and actions rather than variables (e.g. network models, Geographic Information System models of spatio-temporal diffusion, sequence analysis) (see Franzosi, 2010). Traditional, regression-based statistical techniques aim to explain variations in a 'dependent' variable Y as a function of unitary changes in a set of k 'independent' variables X_1, X_2, ... , X_k. QNA and the statistical techniques most homologous with its data (e.g. network models) tackle different research questions: Who did what, when and where, and for what reasons? What was the role of the various social actors in the unfolding of an event (e.g. lynching, strike)? Furthermore, is there a 'typical' sequence of actions in a lynching or strike event?

In an academic world where social scientists are bitterly divided into opposing camps of quality *versus* quantity, QNA provides a way to link quality *and* quantity, words *and* numbers. As such, QNA has much in common with Charles Ragin's QCA approach (Qualitative Comparative Analysis). As Ragin and Rubinson (2009: 13) write:

> the comparative method-sometimes referred to as 'small-*N* comparison-constitutes a distinctive approach to understanding social phenomena. Frequently, comparative methods

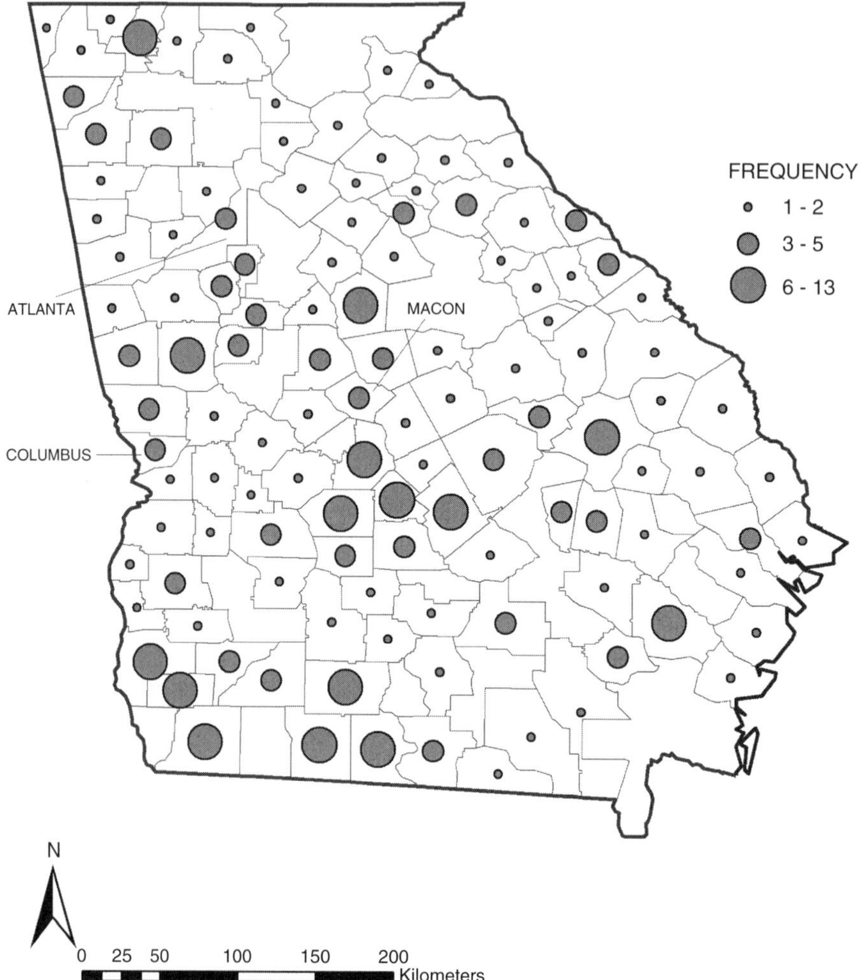

Figure 19.2 Geographic distribution of lynching events by county (Georgia, 1875–1930)

are portrayed as a 'bridge' between qualitative, case-oriented research and quantitative, variable-oriented research.

After all, like QCA, QNA is also 'fundamentally *set theoretic* in nature' (Ragin and Rubinson, 2009: 1; original emphasis) (on QNA and set theory see Franzosi, 1994, 2004: 89–91, 97–100, 109–113). Furthermore, like QCA, QNA is also fundamentally comparative. Contrary to QCA, however, QNA's comparisons are typically carried out on thousands (rather than tens) of cases (i.e. event narratives, with each event narrative providing a case).

NOTES

1 Consequential actions have also been called dynamic motifs (Tomashevski, 1965: 70), cardinal functions (or nuclei) (Barthes, 1977: 93–4), and kernels (Chatman, 1978: 32, 53–6; Rimmon-Kenan, 1983: 16), while sequential actions are static motifs, catalysers, and satellites.

2 Story grammars have a long tradition, starting from Propp's seminal work (1958/1928), Greimas (1966, 1971), van Dijk (1972), Halliday (1994); see also, Todorov (1969: 27–8; more generally, Todorov, 1969: 27–41; 1977: 218–33; 1981: 48–51; Chatman, 1978: 91; Prince, 1973: 32, 92–3); on story grammars, see Franzosi (1989, 1994, 2004: 43–51).

3 The angular brackets < > denote elements that can be further rewritten; while 'terminal elements', i.e. the words or linguistic expressions found in the text, have no < >. Curly brackets { } denote elements that can occur more than one time; while square brackets [ ] denote optional elements. Thus, in the clause 'victim screams' there is only one participant (the agent), while the clause 'mob kills negro' has two participants (the agent, mob, and the goal or patient, negro). As a result, the grammar requires only the first participant; the second is optional.

4 PC-ACE is an application of Microsoft Access 2007. The current release is available in the public domain for free download at www.pc-ace.com.

5 It is possible to implement a very basic story grammar in qualitative data analysis software such as ATLAS.ti (see Franzosi, 2010).

6 In PC-ACE, each item of information stored, is cross-referenced to a specific source of information (newspaper name, date, page, column). In the case of multiple stories on the same event, irreconcilable, contradictory information can be coded as such, thus allowing multiple analyses for the same events from the standpoint of different sources.

7 Newspapers have long been relied upon by historians and social scientists as sources of historical data (on this issue, see Franzosi, 1987, 2004: 167–72, 180; Earl et al., 2004; Ortiz et al., 2005).

8 The sequential nature of narrative data collected on the basis of a story grammar (basically, ordered skeleton narrative sentences) also points to a one-to-one correspondence between story grammars and sequence analysis (Abbott and Barman, 1997; Abbot and Tsay, 2000; Bison, 2010; for an application of sequence analysis to lynching data, see Stovel, 2001). The technique can be used to test the existence of predictable sequences in the unfolding of events (e.g. Franzosi, 2010).

REFERENCES

Abbot, Andrew and Emily Barman (1997). 'Sequence comparison via alignment and gibbs sampling'. *Sociological Methodology*, 27: 47–87.

Abbot, Andrew and Angela Tsay (2000). 'Sequence analysis and optimal matching methods in sociology'. *Sociological Methods and Research*, 29: 3–33.

Barthes, Roland (1977) (1966). 'Introduction to the Structural Analysis of Narratives'. In Roland Barthes, *Image Music Text.* Essays Selected and Translated by Stephen Heath, pp. 79–124. London: Fontana Press.

Beck, E.M. and Stewart E. Tolnay (1990). 'The killing fields of the deep south: The market for cotton and the lynching of blacks, 1882–1930'. *American Sociological Review*, 55(4): 526–39.

Bal, Mieke (1977). 'Narratologie'. *Essais sur la signification narrative dans quatre romans modernes.* Paris: Editions Klincksieck.

Bison, Ivano (2010). 'Lexicographic index: A new measurement of resemblance among sequences'. In Malcolm Williams and W. Paul Vogt (eds) *Handbook of Methodological Innovations in the Social Sciences.* Thousand Oaks, CA: Sage.

Chatman, Seymour (1978). 'Story and Discourse'. *Narrative Structure in Fiction and Film.* Ithaca, NY: Cornell University Press.

Cohan, Steven and Linda M. Shires (1988). *Telling Stories: A Theoretical Analysis of Narrative Fiction.* New York: Routledge.

Dijk, Teun A. van (1972). *Some Aspects of Text Grammars: A Study in Theoretical Linguistics and Poetics.* Paris: Mouton.

Earl, Jennifer, Andrew Martin, John D. McCarthy, and Sarah A. Soule (2004). 'The use of newspaper data in the study of collective action'. *Annual Review of Sociology,* 30: 65–80.

Fantasia, Rick (1988). *Cultures of Solidarity: Consciousness, Action, and Contemporary American Workers.* Berkeley, CA: University of California Press.

Franzosi, Roberto (1987). 'The press as a source of socio-historical data: Issues in the methodology of data collection from newspapers'. *Historical Methods,* 20(1): 5–16.

Franzosi, Roberto (1989). 'One hundred years of strike statistics: Methodological and theoretical issues in quantitative strike research'. *Industrial and Labor Relations Review,* 42(3): 348–62.

Franzosi, Roberto (1994). 'From words to numbers: A set theory framework for the collection, organization, and analysis of narrative data'. In Peter Marsden (ed.) *Sociological Methodology,* 24: 105–36. Oxford: Basil Blackwell.

Franzosi, Roberto (1995). *The Puzzle of Strikes: Class and State Strategies in Postwar Italy.* Cambridge: Cambridge University Press.

Franzosi, Roberto (1996). 'A sociologist meets history. Critical reflections upon practice'. *The Journal of Historical Sociology,* 9(3): 354–92.

Franzosi, Roberto (1997). 'Mobilization and Counter-Mobilization Processes: From the `Red Years' (1919–20) to the 'Black Years' (1921–22) in Italy. A New Methodological Approach to the Study of Narrative Data'. In John Mohr and Roberto Franzosi (eds) Theory and Society. Special double issue on *New Directions in Formalization and Historical Analysis,* 26(2–3): 275–304.

Franzosi, Roberto (1998a). 'Narrative as data. Linguistic and statistical tools for the quantitative study of historical events'. In Marcel van der Linden and Larry Griffin (eds) New methods in historical sociology/social history. Special issue of *International Review of Social History,* 43: 81–104.

Franzosi, Roberto (1998b). 'Narrative analysis – Why (and how) sociologists should be interested in narrative'. In John Hagan (ed.) *The Annual Review of Sociology,* pp. 517–54. Palo Alto: Annual Reviews.

Franzosi, Roberto (1999). 'The Return of the Actor. Networks of Interactions among Social Actors during Periods of High Mobilization (Italy, 1919–22)'. In Dieter Rucht and Ruud Koopmans (eds), 'Protest Event Analysis'. Special issue of *Mobilization,* 4(2): 131–49.

Franzosi, Roberto (2004). *From Words to Numbers: Narrative, Data, and Social Science.* Cambridge: Cambridge University Press.

Franzosi, Roberto (2008). *Content Analysis.* 4 Vols. Thousand Oaks, CA: Sage.

Franzosi, Roberto (2010) (in press). *Quantitative Narrative Analysis.* Thousand Oaks, CA: Sage.

Ginzburg, Ralph (1962). *100 Years of Lynchings.* Baltimore, MD: Black Classic Press.

Greimas, Algirdas Julien (1966). *Semantinque structurale. Recerche de methode.* Paris: Larousse.

Greimas, Algirdas Julien (1971). 'Narrative Grammar: Units and Levels'. *Modern Language Notes,* 86: 793–806.

Griffin, Larry (1993). 'Narrative, event-structure analysis, and causal interpretation in historical sociology', *American Journal of Sociology,* 98(5): 1094–133.

Gurr, Ted Robert (1974). 'The neo-Alexandrians: a review essay on data handbooks in political science'. *American Political Science Review,* 68: 243–52.

Halliday, M.A.K. (1994) (1985). *An Introduction to Functional Grammar.* London: Edward Arnold.

Labov, William (1972). *Language in the Inner City.* Philadelphia: University of Pennsylvania Press.

Ortiz, David G., Daniel J. Myers, Eugene N. Walls, and Maria-Elena D. Diaz (2005). 'Where do we stand with newspaper data?'. *Mobilization: An International Quarterly,* 10(3): 397–419.

Prince, Gerald (1973). A Grammar of Stories; an Introduction. D*e proprietatibus litterarum; Series minor,* Vol. 13. Paris: Mouton.

Propp, Vladimir 1958 [1928]. *Morphology of the Folktale.* Edited with an introduction by Svatava Pirkova-Jakobson. Translated by Laurence Scott. Indiana University Research Center in Anthropology, Folklore, and Linguistics, Publication 10. Bloomington, *Indiana. International Journal of American*

Linguistics, 14(4). Bibliographical and Special Series of the American Folklore Society 9. Philadelphia.

Ragin, Charles C. and Claude Rubinson (2009). 'The distinctiveness of comparative research'. In Todd Landman and Neil Robinson (eds) *The Sage Handbook of Comparative Politics*, pp. 13–34. Thousand Oaks, CA: Sage.

Raper, Arthur F. (1933). *The Tragedy of Lynching*. Chapel Hill, NC: The University of North Carolina Press.

Rimmon-Kenan, Slomith (1983). *Narrative Fiction: Contemporary Poetics*. London: Methuen.

Scott, John (1992). *Social Network Analysis: A Handbook*. Thousand Oaks, CA: Sage.

Stovel, Katherine Wellesley (2001). 'Local sequential patterns: The structure of lynching in the deep south, 1882–1930'. *Social Forces*, 79(3): 843–80.

Tilly, Charles (1978). *From Mobilization to Revolution*. Englewood Cliffs, NJ: Prentice–Hall.

Tilly, Charles (1995). *Popular Contention in Great Britain, 1758–1834*. Cambridge, MA: Harvard University Press.

Tilly, Charles (2007). *Contentious Performances*. Columbia University: Unpublished book manuscript.

Todorov, Tzvetan (1969). *Grammaire du Décaméron*. Paris: Mouton.

Todorov, Tzvetan (1981) (1968). *Introduction to Poetics*. Sussex: The Harvester Press.

Todorov, Tzvetan (1977) (1971). *The Poetics of Prose*. Oxford: Basil Blackwell.

Todorov, Tzvetan (1990) (1978). *Genres in Discourse*. Cambridge: Cambridge University Press.

Tomashevski, Boris (1965) (1925). 'Thematics'. In Lee Lemon and Marion Reis (eds) *Russian Formalist Criticism: Four Essays*, pp. 61–95. Lincoln: University of Nebraska Press.

Toolan, Michael (1988). *Narrative: A Critical Linguistic Introduction*. London: Routledge.

Wasserman, Stanley and Katherine Faust (1994). *Social Network Analysis in the Social and Behavioral Sciences*. Cambridge: Cambridge University Press.

20

Lexicographic Index: A New Measurement of Resemblance Among Sequences

Ivano Bison

WHY SEQUENCE ANALYSIS?

Sequence analysis is for many things. It is to inquire *why people have certain kinds of careers* and not others (Abbott, 1990). It is to observe a single whole social phenomenon as it unfolds over time (Abbott, 1990). It is to believe that certain careers can be produced by certain initial conditions, and that certain careers can explain, in their turn, the choices of people and groups. It is a body of questions about social processes and a collection of techniques available to answer them (Abbott, 1995: 94). It is to adopt a theoretical, methodological and technical perspective to investigate the underlying generative mechanisms that regulate the formation of the life cycles of individuals and groups. It returns us a reality not mediated by the statistical parameter. It is to set order on chaos. It is to discover that the world is less strange, bizarre and complex than we believe and than it could be.

For example, consider the following eight conditions of labor market participation: self-employment; pseudo-self-employment; training; fixed contract employment; fully protected employment; employment without a contract; unemployment; not in the labor force. Nothing prevents these eight conditions from combining freely in time. If 60 months (five years) are considered, the number of the possible orders that a working career could assume is around 15 followed by 53 zeros. In other words, if for every second that passes the actual world population of 6.7 billion people was entirely replaced by as many people, and every single person followed an order different from all those that had preceded, and within this one second there unfolded a 60-month-long sequence, then completing the entire number of possible sequences would require a number of years equal to 72 followed by 35 zeros; around 528259447303585533447899551 times the actual age of the universe. Moreover, but with a probability of 4×10^{-108}, there is no possibility of observing two people with the same working career.

Is this impressive? Absolutely not! We are considering only the possible combinations that eight conditions can assume in a brief time-span of 60 months and not in the subject's entire lifetime, where other events (educational, familial, etc.) enter in action and in combination with a job or career, producing a very large number of combinations.

This is obviously if the system were without constraints and the elements that compose it could randomly combine with each other. However, this is not the case. The number of possible combinations is much smaller. An individual cannot change jobs every day, cannot get married and divorced every month, cannot have more than a certain number of children, cannot have more than a certain number of friendship relationships.

If this were not true, if indeed all the possible elements that make up social reality could freely combine with each other, without any constraints, without any rules, we would have perhaps neither a social system nor a social structure. We would have a set of monad-individuals for whom the knowledge accumulated in interaction with one subject would not be of help in understanding another subject. We would recognize nobody and nobody could recognize us.

Biological, physiological, environmental, social, and cultural bonds drastically reduce the number of possible combinations with which social reality manifests itself. However, this is still not enough to explain why this happens. We can only obtain the answer if we consider time; that same time which is itself a potential cause of complexity.

Every event, every episode, every career is the result of processes that began in the past, each with its own timing, each with its own regularity, each with its own causal pace. Over time, every event is influenced by the prior event and in turn, over time, it will influence future events. From this perspective, time can no longer be understood as a simple organizer of events, but rather as an orchestra conductor who imposes order and rhythm on events. We may say that 'Time is a device to prevent everything happening at once'. (cited in Bernstein, 2004).

Like physical reality, social reality also admits to only a certain number of possible combinations among elements. These in their turn do not give rise to an endless and random number of orders but to a finite number of coherent possible patterns or sequences in which we can recognize similarity and regularity; and in which we can seek the underlying generative mechanisms, constraints and constants that regulate the formation of the life histories of individuals and the groups.

In this scenario, sequence analysis is a powerful theoretical, methodological and technical tool with which to understand, interpret and analyze the world around us, starting from direct observation of the realizations of single individuals, not from the analysis of their attributes (the variables), and seeking similarities, regularities, patterns. 'Is to observe the temporal facet of this move towards context, a turn towards process and events that has taken shape in something called "sequence analysis"?' (Abbott, 1995: 95).

WHY A NEW MEASURE OF RESEMBLANCE?

As already pointed out in the chapter in this volume by Martin and Wiggins, many doubts and criticisms have been expressed in respect of Optimal Matching Analysis (OMA) (Dijkstra and Taris, 1995; Wu, 2000; Levine, 2000; Elzinga 2003). These criticisms have in some way seriously undermined the credibility of the entire theoretical and methodological framework at the base of the sequences analysis developed by Abbott.[1] As Elzinga (2003) rightly points out, optimal matching has over time become the standard technique, so much so that the terms 'sequence analysis' and 'optimal matching technique' are used synonymously. As a result of this terminological confusion, criticisms against optimal matching have been implicitly extended to the entire range of sequence analysis.

Since then, all studies that use the OMA devote at least a paragraph to defending and justifying it. Yet the criticisms have had an indubitable role in inducing researchers to find both solutions to the problems of the OMA, for example new methods of costs definition, and other ways to measure the resemblance among sequences (Dijkstra and Taris, 1995; Dijkstra, 2001; Elzinga, 2003; Bison, 2004, 2006).

The OMA's main problem lies precisely in its main strength: that is, the possibility of defining a distance among sequences according to their degree of similarity. As shown by Dijkstra and Taris (1995) and Elzinga (2003), even if two sequences have some elements in common but in different positions, they may be as dissimilar as a third sequence without any element in common with the other two.

This problem is not resolved with an appropriate substitution cost matrix. Instead, everything becomes more complicated. Serious doubts have been raised concerning: (a) the arbitrariness of the definition of the substitution cost matrix; (b) the assumption of symmetry of distance between two states[2]; (c) the impossibility of capturing both the inner timing of every single sequence and the general timing of the entire system. Substitution cost matrix and indel cost are blind to time and memory loss.

Nor convincing are the solutions proposed in recent years, although they are of a certain interest. The adoption of a substitution cost matrix obtained as the inverse of the probability of observing a transition between two states is as risky as the previous proposals. If on the one hand, the proposal reduces the arbitrariness of the researcher in defining the costs, on the other it does not consider that unlikely events may be highly probable under specific conditions. Probabilities can change over time. For instance, the probability of fertility, marriage, job event can have a different temporal shape across age, cohort, and period. Probability may differ within different groups. The probability of entering unemployment among a group of graduates is less than among a group of low educated people. Yet both groups will be assigned the same probability obtained as the 'mean' of the probabilities of the two separate groups. This penalizes both the group in which the transition is most probable and the group in which this transition is less or not at all probable.

The second problem concerns the inability of the OMA to handle complex events of multiple, parallel tracks of sequence. Suppose that we want to study a working couple's careers. In this case, His career and Her career interact in time to give rise to the couple's career. Taken individually, each of these two sequences takes the form of a series of mutually exclusive episodes. The problem is therefore how to codify two interacting sequences composed of a plurality of mutually exclusive events.

The only strategy available for dealing with multiple, parallel tracks of sequence information in the OMA framework is to create sequences of complex 'events' by cross-classifying a number of simple events. This operation has a number of consequences. First, as Abbott pointed out, using combinations of events requires one to pay '... the price of losing all information about the temporal "shape" of events – their duration and their intensity in terms of producing occurrence – in short their time horizon'. (Abbott, 1990: 146). Second, there is the risk that distinct careers will be tied together, although the order of causality may be bi-directional. Third, 'these various combinatory codings of events create serious complexities in the setting of replacement costs' (Abbott and Tsay, 2000). Finally, reducing everything to a combination of events means losing large part of the variability inherent in each single career.

The third problem concerns the output. The OMA outcome is a symmetric distance matrix between sequences themselves. This symmetric matrix can be used as input in a limited number of data reduction techniques like hierarchical classification (hierarchical cluster) and multidimensional scaling (MDS). This excludes a wide range of techniques with strongest heuristics of classification, such as the 'Fuzzy Cluster' and the 'Self-Organize Map', which do not require distance matrix in input.

It is therefore easy to understand that the limits, doubts, the theoretical perplexities concerning OMA, as well as its techniques applied to the social sciences require us to find new approaches and new ideas. In what follows I shall put forward a proposal.

ORDER AS DISTANCE

In the above paragraph, I have underlined that the first main problem of OMA derives from the way in which similarity between two sequences are defined.

In general, two sequences are equal when they comprise the same elements in the same order and two sequences are maximally different when they have no elements in common (as regards order and type of elements). In other words, imagine that four women are being observed for a period of length 2, and that whether or not they give birth to a child in each time interval is recorded, thus obtaining the following four different sequences: A {0,0}; B {0,1}; C {1,0} and D {1,1}.

With the methods proposed, the distances between sequences BC and AD are greater than the distances between the sequences AB, AC, DB and DC. In fact, A and D do not have elements in common; nor do – in the same order – B and C.

But what is meant by 'maximally dissimilar'? Whilst it is evident that if two sequences share the same number of elements in the same order they are maximally similar, it is less clear what 'maximally dissimilar' signifies. In other words, is the number of shared elements the only possible way in which we can establish the distance between two sequences?

In the above example, woman A had no fertility events during the observation period; woman B had a fertility event immediately before the conclusion of the observation period; woman C had a fertility event at the beginning of the observation period; and woman D had two fertility events, one at the beginning and one at the end of the observation period. It is clear that in this case it is difficult to say that the women B and C are maximally distant: both had just one child, the only difference being that they did so at different moments of the observation period, while it is reasonable to believe that the distance between A and D is maximum. The problem therefore resides in the importance given to the temporal order of the events, their numerousness, and the presence of shared elements when the distance is calculated.

The principal focus of the above-cited studies is the search by means of pairwise comparison for common elements, but this may not be the only way to establish distances (similarities or differences) between sequences. If the sequences are ordered according to the number of observed events and, all observed events being equal, an order is established along the temporal axis in which the events have occurred, then woman B, who had her fertility event immediately before conclusion of the observation, follows (is logically closer to) woman A, who had no fertility event during the observation period;[3] woman C follows A and B in that she also had only one child, but did so before B, and obviously before A. Finally, comes, woman D, who had two fertility events and is therefore more distant from the woman who did not have any, but also from those who had only one. Hence, on considering numerousness and the order of occurrence of the events, one obtains a unilinear structure with the order A, B, C, D of the four sequences. The similarity between sequences and their proximity thus results from the order in which the events occur, not from the common elements. The order itself exhibits that the more elements there are in common, the closer the two sequences, without requiring complicated and not always clear measures to compute the weights and contributions for comparison.

The problem is therefore how to find a simple and rapid way to compute this order.

A FIRST DEFINITION OF LEXICOGRAPHIC INDEX

I can define a generic sequence as a list of episode-states observed in a particular time interval. Ideally, but also graphically, this list develops along a single dimension, that of time. For instance, suppose that one is observing labor market participation by subject A for six months. Assume that at any particular time subject A can exhibit only one of the followings three states: 1 = employed; 2 = unemployed; 3 = inactive. At the end of the six months of observation, sequence A is [123321]. Graphically, this sequence is a list of the episodes experienced by the subject in a one-dimensional space. At the beginning of the observation, A spends the first month in employment and in the second month is unemployed. At the end of the second month, s/he exits the labor market and only returns in the fifth month to seek a job. Finally, in the sixth month s/he is once again employed. Now, the question is: can we reduce a multinomial sequence to a one-dimensional list of different episodes linked in time? The answer is no. Indeed, a multinomial sequence cannot be represented by any list at all. A multinomial sequence does not exist as such; rather, it results from the co-action of the states of which it is composed. A multinomial sequence is a point in the space-time defined by the states space. The problem now is how to represent a multinomial sequence.

It is said above that every state has its own generating mechanism, which operates independently of the others. In geometric terms this signifies that each individual state defines an axis of a $\boldsymbol{q}$-dimensional space, where $\boldsymbol{q}$ is the size of the state space, that is the set of values defined in the state space that the generic sequence can assume. Each axis in its turn represents the state space of the set of all the possible orders in which a state can occur in a sequence of length $\boldsymbol{t}$. Put otherwise: a space will have as many dimensions, each orthogonal to the others, as there are states defined in $\boldsymbol{q}$. Taken individually, each dimension of this space will represent the set of all the possible realizations with which every state may occur in a binary sequence of length $\boldsymbol{t}$.

Now suppose that it is possible to attribute a value to all the elementary sequences observed so that they can be arranged along their axis. Suppose also that it is possible to draw as many orthogonal straight lines as there are axes starting from each point defined by each elementary sequence making up the multinomial sequence. The point in space defined by the intersection of all these straight lines will be the multinomial sequence. A multinomial sequence is therefore a point in the $\boldsymbol{q}$-dimensional space of the states, and its coordinates are the values of the individual elementary sequences of which it is composed.

In this way, three things are obtained. The first is that a multinomial sequence consisting of manifold states is reduced to a single point in space. The second is that the multinomial sequence is no longer a series of realizations along a one-dimensional line in which the different mechanisms that have produced it are confused in a whole. Rather, each individual state, each individual event, is free to define the form and the length of the individual lines, which in turn are free to interweave with each other to form the complicated plot of a story which has a logical narrative. Finally, and perhaps most interestingly, the distance between two multinomial sequences is the distance between two points in a Euclidean space. It will be only necessary to decide what method one wants to adopt for calculating the distance.

Moving from a multinomial sequence to its elementary sequences is straightforward. Just as a qualitative variable of k modality can be represented by k-dummy variables, so a multinomial sequence of q-states can be represented by q binary sequences. For example, the sequence A = [123321] can be represented into the following three sequences A_1 = [100001]; A_2 = [010010]; A_3 = [001100].

Still to be defined is a method to calculate the coordinates, and therefore a method to attribute univocal values to the elementary sequences. The next section provides a possible solution.

THE LEXICOGRAPHIC INDEX

The index now introduced derives from the example in the third section. The goal is instead to attribute a univocal value to each different binary sequence of length t. The intention is also for the index in question to have the properties of triangularity, symmetry and positivity proper to a distance; and even more importantly for it to take account of time; that is, of the different ways in which a state can come about in time within a binary sequence. For these various purposes, we must impose an order of all the possible binary sequences of length t. However, the problem is deciding what order to impose.

Take, for instance, the following binary sequence relative to labor market participation by A = [0101] in a period of four months. This sequence gives us two items of information. The first is that A was employed for two months. The second is that A was employed at the time t_2 and at the time t_4. A binary sequence, therefore, responds to two distinct ways of observing time. The first concerns the quantity of time and answers the question 'how long'. The second concerns the moments in which the states are realized and answers the question 'when', 'at what time'. This twofold nature of the binary sequence forms the basis of the sorting order introduced here.

The index is based on the sorting order of these two different modes of observing time. The first order is given by the quantity of time and is therefore based on the number of times that state q is observed in the sequence. The second order is given – the quantity of observed time being equal – by the 'moment' or 'moments' in the sequence when state q occurs. This second sorting order is also based on a twofold order. The first is the reverse order in which the events occur in time. It thus puts first the events that occurred last and then the events that occurred first. This solution is adopted in light of the discussion in the third section. It will be recalled that woman B with sequence [0, 1] followed woman A with sequence [0, 0]. The two sequences were considered to be closer to each other than the others because B's fertility event occurred immediately before the end of the observation period, with it being hypothesized that A would have had her own fertility event immediately after conclusion of the observation. The second order is a direct consequence of the first. The events that occur last will vary more slowly in the order than those that occurred first.

Because the nature of the sorting order is double, also the proposed index consists of two distinct parts summed together. The first part is an integer and takes account of the different amount of time recorded in each sequence. It is easy to determine the integer part $(x_i') = 2u - 1$ for $u > 0$ and 0 for $u = 0$. Hence, sequences with $u = 1$ are comprised between 1 and 2, and sequences with $u = 2$ are comprised between 3 and 4, and so on. The second part is a decimal number ranging from 0 and 1 which takes account of the different numbers of combinations displayed by the sequences with variation in the amount of time. Calculation of the decimal part is slightly more elaborate.

Suppose that there is a binary sequence x_i containing the observations of T time periods. Observation x_i can assume only two modalities represented by the numbers 0–1. These modalities we shall call absence/presence. Consider the case in which exactly u realizations equal to 1 occur. There are obviously several sequences that have this characteristic. For example (Table 20.1) sequences from 6 to 11 have $u = 2$.

The problem now is to allocate to each sequence x_i a number (x_i'') representing its position, normalized between 0 and 1, in the sorting order of the sequences. An example will aid understanding of the computational procedure. The set of the possible binary sequences x_i of length $T = 4$ are exactly $2^4 = 16$, and they are represented in Table 20.1.

Consider, for simplicity, only the

$$x_i = \binom{T}{u} = \binom{4}{2} = 6$$

sequences for $u = 2$, which are denoted in Table 20.1 by the numbers from 6 to 11. Following the chronological order, the first and second realization (the 1s) of the sequence are called s_1 and s_2. We calculate for every realization u of the sequence x_i three values $s_k\{A_k, B_k, C_k\}$, where:

$\boldsymbol{A_k}$ is the exact position of s_k in the sequence. For instance, in the sequence 6, for $\boldsymbol{s_1}$: $\boldsymbol{A_1} = 3$, and for $\boldsymbol{s_2}$: $\boldsymbol{A_2} = 4$; in the sequence 13, $\boldsymbol{s_1}$: $\boldsymbol{A_1} = 1$, $\boldsymbol{s_2}$: $\boldsymbol{A_2} = 3$, $\boldsymbol{s_3}$: $\boldsymbol{A_3} = 4$;

$\boldsymbol{B_k}$ is the maximum position that s_k can occupy within the sequence. For example, for the sequences 6, 7, 8, $\boldsymbol{s_1}$ can occupy at most position t_3 because position t_4 is occupied by $\boldsymbol{s_2}$, so that $\boldsymbol{B_1} = 3$,

Table 20.1 State space of the sequences length $T = 4$ ordered by lexicographic indices and value of both lexicographic indices

i.	t_1	t_2	t_3	t_4	$r(x_i)$	$d'(x_i)$	$d''(x_i)$
1	0	0	0	0	0.00	0.00	0.50
2	0	0	0	1	1.25	0.25	0.20
3	0	0	1	0	1.50	0.25	0.40
4	0	1	0	0	1.75	0.25	0.60
5	1	0	0	0	2.00	0.25	0.80
6	0	0	1	1	3.17	0.50	0.14
7	0	1	0	1	3.33	0.50	0.29
8	1	0	0	1	3.50	0.50	0.43
9	0	1	1	0	3.67	0.50	0.57
10	1	0	1	0	3.83	0.50	0.71
11	1	1	0	0	4.00	0.50	0.86
12	0	1	1	1	5.25	0.75	0.20
13	1	0	1	1	5.50	0.75	0.40
14	1	1	0	1	5.75	0.75	0.60
15	1	1	1	0	6.00	0.75	0.80
16	1	1	1	1	7.00	1.00	0.50

while for sequences 9 and 10, $\boldsymbol{B}_1 = 2$, because $\boldsymbol{s}_2$ now occupies position t_3. Finally, for sequence 11, $\boldsymbol{B}_1 = 1$. For $\boldsymbol{s}_2$ in all six sequences considered, $\boldsymbol{B}_2 = 4$;

C_k is the minimum position s_k that can occupy. In this case, for all six sequences considered $\boldsymbol{C}_1 = 1$ and $\boldsymbol{C}_2 = 2$.

At this point, the calculation of the decimal part of any binary sequence of length $\boldsymbol{t}$, for any number of realizations u, will be:

$$x_i'' = \frac{1 + \binom{T}{u} - \left[\binom{B_u}{C_u} - \sum_{s_k=1}^{s_k} \binom{B_k}{C_k} - \binom{A_k}{C_k} \right]}{\binom{T}{u}} \tag{1}$$

The decimal part of the lexicographical index is one plus the difference between the set of all the possible realizations of a given value of u minus the difference between the set of the possible realizations for the maximum position (s_k) reach of u minus the summation of the difference between the set of all the possible realizations of s_k taking account of the upper and lower limits within which s_k can occur and the position in which s_k is observed divided by the binomial coefficient of all the sequences that can be realized for a given value of u.

The decision to normalize $\left(x_i''\right)$ is taken because the number of sequences varies with the value of u. Thus, independently of the value of u, the distance between the first and the last sequence defined will be at most 1. Having defined the integer part as $2u$–1, the least distance between two sequences belonging to contiguous sets of u will also be at least 1.

Finally, the binary lexicographic index '$>_{b1}$' comprising the integer part and the decimal part will therefore be:

$$r\left(x_i\right) = x_i' + x_i'' = \left(2u-1\right) + \frac{1 + \binom{T}{u} - \left[\binom{B_u}{C_u} - \sum_{s_k=1}^{s_k} \binom{B_k}{C_k} - \binom{A_k}{C_k}\right]}{\binom{T}{u}} \tag{2}$$

For example, for sequence 7 [0101], with: $T = 4$, $u = 2$, $\boldsymbol{s}_1$ $\{\boldsymbol{A}_1 = 2, \boldsymbol{B}_1 = 3, \boldsymbol{C}_1 = 1\}$ and $\boldsymbol{s}_2$ $\{\boldsymbol{A}_2 = 4, \boldsymbol{B}_2 = 4, \boldsymbol{C}_2 = 2\}$ the value of the lexicographical index is:

$$r\left(x_7\right) = \left(2u-1\right) + \frac{1 + \binom{T}{u} - \left\{\binom{B_2}{C_2} - \left[\left(\binom{B_1}{C_1} - \binom{A_1}{C_1}\right) + \left(\binom{B_2}{C_2} - \binom{A_2}{C_2}\right)\right]\right\}}{\binom{T}{u}}$$

$$r\left(x_7\right) = \left(2\cdot 2-1\right) + \frac{1 + \binom{4}{2\cdot(4-2)} - \left\{\binom{4}{2\cdot(4-2)} - \left[\left(\binom{3}{1\cdot(3-1)} - \binom{2}{1\cdot(2-1)}\right) + \left(\binom{4}{2\cdot(4-2)} - \binom{4}{2\cdot(4-2)}\right)\right]\right\}}{\binom{4}{2\cdot(4-2)}}$$

$$r\left(x_7\right) = 3 + \frac{1 + 6 - \left\{6 - \left[\left(3-2\right) + \left(6-6\right)\right]\right\}}{6} = 3 + \frac{2}{6} = 3.33\overline{3}$$

Possible criticisms of this index might concern its use in clustering procedures where the algorithms are designed to find distinct groups of clouds of points and not gatherings along a continuum.

The solution to this problem is to transform the index '$>_{b1}$' from a measure of distance to an index formed by a couple of distances/coordinates on a Cartesian space (Graph 20.1). The theoretical framework discussed here does not change. I do no more than return to a double measure of distance. The first $d'\left(x_i\right)$ concerns the quantity of time. The second $d''\left(x_i\right)$ concerns the moments (the timing) in which the states are realized.

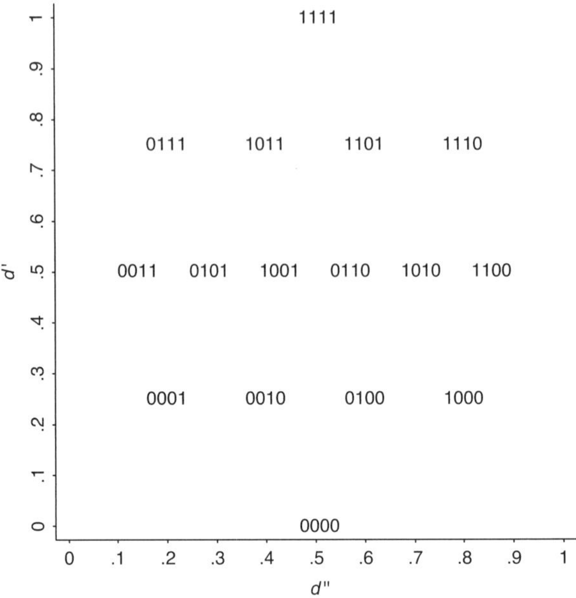

Graph 20.1. Spatial distribution of the 16 sequences of length $T = 4$ by the coordinate $d'(x_i)$ and $d''(x_i)$.

Thus, this new lexicographic index '$>_{b2}$' based on a double measure of distance/coordinate will therefore be:

$$d'(x_i) = \frac{u}{T} \tag{3}$$

$$d''(x_i) = \frac{\binom{T}{u}}{\binom{T}{u}+1} \cdot \frac{1+\binom{T}{u} - \left[\binom{B_u}{C_u} - \sum_{s_k=1}^{s_k}\left(\binom{B_k}{C_k} - \binom{A_k}{C_k}\right)\right]}{\binom{T}{u}} \tag{4}$$

Both the coordinates/distances are normalized between 0 to 1. The upper and lower boundary of the order, that is, for $\boldsymbol{u} = 0$ and $\boldsymbol{u} = T$, $d''(x_i) = d''(x_i) + 0.5$. The measure of distance $d''(x_i)$ is centered on the center of the system, so that the distance between sequences is proportional to the number of $\boldsymbol{\upsilon}$ realizations.

The similarity/distance between two sequences (x_i, x_j) is the Euclidean distance between a couple of lexicographic indices '$>_{b2}$'.

$$r(x_i, x_j) = \sqrt[2]{\sum (d'(x_i) - d'(x_j))^2 + (d''(x_i) - d''(x_j))^2} \tag{5}$$

From binary to multinomial sequences

The next step is to pass from a binary sequence to a multinomial sequence: that is, the case in which there are more than two states (for example, 'employed', 'unemployed', 'never worked', etc.). In the above paragraph I underlined that just as a qualitative variable of $\boldsymbol{k}$ modality can be represented by $\boldsymbol{k}$-dummy variables, so a multinomial sequence of $\boldsymbol{q}$-states can be represented by $\boldsymbol{q}$ binary sequences with values 0–1. So for element $x_{qi}(t)=1$ the ith unit assumes the qth modality in the tth instant, otherwise $x_{qi}(t)=0$. It is possible to apply both the lexicographical indices to each of these sequences and compute the distance measure $r_q(x_i)$ or the coordinate/distance numbers $\left(d'_q(x_i), d''_q(x_i)\right)$. The multinomial sequence x_i is therefore described by a vector to real numbers. The distance function between two multinomial sequences x_i and x_j is the Euclidean [4] distance between their transformations $r_q(x_i)$ and $r_q(x_j)$. Formally if we use the first lexicographic index ($>_{B1}$) the distance is:

$$D\left(x_i, x_j\right) = \sqrt[2]{\sum_{q=1}^{Q}\left(r_q(x_i) - r_q(x_j)\right)^2} \tag{6}$$

while, if we use the coordinate/distance lexicographic index ($>_{B2}$) the distance is:

$$D\left(x_i, x_j\right) = \sqrt[2]{\sum_{q=1}^{Q}\left(d'_q(x_i) - d'_q(x_j)\right)^2 + \left(d''_q(x_i) - d''_q(x_j)\right)^2} \tag{7}$$

Note that it is easy to show that (2), (3), (4), (6), and (7) are effective distances: that is, they satisfy the properties of triangularity, symmetry, and positivity required for a distance measure.

LEXICOGRAPHIC INDICES AND OM. A SHORT COMPARISON

Space does not permit the itemization of the specific differences between the lexicographic indices and between these and the OM procedure. I restrict my discussion to three tests conducted on the working histories of a sample of 1,283 subjects who entered the labor market for the first time between 1990 and 2000 and were observed every month for the five years beginning with the first month of work. The labor market conditions of the subjects were encoded in the same eight classes listed in the first section.

Calculated on the 1,283 multinomial sequences of length $t = 60$ were the lexicographical indices '$>_{b1}$' and '$>_{b2}$' and the OM symmetric distance matrix[5] (henceforth OM).

The two lexicographical indices were analyzed with a k-mean fuzzy cluster[6] while OM was analyzed by a hierarchical cluster[7] using both the 'Wards Linkage' and 'Single Linkage' methods. To guarantee comparability between analyses, I decided to adopt a twelve-class classification.

Table 20.2 Frequencies distribution of the fuzzy clusters on lexicographic index '$>b_1$' and '$>b_2$' and hierarchical 'Wards linkage' and 'Single linkage' clusters on the OM symmetric distance matrix. ($N = 1283$)

*Cluster Number**	*Fuzzy clusters $>_{b1}$*	*Fuzzy clusters $>_{b2}$*	*H. Clusters Wards linkage*	*H. Clusters Single linkage*
1	98	46	187	1270
2	43	115	35	2
3	80	170	69	1
4	32	44	45	1
5	59	54	114	1
6	59	81	84	1
7	171	358	88	1
8	117	62	101	2
9	103	101	38	1
10	79	100	22	1
11	46	76	445	1
12	396	76	55	1

Three clusters analyses (Table 20.2) found separate groups of sequences; but the fourth of them, the 'Single Linkage' hierarchical cluster, classified 99.0% of the sequences in one single class.

There may have been several reasons for this wrong result. It is well known that different algorithms produce different solutions according to the type of data and the heuristic classification adopted. This has various consequences. We do not know what is the minimum number of cluster to extract, or if the result obtained is better than another in representing the system. In our case, for instance, which is the reality? Is it that obtained using the 'Wards linkage' method, which leads us to conclude that there are twelve separate career patterns? Or is it that obtained using the 'Single linkage' method, with which we conclude that there are no common career patterns? The debate is open.

Instead, what is reasonable is the frequency distribution of the sequences within the classes in the other three clusters. The graphic visualization with the sequence index plot showed a substantial coherence within the classes and the existence of distinct patterns.

Nevertheless, the existence of a substantial internal coherence and separate patterns does not guarantee that the three clusters have grouped the same sequences. For instance, sequences that in one cluster analysis belong to a single class, in another may belong to several different classes. There is no clear method

Table 20.3 Mean of the Euclidean distance and mean numbers of different element in the sequence by the three clusters analysis

Cluster Number	*Euclidean Distance on* $>_{b1}$	*Different Elements* $>_{b1}$	*Euclidean Distance on* $>_{b2}$	*Different Elements* $>_{b2}$	*Euclidean Distance on OM*	*Different Elements OM*
1	2.1	5.5	1.8	8.2	0.8	3.3
2	5.9	37.3	1.8	7.9	4.9	25.4
3	2.7	9.1	0.4	1.6	5.6	33.0
4	4.8	25.1	3.8	16.9	5.4	30.0
5	6.0	38.0	4.9	25.9	4.5	21.0
6	3.8	16.6	2.0	8.3	6.0	37.5
7	1.2	2.0	0.0	0.1	3.5	14.0
8	5.4	30.9	4.2	20.0	3.9	17.3
9	4.3	19.5	4.4	21.4	4.8	26.1
10	3.0	11.3	4.6	23.3	3.9	16.5
11	3.2	11.9	1.9	8.3	3.9	15.8
12	1.2	1.7	4.6	22.1	4.2	19.6

with which to establish when a group of sequences has been correctly classified. Nevertheless, we can test the proportion of jointly classified sequences using different classification techniques. It is possible to define the degree of overlap as the ratio between the amounts of the jointly classified sequences on the total of the observed sequences. The greater the degree of overlap, the greater will be the proportion of sequences that are classified in the same class. The comparisons do not show significant differences. The degree of overlap between '$>_{b1}$' and '$>_{b2}$' is 81.2%, that between '$>_{b1}$' and OM is 85.5%, and that between '$>_{b2}$' and OM is 83.9%.

The third test measures the similarity degree of the sequences within a class. In this case, we use two different methods. The first is the mean of the Euclidean distances between the sequence nearest to the class centroid and the other sequences of the class. The second is the mean number of different elements between the sequence nearest to the class centroid and the other sequences of the class. For both measures, the smaller the mean of the two measures, the greater the degree of similarity.

The comparison (Table 20.3) shows that the lexicographical index '$>_{b2}$' has more similarity and less heterogeneity with the classes than do the other two clusters. The mean distance is two thirds less than that within the classes with OM. The number of different elements in the sequences, too, is clearly less than that in OM. In '$>_{b2}$' only six of the twelve classes have in mean more than

15% of elements in different positions in comparison to the ten on twelve classes of the OM.

The index ‘$>_{b1}$’ is closer to ‘$>_{b2}$’ than to OM. The mean Euclidean distance is slightly more than ‘$>_{b2}$’ while the number of classes (six on twelve) that have a number of different elements greater than 15% is equal.

It is clear from the tests that the lexicographical indices proposed are just as able to find similar sequences as the OM used here.[8] Nevertheless, these indices have a series of characteristics that in my opinion make them superior to the OM, as we shall see in the concluding section. However, there are two things to be stressed immediately.

First, it has been shown that the coherence within the classes is greater when using the measures of distance defined by the index than when using OM. This is an important finding. Few sequences classed in one class rather than another may modify the heterogeneity of the class. This in turn, may condition the results of the analyses that will subsequently use the patterns as dependent variables and as independent variables. This may ultimately make the difference between finding ‘causal’ relationships and not finding any at all, between finding regularity and surrendering to vagueness, to complexity.

Second, the two indices augment the statistical tools available to the researcher, who thus has access to new and more powerful and useful statistical tests with which to establish both the number of clusters to extract and the degree of uncertainty in the system. Whilst with the classic clustering techniques the decision of how many classes to extract was left to the ability of the researcher, with these new techniques the decision is assisted by a series of measures specifically designed to find the best solution with the smallest possible loss of information. The outcome of this process is the transformation of research from alchemic to scientific, and the researcher from wizard to scientist.

SOME FINAL CONSIDERATIONS ON THE INDICES

I shall conclude this chapter by briefly discussing both the indices (henceforth index) just presented. First, the lexicographic index is a measure defined *a priori*, independently of the sequences observed. Hence, it is not comparison between the sequences that defines their distance; instead, their distance is given by definition in an independent system of measurement. The index has a known beginning and end; each point of the measure is univocal and identifies one and only one combination of states in sequence. Two sequences which differ in the position of only one element will have different positions. Two sequences with the same number of realizations in the same order will share exactly the same point in the index. None of the information contained in the sequences is lost. From every point one can retrace the exact sequence that has produced it.

The index does not insert, cancel, or replace elements; it does not change the positions; it does not reverse the order (and the time) of the events; it does not define costs *a priori*; it does not require arbitrary assumptions. Each sequence is treated as a whole: it is a point in the states space. The timing that generates and defines the sequence also defines the index.

Similarity between two sequences is therefore the direct product of comparison between two whole realizations, and their distance is smaller, the more elements they have in common in the same order; the larger is the number of shared transitions between the same states, the more similar is their timing.

A second characteristic of the index concerns the treatment of multinomial sequences as a set of binary sequences. This makes it possible to take account of the generative mechanisms of every single state and the entire timing of the system observed. It is possible, in effect, to think that each state (i.e. unemployment, marriage, education, etc.) has its own underlying generating mechanism that determines the timing and the duration of its episodes. These generating mechanisms operate independently of each other, and they interact over time: they stand in a relationship of coexistence. The occurrence of one or other event-state in time within a multinomial sequence is therefore the result of co-action among these various underlying generative mechanisms and of the elementary sequences that they define. Hence, a multinomial sequence does not exist as such; what instead exist are its states and the sequences defined by them. This means that every state has its own generating mechanism that operates independently of the others. A multinomial sequence is not a series of realizations along a one-dimensional line where different mechanisms are confused in a whole. Rather, each single state, each single event, is free to define the form and the length of the individual lines, which in turn are free to interweave with each other to form the complicated plot of a story which has a logical narrative.

A third characteristic of the index concerns the treatment of multiple, parallel tracks of sequences. There are many papers in the OMA literature where parallel sequences are combined: sphere of activity and particular jobs (Abbott and Hrycak, 1990); household status across educational status across job status (Dijkstra and Taris, 1995); and types of jobs and sizes of firms (Blair-Loy, 1999). In all these examples it is possible to hypothesize that these parallel sequences, and the states of which they are composed, have their own underlying generating mechanisms that establish the timing and duration of episodes. These generating mechanisms work independently of each other and interact in time: they stand in a coexistence relationship. The work career, the household career, the couple's career is therefore the result of a complex process of co-action between two or more sequences regulated by different generative mechanisms resulting from the co-action between different generative mechanisms underlying each state. Consequently, reducing everything to a combination of events is to lose a large part of the variability inherent in each single career.

A way to solve this problem is to define a multiple, parallel track of sequences as a point in a $\boldsymbol{q}_j$-dimensional space, as proposed for a multinomial sequence (Bison, 2006). For example, let us suppose that we want to study the couple's careers. In the reality, a couple's career does not exist as such, we cannot observe and we cannot measure it. Every couple's career is made up of two paired multinomial sequences, one for Him and one for Her.[9] For each of the two sequences it is possible to calculate the group of indices that describe the His sequence and the group of indices that describe the Her sequence. These two groups of indices, besides describing the career of His and Her also describe the couple's career as the result of the co-action of the careers of the two partners. Nothing prevents us from defining the couple's career/sequence as a point in the state space whose coordinates are the indices of Her and Him. The distance between two careers in a couple will therefore be the Euclidean distance between two points in the space q_m, q_f-dimensional defined by the four individual sequences produced by the two couples.

First, this simple passage obviates the need to resort to complex cross-classification procedures to combine different sequences with different states. Second, it preserves the individual mechanisms that have produced the His sequence, the Her sequence and the resulting common sequence of the couple. In this way, no information about the temporal 'shape' of events is lost, and there is no confusion about the direction of causality between carriers.

A fourth characteristic of the index concerns its outcome. With current methods, the outcome is a symmetrical matrix of distances that can be used only in hierarchical clusters and multidimensional scaling. The outcome of the lexicographical index is cases by variables format, where the cases are the subject/sequences, and the variables are the lexicographical indices of the states that shape a sequence. Each value of the index can be conceived as a coordinate in the space of the multinomial sequence. This characteristic enables the researcher to adopt different methods to calculate the distance, but also to define forms of space other than Euclidean. Moreover, the index can also be used with other statistical analysis programs, like the *k*-mean cluster or the fuzzy *k*-means cluster or SOM, plus obviously all statistical procedures based on matrixes of distance used with OM. In this case, the matter is not only technical but also substantive. When applying a hierarchical cluster, one implicitly assumes that the phenomenon studied is organized into successive specializations. But this is only one of the possible ways in which a phenomenon may structure itself; the hierarchical model is only one of the possible ways in which a relationship model can be structured.

Being able to adopt other methods of statistical analysis allows one to extend both theoretical and technical horizons of the study of the sequences. Adopting a fuzzy cluster perspective, for instance, does not mean 'following the fashion' nor being academically 'trendy'. It is to change the way in which uncertainty is interpreted from a probabilistic to a fuzzy perspective. Whilst the former uses probabilistic models to quantify the uncertainty associated with the prediction of the phenomenon, and to measure incomplete knowledge through objective modeling (Chen and Hwang, 1992), the latter models uncertainty based on expert knowledge and measures incomplete knowledge through subjective modeling (Gorsevski et al., 2003). By providing class overlap, the fuzzy set classification extends the classic theory of classification towards a continuous classification of entities. In this way, it captures social phenomena in a more realistic way: in their unfolding through time across the variation of complex attributes.

Using the fuzzy cluster approach is then to recognize that there is a certain degree of uncertainty between the sequences. Similar sequences may belong to the same pattern but vary from it by a certain amount due to small variations in the timing. Reducing a group of sequences to simple inclusion/exclusion from a cluster means losing the system's intrinsic variability and richness. It is also to recognize that for some clusters there are no clear boundaries. The passage from one to the other one can be gradual because they share the same semantic space, or because they have a common part of pattern, or because they are produced by similar mechanisms.

Technical-statistic tools to determine the solution that best adapts the system analysed have been developed in the past 20 years. There therefore exist specific tests that enable one to: (a) find the minimum number of classes able to represent the system in analysis in the best possible way; (b) find the maximum quantity of uncertainty admissible from the system without losing information; (c) test the system's stability through the random generation of different starting points; and (d) test the discriminating capacity of the single clusters using Jack-knife/ Bootstrap procedures.

After finding which pattern exists among sequences, the last crucial point to note is the usability of the typology as dependent and independent variables in further analysis. That means to answer two main questions: what determines the sequence and what they in turn determine. As Abbott and Tsay (2000) point out, there have been some successful searches for independent effects of sequence, but no success with sequence as a dependent variable.

Empirical evidence shows the powerful of the indices combined with the fuzzy cluster to find sequences typology which can be treat as dependent and independent variables. In several articles (Bison, 2006, 2009; Bozzon, 2008) the sequences typology identified could be used both as dependent variables, in a multinomial logistic regression, and as independent variables in linear logistic regression models and event history models. In another article (Bison et al., 2009), on the effects of labor market reforms on work contract relationships career, the propensity score matching is used to test the probability to enter into specific sequences typology after and before reforms. Lastly, the index '$>_{b2}$' is used to analyze narrative sequences in Quantitative Narrative Analysis (Franzosi, 2009). The preliminary results (Franzosi, 2009) seem decidedly encouraging. In fact, the tests conducted on a large dataset on the fascist violence in Italy (Franzosi, 1997) made up of more than 9000 triplets gathered in more than 900 narrative histories have found ten different narrative structures of violence. This entire narrative pattern, moreover, varies across time during the 'black' biennial (1921–1922).

In conclusion, sequence analysis is not meant to be a confirmatory statistical tool as pointed out by MacIndoe and Abbott (2004). Rather, it serves an exploratory purpose. It points to patterns that require explanations. It generates research questions. It is to overcome a certain analytical perspective, to open new doors, to access what has been precluded. It is to provide the researcher with new and more powerful tools of analysis in search of the inherent telos that is at the basis of every narrative.

NOTES

1 For a summary of theoretical and methodological approach see Abbott (2001).

2 For instance, the cost of passing from social class A (Bourgeoisie) to social class B (Working class) is exactly the same as passing from B (Working class) to A (Bourgeoisie).

3 Although this is not to say that in the following, not immediately observed, period also A will have a fertility event.

4 Gives the metric nature of the two lexicographical indices, the Euclidean distance is only one of the possible ways of defining the distance between two sequences. It is possible to adopt both measures of Euclidean distance to define other geometric spaces different from that of Euclidean.

5 Not having a hypothesis on the costs, I used the default parameters of the tool 'sqom, k(2) full' implemented in Stata.

6 For this analysis I used the FuzMe program. This is a free software downloadable from the web site http://www.usyd.edu.au/su/agric/acpa/fkme/program.html and it is implemented to Minasny and McBratney (2002).

7 For the Optimal Matching analysis, and the cluster analysis, I used the Stata tools (Brzinsky-Fay et al., 2006).

8 Other analyses have shown that when the complexity of the system increases the capacity of the OM to discriminate drastically reduces (Bison, 2004).

9 Or of course in the case of same sex couples Him/Him; Her/Her.

REFERENCES

Abbott, A. (1990). 'A primer on sequence methods'. *Organization Science*, 1: 373–92.

Abbott, A. (1995). 'Sequence analysis'. *Annual Review of Sociology*, 21: 93–113.

Abbott, A. (2001). *Time Matters: On Theory and Method.* Chicago: University Chicago Press.

Abbott, A. and Hrycak, A. (1990). 'Measuring resemblance in social sequences'. *American Journal of Sociology*, 96:144–85.

Abbott, A. and Tsay, A. (2000). 'Sequence analysis and optimal matching methods in sociology'. *Sociological Methods and Research*, 29(1): 3–33.

Bernstein, W.J (2004). *The Birth of Plenty: How the Prosperity of the Modern World was Created.* New York: McGraw-Hill.

Bison, I. (2004). *Time, Event, Sequence.* University of Trento. (unpublished paper).

Bison, I. (2006). 'When she helps him to the top'. *Intergenerational Transmissions: Cultural, Economic or Social Resources?* RC28 Spring meeting Nijmegen, 11–14 May, 2006.

Bison, I. (2009). 'Class (im)mobility and work (im)mobility: A lexicographic index application'. *Equalsoc Meeting*, Trento, 17–18 February.

Bison, I., Rettore, E., and Schizzerotto, A. (2009). 'La riforma Treu e la mobilità contrattuale degli italiani. Un confronto tra coorti'. In A. Checchi (ed.) *La mobilità sociale in Italia.* Bologna: Il Mulino, (forthcoming).

Blair-Loy, M. (1999). 'Career patterns of executive women in finance'. *American Journal of Sociology,* 104: 1346–97.

Brzinsky-Fay, C., Kohler, U., and Luniak, M. (2006). 'Sequence analysis with Stata'. *Stata Journal,* 6(4): 435–60.

Chen, S.-J., and Hwang, C.-L. (1992). *Fuzzy Multiple Attribute Decision Making.* Berlin: Springer-Verlag.

Dijkstra, W. (2001). 'How to measure the agreement between sequences: A comment'. *Sociological Methods & Research*, 29(4): 532–5.

Dijkstra, W. and Taris, T. (1995). 'Measuring the agreement between sequences'. *Sociological Methods & Research*, 24(2): 214–31.

Elzinga, C.H. (2003). 'Sequence similarity: A non aligning technique'. *Sociological Methods & Research*, 32(1): 3–29.

Franzosi, R. (1997). 'Mobilization and counter-mobilization processes: From the 'Red Years' (1919–20) to the 'Black Years' (1921–22) in Italy. A new methodological approach to the study of narrative data. In J. Mohr and R. Franzosi (eds) *Theory and Society*, 26(2–3): 275–304.

Franzosi, R. (2009). Quantitative narrative analysis. *Quantitative Applications in Social Science*. Sage (Forthcoming).

Gorsevski, P.V., Paul, E. Gessler, P.E., and Jankowski, P. (2003). 'Integrating a fuzzy *k*-means classification and a Bayesian approach for spatial prediction of landslide hazard'. *Journal of Geographical System*, 5: 223–51.

Levine, J.H. (2000). 'But what have you done for us lately? Commentary on abbott and Tsay'. *Sociological Methods & Research*, 29: 34–40.

Macindoe, H. and Abbott, A. (2004). 'Sequence analysis and optimal matching techniques for social science data'. In M. Hardy and A. Bryman (eds) *Handbook of Data Analysis*, pp. 387–406. Thousand Oaks, CA: Sage.

Minasny, B. and McBratney, A.B. (2002). FuzME version 3.0, Australian Centre for Precision Agriculture, The University of Sydney, Australia. http://www.usyd.edu.au/su/agric/acpa (accessed 17/02/10)

Wu, L.L. (2000). 'Some comments on "Sequence analysis and optimal matching methods in sociology: Review and prospect"'. *Sociological Methods and Research*, 29(1): 41–64.

21

Geographic Information Systems (GIS) and Spatial Analysis

Elizabeth Griffiths

Over the past two decades, the notion that 'space matters' has gained popularity in social science scholarship across a broad array of disciplines. This is due in part to increased access to geographically-referenced data and the introduction of user-friendly Geographic Information Systems (GIS) software packages enabling manageable and efficient computerized desktop mapping. While quantitative geographers were at the forefront in employing GIS to capture, analyze, illustrate, and model geographic data beginning in the 1980s, the idea that geography matters was gaining a foothold in other social sciences as well – disciplines traditionally less focused on explicitly conceptualizing and modeling geographic space. Scholars in anthropology, political science, public health, sociology, social work, and urban planning, among other disciplines, now rely upon GIS technology and spatial analytic techniques as both methodological and theoretical tools for investigating and understanding the social world (Berry and Baybeck, 2005; Downey, 2003; Entwisle et al., 1997; Kwan, 2007; McLafferty and Grady, 2005; Nyerges and Green, 2000; Queralt and Witte, 1998).

The National Center for Geographic Information Analysis (NCGIA) defines GIS as 'a system of hardware, software, and procedures designed to support the capture, management, manipulation, analysis, modeling, and display of spatially referenced data for solving complex planning and management problems' (Heikkila, 1998: 351). This definition, like the ones endorsed by other scholars and organizations (ESRI, 1990; Levine and Landis, 1989; Marble, 1990), tends to characterize GIS as principally a vehicle for manipulating and analyzing both geographic coordinate data (precise cartographic locations of incidents, populations, or features) and attribute data (describing the nature of the incidents, populations, or features) (Cox, 1995). The display and organization capabilities for spatially-referenced data make GIS programs attractive for *exploratory* spatial data analysis via mapping or data visualization. However, GIS is also valuable in that it prepares spatial data for the *explanatory* modeling of sociospatial processes through a procedure known as geocoding (Heikkila, 1998).

Incorporating space in social science research is important, as social activities and interpersonal interactions take place in space and time. Yet social scientists have traditionally ignored or neglected spatial aspects of the social world because the available tools necessary to account for space in quantitative research were limited and constraints on access to geographically-referenced data were large. Two important developments have encouraged social scientists to adopt spatial methods of late. First, GIS software is being marketed to a larger academic audience and, consequently, spatial analysis techniques, in menu-driven formats, are more user-friendly. Second, public access to spatial data in the form of street map files and census variables at smaller geographic units-of-analysis (www.census.gov/geo/www/tiger/) has expanded. As a result, attention to the geographic distribution of people across space is being incorporated more systematically in social research.

In the coming years, scholars will be able to use GIS to analyze space as more than simple geographic territories or boundaries, and as more than bundles or clusters of individuals circumscribed by geography. The idea that 'space matters' in the social sciences assumes that 'place matters' and '[p]lace is, at once, the buildings, streets, monuments, and open spaces assembled at a certain geographic spot *and* actors' interpretations, representations, and identifications (Gieryn, 2000: 466–7; emphasis in the original). If researchers begin to incorporate spatial analytic techniques in innovative ways in their research, GIS will offer rich potential for describing and explaining the role of place and space in the social world.

The remainder of the chapter is organized as follows. First, I provide a short overview of recent uses of GIS in social science scholarship, highlighting how GIS and spatial regression has significantly expanded our knowledge base in these fields. This is followed by a brief, non-technical description of two of the most common spatial methods employed in the social sciences: Exploratory Spatial Data Analysis (ESDA) and spatial regression models. Typical problems or issues faced by researchers using spatial methods are then identified, including the Modifiable Areal Unit Problem (MAUP), methodological assumptions of these techniques, and ethical concerns in data collection and dissemination. The chapter concludes with a discussion of the most promising avenues of spatial inquiry in the coming years.

AN ABBREVIATED SURVEY OF GIS IN SOCIAL SCIENCE SCHOLARSHIP

The power of geography for understanding diffusion processes was understood long before the appropriate technology to accomplish such modeling was available. For example, Dr John Snow produced the first known epidemiological study using geographic information on cholera outbreaks during the mid-nineteenth century (Wieczorek and Hanson, 1997). Snow tracked the transmission of cholera across a London neighborhood and, in mapping individual cases, he was able to identify a specific water pump on Broad Street as the source of the outbreak. Disease transmission, as something that occurs in time and space as a result of physical contact between individuals, provides a clear example of the utility of spatial analysis for public health specialists in developing intervention and prevention efforts (Geanuracos et al., 2007).

Just as distance to the water source affected the spread of disease in this case, proximity and ease of accessibility (including transportation, road construction, etc.) to medical clinics can influence health-related behaviors and outcomes (Entwisle et al., 1997). For example, in a much more recent application of GIS in public health research, McLafferty and Grady (2005) demonstrate that generating access to prenatal care is not dependant solely on expanding medical coverage to low-income women, but also on the residential patterns of immigrant women in Brooklyn, New York. Women from Pakistan and Bangladesh, in particular, face barriers to prenatal care as a consequence of distance to medical clinics. Therefore, GIS analysis has the potential to 'identify geographical areas with the greatest unmet service needs', including non-medical social services like community-based prevention programs to combat homelessness (Wong and Hillier, 2001: 21) and accessibility to licensed childcare facilities (Queralt and Witte, 1998).

The exploratory mapping of social phenomena has resulted in important theoretical discoveries in other disciplines as well. For example, two University of Chicago sociologists, Clifford Shaw and Henry McKay (1942), developed social disorganization theory after examining the residential locations of all juvenile delinquents adjudicated by the courts in Chicago, Illinois, at three periods between 1900 and 1933. These researchers plotted the residential addresses of juveniles in conflict with the law by hand, using push pins on large paper maps of the city. In doing so, Shaw and McKay proved that the 'transitional' zone immediately adjacent to the downtown core maintained the highest juvenile delinquency rates in Chicago over three decades despite turnover in the residential population. This discovery confirmed that *places* could be criminogenic, independent of the criminality of neighborhood inhabitants. Shaw and McKay's early study stimulated a long line of criminological research on the social disorganization of urban areas; a research tradition that has been reinvigorated with the application of GIS and related spatial techniques to explore neighborhood effects on crime and delinquency (Sampson et al., 2002).

Spatial concepts have always been critical to theory development in urban sociology, even during periods in which GIS technology was less available. For example, Massey's (1985) spatial assimilation theory posits that immigrant groups initially settle in urban ethnic enclaves, moving to suburban areas only after their socioeconomic prospects improve. This residential mobility is interpreted as an attempt by parents to acculturate or assimilate immigrant children into the majority. Similarly, Wilson (1987) relied upon the concept of 'spatial mismatch' – or the divergence between where workers live and where jobs are located (Kain, 1968) – as a means of understanding the growth of poor, urban ghettos in Chicago during the 1970s and 1980s. The restructuring of the economy through the post-industrial period led to a shrinking number of employment opportunities within urban areas and an associated expansion of jobs in suburbia. Such changes had severe economic consequences for disadvantaged urban residents who experienced pronounced isolation from, and barriers to employment.

While urban sociologists have long been concerned, then, with spatial processes, there have been few efforts to measure 'space' explicitly in the extant literature until recently. Downey (2003) argues for the utility of GIS in examining these spatial processes, and in doing so, clarifies the reach of Wilson's spatial mismatch argument. According to Downey, environmental racial inequalities – in the form of residential proximity to polluting manufacturing facilities – has declined over the post-industrial period as manufacturers relocated outside of the urban core, just as Wilson would predict. However, in mapping racial segregation across Detroit neighborhoods over time, Downey (2003) was able to demonstrate that, contrary to Wilson, this process was the outcome of selective black suburban migration patterns into suburbs devoid of manufacturing facilities rather than, or at least in addition to, social or economic confinement of African Americans to urban ghettos. Through utilizing GIS mapping capabilities, then, the nature of the social processes producing increased environmental equality by race can be better understood.

Like sociologists, political scientists and political geographers have utilized spatial analytic methods to address pressing questions about voter behavior, campaign contributions, and interstate policy adoption, among other issues (Berry and Baybeck, 2005; Gomez et al., 2007; Shin and Agnew, 2007). In a longitudinal examination of the changing political landscape during the 1990s in Italy – a period during which the traditional party system collapsed and new parties emerged – Shin and Agnew (2007) show that the process of party replacement represents more than simple substitution; electoral processes are geographically dependant on the social and economic features of smaller regions in Italy. Likewise, studies on the effect of weather (Gomez et al., 2007), gentrification (Gibbs Knotts and Haspel, 2006), and distance to precinct (Dyck and Gimpel, 2005) on voter turnout have utilized GIS to illustrate predictors of, and impediments to voting among the electorate. In each case, geography is purported to affect political behavior to the extent that the attributes of geographic spaces influence the actions of inhabitants. Exploratory spatial data analysis techniques are useful in illuminating these patterns.

Yet space may represent more than a 'context' comprised of like-attributes or experiences that encourage or constrain the behaviors of residents; instead, geography may actually shape or generate social processes. For example, Berry and Baybeck (2005) report that states develop social policies in one of two way: they either look to the policies and experiences of neighboring states (policy learning) or they seek to enact policies that will provide a competitive edge over neighboring states (economic competition). The diffusion of welfare policies across contiguous states is consistent with the learning model and, according to Berry and Baybeck (2005), states tend to emulate the welfare policies of the majority of their neighbors. The authors find, however, that the propensity to adopt state lotteries is more consistent with an economic competition model. That is, the probability that states will establish state lotteries is higher when state officials express concern that residents will travel to neighboring states to play the lottery, in the absence of adoption. In this case, the spread or diffusion of policy decisions across states is overtly dependent upon geographic contiguity, with an eye toward generating a competitive economic advantage. Specifying the nature of diffusion processes by incorporating GIS in research has extended and enriched explanations of political behavior.

All social science disciplines are interested, to a greater or lesser extent, in the analyses of human beings either in interaction with one another, in interaction with their environment, or both. Anthropologists use GIS to examine the physical environments of societies around the globe focusing, for example, on changes in landscape and deforestation (Nyerges and Green, 2000). Urban planners use GIS to capture the complex interplay of social and physical features of neighborhoods, including socioeconomic characteristics, demographics, land use, commuting patterns, housing stock, neighborhood amenities, school presence, crime rates, and landmarks both simultaneously and over time (Talen and Shah, 2007). Even feminist scholars have, be it somewhat cautiously, embraced some of the analytic methods made possible through GIS (Cieri, 2003; Kwan, 2007). Spatial methods allow researchers to incorporate specific information about the kinds of environments in which individuals are embedded, offering greater precision in the investigation of a wide range of social problems.

Spatially-sensitive research designs can likewise reduce the coverage bias associated with probability sampling in survey research. For example, Landry and Shen (2005) argue that Global Positioning System (GPS) technology can be used to generate more accurate and reliable population sampling frames. The authors note that the use of official enumeration systems is problematic because official lists or census counts systematically exclude certain populations, including illegal migrants, the homeless, and minority populations. Instead, the authors advocate delineating the geographic space into equidistant spatial units according to precise coordinates of longitude and latitude, using a probability sampling frame to select some proportion of those spatial units, and then randomly sampling households or individuals from the selected spatial units for inclusion in the survey. Landry and Shen (2005) show that their GPS sampling frame produces substantively different results in quantitative analyses compared to traditional probability sampling based on official lists or censuses. As much of the extant research demonstrates, then, spatially-sensitive research designs provide important methodological *and* theoretical advantages for social scientists.

TWO COMMON ANALYTIC TECHNIQUES

I do not attempt to provide a technical overview of all of the uses of GIS in social science scholarship in this section of the chapter. Rather, I provide a brief description of two kinds of analytic techniques that have been increasingly utilized by social scientists across a variety of disciplines: exploratory spatial data analysis and spatial regression models. For a more comprehensive technical explanation of these, other GIS techniques, and spatial econometrics, refer to Anselin et al. (2004), Fotheringham et al. (2000), Getis et al. (2004), Griffith (1988), Haining (2003), and Schabenberger and Gotway (2005).

Exploratory spatial data analysis

Exploratory data analyses allow researchers to visualize univariate and bivariate patterns in their data. When the data are spatial in nature, the appropriate term for such analyses is exploratory spatial data analysis or ESDA (Unwin and Unwin, 1998). GIS mapping capabilities facilitate the 'premodeling exploration' of data that are expected to be patterned non-randomly across space (Fotheringham et al., 2000: 10). Though a variety of exploratory analytic techniques are available, point pattern analysis and Moran Scatterplot maps provide the tools for making an initial assessment of the presence of spatial patterns in variables of interest.[1]

Point pattern maps graphically illustrate the location of data points in geographic space wherein each individual case is linked by coordinates of latitude and longitude to a specific point in the study area. The individual cases are geocoded using GIS software; a process that attaches precise coordinates of latitude and longitude to each case based on address information. Visualizing the data in this manner can provide some indication of the non-random clustering or dispersion of data points across the study area, as well as identify spatial outliers. Figure 21.1 provides a point pattern map of the locations of 569 of the 575 homicides known to and investigated by the Buffalo, New York, police department during the 1990s[2] (Gartner and McCarthy, n.d.; Griffiths, 2007). The location of each homicide is layered over a digitized tract-level census map of the city. On initial inspection, the Westside, bordering Lake Erie, and the geographic center of the city, known as the Eastside, evidence some clustering of homicide incidents relative to areas in the north and south of the city of Buffalo proper.

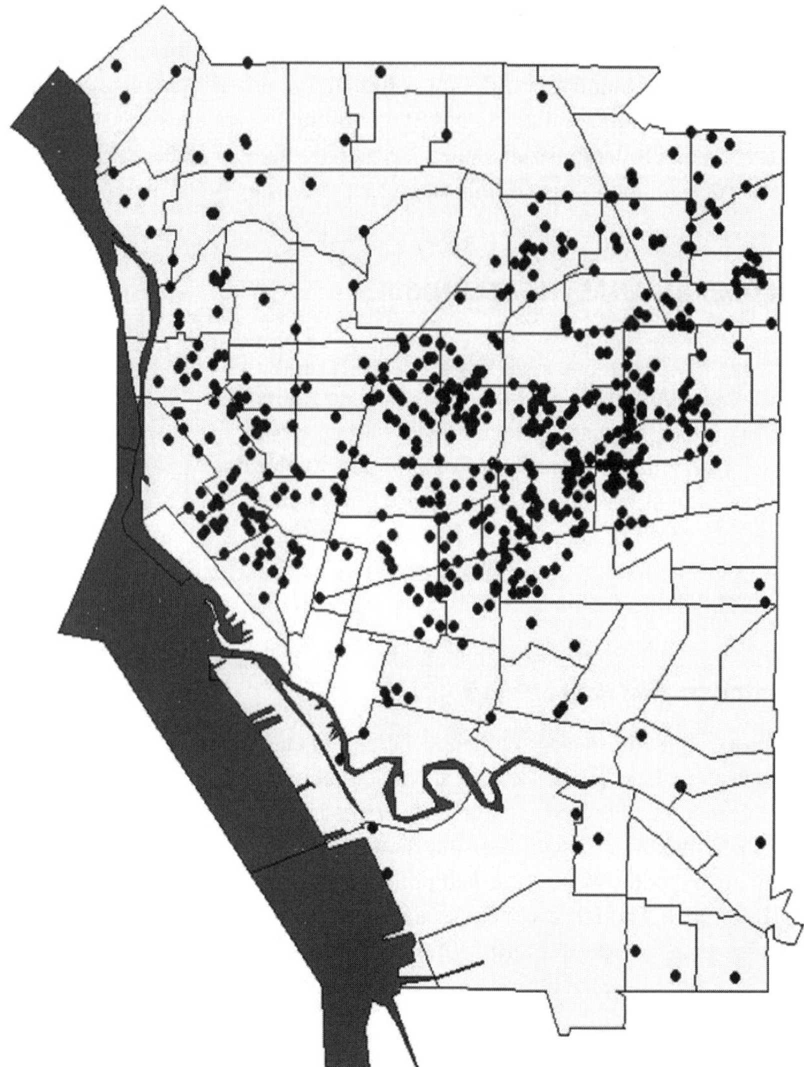

Figure 21.1 Point pattern map of Buffalo homicide incidents in the 1990s (*N* = 569) across census tracts

Such exploratory analyses can be instructive, yet visualizing the data in this manner alone does not provide a formal method for determining the extent to which the observed pattern deviates from spatial randomness. One way to accomplish this is to quantify the total – or in this case, citywide – spatial autocorrelation present in the data by estimating a global measure of spatial autocorrelation, such as a Moran's I statistic (Boots and Getis, 1988). Like the Pearson correlation coefficient, the Moran's I is a cross-product coefficient that is widely used as a summary measure of spatial clustering (Anselin et al., 2000; Cliff and Ord, 1973).

This statistic provides an estimate of the total amount of spatial autocorrelation, or departures from spatial randomness, for variable x distributed across n spatial units.[3] To compute the Moran's I statistic, the adjacency of spatial units must be specified *a priori* by the researcher in a spatial weights matrix (**W**), typically based on an inverse distance-based designation of connectivity or defined according to some binary shared boundary rule[4] (Anselin, 1995; Fotheringham et al., 2000).

In the Buffalo example, homicide incidents are first converted to tract-level rates to formally assess the significance of the observed spatial clustering across neighborhoods in Figure 21.1.[5] This is important because the population at risk (in this case, tract populations) can vary dramatically, making the presence of perceived 'hotspots' and 'coldspots' for homicide more of a product of the population size or land use characteristics (such as parks or industrial areas) than actual danger or safety zones. The decennial homicide rate in each tract is calculated using a linear extrapolation of the population at the mid-point of the decade (1995) in the denominator and the total number of homicides in the tract for the decade as the numerator. In this case, contiguity in the spatial weights matrix is specified according to the 'queen' criterion. The resulting Moran's I statistic is 0.508 ($p < = 0.001$), indicating that homicide rates exhibit significant positive spatial autocorrelation in Buffalo. Positive spatial autocorrelation signifies that like-values tend to cluster with like-values across space, while negative spatial autocorrelation indicates that 'unlike'-values demonstrate greater contiguity. Recall, however, that the Moran's I statistic is a *global* assessment of the degree of spatial autocorrelation present in the data. It does not provide any indication of *local* variations in statistically significant clustering at particular locations across the city.

To the extent that space matters, different effects are expected at different places within the study area. The Moran Scatterplot map illuminates areas of local spatial autocorrelation using Local Indicators of Spatial Association (LISA) statistics[6] (Anselin, 1995). These maps graphically illustrate the specific regions of the study area in which like-values (in this case, tract homicide rates) cluster with like-values (positive spatial autocorrelation), and where different values cluster together (negative spatial autocorrelation) (Anselin et al., 2000; Messner et al., 1999). Two categories describe positive spatial association in the data: tracts that are above average in their homicide rate surrounded by neighbors that are also above average (labeled 'high-high'), and tracts that are below average surrounded by neighboring tracts that are also below average (labeled 'low-low'). Negative spatial association is suggested when above average tracts have below average neighbors (labeled 'high-low'), and when below average tracts are surrounded by above average tracts (labeled 'low-high').

A Moran Scatterplot map of neighborhood homicide rates in Buffalo is provided in Figure 21.2.[7] This map illustrates the locations in the city where high homicide rate tracts tend to cluster with other high rate tracts and low rate tracts tend to cluster with other low rate tracts. As suggested by the point pattern maps,

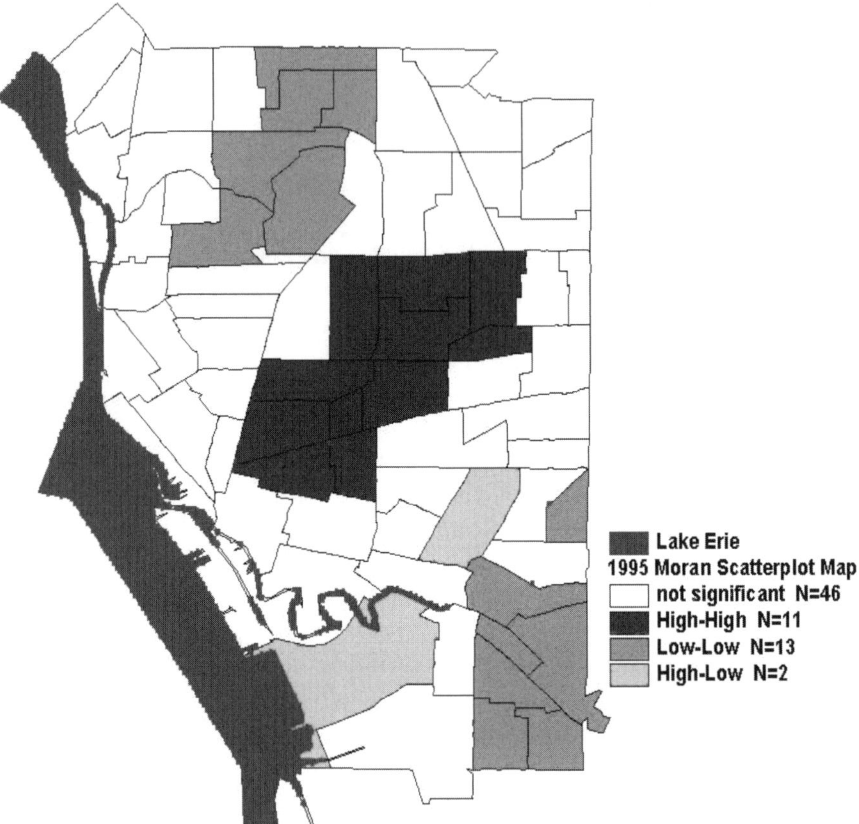

Figure 21.2 Moran scatterplot map of Buffalo homicide rates in the 1990s

neighborhoods in both North and South Buffalo are characterized by a significant clustering of low rate tracts, while the Eastside exhibits significant spatial clustering of high rate tracts. During the 1990s, very few incidents occurred in one of the two 'high-low' tracts in the southwestern part of the city. This tract comprises the Tifft Nature Preserve and is largely non-residential; therefore, the homicide rate in this tract is distorted by the low population estimate in the denominator. Note that the apparent clustering of homicide incidents on the Westside in Figure 21.1 did not rise to the level of statistically significant clustering of homicide rates across tracts in Figure 21.2.

Spatial regression models

While statisticians have generated a variety of complex explanatory modeling strategies for dealing with spatial data, two of the most common techniques include spatial regression modeling (Anselin, 1988; Anselin and Bera, 1998) and geographically weighted regression (Fotheringham et al., 2002). Both types of spatial explanatory modeling recognize that the fundamental assumptions of ordinary least squares regression models are violated when spatial relationships exist in the data. This is because independence of observations cannot be assumed. A technical description of these methods is beyond the scope of this chapter; rather, in this section I briefly describe the key distinction between spatial regression and geographically weighted regression. Readers are encouraged to consult Anselin (1988), Anselin and Bera (1998), Anselin et al. (2004), and Fotheringham et al. (2002) for statistical descriptions and applications of the regression methods outlined below.

Spatial regression models first distinguish the kind of spatial dependence present in the data: spatial error (wherein spatial autocorrelation is a 'nuisance' affecting statistical inference that requires transformation, filtering, or correction) or spatial lag (in which there is substantive spatial dependence between the values of variables in contiguous spatial units). One way to distinguish the type of spatial dependence (error or lag) that requires modeling is the Lagrange multiplier test performed on the residuals of ordinary least squares regression (Anselin, 1988). In the case of spatial error, regression residuals are correlated and thus the standard errors of variables in regular regression models are inflated. Models that ignore this spatial error are thus inefficient. When a spatial lag model is required, parameter estimates in standard regression models are actually biased, leading to incorrect assumptions about the size and nature of effects. Failure to appropriately identify and model spatial effects, then, has important consequences for multivariate results.

Spatial regression models are particularly useful for detecting and modeling spatial diffusion processes. Namely, a significant spatial lag in a regression model is consistent with, and generally interpreted as representing the diffusion of the lagged variable across geographic space (Baller et al., 2001). This is because the value of a variable in one spatial unit is predicted by the value of the same variable in neighboring spatial units, controlling for other covariates in the model. Normally the dependent variable is spatially lagged; though it is also possible to model spatial dependence in independent variables (Morenoff, 2003). Note that only one coefficient is estimated for the spatial lag, providing a 'global' estimate of the presence of diffusion (or related spatial processes) operative in the area under study.

By contrast, geographically weighted regression explicitly models local variation in spatial regression coefficients. This technique treats the study area as a continuous surface in which spatial processes operating in one region of the study area need not be present, or may operate differently, in other regions of the study area (Fotheringham et al., 2000, 2002). In effect, a unique parameter estimate is produced for each geographical unit in the study area on independent variables that are 'spatial' in nature. These parameter estimates can then be mapped to illustrate variation in local spatial effects. Consequently, this method focuses on

> understanding *differences* across space rather than *similarities*. The [local] movement encompasses the dissection of global statistics into their local constituents; the concentration on local exceptions rather than the search for global regularities; and the production of local or mappable statistics rather than on 'whole-map' values. (Fotheringham et al., 2000: 11; emphasis in the original)

REMAINING PROBLEMS

As is true of any novel or innovative analytic technique, both exploratory and explanatory spatial methods have been the subject of criticism. Without providing a comprehensive overview of all of the potential critiques that have been raised, I describe three key issues that confront researchers who employ spatial methods in this section of the chapter. First, questions around defining the number (the *scale* of the analysis) or the size (the *zoning* or partitioning of the units at a given scale) of relevant spatial units are captured in the debate known as the MAUP (Haining, 2003). Second, spatial analytic techniques, like most other quantitative methods, are dependent upon assumptions that may be invalid. Finally, spatial analytic techniques raise ethical concerns over the collection and dissemination of geographically-referenced data. Privacy considerations are paramount to Institutional Review Boards who are charged with protecting human subjects; but unduly restrictive regulations on data collection and dissemination represent significant obstacles to expanding our understanding of how the social world operates. Despite these unresolved issues in spatial analyses, Fotheringham and colleagues (2000: 5) perhaps say it best when they claim that 'the appropriate question to ask of quantitative research … is "How useful is it?" and not "Is it completely free of error?"' I suggest that the weight of the evidence is on the side of spatially-sensitive research designs.

The modifiable areal unit problem

Spatial data are typically situated in larger spatial units, such as block groups, census tracts, ward boundaries, policing areas, and the like. In an effort to observe spatial patterns or trends, however, there may be a mismatch between the scale at which spatial processes are thought to operate and the scale at which data are available. According to Openshaw and Rao (1995), researchers should designate the 'appropriate' or 'optimal' spatial unit to which individual- or incident-level data will be aggregated based on a decision about the level of aggregation that is most suitable for the research question under investigation. However, researchers are often hampered by data constraints in making decisions about the scale of the spatial units to be employed (Smith, 2004). Because these decisions can produce results that are dependent upon the size of the spatial unit that is examined, social scientists conducting spatial analyses routinely confront what is known as the MAUP (Openshaw, 1984; Openshaw and Taylor, 1979).

The title of Openshaw and Taylor's (1979) chapter – 'A Million or So Correlation Coefficients: Three Experiments on the Modifiable Areal Unit Problem' – aptly captures the idea that variability in the results obtained at different levels of aggregation may be, unfortunately, limited only by the number of levels examined and, thus, arbitrary. Therefore, it is incumbent upon researchers to measure 'space' in a manner that is theoretically justifiable, yet studies in the social sciences provide only scant description and explanation about the operationalization of spatial units. Recognizing this as a problem, Hipp (2007: 677) recently argued that 'failure to properly consider the appropriate level of aggregation leaves open the possibility that nonsignificant findings occur because of inappropriate measure[ment] of the aggregated construct, rather than a failing of the theory'. Essentially, then, how one defines the spatial units to be used in the analyses can have a dramatic influence on the substantive findings presented and the consequences for theory-testing.

Downey (2006: 570) provides an innovative approach to addressing the MAUP using GIS by modeling 'physical space as a continuous, unbounded surface in which variable values can vary continuously rather than being tied to specific analysis units'. He argues that vector maps, which use lines, points, and polygons to represent geographic space, should be converted to raster maps, which store data in rectangular grids composed of small square cells of equal area. Raster maps can then be converted back to vector maps as necessary. In making these conversions, researchers can reapportion data according to census boundary changes over time rather than merging data into larger and larger spatial units. They can also avoid assuming that the impact of observations is distributed evenly within administrative units. By 'rasterizing' the data, Downey (2006: 601) contends that problems associated with the MAUP can be reduced or corrected. Ultimately, those employing spatial analytic techniques should routinely conduct, and report on, sensitivity analyses at different resolutions of spatial units to gauge the robustness of their findings.

Methodological assumptions

Spatial regression models provide more precise estimates of both 'aspatial' and 'spatial' variables in predicting the outcome of interest when the observations in the dataset are spatially interdependent. This is because failure to account for spatial dependence produces omitted variable bias in model estimation. Yet even when a significant effect is found for a spatial lag variable, the underlying socio-spatial process responsible for the effect is not explicitly measured. A significant spatial lag *implies* that a diffusion process is responsible for producing the observed spatial dependence; nevertheless, the 'vector of transmission' or the social process through which diffusion occurs is not directly identified (Baller et al., 2001). To use homicide as an example, contiguous neighborhoods may share similar rates of homicide because rival gang territories are geographically concentrated, because drug markets span multiple neighborhoods, or because violence in neighboring areas prompts residents to carry and use weapons more readily in the face of perceived aggression (Tita and Greenbaum, 2008). Ultimately, the spatial lag may represent little more than a '... "catch all" for any number of unobserved, residual processes' (Tita and Greenbaum, 2008: 152) yet it is often assumed to represent clear evidence of diffusion.

A second critique based on the assumptions of spatial regression models is related to time. Spatial regression models rely on cross-sectional data, despite the logical assumption that sociospatial processes occur in time as well as across space. For example, regardless of the vector of transmission, diffusion of violence across neighborhoods generally exhibits some temporal ordering (Cohen and Tita, 1999). The spatial regression methods described earlier in the chapter are based on the assumption that the spatiotemporal processes producing the observed distribution of events across space is complete; that is, the relationship is in a state of equilibrium. Consequently, the snapshot of observations comprising the dataset is assumed to capture the final outcome of whichever spatial processes were responsible for producing the observed distribution. This is a tenuous assumption at best.

Ethical concerns

A final concern for researchers working with spatial analytic methods is related to the ethics of data collection and dissemination. Unlike other multivariate analyses in which the data are derived from one large, unpartitioned city, county, nation, or other administrative unit(s), spatial analyses are conducted on specific places with an identifiable shape and particularistic features. Moreover, to adequately analyze spatial patterns in the data, the study area is partitioned into even smaller units such as block groups, census tracts, policing areas, or 'rasterized' cells, and the like. As a consequence, the potential for identification of specific cases (persons, incidents, etc.) in the data increases, raising concerns about privacy issues.

Two points related to spatial data collection and dissemination warrant special attention. In the first place, the decision to undertake data collection, the storage of sensitive data, and researcher access to the data each raise ethical concerns, particularly when the data cannot be de-identified. Various agencies have established requirements for the ethical treatment of human subjects in research, including the Nuremberg Code, the Helsinki Declaration, the Belmont Report, and other national, international, and discipline-specific codes of conduct to ensure confidentiality of private information and protection from harm for human subjects (Meltzoff, 2005a). Institutional Review Boards (IRBs) are, not surprisingly, concerned about the privacy rights of subjects and the extent to which confidentiality can be guaranteed. Spatially referenced data presents some obstacles to anonymity when each subject or case (for example, residential address or location of victimization) can be located in space via precise coordinates of latitude and longitude. This problem is heightened by the fact that many important studies utilizing spatial techniques have focused on sensitive issues like criminal offending, criminal victimization, sexual practices, and disease incidence and transmission. Researchers are obligated to balance the confidentiality concerns of human subjects with the benefit to society of publication of the research findings.

Second, graphical presentations of data can be manipulated and distorted based upon small changes in scale or perspective (Meltzoff, 2005b; Monmonier, 1996). There is no doubt that spatial analysts have a vested interest in exploring spatial patterns and explaining the reality of spatial processes accurately, rather than in mischaracterizing the results. However, given (1) the existence of the MAUP, (2) the possibility that the aggregate unit at which some spatial processes operate is unknown, and (3) the necessary *a priori* researcher-defined decision rules stipulating, for example, contiguity in spatial weights matrices or defining kernel bandwidth for point pattern analyses, the potential for the 'best' results or the best story to be published – rather than the most accurate results *per se* – is a worrying possibility.

An illustrative example provided by Anselin et al. (2008: 105) clarifies that 'the choice of the bandwidth has important repercussions for results' in kernel density functions. Figures 21.3 and 21.4 illustrate two different kernel maps of the Buffalo homicide data: the Gaussian kernel density function with a larger bandwidth is shown in Figure 21.3 and the triangular kernel function with a smaller, 'spikier' bandwidth is provided in Figure 21.4 (Anselin et al., 2008). Clearly, the two kernel density maps show distinctive patterns, but which map is 'correct'? Which map best represents the reality of homicide clustering in Buffalo? The answer may be both, or it may be neither. Ultimately, the decisions of researchers to use one measurement strategy over another will influence the conclusions reached by readers about the social and spatial distribution of the data. It is incumbent upon researchers using spatial methods, then, to rely on existing empirical findings, theory, or their own understanding of the research site to guide analytic decisions about the appropriate size and shape of spatial units. Given the increasing tendency to use GIS and spatial analytic techniques across a host of disciplines, ethical concerns about data collection, storage, dissemination, and presentation of analyses are likely to become increasingly salient.

THE FUTURE OF GIS AND SPATIAL ANALYSIS IN THE SOCIAL SCIENCES

According to Waldo Tobler's (1970: 236) First Law of Geography, 'everything is related to everything else, but near things are more related than distant things'. As Anselin (1989) notes, however, defining 'near' and 'distant' requires special techniques that can reference data in geographic space. What is more, the

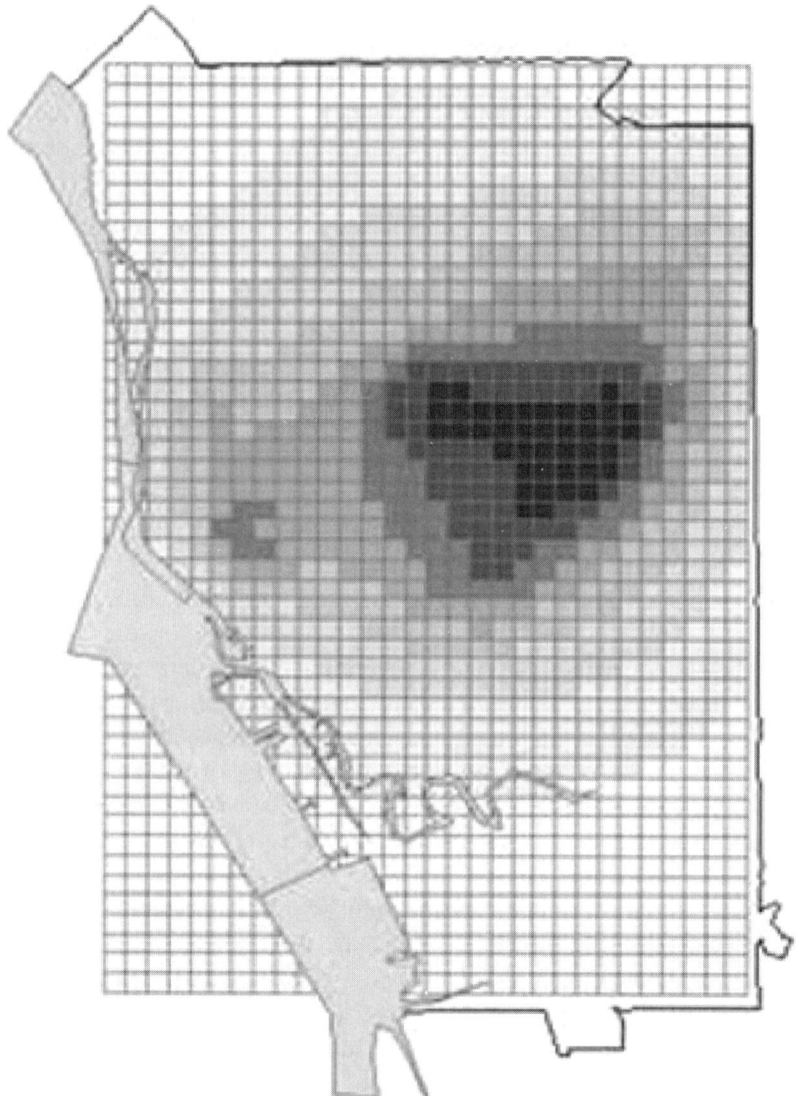

Figure 21.3 Buffalo homicides in the 1990s, Gaussian kernel density function
***Source*: Anselin et al., 2008.**

interpretation of 'near' and 'distant' is not always straightforward. Nonetheless, social science scholarship has and will benefit from continued emphasis on, and innovative approaches to, understanding and modeling space. Two particularly important lines of inquiry are expected to stimulate a flurry of social scientific research using spatial analytic approaches in the near future. The first involves an expanded definition of what constitutes contiguity or adjacency; the second relates to the role of time in spatial analyses.

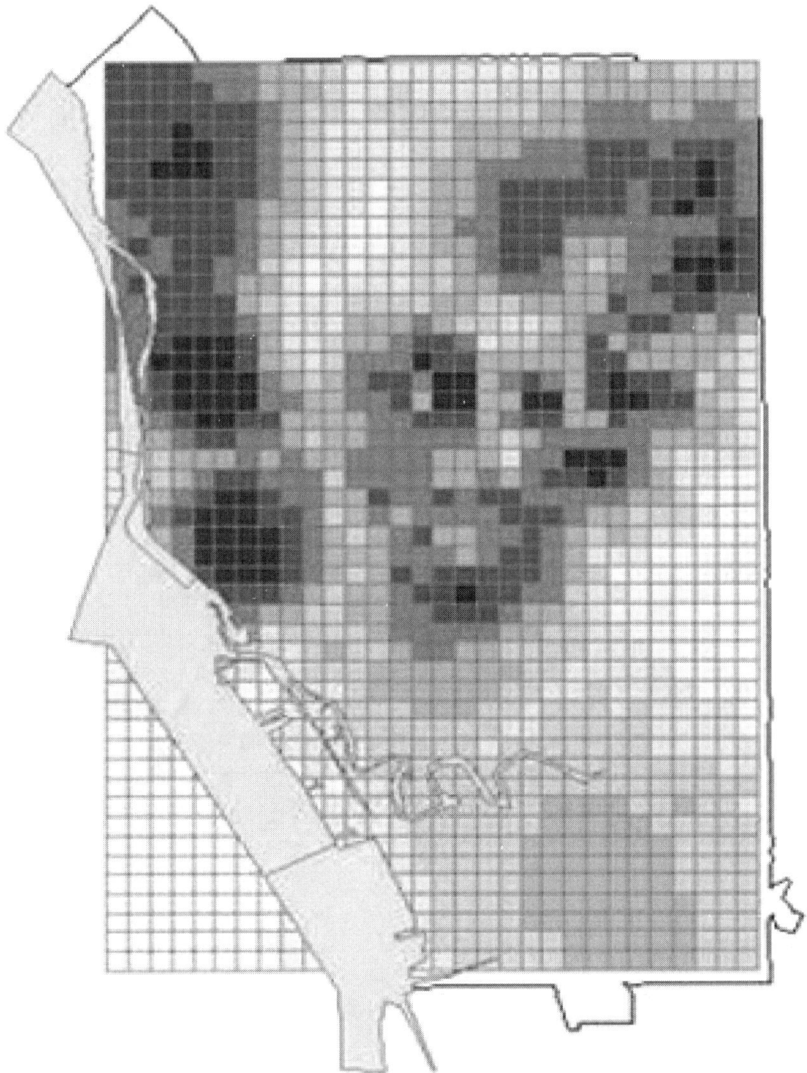

Figure 21.4 Buffalo homicides in the 1990s, triangle kernel density function
***Source*: Anselin et al., 2008.**

Designing the spatial weights matrix (W)

The key to any spatial analytic technique is the representation of the spatial structure of the data, formally expressed in the spatial weights matrix (**W**) (Getis and Aldstadt, 2004). This is because the spatial weights matrix is purported to capture the manner in which 'space matters'; it captures the spatial dependence between observations in the dataset (Anselin, 1988). In the extant social scientific literature, the spatial weights matrix is generally defined as a row standardized contiguity or inverse distance-based matrix composed of n by n cells (w_{ij}) in which each 'connected' cell is non-zero when i and j are neighbors, and zero otherwise. Therefore, **W** is defined *a priori* by the researcher.

The structure of **W** should be specified so as to best approximate the spatial dependency structure in the data and the unit at which spatial processes are thought to operate. However, mathematical convenience and the level at which aggregated data are available tend to influence how **W** is defined much more so than do theoretical considerations. Getis and Aldstadt (2004) outline a number of 'schemes' for constructing **W**, including contiguity measures, ranked distances, lengths of shared borders, and n nearest neighbors, among others; yet each of these schemes requires *a priori* decisions by researchers. A variety of additional specification procedures suggested by Getis and colleagues (Getis, 1995; Getis and Griffith, 2002; Griffith, 1996) are 'designed to find a **W** that 'extracts' or filters the spatial effects from the data' (Getis and Aldstadt, 2004: 91). Nevertheless, construction of the spatial matrix should be, first and foremost, theoretically-driven.

At the cutting edge of spatial research is a focus on moving 'beyond geography' in specifying **W**. Ideally, the spatial weights matrix should be constructed according to a theoretical premise about the nature of the connections between units in the data; that is, theory should drive the assignment of 'neighbors', which may or may not be based on simple geographic adjacency or distance decay alone (Anselin et al., 2004; Leenders, 2002; Mears and Bhati, 2006). In a recent study, Tita and Greenbaum (2008) provide an innovative example of how defining the spatial weights matrix through a deductive process, akin to social network analysts' influence models, can better capture spatial dependence in data as a function of sociospatial processes. The authors compare the results of two spatial regression models predicting the number of gunshots fired across census block groups in Pittsburgh, Pennsylvania. In the first model, **W** is treated as a simple geographic contiguity matrix based on a shared border (rook) criterion, whereas the second model uses a network-based criterion for specifying connections between block groups. That is, block groups containing the turf of gangs are defined as 'neighbors' of block groups containing rival gang turf, despite geographic distance between the territories. The results show that the second spatial weights matrix constructed deductively, and based on sociospatial connections hypothesized to account for underlying spatial dependencies in the data, better captures the role of space in gang studies. The design of theoretically sound spatial weights matrices should be a major preoccupation of researchers as spatial analyses continue to penetrate the social sciences.

Time and space

Spatial and temporal analytic techniques share many commonalities. Time series analyses are used when the data exhibit serial autocorrelation, which is present when information is collected on the same individuals, products, or other units over time. Spatial models are used when data exhibit spatial autocorrelation, which is present when information is collected at the same time on geographical units that are patterned in space. In each case, the value of the dependent variable is a function of the independent variables specified in the model *and* the value of the dependent variable at an earlier point in time (time series) or of neighboring areas (spatial regression). In both cases, the assumptions required for ordinary regression models are violated.

Human activity is fundamentally spatiotemporal activity to the extent that actions are constrained by location in space at any given moment in time (Golledge and Stimson, 1997). Yet the ability to model space and time simultaneously is, as yet, relatively limited (Lesage and Pace, 2004). Indeed, most studies that have attempted to incorporate space and time have done so consecutively rather than concurrently. For example, Griffiths and Chavez (2004) used a semi-parametric, group-based trajectory procedure to identify the number and shape of trajectories describing homicide rate changes in Chicago census tracts for the period of 1980 to 1995. The authors then mapped trajectory groups in geographic space using GIS. These analyses showed that tracts following the same trajectories over the period tended to cluster in certain areas of the city. In the case of explanatory modeling, Elhorst (2004) argues that most previous studies attempting to lag regressands in both space and time did so sequentially, not simultaneously. While some estimation procedures can handle one sparse dimension (few time points or few spatial units) within the context of rich variation on the remaining dimension (de Luna and Genton, 2004), the development of appropriate spatiotemporal modeling strategies represent the next major challenge for researchers.

CONCLUSIONS

The spatial analytic methods made possible by GIS have the potential to considerably advance the research programs of scholars across the social sciences. In reviewing some of the more common ESDA and spatial regression techniques in this chapter, I suggest that three key advantages extend from their use. In the first place, spatial methods underscore variation in effects across study areas. That is, both global spatial patterns and local variations can be observed and modeled. Because people respond to visual stimuli differently than, for example, they respond to numbers, mapping data is a powerful tool for discovering important spatial patterns. As a consequence, scholars are able to identify substantively interesting spatial interactions, target hotspots for intervention, and develop theoretical perspectives that better capture the spatial dimensions of social phenomena.

Second, sociospatial processes, such as diffusion or contagion, can be visualized and estimated quantitatively. To the extent that traditional methods fail to identify the effects of contiguous areas on one another, important social processes like diffusion have been ignored or under-theorized. Finally, spatial analytic methods have the potential to contradict or extend the findings of previous research. Quantitative analyses that neglect spatial effects run the risk of generating inefficient and/or biased results. Therefore, more precise modeling of social phenomena is made possible with GIS technology and associated spatial methods.

Can a new analytic technique or methodology represent a scientific paradigm shift? Does a growing awareness of spatial patterns and processes in the social world signify the coming of a scientific revolution? Kuhn (1962: 6) describes a paradigm shift as a change in the theoretical perspectives ascribed to by the scientific community so sweeping that it 'subvert[s] the existing tradition of scientific practice'. Spatial methods are tools, not theories of how the social world operates; thus, while specialist journals have developed, scholarly organizations have emerged, and research published in major disciplinary journals has incorporated space more explicitly, the notion that 'space matters' does not in and of itself represent a scientific revolution. Nonetheless, spatial analytic methods have fundamentally transformed our ability to model and understand social processes, and more fully explore the effect of the larger social and environmental context on human behavior. A symbiosis of technology and social scientific theory is possible with continued innovation in the uses of GIS technology and associated spatial analytic methods. Perhaps a revolution is on the horizon.

ACKNOWLEDGEMENTS

I would like to thank Breda McCabe and George Tita for helpful feedback on an earlier version of this chapter.

NOTES

1 Other ESDA techniques used to explore spatial patterns in data include, but are not limited to, scatterplots, boxplots, kernel density maps – which illustrate the weighted average of events in a moving window of a designated bandwidth across the study area – and spatial scan statistics (Anselin et al., 2008; Kulldorff, 1997; Openshaw et al., 1987; Waller and Gotway, 2004).

2 Six of the homicides (1.04 per cent) could not be geocoded due to missing or incomplete address information.

3 The formula for computing the Moran's I statistic is:

$$I = \left(\frac{n}{\sum_i \sum_j w_{ij}} \right) \left(\frac{\sum_i \sum_j w_{ij} (x_i - \bar{x})(x_j - \bar{x})}{\sum_i (x_i - \bar{x})^2} \right)$$

where i and j represent any two of n spatial units, $\bar{x}$ is the mean of x (the observed value at each location) and w_{ij} defines the weight of i and j which is non-zero when i and j are neighbors, and zero otherwise.

4 The spatial weights matrix, **W**, may be defined a number of different ways depending on the study topic and goals of the researcher. Generally these designations are based on contiguity (known as the *rook* criterion when the units share a common boundary and the *queen* criterion when the units share any common boundary or point), an inverse distance-decay function, or semivariogram models (Getis and Aldstadt, 2004).

5 Census tracts are a common proxy measure of neighborhoods in community-level research, though other levels of aggregation including block groups and neighborhood planning units have also been employed (Hipp, 2007).

6 A variety of alternative statistics for measuring global and local spatial autocorrelation are available, including G and G* (Ord and Getis, 1995).

7 SpaceStat 1.90 software was used to create spatial weights based on the 'queen' criterion for the Moran Significance maps procedure in Arcview 3.2.

REFERENCES

Anselin, Luc (1988) *Spatial Econometrics: Methods and Models*. Boston: Kluwer Academic Publishers.

Anselin, Luc (1989) 'What is Special about Spatial Data? Alternative Perspectives on Spatial Data Analysis', paper presented at the Symposium on *Spatial Statistics, Past, Present, and Future*, Syracuse University.

Anselin, Luc (1995) 'Local Indicators of Spatial Association – LISA'. *Geographical Analysis*, 27(2): 93–115.

Anselin, Luc and Bera, Anil (1998) 'Spatial Dependence in Linear Regression Models with an Introduction to Spatial Econometrics'. In Amman Ullah and David E.A. Giles (eds) *Handbook of Applied Economic Statistics*. New York: Marcel Dekker, Inc., pp. 237–90.

Anselin, Luc, Cohen, Jacqueline, Cook, David, Gorr, Wilpen and Tita, George (2000) 'Spatial Analyses of Crime'. In National Institute of Justice, *Criminal Justice 2000, Volume 14, Measurement and Analysis of Crime and Justice*. Washington, DC: US Department of Justice.

Anselin, Luc, Florax, Raymond J.G.M. and Rey, Sergio J. (eds) (2004) *Advances in Spatial Econometrics: Methodology, Tools and Applications*. New York: Springer.

Anselin, Luc, Griffiths, Elizabeth and Tita, George (2008) 'Crime Mapping and Hot Spot Analysis'. In Richard Wortley, and Lorraine Mazerolle (eds) *Environmental Criminology and Crime Analysis*. Devon: Willan Publishing, pp. 97–116.

Baller, Robert D., Anselin, Luc, Messner, Steven R., Deane, Glenn and Hawkins, Darnell F. (2001) 'Structural Covariates of US County Homicide Rates: Incorporating Spatial Effects'. *Criminology*, 39(3): 561–90.

Berry, William D. and Baybeck, Brady (2005) 'Using Geographic Information Systems to Study Interstate Competition'. *American Political Science Review*, 99(4): 505–19.

Boots, Barry N. and Getis, Arthur (1988) *Point Pattern Analysis*. Newbury Park, CA: Sage Publications.

Cieri, Marie (2003) 'Between Being and Looking: Queer Tourism Promotion and Lesbian Social Space in Greater Philadelphia'. *ACME*, 2(2): 147–66.

Cliff, A.D. and Ord, J.K. (1973) *Spatial Autocorrelation*. London: Pion.

Cohen, Jacqueline and Tita, George (1999) 'Diffusion in Homicide: Exploring a General Method for Detecting Spatial Diffusion Processes'. *Journal of Quantitative Criminology*, 15(4): 451–93.

Cox, Allen B. (1995) 'An Overview to Geographic Information Systems'. *The Journal of Academic Librarianship*, 21(4): 237–49.

de Luna, Xavier and Genton, Marc G. (2004) 'Spatio-Temporal Autoregressive Models for U.S. Unemployment Rate'. In James P. Lesage and R. Kelley Pace (eds) *Spatial and Spatiotemporal Econometrics: Advances in Econometrics, Volume 18*. New York: Elsevier, pp. 279–94.

Downey, Liam (2003) 'Spatial Measurement, Geography, and Urban Racial Inequality'. *Social Forces*, 81(3): 937–52.

Downey, Liam (2006) 'Using Geographic Information Systems to Reconceptualize Spatial Relationships and Ecological Context'. *American Journal of Sociology*, 112(2): 567–612.

Dyck, Joshua J. and Gimpel, James G. (2005) 'Distance, Turnout, and the Convenience of Voting'. *Social Science Quarterly*, 86(3): 531–48.

Elhorst, J. Paul (2004) 'Serial and Spatial Error Dependence in Space-Time Models'. In Arthur Getis, Jesús Mur, and Henry G. Zoller (eds) *Spatial Econometrics and Spatial Statistics*. New York: Palgrave Macmillan, pp. 176–93.

Entwisle, Barbara, Rindfuss, Ronald R., Walsh, Stephen J., Evans, Tom P. and Curran, Sara R. (1997) 'Geographic Information Systems, Spatial Network Analysis, and Contraceptive Choice'. *Demography*, 34(2): 171–87.

ESRI (1990) *Understanding GIS: The Arc/Info Method.* Redlands, CA: Environmental Systems Research Institute.

Fotheringham, A. Stewart, Brunsdon, Chris and Charlton, Martin (2000) *Quantitative Geography: Perspectives on Spatial Data Analysis.* London: Sage Publications.

Fotheringham, A. Stewart, Brunsdon, Chris and Charlton, Martin (2002) *Geographically Weighted Regression: The Analysis of Spatially Varying Relationships.* England: John Wiley & Sons Ltd.

Gartner, Rosemary and McCarthy Bill (n.d.) *Homicide in Four Cities Data Set.* Social Sciences and Humanities Research Council of Canada (SSHRC), Grant # 410-94-0756.

Geanuracos, Catherine G., Cunningham, Shayna D., Weiss, George, Forte, Draco, Henry Reid, Lisa M. and Ellen, Jonathan M. (2007) 'Use of Geographic Information Systems for Planning HIV Prevention Interventions for High-Risk Youth'. *American Journal of Public Health,* 97(11): 1974–81.

Getis, Arthur (1995) 'Spatial Filtering in a Regression Framework: Examples Using Data on Urban Crime, Regional Inequality, and Government Expenditures'. In Luc Anselin and Raymond J.G.M. Florax (eds) *New Directions in Spatial Econometrics.* New York: Springer, pp. 172–85.

Getis, Arthur and Griffith, Daniel A. (2002) 'Comparative Spatial Filtering in Regression Analysis'. *Geographical Analysis,* 34(2): 130–40.

Getis, Arthur and Aldstadt, Jared (2004) 'Constructing the Spatial Weights Matrix Using a Local Statistic'. *Geographical Analysis,* 36(2): 90–104.

Getis, Arthur, Mur, Jesús and Zoller, Henry G. (eds) (2004) *Spatial Econometrics and Spatial Statistics.* New York: Palgrave Macmillan.

Gibbs Knotts, H. and Haspel, Moshe (2006) 'The Impact of Gentrification on Voter Turnout'. *Social Science Quarterly,* 87(1): 110–21.

Gieryn, Thomas F. (2000) 'A Space for Place in Sociology'. *Annual Review of Sociology,* 26: 463–96.

Golledge, Reginald G. and Stimson, Robert J. (1997) *Spatial Behavior: A Geographic Perspective.* New York: The Guilford Press.

Gomez, Brad T., Hansford, Thomas G. and Krause, George A. (2007) 'The Republicans Should Pray for Rain: Weather, Turnout, and Voting in U.S. Presidential Elections'. *The Journal of Politics,* 69(3): 649–63.

Griffith, Daniel A. (1988) *Advanced Spatial Statistics: Special Topics in the Exploration of Quantitative Spatial Data Series.* New York: Springer.

Griffith, Daniel A. (1996) 'Some Guidelines for Specifying the Geographic Weights Matrix Contained in Spatial Statistical Models'. In Sandra L. Arlinghaus (ed.) *Practical Handbook of Spatial Statistics.* Boca Raton: CRC, pp. 65–82.

Griffiths, Elizabeth (2007) *The Diffusion of Homicide across Neighbourhoods: A Social Ecological Case Study of Buffalo, New York, 1950–1999.* PhD dissertation, University of Toronto.

Griffiths, Elizabeth and Chavez, Jorge (2004) 'Communities, Street Guns, and Homicide Trajectories in Chicago, 1980–1995: Merging Methods for Examining Homicide Trends across Space and Time'. *Criminology,* 42(4): 941–78.

Haining, Robert (2003) *Spatial Data Analysis: Theory and Practice.* Cambridge: Cambridge University Press.

Heikkila, Eric J. (1998) 'GIS is Dead; Long Live GIS!'. *Journal of the American Planning Association,* 64(3): 350–60.

Hipp, John R. (2007) 'Block, Tract, and Levels of Aggregation: Neighborhood Structure and Crime and Disorder as a Case in Point'. *American Sociological Review,* 72(5): 659–80.

Kain, John F. (1968) 'Housing Segregation, Negro Employment, and Metropolitan Decentralization'. *Quarterly Journal of Economics,* 82(2): 175–97.

Kuhn, Thomas S. (1962) *The Structure of Scientific Revolutions,* 3rd edn. Chicago: The University of Chicago Press.

Kulldorff, M. (1997) 'A Spatial Scan Statistic'. *Communications in Statistics: Theory and Methods,* 26(6): 1487–96.

Kwan, Mei-Po (2007) 'Affecting Geospatial Technologies: Toward a Feminist Politics of Emotion'. *The Professional Geographer,* 59(1): 22–34.

Landry, Pierre F. and Shen, Mingming (2005) 'Reaching Migrants in Survey Research: The Use of the Global Positioning System to Reduce Coverage Bias in China'. *Political Analysis,* 13(1): 1–22.

Leenders, Roger Th. A.J. (2002) 'Modeling Social Influence through Network Autocorrelation: Constructing the Weight Matrix'. *Social Networks,* 24(1): 21–47.

Lesage, James P. and Pace, R. Kelley (2004) *Spatial and Spatiotemporal Econometrics: Advances in Econometrics, Volume 18.* New York: Elsevier.

Levine, Jonathan and Landis, John (1989) 'Geographic Information Systems for Local Planning'. *Journal of the American Planning Association,* 55(2): 209–20.

Marble, Duane F. (1990) 'Geographic Information Systems: An Overview'. In Donna J. Peuquet and Duane F. Marble (eds) *Introductory Readings in Geographic Information Systems.* London: Taylor and Francis, pp. 8–17.

Massey, Douglas (1985) 'Ethnic Residential Segregation: A Theoretical Synthesis and Empirical Review'. *Sociology and Social Research,* 69(3): 315–50.

McLafferty, Sara and Grady, Sue (2005) 'Immigration and Geographic Access to Prenatal Clinics in Brooklyn, NY: A Geographic Information Systems Analysis'. *American Journal of Public Health,* 95(4): 638–40.

Mears, Daniel P. and Bhati, Avinash S. (2006) 'No Community is an Island: The Effects of Resource Deprivation on Urban Violence in Spatially and Socially Proximate Communities'. *Criminology,* 44(3): 509–48.

Meltzoff, Julian (2005a) 'Ethics in Research'. *Journal of Aggression, Maltreatment & Trauma,* 11(3): 311–36.

Meltzoff, Julian (2005b) 'Ethics in Publication'. *Journal of Aggression, Maltreatment & Trauma,* 11(3): 337–55.

Messner, Steven F., Anselin, Luc, Baller, Robert D., Hawkins, Darnell F., Deane, Glenn and Tolnay, Stewart E. (1999) 'The Spatial Patterning of County Homicide Rates: An Application of Exploratory Spatial Data Analysis'. *Journal of Quantitative Criminology,* 15(4): 423–50.

Monmonier, Mark (1996) *How to Lie with Maps,* 2nd edn. Chicago: University of Chicago Press.

Morenoff, Jeffrey D. (2003) 'Neighborhood Mechanisms and the Spatial Dynamics of Birth Weight'. *American Journal of Sociology,* 108(5): 976–1017.

Nyerges, A. Endre and Martin Green, Glen (2000) 'The Ethnography of Landscape: GIS and Remote Sensing in the Study of Forest Change in West African Guinea Savanna'. *American Anthropologist,* 102(2): 271–89.

Openshaw, Stan (1984) *The Modifiable Areal Unit Problem,* CATMOG 38. Norwich, England: GeoBooks.

Openshaw, Stan and Rao, Liang (1995) 'Algorithms for Re-engineering 1991 Census Geography'. *Environment and Planning A,* 27(3): 425–46.

Openshaw, Stan and Taylor, P.J. (1979) 'A Million or So Correlation Coefficients: Three Experiments on the Modifiable Areal Unit Problem'. In N. Wrigley (ed.) *Statistical Applications in the Spatial Sciences.* London: Pion, pp. 127–44.

Openshaw, Stan, Charlton, Martin, Wymer, Colin and Craft, Alan (1987) 'A Mark I Geographical Analysis Machine for the Automated Analysis of Point Data Sets'. *International Journal of Geographical Information Systems,* 1(4): 359–77.

Ord, J.K. and Getis, Arthur (1995) 'Local Spatial Autocorrelation Statistics: Distributional Issues and an Application'. *Geographical Analysis,* 27(4): 286–306.

Queralt, Magaly and Witte, Ann D. (1998) 'A Map for You? Geographic Information Systems in the Social Services'. *Social Work,* 43(5): 455–69.

Sampson, Robert J., Morenoff, Jeffrey D. and Gannon-Rowley, Thomas (2002) 'Assessing "Neighborhood Effects": Social Processes and New Directions in Research'. *Annual Review of Sociology,* 28: 443–78.

Schabenberger, Oliver and Gotway, Carol A. (2005) *Statistical Methods for Spatial Data Analysis.* Florida: CRC Press.

Shaw, Clifford R. and McKay, Henry D. (1942) *Juvenile Delinquency in Urban Areas.* Chicago: University of Chicago Press.

Shin, Michael E. and Agnew, John (2007) 'The Geographical Dynamics of Italian Electoral Change, 1987–2001'. *Electoral Studies,* 26(2): 287–302.

Smith, Tony (2004) 'Aggregation Bias in Maximum Likelihood Estimation of Spatial Autoregressive Processes'. In Arthur Getis, Jesús Mur, and Henry G. Zoller (eds) *Spatial Econometrics and Spatial Statistics.* New York: Palgrave Macmillan, pp. 53–88.

Talen, Emily and Shah, Swasti (2007) 'Neighborhood Evaluation Using GIS: An Exploratory Study'. *Environment and Behavior,* 39(5): 583–615.

Tita, George E. and Greenbaum, Robert T. (2008) 'Crime, Neighborhoods and Units of Analysis: Putting Space in its Place'. In David Weisburd, Wim Bernasco, and Gerben J.N. Bruinsma (eds) *Putting Crime in its Place: Units of Analysis in Geographic Criminology.* New York: Springer, pp. 145–70.

Tobler, Waldo R. (1970) 'A Computer Movie Simulating Urban Growth in the Detroit Region'. *Economic Geography,* 46(June Supplement): 234–40.

Unwin, A. and Unwin, D. (1998) 'Exploratory Spatial Data Analysis with Local Statistics'. *The Statistician,* 47(3): 415–23.

Waller, Lance A. and Gotway, Carol A. (2004) *Applied Spatial Statistics for Public Health.* New Jersey: Wiley.

Wieczorek, William F. and Hanson, Craig E. (1997) 'Geographic Information Systems and Spatial Analysis'. *Alcohol Health & Research World,* 21(4): 331–39.

Wilson, William Julius (1987) *The Truly Disadvantaged: The Inner City, the Underclass, and Public Policy.* Chicago: University of Chicago Press.

Wong, Yin-Ling Irene and Hillier, Amy E. (2001) 'Evaluating a Community-Based Homelessness Prevention Program: A Geographic Information System Approach'. *Administration in Social Work,* 25(4): 21–45.

PART 4

Sampling, Inference and Measurement

Introduction

W. Paul Vogt and Malcolm Williams

Modern statistical theory is built upon assumption of random sampling from a known population. It can also be based upon the assumption of random assignment of research subjects to control/experimental groups. Ideally the pool of research subjects randomly assigned would have been drawn from a random sample of a clearly defined population. Further, the statistical theory that justifies making inferences from random samples and randomly assigned groups is based on the assumption of a complete data set – samples and control/experimental groups with no missing data. Finally, it is assumed that the data are measured reliably and validly with no systematic error. Of course, this is a formidable set of impossibly ideal assumptions. It is never met in social research. Innovation in research on quantitative data is driven by the need to find ways to make the real world approximate the ideal world of statistical assumptions.

Real world messiness intrudes on the theoretical world of mathematical assumptions in several ways. Populations may be unknown so that identifying a sampling frame from which to draw a random sample is not feasible. Sampled individuals often refuse to participate. Random assignment may be impossible for practical or ethical reasons, or, if possible, potential research subjects may resist being assigned at random. Variables may not be manipulable; this means that even when groups can be randomly assigned, researchers cannot control the treatments that are delivered to them. And data are almost always missing – even in modern, randomized controlled trials (Baccini et al., 2010). Program or experimental participants withdraw. Survey respondents skip particular questions. Variables of interest are often 'latent' meaning that there is no direct way to measure them; one makes do with more or less satisfactory indicators. We all know that the assumptions on which typical textbook descriptions of research methods are based are unrealistic. Much of what is innovatory in modern research methods has arisen to meet the challenge of conducting valid and reliable research in circumstances that are far less than ideal. The six chapters in this section address aspects of these less than ideal circumstances and propose innovative solutions – or, at least, 'work arounds'.

Respondent-driven sampling (RDS), as described by Wejnert and Heckathorn in Chapter 22, provides rigorous sampling and estimation procedures for use when the populations are unknown or difficult to reach – classic examples being homeless people, illegal drug users, and individuals with HIV/AIDS. RDS builds on the idea of snowball sampling in which initial respondents give the researcher suggestions for finding subsequent respondents. Briefly the procedure is as follows: A small number of initial respondents, called *seeds*, are recruited. These in turn recruit others, who recruit still others until an *equilibrium* point is reached. Of course, such networks of respondents are not random, but by using information about who recruited whom, researchers can adjust for sample bias. A major assumption of RDS, one that has been shown to be reasonable in many circumstances, is that such adjustments yield unbiased samples. Another method for sampling populations that are hard to contact, are rare, and/or whose membership is unknown is the so-called 'contact–recontact' method. The basic idea of contact–recontact method was developed in the study of animal populations, where it is usually known as capture–recapture. For instance, to study the fish population of a lake, researchers capture, mark, and release a sample of fish. By doing so repeatedly and noting how many of subsequent captures had been previously captured, it is possible to estimate the size and composition of the lake's population of fish. Adapting this method to human populations has not been easy (see Hay et al., 2009 and Williams and Cheal, 2002 for examples). The capture–recapture method seems to be more widespread in the UK while RDS is more discussed in the US. Both address the problem that populations of interest to social researchers are often not accessible under the assumptions of classical sampling theory. This example reminds us that innovation on the same problem may proceed along different paths in different national contexts.

A growing issue in research based on sampling, such as survey research, is the phenomenon of declining response rates. Potential respondents are getting harder to contact and are more likely to refuse to participate when contacted. This is a pervasive and persistent problem in surveys of all types and in all nations (Groves, 2006). How serious a problem is it, how much bias does it introduce into the results, and what can researchers do to counteract this bias? Non-response is a problem because inferences are made based on a sampling theory which assumes a 100% response rate. That target is being missed by ever-wider margins. The best approach is to use imputation techniques to adjust for the missing data coming from non-response. To use imputation techniques, researchers need to include auxiliary variables that are related both to the propensity to respond and to the key variables of interest in the survey. Carpenter and Plewis in Chapter 23 provide a set of innovative options for handling the problems of missing data, especially when data are missing in longitudinal research. This is an especially important area of investigation because the problem of missing data tends, for obvious reasons, to be much greater in longitudinal social surveys than in cross-sectional surveys.

Missing data problems are not confined to longitudinal survey research of course. Indeed, they pervade all forms of research. As Rubin eloquently explains in Chapter 24, missing data problems are at the heart of all inference, including causal inference. For example, in an experiment, we have data about effects on those receiving a treatment, but we do not, and cannot, have data about outcomes when they did not receive the treatment. Hypothetical data about what we can reasonably *assume* would have happened had they not received treatment is available from the control group. We use data from a control group to infer missing data from individuals whom we cannot compare in two simultaneous states, both in and out of treatment. We compare two outcomes, the first actual, the second counterfactual to make assumptions about the counterfactual state. As Rubin says, 'there is no assumption-free causal inference'. Rubin's causal model (RCM) has been around since the 1980s, but it is still innovative in the sense that researchers continue to switch to it. It is new for them as is the greater accessibility of its Bayesian (rather than frequentist) foundations. One of the RCM's important features is that it unifies the notation for analyzing causal outcomes in experimental and observational studies. Missing data imputation is important for inference in both. As Rubin explains, Bayesian/likelihood methods for estimating missing data, such as multiple imputation, are increasingly improved. The necessary software, rooted in MCMC simulations, is better than just a decade ago, and the methods and the software continue to be under innovative development.

Many social research concepts are too abstract to study directly. To gather empirical data, concepts usually need to be made more concrete. One method is to stipulate *operational definitions*, which are the concrete steps (operations) one takes to decide how to categorize or measure a concept. A second method is to specify the *indicators* one will use to determine whether something is present or absent and, if present, how much of it there is. The ways we code and measure often imply something substantive about what we are studying. The indicators or operational definitions can be substantively related to the concept in several, partly overlapping ways. They can be: components, conditions, symptoms, or causes. First, an indicator can be a *component*, part of the definition of the concept, as many theorists see free elections to be a definitional component of democracy. Second, the components can be conditions of a concept. They may be sufficient conditions, necessary conditions, or a group of necessary conditions which are, together, sufficient. Third, an indicator can be a *symptom*, caused by the concept. This approach is the basis of most structural equation modeling (SEM), but it is much older than that. A classic example is Durkheim's study of the history of morality by studying the history of law. His theory was that, in the long run, a society's moral values shape its laws. A society's laws are a symptom (indicator) of its moral values. Note that, like many indicators, this is a substantive assertion, not merely a measurement convenience. Fourth, an indicator can be a *cause* of the concept. For example, a standard definition of prejudice is: an irrational negative belief about someone or something in the face of evidence to the contrary. One indicator of prejudice is irrationality. That is because irrationality is a component of prejudice, *and* because irrationality causes prejudice.

These relations between concepts, indicators, and operational definitions are the subject of our next three chapters (25, 26, and 27). One of the most rapidly expanding areas of applied research in which (manifest) indicators of (latent) variables or concepts is crucial is the field of test development. Testing and measurement of knowledge and ability requires a way to generate multiple indicators that are valid and reliable. The spread of high-stakes testing stimulates this demand. Embretson and McIntyre in Chapter 25 provide the background and introduce us to the most recent approach – automatic item generation (AIG), which is a computerized method to write items. The old approach to test item construction (and the current approach to most survey question writing) was to use the knowledge and experience of the test writers to draft some items, try them out, and analyze how they worked in practice. It is possible to do much better using techniques based on structural modeling and especially on item response theory (IRT). IRT is a group of methods for assessing the reliability, validity, and difficulty of items on tests. The assumption is that each of the items is measuring some aspect of the same underlying (latent) ability, trait, or attitude. IRT is important for determining equivalency of tests, the difficulty of test items, and the ability or knowledge of the individuals responding to those items. Simply put, the difficulty of items is judged by the number of individuals who get them right and the knowledge of individuals is judged by how many items they got right. Good test items discriminate among the ability levels of the test takers. For example, a valid difficult item should be answered correctly mostly by individuals who scored well on the other items. An example of a poor item would be one that only high-ability test takers answered incorrectly. IRT uses a version of logistic regression as its basic tool; the dependent variable is the log of the odds of answering questions correctly. What Embretson and McIntyre illustrate is how the theoretically rich procedures of IRT are being incorporated into an area of work all but inconceivable until recently: computer-intensive methods to generate test items.

The final two chapters in this section introduce us to some of the more exciting developments in structural equation modeling and multi-level modeling (MLM). Both emerged in the closing decades of the twentieth century and rapidly became standard items in the advanced researcher's toolkit. And both are still under rapid development.

SEM (also called analysis of covariance structures) is a sophisticated statistical method for testing complex causal models in which the dependent and independent variables are latent. A latent variable is a construct, or a theoretical entity, inferred from a pattern of relations (a structure) among observable variables.

SEM combines the techniques of factor analysis, path analysis, and multiple regression thus allowing researchers to study the effects of latent variables on each other. SEM is used to analyze causal models with multiple indicators of latent variables and structural relations among latent variables. It is more powerful than simple path analysis, because bias due to random measurement error in the multiple indicators of the latent variables is corrected. It goes beyond the more typical exploratory factor analysis, and allows the researcher to conduct confirmatory factor analyses.

Multi-level modeling is also called hierarchical linear modeling (HLM) after the widely used software package used to conduct these analyses. It is also called 'covariance components models', and, mostly by economists, 'random coefficients models'. MLMs are also called mixed models or 'mixed effects models' (not to be confused with mixed-methods research), because they always include both fixed and random effects. The proliferation of names for identical or highly similar techniques is due to the relative newness of the techniques, the fact that they were created more or less simultaneously by several researchers in different disciplines, and, perhaps, to the desire of software creators to come up with distinctive brand names. Multi-level modeling is probably the most generic term, but the others are both descriptive and widely used.

MLM is an alternative to OLS regression models used when data are in nested categories or levels, such as, to use the most frequent example, students in a classroom, which is in a school, which is in a neighborhood. With MLM it is possible to separate the variance into components explaining the effects of different levels of analysis, such as the effects of a classroom, a school, and a neighborhood. Usually a single dependent variable at one level is explained with predictor variables at more than one level. For example, a multi-level study of the effects of schooling on academic achievement could study the effects on student learning (Level 1) of a particular classroom (Level 2), which is located in a given school (Level 3). Models with more than three levels are possible but rare. MLMs can also be used to study repeated observations of individuals over time, in which case the observations (Level 1) are nested within the individuals (Level 2). MLMs are often considered more realistic because they explicitly incorporate social context into explanations of outcomes.

Some of the most exciting developments in these two rapidly evolving suites of methods involve efforts to combine them. There is a tendency for MLM to be more interesting to sociologists and economists and SEM to be more interesting to psychologists and others working in psychology-based disciplines. Some of that is understandable because of the research questions of interest to investigators in these fields, but methodologically, this is unfortunate since the SEM and MLM are related in many ways. Kline in Chapter 26 and Pituch and Stapleton in Chapter 27 introduce us to the innovative ways in which the two are being combined.

Kline points out that the SEM and HLM 'families of techniques have some complementary strengths and weaknesses' and that they are 'more closely related to each other' than it might at first seem. He also reviews the software applications for conducting one or both of them. Pituch and Stapleton also review the advantages and disadvantages associated with the two approaches to modeling, MLM (which they call HLM) and SEM. While Kline discusses MLM and SEM more generally, Pituch and Stapleton focus on their specific applications to research involving large-scale experimental designs, especially randomized field trials. In brief, both authors agree that SEM improves the study of constructs with multiple indicators and, in Pituch and Stapleton's words, MLM/HLM 'is more useful when additional levels are present in the data structure, such as student, class, and school'.

The complications to using either method are formidable, and integrating the two is even more challenging, despite recent software advances. But the reward for mastering them is great. Many and probably most of the problems social researchers are interested in are in fact multi-level problems. And many of the constructs social researchers study are best measured as latent variables with multiple indicators. SEM and MLM, and especially the innovations that have led to their integration, better enable us to study the world as it is. With the integration of SEM and MLM our methods better match our ambitions and are in greater accord with what we believe to be true about the world we are trying to study.

REFERENCES

Baccini, Michela, Sam Cook, Constantine Frangakis, Fan Li, Fabrizia Mealli, Don Rubin, and Elizabeth Zell (2010) Multiple imputation in the anthrax vaccine research program. *Chance,* 23(1): 16–23.

Groves, Robert M. (2006). Nonresponse rates and nonresponse bias in household surveys. *Public Opinion Quarterly,* 70(5): 646–75.

Hay, Gordon, Maria Gannon, Jane MacDougall, Catherine Eastwood, Kate Williams, and Tim Millar (2009). Capture–recapture and anchored prevalence estimation of injecting drug users in England: National and regional estimates. *Statistical Methods for Medical Research,* 18: 323–39.

Williams, Malcolm and Brian Cheal (2002) Can we measure homelessness? A critical evaluation of the method of 'capture–recapture'. *International Journal of Social Research Methodology,* 5(4): 313–31.

22

Respondent-Driven Sampling: Operational Procedures, Evolution of Estimators, and Topics for Future Research

Cyprian Wejnert and Douglas Heckathorn

INTRODUCTION

Respondent-driven sampling (RDS) is a method for drawing and analyzing probability samples of hidden, or 'hard-to-reach', populations. Populations such as these can be difficult to sample using standard survey research methods for two reasons: First, they lack a sampling frame, that is, an exhaustive list of population members from which the sample can be drawn. Second, constructing a sampling frame is not feasible because one or more of the following are true: (a) the population is such a small part of the general population that locating them through a general population survey would be prohibitively costly; (b) because the population has social networks that are difficult for outsiders to penetrate, access to the population requires personal contacts; and/or (c) membership in the population is stigmatized, so gaining access requires establishing trust. Populations with these characteristics are important to many research areas including public health studies of HIV and other infectious diseases, sociological studies of the welfare of marginalized or low income groups, and network studies of large populations.

RDS is now widely used to study a wide range of hidden populations in the US including jazz musicians (Heckathorn and Jeffri, 2001), aging artists (Spiller et al., 2008), drug users (Abdul-Quader et al., 2006), men who have sex with men (Ramirez-Valles et al., 2005), and Latino migrant workers (Kissinger et al., 2008). Internationally, over 120 studies in 30 countries have used RDS to study HIV/AIDS and other sexually transmitted infections (Malekinejad et al., 2008).

RDS accesses members of hidden populations through their social networks, employing a variant of a snowball or 'chain-referral' sampling. As in all such samples, the study begins with a set of initial respondents who serve as *seeds*. These seeds then recruit their acquaintances, friends, or relatives who qualify for inclusion in the study to form the first 'wave'. The first wave respondents then recruit the second wave, who in turn recruit the third wave, and so forth. By allowing respondents to recruit new participants directly, RDS removes the need for researchers to locate population members, penetrate social networks through personal contacts, or establish trust within stigmatized populations.

While snowball sampling has been used for decades (Coleman, 1958), the resultant data have generally been viewed as convenience samples because respondents are not sampled in a random way. RDS challenges this view by applying a mathematical model that weights the sample to compensate for the fact that it was not obtained in a simple random way (Salganik and Heckathorn, 2004). Consequently, RDS provides researchers a method of harnessing the advantages of snowball sampling without sacrificing the ability to make unbiased population estimates.

In this chapter we first present operational procedures used in collecting RDS data. We then outline the progression of two families of the RDS estimator and discuss RDS network analysis techniques. The chapter concludes with a discussion of limitations, ongoing projects, and directions for future RDS development.

OPERATIONAL PROCEDURES OF RDS

RDS operational procedures primarily consist of recruiting seeds, setting incentives, and collecting data necessary for RDS analysis. Additionally, it is important for operating procedures to promote long recruitment changes and minimize recruitment by strangers. Figure 22.1 shows an RDS recruitment network of university undergraduates by gender and fraternity/sorority membership. The sample starts with nine seeds from which 378 additional respondents are gathered. As is common in RDS studies, a small number of seeds produce a majority of recruitments.

Seed selection

As in all chain-referral samples, the sampling process in RDS begins with the selection of an initial set of respondent group members or seeds (Heckathorn, 1997).

Figure 22.1 RDS recruitment chains of university undergraduates by gender and fraternity/sorority membership. The sample includes nine seeds, however over 80% of sample originates from two 'super seeds'

The seeds complete the survey interview and are then asked to recruit a specified number of additional respondents to be interviewed, who in turn recruit a subsequent wave of respondent group members, and so on until a target sample size has been reached. Because the ultimate sample composition under RDS does not depend upon the characteristics of the seeds chosen, it is not necessary that the seeds be randomly chosen. However, because the rate at which sample composition becomes independent of seeds is increased if the seeds chosen are diverse with regard to key characteristics, choosing a diverse set of seeds increases the efficiency of the sampling operation.

Given that recruitment chains grow only if seeds actually recruit, it is also important that seeds be well motivated. Ideally, seeds should be sociometric stars that are committed to the goals of the study. These characteristics fit the 'volunteers' with which many snowball samples begin, and have traditionally been seen as a source of bias in these samples. In contrast, in RDS, given that seed selection becomes irrelevant only if seeds succeed in spawning expansive recruitment chains, starting with high energy seeds does not add to bias but instead reduces it by speeding the recruitment process.

Incentives

RDS relies on dual incentives to encourage participation and achieve sufficiently long referral chains (Heckathorn, 1997). First, respondents are rewarded for participating in an interview. Second, respondents are given a modest reward for each peer they recruit into the study. For example, in a recent US study of drug users conducted by De Jarlais et al. (2007), respondents were paid $20 for participating in a survey interview and an additional $10 for each drug user they successfully recruited (i.e. whose recruits subsequently appear to be interviewed and fulfill the study criteria for inclusion). These recruits were in turn paid to be interviewed and for each successful recruit.

The size of incentive is determined on a setting-by-setting basis, but in general should be of sufficient size to encourage participation by respondent group members, but not so large as to encourage participation by imposters. Excessive rewards could also encourage coercive recruitment.

Idealistic motives for recruiting peers are also emphasized. In this way, respondents are provided not only with a means to earn respondent fees, but also a means to help peers by giving them the opportunity to benefit from participation in the study. It is emphasized to subjects that by recruiting peers, they are undertaking a task that in most other studies is carried out by public health professionals; and the rewards they receive are recognition for their having succeeded at this important task. Rewards for recruiters are a useful means for promoting peer recruitment and thereby producing the large recruitment chains upon which the RDS method depends.

Recruitment quotas and the referral process

As discussed below, sampling bias is minimized in RDS by having long referral chains. In order to encourage longer referral chains and promote greater socio-metric depth, recruitment quotas are used in order to limit the ability of population members with large personal networks to dominate a given sample

(Heckathorn, 1997). Consider, for example, what would happen without quotas. If one respondent recruited 10 peers, each of whom recruited 10 peers, the sample size would quickly grow huge, for example starting from a single seed (wave 0) to 10, then 100, then 1,000, and 10,000 by wave 4. In contrast, if each recruited only 2 peers, the growth would be much slower, for example from the single seed, to 2, then 4, then 8, and then 16 by wave 4. Thus, for any given sample size, restrictive recruitment quotas produce recruitment chains with more waves. Quotas are also useful because they make recruitment rights scarce and hence too valuable to waste on strangers.

Choosing the proper recruitment quota involves a trade-off. If the quota is too small, recruitment may die out because some subjects fail to recruit and others do not fulfill their quotas. Furthermore, restrictive recruitment quotas slow the recruitment process, because they prevent energetic recruiters from contributing as much as they could. Therefore, quotas should be small, but not oppressively so. In most RDS applications in the US to date, the quota has been set at 3 or 4 recruits per recruiter, and only about two-thirds of recruitment rights have usually been exercised, so when the quota is 3, the average number of recruits per subject is 2. In general, an initial quota of 3 recruits per respondent group member is recommended.

In many applications of RDS, recruitment quotas have been implemented by providing subjects with paper money-sized recruitment coupons (see Figure 22.2). The coupon includes information on how to contact the project and a map to the interview site. Each coupon also includes a unique serial number. This is useful for determining how much each subject should be paid for recruitment. More importantly, it is also useful for documenting who recruited whom, a piece of information that is crucial for calculating RDS population estimates. The serial number also ensures that only the subject to whom it was given can be rewarded for the recruitment, so the recruitment coupons cannot circulate as though they were an alternative form of money.

Data requirements

RDS analysis has special data requirements because each analysis requires not only information on the focal variable, but also two additional items of information that function to provide the sampling frame from which post-stratification weights are calculated. These are:

- Cross-group recruitment (e.g. proportional recruitment of HIV positives by HIV negatives, and recruitment of HIV negatives by HIV positives).
- Estimated mean network sizes (e.g. the estimated mean network sizes of HIV positives and negatives).

The reason why every RDS study must keep track of who recruited whom is so that these cross-group recruitment proportions can be calculated, and the reason

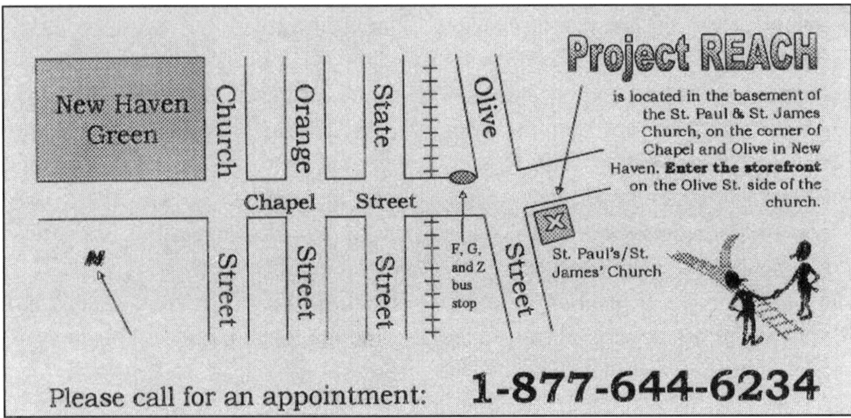

Figure 22.2 Example of a recruitment coupon employed in an RDS study of Connecticut injection drug users (IDUs). Note that the front includes a serial number, and the back includes a map to the interview site

why each respondent must be asked about their personal network size, termed *degree,* is so that estimated mean degree by group can be calculated. These are then used to calculate unbiased population estimates.

A typical question for measuring personal degree in a study of IDUs is: 'How many people do you know personally who inject, that is people you know, who also know you, and that you have seen at least once in the last 6 months?' Note that it is essential that this question be framed so subjects are asked about the number of peers they know who fit the screening criteria for the study, because the aim of this question is to find out how many potentially recruitable persons the respondent knows. It is also important that the question make clear that these are not people the respondent has heard about, but persons with whom the respondent has a personal relationship. Finally, an interval for most recent contact should be specified to exclude persons known only in the distant past.

In order to provide a test of two key assumptions for analysis (discussed below) two additional items of information are collected:

- Relationship of recruit to recruiter. This can be assessed using the following question asked from each recruit: How can your relationship to your recruiter be best described: As closer than a friend; As a friend; As an acquaintance; As a stranger; etc.?
- Proportional distribution of networks. This is generally added as a follow up to the degree question by asking: How many of these [answer to network question] people are White? Black? Hispanic? Male? Female? etc.

These last items allow the researcher to test two key assumptions of RDS: reciprocity (that each respondent knows his or her recruiter) and random recruitment from among one's peers (that the composition of recruitment is representative of the composition of personal networks).

WebRDS

Wejnert and Heckathorn (2008) introduce an online version of RDS, termed *WebRDS*. WebRDS studies follow similar operating procedures as regular RDS, except the interview is replaced by a web-based survey and recruitment occurs through an electronic medium such as email. Among populations that are well connected electronically, WebRDS provides several advantages over regular RDS. First, because there is no need for an interview location or staff, the operating cost in terms of manpower and capital is minimal. Once seeds have been contacted and the survey has been set up, the researcher need to only distribute incentives and download the data. Second, because respondents can be recruited, complete the survey, and recruit peers from their personal computer, the sampling speed can be especially fast. In their WebRDS study of university undergraduates, Wejnert and Heckathorn (2008) were able to collect a sample of 159 surveys in 72 hours. While not yet tested, WebRDS also has the potential to sample online communities without geographical limitation.

WebRDS has several limitations. First, the anonymity of the internet makes uniquely identifying respondents and therefore preventing study exploitation through repeat participation difficult. Similarly, limiting false positives, that is respondents who are not members of the target population, presents a challenge. Finally, because respondents are never physically in contact with the researcher, distribution of incentives can be problematic. While further research is needed to fully remove these limitations, incentives and distribution can be designed to provide some safeguards. For example, in a WebRDS study of university undergraduates, Wejnert and Heckathorn (2008) required respondents to pick up incentives in person and present a valid university student ID. Alternately, online studies could provide gift cards to sellers who only sell products of interest to the target population.

ANALYSIS AND ESTIMATION

RDS is based on a mathematical model of the recruitment process which functions somewhat like a corrective lens, controlling the distorting effects of network structure on the sampling process to produce an unbiased estimate of population characteristics. This procedure includes controls for four biases that are inherent in any snowball sample:

1 The seeds cannot be recruited randomly, because if that were possible, the population would not qualify as 'hidden' in the first place. Generally, the seeds are respondents to whom researchers have easy access, a group that may not be representative of the full target population. Consequently, the seeds introduce an initial bias.
2 Respondents recruit their acquaintances, friends, and family members, whom they tend to resemble in income, education, race/ethnicity, religion, and other factors. The implication of this 'homophily' principle is that by recruiting those whom they know, respondents do not recruit randomly. Instead recruitments are shaped by the social network connecting the target population.
3 Respondents who are well-connected tend to be over-sampled, because more recruitment paths lead to them. Therefore, respondents who have larger social networks are over-sampled.
4 Population subgroups vary in how effectively they can recruit, so the sample reflects disproportionately the recruitment patterns of the most effective recruiters. For example, in AIDS prevention research, HIV positives generally recruit more effectively, and also tend to recruit other positives, so positives tend to be over-sampled.

RDS employs a Markov chain model to approximate the recruitment process. This model is based on two observations (Heckathorn, 2002): (1) if recruitment chains are sufficiently long, an equilibrium is reached in which the sample composition is independent of the initial seeds; (2) information gathered during the sampling process can be used to account for sampling bias.

Equilibrium

The first observation is recognizing that if referral chains are sufficiently long; that is, if the chain-referral process consists of enough waves or cycles of recruitment, the composition of the final sample with respect to key characteristics and behaviors will become independent of the seeds from which it began. In other words, after a certain number of waves, the sample compositions stabilize, remaining unchanged during further waves, and this sample composition is independent of the seeds from which sampling began. This point at which the sample composition becomes stable is termed the 'equilibrium'.

Figure 22.3 illustrates this process, based on the sample shown in Figure 22.1. Figure 22.3(a) uses data on peer recruitment by gender and fraternity/sorority membership to project what the sample composition would have been had sampling begun with only non-fraternity males. The seeds (wave 0) would have all been non-fraternity males, but their percentage would decline to 51% in wave 1, 30% in wave 3, and stabilize at 26%. Figure 22.3(b) projects what would have happened had all the seeds been from sorority members. The percentage of non-fraternity males among the seeds (wave 0) would have been 0%, but this would increase to 9% in wave 1, 19% in wave 3, 24% in wave 5, and stabilize at 26%. Note that after the first several waves, the sample composition is the same whether

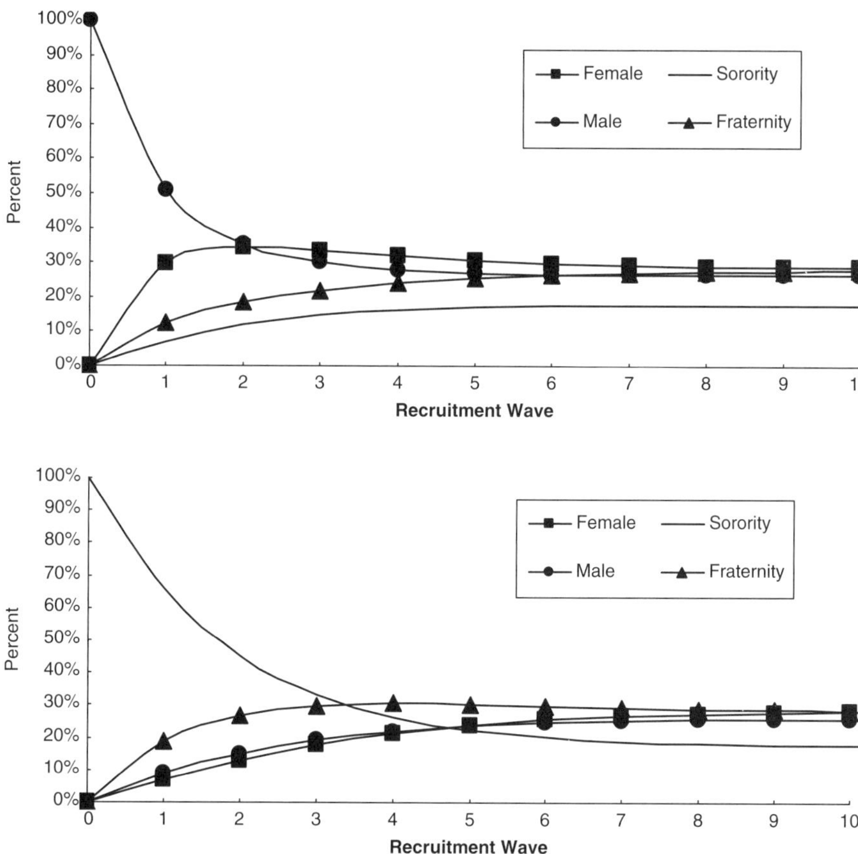

Figure 22.3 Simulated equilibrium of RDS sample composition. In the top graph the sample begins with 100% males. In the bottom graph, sample begins with 100% sorority members. However, the sample reaches equilibrium after only a few waves in both graphs and the subsequent sample composition is the same, regardless of starting point

the seeds were all non-fraternity males or all sorority members. The same would be true had all the seeds been drawn from other groups, or any combination of groups. The implication is that if recruitment chains are sufficiently long, the selection of seeds becomes irrelevant, so lengthening recruitment chains provides the means for overcoming bias from the choice of seeds (Ramirez-Valles et al., 2005).

The number of waves required to reach equilibrium varies based on the level of segmentation, or *homophily* (discussed in detail below), present in the population. Figure 22.4 shows the relationship between homophily and the number of waves required for equilibrium to be attained when all the seeds are drawn from the same group. The curve is accelerating (that is, as one moves to the right it becomes steeper). When homophily is zero, equilibrium is attained in only a single wave, because irrespective of group membership, each subject recruits randomly from the target population. As homophily grows, so does the number of

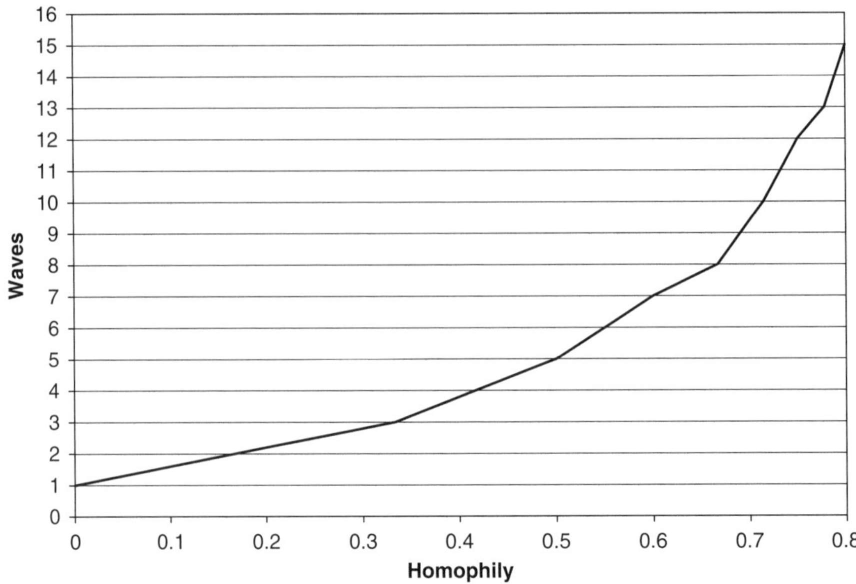

Figure 22.4 Waves required for sample composition to reach equilibrium: A worst case projection based on drawing all seeds from a single group

waves required for equilibrium to be attained, because it takes an increasing number of waves to break out of the initial group. In the extreme case of 100% homophily, recruitment chains could never break out of that group, so equilibrium would never be attained (such a case is a violation of assumption 2, discussed below). In Figure 22.3, homophily ranges from 0.233 among non-fraternity males to 0.628 among fraternity males and equilibrium is reached in five waves.

Fortunately for RDS analysis, homophily levels tend not to be extreme. For example, based on the limited number of currently available studies of US injection drug users (IDUs), homophily tends to be greatest by race and ethnicity, in the 0.3 to 0.55 range. Homophily among US IDUs tends to be lower for HIV risk behavior, such as syringe sharing and condom use, where homophily is in the 0.1 to 0.3 range, and homophily by HIV status is generally less than 0.1. Therefore, only a modest number of waves would be required for equilibrium to be attained, even if one were to adopt the worst possible strategy for selecting seeds, taking them all from the most insular (i.e. most homophilous) group. Of course, fewer waves are required if the seeds are diverse.

While equilibrium is necessary for analysis to occur, reaching equilibrium should not determine when sampling stops. That is, sampling should continue beyond equilibrium whenever possible. Some scholars suggest data collected before equilibrium is reached could be biased and estimates may benefit if only data collected after equilibrium is used in their calculation (Salganik, 2006). However, in an empirical test on a population with known parameters, Wejnert (2009) finds no evidence to support such a hypothesis (see also Wejnert and Heckathorn, 2008).

Recruitment information

The second observation upon which RDS is based is that gathering information during the sampling process can provide the means for constructing a sampling frame from which inclusion probabilities can be calculated. This in turn provides the means to verify that population estimates are unbiased and to determine the variability of these indicators.

Recall that in traditional sampling methods such as cluster sampling, construction of the sampling frame comes before the first respondent is selected. In a simple random sample, selection probabilities are equal, and in a stratified sample subgroups of special interest are over-sampled so selection probabilities are unequal. In either case, the sample is pre-stratified because selection probabilities are determined before the first respondent is selected. The effects of stratification are then taken into account when data are analyzed using sampling weights that are equal for a simple random sample and unequal for stratified samples (Ramirez-Valles et al., 2005)

In contrast, in RDS, the sampling frame is created during the sampling process based on special information gathered during the sampling process. This special information involves three elements:

- Who recruited whom? This provides the basis for controlling bias introduced by the tendency of subjects to recruit those like themselves. Therefore, an important element in the RDS research design is documenting recruiter/recruit relationships.
- How well connected is each respondent within the target population, that is, what is the subject's personal degree? Information on how many persons each subject knows who fit the eligibility criteria for the study provides the means for controlling bias toward over-sampling those with larger personal networks.
- Do the recruiter and recruit know one another, or are they strangers? The analytics upon which RDS population estimates are based depends on the recruiter and recruit knowing one another, so the RDS research design includes means for encouraging subjects to recruit those they already know. This includes rewards for recruiters and making recruitment rights scarce through quotas, so valuable recruitment rights will not be wasted on strangers. Asking recruits about their relationship to their recruiter is also useful so recruitments by strangers can be flagged for possible elimination from the data set.

Based on this information, relative inclusion probabilities in the form of sampling weights are calculated using the statistical theory upon which RDS is based. This occurs only after sampling has been completed, a process known as post-stratification. Because RDS does not require a sampling frame before sampling can begin, it can be implemented quickly. Because a sampling frame is available when RDS data are analyzed, the RDS method provides the benefits of other probability sampling methods. However, because RDS relies on relative inclusion probabilities, it provides estimates of relative group size (proportions), but cannot directly produce estimates of absolute population size. Absolute population size can be calculated if RDS analysis is combined with additional information. For example if RDS estimates 25% of population members belong to a specific club and the researcher knows the club has 100 members, then the overall population size can be estimated at 400 members.

Assumptions

It has been shown that if the assumptions upon which RDS is based are satisfied, RDS estimates are asymptotically unbiased (Salganik and Heckathorn, 2004). The model is based on five assumptions. The first three specify the conditions under which RDS is an appropriate sampling method:

1 Respondents must know one another as members of the target population. Peer recruitment is a feasible sampling strategy only if this condition is satisfied. Consequently, RDS would not be suitable for sampling tax cheats, who can be friends and not know they share membership in that hidden population. On the other hand, it is suitable for sampling populations linked by a 'contact pattern', such as musicians who perform together or drug users who purchase drugs together.
2 Ties must be reciprocal and dense enough to sustain the chain-referral process. For populations linked by a contact pattern or those that form a single community, this is rarely problematic.
3 Sampling is assumed to occur with replacement, so recruitments do not deplete the set of respondents available for future recruitment. Consequently, the sampling fraction should be small enough for a sampling-with-replacement model to be appropriate.

The final two assumptions are required by the statistical model on which estimation is based:

4 Respondents can accurately report the number of peers they could potentially recruit for the study. Studies of the reliability of network indicators suggest that the RDS network question is one of the more reliable indicators (Marsden, 1990); furthermore, the RDS population estimator depends not on absolute but on relative degree, so variations that inflate or deflate the reports in a linear manner have no effect on the estimates. However, violation of this assumption is a source of potential bias (Wejnert and Heckathorn, 2008).
5 Respondents are recruited as though they are choosing randomly from their networks. That is the composition of recruitment is representative of the composition of personal networks. This is based on the expectation that respondents would lack an incentive or ability to coordinate to selectively recruit any particular group. The plausibility of this assumption is enhanced, in part, by appropriate research design. For example, if a research site were located in a high-crime neighborhood, recruiting residents of the neighborhood might be easy, but recruiting peers from more comfortable neighborhoods might prove difficult, so sampling would be non-random because it excluded the latter group. However, if research identifies neutral turf in which all potential respondents feel safe, the random recruitment assumption is made more plausible. Similarly, if incentives are offered that are salient to respondents from all income groups (e.g. a choice between receiving a monetary reward and making a contribution to a charity of the respondent's choice), the random recruitment assumption is made more plausible (Ramirez-Valles et al., 2005).

There is no direct way to test if respondents accurately report their number of peers or if they then recruit randomly from that pool. However, it is possible to test if respondents' recruitment patterns accurately reflect their self-report network composition by gathering additional data on personal network composition based on easily identifiable traits, such as gender or race (discussed above). While, some studies have found strong association between recruitment patterns and self-reported network composition (Heckathorn et al., 2002; Wang et al., 2005), others have found significant differences between self-report network composition and recruitment patterns (Wejnert and Heckathorn, 2008; Wejnert, 2009). Whether these differences are due to a failure of random recruitment or a failure of accurate reporting of network composition requires further research.

RDS estimators

Over a decade of research has gone into refining and enhancing RDS-population proportion point estimators. Table 22.1 compares seven published RDS estimators and their contributions to RDS theory.

The first RDS estimator, described by Heckathorn (1997), is limited to nominal variables and uses the Markov chain equilibrium proportion, $\widehat{E_X}$, as the estimator.

$$\widehat{E_X} = \frac{\widehat{S_{YX}}}{\widehat{S_{YX}} + \widehat{S_{YX}}}, \tag{1}$$

where $\widehat{S_{XY}}$ is the transition probability (discussed below) from group X to group Y. Heckathorn (1997) also showed that an RDS sample is self-weighting if homophily is uniform across groups. While this estimator paved the way for future RDS estimators it does *not* account for all major sources of sampling bias and is no longer used as a method of population estimation with RDS data.

RDS I estimators

In 2002, Heckathorn introduced the reciprocity model, which assumes a reciprocal relationship between recruiter and recruit. That is, if X recruited Y there is a non-zero probability that Y could have recruited X. Using this model, Heckathorn (2002) presents an improved estimator that controls differences in homophily and average degree across groups. In the first version of this estimator, 2002A, linear least squares are used to solve a system of over determined equations to calculate estimates for variables of more than two categories. In a second estimator, 2002B, the reciprocity model provides means for calculating multi-category estimates. Under reciprocity, the number of ties or recruitments from group X to group Y equals the number of ties or recruitments from group Y to group X. However, in a finite sample, this is not always the case. Thus, Heckathorn (2002) improves the estimate of cross-group ties through a process known as *data-smoothing,* in which the number of cross-group recruitments from X to Y and Y to X are averaged such that the recruitment matrix is symmetric. The data-smoothed recruitment matrix is then used to calculate transition probabilities, $\widehat{S_{XY}}$. The data-smoothing method is recommended over linear least squares because it produces narrower confidence intervals around RDS estimates.

Table 22.1 RDS estimators

RDS estimator	*Information employed*	*Type of estimator*	*Limitations*	*Variance estimation*	*Distinctive contribution*
Heckathorn (1997)	Recruitment matrix	Markov equilibrium	Limited to nominal variables; does not control for differences in degree	None	Shows that sample is self-weighting when homophily is uniform across groups
Heckathorn (2002A)	Recruitment matrix; self-reported degrees	Reciprocity model-based estimator (RDS I); Linear least squares used for >2 categories	Limited to nominal variables	Bootstrap	Introduces controls for differences in degree and homophily across groups
Heckathorn (2002B)	Recruitment matrix; self-reported degrees	Reciprocity model-based estimator (RDS I); Data-smoothing used to estimate >2 categories	Limited to nominal variables	Bootstrap	Data-smoothing yields narrower confidence intervals than linear least squares
Salganik and Heckathorn (2004)	Recruitment matrix; self-reported degrees	Reciprocity model-based estimator (RDS I)	Limited to nominal variables	Bootstrap	Proof that estimate is asymptotically unbiased; provides estimate of average group degree
Heckathorn (2007)	Recruitment matrix; self-reported degrees	Dual-component estimator (RDS I)	As other estimators, limited by RDS assumptions	Bootstrap	Allows analysis of continuous variables; controls for differential recruitment
Volz and Heckathorn (2008A)	Recruitment matrix; self-reported degrees	Probability-based estimator (RDS II)	Does not control for differential recruitment	Analytic	Introduces new, analytically tractable estimator; permits analysis of continuous variables
Volz and Heckathorn (2008B)	Recruitment matrix; self-reported degrees	Probability-based estimator with data-smoothing (RDS II)	Limited to nominal variables	Analytic	Demonstrates convergence between reciprocity and probability-based RDS estimators; uses data-smoothing to control for differential recruitment

These reciprocity-based estimators provide the foundation for a family of RDS estimators, termed *RDS I* estimators. RDS I estimators employ a two-stage estimation process where the data are first used to make inferences about network structure in the form of transition probabilities (based on the recruitment matrix) and estimates of average group degree (based on self-reported degrees). These inferences are then used to calculate a population proportion estimate for each group, $\widehat{P_X^{RDS\ I}}$.

$$\widehat{P_X^{RDS\ I}} = \frac{\widehat{S_{YX}}\,\widehat{D_Y}}{\widehat{S_{YX}}\,\widehat{D_Y} + \widehat{S_{XY}}\,\widehat{D_X}}, \tag{2}$$

where $\widehat{D_X}$ is the estimated average degree of group *X*. These all estimators control for differences in average degree and homophily across groups and thus differ substantially from the estimator developed by Heckathorn (1997). Unfortunately, the two-stage estimation process complicates variance calculations. To date, RDS I estimates rely on a bootstrap algorithm to estimate confidence intervals around the estimate (Heckathorn, 2002; Salganik, 2006).

While Heckathorn (2002) details much of the underlying theory and estimation procedures for RDS I estimation, several improvements have been made. Salganik and Heckathorn (2004) derive an unbiased estimate of average group degree and prove that the RDS I estimator is asymptotically unbiased, which means that bias is on the order of 1/[sample size], so bias is trivial in samples of meaningful size (Cochran, 1977). In 2007, Heckathorn developed a dual-component version of the RDS I estimator which calculates a sampling weight based on equation (2) that can be applied to the sample proportion to estimate population proportion. This estimator not only controls for differences in degree and homophily across groups, but also separates their effects on the sampling weight into recruitment (homophily) and degree components. The dual-component estimator allows for analysis of continuous variables and controls for differential recruitment that occurs if some groups recruit more effectively than others (Heckathorn, 2007).

In a study of IDUs, Frost et al. (2006) compare estimates generated using data-smoothing (Heckathorn, 2002) and degree adjustment (Salganik and Heckathorn, 2004) to those based on unadjusted data and find that RDS I estimates are sensitive to differences in the estimation model applied. Such sensitivity to adjustments is not unexpected because both adjustments represent a theoretical improvement in estimation for which there would be no need without sensitivity to them. Consequently, estimates based on Frost et al.'s (2006) 'smoothed-adjusted' model, which corresponds to Heckathorn's (2007) dual-component estimator are likely the most reliable.

RDS II estimators

Using a probability-based estimation approach, Volz and Heckathorn (2008) introduce a second family of RDS estimators, $\widehat{P_X^{RDS\ II}}$, termed *RDS II* estimators.

$$\widehat{P_X^{RDS\ II}} = \left(\frac{n_X}{n}\right)\left(\frac{\widehat{D}}{\widehat{D_X}}\right), \tag{3}$$

where n_X is the number if respondents in group X, n is the total number of respondents, and $\widehat{D}$ is the overall average degree. Essentially, the estimate is the sample proportion, (n_X/n), weighted by a correction for network effects, $(\widehat{D}/\widehat{D_X})$. RDS II estimators are calculated directly from the data, removing the middle step of making inference about network structure necessary in RDS I. More importantly, the mathematical approach used to calculate RDS II estimates allows for analytical variance calculation. Currently, there are two versions of the RDS II estimator. The first, 2008A, allows analysis of continuous variables, but does not adjust for differential recruitment. The second, 2008B, uses data-smoothing to adjust for differential recruitment, but cannot be used to analyze continuous data (data-smoothing is only applicable to nominal data).

RDS I vs. RDS II estimation

As expected of two unbiased estimators of the same parameter, Volz and Heckathorn (2008) show that when data-smoothing is used, RDS I and RDS II estimators are convergent. Consequently, beyond the mathematical approach used in their calculation, the primary difference between RDS I and RDS II estimation is the method in which estimate variance and confidence intervals are calculated.

Confidence intervals for RDS I are estimated using a specialized bootstrap algorithm (Heckathorn, 2002; see also Salganik, 2006). The algorithm generates a resample of dependent observations based on the sample transition matrix. That is, if 70% of type A recruitments are other As and the current observation is of type A, the algorithm will generate an A as the next observation in the resample with probability 0.7. This process continues until the resample reaches the original sample size. RDS I estimates are then calculated and the process is repeated until the specified number of resamples has been reached. Confidence interval tails are then taken from the distribution of these bootstrapped estimates. For example, the upper bound of a 95% confidence interval is defined as the value above which 2.5% of the bootstrapped estimates fall. Consequently, the bootstrap algorithm allows for non-symmetric confidence intervals and does not provide a direct estimate of variance.

Confidence interval bounds for RDS II estimates are based on the RDS II variance estimator (Volz and Heckathorn, 2008):

$$Var\left(\widehat{P_X^{RDS\ II}}\right) = \widehat{V}_1 + \frac{\widehat{P_X^{RDS\ II}}^2}{n.}\left((1-n.) + \frac{2}{n_X}\sum_{i=2}^{n}\sum_{j=1}^{i-1}\left(\widehat{S.}^{i-j}\right)_{xx}\right), \tag{4}$$

where

$$\widehat{V}_1 = \frac{\widehat{Var(Z_i)}}{n.} = \frac{1}{n.(n.-1)} \sum_{i=1}^{n} \left(Z_i - \widehat{P_X^{RDS\ II}} \right)^2 \tag{5}$$

and

$$Z_i = d_i^{-1} \widehat{D}.I_X(i), \tag{6}$$

where d_i is the degree of respondent i, $\widehat{S}.$ is the matrix of transition probabilities, and $I_X(i)$ is an indicator function which takes the value 1 if $i \in X$ and 0 otherwise. While the estimate is not unbiased, Volz and Heckathorn (2008) find that it closely approximates unbiased estimates of variance in their simulations.

To date, few studies have directly compared the two methods. However, a study by Wejnert (2009), which compares 95% confidence intervals generated by RDS I and RDS II for real data with known parameters, finds both variance estimation methods lacking, albeit in different ways. That is, confidence intervals based on RDS II are generally wider, more consistent across variables, and more likely to capture population parameters than their RDS I counterparts, however, analysis of design effects suggests RDS II overestimates variance, in some cases by a large amount. Furthermore, the RDS I bootstrap procedure used to estimate confidence intervals was found to underestimate variance, especially for small groups. In Wejnert's (2009) analysis, 95% confidence intervals calculated based on bootstrapped variance fail to capture the parameter more often than the 5% suggested by the interval, while those calculated using RDS II display a capture rate that resembles what would be expected from an ideal variance estimate (Wejnert, 2009).

More generally, computational work testing both RDS I (Salganik and Heckathorn, 2004) and RDS II (Volz and Heckathorn, 2008) estimators suggests they perform well. Using real data on men who have sex with men, Kendall et al. (2008) find that RDS produce a sample with wider inclusion of relevant demographic groups than time-location sampling or other snowball methods. When comparing RDS I estimates to known population parameters, Wejnert and Heckathorn (2008) conclude that RDS estimation is reasonable, but not precise. Using two data sets, including that used by Wejnert and Heckathorn (2008), Wejnert (2009) tests both RDS I and RDS II estimates and find both to be reasonably accurate and that problems with confidence intervals described by Wejnert and Heckathorn (2008) are likely due to variance estimation procedures and not point estimation.

Social network analysis with RDS

A currently underused feature of RDS data is the presence of network information ideal for analysis of social network structure (Wejnert, 2010). RDS has two advantages that make it especially efficient for social network analysis.

First, estimates of homophily and average degree allow inferences on large networks using survey data. Studying large networks with current techniques is problematic; ego-centric samples are unlikely to include connected respondents; database records, such as email networks, often lack important demographic variables; and saturated data are simply impractical for large networks. The second advantage is that every respondent has at least one documented behavioral tie (recruitment) to another respondent in the data. Including respondents' alters in the data allows for analysis of network structure based on private characteristics unknown to a respondent's immediate ties, avoiding what Erickson (1979) calls *masking*, where respondents project their own views onto their friends in self-report studies. RDS also provides greater range of analysis because tie and node characteristics can be collected independently and combined during analysis. Finally, because respondents are only asked information about themselves or their recruiters, who have already provided informed consent through their own participation, many ethical human subjects concerns often associated with network analysis are avoided (Kadushin, 2005; Klovdahl, 2005).

Average group degree

Salganik and Heckathorn (2004) derive an average group degree estimator that is the ratio of two Hansen–Hurwitz estimators, which are known to be unbiased (Brewer and Hanif, 1983). The ratio of two unbiased estimators is asymptotically unbiased with bias on the order of n^{-1}, where n is the sample size (Cochran, 1977; Salganik and Heckathorn, 2004). In addition to providing a correction for degree bias in RDS estimation of categorical variables, the estimator provides a measure of group centrality.

$$\widehat{D_X} = \frac{n_X}{\sum_{i=1}^{n_X} \frac{1}{d_i}}, \tag{7}$$

where $\widehat{D_X}$ is the average degree of group X, n_X is the sample size of nodes in group X, and d_i is the self reported personal degree of individual i (Salganik and Heckathorn, 2004).

This estimator can be used to study important network characteristics, such as connectedness and centrality. For example, in a study of New York City aging artists, Spiller et al. (2008) find that artists tend to lose connections to the art community as they age. However, a small proportion of aging artists remain involved in the community and maintain far reaching contact networks, such that even those maintaining less than five network ties are likely associated with someone who is very well connected.

Homophily and affiliation

As stated above, network-based samples, like RDS, are biased by the nonrandom nature of social network ties used to make recruitments. RDS network analysis makes use of this bias to measure a common friendship tendency constraining social network structure: the tendency for individuals to associate with specific alters based on the characteristics of those alters. A special form of this tendency, termed *homophily*, concerns 'the principle that contact between similar people occurs at a higher rate than among dissimilar people' and has been shown to be a powerful mechanism by which affiliations deviate from random mixing (McPherson et al., 2001: 416). Evidence for the homophily effect is extensive across a wide range of variables. Strong instances of homophily have been found according to race and ethnicity, age, gender, educational aspiration, drug use, musical tastes, political identification, religion, and behavior (see McPherson et al., 2001 for an extensive review).

RDS homophily can be calculated for any variable in the data set by comparing a standardized measure of the difference between affiliation patterns observed among respondents and the affiliation patterns that would result from random mixing (Heckathorn, 2002). Specifically, homophily is calculated from the estimated proportion of in-group ties and that which would be expected from random mixing, in which in-group ties would merely reflect the group's proportional size (Heckathorn, 2002).

$$\widehat{H_X} = \frac{\widehat{S_{XX}} - \widehat{P_X}}{1 - \widehat{P_X}} \quad if\ \widehat{S_{XX}} \geq \widehat{P_X},$$
$$\widehat{H_X} = \frac{\widehat{S_{XX}} - \widehat{P_X}}{\widehat{P_X}} \quad if\ \widehat{S_{XX}} < \widehat{P_X}, \tag{8}$$

where $\widehat{S_{XX}}$ is the transition probability of in-group recruitments made by group *X*, $\widehat{P_X}$ is the estimated proportion of the population contained in group *X*, and $\widehat{H_X}$ is the homophily of group *X*. The measure was first introduced by Coleman (1958) as what he termed an index of 'inbreeding bias' and later independently derived by Fararo and Sunshine (1964) as part of their work on biased net theory. RDS homophily can be calculated for any partition of categorical variables and ranges from negative one to positive one. Positive homophily indicates a group with disproportionate in-group ties, suggestive of preference. Homophily near zero indicates a non-group, that is the variable in question is not of social importance to the network structure. Negative homophily, or *heterophily,* indicates disproportionately few in-group ties, suggestive of avoidance (Heckathorn, 2002).

Intermediate levels of homophily are defined in a parallel manner. For example, a homophily of 0.12 means that the respondents form their networks as though 12% of the time form a tie to another person like themselves, and the rest of the time they form ties through random mixing, that is, forming ties in proportion to population composition. Negative homophilies are defined similarly. For example, a homophily of –0.16 means that the respondents form their networks as though 16% of the time form a tie to someone unlike themselves, and the rest of the time form network connection in proportion to population composition.

The RDS homophily measure depends on the population proportion of each group, providing a better measure of departure from random mixing than earlier methods, such as Krackhardt and Stern's (1988) E–I index, which depend on the proportion of in-group ties compared to that of out-group ties. In studies where groups represent equal portions of the population these methods are not problematic; however, in populations where group sizes differ, random mixing will generate more ties to individuals in larger groups than smaller groups.

In RDS theory, the homophily estimator reflects the strength of association to one's own group beyond random mixing. A generalization, termed *affiliation*, expresses the strength of association between differing groups, where a positive value for two groups indicates a greater proportion of cross-linking ties than random mixing would produce and a negative value indicates fewer cross-linking ties (Heckathorn, 2002). Hence, the affiliation index provides a measure of preference or avoidance for any cell in the matrix. It can measure, for example, not only whether Whites prefer or avoid other Whites (homophily or heterophily), but whether and to what extent they interact with Blacks, Asians, or Hispanics. RDS network measures differ from other indices, which identify groups by structural measures, such as density and transitivity (Wasserman and Faust, 1994), by focusing on actor characteristics and identifying which characteristics significantly influence the network.

$$\begin{aligned} \widehat{A_{XY}} &= \frac{\widehat{S_{XY}} - \widehat{P_Y}}{1 - \widehat{P_Y}} \quad \textit{if } \widehat{S_{XY}} \geq \widehat{P_Y}, \\ \widehat{A_{XY}} &= \frac{\widehat{S_{XY}} - \widehat{P_Y}}{\widehat{P_Y}} \quad \textit{if } \widehat{S_{XY}} < \widehat{P_Y}, \end{aligned} \tag{9}$$

where $\widehat{A_{XY}}$ is the affiliation preference of group X for group Y. In calculating homophily, the $\widehat{S_{XX}}$ term is simply the transition probably from group X to itself observed in the data. In calculating the affiliation, RDS' assumption of reciprocity between recruiter and recruit becomes significant for the $\widehat{S_{XY}}$ term. Consequently, data-smoothing is used in calculation of the $\widehat{S_{XY}}$ term in equation (9). Note that because data-smoothing does not alter the diagonal entries of the transition matrix, it does not alter calculation of homophily.

These measures can be used to analyze macro-level social network structures. For example, in the aging artist study, Spiller et al. (2008) find distinctly different structures between professional and non-professional artists. Affiliation of professional artists is centered on participation in the artistic community whereas affiliation patterns of non-professional artists resemble those of the general population.

Ego-centric network analysis

Additionally, the random sample of network ties and presence of both recruiter and recruit allow for micro-level network analysis. For example, in a study of racial integration among university undergraduates, Wejnert (2010) finds that while cross-race ties are less frequent than some-race ties, those that do occur do not differ from same-race ties in terms of quality or closeness.

In summary, RDS provides a random sample of ties based on *behavioral* network data, that is recruitments (Salganik and Heckathorn, 2004), that can be used to make social network inferences at the micro level by comparing characteristics of certain types of ties with others, at the group level through estimates of average group degree, and at the macro level through homophily and affiliation analysis.

THE FUTURE OF RDS

In little over a decade its effectiveness and ease of use has made RDS the emerging *de facto* method for sampling hard-to-reach populations worldwide. RDS data has been collected in hundreds of studies in over 30 nations on six continents. However, while new data sets and sampling lessons continue to emerge, the development and enhancement of methods to statistically analyze such data is limited to a small handful of researchers and RDS-specific analytical techniques remain largely underdeveloped. While the first decade of research has been dedicated to optimizing RDS sampling procedures, current research is focused on expanding RDS statistical analysis in three directions: variance estimation, multivariate analysis, and network analysis. Additionally, the uses and applications of WebRDS, especially its potential for very fast sampling and researching online communities, need to be further tested.

Variance estimation

Developing an improved estimate of variance is the primary motivation behind the RDS II family of estimators. By recalculating the estimate using a probability based approach, RDS II opened the door for analytical calculation of varian (Volz and Heckathorn, 2008). While the variance estimator presented by and Heckathorn (2008) is not without problems (Wejnert, 2009), it represe crucial first step toward an analytical variance estimate.

One problem affecting both RDS I and RDS II variance estimatio is multiple recruitment. The RDS II analytical variance formul maximum of one recruitment per respondent. Similarly, the RD method, simulates samples following a chain in which each re one recruitment. Projects are currently under way to impr measures by removing the single recruitment assumption.

Multivariate analysis

A major limitation of RDS is the lack of RDS-specific methods of multivariate analysis. Heckathorn's (2007) dual-component estimator makes an important contribution to future multivariate analysis techniques by splitting the sampling weight and deriving an individual-level degree component. However, because the recruitment component is based on group-level calculations, the method falls one step short of the holy grail of multivariate RDS analysis: an individual-level sampling weight applicable across all variables.

Multivariate analysis with RDS data is currently the most widely anticipated and researched next step for RDS research. Several methods are under development (e.g. Platt et al., 2006; Philbin et al., 2008); however, the current recommendation is to apply sampling weights based on the dependent variable as an overall sampling weight. In addition, work by Winship and Radbill (1994) finds that under certain conditions, regression analysis based on unweighted data provides greater precision than analysis using weighted data. Such an approach is employed by Ramirez-Valles et al. (2008) in an RDS study of Latino men who have sex with men. More research is needed to validate these techniques and further develop new multivariate analysis techniques for RDS data.

Social network analysis

Currently, RDS researchers can easily make inferences regarding group-level network structure and centrality using the RDS degree and homophily/affiliation measures based on only the information required for normal RDS analysis (Heckathorn, 2002). Unfortunately, this information is greatly underused in many RDS studies, including research in which networks play a vital role in the research topic, such as studies of HIV transmission.

While multiple RDS network inferences exist, the full potential of RDS as a method of network analysis has yet to be developed (Wejnert, 2010). Research is currently being conducted to improve the network analysis capacity of RDS. In one project, Heckathorn, Frost, and others are building a simulation environment to understand what information about network structure can be ascertained from the RDS sampling process. By using observed network information to construct a family of model networks with consistent structural features researchers hope to provide new information about network attributes that can be incorporated into RDS estimates, providing improved variance estimates.

WebRDS

The potential of WebRDS is yet to be fully explored. Projects are currently underway using WebRDS to study both online and electronically connected real-world communities. The data and lessons learned from these projects will provide information on the method's ability to sample various populations, the speed with which samples can be collected, and the factors influencing efficiency and efficacy of the method.

Validation of existing techniques

Finally, empirical and computational testing and validation of analytical techniques are being conducted. For example, researchers are using simulation experiments to explore the performance of the RDS sampling process and RDS estimators on empirical and simulated networks when assumptions about network structure and recruitment behavior are systematically relaxed. Simulating RDS with parameters drawn from real RDS data sets will be used to further refine estimates and guidelines about when RDS can be successfully applied. Additionally, more empirical work in which RDS is applied to known populations and estimates are compared to true population parameters is needed to confirm that RDS estimation provides valid estimates in practice as well as in theory.

CONCLUSION

RDS combines an efficient chain-referral sampling method with a statistical method of analysis that corrects the fact data collected in a non-random way to provide unbiased population estimates. It has been widely used in the fields of public health and sociology to study hidden populations such as those at risk for HIV, artistic communities, and impoverished groups. Additionally, RDS has been shown to be an effective method of analyzing social network structure and has been successfully implemented as an online sampling method. Further information, along with specialized software for conducting RDS analysis, is available, free of charge from the RDS website: respondentdrivensampling.org.

REFERENCES

Abdul-Quader, Abu S., Douglas D. Heckathorn, Courtney McKnight, Heidi Bramson, Chris Nemeth, Keith Sabin, Kathleen Gallagher, and Don C. Des Jarlais (2006). Effectiveness of respondent driven sampling for recruiting drug users in New York City: Findings from a pilot study. *AIDS and Behavior*, 9: 403–8.

Brewer, K.R.W. and Muhammad Hanif (1983). *Sampling with Unequal Probability.* New York: Springer-Verlag.

Cochran, William G. (1977). *Sampling Techniques*, 3rd edn. New York: Wiley.

Coleman, James S. (1958). Relational analysis: The study of social organization with survey methods. *Human Organization*, 17: 28–36.

Des Jarlais, Don C., Kamyar Aresteh, Theresa Perlis, Holly Hagan, Abu Abdul-Quader, Douglas D. Heckathorn, Courtney McKnight, Heidi Bramson, Chris Nemeth, Lucia V. Torian, and Samuel R. Friedman (2007). Convergence of HIV seroprevalence among injecting and non-injecting drug users in New York City. *AIDS,* 21: 231–5.

Erickson, B.H. (1979). Some problems of inference from chain data. *Sociological Methodology,* 10: 276–302.

Fararo, T. J. and M.H. Sunshine (1964). *A Study of a Biased Friendship Net.* Syracuse, NY: Syracuse University Youth Development Center.

Frost, Simon D.W., Kimberly C. Brouwer, Michelle A. Firestone Cruz, Rebeca Ramos, Maria Elena Ramos, Remedios M. Lozada, Carlos Magis-Rodriques, and Steffanie A. Strathdee (2006). Respondent-driven sampling of injection drug users in two US–Mexico border cities: Recruitment dynamics and impact on estimates of HIV and syphilis. *Journal of Urban Health*, 83: i83–i97.

Heckathorn, Douglas D. (1997). Respondent-driven sampling: A new approach to the study of hidden populations. *Social Problems*, 44: 174–99.

Heckathorn, Douglas D. (2002). Respondent-driven sampling II: Deriving valid population estimates from chain referral samples of hidden populations. *Social Problems*, 49: 11–34.

Heckathorn, Douglas D. (2007). Extensions of respondent-driven sampling: Analyzing continuous variables and controlling for differential degree. *Sociological Methodology*, 37*:* 151–207.

Heckathorn, Douglas D. and Joan Jeffri (2001). Finding the beat: Using respondent-driven sampling to study jazz musicians. *Poetics*, 28: 307–29.

Heckathorn, Douglas D., Salaam Semaan, Robert S. Broadhead, and James J. Hughes (2002). Extensions of respondent-driven sampling: A new approach to the study of injection drug users aged 18–25. *AIDS and Behavior*, 6: 55–67.

Kadushin, C. (2005). Who benefits from network analysis: Ethics of social network research. *Social Networks*, 27: 139–53.

Kendall, Carl, Ligia R.F.S. Kerr, Rogerio C. Gondim, Guilherme L. Werneck, Raimunda Hermelinda Maia Macena, Marta Ken Pontes, Lisa G. Johnston, Keith Sabin, and Willi Farland (2008). An empirical comparison of respondent-driven sampling, time location sampling, and snowball sampling for behavioral surveillance in men who have sex with men, Fortaleza, Brazil. *AIDS and Behavior*, 12: s97–s104.

Kissinger, Patricia, Nicole Liddon, Lisa Longfellow, Erin Curtin, Norine Schimdt, Oscar Salinas, Jaun Cleto, and Douglas Heckathorn (2008). HIV/STI risk among Latino migrant workers in New Orleans post-hurricane Katrina. Presented at the *Annual CDC STD Prevention Conference*, Chicago, IL.

Klovdahl, A.S. (2005). Social network research and human subjects protection: Towards more effect infectious disease control. *Social Networks*, 27: 119–37.

Krackhardt, D. and R. Stern (1988). Informal networks and organizational crises: An experimental simulation. *Social Psychology Quarterly,* 51: 123–40.

Malekinejad, Mohsen, Lisa G. Johnston, Carl Kendall, Ligia R.F.S. Kerr, Marina R. Rifkin, and George W. Rutherford (2008). Using respondent-driven sampling methodology for HIV biological and behavioral surveillance in International settings: A systematic review. *AIDS and Behavior,* 12: 105–30.

Marsden, Peter V. (1990). Network data and measurement. *Annual Review of Sociology*, 16: 435–63.

McPherson, M., L. Smith-Lovin, and J.M. Cook (2001). Birds of a feather: Homophily in Social networks. *Annual Review of Sociology,* 27: 415–44.

Philbin, Morgan, Robin A. Pollini, Rebecca Ramos , Remedios Lozada, Kimberly C. Brouwer, Maria Elena Ramos, Michelle Firestone-Cruz, Patricia Case, Steffanie A. Strathdee (2008). Shooting gallery attendance among IDUS in Tijuana and Ciudad Juarez, Mexico: Correlates, prevention opportunities, and the role of the envirnoment. *AIDS and Behavior,* 12: 552–60.

Platt, Lucy, Natalia Bobrova, Tim Rhodes, Anneli Uuskula, John V. Parry, Kristi Ruutel, Ave Talu, Katri Abel, Kristina Rajaleid, and Ali Judd (2006). High HIV prevalence among injecting drug users in Estonia: Implications for understanding the risk environment. *AIDS*, 20: 2120–3.

Ramirez-Valles, Jesus, Douglas D. Heckathorn, Raquel Vázquez, Rafael M. Diaz, and Richard T. Campbell (2005). From networks to populations: The development and application of respondent-driven sampling among IDUs and Latino gay men. *AIDS and Behavior*, 9: 387–402.

Ramirez-Valles, Jesus, Dalia Garcia, Richard T. Campbell, Rafael M. Diaz, and Douglas D. Heckathorn (2008). HIV infection, sexual risk behavior, and substance use among Latino gay and bisexual men and transgender persons. *American Journal of Public Health*, 98: 1036–42.

Salganik, Mathew J. (2006). Variance estimation, design effects, and sample size calculations for respondent-driven sampling. *Journal of Urban Health,* 83: i98–i112.

Salganik, Mathew J. and Douglas D. Heckathorn (2004). Sampling and estimation in hidden populations using respondent driven sampling. *Sociological Methodology*, 34: 193–239.

Spiller, Michael W., Douglas D. Heckathorn, and Joan Jeffri (2008). The social networks of aging visual artists. In *Above Ground: Information on Artists III: Special Focus on New York City Aging Artists.* Research Center for Arts and Culture, pp. 29–69. New York.

Volz, Erik, and Douglas D. Heckathorn (2008). Probability-based estimation theory for respondent-driven sampling. *Journal of Official Statistics*, 24: 79–97.

Wang, Jichuan, Robert G. Carlson, Russell S. Falck, Harvey A. Siegal, Ahmmed Rahman, and Linna Li (2005). Respondent driven sampling to recruit MDMA users: A methodological assessment. *Drug and Alcohol Dependence*, 78: 147–57.

Wasserman, Stanley and Katherine Faust (1994). *Social Network Analysis.* Cambridge, MA: Cambridge University Press.

Wejnert, Cyprian (2009). An empirical test of respondent-driven sampling: Point estimates, variance, measures of degree, and out-of-equilibrium data. *Sociological Methodology*, 39: 73–116.

Wejnert, Cyprian (2010). Social network analysis with respondent-driven sampling data: A study of racial integration on campus. *Social Networks*, 32: 112–24.

Wejnert, Cyprian and Douglas D. Heckathorn (2008). Web-based networks sampling: Efficiency and efficacy of respondent-driven sampling for online research. *Sociological Methods and Research*, 37: 105–34.

Winship, Christopher and Larry Radbill (1994). Sampling weights and regression analysis. *Sociological Methods and Research*, 23: 230–57.

23

Analysing Longitudinal Studies with Non-response: Issues and Statistical Methods

James Carpenter and Ian Plewis

INTRODUCTION

Just as the advantages of longitudinal studies in terms of their potential for measuring and understanding change are well known, so is their one major drawback: members of the target sample are lost over time and that this loss is usually cumulative. Hence, researchers using longitudinal studies need to recognise that inferences from the observed sample (i.e. those cases that remain) will not necessarily be accurate inferences about the parameters of interest in the target population.

The aim of this chapter is to provide an overview of the implictions of non-response, and methods that can be used to analyse data affected by non-response. We begin by discussing the kinds of non-response that are common to all social investigations and those that are particular to longitudinal studies. We then review preventative strategies for minimising non-response in longitudinal studies. Important as prevention is, it is unlikely to be sufficient on its own, so we also discuss strategies for valid analysis of data sets with missing observations. The latter half of the chapter is concerned with methods for the analysis of longitudinal data sets with selectively missing data of different kinds. We focus on three methods: (i) inverse probability weighting, (ii) multiple imputation and

(iii) joint modelling. This is an area of considerable methodological innovation with an increasing emphasis on what are often referred to as 'statistically principled' methods. It is still relatively unusual in the social sciences, although it is becoming more common in epidemiology, for substantive analyses to do much more than describe the patterns of missing data in a study. Our hope is that this chapter will encourage quantitative social researchers to consider more carefully the implications for their inferences and conclusions of the data that they intended to use in their analyses, but were in fact unable to, because they were unobserved. To this end, we illustrate the three approaches using a data set from the National Child Development Study (NCDS), the second of the four UK birth cohorts described by Ferri et al. (2003). We conclude with a discussion of the pros and cons of these methods.

TOWARDS A STRATEGY FOR ANALYSING PARTIALLY OBSERVED DATA

It is, of course, the case that most quantitative investigations are based on data that are incomplete by design; cases are sampled from a known population in such a way that inferences about the population can be made from the sample with a known degree of uncertainty. Unfortunately, data are often missing for other reasons, particularly as a result of failing to measure all the sampled cases, either completely or partially. We can regard the process, or mechanism, that causes the missing data as a second stage of sampling which stands between the data we wish to observe and those data we actually observe. Unfortunately, this missing data mechanism is usually neither within our control nor fully known. If we do not fully understand the sampling process it is difficult, in general, to make reliable inferences. Therefore, a non-trivial proportion of missing data introduces additional ambiguity into our inferences, qualitatively different from the variation generated by statistical sampling.

In order to carry out analyses, and draw inferences, we thus first need to consider processes that cause the data to be missing, which we term *the missingness mechanism*. In particular, is the missingness mechanism unconnected with values of the data we wish to collect for our analysis, or is it systematically linked to these values in some way? If we can make the former assumption, the (partially) observed data will give unbiased estimates for the target population (although these may be less precise than we intended); in the latter case this will generally not be so.

Summarising the above, when analysing partially observed data, we are forced to make assumptions about the missingness mechanism. Although we can sometimes see whether these assumptions are consistent with our observed data (e.g. are older people less likely to be observed) we cannot definitively identify the missingness mechanism from the observed data. As different assumptions about the missingness mechansim may imply different inferences and conclusions, our strategy should, ideally, be based on the following steps:

1 In discussion with experts, preferably those with experience of actually collecting data, identify likely missingness mechanisms (these should also be consistent with the pattern of observed and missing data).
2 For each of these mechanisms in turn, perform a valid statistical analysis and draw conclusions. In other words, carry out an analysis that gives valid inferences for the target population under the assumed missingness mechanism.
3 If the conclusions from the various analyses in (2) are similar, we can be confident that the ambiguity caused by the missing data is minimal. If they are different, then we must communicate this to the users of our research.

Steps (1)–(3) therefore represent the ideal analysis in the presence of missing data. In practice, it will often be hard to realise this goal. Nevertheless, it is still useful to be clear about the direction we should be going in.

The next stage is thus to consider how data come to be missing, that is, plausible missingness mechanisms. For ease of exposition, we focus on data collected in surveys of different kinds although the ideas can be extended to data from experiments and from administrative sources.

CATEGORIES OF NON-RESPONSE

In surveys, missing data arises because of non-response, which we can divide into four main categories:

1 Unit non-response – when nothing is known about a particular unit other than the very limited information that might be available from the sampling frame. This is a problem for observational studies of all types.
2 Item non-response – when the data from a unit are incomplete. For example, a respondent to a survey might not have answered one or more questions. Again, this can apply to both cross-sectional and longitudinal studies.
3 Wave non-response – this is specific to longitudinal studies and refers to those situations where (whether by design or not) units move into and out of the target sample over time.
4 Attrition – again specific to longitudinal studies, this refers to units which drop out never to return at subsequent waves. It is not always possible to distinguish unit attrition from wave non-respondents until the end of a study. Whether a case deemed lost due to attrition can be regarded as no longer part of the longitudinal target sample depends on decisions made at the outset of the study. These depend on a study's aims. For example, studies of children such as the UK birth cohort studies usually regard deaths and emigrations from the UK as losses from the population and not from the sample, whereas epidemiological studies of older people sometimes treat death as another kind of sample loss.

We can sub-divide unit non-response into non-contact and non-cooperation (or refusal); item non-response can arise as a result of the respondent not knowing the answer to a question, refusing to answer it, or the interviewer forgetting or choosing not to ask the question; wave non-response and attrition can both be sub-divided into not being located (as a result of residential mobility), non-contact and refusal (Lepkowski and Couper, 2002). Ideally, we would like to tailor our analysis to the missing data arising due to these different categories of non-response.

Given the categories above, when confronted by missing data in a survey, we are clearly confronted with multiple missingness mechanisms working in different ways. Comprehensively taking them into account is thus not possible; the art lies in identifying those likely to cause non-trivial bias or loss of power, and addressing those. Inevitably, this is related to the analysis question.

In the light of this we need to think about the possible impact of reasons for missing data (missingness mechanisms) on estimates and inferences. The typology originally developed by Rubin (1976), and presented with mathematically precise definitions by Little and Rubin (2002), is helpful here, as it casts light on the likely effect of missingness mechanisms on inference.

TYPOLOGY OF MISSINGNESS MECHANISMS

(A) Missing Completely At Random (MCAR) – the mechanism causing the missing data is unrelated to the analysis question. It may be due to chance, or it may be associated with some variables in the survey. If the latter, the values of these variables do not affect our analysis.

For example, data may be more likely to be missing because of a change of local administrative procedure; this may be documented in the survey, but would be unrelated to analysis concerned with, say, marital status.

When data are MCAR, analysis of those cases with no missing observations – so-called complete cases (CC) – will be unbiased, but it may be imprecise.

(B) Missing At Random (MAR) – essentially this says that, given the observed data, the mechanism causing the missing data is independent of the unobserved values. In other words, for a particular unit the chance of seeing a variable may depend on its value, but given the observed variables on that unit, this association is broken.

For example, suppose we intend to collect data on income from 200 people, but only obtain data from 157 of these. Suppose further that the chance of observing income is lower for higher incomes. This is illustrated in Figure 23.1, where we observe 68% of the people with higher incomes (those with job A) and 89% of those with lower incomes (those with job B). This figure is artifically generated, so we know the true mean income is £45,000. However, because of the missing data mechanism, the mean of the 157 observed incomes is £43,149. Clearly the chance of observing income depends on income.

However, income is MAR *given job* if, for each job type, *the chance of seeing income does not depend on income*. In other words, job type has broken the dependence between the chance of seeing income and the actual income. In this case, we can get a valid estimate of income *within each job type* by simply averaging

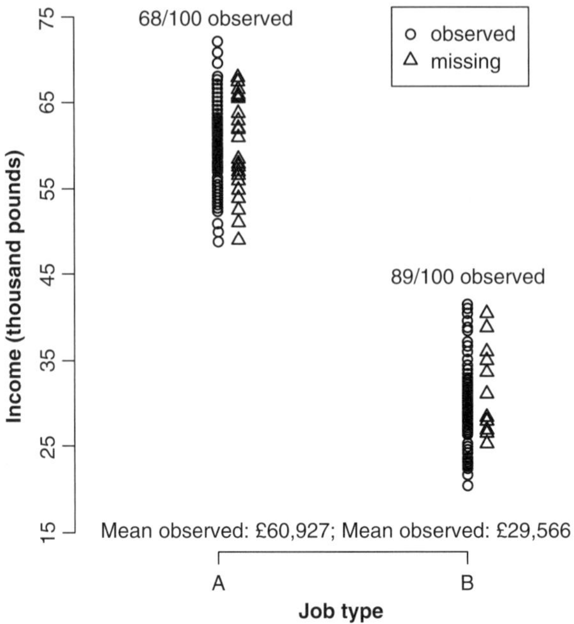

Figure 23.1 Illustration of missing at random. Details in text.

the observed incomes for that job type. This is shown just above the *x*-axis in Figure 23.1. Now we can obtain a valid estimate of mean income by weighting by the number of patients with each job type:

$$(100 \times £60{,}927 + 100 \times £29{,}566)/200 = £45{,}246,$$

which is less biased.

The important point to note is the following. If responses Y (here income) are MAR given observed covariates X (here job type) this implies the distribution of Y given X is identical *whether or not Y is actually observed.*

This is a key observation, because its implication is that, assuming MAR, we can use units with observed y to validly estimate the distribution of Y given X. Then we can sample the missing response data from this distribution, and so 'complete' our data set. This provides a key to multiple imputation.

(C) Missing Not At Random (MNAR) – the data are neither MCAR nor MAR. In other words, the distribution of the unobserved data is not only estimable from the observed data but also critically depends on what would have been (but was not) observed. This is the most difficult situation to adjust for, because now if Y is partially observed, the distribution of Y given X *is* different depending on whether or not Y is observed. Thus, this difference has to be specified in some way for analysis to proceed.

For example, in longitudinal studies, Y is MNAR can mean that whether or not y is missing at time t (y_t) depends not only on y_{t-1} but also on the change in y from time t-1 to time t. Contrast this with MAR, where it is sufficient to know y_{t-1} in order to make valid inferences about y_t (because we can estimate the distribution of y_t given y_{t-1} from those with both observed).

Types of missingness (A) and (B) are sometimes referred to as non-informative or ignorable missingness, type (C) as informative or non-ignorable missingness. The ignorable here relates not to whether we can 'ignore' the missing data (in the colloquial sense) but whether we can 'ignore' thinking about differences between (in the example of the previous paragraph) the distribution of y_t given y_{t-1} depending on whether y_t is observed or not.

While we use MCAR, MAR, MNAR – the terms found in the literature – we freely admit that they are not the most felicitous terms in the statistical lexicon. MAR is a conditional independence statement; it does not mean data are missing 'at random' in the colloquial sense. Further, as we show later, the fact that the missing data are ignorable does not necessarily mean that consideration of the missing data mechanism has no role to play in the analysis.

Another useful way of categorising non-response is in terms of its pattern; in particular, whether it follows a monotone or non-monotone pattern. For longitudinal studies, missing data at the case level are monotone if there is no wave non-response. In other words, once a case has left the study it does not return. This can happen if, for example, refusals at wave t are not reissued to the field at subsequent waves or if no attempt is made to locate non-contacted cases after the end of a wave of data collection.

Analytically, it can be easier to adjust for non-response if the pattern is monotone but, as we illustrate later, most missing data patterns are non-monotone, both at the case level and even more so at the item level within a particular survey. Our methods need to recognise this reality.

EXAMPLE: NATIONAL CHILD DEVELOPMENT STUDY (NCDS)

Later in this chapter, we illustrate ways of adjusting for missing data by using data from the NCDS. Here, we introduce the study in the light of our previous discussion of categories of non-response. The NCDS target sample size at birth in 1958 was 17,634 and this had reduced, as a result of death and permanent emigration, to 15,885 by age 23. The size of the observed sample at age 23 was 12,044 with 1,837 cases lost from the target sample as a result of attrition and 2001 wave non-respondents (plus three cases whose status was not known). In other words, 24% of the target sample at age 23 were missing, far from non-trivial percentage. The pattern of missing data in NCDS is not monotone with more than half the missing cases at age 23 reappearing in the observed sample at later waves. Of the missing cases at age 23, about one-third were due to non-cooperation, while two-thirds were either not located or not contacted. For more details about how the NCDS population and sample changed over time, see Plewis et al. (2004).

Table 23.1 NCDS data: missing data for model of interest

Care	*Social housing*	*Birth weight*	*Mother's age*	*Educational qualifications age 23*	*Frequency*	*% N = 15,882*
+	+	+	+	+	10,279	65
+	+	+	+	–	2,824	18
–	–	+	+	+	1,153	7.3
–	–	+	+	–	765	4.8
+	+	–	+	+	349	2.2
+	+	–	–	+	109	0.67
+	+	–	+	–	97	0.61
+	–	+	+	+	59	0.37
+	–	+	+	–	52	0.33
–	–	–	–	+	44	0.28
–	–	–	+	+	37	0.23
		Other patterns			114	0.72

Note: +: observed; –: not observed.

The substantive question that drives our analysis is how well the probability of having any educational qualifications at age 23 (wave 4) can be predicted by four variables measured at birth (wave 0) and in early childhood (wave 1): birth weight, mother's age, living in social housing and spending a period in care. As well as attrition and wave non-response, further 1,765 cases exhibited at least some item non-response so that the 'complete case' analysis was based on 10,279 cases, just 65% of the target sample. This raises the question of whether inferences based on these complete cases differ from those that might have been obtained for the complete target sample of 15,885. Table 23.1 shows the patterns of item non-response and indicates that 65% (1153/1765) of the item non-response comes from just one pattern – missing information on the 'in care' and 'social housing variables' measured at wave 1.

PREVENTING NON-RESPONSE AND MINIMISING ITS IMPACT

Unit non-response, item non-response and attrition are all facts of life for most observational studies; nevertheless steps can be taken to keep them to a minimum. In particular, there is a considerable literature about preventing non-response in cross-sectional studies. Recurrent themes include the selection and training of interviewers in face-to-face surveys, the value of reminders in mail surveys and the efficacy of incentives to improve response rates. Groves et al. (2002, 2004) are useful references.

The literature on preventing non-response in longitudinal studies after the first wave of data collection is less extensive. Cases lost from longitudinal surveys are likely to be different from non-respondents in cross-sectional surveys because they are known to have participated in one or more earlier sweeps, so some information about them is available. Agencies responsible for large, long-running longitudinal studies like the UK birth cohorts, the British Household Panel Survey (BHPS), the Panel Survey of Income Dynamics in the US and the German Socio-Economic Panel invest substantial survey resources to maintain contact and cooperation (panel maintenance). Laurie et al. (1999) describe the strategies used in the BHPS and Shepherd (1995) describes the tracing methods (e.g. the use of birthday cards to cohort members) used in the NCDS up to wave 5. One issue that remains unresolved in the literature is whether panel maintenance, especially the resources devoted to tracing very mobile households, is cost-effective in terms of the numbers and kinds of households which are retained in the study.

With thought, we can also design our study to minimise the ambiguity caused by the inevitable non-response. To do this we draw on the discussion above, noting that missing data do not cause ambiguity *per se* but because we are inherently unsure about the mechanism generating the missing data. Further, if the mechanism causing the missing data is MAR, then we can use the methods discussed below to obtain valid inferences. The idea is to design any study so that we maximise the chances that missing data are MAR. Thus, at the design stage we want to think about possible predictors of non-response to the key survey questions and think about strategies for maximising the chance of recording those predictors. In other words, we want to design the study so that missing data are likely to be MAR. Then, the ambiguity caused by the missing data is greatly reduced, and we can employ one of the methods below to obtain valid inferences from the partially observed data.

THREE METHODS FOR THE ANALYSIS OF PARTIALLY OBSERVED DATA

We now consider three methods for analysing partially observed data. These are:

1 inverse probability weighting (IPW),
2 multiple imputation (MI), and
3 joint modelling.

IPW and MI are typically used when the data are MAR; a joint model of the substantive process and the missingness mechanism can be used when the data are MNAR. We illustrate the use of each of these with the NCDS data.

Inverse probability weighting

Weighting to adjust for unit and wave non-response and attrition is probably the most common method of adjustment. It is predicated on the idea that each sample member has a propensity to respond that can be predicted from their observed characteristics.

Ignoring for the moment different kinds of non-response, we estimate a model – a logit or a probit model – for the probability, π_{it}, that a case i responds at wave t. Algebraically,

$$\text{logit/probit}\pi_{it} = \beta_0 + \sum_p \beta_p x_{pi,t-k} + \sum_r \delta_r z_{rit}$$

where $x_{pi,t-k}$ are covariates measured at wave $t-k$ $(k \geq 1)$ and z_{rit} are aspects of the data collection process at wave t. See Hawkes and Plewis (2006) for an example. Once this model is fitted, the predicted probability (p) of responding for the cases that actually responded can easily be computed. The lower the predicted probability, the greater the proportion of cases with these characteristics that do not respond. We therefore give these cases more weight in any analysis. In other words, we upweight the observed units to represent both themselves and similar unobserved units. Specifically, all cases are weighted by the inverse of their predicted probability of responding, that is $1/p_{it}$. Our hope is that, by making this adjustment, we essentially reintroduce into the analysis the information lost as a result of non-response. The principle is the same as that developed for sampling schemes that do not give an equal probability of selection to all members of the population. Indeed, it is possible to combine these sampling weights with the non-response weights to generate an overall weight as has been done for another of the UK birth cohort studies, the Millennium Cohort Study (Plewis, 2007).

Adjusting for missingness by weighting is relatively easy to apply, and the weights can be made available for secondary analysts to use. These are two important practical advantages of the method. There are, however, a number of drawbacks:

1 The model for the probability of responding needs (a) to include all the important predictors and (b) not to be affected by item non-response among the explanatory variables in the weighting model. Condition (b) can be difficult to satisfy in the presence of wave non-response and attrition. More generally, the combination of these two kinds of non-response can lead to difficulties in the construction of weights for successive waves.
2 The weights are estimated from the data rather than being known and are therefore subject to error which should be reflected in the standard errors of estimated parameters in the analyses of substantive interest. Also, inverse probability weights can be very large if the probability of responding is very low and this variability in the weights leads to a loss of precision. For this reason, weights should be graphed as part of the analysis. One solution to the problem of 'exploding' weights is to group the predicted probabilities into quintiles and use the median weight within each group. This reduces variability but the trade off is a possible increase in bias.
3 Weighting (at least as often applied) implicitly assumes that the same adjustment procedure is optimal for all kinds of substantive analysis.
4 Estimation can be imprecise, because information from units with partial data is not directly incorporated; only fully observed units are weighted.

Multiple Imputation

Multiple imputation (MI) is a Monte Carlo method with two stages for fitting models to partially observed data. Stage one estimates the distribution of the missing data given the observed data, and stage two fits the user's model of interest to data drawn from this distribution, and averages the results for final inference. It can be viewed as allowing units with partial data to make a statistically valid contribution to the analysis.

To illustrate, suppose that income and age are partially observed, that sex is fully observed, and that our model of interest regresses income on age and sex. Multiple imputation would proceed as a series of steps as follows:

A1 Fit a multivariate response model with the partially observed data (age and income) as responses and any fully observed data (here sex) as covariates.[1] This is known as the *imputation model.* We discuss how to do this below.

A2 Create K 'completed' data sets by drawing the unseen data from the multivariate response model fitted in A1 that is from the estimated distribution of the missing data given the observed data. Essentially, creating multiple imputed data sets provides a computationally convenient way of taking into account the uncertainty in estimating the model in step A1.

A3 Fit the model of interest to each imputed data set, giving K sets of parameter estimates and their standard errors. For a particular (scalar) parameter estimate, denote these by $\hat{\theta}_k, \hat{\sigma}_k^2$, $k = 1, \ldots K$.

A4 The multiple imputation estimate of θ is calculated as:

$$\hat{\theta}_{MI} = \frac{1}{K}\sum_{k=1}^{K} \hat{\theta}_k,$$

with variance

$$\hat{\sigma}_{MI}^2 = \hat{\sigma}_w^2 + \left(1 + \frac{1}{K}\right)\hat{\sigma}_b^2,$$

where

$$\hat{\sigma}_w^2 = \frac{1}{K}\sum_{k=1}^{K} \hat{\sigma}_k^2, \text{ and } \hat{\sigma}_b^2 = \frac{1}{K-1}\sum_{k=1}^{K} (\hat{\theta}_k - \hat{\theta}_{MI})^2.$$

To test the hypothesis $\theta = \theta_0$, compare $\frac{\hat{\theta}_{MI} - \theta_0}{\hat{\sigma}_{MI}}$ to a t-distribution with v degrees of freedom where

$$n = (K-1)\left[1 + \frac{\hat{\sigma}_w^2}{(1+1/K)\hat{\sigma}_b^2}\right]^2.$$

These rules for combining the results of the K imputations for inference were derived by Rubin (e.g. Rubin, 1987) and are commonly referred to as 'Rubin's rules'.[2] Almost all softwares for multiple imputation do the calculations automatically. Note that we have given the formulae for a single (scalar) parameter; analogous formulae for parameter vectors exist (e.g. Rubin, 1987; Schafer, 1997a).

Steps A1 and A2 are critical. Fitting the imputation model referred to in A1 is not always easy. We sketch one approach, most suitable for cross-sectional data, which we employ in the analysis below. This effectively fits the multivariate or 'joint' model we refer to, but indirectly, through a series of univariate regression models. This approach is known as 'imputation using chained equations' or, equivalently 'full conditional specification' (see, for example van Buuren et al., 2006; Kenward and Carpenter, 2007). For our problem with income, age and sex we would proceed as follows:

B1 Initialisation: for each variable, get started by replacing missing values by sampling with replacement from observed values for that variable.
B2 Return to the observed income data (i.e. set the values for income substituted in the initialisation *or* last imputation stage to be missing). Regress income on age and sex, and then impute the missing income values (taking full account of the uncertainty in estimating the model).
B3 Return to the observed age data (set all initialised or previously imputed values as missing). Regress age on income and sex, then impute missing age.
B4 Return to the observed sex data. Regress (using logistic regression) sex on income and age, then impute missing sex values (if not fully observed).

In our example with three variables, steps B2 to B4 form one cycle. Note that as we said there were no missing sex observations, step B4 is unnecessary here. We typically run the process for 10–20 cycles, then at the end of step B4 collect our first 'imputed data set'. We then carry on running the process for another 10–20 cycles, then collect our second imputed data set, and so on until we have K imputed data sets with K equal to at least five.

Note that for valid inference, our imputation model, whether explicitly set up and fitted as a multivariate response model, or implicitly fitted via the chained equations approach, must be such that (i) the missing data are plausibly MAR (although not every case must have the same MAR mechanism) and (ii) be consistent with the model of interest. Both points are critical in the NCDS analysis, and we discuss them further below.

It is also worth stressing that in step A2 of the original algorithm (and by implication each time data are imputed in steps B2 to B4 of the chained equation process above), the imputed data must reflect the uncertainty in estimating the parameters in the imputation model, not just the model's residual variance. For each new imputed set of data (K in all), we therefore need to:

(i) draw a new parameter vector (parameters of the imputation model) from its estimated sampling distribution;
(ii) use this in calculating the conditional mean for the missing data and;
(iii) add on residual error to arrive at the imputed data.

Steps (i) to (iii) are important and ensure that MI does not underestimate the uncertainty about the missing data, which would in turn lead to standard errors in the model of interest that were too small. Most users need not be too concerned about these details, though, as they are usually taken care of by the software.

More details of MI, spelt out in Rubin (1987) and Schafer (1997a), give algorithms; for a review of the state of the art, see Kenward and Carpenter (2007).

The attraction of MI is that it is very general. Rubin's rules are simple, and apply in a very wide variety of settings – essentially whenever (in the absence of missing data) the asymptotic sampling distribution of the parameter estimators is multivariate normal. Further, Rubin's rules give an estimate of the variance, which is often relatively hard to get with other methods such as those based on the EM algorithm (Dempster et al., 1977) and mean-score imputation (Clayton et al., 1998). In particular, it is not possible to derive the correct variance formula in general for a single imputed data set, although formulae for particular situations may be calculated with some difficulty. Use of the usual variance formulae with a single imputed data set usually dramatically underestimates the loss of information caused by the missing data, and should be avoided.

Assuming the user has a model of interest in mind, once the imputation model (in step A1) is chosen, the method is automatic, and hence readily programmable. The choice of imputation model is therefore the key to reliable results. While this model is a multivariate response model (in which partially observed variables are responses) it can, as discussed above, be specified as a series of univariate regression models (see also the software description below). Besides the formal specification of the imputation model, there are two criteria that need to be satisfied:

C1 for each case, their missing data need to be MAR given their observed data (this is the minimal mathematical requirement for a valid MAR analysis) and
C2 all the structures we are investigating in our model of interest need to be present in the imputation model.

Point C1 needs to hold for valid inference with data imputed from the imputation model. In practice, this means we may need to include additional (termed auxiliary) variables in the imputation model, on top of those in the model of interest. In our hypothetical example above we may want to add social class to the imputation model, as income data are more likely to be MAR given social class.

Such auxiliary variables need to be (i) predictive of missing data and (ii) correlated with variables in our model of interest. In practice (as in the NCDS analysis below) they are usually identified by:

(a) a logistic regression of the probability of seeing partially observed variables on (almost) fully observed ones and
(b) looking to see if the variables identified in (a) are correlated with variables in the model of interest.

Notice that we can also include auxiliary variables in the imputation model which are predictive of the partially observed variables, even if they are not predictive of the chance of observing these variables. In this latter case, we may gain precision through multiple imputation, but our parameter estimates will be little changed.

Point C2 is also very important in practice. First, it requires that all the variables (including the response) in our model of interest need to be included in the imputation model. While including the response may appear surprising, on reflection it makes sense, as if we do not do this our imputed data will not have the correct association with the response. In the example above, we said income and age had missing data. If our model of interest regresses income on age and sex, income and sex must be included in our imputation model, otherwise imputed age values will be unassociated with both income and sex. It follows from this point that any non-linear terms and interactions in our model of interest should be in the imputation model; otherwise the imputed data cannot have the non-linear structure or interactions.

Software

Although there are a number of approaches and corresponding software packages for multiple imputation, three are broadly established at this time:

1 Assume multivariate Normality for the imputation model. That is to say the imputation model is an unstructured multivariate Normal distribution for the fully and partially observed data. This approach is used in SAS PROC MI (with the MCMC option) and also in Shafer's NORM software.

This approach is theoretically well grounded, fast, and handles large data sets fairly reliably. For most accurate results, variables should be transformed to be approximately Normal beforehand, and back transformed afterwards, that is before steps A3 and A4 above. Perhaps surprisingly, binary data can quite often be treated as Normal for imputation and rounded back afterwards, with minimal bias (Bernaards et al., 2007). Problems can arise with unordered categorical variables with more than two levels, though.

2 Instead of specifying a joint model explicitly, specify a regression model for each variable on all the others in turn, as described above with the income, age and sex example.

This approach is the so-called 'full conditional specification' (also known as the 'chained equations' approach). While its theoretical basis is less well established, its attraction is that the need to transform variables is avoided. A drawback in data sets with many variables is that the regression models can become over-specified (i.e. with 100 variables each of the 100 regression imputation models has 99 covariates), leading to over-fitting and unpredictable results. This is especially likely for categorical variables (e.g. Carpenter and Kenward, 2008: 110); in this respect this method is less robust than the multivariate Normal approach above. The approach is available in R (mice: Van Buuren and Oudshoorn, 2000, mi: Su et al., 2010), Stata (ice: Royston, 2007) and SAS (iveware macro: Raghunathan et al., 2009).

3 The third approach again uses the multivariate Normal model, but now allows for multilevel structure. This has been implemented in Schafer's PAN package (Schafer, 1997b) and in *MLwiN* (www.cmm.bristol.ac.uk; see Carpenter and Goldstein, 2005). As with approach one, we need to transform to and from approximate Normality before and afterwards. We have already mentioned the importance of the imputation model being consistent with the model of interest, and allowing for the multilevel structure can be an important part of this (Carpenter and Goldstein, 2005), particularly if data are (i) unbalanced and/or (ii) if there is a high intra-class correlation (so clustering is an important issue) and/or (iii) there are partially observed variables at the cluster level (i.e. level two). This approach has been further developed for multivariate mixed response types with potentially missing data at two levels, although the software is more experimental (Goldstein et al., 2009).

The above overview of MI gives an idea of its flexibility and the key points to bear in mind when using it. These are explored further in the example from the NCDS. In essence, MI is a Bayesian method, though if it is done properly (i.e. as outlined above) reliable frequentist inferences can be drawn. As a Bayesian approach, it could be programmed in a Bayesian software package, such as WinBUGS (Spiegelhalter et al., 1999); in practice, we have found this is often prohibitively slow for models of reasonable complexity with more than 3–5000 observations.

Joint modelling

The key difference from the above is that we do not assume that the data are MAR. Instead, the possibility that there are unobserved variables that affect both the outcome and missingness is accommodated by allowing the residual terms from the two models (for outcome and missingness) to be correlated. A particular form of these joint models which we explore here – often known as Heckman models (Heckman, 1979) – can be set out as follows.

The model of interest for a discrete outcome is usually a generalised linear model. For a binary outcome, it can be written as:

$$P\left(\sum_p \beta_p x_{pi} + u_{1i} > 0\right) = \Phi\left(\sum_p \beta_p x_{pi}\right),$$

where Φ is the standard Normal distribution function so $u_{1i} \sim N(0,1)$.

The model of missingness, also known as the selection model, is:

$$P\left(\sum_q \alpha_q z_{qi} + u_{2i} > 0\right) = \Phi\left(\sum_q \alpha_q z_{qi}\right)$$

with $u_{2i} \sim N(0,1)$. See Freedman (2005: Ch. 6) for a more detailed explanation of the way these so-called probit models are specified.

The key aspect of the specification of the joint model is that u_{1i} and u_{2i} are not independent, that is $E(u_1 u_2) \neq 0$. This implies that unobserved variables (contained in u_2) that are correlated with being missing are also correlated with the outcome via u_1 and its correlation with u_2.

The joint model can be estimated using maximum likelihood providing the model is identified. Stata has two procedures: *heckman* when the outcome is continuous and *heckprob* when it is binary, and these have been extended to survey data that are stratified and clustered (*svy:heckman* etc.). Identification is achieved by including in the selection model variables (often called 'instruments') that are not in the model of interest. These instruments need to be variables that are associated with missingness but are not associated with the outcome of interest. It is not always easy to find suitable instruments (Fitzgerald et al., 1998).

NCDS DATA ANALYSIS: FACTORS AFFECTING EDUCATIONAL QUALIFICATIONS AT AGE 23

Hawkes and Plewis (2006) show that the best predictors of attrition and wave non-response at wave 4 (age 23) are sex, two variables measured at wave 3 (reading score and number of residential moves from birth to age 16) and one variable measured at wave 2 (social adjustment at age 11). The estimated coefficients from the multinomial logistic model are given in Table 23.2 and show that the estimates are, apart from number of moves, greater for attrition than they are for wave non-response, suggesting that the missing mechanism for attrition is different from and more systematic than it is for wave non-response. As described above, we can generate inverse probability weights from the information in Table 23.2 and apply them to our substantive model based on the probit of having an educational qualification. The comparisons between the unweighted and weighted estimates are given in Table 23.3.

Looking first at the actual estimates, we see some changes: stronger effects for in care and inverse birth weight, weaker effects for social housing, mother's age

Table 23.2 Estimates from multinomial logistic model for response at age 23

Explanatory variable	*Attrition*		*Wave non-response*	
	Estimate	*s.e.*	*Estimate*	*s.e*
Constant	–1.7	0.20	–2.1	0.18
Sex	–0.33	0.098	–0.20	0.076
Social adjustment, wave 2	0.021	0.0052	0.016	0.0044
No. moves, birth to wave 3	0.083	0.025	0.13	0.019
Reading score, wave 3	–0.046	0.0067	–0.012	0.0057

Note: Sample size = 8,072.
Here, and subsequently, sex is coded 1 for female and 0 male.

Table 23.3 Inverse probability weights (1) applied to model of interest

Explanatory variable	*Estimate*		*s.e.*	
	No weights	*Inverse probability weights* (1)	*No weights*	*Inverse probability weights* (1)
Constant	−1.6	−1.7	0.078	0.11
In care	0.65	0.73	0.096	0.14
Social housing	0.58	0.51	0.035	0.046
Inverse birth weight	73	80	8.5	12
Mother's age (at birth)	−0.017	−0.011	0.0037	0.0053
Mother's age squared	0.0020	0.00083	0.00047	0.00066
Age * housing	0.013	0.0026	0.0054	0.0075
Age squared * housing	−0.00078	−0.00017	0.00068	0.00094

Note: Sample sizes = 10,279 (no weights); 5,996 (inverse probability weights).
Here, and subsequently, birth weight is in ounces and mother's age at child's birth is in years (centred at 28 years).

and their interactions. The bigger changes are, however, in the standard errors which are about 40% higher for the model using weights. This decrease in precision is mostly due to the fact that the weighted model is estimated on 5,996 cases, just 58% of the number in the unweighted model. This diminution of the sample arises partly because the model for generating the weights has only 8,072 cases and partly because these 8,072 cases are not a subset of the 10,279 complete cases. This illustrates one of the difficulties with using non-response weights in this way: the most complete model in terms of predicting non-response (and hence the model that comes closest to meeting the MAR assumption) itself suffers from item non-response and so any gains in terms of reducing bias can be dissipated by the loss of precision (see also discussions in Carpenter et al., 2006; Vansteelandt et al., 2009).

If we look at the patterns of missing values for the non-response model we find that 1,899 cases are missing information just on number of moves, 1,581 just on the reading test and 994 just on the social adjustment measure (and none just on sex). Consequently, we can estimate three more sets of weights based on the models that exclude just one of these variables, examine the relation of the weights from the incomplete (i.e. misspecified) models for response with those from the full model and then, if the association is reasonably good, calibrate the weights from the full model against those from the incomplete models and replace the missing weights by the estimated weights from the calibrations. As before, it is important to examine the properties of the weights so generated graphically.

We find that the weights from the three incomplete models are highly correlated with the weights from the full model estimated on 8,072 cases. The correlations are 0.82 (excluding number of moves), 0.89 (excluding the reading test) and 0.90 (excluding social adjustment). We therefore replace the missing weights in the following way:

1 Replace, where possible, missing weights by predicted values using estimates from the linear regression of the weight from the full model against the weight for the model omitting social adjustment.
2 Replace, where possible, weights that are still missing by predicted values using estimates from the linear regression of the weight from the full model against the weight for the model omitting the reading test.
3 Finally replace, where possible, weights that are still missing by predicted values using estimates from the linear regression of the weight from the full model against the weight for the model omitting the number of moves.

These steps allow us to estimate a weighted model with 8,841 rather than 5,996 cases and the results are given in Table 23.4. We see that the estimates that use these additional cases are closer to the estimates in the complete case analysis, suggesting that the restriction of only using weights where there is no item non-response could be leading to an over-adjustment in this case. We also gain quite a lot of precision.

Analysis using multiple imputation

We now repeat the above analysis using multiple imputation (MI). For this analysis, all the calculations were carried out using the *ice* software (Royston, 2007) in Stata 10.

We use the same model of interest as before; that is to say a probit regression of an indicator for educational qualifications at age 23 on sex, mother's age at

Table 23.4 Inverse probability weights (2) applied to model of interest

Explanatory variable	*Estimate*		*s.e.*	
	No weights	*Inverse probability weights (2)*	*No weights*	*Inverse probability weights (2)*
Constant	−1.6	−1.6	0.078	0.088
In care	0.65	0.64	0.096	0.11
Social housing	0.58	0.57	0.035	0.038
Inverse birth weight	73	75	8.5	9.5
Mother's age (at birth)	−0.017	−0.014	0.0037	0.0042
Mother's age squared	0.0020	0.0017	0.00047	0.00052
Age * housing	0.013	0.0065	0.0054	0.0059
Age squared * housing	−0.00078	−0.00054	0.00068	0.00075

Note: Sample sizes = 10,279 (no weights); 8,841 (inverse probability weights).

child's birth, birth weight, whether the child was in care before age 7, and whether the mother and child lived in social housing at age 7. In the regression, we use inverse birth weight and explore a non-linear relationship with mother's age, and the interaction of mother's age with social housing. Parameter estimates and standard errors from fitting the model to the 10,279 cases with no missing data are shown in second and sixth columns respectively of Table 23.5 (these are the same as the 'no weights' analysis in Table 23.3).

Before performing multiple imputation, we discuss its likely benefits and difficulties (Sterne et al., 2009). First, we note that if we do not include any auxiliary variables, just putting the variables in the model of interest into the imputation model, cases with a missing response (educational qualifications at age 23), will not contribute information through the MI analysis, whether or not they have covariates observed. However, cases with an observed response but missing covariates will contribute through the MI analysis.

Table 23.1 therefore suggests that most of the extra information will come from the 1,153 individuals with no 'care' or 'social housing' data, but otherwise observed, and the 349 with no birth weight, but otherwise observed.

Second, if the mechanism causing the missing data depends on the covariates in the model of interest and, given these, not on the response, then a complete case analysis will not be biased, though it may be inefficient. In this example, though, the reason for missing values depends critically on additional variables mentioned above – reading ability at age 16, behaviour measure at age 11, number of family moves between birth and age 16 and sex. Since these auxiliary variables are also strongly correlated with the covariates and the response in the model of interest, we need to include them in the imputation model to increase the plausibilty of the missing at random assumption. Thus, in the MI analysis including these auxiliary variables, it is very possible that the parameter estimates will be different from those from the analysis which includes only the 10,279 complete cases.

An additional advantage of including auxiliary variables, *even if they are not predictive of a variable being missing* is that they can recover information about that variable, particularly if they are good surrogates for the response. Thus, in MI, when imputing we can include auxiliary variables on the causal pathway, which we would not want to include in our model of interest. It follows that an MI analysis with auxiliary variables is usually preferable to one without.

Lastly, we commented above that the structure in the model of interest should be reflected in the imputation model. In our analysis of the NCDS data, we are exploring (i) the possibility of a non-linear relationship between mother's age and the child's educational qualifications at age 23 and (ii) an interaction between mother's age and living in social housing at age 7. Ideally, the imputation model should reflect this structure although, as we shall see, this is not always straightforward and may be beyond current software.

Results of imputation analyses

We now describe three MI analyses of these data under the MAR assumption, highlighting their strengths and weaknesses. We indicate where we would expect these to conincide with results from other packages which do not use the full conditional specification approach; we would expect similar results from the SAS macro IVEware and the R macro *mice* for all analyses. All analyses reported below used 30 cycles between each of the 50 imputations, and included the following four auxillary variables: reading ability at age 16, behaviour measure at age 11, number of family moves between birth and age 16 and sex.

(I) Analysis I uses linear regression for all the imputation models, regardless of whether the response is continuous or discrete. As the imputation model has nine variables (including the auxiliary variables and the response from the model of interest, but before calculating derived variables) the chained equation specification has nine linear regressions, each of one variable on the other eight. Note that each of these models only has a linear relationship of the response on the covariates (no quadratic term or interaction). Thus, this analysis could equally well be done in SAS, using PROC MI with the MCMC option, or using Schafer's NORM package, as they both rely on multivariate Normality. Variables could be transformed to improve marginal Normality before this analysis, and back transformed afterwards, but apart from using inverse birth weight instead of birth weight we have not done this.

After performing the imputations, for the continuous variables mother's age and birth weight, imputed values for these variables outside the maximum/minimum in the observed data were set to the maximum/minimum in the observed data (typically six changes per imputed data set). Imputed values for binary variables were rounded to zero if < 0.5, and to one if >0.5.

The results of this analysis are shown in Table 23.5, third column; the complete case (CC) analysis is shown in second column; standard errors are shown in sixth and seventh columns. We see that while, as is typically the case, standard errors are substantially smaller (as we are making use of the partial information), point estimates are similar, though they are mostly slighly attenuated. In particular, the non-linear and interaction terms (the last three) are all attenuated. This is to be expected, as none of the imputed data has this non-linear or interaction structure.

(II) Analysis II attempts to address the omission of the non-linear term (age squared) from the imputations. For these imputations, in the chained equation specification we use linear regression where the response is continuous, and logistic regression where it is discrete. We also use the square of mother's age in all imputation regressions, except the imputation regression where mother's age is itself the response. At each iteration (cycle) of the chained equations algorithm, after fitting this last model, the square of mother's age was calculated deterministically by squaring mother's age.

The results are shown in Table 23.5, MI(II). Again, a small minority of imputed values of the continuous variables birth weight and mother's age that lay beyond

Table 23.5 Results of multiple imputation

Explanatory variable	*Estimate*				*s.e.*			
	CC	*MI(I)*	*MI(II)*	*MI(III)*	*CC*	*MI(I)*	*MI(II)*	*MI(III)*
Constant	−1.6	−1.4	−1.5	−1.5	0.078	0.072	0.067	0.075
In care	0.65	0.65	0.69	0.70	0.096	0.091	0.086	0.090
Social housing	0.58	0.53	0.58	0.58	0.035	0.032	0.032	0.033
Inverse birth weight	73	70	74	75	8.5	7.7	7.2	8.6
Mother's age (at birth)	−0.017	−0.014	−0.15	−0.017	0.0037	0.0033	0.0035	0.0037
Mother's age squared	0.0020	0.0016	0.0018	0.0019	0.00047	0.00042	0.00041	0.00048
Age* housing	0.013	0.012	0.012	0.015	0.0054	0.0048	0.0048	0.0051
Age squared* housing	−0.00078	−0.00068	−0.00069	−0.00094	0.00068	0.00061	0.00061	0.00065

Note: CC: complete case analysis ($N = 10{,}279$).
MI(I): omitting non-linear and interaction terms from the imputation model.
MI(II): including mother's age squared in the imputation model.
MI(III): MI(II) plus the interaction between social housing and mother's age.

the maximum/minimum in the observed data were set at these values. Comparing the CC analysis and MI(I), we see a similar gain in precision. Now, however, not all point estimates from MI(II) are attenuated; in particular the non-linear term in mother's age is closer to the observed value; however the interaction terms are still attenuated. Although MI(II) goes some way to addressing the non-linearity issue in the imputations, it is not perfect because including mother's age squared in all the imputation models except that with mother's age as a response means that the implied relationships within the data are not consistent. In practice, unless we are specifically concerned with the non-linear coefficients, this may not be too important.

(III) Analysis III seeks to handle the interactions by (i) dropping those cases with missing social housing and (ii) imputing separately in each social housing category using the same imputation model as MI(II).

The results are shown in Table 23.5. Compared with the CC analysis, we have a slightly stronger effect of 'in care', but most noticeably stronger interaction terms. This analysis results in a smaller p-value for both the linear and non-linear interaction between mother's age and social housing, though the non-linear term is still not significant.

However, the potential drawback with MI(III) is that we have discarded cases with missing social housing, in order to impute allowing a different structure in the two social housing categories. While this does not seem to have had much of an effect on the standard errors, it may cause bias. To assess this, we first look at the reasons for missing social housing. A logistic regression of the chance of observing social housing shows that the only predictor is in care; after allowing for this no others (including the auxiliary variables) approach significance (smallest p-value 0.16).

Further, the significant association with care rests on 121 cases where social housing is missing but care is observed. Thus, for those cases where social housing is missing, assuming it is not MNAR, it appears to be either MCAR or MAR depending on the 'in care' variable (another covariate in the model of interest). In neither of these two cases would we expect the point estimates from an analysis where we leave out cases with missing social housing values to be markedly biased. Therefore, we conclude that assuming data are MAR, our preferred estimates are from MI(III). The gain of MI is both improved precision and confirmation of the interesting interaction between mother's age and social housing.

Results from the joint model

Turning to the results from jointly modelling the outcome of interest and missingness, we use sex and number of family moves from birth to age 7 as our instruments in the selection model. In principle, we can use all the explanatory variables that appear in the model of interest in the selection model but, in fact, only in care and inverse birth weight are important; mother's age and social housing do not make an additional contribution to the explanation of missingness. We do not use variables like reading score and social adjustment because they are on the causal path linking earlier states to qualifications at age 23 even though they are not used in this substantive analysis.

Table 23.6 gives the estimates for the model of interest and the selection model. We see that, compared with the CC analysis for the model of interest, a substantial increase in the estimate for 'in care', a decrease for the social housing variable but little difference in the point estimates and their standard errors for the other variables. The estimates for the selection model show that the probability of being included at age 23 are smaller if the child was 'in care' early in their lives, increases as birth weight increases, are higher for female children, and decline with the number of moves. The estimated residual correlation (–0.58; $\chi_1^2 = 6.52$, $p < 0.02$) shows that there is a strong negative correlation between the two residuals u_1 and u_2 such that the unobserved variables that make inclusion more likely are associated with a better chance of qualifications at age 23 (and thus negatively associated with the unobserved variables that predict having no qualifications at age 23). It is, however, important to bear in mind the general point that estimates for the model of interest are sensitive to the specification of the selection model, in particular to the choice of instruments, and, although not shown here, this is true for the models used in this example (Little, 1986).

Table 23.6 Results from joint model

Explanatory variable	*Outcome model*		*Selection model*	
	Estimate	*s.e.*	*Estimate*	*s.e.*
Constant	–1.3	0.15	0.90	0.069
In care	0.80	0.10	–0.22	0.092
Social housing	0.53	0.047	n.a.	
Inverse birth weight	72	8.8	–15	7.8
Mother's age (at birth)	–0.017	0.0035	n.a.	
Mother's age squared	0.0020	0.00045	n.a.	
Age * housing	0.012	0.0051	n.a.	
Age squared * housing	–0.00077	–0.00064	n.a.	
Sex	n.a.		0.17	0.024
Moves, birth to age 7	n.a.		–0.051	0.0086

Note: Combined $N = 12{,}950$.

Reporting the analysis of partially observed data

The analysis of the NCDS data highlights several general points for reporting the analysis of a partially observed data set (see also Sterne et al., 2009). First, patterns of missing data should be reported, in a way similar to our Table 23.1, to give readers a feeling for what information is missing. Second, an indication should be given of plausible mechanisms for the missing data, including relevant auxiliary variables. Third, the CC analysis should be presented alongside the results of other methods as a benchmark. If, for cases with missing responses, these are plausibly MAR given observed covariates in the model of interest, and for cases with observed response but missing covariates, these covariates are plausibly MAR given the observed covariates (but not the response), then point estimates from the CC analysis are likely to be relatively unbiased. Further, as here with MI(I), comparing with CC analysis can highlight problems with MI analysis that need to be addressed.

CONCLUSION

Analysis of partially observed data from cohort studies such as the NCDS is nontrivial, requiring careful reflection about likely mechanisms causing missing data and their impact on the inferential question at hand.

We have reviewed three approaches: inverse probability weighting, multiple imputation under MAR and joint modelling. Inverse probability weighting is relatively inefficient, but can nevertheless provide a useful cross-check on multiple imputation. We recommend trying our calibration approach to maximse the number of cases in the analysis. MI is our preferred analysis under MAR, but note that its use was far from automatic. Comparing the CC analysis with our preferred MI analysis (MI III) we have some gain in precision overall, though not as dramatic as in some data sets. There is a slightly stronger adverse effect of 'in care' (0.65 for CC to 0.70). There is also a suggestion of a stronger and more significant estimate of the interesting interaction of mother's age and social housing. This suggests that the gain in the chance of the child obtaining educational qualifications by age 23 with increasing mother's age is all but cancelled out if the family is in social housing. This is probably indicative of more disadvantaged circumstances. The Heckman model needs to be interpreted cautiously, but suggests that *under this model* (whose assumptions, as is typical in these situations, we cannot check) there is some evidence of MNAR so that relative to MAR, individuals who are more likely to have missing data have a lower chance of obtaining qualifications at age 23. Looking at the standard errors suggests the Heckman and MI(III) analysis are essentially consistent. However, there is a suggestion that relative to the MI analysis, the Heckman analysis (i) increases the adverse effect of being in care (0.7 to 0.8) but (ii) decreases the interaction between mother's age and social housing (0.015 to 0.012, similar to the CC analysis).

In summary, our additional analyses clearly show that data are not MCAR. Analysis under MAR via MI using auxiliary variables suggests (i) the detrimental effect of being 'in care' is underestimated by the CC analysis and (ii) the beneficial effect of increasing mother's age is diluted by being in social housing at age 7. Both are consistent with the Heckman model.

Our analysis highlights the need for the research called for by Kenward and Carpenter (2007): outstanding questions include establishing more fully the theoretical basis for the chained equations method used here, and handling non-linearities, multilevel structure and sampling weights properly in the imputation. A start has been made with multilevel MI using *MLwiN* (Carpenter and Goldstein, 2005) and allowing for multilevel discrete data (Goldstein et al., 2009) but further important work remains. This includes allowing for survey weights in multiple imputation, allowing for interactions and non-linearities, and building robust software for a large number of variables. Joint modelling offers one way out of the restrictions imposed by the MAR assumption but at the cost of extra assumptions about distributions and specifications that might not be realistic. A more attractive option may well be the pattern mixture approach, implemented through multiple imputation (Little and Yau, 1996). For this we first impute under MAR. Then, we change these imputations to reflect possible departures from MAR. Different groups, or patterns, of missing data can have different departures. Finally, we use the usual MI rules to analyse the imputed data. If our assumptions about departures from MAR are valid, so will our inference be. A key attraction of this approach is that a range of researchers can engage meaningfully with departures from MAR imputations (which can often be displayed graphically, in terms of variable means under MAR and under MNAR) in a way they cannot with selection models in joint modelling.

As we noted in our introduction, it is unusual to find reports of quantitative social science investigations that explicitly explore the possible effects of missing data on inferences. This is a weakness across the board but it is an especially important omission from analyses that use longitudinal data as these data are particularly prone to missingness. Our NCDS example has shown what can be gained, particularly in terms of increased precision, by adjusting for non-response. With a range of 'statistically principled' tools now available for analysis it should be possible to build up a series of examples that demonstrate that MI, for example, can reduce bias and increase precision over a CC analysis. This chapter sets out how these analyses can be carried out and reported. Our hope is that it will encourage researchers to take these problems more seriously and address them.

ACKNOWLEDGEMENT

James Carpenter is fully supported by Economic and Social Research Council Research Fellowship grant RES-063-27-0257 from January 2009–December 2011.

NOTES

1 Although, in many cases,. fully observed variables could equally be included as an additional response, this may create unnecessary modelling complexity.

2 To apply them, we also need that, in the absence of missing data, our estimator has a Normal sampling distribution. Thus, for example, we apply Rubin's rules to log-odds ratios, not odds ratios. Most software handles this automatically.

REFERENCES

Bernaards, C.A., Belin, T.R., and Schafer, J.L. (2007) 'Robustness of a multivariate normal approximation for imputation of incomplete binary data'. *Statistics in Medicine*, 26: 1368–82.

Carpenter, J.R. and Goldstein, H. (2005) 'Multiple imputation in *MLwiN'. Multilevel Modelling Newsletter,* 16: 9–18.

Carpenter, J.R. and Kenward, M.G. (2008) *Missing Data in Randomised Controlled Trials – A Practical Guide.* Birmingham: National Institute for Health Research, Publication RM03/JH17/MK. Available at: http://www.pcpoh.bham.ac.uk/publichealth/methodology/projects/RM03_JH17_MK.shtml

Carpenter, J.R., Kenward, M.G., and Vansteelandt, S. (2006) 'A comparison of multiple imputation and inverse probability weighting for analyses with missing data'. *Journal of the Royal Statistical Society, Series A,* 169: 571–84.

Clayton, D., Spiegelhalter, D., Dunn, G., and Pickles, A. (1998) 'Analysis of longitudinal binary data from multi-phase sampling (with discussion)'. *Journal of the Royal Statistical Society, Series B*, 60: 71–87.

Dempster, A.P., Laird, N.M., and Rubin, D.B. (1977) 'Maximum likelihood for incomplete data via the EM algorithm (with discussion)'. *Journal of the Royal Statistical Society, Series B*, 39: 1–38.

Ferri, E., Bynner, J., and Wadsworth, M. (eds) (2003) *Changing Britain, Changing Lives: Three Generations at the Turn of the Century*. London: Institute of Education, University of London.

Fitzgerald, J., Gottschalk, P., and Moffitt, R. (1998) 'An analysis of sample attrition in panel data'. *Journal of Human Resources*, 33: 251–99.

Freedman, D.A. (2005) *Statistical Models: Theory and Practice*. New York: Cambridge University Press.

Goldstein, H., Carpenter, J.R., Kenward, M.G., and Levin, K.A. (2009) 'Multilevel models with multivariate mixed response types'. *Statistical Modelling*, 9: 173–97.

Groves, R.M., Dillman, D.A., Eltinge, J.A., and Little, R.J.A. (eds) (2002) *Survey Nonresponse*. New York: John Wiley.

Groves, R.M. F.J. Fowler, M.P. Couper, J.M. Lepkowski, E. Singer, and R. Tourangeau (2004) *Survey Methodology*. New York: John Wiley.

Hawkes, D. and Plewis, I. (2006) 'Modelling non-response in the National Child Development Study'. *Journal of the Royal Statistical Society, Series A*, 169: 479–91.

Heckman, J.J. (1979) 'Sample selection bias as a specification error'. *Econometrica*, 47: 153–61.

Kenward, M.G. and Carpenter, J.R. (2007) 'Multiple imputation: current perspectives'. *Statistical Methods in Medical Research*, 16: 199–218.

Laurie, H., Smith R., and Scott, L. (1999) 'Strategies for reducing nonresponse in a longitudinal panel survey'. *Journal of Official Statistics*, 15: 269–82.

Lepkowski, J.M. and Couper, M.P. (2002) 'Nonresponse in the second wave of longitudinal household surveys'. In R.M. Groves D. A. Dillman, J. L. Eltinge, and R. J. Little (eds) *Survey Nonresponse*. New York: John Wiley.

Little, R.J.A. (1986) 'A note about models for selectivitiy bias'. *Econometrica*, 53: 1469–74.

Little, R.J.A. and Rubin, D.B. (2002) *Statistical Analysis with Missing Data*, 2nd edn. Chichester: Wiley.

Little, R.J.A. and Yau, L. (1996) 'Intent-to-treat analysis for longitudinal studies with drop-outs'. *Biometrics*, 52: 471–83.

Plewis, I. (2007) 'Non-response in a birth cohort study: the case of the Millennium Cohort Study'. *International Journal of Social Research Methodology*, 10: 325–34.

Plewis, I., Calderwood, L., Hawkes, D., and Nathan, G. (2004) *National Child Development Study and 1970 British Cohort Study Technical Report: Changes in the NCDS and BCS70 Populations and Samples over Time*, 1st edn. London: Institute of Education, University of London.

Raghunathan, T.E., Solenberger, P.W., and Van Hoewyk, J. (2009) *IVEware: Imputation and Variance Estimation Software*. Survey Methodology Program, Survey Research Center, Institute for Social Research, University of Michigan. Available from http://www.isr.umich.edu/src/smp/ive/ (viewed 6 Jan 2009)

Royston, P. (2007) 'Multiple imputation of missing values: further update of ice, with an emphasis on interval censoring'. *Stata Journal*, 7: 445–64.

Rubin, D.B. (1976) 'Inference and missing data'. *Biometrika*, 63: 581–92.

Rubin, D.B. (1987) *Multiple Imputation for Nonresponse in Surveys*. New York: Wiley.

Schafer, J.L. (1997a) *Analysis of Incomplete Multivariate Data*. London: Chapman and Hall.

Schafer, J.L. (1997b) *Imputation of Missing Covariates under a General Linear Mixed Model*. Technical report, Dept. of Statistics, Penn State University. Software and report from http://www.stat.psu.edu/~jls/misoftwa.html (accessed 6 Jan 2009)

Shepherd, P. (1995) *The National Child Development Study (NCDS). An Introduction to the Origins of the Study and the Methods of Data Collection*. NCDS User Support Group Working Paper 1. London: Social Statistics Research Unit, City University.

Spiegelhalter, D.J., Thomas, A., and Best, N.G. (1999) *WinBUGS version 1.2 user manual*. Cambridge: MRC Biostatistics Unit.

Sterne, J.A.C., White, I.R., Carlin, J.B., Spratt, M., Royston, P., Kenward, M.G., Wood, A., and Carpenter, J. R. (2009) `Multiple imputation for missing data in epidemiological and clinical research: Potential and pitfalls'. *British Medical Journal*, 338: b2393.

Su, Y., Gelman, A., Hill, J., and Yajima, M. (in press) 'Multiple imputation with diagnostics (mi) in R: opening windows into the black box'. *Journal of Statistical Software*.

Vansteelandt, S., Carpenter, J.R., and Kenward, M.G. (2009) 'Analysis of incomplete data using inverse probability weighting and doubly robust estimators'. *European Journal of Research Methods for the Behavioral and Social Sciences*, 6: 37–48.

Van Buuren, S. and Oudshoorn, C.G.M. (2000) *Multivariate Imputation by Chained Equations: MICE V1.0 User's manual.* Report PG/VGZ/00.038, TNO Prevention and Health, Leiden.

Van Buuren, S., Brand, J.P.L., Groothuis-Oudshoorn, C.G.M., and Rubin, D.B. (2006) 'Fully conditional specification in multivariate imputation'. *Journal of Statistical Computation and Simulation*, 76: 1049–64.

24

Statistical Inference for Causal Effects, with Emphasis on Applications in Psychometrics and Education

Donald B. Rubin

CAUSAL INFERENCE PRIMITIVES

We begin with the description of the first part of a framework for causal inference that is now commonly referred to as 'Rubin's Causal Model' (RCM; Holland, 1986) for a series of articles developing this framework (Rubin, 1974, 1975, 1976, 1977, 1978). The RCM has three parts. The first part is the use of potential outcomes to define causal effects in general; Neyman (1923) introduced this concept in the context of randomized experiments and randomization-based inference. The second part of the RCM framework is a formal model for the assignment mechanism and associated assumptions, which is described in the second section. The use of the framework for classical inference in randomized experiments, initially due to Neyman (1923) and Fisher (1925), is described in the third section, as is its use for the analysis of observational data for causal effects using propensity scores, due to Rosenbaum and Rubin (1983). The use of the framework for Bayesian inference for causal effects, due to Rubin (1975, 1978), is also described in the third section, and this is the third defining part of the RCM. The remaining section very cursorily discusses some extensions and complications. Other approaches to causal inference, such as graphical ones (e.g. Pearl, 2000), I find conceptually less satisfying, for reasons discussed, for instance, in Rubin (2004a) and Rubin (2005). The presentation here is essentially a very shortened and compact version of the perspective presented in the text by Imbens and Rubin (2009); summaries even briefer than this can be found in Imbens and Rubin (2011), and other ones that are relatively similar to this include Rubin (2006a, 2008a, b).

Units, Treatments, Potential Outcomes

A 'unit' is a physical object (e.g. a person) at a particular point in time t_0, and a 'treatment' is an action that can be applied or withheld from that unit at t_0. We focus on the case of two treatments, although the extension to more than two treatments is simple in principle although not necessarily so with real problems. Associated with each unit are two 'potential outcomes': the value of an outcome variable Y at a point in time $t_1 > t_0$ when the active treatment is applied at t_0 and the value of that outcome variable at t_1 when the active treatment is withheld at t_0. The objective is to learn about the causal effect of the application of the active treatment relative to the control (the withholding of the active treatment) on Y. For example, the unit could be 'you now' with your headache, the active treatment could be your taking aspirin for your headache, the control treatment could be your not taking aspirin, and the outcome Y could be the intensity of your headache in two hours, with the potential outcomes being your headache intensity if you take aspirin and if you do not take aspirin. Formally, let W indicate which treatment the unit, you, received: $W = 1$ for the active treatment, $W = 0$ for the control treatment. Also let $Y(1)$ be the intensity of your headache in two hours if you received the aspirin, and $Y(0)$ the value in two hours if you received no aspirin. The causal effect of the active treatment relative to the control is the comparison of $Y(1)$ and $Y(0)$ – typically the difference, $Y(1) - Y(0)$, or perhaps the difference in logs, $\log[Y(1)] - \log[Y(0)]$. We can observe only one or the other, $Y(1)$ or $Y(0)$, as indicated by W. The fundamental problem facing causal inference (Rubin, 1978; Holland, 1986) is that, for any individual unit, we observe the potential outcome under only one of the possible treatments, namely the treatment actually assigned, and the potential outcome under the other treatment is missing. Thus, inference for causal effects is inherently a missing-data problem.

Relating this definition of causal effect to common usage

This definition of causal effect as the comparison of potential outcomes is intuitive and implicitly used frequently. Most of us have probably seen parts of the movie 'It's A Wonderful Life' with Jimmy Stewart as George Bailey. At one point in George's life, he becomes very depressed and sincerely wishes he had never been born, but then a wingless angel named 'Clarence' shows him exactly what the world would be like if, contrary to fact, he had not been born. The actual world is the real observed potential outcome, but Clarence shows George the other potential outcome, the counterfactual unobserved one, and George sees this other world as a real phenomenon, just as real as his actual world. Not only are there obvious consequences, like his own children not being born, but there are many other untoward events. For example, his younger brother, Harry, who was, in the actual world, a Second World War hero, in the counterfactual world drowned in a skating accident at the age of eight, because George was never born, and thus was not there to save Harry as he did in the actual world. The causal effect of George not being born is the comparison of (a) the entire stream of events in the actual world with him in it, to (b) the entire stream of events in the counterfactual world without him in it. Fortunately for George, he had Clarence to show him both potential outcomes, and George regretted ever having wished he'd never been born, and he returned to the actual world no longer depressed.

Another example is legal damages settings. Suppose that you acted in a way that you should not have, *and as a result of that action*, someone else suffered damages. The causal effect of your action relative to the absence of that action is the comparison of potential outcomes, the first the actual, the second the counterfactual. For example, suppose that because you were driving and talking on a cell phone, you ran a stop sign, hitting another car. 'But for' your negligence, the other car would not have been involved in any accident. The causal effect of your action is the amount of damage in this accident. The legal 'but-for' analysis compares the observed potential outcome in the actual world to the potential outcome in the counterfactual world without your negligence, and the difference between the monetary values in these two worlds is the damages that you owe.

Learning about causal effects: Replication and the stable unit treatment value assumption– SUTVA

We learn about causal effects through replication, more units, some exposed to the active treatment and some to the control treatment. For example, if I want to learn about the effect of my taking aspirin on headaches, I look for times in the past when I did and did not take aspirin to relieve my headache, thereby having some observations of $Y(0)$ and some of $Y(1)$. When we want to generalize to units other than ourselves, we typically use a collection of physical objects for units, some exposed to the active treatment and some exposed to the control treatment. But more than one unit brings complications. Suppose we have two units. Now in general we have at least four potential outcomes for each unit: the outcome for unit 1 if both unit 1 and unit 2 received the control treatment, the outcome for unit 1 if both units received the active treatment, the outcome for unit 1 if unit 1 received control and unit 2 active, and the outcome for unit 1 if unit 1 received active and unit 2 received control, and analogously for unit 2. In fact, there are even more potential outcomes because there have to be at least two 'doses' of the active treatment available to contemplate all possible assignments, and which one was taken could make a difference. For example, in the aspirin case, one tablet may be very effective and the other quite ineffective.

Clearly, replication does not help causal inference unless we can restrict the explosion of potential outcomes. As in all theoretical work with utility, simplifying assumptions are crucial. The most straightforward assumption to make is the 'stable unit treatment value assumption' (SUTVA – Rubin, 1980, 1990) under which the potential outcomes for the *i*th unit depend only on the treatment the *i*th unit received. That is, there is 'no interference between units' and there are 'no versions of treatments'. Then, all potential outcomes of N units with two possible treatments can be represented by an array with N rows and two columns, the *i*th unit having a row with two potential outcomes, $Y_i(0)$ and $Y_i(1)$. Under SUTVA, this N-row matrix represents all possible values of Y that could be observed under all possible assignments. Obviously, SUTVA is a major assumption. But there is no assumption-free causal inference, and nothing is wrong with this. It is the quality of the assumptions that matters, not their existence or even their absolute correctness. For example, SUTVA becomes more plausible when units are isolated from each other, as when using, for the units, intact schools that are geographically isolated rather than students in the schools when studying an educational intervention, such as a smoking prevention program (e.g. see Peterson et al., 2000).

Covariates

In addition to (1) the vector indicator of treatments for each unit in the study, $W = \{W_i\}$, (2) the array of potential outcomes when exposed to treatment, $Y(1) = \{Y_i(1)\}$, and (3) the array of potential outcomes when not exposed, $Y(0) = \{Y_i(0)\}$, we have (4) an array of covariates $X = \{X_i\}$, which are, by definition, unaffected by treatment, such as pretest scores, age, sex, race, etc. All causal estimands involve comparisons of $Y_i(0)$ and $Y_i(1)$ on either all N units, or a common subset of units; for example, the average causal effect across all units that are female, as indicated by X_i, or the median causal effect for units with X_i indicating male, and $Y_i(0)$ indicated failure on the post-test. Under SUTVA, all causal estimands can be calculated from the matrix of 'scientific values' with *i*th row $(X_i, Y_i(0), Y_i(1))$. By definition, all relevant information is encoded in X_i, $Y_i(0)$, $Y_i(1)$, and so the labeling of the N rows is a random permutation of 1, …, N. In other words, the N-row array $(X, Y(0), Y(1))$ is row exchangeable.

Covariates play a particularly important role in observational studies for causal effects, where they are variously known as 'confounders' or 'risk factors' or 'disturbing variables'. In some studies, the units exposed to the active treatment systematically differ on their distribution of covariates in important ways from the units not exposed. To see how this issue influences our formal framework, we must define the 'assignment mechanism', the probabilistic rule that determines which units are exposed to the active version of treatment and which units are exposed to the control version. The assignment mechanism is the topic of the second section.

A brief history of the potential outcomes framework

The basic idea that causal effects are the comparisons of potential outcomes must have ancient roots, and we can find elements of this definition of causal effects among both experimenters and philosophers. See, for example, the philosopher John Stuart Mill, when discussing Hume's views (Mill, 1973: 327) and Fisher (1918: 214). Nevertheless, there appears to be no formal notation for potential outcomes until Neyman (1923), which appears to have been the first place where a mathematical analysis is written for a randomized experiment. After about 1935, this notation became standard for work in randomized experiments from the randomization-based perspective (e.g. Pitman, 1938; Welch, 1937), and the notation was a major advance because it allowed explicit frequentist probabilistic causal inferences to be drawn from data obtained by a randomized experiment, approaches briefly discussed in the third section. The notion of the central role of randomized experiments seems to have been 'in the air' in the 1920s, but Fisher (1925) was apparently the first to recommend the actual physical randomization of treatments to units. Despite the almost immediate acceptance in the late 1920s of Fisher's proposal for randomized experiments, and Neyman's notation for potential outcomes in randomized experiments, this same framework was not used outside randomized experiments for a half century thereafter, apparently not until Rubin (1974), and the consequential insights from using the potential outcome notation therefore were entirely limited to randomization-based frequency inference in randomized experiments.

The approach used in nonrandomized settings during the half century following the introduction of Neyman's seminal notation for randomized experiments was based on mathematical models (e.g. least squares regression models) relating the observed value of the outcome variable $Y_{obs} = \{Y_{obs,i}\}$ to covariates and indicators for the treatment received, and then to define causal effects as parameters in these models; here, $Y_{obs,i} = Y_i(1)\ W_i + Y_i(0)(1-W_i)$. The same statistician would simultaneously use Neyman's potential outcomes to define causal effects in randomized experiments and the observed outcome set up in observational studies. This led to substantial confusion because the role of randomization cannot even be stated using the observed outcome notation.

This RCM perspective conceives of all problems of statistical inference for causal effects as missing data problems with an explicit model that creates missing data in the potential outcomes (Rubin, 1976). Of course, there were seeds of the RCM before 1974. Already mentioned is Neyman (1923) in the context of randomized experiments. In economics there is Tinbergen (1930), Haavelmo (1944), and Hurwicz (1962), in the context of nonrandomized studies, but these contributions did not have explicit notation for the potential outcomes. The potential outcomes framework seems to have been basically accepted and adopted by most workers by the end of the twentieth century. Sometimes the move was made explicitly, as with Pratt and Schlaifer (1984). Sometimes it was made less explicitly, as with those who were still trying to make a version of the observed outcome notation work in the late 1980s (e.g. see Heckman and Hotz, 1989), before fully accepting the RCM in subsequent work (e.g. Heckman, 1989, after discussion by Holland, 1989).

THE ASSIGNMENT MECHANISM

Even with SUTVA, inference for causal effects requires the specification of an assignment mechanism: a probabilistic model for how some units were selected to receive the active treatment and how other units were selected to receive the control treatment. We illustrate the importance of the assignment mechanism in two artificial examples, and then present formal notation for it.

Illustrating the criticality of the assignment mechanism

Consider a teacher who is considering one of two treatments to apply to each of his eight students, a standard and a new one. This teacher is a great teacher: he chooses the treatment that is best for each student! When they are equally effective for a student, he tosses a coin. The left part of Table 24.1 gives the hypothetical potential outcomes in final test scores under both treatments for these students, and so implicitly also gives their individual causal effects. The right half of Table 24.1 shows the chosen treatment for each of the students and their observed potential outcomes.

Notice that the actual causal effects indicate that the typical student will do better with the standard treatment: the average causal effect is two points in favor of the standard. But the teacher, who is conducting ideal educational practice, reaches the opposite conclusion from an examination of the observed data: the students assigned the new treatment do, on average, twice as well as the students assigned the control, with absolutely no overlap in their outcome distributions! Moreover, if the teacher now applies the new treatment to all students in a population of students like the eight in this study, he will be disappointed: the average test score will be close to five points under the new treatment rather than the eleven points seen in the earlier study, and even smaller than the average of seven points seen in the standard treatment of this study.

What went wrong? The simple comparison of observed results assumes that treatments were *randomly assigned*, rather than as they were, to provide maximal benefit to the students. The point here is simply that the assignment mechanism is crucial to valid inference about causal effects, and the teacher used a 'nonignorable' assignment mechanism (defined shortly). With a known, or even posited, assignment mechanism, it is possible to draw causal inferences; without one, it is impossible. It is in this sense that when drawing causal inferences, a model for the assignment mechanism is more fundamental than a model for the potential outcomes: Without positing an assignment mechanism, we cannot draw

Table 24.1 Perfect teacher

	Potential outcomes		*Observed data*		
	$Y(0)$	$Y(1)$	W	$Y(0)$	$Y(1)$
	13	14	1	?	14
	6	0	0	6	?
	4	1	0	4	?
	5	2	0	5	?
	6	3	0	6	?
	6	1	0	6	?
	8	10	1	?	10
	8	9	1	?	0
True averages	7	5	Observed averages	5.4	11

valid causal inferences, valid in the sense of being correct under the explicitly stated assumptions, not in the impossible sense of being absolutely correct.

More precisely, notice that the teacher, by comparing observed means, is using the three observed values of $Y_i(1)$ to represent the five missing values of $Y_i(1)$, effectively imputing (or filling in) the observed mean in the treatment group, $\bar{y}_1$, for the five $Y_i(1)$ question marks, and analogously effectively filling in $\bar{y}_0$ for the three $Y_i(0)$ question marks. This process makes sense for point estimation if the three observed values of $Y_i(1)$ were randomly chosen from the eight values of $Y_i(1)$, and analogously if the five observed values of $Y_i(0)$ were randomly chosen from the eight values of $Y_i(0)$. But under the actual assignment mechanism, filling in these means does not make any sense, and so neither does using the observed means to compare treatments. It would obviously make much more sense, under the actual assignment mechanism, to impute the missing potential outcome for each student to be some value less than, or equal to, that student's observed potential outcome.

Lord's paradox

We now consider a 'paradox' in causal inference in education that was easily resolved with the simple ideas we have already presented, despite the controversy that it engendered in some literatures. This example illustrates how important it is to keep this perspective clearly in mind when thinking about causal effects of interventions. Lord (1967) pvoposed the following example:

> A large university investigating the effects on the students of the diet provided in the university dining halls and any sex differences in these effects. Various types of data are gathered.

In particular, the weight of each student at the time of arrival in September and the following June are recorded.

The result of the study for the males is thet their average weight is identical at the end of the school year to what it was at the beginning; in fact, the whole distribution of weights is unchanged, although some males lost weight and some males gained weight – the gains and losses exactly balance. The same thing is true for the females. The only difference is that the females started and ended the year lighter on average than the males. On average, there is no weight gain or weight loss for either males or females. From Lord's description of the problem quoted above, the quantity to be estimated, the estimand, is the difference between the causal effect of the university diet on males and the causal effect of the university diet on females. That is, the causal estimand is the difference between the causal effects for males and females, the 'differential' causal effect.

The paradox is generated by considering the contradictory conclusions of two statisticians asked to comment on the data. Statistician 1 *observes* that there are no differences between the September and June weight distributions for either males or females, and so Statistician 1 concludes that there is no evidence of any effect of diet on student weight because neither group shows any systematic change. Statistician 2 looks at the data in a more 'sophisticated' way. Effectively, he examines males and females with nearly the same initial weight in September, say a subgroup of 'overweight' females (meaning simply above-average-weight females) and a subgroup of 'underweight' males (analogously defined), and notices that these males tended to gain weight on average and these females tended to lose weight on average. He also notices that this result is true no matter what value of initial weights is chosen to focus on, and so concludes that after 'controlling for' initial weight, the diet has a differential positive effect on males relative to females because, for males and females with the same initial weight, on average the males gain more than the females. Notice the focus of both statisticians on gain scores, but gain scores are not causal effects because they do not compare potential outcomes at the same point in time, but rather compare before and after values. Both statisticians are wrong because these data cannot support any causal conclusions about the effect of the diet without making some very strong unstated assumptions.

Back to the basics. The units are obviously the students, and the time of application of treatment (the university diet) is clearly September and the time of the recording of the outcome Y is clearly June; accept the stability assumption. Notice that Lord's statement of the problem has reverted to the already criticized observed variable notation, $Y_{\text{obs}} = \{Y_{\text{obs},i}\}$, rather than the potential outcome notation being advocated. The potential outcomes are June weight under the university diet $Y_i(1)$ and under the 'control' diet $Y_i(0)$. The covariates are sex of students, male versus female, and September weight. But the assignment mechanism has assigned everyone to the university diet! There is no one, male or female, who is assigned to the control diet. Hence, there is absolutely no purely empirical basis on which to estimate the causal effects, either raw or differential, of the university diet versus the control diet. By making the problem complicated with the introduction of the covariates 'male/female' and 'initial weight', Lord has created partial confusion.

For more statistical details of the resolution of this paradox, see Holland and Rubin (1983), and for earlier related discussion, see for example, Lindley and Novick (1981), or Cox and McCullagh (1982). But the point here is that the 'paradox' is immediately resolved through the explicit use of potential outcomes and the explicit consideration of the assignment mechanism. Either statistician's answer could be valid for causal inference depending on what we are willing to assume about the potential outcomes under the control diet.

Unconfounded and strongly ignorable assignment mechanisms

We have seen that a model for the assignment mechanisms is needed for valid inference for causal effects. The assignment mechanism gives the conditional probability of each vector of assignments given the covariates and potential outcomes:

$$\Pr(W \mid X, Y(0), Y(1)). \tag{1}$$

Here W is an N by 1 vector and X, $Y(1)$ and $Y(0)$ are all matrices with N rows. A specific example of an assignment mechanism is a completely randomized experiment, where n units are randomly assigned to the active treatment and $N - n$ units to the control treatment.

$$\begin{aligned} \Pr(W \mid X, Y(0), Y(1)) = 1 / C_n^N & \text{ if } \Sigma W_i = n \\ 0 & \quad \text{otherwise.} \end{aligned} \tag{2}$$

More generally, an 'unconfounded assignment mechanism' is free of dependence on either $Y(0)$ or $Y(1)$:

$$\Pr(W \mid X, Y(0), Y(1)) = \Pr(W \mid X). \tag{3}$$

With an unconfounded assignment mechanism, at each set of values of X_i that has a distinct probability of $W_i = 1$, there is effectively a completely randomized experiment. That is, if X_i indicates sex, with males having probability 0.2 of receiving the active treatment and females having probability 0.5 of receiving the active treatment, then essentially one randomized experiment is prescribed for males and another for females. The assignment mechanism is 'probabilistic' if each unit has a positive probability of receiving either treatment:

$$0 < \Pr(W_i = 1 \mid X, Y(0), Y(1)) < 1. \tag{4}$$

Because unconfounded probabilistic assignment mechanisms allow particularly straightforward estimation of causal effects, these assignment mechanisms form the basis for inference for causal effects in more complicated situations, such as when assignment probabilities depend on covariates in unknown ways. Unconfounded probabilistic assignment mechanisms are called 'strongly ignorable' (Rosenbaum and Rubin, 1983). This structure will form our bridge to the analysis of observational studies, discussed briefly later.

Confounded and ignorable assignment mechanisms

A confounded assignment mechanism is one that depends on the potential outcomes:

$$\Pr(W \mid X, Y(0), Y(1)) \neq \Pr(W \mid X). \tag{5}$$

A special class of confounded assignment mechanisms are ignorable assignment mechanisms (Rubin, 1978), which are defined by their freedom from dependence on any missing potential outcomes:

$$\Pr(W \mid X, Y(0), Y(1)) = \Pr(W \mid X, Y_{\text{obs}}). \tag{6}$$

Ignorable confounded assignment mechanisms arise in practice, for example, in sequential experiments, where the next unit's probability of being exposed to the active treatment depends on the success rate of those units previously exposed to the active treatment versus the success rate of those units exposed to the control treatment, as in 'play-the-winner' designs (e.g. Efron, 1971): expose the next patient with higher probability to whichever treatment appears to be more beneficial.

All unconfounded assignment mechanisms are ignorable, but not all ignorable assignment mechanisms are unconfounded. The reasons why strongly ignorable assignment mechanisms play a critical role in causal inference were seen in the two examples that started this section, the first involving a nonignorable treatment assignment mechanism (perfect teacher), and the second involving an unconfounded but nonprobabilistic assignment mechanism (Lord's paradox), and therefore not strongly ignorable, but formally ignorable.

MODES OF CAUSAL INFERENCE

Fundamentally, there are three formal statistical modes of causal inference; two that are based only on the assignment mechanism, which treat the potential outcomes as fixed but unknown quantities, and Bayesian, discussed last, which treats the 'science' as random variables. After introducing the first two, based on the assignment mechanism, we discuss their nontraditional use in nonrandomized studies.

Fisherian randomization-based inference

Fisher's approach is closely related to the mathematical idea of proof by contradiction. It basically is a 'stochastic proof by contradiction' giving the significance level (or p-value) – really, the plausibility – of a 'null hypothesis'. The first element in Fisher's mode of inference is the null hypothesis, which is usually $Y_i(1) \equiv Y_i(0)$ for all units: the active treatment versus the control has absolutely no effect on the potential outcomes. Under this null hypothesis, all potential outcomes are known from the observed values of the potential outcomes, Y_{obs}, because $Y(1) \equiv Y(0) \equiv Y_{obs}$. It follows that, under this null hypothesis, the value of any statistic such as the difference of the observed averages for units exposed to treatment 1 and units exposed to treatment 0, $\bar{y}_1 - \bar{y}_0$, is known, not only for the observed assignment, but for all possible assignments W.

Choose a statistic, S, such as $\bar{y}_i - \bar{y}_0$, and calculate its value under each possible assignment (assuming the null hypothesis), and also calculate the probability of each assignment under the randomized assignment mechanism. In many classical experiments, these probabilities are either 0 or a common value for all possible assignments. For example, in a completely randomized experiment with $N = 2n$ units, n are randomly chosen to receive treatment 1 and n to receive treatment 0, and so any assignment W that has n 1's and n 0's has probability $1/C_n^N$, and all other W's have zero probability. Knowing the value of S for each W and its probability, we can then calculate the probability (under the assignment mechanism and the null hypothesis) that we would observe a value of S as 'usual' as, or more unusual than, the observed value of S, S_{obs}. 'Unusual' is defined *a priori*, typically by how discrepant S_{obs} is from the typical value of S. This probability is the plausibility (p-value or significance level) of the observed value of the statistic S under the null hypothesis: the probability of a result (represented by the value S_{obs} of the statistic, S) as rare, or more rare, than the actually observed value if the null hypothesis were true, where the probability is over the distribution induced by the assignment mechanism.

Neymanian randomization-based inference

Neyman's form of randomization-based inference can be viewed as drawing inferences by evaluating the expectations of statistics over the distribution induced by the assignment mechanism in order to calculate a 'confidence interval' for the typical causal effect. Typically, an unbiased estimator of the causal estimand (the typical causal effect, e.g. the average) is sought, and an unbiased, or upwardly biased, estimator of the sampling variance of that unbiased estimator is also sought (bias and sampling variance both defined with respect to the randomization distribution). Then, an appeal is made to the central limit theorem for the normality of the estimator over its randomization distribution, whence a confidence interval for the causal estimand is obtained.

To be more explicit, suppose the causal estimand is the average causal effect $\overline{Y(1)} - \overline{Y(0)}$, where the averages are over all units in the population being studied, and the statistic for estimating this causal effect is the difference in sample averages for the two groups, $\bar{y}_1 - \bar{y}_0$, which can be shown to be unbiased for $\overline{Y(1)} - \overline{Y(0)}$ in a completely randomized design, as well as in other common experimental designs. A common choice for estimating the sampling variance of $\bar{y}_1 - \bar{y}_0$ over its randomization distribution, in completely randomized experiments with $N = n_1 + n_0$ units, is $se^2 = s_1^2 / n_1 + s_0^2 / n_0$, where s_1^2, s_0^2, n_1, and n_0 are the observed sample variances and sample sizes in the two treatment groups. Neyman (1923) showed that se^2 overestimates the actual sampling variance of $\bar{y}_1 - \bar{y}_0$, unless additivity holds (i.e. unless all individual causal effects are constant), in which case se^2 is unbiased for the sampling variance of $\bar{y}_1 - \bar{y}_0$. The standard 95% confidence interval for $\overline{Y(1)} - \overline{Y(0)}$ is $\bar{y}_1 - \bar{y}_0 \pm 1.96se$, which in large samples, includes $\overline{Y(1)} - \overline{Y(0)}$ in at least 95% of the possible random assignments.

Propensity scores and the bridge to observational studies

Before discussing Bayesian inference, we discuss propensity scores and their use in observational studies to try to approximate hypothetical underlying randomized experiments.

Suppose that the assignment mechanism is unconfounded; then for all W that have positive probability, we can, with essentially no loss of practical generality, write $\Pr(W|X)$ as "individualistic" in the sense that

$$\Pr(W \mid X) \propto \int \prod_{1}^{N} e(X_i \mid \phi) p(\phi) d\phi, \tag{7}$$

where the function $e(X_i \mid \phi) = \Pr(W_i = 1 \mid X_i, \phi)$ gives the probability that each unit with covariate value X_i of the covariate is assigned $W_i = 1$ as a function of some possibly unknown parameter ϕ. The unit level assignment probabilities, $e_i = e(X_i \mid \mathbf{f})$, are called propensity scores (Rosenbaum and Rubin, 1983). With an observational data set, we try to structure the problem so that we can conceptualize the data as having arisen from an underlying unconfounded assignment mechanism.

When the propensity scores are known, the assignment mechanism is essentially known. As a result, simple generalizations of Fisherian and Neymanian modes of inference can be applied, for example, by considering the number of treated ΣW_i and number of controls $\Sigma(1 - W_i)$ to be fixed by design. As the overlap in propensity scores in the treatment and control groups becomes more limited (i.e. as propensity scores approach 0 or 1), the Neymanian sampling variance of estimators for the average causal effect increases, with the result that confidence intervals become very wide, and the Fisherian randomization distribution has more of its probability mass on the observed randomization, with the result that it becomes very difficult to get a 'significant' p-value. If there is no, or little, overlap of the propensity scores in the two treatment groups, no sharp causal inference is possible using the basic Fisherian or Neymanian assignment-mechanism-based perspectives.

In general, with the assignment-based modes of inference and known propensity scores that take many values, it is often acceptable to create several (e.g. 5–10) subclasses of propensity scores, with relatively constant propensity scores within each subclass, effectively to reconstruct a randomized block experiment (i.e. a series of completely randomized experiments with different propensities across the blocks; see Cochran (1968)). Units with extreme propensity scores may have to be discarded to create such subclasses. Alternatively, pairs of treatment-control units can be created that are matched on the propensity scores, thereby recreating a paired comparison experiment (e.g. see Rubin, 2006b, for articles on such matching methods).

When the propensity scores are unknown, the first step is to estimate them. Various methods can be used to do this (e.g. discriminant analysis, logistic regression, probit regression). Typically estimated propensity scores are used as if they were known, and often this leads to more precision than using true propensity scores (Rubin and Thomas, 1992). The issues that arise with estimated propensity scores are the same as with known ones, and the reduction to a hypothetical paired-comparison or randomization-block design can be acceptable when there is enough overlap in the estimated propensity scores.

With observational studies, we attempt to assemble data with enough covariates that it becomes plausible that the unknown assignment mechanism is unconfounded given these covariates. If there is little or no overlap in the distributions of the estimated propensity scores in the treatment and control groups, there is no hope of drawing valid causal inferences from these data without making strong external assumptions. The message that sometimes a data set cannot support a decent causal inference is very important. Good observational studies are designed, not simply 'found'. Even if outcome data are available at the design stage, they should be put aside: Rubin (2007, 2008c) provides some guidance, and the text by Imbens and Rubin (2009) has several chapters illustrating the entire process in real examples.

Because observational studies are rarely known to be unconfounded, we should be concerned with sensitivity of answers to unobserved covariates. Although in my view this and other complications are better dealt with from the model-based (Bayesian) perspective, methods described by Rosenbaum (2002) are appropriate from the randomization-based perspective.

Bayesian posterior predictive causal inference

Bayesian causal inference for causal effects requires a model for the underlying science, $\Pr(X, Y(0), Y(1))$. A great virtue of the RCM framework being advocated is that it separates the science – a model for the underlying data, from what we do to learn about science – the assignment mechanism, $\Pr(W|X,Y(0),Y(1))$. The Bayesian approach directly and explicitly confronts the missing potential outcomes, $Y_{mis} = \{Y_{mis,i}\}$, where $Y_{mis,i} = W_iY_i(0) + (1-W_i)Y_i(1)$. The perspective takes the specification for the assignment mechanism and the specification for the underlying data, and derives the posterior predictive distribution of Y_{mis}, that is, the distribution of Y_{mis} given all observed values:

$$\Pr(Y_{mis} \mid X, Y_{obs}, W).$$

From this distribution, the posterior distribution of any causal effect can, in principle, be obtained. This conclusion is immediate if we view the posterior predictive distribution of Y_{mis} as specifying how to take a random draw of Y_{mis}. Once a value of Y_{mis} is drawn, any causal effect can be directly calculated from the drawn value of Y_{mis} and the observed values of W, X, and Y_{obs}. Repeatedly drawing values of Y_{mis} and *calculating* the causal effect for each draw and the observed values generates the posterior distribution of the desired causal effect. Thus, as in Rubin (1975, 1978), we can view causal inference entirely as a missing data problem, where we multiply-impute (Rubin, 1987, 2004b) the missing potential outcomes to generate a posterior distribution for the causal effect.

In general:

$$\Pr(Y_{mis} \mid Y, Y_{obs}, W) = \frac{\Pr(X, Y(0), Y(1)) \Pr(W \mid X, Y(0), Y(1))}{\int \Pr(X, Y(0), Y(1)) \Pr(W \mid X, Y(0), Y(1)) dY_{mis}}.$$

With an ignorable treatment mechanism assignment (equation (6)), this becomes:

$$\Pr(Y_{mis} \mid X, Y_{obs}, W) = \frac{\Pr(W, Y(0), Y(1))}{\int \Pr(X, Y(0), X(1)) dY_{mis}},$$

which reveals that, under ignorability, all that we need to model is the science $\Pr(X, Y(1), Y(1))$, and we can ignore the assignment mechanism. The great strength of this model-based approach is that it allows us to conduct causal inference by explicitly predicting the missing potential outcomes from observed values. The problem with this approach is the need to specify the distribution $\Pr(X, Y(0), Y(1))$, which sometimes can implicitly involve extrapolations that are extremely unreliable. With a nonignorable treatment assignment mechanism, the simplifications previously described do not follow in general, and the analysis typically becomes far more difficult and speculative. More details of this approach are beyond the scope of this entry. Again, Imbens and Rubin (2009) provides many details and examples, and Rubin (2006a) provides some illustrative examples.

COMPLICATIONS

There are many complications that occur in real world studies for causal effects, many of which can be handled much more flexibly with the Bayesian approach than with randomization-based approaches. Of course, the models involved, including associated prior distributions, can be very demanding to formulate in a practically reliable manner. Also, Neymanian evaluations are still important. Here I mention just some of these complications, most of which can arise even in randomized experiments, especially with people. The citations that follow are somewhat idiosyncratic in the sense of reflecting my experiences rather than a full range of more general complications.

When there are more than two treatments, the notation becomes more complex but is still straightforward under SUTVA. Without SUTVA, however, both the notation and the analysis can become very involved. Most of the field of classical experimental design is devoted to issues that arise with more than two treatment conditions (e.g. Kempthorne, 1952; Cochran and Cox, 1957; Cox, 1958; Box et al., 2005). For more recent work, see, for example, Cheng and Bulutoglu (2003) and Bailey and Williams (2007).

Missing data, due perhaps to unit dropout, can complicate analyses more than one would expect based on a cursory examination of the problem. Fortunately, Bayesian/likelihood tools for addressing missing data such as multiple imputation (Rubin, 1987, 2004b) or the EM algorithm (Dempster et al., 1977) and its relatives, including data augmentation (Tanner and Wong, 1987) and the Gibbs sampler (Geman and Geman, 1984) are fully compatible with the Bayesian approach to causal inference. For a general reference on missing data, see Little and Rubin (2002), and for the multiple imputation approach, see Rubin (1987, 2004b).

Another complication, common when the units are people, is noncompliance. For example, some of the subjects assigned to take the active treatment take the control treatment instead, and some assigned to take the control manage to take the active treatment. A simple example of this is given in Sommer and Zeger (1991). Initial interest focuses on the effect of the treatment for the subset of people who will comply with their treatment assignments. Early work related to this issue can be found in economics (e.g. Tinbergen, 1930; Haavelmo, 1944) and elsewhere (e.g. Zelen, 1979; Bloom, 1984). Much progress has been made in recent years on this topic (e.g. Baker, 1998; Baker and Lindeman, 1994; Goetghebeur and Molenberghs, 1996; Angrist et al., 1996; Imbens and Rubin, 1997; Little and Yau, 1998; Hirano et al., 2000; Jin and Rubin, 2008a). With noncompliance, sensitivity of inference to prior assumptions can be severe, and the Bayesian approach is well-suited to revealing not only this sensitivity, but also to formulating reasonable prior restrictions.

A further complication is 'truncation due to death'. Consider an educational intervention designed to improve final high school test scores, but some students drop out of school before taking the final test, and so effectively have their data 'truncated by death'. This problem is far more subtle than it may appear to be, and valid approaches to it have only recently been formulated (Rubin, 2002; Zhang and Rubin, 2003). The models also have applications in economics (Zhang, Rubin and Mealli, 2008), such as the evaluation of job-training programs on wages (Zhang et al., 2009).

Another topic that is more subtle than it first appears to be involves direct and indirect causal effects, for example, the separation of the 'direct' effect of a vaccination on disease from the 'indirect' effect of the vaccination that is due solely to its effect on blood antibodies and the 'direct' effect of the antibodies on disease. I feel that this language turns out to be too imprecise to be useful within our formal causal effect framework. This problem is ripe for Bayesian modeling, as briefly outlined in Rubin (2004a, 2005).

The examples just discussed can be viewed as special cases of 'principal stratification' (Frangakis and Rubin, 2002), where the principal strata are defined by partially unobserved intermediate potential outcomes, namely in our examples: compliance behavior under both treatment assignments, survival under both treatment assignments, and antibody level under both treatment assignments. This appears to be an extremely fertile area for research and application of Bayesian methods for causal inference, especially using modern simulation methods such as MCMC (Markov Chain Monte Carlo); see, for example, Gelman et al. (2003) and Gilks et al. (1995).

In the real world, complications typically do not appear simply one at a time. For example, a randomized experiment in education evaluating 'school choice' suffered from missing data in both covariates and longitudinal outcomes; also, the outcome was multicomponent at each point in time. Moreover, it suffered from noncompliance that took several levels because the years could be spent in different schools. Some of these combinations of complications are discussed in Barnard et al. (2003) and Jin and Rubin (2008b) in the context of the school choice example.

In general, I feel that real world complexities require the Bayesian model-based approach. Two important points must be kept in mind, however, when using the Bayesian approach, because, as George Box says, all models are wrong but some are useful. First, studies for causal effects must be carefully designed in an outcome-free way to ensure, to the extent possible, similar distributions of covariates across treatment groups. Second, chosen models must be assessed using posterior predictive checks (Rubin, 1984; Gelman et al., 2004) to ensure that the models could have generated the observed data and can generate scientifically reasonable data. Often, frequentist evaluations of the long-run operating characteristics of the procedures generated by Bayesian models will also be enlightening.

REFERENCES

Angrist, J.D., Imbens, J.W., and Rubin, D.B. (1996). Identification of causal effects using instrumental variables. *Journal of the American Statistical Association*, 91: 444–72.

Bailey, R.A. and Williams, E.R. (2007). Optimal nested row-column designs with specified components. *Biometrika*, 94: 459–68.

Baker, S.G. (1998). Analysis of survival data from a randomized trial with all-or-none compliance: Estimating the cost-effectiveness of a cancer screening program. *Journal of the American Statistical Association*, 93: 929–34.

Baker, S.G. and Lindeman, K.S. (1994). The paired availability design: a proposal for evaluating epidural analgesia during labor. *Statistics in Medicine*, 13: 2269–78.

Barnard, J., Hill, J., Frangakis, C., and Rubin, D. (2003). School choice for NY City: A Bayesian analysis of an imperfect randomized experiment. In C. Gatsonis, B. Carlin and A. Carriguiry (eds) *Case Studies in Bayesian Statistics*, Vol. V, pp. 3–97. New York: Springer-Verlag.

Bloom, H.S. (1984). Accounting for no-shows in experimental evaluation designs. *Evaluation Review*, 8: 225–46.

Box, G.E.P, Hunter, J.S., and Hunter, W.G. (2005). *Statistics for Experimenters: Design, Innovation, and Discovery*, 2nd edn. New York: Wiley.

Cheng, C.-S. and Bulutoglu, D.A. (2003). Hidden properties of some nonregular fractional factorial designs and their applications. *Annals of Statistics*, 31: 1012–26.

Cochran, W.G. (1968). The effectiveness of adjustment by subclassification in removing bias in observational studies. *Biometrics*, 24: 295–313.

Cochran, W.G. and Cox, G.M. (1957). *Experimental Designs*, 2nd edn. New York: Wiley. Reprinted as a 'Wiley Classic' (1992).

Cox, D.R. (1958). *The Planning of Experiments*. New York: Wiley.

Cox, D.R. and McCullagh, P. (1982). Some aspects of covariance. *Biometrics*, 38: 541–61.

Dempster, A.P., Laird, N., and Rubin, D.B. (1977). Maximum likelihood from incomplete data via the EM algorithm. *Journal of the Royal Statistical Society, Ser. B*, 39: 1–38.

Efron, B. (1971). Forcing a sequential experiment to be balanced. *Biometrika*, 58: 403–17.

Fisher, R.A. (1918). The causes of human variability. *Eugenics Review*, 10: 213–20.

Fisher, R.A. (1925). *Statistical Methods for Research Workers*. Edinburgh: Oliver and Boyd.

Frangakis, C.E. and Rubin, D.B. (2002). Principal stratification in causal inference. *Biometrics*, 58: 21–9.

Geman, S. and Geman, D. (1984). Stochastic relaxation, Gibbs distributions, and the Bayesian restoration of images. *IEEE Transactions on Pattern Analysis and Machine Intelligence*, 6: 721–41.

Gelman, A., Carlin, J., Stern, H., and Rubin, D. (2004). *Bayesian Data Analysis*, 2nd edn. New York: CRC Press.

Gilks, W.R., Richardson, S., and Spiegelhalter, D.J. (1995). *Markov Chain Monte Carlo in Practice*. New York: CRC Press.

Goetghebeur, E. and Molenberghs, G. (1996). Causal inference in a placebo-controlled clinical trial with binary outcome and ordered compliance. *Journal of the American Statistical Association*, 91: 928–34.

Haavelmo, T. (1944). The probability approach in econometrics. *Econometrica*, 15: 413–419.

Heckman, J.J. (1989). Causal inference and nonrandom samples. *Journal of Educational Statistics*, 14: 159–68.

Heckman, J.J. and Hotz, V.J. (1989). Alternative methods for evaluating the impact of training programs. *Journal of the American Statistical Association*, 84: 862–74.

Hirano, K., Imbens, G., Rubin, D.B., and Xhou, X. (2000). Assessing the effect of an influenza vaccine in an encouragement design. *Biostatistics*, 1: 69–88.

Holland, P.W. (1986). Statistics and causal inference. *Journal of the American Statistical Association*, 81: 945–70.

Holland, P.W. (1989). It's very clear. Comment on 'Choosing among alternative nonexperimental methods for estimating the impact of social programs: the case of manpower training' by J. Heckman and V. Hotz. *Journal of the American Statistical Association*, 84: 875–7.

Holland, P.W. and Rubin, D.B. (1983). On Lord's paradox. In H. Wainer and S. Messick (eds) *Principals of Modern Psychological Measurement: A Festschrift for Frederic M. Lord*, pp. 3–25. Hillsdale, NJ: Earlbaum.

Hurwicz, L. (1962). On the structural form of interdependent systems. In E. Nagel, P. Suppes and A. Tarski (eds) *Logic, Methodology, and Philosophy of Science*. Proceedings of the 1960 International Congress. Stanford, CA: Stanford University Press.

Imbens, G.W. and Rubin, D.B. (1997). Bayesian inference for causal effects in randomized experiments with noncompliance. *Annals of Statistics*, 25: 305–27.

Imbens, G.W. and Rubin, D.B. (2008). Rubin causal model. In S.M. Durlauf and C.E. Blume (eds) *The New Palgrave Dictionary of Economics*, 2nd edn, vol. 7, pp. 255–62. New York: Palgrave McMillan.

Imbens, G.W. and Rubin, D.B. (2011). *Causal Inference in Statistics, and in the Social and Biomedical Sciences.* New York: Cambridge University Press.

Jin, H. and Rubin, D.B. (2008a). Principal stratification for causal inference with extended partial compliance: Application to Efron–Feldman data. *Journal of the American Statistical Association*, 103: 101–111.

Jin, H. and Rubin, D.B. (2008b). Public schools versus private schools: causal inference with extended partial compliance. *The Journal of Educational and Behavioral Statistics*, on-line early print, March 2008: 1076998607307475v1.

Kempthorne, O. (1952). *The Design and Analysis of Experiments.* New York: Wiley.

Lindley, D.V. and Novick, M.R. (1981). The role of exchangeability in inference. *Annals of Statistics*, 9: 45–58.

Little, R.J. and Rubin, D.B. (2002). *Statistical Analysis with Missing Data*, 2nd edn. New York: Wiley. Translated into Chinese in 2003: China Statistics Press, People's Republic of China.

Little, R.J. and Yau, L. (1998). Statistical techniques for analyzing data from prevention trials: Treatment of no-shows using Rubin's causal model. *Psychological Methods*, 3: 147–59.

Lord, F.M. (1967). A paradox in the interpretation of group comparisons. *Psychological Bulletin*, 68: 304–05.

Mill, J.S. (1973). A system of logic. In *Collected Works of John Stuart Mill*, 7. Toronto: University of Toronto Press.

Neyman, J. (1923). On the application of probability theory to agricultural experiments: essay on principles, section 9. Translated in *Statistical Science*, 5: 465–80, 1990.

Pearl, J. (2000). *Causality: Models, Reasoning and Inference.* Cambridge: Cambridge University Press.

Peterson, A.V. et al. (2000). Hutchinson smoking prevention project: Long-term randomized trial in school-based tobacco use prevention-results on smoking. *Journal of the National Cancer Institute*, 92: 1979–91.

Pitman, E.J.G. (1938). Significance tests which can be applied to samples from any population. III. The analysis of variance test. *Biometrika*, 29: 322–35.

Pratt, J.W. and Schlaifer, R. (1984). On the nature and discovery of structure. *Journal of the American Statistical Association*, 79: 9–33

Rosenbaum, P.R. (2002). *Observational Studies*, 2nd edn. New York: Springer-Verlag.

Rosenbaum, P.R. and Rubin, D.B. (1983). The central role of the propensity score in observational studies for causal effects. *Biometrika*, 70: 41–55.

Rubin, D.B. (1974). Estimating causal effects of treatments in randomized and nonrandomized studies. *Journal of Educational Psychology*, 66: 688–701.

Rubin, D.B. (1975). Bayesian inference for causality: the importance of randomization. *Proceedings of the Social Statistics Section of the American Statistical Association*, 233–39.

Rubin, D.B. (1976). Inference and missing data. *Biometrika*, 63: 581–92.

Rubin, D.B. (1977). Assignment of treatment group on the basis of a covariate. *Journal of Educational Statistics*, 2: 1–26.

Rubin, D.B. (1978). Bayesian inference for causal effects: The role of randomization. *Annals of Statistic*, 7: 34–58.

Rubin, D.B. (1980). Comment on 'Randomization analysis of experimental data: The Fisher randomization test' by D. Basu. *Journal of the American Statistical Association*, 75: 591–93.

Rubin, D.B. (1984). Bayesianly justifiable and relevant frequency calculations for the applied statistician. *Annals of Statistics*, 12: 1151–72.

Rubin, D.B. (1987). *Multiple Imputation for Nonresponse in Surveys.* New York: Wiley.

Rubin, D.B. (1990). Comment: Neyman (1923) and causal inference in experiments and observational studies. *Statistical Science*, 5: 472–480.

Rubin, D.B. (2002). Using propensity scores to help design observational studies: application to the tobacco litigation. *Health Services & Outcomes Research Methodology*, 2: 169–88.

Rubin, D.B. (2004a). Direct and indirect causal effects via potential outcomes. *The Scandinavian Journal of Statistics*, 31: 161–70, 195–8.

Rubin, D.B. (2004b). *Multiple Imputation for Nonresponse in Surveys.* New York: Wiley. Reprinted with new appendices as a 'Wiley Classic'.

Rubin, D.B. (2005). Causal inference using potential outcomes: Design, modeling, decisions. 2004 Fisher Lecture. *Journal of the American Statistical Association*, 100: 322–31.

Rubin, D.B. (2006a). Statistical inference for causal effects, with emphasis on applications in psychometrics and education. In C.R. Rao and S. Sinharay (eds) *Handbook of Statistics, Volume 26: Psychometrics*, pp. 769–800. The Netherlands: Elsevier.

Rubin, D.B. (2006b). *Matched Sampling for Causal Effects.* New York: Cambridge University Press.

Rubin, D.B. (2007). The design versus the analysis of observational studies for causal effects: parallels with the design of randomized trials. *Statistics in Medicine*, 26: 20–30.

Rubin, D.B. (2008a). Statistical inference for causal effects, with emphasis on applications in epidemiology and medical statistics. In C.R. Rao, J.P. Miller and D.C. Rao (eds) *Handbook of Statistics: Epidemiology and Medical Statistics*, Chapter 2, pp. 28–63. The Netherlands: Elsevier.

Rubin, D.B. (2008b). Statistics: Causal inference. To appear in E. Baker, B. McGaw and P. Peterson (eds) *International Encyclopedia of Education*, 3rd edn. Oxford, U.K.: Elsevier.

Rubin, D.B. (2008c). For objective causal inference, design trumps analysis. *Annals of Applied Statistics*, 2: 808–40.

Rubin, D.B. and Thomas, N. (1992). Characterizing the effect of matching using linear propensity score methods with normal covariates. *Biometrika*, 78: 797–809.

Sommer, A. and Zeger, S. (1991). On estimating efficacy from clinical trials. *Statistics in Medicine*, 10: 45–52.

Tanner, M.A. and Wong, W.H. (1987). The calculation of posterior distributions by data augmentation. *Journal of the American Statistical Association*, 82: 528–50.

Tinbergen, J. (1930). Determination and interpretation of supply curves: An example. *Zeitschrift fur Nationalokonomie*. Reprinted in *The Foundations of Econometric Analysis* D.F. Hendry and M.S. Morgan (eds), 1995; New York: Cambridge University Press.

Welch, B.L. (1937). On the z test in randomized blocks and Latin squares. *Biometrika,* 29: 21–52.

Zelen, M. (1979). A new design for randomized clinical trials. *New England Journal of Medicine* 300: 1242–5.

Zhang, J. and Rubin, D.B. (2003). Estimation of causal effects via principal stratification when some outcomes are truncated by 'death'. *Journal of Educational and Behavioral Statistics*, 28: 353–68.

Zhang, J., Rubin, D.B., and Mealli, F. (2008). Evaluating the effects of job training programs on wages through principal stratification. *Advances in Economics*, 21: 93–118.

Zhang, J., Rubin, D.B., and Mealli, F. (2009). Likelihood-based analysis of causal effects of job-training programs using principal stratification. *Journal of the American Statistical Association*, 104: 166–76.

25

Automatic Item Generation: An Innovation for Developing Complex Cognitive Tests

Susan E. Embretson and Heather H. McIntyre

Researchers have often noted that principles for writing test items were weak throughout most of the twentieth century (e.g. Bejar, 2002; Bormuth, 1970; Haladyna, 1999; Hornke, 2002; Thorndike, 1971). Indeed, item design was even regarded as more art than science to the very scientists devoted to its practice. As stated by Wesman (1971), 'Just as there can be no set of formulas for producing a good story or a good painting, so there can be no set of rules that guarantees the production of good test items' (p. 81). At the same time, Irvine et al. (1990) note that this era of psychological testing relied heavily on the results of empirical tryouts and factor analytic methodology to build tests. Thus, item design principles were given relatively little consideration, and the (theoretical) meaning behind a test score represented the last step in the process of test development: validation.

Interestingly, the earliest forms of systematic item design were not empirically-based. Several researchers converged on the idea of using templates for item writing. For example, Guttman (1969) constructed items from 'mapping sentences' in order to explore the 'universe' of operationalized behaviors within a content domain. At about the same time, Hively et al. (1968) used 'item forms', also referred to as 'item shells' (Haladyna and Shindoll, 1987) to boost the production (i.e. in the hundreds) of math word problem items. However, these items varied only in surface features such as the actors and objects in the storyline. The impact of item features on item psychometric properties were generally not considered at the outset of item design. Item forms and item shells were often capable of producing large numbers of items, but empirical tryout was required to establish psychometric properties. This approach to item generation has since been termed 'functional' (Bejar, 2002).

Another important development in item generation for measuring abilities was developing tests from cognitive tasks that had been studied by experimental psychology methods. For example, Irvine et al. (1990) developed some tests for the *British Army Recruit Battery* that were both referenced to the psychometric literature as abilities and that had a cognitive performance model. Similarly, tests in the Cognitive Abilities Measurement (CAM) were developed for possible use by the United States military based on contemporary cognitive psychology principles (Kyllonen and Cristal, 1990; Kyllonen, 1995). The primary advantage of this approach is that the design principles for the items were well supported by empirical results from laboratory and test development studies. However, the tasks represent more narrow aspects of cognition, which may limit the correlations of the tests with other measures and criteria.

Over the last two decades, starting with research noted by Frederiksen et al. (1993), developing item generators for complex cognitive items, such as found on high stakes ability and achievement tests, has been a major focus. These item generators have been characterized as model-based (Bejar, 2002). However, it is important to note that Bejar's term 'model-based' has two rather different meanings in this context.

In the *item model approach*, operational items from an established test provide models for developing new items. In this approach, the term model refers to a template. The item model approach is somewhat like the item shell approach, in that parts of the item become variables. That is, syntactical structures for the items are identified and some features within the items are converted to variables that are systematically manipulated to produce new items.

For example, surface features of the following mathematics word problem can become variables, as shown in italics:

> In a certain *store*, each *record* costs x dollars and each *tape* costs y dollars. *Bob* bought 3 *records* and 2 *tapes* for a total cost of \$39. What is the relationship of the cost of the *record* to the cost of the *tape*?

These several surface features (store, record and tape) can be substituted for (*supermarket*, *appetizers*, *steaks* and *Mindy*) with no real change in the problem requirements; the name of the actor, the objects that are bought, where they are bought, etc. The numerical values also could be substituted given some constraints so that the same procedural level (whole numbers) is maintained. Unlike the functional approach, the task here is not to flush out an item domain but to produce *isomorphs* that have very similar psychometric properties. This approach to item generation has facilitated the production of test items via rigorously developed computer algorithms (e.g. Mathematics Test Creation Assistant; TCA; Singley and Bennett, 2002) and contributed to the banking of items that have undergone quality control inspections regarding item content (Singley and Bennett, 2002). However, in the item model approach, the sources of item difficulty are often not explained.

The other model-based approach is the *structural modeling approach*. In this approach, the term model refers to a statistical model. That is, the empirical properties of items, such as item difficulty, discrimination or response time, are predicted from statistical models. The predictors are scores for items on content features that are believed to be important in their empirical properties. Thus, the goal is to statistically model item *variants* in the item domain. In some applications, the features are related to theoretical models of task complexity.

An example of a structural model approach is Embretson's (1998) cognitive design systems approach. Embretson (1998) developed a cognitive model for abstract reasoning items based on previous cognitive psychology research (Just et al., 1990). Variables were scored on items to represent variations in the stimulus features that determined cognitive complexity and then statistical models were applied to predict item psychometric properties and item response times. Specifying the sources of cognitive complexity in theoretically and empirically plausible cognitive models explicates the substantive aspect of construct validity (Messick, 1995). If the model is plausible, then an item generator can be developed by defining unique combinations of the model variables to define item structures. The generator then can generate items by selecting exact item content to fulfill the structure.

The *item model* and the *item structure* approach differ in several ways. First, they differ in the nature of the items that are produced. In the *item model* approach, *isomorphs* are produced such that the new items have approximately the same psychometric properties as the parent. Thus, the parent and isomorphs form a family. In the *item structure* approach, *variants* are produced as combinations of stimulus features that are related to cognitive complexity. Consequently, statistical models are needed to predict the psychometric properties of the new items.

Second, according to Bejar (2002), the broadness of the construct domain being captured in the test items also can differ between the two approaches. For example, item models that generate isomorphs are necessarily narrow in content and, reminiscent of the functional approach, entail variations in relatively superficial item features so that the psychometric properties of the parent are applicable to the new items. Indeed, a commonly cited problem with item models is their degree of overlap and overuse in wide scale testing applications, resulting in potential item familiarity among respondents which could compromise in test validity (Bejar, in press; Bejar, 2002). This problem, as well as narrowness of a construct domain, may be avoided by increasing the number and variability in features among item models, as well by the mixture of items on a particular test (Morley et al., 2008). In contrast, the item structure approach can permit the generation of a broad domain of items as new combinations of sources of complexity provide a generating structure.

Third, and somewhat related to the latter distinction, the two approaches typically differ in the strength of the theory guiding item models or structures, that is strong versus weak theory (Drasgow et al., 2006). The strong theory approach can only be used to develop automatic item generators in the *structural model* approach to item generation when the item stimulus features have substantial impact on item psychometric properties (e.g. Embretson, 1998). However, when the construct domain is broad or theory has not yet been developed, the weak theory approach is more feasible for guiding item structures (e.g. Bejar, 2002). Hypothetically, weak theory may also be useful in the *item model* approach if each isomorph-producing item model is designed to fit, for example, a cell within a two-way (or more) test blueprint. Indeed, this hypothetical scenario also represents a potential exception to the previous distinction made between the two model-based approaches – namely, broadness of construct. However, an empirical test of item generation based on this particular arrangement has not been reported.

A higher level of item generation has been envisioned as a grammatical approach. According to Bejar (2002: 200), 'At this level the item generation and psychometric modeling are completely intertwined in such a way that it becomes possible to not only generate items but also "parse" any item to characterize its psychometric properties'. Further, in the grammatical approach, the item generator would have not only the capacity to produce the full domain of items, but also the capacity to produce operational test items 'on-the-fly' during test administration. The latter capability was demonstrated with the *item model* approach applied to mathematical reasoning (Bejar, 2002), while the former capability has been approached in analytic reasoning (Newstead et al. (2006); Embretson, 1999) and spatial ability (Bejar and Yocom, 1991; Embretson and Gorin, 2001), using the *item structure* approach. Developing item generators with the full set of capabilities of the grammatical approach is the final stage of a technological evolution in testing; that is a fully automated procedure. However, none of the current approaches are yet fully grammar-based.

Features that characterize differences between the current item generators include (1) the approach to item generation, the *item model* versus the *item structure* approach, (2) the scope of the item domain produced, ranging from broad to narrow, (3) the predictability of item psychometric properties, and (4) the amount of support for the various aspects of construct validity for the generated items, such as the substantive aspect, the structural aspect, and the external aspect of validity. The latter three qualities are especially important in determining the degree of methodological innovation that is represented by an item generator. That is, an item generator that produces items with predictable psychometric properties that measure a broad trait, along with strong support for construct validity, represents a high level of innovation. The predictability of psychometric properties is crucial to innovation, because if obtained, the need for item tryouts before operational test administration is minimized. In the case of established tests, predictable item properties also implies that the generated items can inherit the validity of the established test. Preceding this review is a presentation of item response theory (IRT) models that serve as the statistical foundation for testing construct representation in item models.

IRT MODELS

Three IRT models that are germane to automatic item generation (AIG), and thus will be discussed here, are Fischer's (1973) linear logistic test model (LLTM), Embretson's (1999) 2PL-Constrained model and Glas and van der Linden's (2003) hierarchical model. The purpose of these IRT models is to estimate either (1) parameters that reflect the impact of stimulus features on item psychometric properties (i.e. difficulty, discrimination, etc.) or (2) psychometric parameters that apply to all items produced by the same item model. The LLTM belongs to the Rasch family of IRT models; thus, difficulty is the only item parameter being predicted by the item stimulus features. However, the difficulty parameter is replaced in the model with a weighted set of linear predictors. According to this model, the probability that the person *j* passes item *i*, $P(X_{ij} = 1)$ is given as follows:

$$P(X_{ij} = 1 \mid \theta_j, \mathbf{q}, \eta) = \frac{\exp\left(\theta_j - \sum_{k=1}^{K} q_{ik}\eta_k\right)}{1 + \exp\left(\theta_j - \sum_{k=1}^{K} q_{ik}\eta_k\right)}, \tag{1}$$

where q_{ik} is the score of item *i* on stimulus feature *k*; η_k , the weight of stimulus feature *k* in item difficulty; and θ_j , the ability of person *j*. It is also important to note that q_{i1} is valued at unity and 0_1 symbolizes an intercept. As compared to the Rasch model, which is widely used to calibrate new items, no parameter for item difficulty appears in the LLTM; instead, item difficulty is predicted from a weighted combination of stimulus features that represent the cognitive complexity of the item. In the past, LLTM was difficult to estimate for large item sets, due to the heavy computational demands required for the conditional maximum likelihood algorithm that was available. However, LLTM now may be estimated by a variety of procedures (e.g. see DeBoeck and Wilson, 2004).

The 2PL-Constrained model (Embretson, 1999) includes cognitive complexity models for both item difficulty and item discrimination. The 2PL-Constrained model gives the probability that person *j* passes item *i* as follows:

$$P(X_{ij} = 1 \mid \theta_j, \mathrm{q}, \eta, \tau) = \frac{\exp\left(\sum_{m=1}^{M} q_{im}\tau_m\left(\theta_j - \sum_{k=1}^{K} q_{ik}\eta_k\right)\right)}{1 + \exp\left(\sum_{m=1}^{M} q_{im}\tau_m\left(\theta_j - \sum_{k=1}^{K} q_{ik}\eta_k\right)\right)}, \tag{2}$$

where, q_{ik} and q_{im} are scores of stimulus factors, for item difficulty and item discrimination, respectively, in item *i*; 0_k is the weight of stimulus factor *k* in the difficulty of item *i*, ϑ_m is the weight of stimulus factor *m* in the discrimination of item *i* and θ_i is defined as in equation (1). ϑ_1 and 0_1 serve as intercepts, as q_{i1} is unity for all items. The 2PL-Constrained is essentially an extension of the two parameter logistic (2PL) model, which includes both item difficulty parameters, b_i, and item discrimination parameters, a_i. In the 2PL-Constrained model, these parameters are replaced with regression models for the stimulus features.

A different set of models estimate base parameters that characterize groups of items, along with variability among items with the group. Each group of items (e.g. an item model and its isomorphs) constitutes a family. One IRT model amenable to this arrangement is Glas and van der Linden's (2003) hierarchical IRT model. In addition, Bayesian approaches can be customized to estimate parameters for generated items (see Bradlow et al., 1999; Fox and Glas, 1998), though these models will not be elaborated here.

The hierarchical IRT model (Glas and van der Linden, 2003) is similar to the three parameter (3PL) model, except that the parameters represent a common value for a family of items. This model can be considered explanatory when item categories reflect substantive combinations of features, such as when generative item models reflecting variations in difficulty as a function of a particular pattern of stimulus features weights. The item parameters are given for the item family, as follows:

$$P\left(X_{ij_p}=1\,|\,\theta_j,a_{i_p},b_{i_p},c_{i_p}\right)=c_{i_p}+\left(1-c_{i_p}\right)\frac{\exp\left(a_{ip}\left(\theta_j-b_{ip}\right)\right)}{1+\exp\left(a_{ip}\left(\theta_j-b_{ip}\right)\right)}, \tag{3}$$

where *P*(*X*...) is the probability of passing item *i* from family *p* for person *j* ; a_{ip} is item slope or discrimination of item family *p*, b_{ip} is the item difficulty of item family *p*, c_{ip} is lower asymptote of item family *p* and q_j is ability for person *j*. Thus, in this model, items within family *p* are assumed to be characterized by the same parameters, but vary somewhat due to the differing features among generated items. For example, in quantitative word problems, a problem of the same difficulty can be presented with different locations, persons, objects of measurement, etc. Nevertheless, the exact content features of items can instigate variability within a family. The hierarchical model includes estimates of within family variability, under assumptions about the distribution of the parameters within families. Although hierarchical IRT models have been applied to items generated from item models, it is also possible to consider items generated from the same structure as representing an item family.

APPLICATIONS TO GENERATING COMPLEX COGNITIVE ITEMS

Model-based tem generation has been primarily explored in three complex ability domains: (1) spatial ability, (2) abstract or analytical reasoning, and (3) quantitative reasoning/skills. However, only a handful of studies have concerned item generators that cover the full range of predictable psychometric properties, including validity. For example, several item generators produce items from a structure but their psychometric properties were not subsequently compared to operational test of the same, or similar, underlying construct. These latter studies will be briefly summarized for their usefulness in achieving construct representation via modeling of item difficulty components, but the majority of the review will center on those studies which cover the full range of validity testing and, thus are closer to the full stage of grammar-based item generation.

Spatial ability

At the forefront of generative item modeling, Bejar (1990) explored its potential in a spatial ability test composed of mental rotation tasks. Items have a true–false response format, wherein the respondent must determine whether or not the object on the right can be rotated to the orientation of the object pictured on the left. Research has supported one particular feature of these stimuli as consistently contributing to response time and accuracy, that is, angular disparity between the two figures (Shepherd and Metzler, 1971). As the angular disparity between the two figures increases, more time is needed to mentally manipulate (i.e. rotate) the figures, and inaccuracies may increase.

A set of 80 three-dimensional rotation items were constructed, administered to a sample of high school students, and parameters calibrated by dichotomizing response time and fitting a 1PL model for each successive dichotomization. A regression of response time onto angular disparity strongly supported the difficulty hypothesis, though the prediction was stronger for true items than false ones. No comparison was made with an operational test, although multiple choice versions of similar rotation tasks do appear on cognitive test batteries. Nevertheless, this study represents early efforts and preliminary success at linking item stimulus features to item difficulty and thus empirically supporting one aspect of spatial ability: mental rotation.

An item generator for a spatial ability test that is used operationally, the *Assembling Objects* (AO) *Test* of the *Armed Service Vocational Aptitude Battery* (ASVAB) also has been developed (Embretson, 2000; Embretson, in press). The AO test was developed to increase the prediction of job performance by measuring the spatial rotation component of spatial ability. In the AO task (see Figure 25.1), pieces of an object are presented and the examinee selects from four alternatives to identify the object that results from assembling the pieces. The structures in the item generator were based on the variables of a cognitive model that was developed to predict both item difficulty and item response time (Embretson and Gorin, 2001; Embretson, in press) on operational AO items.

The postulated cognitive model combined a visual search process and spatial manipulations, along with a two-stage decision process to accommodate the multiple choice format of AO items. The first stage is encoding of the stem elements, in which item difficulty depends on the number of pieces, the number of

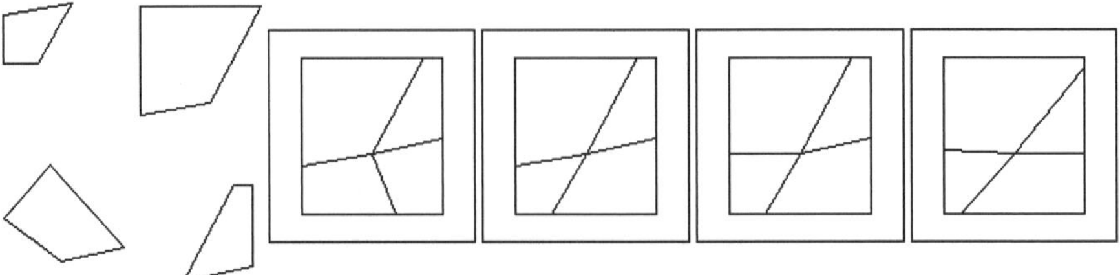

Figure 25.1 An item from the item generator for the Assemblying Objects Test (Embretsn, 2000)

edges and curves, as well as by the availability of verbal labels to describe the piece (i.e. circle, triangle, etc.). The second stage is falsification, which is a visual search process in which the examinee searches for response alternatives that can be eliminated because they have grossly inappropriate features, such as the wrong number of pieces and obviously mismatched pieces as compared to the stem. The final stage is confirmation, which involves searching, rotating, and comparing shapes between the stem and the remaining response alternatives. The difficulty of confirming the key depends on the number of displaced pieces and the number of rotated pieces, as well as its distance from the stem. The difficulty of processing the distractors increases with the expected number of comparisons to detect a mismatched piece, as well as with the number of pieces that are mismatched by small angular disparities. Embretson (in press) presents results from several studies that show strong predictability of psychometric properties for both existing and newly generated items.

Analytical reasoning

Item generation has been applied to two predominant forms of analytical reasoning: verbal (Newstead et al., 2006) and non-verbal (Arendasy, 2005; Embretson, 1998; Hornke and Habon, 1986; Primi, 2001).

Verbal

Newstead et al. (2006) developed an item generator for verbal analytical reasoning (AR) problems, such as found on the *Graduate Record Examination* (GRE). They linked the item generator to item difficulty by structural modeling of the response processes engaged by respondents when devising solutions to these problems. Although verbal AR items are no longer found in the GRE, they are still part of the *Law School Admission Test* (LSAT), and scores on tests of this type have been instrumental for predicting success in higher education (Kuncel et al., 2001). The syntactical structure of each item can be broken down into four components. Each component contained the following two elements: (1) *incidentals*, which define surface content that is not manipulated to define problem difficulty and (2) *radicals*, model elements that are systematically varied across item structures. For example, the first component is the initial scenario that describes a vertical array of elements (e.g. companies) and their range of potential locations (floors of a building), which essentially translates into a set of possible sequences (i.e. orderings) for element-location pairs (e.g. 720). Restrictions on orderings are embedded in the second component, the initial rule set, and these constraints effectively reduce the number of valid sequences. The third component, the item stem, falls into one of the following categories: (a) possible orders ('which order could be true'; e.g. item 1), (b) necessity ('which order must be true'; e.g. item 2), (c) impossibility ('which order cannot be true'; e.g. item 3), and (d) possibility ('which order is the only one that is true'; e.g. item 4). Finally, each of the response options (fourth component) contains a vertical array of elements, by location.

Based on the above layout and findings from previous research, Newstead et al. (2006) hypothesized four possible sources of difficulty to form the basis for the item models. The first source, context effects, refers to both content framing of the problem as well as the location indicators for elements in the array – e.g. 'taller than', 'behind', etc. Second, the number and (linguistic) complexity of AR initial and item-specific rules were anticipated to impact item difficulty. Specifically, simple rules were expected to impact item difficulty considerably less than compound rules, with disjunctive inclusives exceeding disjunctive exclusives. Conditional and bi-conditional statements were also pinpointed as a potential source of added difficulty over simple rules. Mental model theory was hypothesized to account for the impact of representation complexity (i.e. element-location orderings) and memory retrieval for identification of the key (correct answer) within the response set.

Newstead et al. (2006) tested hypotheses regarding the link between item features and difficulty in a series of experiments by regressing item difficulty on the aforementioned predictors. Overall, mental model theory was supported by significant weights for rule-based and model-based factors, though the best predictions were made for impossibility items ($r = 0.80$ between predicted and actual scores). For possible order items, the complexity of the rules was most predictive of item difficulty, suggesting that a dominant strategy for these items was rule checking against each response option. For necessary and impossibility items, however, model variability (differences among models/orderings posed in each response option) most strongly impacted item difficulty. Furthermore, difficulty of all item types was predicted by rule-based factors such as the minimum number of rules needed to confirm or falsify the key and its surrounding distractors within the response set. Thus, support was obtained for a link between cognitive processing and item stimulus features.

Non-verbal

Raven's *Advanced Progressive Matrix* (APM; Raven et al., 1992) test has been used cross-culturally in both research and applied settings for several decades.

The APM contains a series of matrices, each composed of a 3×3 set of objects (elements) and the examinee must infer and apply the relationships in the array to determine the missing elements. Carpenter et al. (1990) developed a cognitive processing theory for matrix problems based on APM items. Relationships (patterns) among the matrix elements include the following: (a) identity relations, in which the attribute(s) of matrix elements is identical across the row or column cells; (b) pairwise progression relations, in which element attributes changes incrementally from cell to cell (e.g. size increases); (c) figure addition or subtraction (e.g. first two elements in a row sum up to the third element in that row); (d) distribution of three relations (e.g. element attribute appears just once in a row or column) and (e) distribution of two relations (e.g. one matching element from the three possible is null or missing). Carpenter et al. (1990) postulated that respondents consider lower-level relationships (e.g. identity) first, then consider the more complex (e.g. distribution of two). Thus, working memory is a crucial process in responding to these items; not only is working memory required to recall which relationships have been previously considered in the response process, but the memory space diminishes as incrementally more complex.

Embretson (1999) developed an item generator for matrix items by extending Carpenter et al.'s (1990) theory to include perceptual principles. The cognitive model included relatively few variables: number of relationships and relational level, as well as three perceptual properties of the item array, but provided good prediction of the psychometric properties of APM items. Item structures that represented unique combinations of the cognitive variables were then used to generate items. Figure 25.2 portrays two items with the same structure; namely, there are three rules: (1) two pairwise rules (e.g. for the changes of shading of the H and the rotation of the H in top item) and (2) a distribution of three (for each shape included once in each row and each column of both items).

Embretson (1998, 2002) found that items from the same structure were not only quite similar, but also that the cognitive model predicted item difficulty and item response time, thus supporting construct validity. For a set of 150 newly-generated items, all cognitive variables (item stimulus features) yielded significant weights for predicting item difficulty. Memory load accounted for approximately 49% of variance in difficulty, and perceptual organization and key position significantly improved prediction. The overall model demonstrated a multiple correlation of 0.81 with item difficulty. A similar pattern of findings emerged when predicting response time, for a multiple correlation of 0.72 for the model. In addition, tests developed using the new items yielded similar internal reliabilities to those of the APM ($\alpha = 0.878$ and 0.881, respectively), and the two tests loaded onto the same factor in a confirmatory factor analysis. Furthermore, scores on this test correlated as expected with related measures such as the ASVAB and the APM. Thus, the results support both predictable item properties, adequate internal structure and external validity (Embretson, 1998, 2000).

Other item generators for matrix items and similar non-verbal item types have also been developed (Arendasy, 2005; Hornke and Habon, 2002), although they

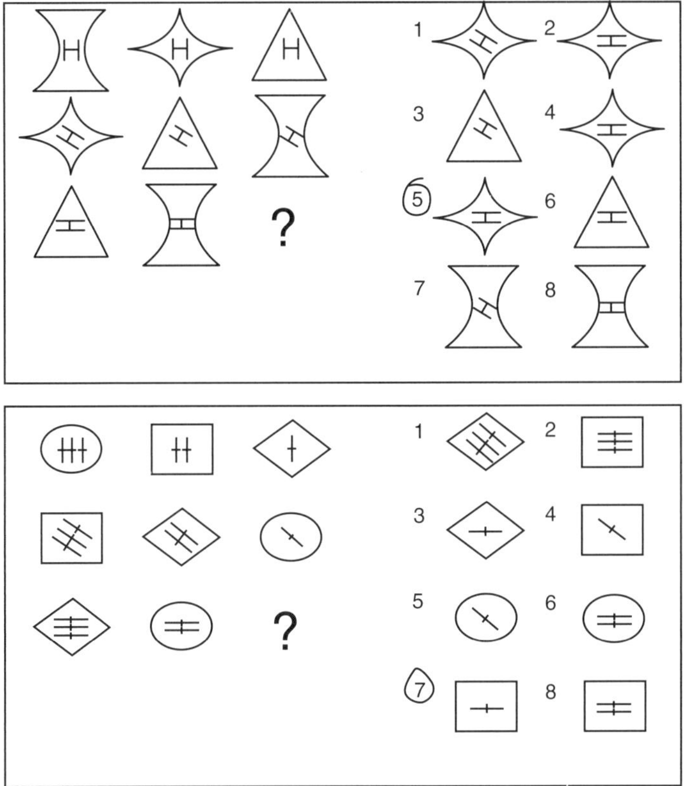

Figure 25.2 Item model for ART items as seen in Figure 1 of Embretson (1998)

are not as closely linked to validity. Hornke and Habon (1986) used a rule set based on the work of Jacobs and Vandeventer (1972) to build item models, each containing a 3×3 matrix that varied in (a) perceptual organization, (b) sequence direction, and (c) cognitive operation (transformation rule). Multiple elements within a matrix cell were perceptually organized as (1) separated components (SC), (2) integrated components (IC), or (3) embedded components (EC). The elements were then arranged in a sequence across (a) rows, (b) columns, or (c) rows and columns, as a function of the following eight cognitive operations (i.e. transformation rules): Identity (I), Addition (A), Subtraction (SU), Intersection (IN), Unique Addition (UA), Seriation (SE), Variation of Closed Gestalts (VC), or Variation of Open Gestalts (VO). These rules overlap somewhat with those incorporated in Embretson's (1998) item structures. For example, the latter two operations resemble the 'distribution of three' rule. Based on the results of a multiple regression analysis, perceptual organization accounted for a significant proportion of variance in item difficulty estimates. In particular, the EC increased the difficulty of items relative to IC and SC, the latter being the least difficult. Of the operations, ID lowered the difficulty of items relative to all operations, and the most difficult operations were IN and UA. Taken together, these components accounted for approximately 40% of the variance among items, which is somewhat lower than Embretson (1998). Based on the results of an analysis conducted on a subsequent sample in 1996, on the same set of 456 items, the same pattern of weights among the components were found along with an R of 0.66 (Hornke, 2002). Furthermore, item difficulty estimates obtained across multiple samples of data obtained for 272 addition items have correlated in the 0.70s to 0.80s (Hornke, 2002: 166).

Primi (2001) attempted to integrate and clarify the findings of Hornke and Habon (1986), who found support for the predominant role of perceptual organization in determining item difficulty, and Embretson (1998), who instead found incremental support for components related to working memory such as number of rules (goal management) and rule type. In particular, variables related to perceptual organization and working memory capacity were more finely distinguished by constructing items that contained orthogonal combinations of these variables. The four variables were: (1) the number of elements in a cell (each cell of the 3 × 3 matrix contained either two or four overlaid objects); (2) the number of rules (two or four); (3) the complexity of the rules (four levels); and (4) the type of perceptual organization (e.g. harmonic, Gestalt principles met, versus non-harmonic, i.e. lack of continuity within a grouping of elements). The four levels of rule complexity, which are based on a reorganization and integration of pre-existing theoretical frameworks (e.g. Carpenter et al., 1990; Jacobs and Vandeventer, 1972) are: (1) simple (SI), (2) spatial (SP), (3) complex (CX) and (4) conceptual (CO). The first two levels involved an incremental change, across rows or columns, in some feature (e.g. size, spatial orientation) of the cell objects; the distinction lies in whether or not this change is quantitative or spatial (levels 1 and 2, respectively). Similarly, levels 3 and 4 differ in terms of the complexity of the transformation across rows or columns (e.g. unique addition versus distribution of three). Thus, 64 items were designed to cross the four, aforementioned variables.

By separating out the effects of number of rules and complexity of rules in a stepwise multiple regression analysis, Primi (2001) was able to demonstrate that perceptual organization explained the largest amount of variance in item difficulty, followed by rule complexity. However, it should be noted that the matrices studied by Primi (2001), Hornke and Habon (1986), and Embretson (1998, 2002) may differ in overall size and complexity of the figures, which could account for the varying role of perceptual organization in these studies. A report on an item generator for Primi's (2001) 64 item types apparently has not yet appeared in the English literature.

Arendasy (2005) constructed non-verbal AR item models without reference to an operational test, although the predictive utility of the item model across a series of studies was compared. The stimuli (elements) contained in an item were referred to as 'geoms', and included squares, circles, triangles, deltoids, hexagons, or rectangles arranged in a 3 × 3 matrix of elements. As with previous studies, the crucial feature of the matrices is the transformation rule (i.e. change in element appearance or attribute, such as size or color) as one moves across a row, column, or both simultaneously. Various rules determine the pattern of elements within the matrix (see Carpenter et al., 1990). For example, a small diamond appears in the same position for every cell, consistent with the simple 'completeness' rule, whereas the change in location of the circle across the top row corresponds with a more complex 'seriality' rule. Items were then generated in GeomGen from models that varied in the following: (1) display format (NV, in which the matrix elements are all the same size, vs. CV, in which the elements range in size and are centered in their respective matrix cell), (2) geom type (shape); (3) number of rules applied; (4) number of geoms (working memory capacity); (5) geom-specific combination rules (e.g. seriality, completeness, subtraction); and (6) task-specific rule direction (horizontal vs. vertical).

The psychometric quality of AR item models was defined as the extent to which generated items exhibited Rasch homogeneity. While the initial 30 items tested failed tests of Rasch homogeneity (based on likelihood ratio test), a subsequently reduced set of 26 items yielded homogeneity. Based on a chi-square model fit comparison and Martin–Lof test statistic, NV and CV items were deemed unidimensional and thus similar to one another in terms of underlying construct measured. When examined separately, however, newly-generated NV items demonstrated stronger evidence of Rasch homogeneity than that of CV items. Thus, additional examination of CV items, particularly with respect to perceptual load, should be considered.

Quantitative reasoning

Mathematical word problems are important in measuring both ability and achievement. Singley and Bennett (2002) describe the *Mathematics Test Creation Assistant* (TCA) that has been used operationally to help item writers create new items. It is based on the item model approach, and the TCA has capabilities for model browsing, model creation, and variant generation. That is, the item writer searches for existing test items as models and then 'variabilizes' surface features that are believed to be unrelated to item psychometric properties. Then, by using lists of permissible substitutions of surface features, new items are created. Although, Singley and Bennett (2002) discuss theoretical accounts of solving mathematical items, particularly schema theory, they are not applied to predict the psychometric properties of items in TCA. Instead, the generated items from TCA are isomorphs and hence, they are assumed to inherit the psychometric properties of their parent model. However, Singley and Bennett (2002) do not report applying these item models to a real testing sample.

Bejar et al. (2003) generalized the item model approach in TCA to 'on-the-fly' item generation, in which the most informative item about a persons' ability can be generated anew while the examinee takes the test. In this research, the similarity of generated items within a family supports the adequacy of the item generator. Item generation models were constructed from 147 pre-existing quantitative GRE items that included 100 quantitative comparison items and 47 problem solving items. Both text-based and figural items (e.g. tables, number lines, geometric figures, and pie charts) were generated. An item model template can be described as follows. Variables are located throughout the template, beginning with the item stem in which, for example, unit of measurement (e.g. centimeters, kilometers) can be manipulated and varied. Moreover, constraints (or rules) are typically specified to place limits on the values of variables. In fact, certain variables do not actually appear in an item; rather, they provide constraints over the values of variables that are visually encountered in the item. The most common rules included in these item model constraints are equities and inequities. Additional control was exerted over distractors, such as the descending or ascending order of values in a particular item model. It is important to note that no specific cognitive design is outlined in the Bejar et al. paper; thus, the innovation for testing rests on the assumption that the isomorphs inherit the psychometric properties of the parent item model.

The parameters for the original 147 GRE items were estimated in a three parameter logistic IRT model and then imputed for the 147 associated item models. Estimation uncertainty arising from variation among instances of an item model was built in to the calibration of the models via the use of expected response functions (ERFs). Thus, the averaging of item characteristic curves (ICCs) from different instances of the same model can be compared to the ERF, paying particular attention to differences in slope between expected and observed cumulative probability functions. Based on the results from a sample ($n = 282$) that was given three test forms, each with 30 items that represented different instances of the same item models, the correlation between previously administered operational GRE test scores and the experimental (newly generated) test scores was 0.87, and the model instances correlated with each other, on average, from 0.77 to 0.87. The correlation among difficulty estimates within a generative item model range from 0.80 to 0.88. Response times among the different experimental test forms were also highly correlated. Thus, these results strongly support the inheritance of the psychometric properties of the item model to the newly generated items.

An item generator for mathematics items with a greater capacity to produce variability is under development. A natural language item generator (Deane and Sheehan, 2003; Deane et al., 2006) has been developed by extending Singley and Bennett's (2002) developments using frame semantics. Although the natural language item generator has been extended to only a few problem types, such as DRT, it provides far greater variation in syntax, vocabulary and substitutions than the previous TCA, more akin to the variability produced by human item writers applying algorithmic item generation methods (Enright et al., 2001).

Finally, from a different perspective, an item generator for algebra word problems was developed to assure quality control (Arendasy et al., 2006). That is, Arendasy et al. (2006) used a structure of radicals to assure a well-defined domain structure for test interpretations and for quality control. Internal evidence is presented to support the generated items as having adequate psychometric properties and relationships of the generated items to other tests that had the predicted structure. In this case, the model-based approach was used for quality control and domain definition rather than to predict the relative psychometric properties of the generated items.

CONCLUSIONS

This chapter has reviewed automatic item generation as a methodological innovation for testing. A review of some earlier developments showed that the roots of automatic item generation date back to the 1960s, with the development of item shells (Hively et al., 1968) and facet theory (Guttman, 1969). Another significant development involved the development of computer programs to produce cognitive tasks as test items (Irvine et al., 1990; Kyllonen and Cristal, 1990). The current state of the art in automatic item generation involves operational test items for complex abilities and achievement. These item generators not only produce items with acceptable psychometric properties, but are also able to produce items to target levels of difficulty. This has led to the possibility of online adaptive testing, where the items are developed anew for each examinee during the testing session (rather than being selected from a pre-existing item bank) (Bejar et al., 2003).

Several item generation programs for complex cognitive abilities have emerged and were reviewed above. Parameters that are appropriate for predicting item psychometric properties arise from calibrating the generating principles through special IRT models such as the LLTM, 2PL-Constrained and hierarchical, family-based models, which were reviewed above.

The current developments for generating items for complex ability and achievement tests have many advantages. First, item development is less expensive and more efficient. Large numbers of items with targeted psychometric properties may be developed from the item generators. If the prediction model is sufficiently strong, the items may be used with little or no tryout, thus eliminating a major bottleneck (empirical tryout) in the test development process. Second, the substantive aspect of construct validity is increased with the structural modeling approach to automatic item generation. That is, cognitive processing theory is directly involved in item production, as items can be developed not only to target difficulty levels, but also to specified sources of cognitive complexity (e.g. Embretson, 1999). Further, automatic item generation may also serve as a context for testing competing theories regarding a particular construct (e.g. Arendasy et al., 2005). Theories can be falsified when the item features demonstrate low, non-significant regression weights for predicting item difficulty or lack of fit to an explanatory IRT model. Indeed, it can be said that one purpose of item design is to explore the theoretical domain of the underlying construct, falsify theories, and determine which theory best accounts for variation in item scores. Third, the ability to spontaneously produce large numbers of items reduces security risks associated with potential exposure to items prior to testing (Morley et al., 2004).

That is, a continual supply of new items minimizes the threat to test security of item exposure and familiarity. If item models and cognitive structures are sufficiently broad, the possible overuse of a particular item model is circumvented so that familiarity and overexposure of certain item structures is also minimized (Bejar et al., 2003).

It is also important to point out a distinction between what item generation researchers have regarded as strong theory and weak theory. Item generation based on strong theory is characterized by the manipulation of specific item stimulus features among test items or test models to differentially impact the cognitive processing components that contribute to item solution. Studies with item generators that conform to strong theory include Bejar (1990), Embretson (1998), and Newstead et al. (2006). Application of weak theory to item generation has involved broad constructs (e.g. quantitative reasoning as depicted on GRE), which may be less amenable than narrow constructs to the use of strong theory. Thus, weak theory may be sufficient for constructing generative item models and attaining adequate prediction and theory-based explanation in these broader constructs. In fact, the most impressive demonstration of automatic item generation, 'on-the-fly' testing, has resulted from the weak theory approach (Bejar et al., 2003).

In conclusion, item generation may be implemented for various purposes, whether it is to generate large numbers of items for new test forms, to explain item difficulty via cognitive processing theory, exert quality control over items, or test competing theoretical processing models. The benefits associated with these uses of item generation are multifold and include, most importantly, improved measurement of the underlying construct and heightened efficiency of testing procedures via spontaneity, and the possibility of automatic and adaptive item generation during testing. Although much more research is needed, the research studies reviewed here, as well as others, reflect a collective movement toward greater precision and efficiency in testing that begins with a more organized, systematic protocol for item design. However, many of these applications have been restricted to the cognitive ability domain. It would be relatively easy to adapt an item generator such as TCA to mathematical achievement, which is widely assessed at many levels. Further, exact specifications of item structures in AIG help assure that the targeted skills in the test blueprints for achievement, and not irrelevant skills, occur in the items. Extensions to domains involving verbal comprehension would be valuable, since this is another important area in achievement testing. This area is particularly challenging for AIG, due to the ambiguities and contextual effects of language. However, a research base for verbal comprehension items is emerging (e.g. Gorin, 2005).

REFERENCES

Arendasy, M. (2005). Automatic generation of Rasch-calibrated items: Figural matrices test GEOM and endless-loops test E^c. *International Journal of Testing*, 5(3): 197–224.

Arendasy, M., Sommer, M., and Ponocny, I. (2005). Psychometric approaches help resolve competing cognitive models: When less is more than it seems. *Cognition and Instruction,* 23(4): 503–21.

Arendasy, M., Sommer, M., Gittler, G., and Hergovich, A. (2006). Automatic generation of quantitative reasoning items: A pilot study. *Journal of Individual Differences,* 27: 2–14.

Bejar, I.I. (1990). A generative analysis of a three-dimensional spatial task. *Applied Psychological Measurement,* 14(3): 237–45.

Bejar, I.I. (1993). A generative approach to psychological and educational measurement. In N. Frederiksen, R.J. Mislevy, and I.I. Bejar (eds) *Test Theory for a New Generation of Tests,* pp. 323–59. Hillsdale, NJ: Erlbaum.

Bejar, I.I. (2002). Generative testing: From conception to implementation. In S.H. Irvine and P.C. Kyllonen (eds) *Item Generation for Test Development,* pp. 199–218. Mahwah, NJ: Erlbaum.

Bejar, I.I. and Yocom, P. (1991). A generative approach to the modeling of isomorphic hidden-figure items. *Applied Psychological Measurement,* 15: 129–37.

Bejar, I.I. (in press). Model-based item generation: A review of recent research.

Bejar, I.I., Lawless, R.R., Morley, M.E., Wagner, M.E., Bennett, R.E., and Revuelta, J. (2003). A feasibility study of on-the-fly item generation in adaptive testing. *Journal of Technology, Learning, and Assessment,* 2(3), Available from http://www.jtla.org.

Bormuth, J.R. (1970). *On the Theory of Achievement Test Items.* Chicago, IL: University of Chicago Press.

Bradlow, E.T., Wainer, H., and Wang, X. (1999). A Bayesian random effects model for testlets. *Psychometrika,* 64(2): 153–68.

Carpenter, P.A., Just, M.A., and Shell, P. (1990). What one intelligence test measures: A theoretical account of processing in the Raven's Progressive Matrices Test. *Psychological Review,* 97: 404–31.

Deane, P. and Sheehan, K. (2003). *Automatic Item Generation via Frame Semantics: Natural Language Generation of Math World Problems* (Unpublished report). Princeton, NJ.

Deane, P., Graf, E.A., Higgins, D., Futagi, Y., and Lawless, R. (2006). *Model Analysis and Model Creation: Capturing the Task-model Structure of Quantitative Domain Items* (Research Report No. RR-06-01). Princeton, NJ: Educational Testing Service.

DeBoeck, P. and Wilson, M. (2004). *Explanatory Item Response Models: A Generalized Linear and Nonlinear Approach.* New York: Springer-Verlag.

Drasgow, F., Luecht, R., and Bennett, R.E. (2006). Technology and testing. In: R.L. Brennan (ed.) *Educational Measurement,* 4th edn, pp. 471–515. Westport, CT: Praeger Publishers.

Embretson, S.E. (1983). Construct validity: Construct representation versus nomothetic span. *Psychological Bulletin,* 93: 179–97.

Embretson, S.E. (1998). A cognitive design system approach to generating valid tests: Application to abstract reasoning. *Psychological Methods,* 3: 380–96.

Embretson, S.E. (1999). Generating items during testing: Psychometric issues and models. *Psychometrika,* 64(4): 407–33.

Embretson, S.E. (2000). Generating Assembling Objects items from cognitive specifications. Final Report for HumRRO: Washington, D.C.

Embretson, S.E. (2006). Item security and automatic item generation in internet testing for selection. Paper presented at the annual meeting of the American Psychological Association. New Orleans, LA, August.

Embretson, S.E. (in press). Cognitive design systems: A structural model approach to generating and calibrating intelligence test items. In S.E. Embretson (ed.) *New Directions in Measuring Psychological Constructs with Model-based Approaches.* Washington, DC: American Psychological Association Books.

Embretson, S.E. and Gorin, J. (2001). Improving construct validity with cognitive psychology principles. Invited article for *Journal of Educational Measurement,* 38: 343–68.

Enright, M.K., Morley, M., and Sheehan, K.M. (2002). Items by design: The impact of systematic feature variation on item statistical characteristics. *Applied Measurement in Education,* 15: 49–74.

Fischer, G.H. (1973). Linear logistic test model as an instrument in educational research. *Acta Psychologica,* 37: 359–74.

Fox, J.P. and Glas, C.E.W. (1998). *Multi-level IRT with Measurement Error in the Predictor Space* (Research Report 98–16). Enschede, The Netherlands: University of Twente.

Glas, C.A.W. and Van der Linden, W. (2003). Computerized adaptive testing with item cloning. *Applied Psychological Measurement,* 27: 247–61.

Gorin, J.S. (2005). Manipulation of processing difficulty on reading comprehension test questions: The feasibility of verbal item generation. *Journal of Educational Measurement,* 42: 351–73.

Guttman, L. (1969). *Integration of Test Design and Analysis.* Proceedings of the 1969 Invitational Conference on Testing Problems. Princeton, NJ: Educational Testing Service.

Haladyna, T.M. (1999). *Developing and Validating Multiple-choice Test Items,* 2nd edn. Mahwah, NJ: Lawrence Erlbaum Associates, Inc.

Haladyna, T.M. and Shindoll, R.H. (1987, April) *Item Shells: Progress and Potential.* Paper presented at the Annual Meeting of the National Council on Measurement in Education, Washington, D.C.

Hively, W., Patterson, H.L., and Page, S.A. (1968). A 'universe-defined' system of arithmetic achievement tests. *Journal of Educational Measurement,* 5: 275–90.

Hornke, L.F. (2002). Item-generation models for higher order cognitive functions. In S.H. Irvine and P.C. Kyllonen (eds) *Item Generation for Test Development,* pp. 199–218. Mahwah, New Jersey: Earlbaum.

Hornke, L.F. and Habon, M.W. (1986). Rule-based item bank construction and valuation framework. *Applied Psychological Measurement,* 10(4): 369–80.

Irvine, S.H., Dann, P.L., and Anderson, J.D. (1990). Towards a theory of algorithm determined cognitive test construction. *British Journal of Psychology,* 81: 173–95.

Jacobs, P.I. and Vandeventer, M. (1972). Evaluating the teaching of intelligence. *Educational and Psychological Measurement,* 32: 235–48.

Kyllonen, P.C. (1995). CAM: A theoretical framework for cognitive abilities measurement. In D. Detterman (ed.) *Current Topics in Human Intelligence: Volume IV, Theories of Intelligence.* Norwood, NJ: Ablex.

Kyllonen, P.C. and Cristal, R.E. (1990). Reasoning ability is (little more than) working memory capacity? *Intelligence,* 14: 389–433.

Kuncel, N.R., Hezlett, S.A., and Ones, D.S. (2001). A comprehensive meta-analysis of the predictive validity of the graduate record examinations: Implications for graduate student selection and performance. *Psychological Bulletin,* 127(1): 162–81.

Loevinger, J. (1957). Objective tests as instruments of psychological theory. *Psychological Reports,* 3: 653–94.

Marshall, S. (1995). *Schemas in Problem Solving.* New York: Cambridge University Press.

Mayer, R.E., Larkin, J.H., and Kadane, J.B. (1984). A cognitive analysis of mathematical problem solving ability. In R.J. Sternberg (ed.) *Advances in the Psychology of Human Intelligence,* pp. 231–73. Hillsdale, NJ: Erlbaum.

Messick, S. (1995). Validity of psychological assessment. *American Psychologist,* 50: 741–9.

Morley, M., Bridgeman, B., and Lawless, R.R. (2004). *Transfer Between Variants of Quantitative Items* (No. RR-04-06). Princeton, NJ: Educational Testing Service.

Newstead, S.E., Bradon, P., Handley, S.J., Dennis, I., and Evans, J.St.B.T. (2006). Predicting the difficulty of complex logical reasoning problems. *Thinking & Reasoning,* 12: 62–90.

Primi, R. (2001). Complexity of geometric inductive reasoning tasks: Contribution to the understanding of fluid intelligence. *Intelligence,* 30: 41–70.

Raven, J.C., Court, J.H., and Raven, J. (1992). *Manual for Raven's Progressive Matrices and Vocabulary Scale.* San Antonio, TX: Psychological Corporation.

Roid, G.H. and Haladyna, T.M. (1982). *A Technology for Item Writing.* New York: Academic Press.

Sebrechts, M.M., Enright, M., Bennett, R.E., and Martin, K. (1996). Using algebra word problems to assess quantitative ability: Attributes, strategies, and errors. *Cognition and Instruction,* 14: 285–343.

Shepherd, R.N. and Metzler, J. (1971). Mental rotation of three-dimensional objects. *Science,* 171: 701–3.

Singley, M.K. and Bennett, R.E. (2002). Item generation and beyond: Applications of schema theory to mathematics assessment. In S. Irvine and P. Kyllonen (eds) *Item Generation for Test Development,* pp. 361–84. Mahwah, NJ: Lawrence Erlbaum Associates, Inc.

Thorndike, R.L. (1971). *Educational Measurement,* 2nd edn. Washington, DC: American Council on Education.

Wesman, A.G. (1971). Writing the test item. In R.L. Thorndike (ed.) *Educational Measurement,* 2nd edn, pp. 81–129. Washington, DC: American Council on Education.

26

Convergence of Structural Equation Modeling and Multilevel Modeling

Rex B. Kline

Everything is related to everything, but near things are more related than distant things.

The quote that opens this chapter is Waldo Tobler's First Law of Geography (quoted in Longley et al., 2005: 65), and it emphasizes that all places are more or less similar, but nearby places are more akin than distant places. This law could also describe the attainment of wisdom about some domain of study, that is, a sense of the big picture about how things that on the surface appear to be unrelated are actually connected on a more fundamental level. Deep learning is another term for this kind of understanding, and it is contrasted with surface learning, which involves more rote memorization than a conceptual reorganization that transfers to other situations and affects future problem solving (Lombardo, n.d.). Many have argued that the ultimate goal of education should be the facilitation of deep learning instead of just the accumulation of facts or situation-specific skills (e.g. Gardner, 1999).

It is also true that part of maturing as a researcher should involve an increasing sense of how many statistical techniques are, despite the use of different names or computer tools for the same basic analytical method, fundamentally related. An example was the realization starting in the 1960s that all forms of the analysis of variance (ANOVA) are nothing more than a restricted case of multiple regression (e.g. J. Cohen, 1968), which itself is just an extension of bivariate regression that analyzes one or more predictors (factors, independent variables) of a continuous criterion (outcome, dependent variable). Any predictor in MR can be continuous or categorical, and both types of predictors can be analyzed together in the same equation. In contrast, it is awkward in ANOVA to include a continuous variable, such as age in years, as a factor in the analysis. One way to do so is to categorize a continuous variable into a dichotomy, such as through a median split, or into three or more discrete levels that make up an ordinal scale (e.g. low, medium, high). However, categorization – Thompson (2006) used the perhaps more apt term mutilation – of a continuous predictor is generally a bad idea for a few reasons. These include the loss of numerical information about individual differences in the original distribution and the possible introduction of statistically-significant-but-artifactual results due to mutilation (e.g. MacCallum et al., 2002). The analysis could be enhanced by the insight that categorization of continuous predictors is unnecessary when using a regression procedure instead of an ANOVA procedure.

Relations among behavioral science statistical methods extend even further. For instance, MR is part of the general linear model (GLM) family of techniques that include canonical correlation and multivariate analysis of variance (MANOVA) when there are multiple outcome variables and also some methods of exploratory factor analysis, such as principle components, when there is no distinction between predictor and outcome variables. All parametric GLM techniques are in turn subsumed under the family of techniques referred to as structural equation modeling (SEM), also known as covariance structure analysis (e.g. Fan, 1997). As a whole, SEM techniques are highly versatile and permit the evaluation of a wide range of hypotheses, such as those about direct or indirect effects, associations between manifest (observed) variables and latent variables (e.g. measurement), or means of observed or latent variables. In part due to their flexibility, SEM techniques have become quite popular among researchers. Indeed, it is increasingly hard to look through an issue of a research journal in the behavioral sciences and not find at least one article in which results of SEM analyses are reported.

A different family of statistical methods known as multilevel modeling (MLM) – also referred to as hierarchical linear modeling, random coefficients modeling, and mixed effects modeling, among other variations – has been emphasized in areas where hierarchical or clustered datasets are routinely analyzed. In such datasets, individuals (cases) are grouped into higher units, such as siblings within families or workers within departments. These larger units may themselves be nested under even higher-order variables, such as families within neighborhoods or departments within companies. Within each level, scores may not be independent. For example, siblings may all be affected by common family characteristics, such as total family income, and family characteristics may be affected by common neighborhood variables, such as community socioeconomic status (SES). Repeated measures datasets are also hierarchical in that multiple scores are clustered under each case, and these scores may not be independent.

Many standard statistical techniques for single-level analyses where cases are not clustered, such as MR and ANOVA for between-subject effects, assume independence of the scores. Statistical tests in MR also generally assume that the residuals (error scores) are not only independent but also normally distributed and homoscedastic, or that their variance is constant across all levels of the criterion. Violation of these assumptions generally results in negatively biased estimates of standard errors, which means that they are on average too small. Because standard errors are the denominators of some statistical tests, such as the *t*-test, then the results of such tests could be statistically significant too often. That is, the actual Type I error rate (e.g. 0.55) could be much higher than the stated level of statistical significance (e.g. $\alpha = 0.05$) when a statistical test that assumes independence is conducted with dependent scores. Estimates of certain population parameters, such as regression coefficients, could be biased too. With the exception of the analysis of repeated measures data, SEM also generally assumes independence. Overall, SEM is better suited for single-level analyses in datasets that are not hierarchical. However, it can be difficult to estimate both direct and indirect effects also effects of latent variables measured by multiple indicators in MLM, but these kinds of analyses pose no special problem in SEM. Thus, the SEM and MLM families of techniques have some complementary strengths and weaknesses.

Just as GLM and SEM can be viewed as extensions of basic principles of MR to the analysis of, respectively, multiple outcomes or latent variables, so too can MLM, but here core MR principles are extended to multilevel analysis of hierarchical data (e.g. Bickel, 2007). This common lineage also implies that SEM and MLM are more closely related to each other than might seem at first glance. For example, there are some specialized computer programs for MLM – including MLwiN 2.02 (Rasbash et al., 2005) and Hierarchical Linear and Nonlinear Modeling (HLM) 6.06 (Raudenbush et al., 2008), among others[1] – but they cannot generally analyze structural equation models with latent variables measured by multiple indicators.

Likewise, it has been awkward until recently to analyze multilevel models with specialized software for SEM,[2] including older versions of LISREL, EQS, and Amos, among others. A notable exception is Mplus, which has been capable of SEM analyses and MLM analyses through its last several versions, the most recent of which is Mplus 5 (L. Muthén and B. Muthén, 1998–2007). Indeed, the analysis of multilevel structural equation models with latent variables measured by multiple indicators is quite straightforward in Mplus. Also, the most recent versions of LISREL (8.8; Jöreskog and Sörbom, 2006) and EQS (6.1; Bentler, 2005) include special syntax and features for analyzing multilevel structural equation models.

Work published over the last two decades by several different authors about commonalities between SEM and MLM has facilitated the development of the computer tools just mentioned. For example, B. Muthén (1994) described how to represent and estimate multilevel confirmatory factor analysis models using (then) standard SEM software and notation. This approach involved exploiting the capability of SEM computer tools to analyze models across multiple groups, but in this case the 'groups' corresponded to within-group variation versus between-group variation in the same hierarchical dataset. McArdle and Hamagami (1996) described how different kinds of multilevel models could be specified as instances of multiple-group structural equation models. More recently, Bauer (2003) and Curran (2003) demonstrated how structural equation models and multilevel models are analytically equivalent for certain kinds of hierarchical datasets. See the two works just mentioned for additional citations of important work about the convergence of SEM and MLM.

A more complete synthesis of the two sets of techniques is described as multilevel structural equation modeling (ML-SEM) (e.g. Heck, 2001; Kaplan, 2000: Chapter 7; Rabe-Hesketh et al., 2007), and it offers potential advantages to researchers who are familiar with either SEM or MLM, but not both. Considered next are the basic rationales of MLM and SEM with emphasis on their complementary strengths and weaknesses. After review of these foundational issues, examples of the kinds of hypotheses and models that can be tested in ML-SEM are considered.

RATIONALE OF MULTILEVEL MODELING

There are two main contexts for the analysis of hierarchical data. The first is in repeated measures designs where scores are clustered under each case. Expected dependence among such scores is accounted for in some standard statistical techniques. For example, the error term in repeated measures ANOVA takes account of score covariances across the levels of repeated measures factors. However, ANOVA assumes that the error variances of repeated measures variables are equal and independent. These restrictive assumptions are often violated in actual repeated measures datasets. The technique of MANOVA can also be applied to repeated measures data, and its assumptions about error variance are less restrictive (e.g. errors may covary). A special strength of SEM is that it allows even greater flexibility in the modeling of error covariances compared with ANOVA or MANOVA, a point that is elaborated later.

The second context is the use of a complex sampling design in which the levels of at least one higher-order variable are selected prior to sampling of individual cases within each level. An example is the method of cluster sampling. Suppose in a study of Grade 2 scholastic skills a total of 100 public elementary schools in a particular geographic region is randomly selected, and then every Grade 2 student in these schools is assessed. Here, students are clustered within schools. A variation for this example is multistage sampling where only a portion of the students within each school are randomly selected (e.g. 10%) for inclusion in the sample. In stratified sampling, a population is divided into homogenous, mutually exclusive subpopulations (strata), such as by gender or ethic categories, and then cases within each stratum are randomly selected. The resulting hierarchical dataset may be representative of the variable(s) selected for stratification.

In a complex sample, scores within each level of a higher-order variable may have some degree of dependence. This means that the application of standard formulas for estimating standard errors that assume independence may not yield correct results. These formulas may be reasonably accurate in a single-level sample, but they tend to underestimate sampling variance for dependent scores. Thus, one motivation for the development of multilevel statistical methods is the need to correctly estimate standard errors in complex sampling designs.

A second motivation for multilevel analysis is the study of effects of contextual variables on scores at lower levels in a hierarchical dataset. Suppose that a researcher wishes to study factors that predict scholastic achievement among Grade 2 students. The researcher will measure characteristics of students, such as their gender, ethnicity, and family income. In a complex sampling design, the students will be selected from within a total of 100 different schools. Characteristics of the students' schools will also be measured, such as their size (total student body) and degree of emphasis on academic excellence. The variables just mentioned are uniquely school-level characteristics.

However, it is also possible to aggregate selected student-level variables up to the school level and to consider these aggregated variables as school-level variables, too. For example, gender is a dichotomous variable for individual students, but the total proportion of students who are girls at each school is a school-level characteristic. Likewise, the average family income over all students who attend the same school is a characteristic of that school. Measured across all schools, the proportion of girl students or average family income could be between-school predictors of student achievement at the individual level. In a multilevel statistical analysis, both student-level and school-level predictors of achievement could be analyzed together in a way that (1) correctly estimates standard errors and (2) simultaneously incorporates data from the two different levels, within groups and between groups. These features lead to (3) separate estimates of between-group effects (e.g. school size) and within-groups effects (e.g. student gender) on variables of interest (e.g. achievement).

Often the first step in analyzing a hierarchical dataset is the calculation of a statistical index of the degree to which observations at the case level, such as students, depend on a grouping or cluster variable, such as schools. One such index is the unconditional intraclass correlation coefficient (UICC), and its value indicates the proportion of total variability explained by the grouping variable. One way to estimate the UICC is to conduct a standard, fixed-effects ANOVA where the grouping variable is the single factor and scores at the case level are the dependent variable. From the results of this analysis, UICC is calculated as

$$\hat{\rho} = \frac{MS_C - MS_W}{MS_C + (df_C) MS_W} \quad (1)$$

where $\hat{\rho}$ is the sample estimate of the UICC, MS_C is the between-groups mean square for the cluster variable (e.g. schools), MS_W is the pooled-within groups mean square (e.g. students within schools), and df_C is the degree of freedom for the grouping variable, which is one less than the number of clusters. An alternative is to conduct a random-effects (variance components) ANOVA where the grouping variable is specified as a random factor:

$$\hat{\rho} = \frac{\hat{\sigma}_C^2}{\hat{\sigma}_C^2 + \hat{\sigma}} \tag{2}$$

where $\hat{\sigma}_C^2$ is the variance component estimate for the grouping variable and $\hat{\sigma}_\varepsilon^2$ is the variance component estimate for error. In SPSS, the value of $\hat{\rho}$ estimated using either equation (1) or (2) within the same hierarchical dataset should be equivalent within rounding error when the estimation method is specified in the Variance Components procedure as 'ANOVA'; otherwise, the two values may be somewhat different.

If the value of $\hat{\rho}$ is high enough, then it may be necessary to employ MLM instead of a standard, single-level statistical technique. Unfortunately, there is no 'gold standard' concerning cut-off values for $\hat{\rho}$ above which would clearly indicate a problem if MLM were not used. Some sources suggest that UICC values as low as 0.10 may be sufficient to result in appreciable bias in standard errors if MLM techniques are not used (e.g. Maas and Hox, 2005). Another standard is that MLM should be conducted if the value of $\hat{\rho}$ is statistically significant, but it is possible that near-zero values of $\hat{\rho}$, such as $\hat{\rho} = 0.01$, could be statistically significant in a large sample. In any event, the decision rule 'if $\hat{\rho} \geq 0.10$, then use multilevel modeling' may be a relatively conservative one; see Bickel (2007: ch. 3) for more information.

An example of the need to separately estimate effects at different levels of analysis described by Stapleton (2006) is considered next. Suppose that a researcher believes that students who spend more time watching television (TV) have lower levels of scholastic achievement (Ach). Both variables are measured among students who attend four different schools; that is, students are clustered within schools. The scatterplots for each of four hypothetical schools are presented in Figure 26. 1. The group centroid – the point that represents the mean on both variables – and the within-group regression line are represented in the figure for each scatterplot with, respectively, a dot or a dashed line. Within each school, the association between TV and Ach is negative; that is, more time spent watching television predicts lower achievement. From the perspective of SEM, the same basic within-group covariance structure holds across schools.

However, there is another aspect of the relation between the variables TV and Ach in Figure 26.1 that is apparent from a between-school perspective: There is a *positive* association between the average number of hours of television watched at a school and the average achievement in a school. This positive covariance is apparent if you draw a line in the figure that connects the four group centroids. The fact that the within-school versus between-school associations between the

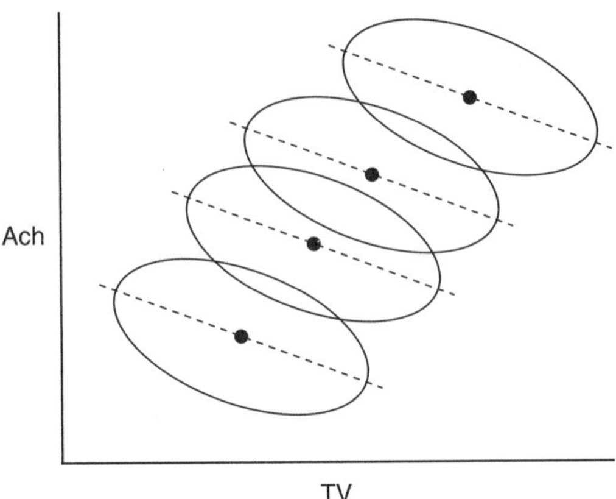

Figure 26.1 Representation of within-school versus between-school variation in the relation between television watching (TV) and scholastic achievement (Ach)

variables TV and Ach are of opposite signs (respectively, negative, positive) is not contradictory. This is because the between-school association is estimated using group statistics (means), but the within-school associations are estimated using scores from individual students.

In Figure 26.1, the within-school slopes are identical, but the within-school intercepts differ across the schools. This particular pattern may be improbable. Specifically, given a more realistic number of schools in a two-level dataset, such as about 100 or so, it may be more likely that (1) both the slopes and the intercepts of the within-school regression lines may vary across schools. Furthermore, it is also possible that (2) part of the variability in slopes or intercepts is explained by at least one contextual variable, such as school size. For example, the relation between television watching and achievement could be stronger in smaller schools but weaker in larger schools, or even close to zero. It is also possible that (3) variability in slopes is related to variability in intercepts, both across schools. For example, a higher school average level of achievement (i.e. a higher intercept) may predict a stronger negative relation between television watching and achievement, and vice-versa. That is, the covariance between intercepts and slopes across schools may not be zero.

Random coefficient regression

Perhaps the most basic multilevel statistical technique is random coefficient regression. Unlike in standard MR for single-level datasets where slopes and intercepts are conceptualized as fixed population parameters, coefficients for slopes and intercepts in random coefficient regression can be specified as random effects that vary (and covary) across subpopulations. In a two-level dataset, these subpopulations correspond to levels of cluster variables, such as schools for the example discussed to this point about the relation between television watching and achievement. Specifically, the researcher could specify in a random coefficient regression that both the within-school slopes and intercepts vary across schools. In contrast to a standard MR analysis where separate sets of slopes and intercepts would be estimated for each and every school, two different types of parameters are estimated in random coefficient regression. These include (1) the variance and covariance of the slopes and intercepts, and (2) the weighted average slope and intercept across all schools. The latter are the fixed components of the randomly-varying slopes and intercepts, and the former are the random components of these parameters.

A related point is that ordinary least squares (OLS) is not the typical estimation method used in random coefficient regression as it is in standard MR. Briefly, if the cluster sizes at the second level are all equal (e.g. the size of every school is the same), then the design is balanced. In this case, it may be possible to use full-information maximum likelihood (FIML) estimation in a random coefficient regression analysis. This assumes that the number of clusters is large, say, > 75 or so (e.g. Maas and Hox, 2005) and also that the total number of cases across all clusters is large, too. In unbalanced designs, it may be necessary to use an approximate maximum likelihood estimator, one that is less computationally intensive but accommodates unequal cluster sizes. An example is restricted maximum likelihood (REML), which is available in the Linear Mixed Models procedure of SPSS for multilevel analyses.

Multilevel regression

In a basic random coefficient regression, there are no predictors of the variances and covariances among within-group slopes and intercept across clusters. There are such predictors in a full multilevel regression analysis, and these predictors are typically contextual variables, or characteristics of groups. Presented next are the equations that specify a hypothetical two-level regression analysis where television watching and achievement are each measured within 100 different schools and where school size is a predictor of within-school regression coefficients. The level-1 within-school regression equation is

$$\text{Ach}_{ig} = \beta_{0g} + \beta_{1g}\,\text{TV}_{ig} + r_{ig} \qquad (3)$$

where Ach_{ig} is the ith student's achievement score in the gth school and TV_{ig} is the student level predictor of amount of television watching. The terms β_{0g} and β_{1g} represent, respectively, the random intercept and slope of the line for the regression of achievement on television watching for the gth school (e.g. Kaplan, 2000: 132–4).

Continuing with same example, there are two equations at level-2, the between-school level, one for each of the random intercepts and slopes from equation (3):

$$\beta_{0g} = \gamma_{00} + \gamma_{01}\,\text{Size}_g + u_{0g} \tag{4}$$

$$\beta_{1g} = \gamma_{10} + \gamma_{11}\,\text{Size}_g + u_{1g} \tag{5}$$

where Size_g is the size of the gth school, γ_{00} is the mean intercept across all schools, and γ_{01} is the slope of the regression line for the relation between school mean achievement and the mean amount of television watching (e.g. see Figure 26.1). The terms γ_{00} and γ_{10} are the fixed components (averages) of the random intercepts and slopes. The terms u_{0g} and u_{1g} in equations (4) and (5) refer to, respectively, variability in the random intercepts and slopes; thus, they are the random components of the slopes and intercepts. The specification of intercepts and slopes as criterion variables in multilevel regression is described as an intercepts- and slopes-as-outcomes model.

Substituting the terms in the right-hand sides of equations (4) and (5) for, respectively, β_{0g} and β_{1g} back into equation (3) generates the full regression model at the student level, which is

$$\text{Ach}_{ig} = \gamma_{00} + \gamma_{01}\,\text{Size}_g + \gamma_{10}\,\text{TV}_{ig} + \gamma_{11}\,\text{Size}_g\,\text{TV}_{ig} + (u_{0g} + u_{1g}\,\text{TV}_{ig} + r_{ig}). \tag{6}$$

In words, the full model specifies that achievement of individual students is a function of the overall intercept (γ_{00}), the main effect of school size ($\gamma_{01}\,\text{Size}_g$), the main effect of the students' time spent watching television ($\gamma_{10}\,\text{TV}_{ig}$), and the cross-level interaction effect where school size moderates the relation between watching television and achievement ($\gamma_{11}\,\text{Size}_g\,\text{TV}_{ig}$). The remaining terms in parentheses in equation (6) correspond to error variance from both levels of the model [see equations (3)–(5)].

Output from a computer tool for a multilevel regression analysis would include the regression coefficients for the terms specified in equation (6) and estimates of the residual (error) variance and also of the variances and covariances of the random slopes and intercepts. A two-level regression model can quickly become quite complicated as additional individual- or group-level predictors are added to the model. Also, the researcher must make many decisions about specification, including the designation of individual-level intercepts or slopes as random versus fixed effects or whether random components covary or not. The specification of covariance patterns among predictor or outcome variables is familiar to those who work mainly with SEM. Also compared with SEM, it is just as crucial in MLM to balance model complexity against parsimony and theoretical justification. That is, the goal in both techniques is to find the simplest model with a sound rationale that also fits the data.

A multilevel regression analysis can be expanded in many ways. For example, it is possible to estimate models with three or more levels (i.e. there are two levels of cluster variables), but the complexity of such models can be daunting. This is in part explains why most multilevel models described in the research literature are two-level models. The analysis of repeated measures from a multilevel perspective also affords much flexibility. An example concerns latent growth models, in which the slopes and intercepts of repeated measures variables are treated as latent outcome variables that are predicted by either time-invariant variables (i.e. they are measured once) or other repeated measures variables. A standard textbook for MLM is Raudenbush and Bryk (2002), but its presentation is mathematically rigorous; see Bickel (2007) for a more-introductory level presentation that emphasizes the connection between MLM and standard OLS regression.

Summarized next are some limitations of MLM (Bauer, 2003; Curran, 2003):

1 Scores on individual- or group-level predictors in MLM are observed variables that are assumed to be perfectly reliable. (The same assumption applies to predictors in single-level MR, too.) This requirement is unrealistic, especially for predictors that are psychological variables measured with questionnaires instead of demographic variables.
2 There is no straightforward way in MLM to represent either predictor or outcome variables as latent variables (constructs) measured by multiple indicators. In other words, it is difficult to specify a measurement model as part of a multilevel model.
3 Although there are methods to estimate indirect effects apart from direct effects in MLM (e.g. Krull and MacKinnon, 2001), they can be difficult to apply in practice.
4 There are statistical tests of individual coefficients or of variances/covariances in multilevel regression, but there is no single inferential test of the model as a whole. Instead, the relative predictive power of alternative multilevel models estimated in the same sample can be evaluated in MLM (e.g. Bickel, 2007: ch. 3).

RATIONALE OF STRUCTURAL EQUATION MODELING

Diagrams of structural equation models are presented next using the reticular action modeling (RAM) symbol set (e.g. McArdle and McDonald, 1984). The RAM symbolism explicitly represents every model parameter that requires a statistical estimate.

Path models

A basic covariance structure consists of a structural model or a measurement model. Presented in Figure 26.2(a) is an example of a structural model for observed variables, or a path model. The observed variables in this model, X_1, Y_1, and Y_3, are each represented with squares (rectangles can also represent observed variables). Each line with a single arrowhead ($\rightarrow$) in Figure 26.2(a) represents a hypothesized direct effect of one variable on another. (Direct effects are also called paths.) The arrowhead points to the presumed effect and the line originates from a presumed cause, such as $X_1 \rightarrow Y_1$ in the figure. Variable X_1 in this model is exogenous because whatever is presumed to cause this variable is not represented in the path model. In contrast, variables Y_1 and Y_3 are endogenous because they are specified as outcomes of other observed variables.

Note in the path model of Figure 26.2(a) the specification $X_1 \rightarrow Y_1 \rightarrow Y_3$, which represents the presumed indirect effect of X_1 on Y_3 through a mediator variable, Y_1. This specification reflects the hypothesis that X_1 has an effect on Y_1 and that part of this effect is then 'transmitted' on to Y_3. Note that the path model in the figure also contains a direct effect of X_1 on Y_3, or $X_1 \rightarrow Y_3$. The separate estimation of direct versus indirect effects is a standard part of path analysis that is referred to as effects decomposition. The circles in the path model of Figure 26.2(a) represent latent variables (ellipses can also represent latent variables), in this case the disturbances of the endogenous variables. Disturbances represent all omitted causes of an endogenous variable, and they are considered in SEM as unmeasured exogenous variables. The numbers (1) that appear in the figure are scaling constants. These specifications assign a scale to each disturbance that is related to that of the unexplained variance of the corresponding endogenous variable. The two-headed curved arrows that exit and reenter the same variable in the figure represent the variances of the exogenous variables, which are also considered model parameters because these variables are free to vary (and covary, too).

Structural-regression models

A limitation of path analysis is that scores on exogenous variables are assumed to be perfectly reliable. Also, measurement error in endogenous variables is reflected in their disturbances along with systematic variance not otherwise explained by predictors. That is, estimation of the proportion of unexplained variance is confounded with that of measurement error in path analysis. An alternative to these restrictive assumptions is to specify a structural-regression (SR) model, which has both a structural model and a measurement model. In the latter, observed variables are specified as multiple indicators of latent variables (constructs, factor). Direct and indirect effects are specified in the structural model, but in SR models these effects are between latent variables. This synthesis of regression analysis and factor analysis allows the separate estimation of measurement error in observed variables from unexplained variance in underlying factors.

The SR model presented in Figure 26.2(b) contains the same basic pattern of structural relations specified in the path model of Figure 26.2(a), but these effects involve latent variables in the SR model. Each latent variable in Figure 26.2(b) is specified as measured by either two or three observed variables, and the direct effects from factors to indicators (e.g. $A \rightarrow X_2$) represent the influences of factors on scores. The scaling constants (1) that appear in the SR model next to the path for one indicator of each factor (e.g. $A \rightarrow X_1$) assign a scale to each factor related to that of the explained variance of the corresponding indicator. Note in Figure 26.2(b) that (1) every indicator has a residual term that represents, in part, measurement error (unreliability); and (2) every endogenous factor (B, C)

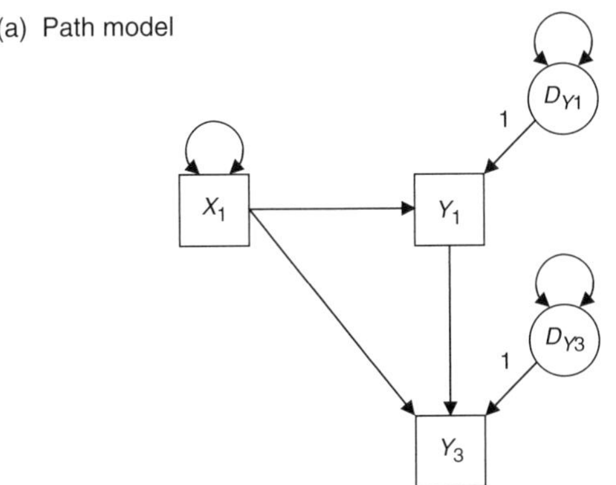

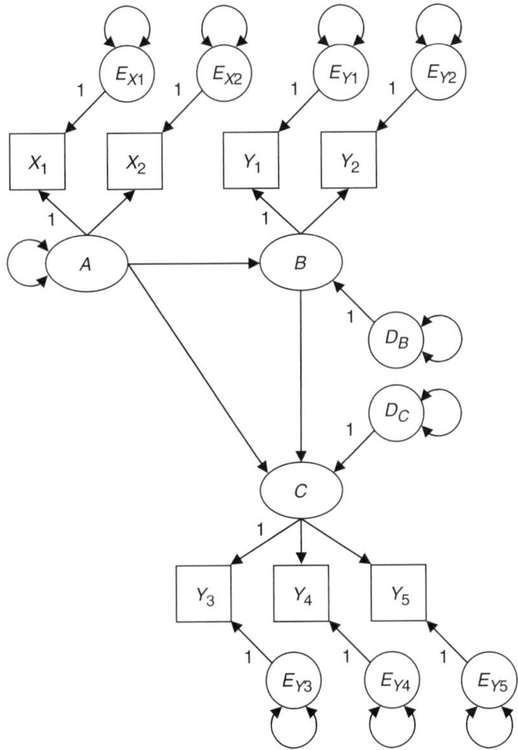

Figure 26.2 Examples of a path model (a) and a structural-regression model (b)

has a disturbance. Through this specification, it is possible to estimate direct and indirect effects between factors (e.g. $A \rightarrow B$), controlling for measurement error in their indicators.

Confirmatory factor analysis models

When analyzing an SR model, it is often important to first verify its measurement model, that is, to test the hypotheses about the correspondence between the indicators and the factors they are supposed to measure. If these hypotheses are wrong, then knowing relations among the factors specified in the structural part of the model may be of little value (Thompson, 2000). For example, if the three-factor measurement model implied by the SR model in Figure 26.2(b) did not explain covariance patterns among the seven indicators, then the fit of the whole SR model may be poor and the path coefficients may have little interpretive value. This is why many researchers use a two-step method to analyze SR models described by Anderson and Gebring (1988), as follows: In the first step, evaluate the measurement model implied by the original SR model. If this model is rejected, then it must be respecified. Given a satisfactory measurement model, the second step involves the testing of hypotheses about direct and indirect effects; that is, the structural part of the SR model is now analyzed.

Confirmatory factor analysis (CFA) is the SEM technique for evaluating pure measurement models. In such models, all associations between the factors are specified as unanalyzed, which implies that the factors covary, but we have no specific explanation about why they do so. An example of a two-factor CFA model is presented in Figure 26.3(a). In this model, the six observed variables are specified as measuring two factors, where indicators X_1–X_3 are presumed to reflect factor A and indicators X_4–X_6 are presumed to reflect factor B. The curved line with two arrowheads in Figure 26.3(a) that connects the factors represents their covariance. If this path were replaced with a direct effect, such as $A \rightarrow B$, then the CFA model in Figure 26.3(a) would be transformed into an SR model.

Latent growth models

A latent growth model as specified in SEM is presented in Figure 26.3(b). In addition to its covariance structure, this model has a mean structure, which is represented in RAM symbolism by the graphical symbol △(1), and here it represents a constant that equals 1 for every case. In SEM, this constant is treated as an exogenous variable (even though its variance is zero) that has direct or indirect effects on other variables in the model except for residual terms. The unstandardized coefficients for effects of the constant are interpreted as either means or intercepts. (This is the same basic method carried out 'behind the scenes' when a modern computer program for regression calculates an intercept.) In the model in Figure 26.3(b), these specifications result in the estimation of the means of the

(a) Confirmatory factor analysis model

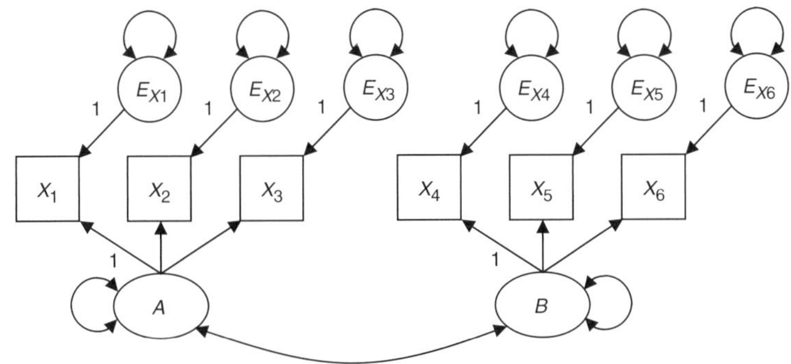

(b) Latent growth model

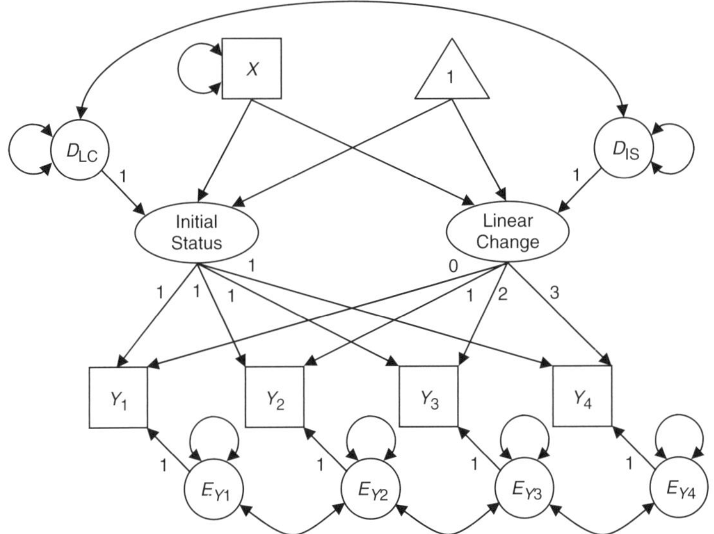

Figure 26.3 Examples of a confirmatory factor analysis model (a) and a latent growth model (b) as specified in structural equation modeling

two factors and also of the intercepts for the repeated measures outcome variable, which is represented as Y_1–Y_4 in the figure.

These variables Y_1–Y_4 in Figure 26.3(b) are specified as the indicators of two latent growth factors, Initial Status (IS) and Linear Change (LC). The IS factor represents the baseline level of variable Y, adjusted for measurement error. Because the IS factor is basically an intercept, loadings of Y_1–Y_4 on IS are all specified as 1. In contrast, loadings on the LC factor are fixed to constants that correspond to the times of measurement, beginning with 0 for the first measurement and ending with 3 for the last. These constants (0, 1, 2, 3) specify a positive linear trend, but one that is adjusted for measurement error when the model is estimated.

In an actual analysis, one would obtain estimates of the factor means and also of their variances and covariances. For example, the mean for the LS factor in Figure 26.3(b) is the weighted average linear change (slope) over time across all cases. This mean is analogous to the fixed component of a random effect in MLM. The estimate of the variance of the LS factor indicates the range of individual difference in slopes across the cases. This variance is akin to the random component of a random effect in MLM. Also, the IS and LC factors in Figure 26.3(b) are specified to covary, and the estimate of this covariance indicates the degree to which initial levels of externalization predict rates of subsequent linear change, again corrected for measurement error.

The model in Figure 26.3(b) also has an error covariance structure, one where the error terms of the repeated measures indicators are allowed to covary across adjacent times (e.g. between E_{Y1} and E_{Y2}). Other patterns are possible, including no error covariances (i.e. the errors are independent over time) or the specification of additional error covariances (e.g. between E_{Y1} and E_{Y3}). Finally, the model in Figure 26.3(b) includes a predictor, variable X, of the IS and LC factors. This predictor could be either a continuous variable, such as family income, or a dichotomous one, such as gender. In this model, X is specified as a predictor of latent intercepts and slopes. The capability to specify observed variables as predictors of intercepts and slopes treated as latent variables in multilevel regression was mentioned earlier.

The analysis of latent growth models in SEM requires (1) a continuous outcome variable measured on at least three occasions; (2) scores that have the same units over time; and (3) data that are time structured, which means that cases are all tested at the same intervals. In contrast, the analysis of latent growth models in MLM does not require time-structured data, so it is even more flexible than SEM for analyzing latent growth models. As noted by Bauer (2003), Curran (2003), and others, latent growth models analyzed in SEM are in fact multilevel (two-level) models, ones that explicitly acknowledge the fact that scores are clustered under individuals (i.e. repeated measures). A latent growth model is specified differently in MLM – specifically, time is treated as a predictor in MLM, but time is represented in SEM via factor loadings that designate measurement occasions (e.g. the set 0, 1, 2, 3 for the LS factor in Figure 26.3(b)) – but SEM and MLM computer programs generate the same basic parameter estimates for the same latent growth model. This point of isomorphism between MLM and SEM is a major basis for relating the two techniques (Curran, 2003).

Multiple-group analysis

Essentially any type of structural equation model can be analyzed across multiple samples. The main question addressed in a multiple-sample SEM is whether values of estimated model parameters vary appreciably across the groups. If so, then (1) group membership moderates the relations specified in the model (i.e. there is a group × model interaction), and (2) separate estimates of some model parameters may be needed for each group. The capability to simultaneously estimate a model across multiple samples adds much flexibility to SEM. This is also another point of contact between SEM and MLM. Specifically, some types of multilevel models can be represented as instances of multiple-group SEM (McArdle and Hamagami, 1996); this point is elaborated in the next section.

Many of the special strengths of SEM correspond to limitations of MLM. For example, it is possible to represent latent variables measured with multiple indicators as either predictor or outcome variables in SEM. As a consequence of this specification, measurement error is controlled in the analysis. Likewise, the estimation of direct or indirect effects is relatively straightforward in SEM. Finally, there are inferential tests of the fit of an entire structural equation model to sample data. This test is based on the familiar model (familiar in SEM) chi-square statistic with degrees of freedom that equal the differences between the number of observations (sample covariances and means) and parameters that require statistical estimates. More parsimonious models have greater degrees of freedom. The same model chi-square statistic can also be used to test the relative fit of two nested models, in this case where one model is a subset of the other. Except when analyzing a particular class of latent growth models, SEM does not directly take account of clustering in a multilevel dataset.

EXTENDING STRUCTURAL EQUATION MODELING TO MULTILEVEL ANALYSES

Early efforts to extend SEM were based on 'tricking' standard computer SEM programs into analyzing two-level models. The trick is to exploit the capability of the software to simultaneously estimate a structural equation model across two groups. However, in this case the 'groups' corresponded to two different models, a within-group or level-1 model and a between-group or level-2 model, both analyzed in the same complex sample. The data matrix for the level-1 model is the pooled within-group covariance matrix based on the variation of scores from individual cases around group means, and for the level-2 model it is the between-group covariance matrix based on the variation of the group means around the grand means. Because older versions of most SEM computer programs had no built-in capabilities for analyzing clustered data, it was usually necessary to calculate these two data matrices using an external program such as SPSS. The two data matrices were then submitted to the SEM computer program as external files or were included as part of the syntax (command) file.

Presented in Figure 26.4(a) is the model diagram for a two-level regression analysis conducted by tricking an SEM computer program into estimating a two-level model. This model corresponds to the hypothetical data represented in Figure 26.1 where the within-school covariance between television watching and achievement is negative, but the between-school covariance is positive. In Figure 26.4(a), the observed variables TV and Ach are each specified as the single indicator of a within-school factor and a between-school factor (e.g. $Ach_W \rightarrow Ach$, $Ach_B \rightarrow Ach$). The scaling constants for the within-school factors both equal 1, but for the between-school factors these constants equal the square root of the cluster n_C, or the number of cases in each school. Group size is constant in a balanced design; otherwise, it is calculated as

$$n_C = \frac{N^2 - \sum_{g=1}^{G} n_g^2}{N(G-1)} \tag{7}$$

where N is the total number of cases across all groups and G is the number of groups. At each level of the model in Figure 26.4(a), the Ach factor is regressed on the TV factor (i.e. $TV_W \rightarrow Ach_W$, $TV_B \rightarrow Ach_B$). This specification tells the computer to derive separate estimates of the within-school and between-school regression coefficients.

Listed in Table 26.1 is EQS syntax for analyzing the two-level regression model in Figure 26.4(a) as a two-group structural equation model. Although EQS 6.1 has special syntax for multilevel analyses, it is not used in this example. Instead, the syntax in the table indicates how to trick EQS into analyzing a two-level model as a two-group structural equation model. I assumed for this analysis, a balanced design where data are collected from $n_C = 50$ students in each of 100 different schools (i.e. $N = 5{,}000$). I also assumed equal and negative slopes of the within-school regression lines across the schools, which is consistent with the scatterplots represented in Figure 26.1.

Listed in the top part of Table 26.1 is syntax that specifies the within-school part of the model in Figure 26.4(a). This syntax also defines the pooled within-school covariance matrix, in which the observed covariance between the variables TV and Ach is –7.1 (see Table 26.1). Syntax for the between-school part of the model in Figure 26.4 is listed in the lower part of Table 26.1. Part of the trick of manual model set-up is to specify the within-school regression as part of the between-school model and to also impose equality constraints across the within- and between-school models on the corresponding parameter estimates. Finally, the between-school syntax in Table 26.1 defines the between-school model covariance matrix, in which the observed covariance between the variables TV and Ach is 10.6.

I submitted the syntax in Table 26.1 to EQS 6.1, and the analysis ran without problem. The model in Figure 26.4 perfectly fits the data because one regression coefficient is estimated between two variables at each level, so the total degrees of freedom are zero. However, what is more interesting here is that EQS calculates different coefficients for the regression of Ach on TV for the within-school versus between-school parts of the model. Specifically, the unstandardized (and standardized) values for the within-school and between-school models are, respectively, –0.710 (–0.502) and 1.180 (0.914). These results are consistent with the data representation in Figure 26.1. See Stapleton (2006) for additional examples.

Table 26.1 EQS syntax for manual set-up of the two-level regression model in Figure 26.4(a)

```
/title
within-school model
/specifications
cases=5000; variables=2; matrix=covariance; groups=2;
/labels
V1=TV; V2=Ach; F1=TV_W; F2=Ach_W;
/equations
V1=F1; V2=F2;
F2=*F1+D2;
/variances
F1=*; D2=*;
/matrix
10.0
-7.1 20.0
/end
/title
between-school model
/specifications
cases=100; variables=2; matrix=cov; method=ml;
/labels
V1=TV; V2=Ach; F1=TV_W; F2=Ach_W; F3=TV_B; F4=Ach_B;
/equations
F2=*F1+D2; F4=*F3+D4;
V1=F1+7.07F3; V2=F2+7.07F4;
/variances
F1=*; D2=*; F3=*; D4=*;
/matrix
25.0
10.6 45.0
/constraints
(1,F1,F1)=(2,F1,F1); (1,D2,D2)=(2,D2,D2);
(1,F2,F1)=(2,F2,F1);
/end
```

Although it is interesting that SEM computer programs can be tricked into analyzing a two-level model, there is a cost in terms of complexity. For example, the model diagram in Figure 26.4(a) and the syntax in Table 26.1 are both rather complicated for what is basically a trivial two-level regression analysis where both the slopes and intercepts do not vary or covary. If we rely on the same trick to analyze more realistic – and interesting – multilevel models, then the degree of complexity can quickly become daunting. For example, Bauer (2003) and Curran (2003) described how to specify and analyze the intercepts- and slopes-as-outcomes model defined by equations (3)–(6) using standard SEM notation and

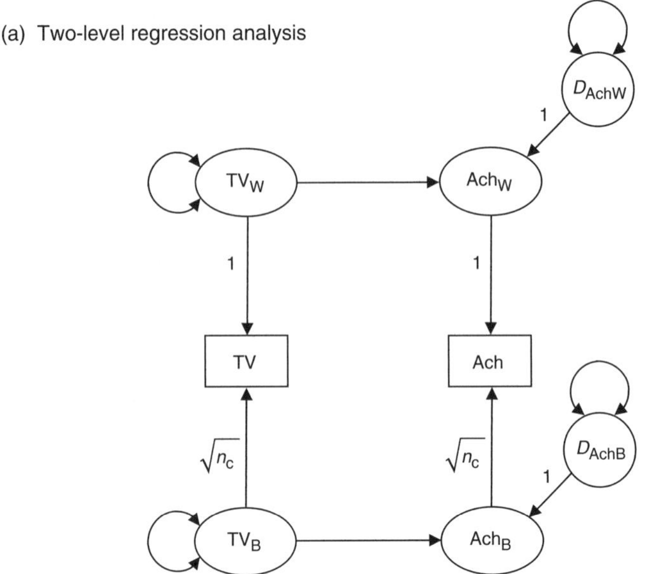

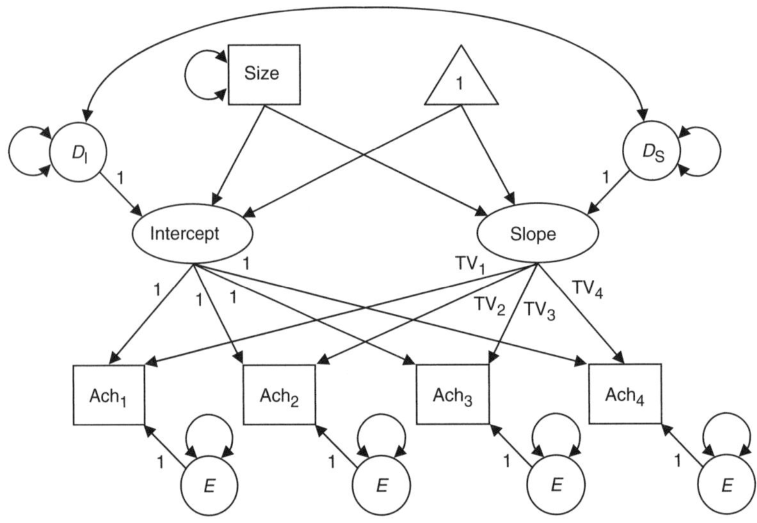

Figure 26.4 Diagrams for manual set-up in a computer program for structural equation modeling for a two-level regression analysis (a) and an intercepts- and slopes-as-outcomes model (b)

software without MLM capabilities (i.e. a variation of the trick). For simplicity's sake, let us assume a balanced design where only four students are selected from each of 100 different schools and also that there are no missing data (i.e. $n_C = 4$, $N = 400$). Scores on the variables TV and Ach are collected from each student as level-1 variables. Also, the size of each school is measured as a level-2 predictor of level-1 slopes and intercepts for the regression of Ach on TV across the schools.

Presented in Figure 26.4(b) is the structural equation model diagram for the multilevel regression analysis just described. At first glance, the model in Figure 26.4(b) resembles the latent growth model in Figure 26.3(b). Both models just mentioned have mean structures, latent variables that correspond to intercept and slope terms, and a predictor of the two terms. However, there are two crucial differences that make the model in Figure 26.4(b) much more difficult to analyze: First, the model in Figure 26.4(b) holds for just four students in a particular school. The achievement scores of the four students are designated in the figure as Ach_1, Ach_2, and so on. Because the ordering of the four scores in the data file is arbitrary, the four error terms associated with each score are constrained to have equal variances. The four achievement scores in Figure 26.4(b) are specified to load on an intercept factor and also on a slope factor. The intercept and slope concern the corresponding terms from the regression of the achievement scores on the television watching variable, TV, within this particular school. In Figure 26.4(b), the higher-order variable school size is specified as a predictor of the within-school intercept and slope. All loadings of the achievement indicators on the intercept factor equal 1, but the loadings on the slope factor are fixed to equal the scores on the television watching variable for each student. For example, the loading TV_1 for the path Slope $\rightarrow$ Ach_1 in Figure 26.4(b) is the score on the television watching variable for the first student.

Second, in an analysis of the model in Figure 26.4(b) across all schools, the computer must apply individual factor loading matrices where 'individual' actually means 'classroom'. That is, the factor loading matrix is unique to each classroom, and the elements of this matrix for the slope factor contain the observed scores on the TV variable for the students in each classroom (Curran, 2003). Not all SEM computer programs allow the specification of individual factor loading matrices, but one that does is Mx (Neale et al., 2002), a freely-available matrix algebra processor and numerical optimizer that can also estimate the full range of structural equation models. Analysis of the model in Figure 26.4(b) becomes even more complicated if the cluster size is a more realistic number (e.g. at least 100 students per school), and it becomes more complex still, if the design is unbalanced with unequal numbers of students in each school. Clearly, trying to trick an SEM computer program to estimate even a relatively simple multilevel regression quickly 'becomes a remarkably complex, tedious, and error-prone task' (Curran, 2003: 557), in other words, a data-management nightmare.

Fortunately, more and more computer programs for SEM feature special syntax that makes it easier to specify and estimate multilevel models. This is because use of this special syntax automates much of the analysis so that the computer, and not you, does most of work when analyzing multilevel models. For example, listed in Table 26.2 is Mplus syntax for the multilevel regression model defined by equations (3)–(6). The raw data are contained in the external

Table 26.2 Mplus syntax for the multilevel regression model defined by equations (3)–(6)

```
title: multilevel regression model
data: file = school.dat;
variable: names = Ach TV School Size;
within = TV;
between = Size;
cluster = School;
centering = grandmean (TV);
analysis: type = twolevel random;
model:
%within%
s | Ach ON TV;
%between%
Ach s ON Size;
Ach WITH s;
```

file called 'school.dat', and the four variables are Ach, TV, School (attended), and Size (total enrollment of school attended). Next, the Mplus syntax in Table 26.2 indicates that TV is the within-group or level-1 predictor, the cluster variable is School, and the between-school or level-2 predictor is Size. Grand-mean centering of the TV variable is specified, and the analysis type is specified as two-level with random coefficients (see the table). Mplus syntax for the within-school part of the model defines the slope, labeled 's', from the regression of Ach on TV as a random variable. Syntax for the between-school part of the model listed in Table 26.2 specifies that the random slopes and random intercepts are regressed on the school size variable and that the random terms just mentioned covary. That's all there is to it. In general, Mplus syntax for both SEM and MLM is concise and straightforward.

Presented in Figure 26.5 are two examples of how diagrams for multilevel models are represented in the Mplus manual (L.K. Muthén and B.O. Muthén, 1998–2010). Compared with RAM symbolism, these abbreviated diagrams are simpler and relatively easy to understand. For example, the model in Figure 26.5(a) is an abbreviated version of the standard SEM model in Figure 26.4(a) for the basic two-level regression analysis where Ach is regressed on TV both within schools and between schools. The model diagram in Figure 26.5(a) indicates that the same basic regression analysis is conducted at both levels. Residual variance in this model is represented by the lines with single arrowheads oriented at 45° angles that point to outcome variables. The model in Figure 26.5(b) is an abbreviated version of the standard SEM model in Figure 26.4(b) for the intercepts- and slopes-as-outcome model defined by equations (3)–(6). In the within part of the model in Figure 26.5(b), the filled circle at the end of the arrow from TV to Ach represents a random intercept, and the filled circle on the arrow from TV to Ach labeled 's' represents a random slope. In the between part of the model in Figure 26.5(b), the random intercept is referred to as Ach, and it appears as a circle because it is conceptualized as a continuous latent variable that varies

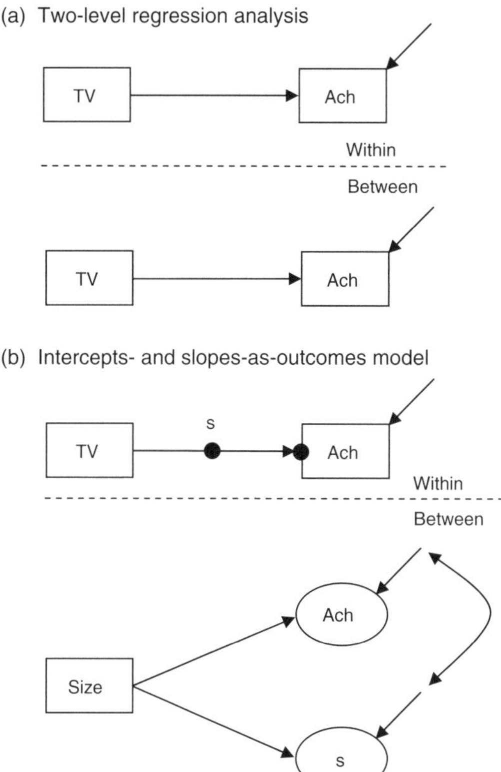

Figure 26.5 Abbreviated diagrams for a two-level regression analysis (a) and an intercepts- and slopes-as-outcomes model (b)

across schools. Also represented in the between part of the model is (1) size as a predictor of random intercepts and random slopes, and (2) a presumed covariance between the two random terms, Ach (intercepts) and 's' (slopes). A mean structure is implied in Figure 26.5(b) because intercepts are estimated, but it is not explicitly depicted as in RAM notation.

MULTILEVEL STRUCTURAL EQUATION MODELING

Multilevel structural equation models are usually estimated in three basic steps. The first involves calculation of UICC values for outcome variables across the levels of the cluster variable. If more than about 10% of the variance is explained by between-group variation, then the need for multilevel structural equation modeling (ML-SEM) may be indicated. The next two steps parallel those of two-step estimation of SR models in SEM, but for ML-SEM these steps correspond to analysis of the within-group model only prior to simultaneous estimation of the within- and between-group models. The goal is to distinguish specification error in either level, within versus between. Specifically, the within model is analyzed using just the pooled-within group covariances and means (i.e. the cluster variable is ignored). Although the fit of the within model may not be satisfactory due to the omission of between-group effects, the basic parameter estimates should nevertheless make sense. Next, the between model is specified, and then both the within and between models are simultaneously estimated using both the pooled within-group and between-group covariances and means. If the model is an intercepts- and slopes-as-outcomes-model, then between-group predictors of these random effects are added at the second step. Otherwise, one could specify the basic same model at the between level as for the within level. Poor model fit in this analysis may indicate the need to specify different models at within versus between levels. See Hox (2002) and Stapleton (2006) for description of additional possible analytic steps. Considered next are examples of ML-SEM.

This example of a multilevel path analysis (ML-PA) concerns a recent study by Wu (2007), who administered within a sample of 333 undergraduate students questionnaires about life satisfaction, what respondents say they want, or amount, and also of the gap between what they have and what they want, or have–want discrepancy. These questionnaires concerned 12 different life facets, including social support, health, physical safety, financial resources, and so on. Because ratings about life facets are repeated measures, Wu conceptualized that facets are nested under individuals. That is, the within-individual level concerns variation among facets for each respondent, and the total number of observations at this level equals 333 × 12, or 3,996. The between-individual level refers to differences across people that may affect ratings at the facet level, and the total number of observations at this level is 333. Values of the UICC across the 12 life facets ranged from 0.18–0.23, which indicate that about 18–23% of variance in life facet ratings is explained by between-individual variation.

At the both within and between levels, Wu hypothesized that both have–want discrepancy and amount have direct effects on life satisfaction and also that the former has an indirect effect through the latter (i.e. Discrepancy → Amount → Satisfaction). The structural model of the presumed direct and effects among these observed variables at the within level is presented in the top part of Figure 26.6(a). However, results of subsequent analyses indicated that a simpler structural model, one with no direct effect from amount to satisfaction, held at the between level, which is presented in the bottom part of Figure 26.6(a). That is, the effect of amount on satisfaction was mediated entirely by have–want discrepancy at the between-individual level, but not at the within-individual level where amount also directly affected satisfaction. Wu interpreted these results as suggesting that life satisfaction involves an explicit have–want comparison, but whether its effect is entirely indirect through its prior impact on overall amount of wants or not depends on the level of analysis, within- versus between-individuals. See Heck (2001) for description of an ML-PA where student characteristics, such as gender and minority status, and school characteristics, such as the degree of school quality, were specified as predictors of math skills

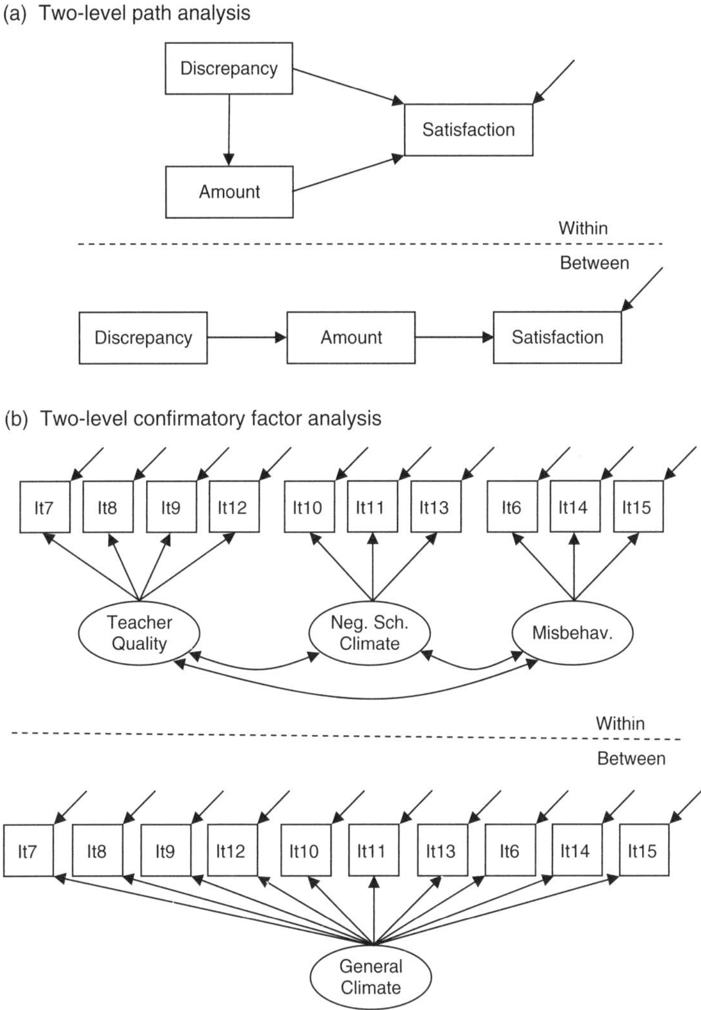

Figure 26.6 A multilevel path analysis model (a) and a multilevel confirmatory factor analysis model (b)

among Grade 8 students in, respectively, a within-school path model versus a between-school path model.

The next example concerns the multilevel analysis of a measurement model, that is, one with latent variables measured by multiple indicators. Using data from a sample of over 10,000 public school Grade 10 students who attended about 1,000 different schools in the United States, Kaplan (2000: 48–53) described the results of a single-level CFA of a 15-item questionnaire about perceptions of school climate. Items included those about perceptions of teacher quality (e.g. teachers seen as interested in students), negative school environment (e.g. feels unsafe at school), and misbehavior on the part of students (e.g. students often disrupt class) (see Kaplan, p. 42, for a complete list of all items). Kaplan found that a measurement model where 11 items were specified as indicators of three factors that corresponded to the three areas just mentioned had adequate fit to the data in the whole sample (i.e. ignoring school as a cluster variable).

In a subsequent analysis, Kaplan (pp. 136–40) conducted a multilevel confirmatory factor analysis (ML-CFA) in which the fact that students are nested under schools was explicitly represented. The ML-CFA model estimated by Kaplan is presented in Figure 26.6(b). The within-school CFA model in the figure is the same basic three-factor measurement model estimated by Kaplan in the single-level CFA. Names of the indicators in this model refer to questionnaire items (e.g. 'It7' in the figure means item no. 7). However, the measurement model at the between-school level in Figure 26.6(a) is a single-factor model where all indicators load one a general school climate factor. That is, this ML-CFA model reflects the hypothesis that within-school variation in student ratings is differentiated along three dimensions, but one general climate factor explains between school variation. This model had adequate fit to the hierarchical data for this analysis. See Dyer et al. (2005) for an example of an ML-CFA where organizational and national variables are included in models of the factor structure of leadership.

There are other many variations of ML-SEMs, including multilevel SR models, multilevel latent growth models, and so on. It is also possible to estimate intercepts- and slopes-as-outcome models where either predictor or outcome variables are latent variables measured with multiple indicators. An example of such a model is presented in Figure 26.7. The within model consists of a path model where the slopes and intercepts associated with all three paths are specified as random effects. In the between model, these slopes and intercepts are specified as outcome variables where the group-level predictor is a factor (A) measured by multiple indicators (X_2–X_4), which controls for measurement error at this level. The whole multilevel model in Figure 26.7 reflects the hypotheses that (1) the magnitudes of the intercepts and slopes associated with the direct effects at the individual level vary as a function of the group variable, and (2) the intercepts and slopes from each direct effect are pairwise correlated. This whole model in Figure 26.7 features the representation of indirect effects (within model) and also takes account of measurement error (between model), a combination relatively unique to the convergence of SEM and MLM.

CONCLUSION

Researchers who know something about both SEM and MLM can test an even wider range of hypotheses compared with those who know about one technique, but not the other. Specifically, the convergence of the two techniques in the form of ML-SEM offers the ability to (1) calculate correct standard errors in

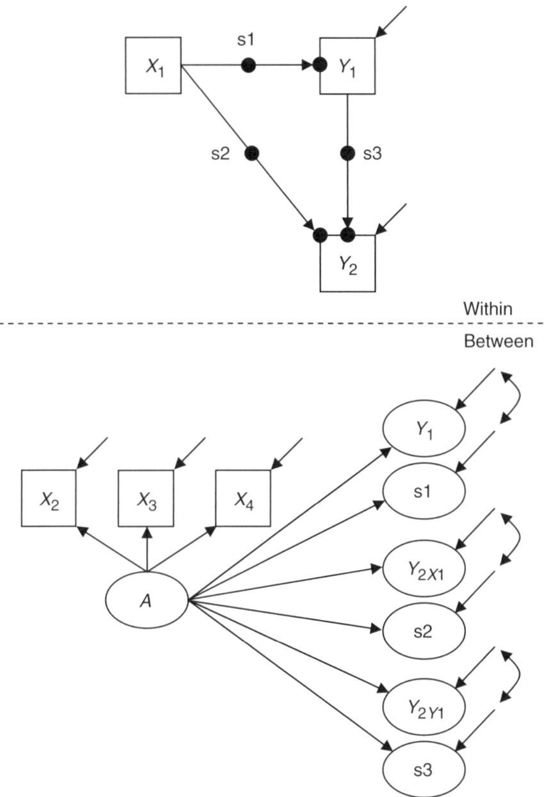

Figure 26.7 A multilevel structural equation model with indirect effects, a latent predictor measured by multiple indicators, and random intercepts and slopes

hierarchical datasets, (2) enter predictors from both the individual level and the group level (contextual effects) in the same analysis, (3) take account of unreliability when latent variables are represented as measured by multiple indicators, and (4) estimate both direct and indirect effects when structural models are analyzed, perhaps all in the same analysis depending on the model. The increasing availability of computer tools that directly support the analysis of multilevel structural equation models analyzed in complex samples is making it easier for researchers to actually reap these potential benefits. The costs for this increased flexibility in hypothesis testing include the need to make informed decisions about an even larger number of specification issues in ML-SEM compared with using either SEM alone or MLM alone. If these decisions are poor, then the results of ML-SEM may have little value, but this is true for any statistical modeling technique. Given good ideas based on relevant theory and results of empirical studies, though, it may be possible to better represent them in ML-SEM compared with either SEM or MLM alone.

NOTES

1 Code for conducting certain types of multilevel analyses in R, a free software environment for statistical computing and graphics production, is available in works such as de Leeuw (2008).

2 There are also examples of R code for SEM analyses; see Fox (2006).

REFERENCES

Anderson, J.C. and Gebring, D.W. (1988). Structural equation modeling in practice: A review and recommended two-step approach. *Psychological Bulletin*, 103: 411–23.

Bauer, D.J. (2003). Estimating multilevel linear models as structural equation models. *Journal of Educational and Behavioral Statistics*, 28: 135–67.

Bentler, P.M. (2005). EQS 6.1 for Windows [computer software]. Encino, CA: Multivariate Software.

Bickel, R. (2007). *Multilevel Analysis for Applied Research: It's Just Regression!* New York: Guilford Press.

Cohen, J. (1968). Multiple regression as a general data-analytic system. *Psychological Bulletin*, 70: 426–43.

Curran, P.J. (2003). Have multilevel models been structural equation models all along? *Multivariate Behavioral Research*, 38: 529–69.

de Leeuw, J. (2008). Multilevel analysis in R with a broken-line example. Retrieved 2 February, 2009, from http://repositories.cdlib.org/cgi/ viewcontent.cgi?article=1316&context=uclastat

Dyer, N.G., Hanges, P.J., and Hall, R.J. (2005), Applying multilevel confirmatory factor analysis techniques to the study of leadership. *The Leadership Quarterly*, 16: 149–67.

Fan, X. (1997). Canonical correlation analysis and structural equation modeling: What do they have in common? *Structural Equation Modeling*, 4: 65–79.

Fox, R. (2006). Structural equation modeling with the sem package in R. *Structural Equation Modeling*, 13: 465–86.

Gardner, H. (1999). *The Disciplined Mind: What all Students Should Understand.* New York: Simon & Schuster.

Heck, R.H. (2001). Multilevel modeling with SEM. In G.A. Marcoulides and R.E. Schumaker (eds) *New Developments in Techniques in Structural Equation Modeling*, pp. 89–127. Mahwah, NJ: Erlbaum.

Hox, J. (2002). *Multilevel Analysis: Techniques and Applications.* Mahwah, NJ: Erlbaum.

Jöreskog, K.G. and Sörbom, D. (2006). LISREL 8.8 for Windows [computer software]. Lincolnwood, IL: Scientific Software International.

Kaplan, D. (2000). *Structural Equation Modeling: Foundations and Extensions.* Thousand Oaks, CA: Sage.

Krull, J.L., and MacKinnon, D.P. (2001). Multilevel modeling of individual and group level mediated effects. *Multivariate Behavioral Research*, 36: 249–77.

Lombardo, T. (n.d.). *The Pursuit of Wisdom and the Future of Education.* Retrieved 29 March 2008, from http://www.odysseyofthefuture.net/pdf_files/Readings/ Pursuit_Wisdom-Short.pdf

Longley, P.A., Goodchild, M.F., Maguire, D.J., and Rhind, D.W. (2005). *Geographic Information Systems and Science*, 2nd edn. New York: Wiley.

Maas, C.J.M., and Hox, J.J. (2005). Sufficient sample sizes for multilevel modeling. *Methodology*, 3: 86–92.

MacCallum, R.C., Zhang, S., Preacher, K.J., and Rucker, D.O. (2002). On the practice of dichotomization of quantitative variables. *Psychological Methods*, 7: 19–40.

McArdle, J.J. and Hamagami, F. (1996). Multilevel models from a multiple group structural equation perspective. In G.A. Marcoulides and R.E. Schumaker (eds) *Advanced Structural Equation Modeling*, pp. 89–124. Mahwah, NJ: Erlbaum.

McArdle, J.J. and McDonald, R.P. (1984). Some algebraic properties of the reticular action model for moment structures. *British Journal of Mathematical and Statistical Psychology*, 37: 234–51.

Muthén, B.O. (1994). Multilevel covariance structure analysis. *Sociological Methods and Research*, 22: 376–98.

Muthén, L., and Muthén, B. (1998–2010). MPlus 6 [computer software]. Los Angeles: Muthén and Muthén.

Neale, M.C., Boker, S.M., Xie, G., and Maes, H.H. (2002). *Mx: Statistical Modeling*, 6th edn. Richmond: Virginia Commonwealth University, Virginia Institute for Psychiatric & Geriatric Genetics.

Rabe-Hesketh, S., Skrondal, A., and Zheng, X. (2007). Multilevel structural equation modeling. In S.-Y. Lee (ed.) *Handbook of Computing and Statistics with Applications: Vol. 1. Handbook of Latent Variable and Related Models*, pp. 209–27. Amsterdam: Elsevier.

Rasbash, R., Steele, F., Browne, W., and Prosser, B. (2005). MLwiN 2.02 [computer software]. Bristol, UK: Centre for Multilevel Modeling, University of Bristol.

Raudenbush, S.W. and Bryk, A.S. (2002). *Hierarchical Linear Models*, 2nd edn. Thousand Oaks, CA: Sage.

Raudenbush, S.W., Bryk, A.S., and Cheong, Y.F. (2008). HLM 6.06 for Windows [computer software]. Lincolnwood, IL: Scientific Software International.

Stapleton, L.M. (2006). Using multilevel structural equation modeling techniques with complex sample data. In G.R. Hancock and R.O. Mueller (eds) *Structural Equation Modeling: A Second Course*, pp. 345–83. Greenwich, CT: Information Age Publishing.

Thompson, B. (2000). Ten commandments of structural equation modeling. In L.G. Grimm and P.R. Yarnold (eds) *Reading and Understanding More Multivariate Statistics*, pp. 261–83. Washington, DC: American Psychological Association Books.

Thompson, B. (2006). *Foundations of Behavioral Statistics: An Insight-Based Approach*. New York: Guilford Press.

Wu, C.-H. (2007, October 25). The role of perceived discrepancy in satisfaction evaluation. *Social Indicators Research Online First*. Retrieved 19 March 2008, from http://www.springerlink.com/content/k2348v012u38620g/fulltext.pdf

27

Hierarchical Linear and Structural Equation Modeling Approaches to Mediation Analysis in Randomized Field Experiments

Keenan Pituch and Laura Stapleton

Experimental designs are often appealing to researchers because of their ability to demonstrate causal relations. For applied researchers and the general public, results of randomized experiments can provide vital information, such as whether a newly developed diabetes drug more effectively reduces blood glucose levels, whether a new therapy approach helps troubled youth to better manage feelings of anger, and whether a new teaching method promotes increased reading comprehension. Because well-executed experiments provide a rigorous test of the impact of a treatment, they are generally considered the 'gold standard' in evaluating the effects of interventions and programs.

To test whether the effects of an intervention hold in real-life settings, such as schools and workplaces, researchers use randomized field trials. As noted by Kellam and Langevin (2003), randomized field trials are especially useful in effectiveness studies. In such a study, the goal is to identify if the effects of a treatment, which had previously been found to be effective in 'ideal' and more local settings, such as in a lab or in one school, work just as well when delivered in multiple and more natural field settings. Randomized field trials have been effectively used to identify successful treatments in such fields as medical research, criminology, health sciences, social policy, and psychology. Although debate continues on the issue of the appropriate role of randomized field trials in some fields, such as education (Chatterji, 2004; Eisenhart and Towne, 2003; Olson, 2004), the demand to use this method, as seen in current federal policy guidelines (Institute of Education Sciences, 2003; What Works Clearinghouse, 2005), ensures the continued use of large-scale randomized studies in educational field settings.

In conducting randomized field trials, researchers have two general large-scale experimental designs from which to choose. In the first, the *cluster-randomized trial*, clusters or groups of people, instead of individuals, are randomly assigned to treatment conditions. This design is used to prevent treatment diffusion, or the 'spread' of the treatment to the control condition(s), which may result when different treatments are implemented in the same setting, such as in schools or workplaces. The design is also a logical choice when an intervention is to be delivered to an entire organization, such as a hospital or community, and when assignment of individuals to treatments is not feasible. The cluster-randomized trial has been used in fields such as public health, education, and sociology (Borman et al., 2005; Boruch, 2005; Donner and Klar, 2000; Murray, 1998; Varnell et al., 2004).

A second large-scale design that is widely used is the *multisite trial* (Finn and Achilles, 1990; Mosteller, 1995; Plewis and Hurry, 1998; Raudenbush and Liu, 2000). In this design, individuals are randomly assigned to treatments within a given site, with this treatment assignment process repeated across many sites. Since treatment and control conditions are implemented at each of several sites, each site provides a potentially unique estimate of the treatment effect. In this design, researchers can then estimate not only the overall effect of the treatment but can determine if treatment effects vary across sites. If effects differ across sites, researchers can test or explore site-level factors that may moderate or change the strength of the treatment. Such knowledge suggests factors that may strengthen or impede the effects of an intervention.

In addition to the overall or total effect of a treatment, the mediating or indirect effect of a treatment is often of interest. For a single-mediator model, a mediator is a variable that is caused by the treatment and is assumed to be causally related to the final outcome of interest. Figure 27.1 shows a basic mediation model, in which the treatment (T) is hypothesized to cause the mediator (M), which is hypothesized to be a cause of the final outcome of interest (Y). In terms of one of the preceding examples, a newly developed diabetes drug (T) is intended to regulate blood glucose levels (M) more effectively than the competing drug, which then leads to a reduced risk of stroke (Y). In Figure 27.1, path a represents the impact of the treatment on the mediator (the impact of the drug on blood glucose levels), path b represents the relation of the mediator to the outcome (between blood glucose levels and risk of stroke), controlling for the treatment, and path c'

represents the effect of the treatment on the outcome (the impact of the drug on the risk of stroke, controlling for the blood glucose). Path c' is also referred to as the direct effect of the treatment. The product of paths a and b is typically used to represent the mediating or indirect effect of the treatment on the outcome (the impact of the drug on risk of stroke via its effect on blood glucose). Given that a treatment effect has been observed, mediation is usually considered to be present when the ab product, or indirect effect, is statistically significant.

For experiments, testing indirect effects and the paths involved in the indirect effects provides vital information to researchers. In essence, a hypothesized mediation model depicts *how* an intervention attains its impact. That is, it is a theory for how the intervention works. Testing the indirect effects of a treatment then provides a test of this theory, which may provide support for the processes or mechanisms thought to be the key to effective treatments. Others wishing to replicate the success of this program may then, wisely perhaps, focus the efforts of the intervention on the mediating variables. As mentioned by MacKinnon (2008: 378), researchers may also wish to design studies where the mediator is manipulated, in order to check on its status as a causal variable.

Further, testing specific paths involved in an indirect effect may lead to improvements in the intervention. For example, if a treatment impacts the mediator but the mediator is not related to the outcome, this finding suggests that the 'wrong' mediator may have been targeted. This information may encourage program developers to rethink how the program attains its effects. Also, if a treatment, unexpectedly, has no impact on a mediator, this 'null' finding may indicate problems in the delivery of the treatment and force program developers to find ways to improve treatment implementation. For these reasons, the importance of testing mediation models has been widely recognized (Judd and Kenny, 1981; MacKinnon, 2008; Pituch, 2004).

The interest in testing mediation models has been extended to large-scale studies. Kenny et al. (1998) and Krull and MacKinnon (1999, 2001) were among the first to present statistical models to test for mediation in large-scale studies, such as the multisite and cluster-randomized experimental designs mentioned above. Similarly, Pituch and others (2005, 2006, 2008), extending the work largely of MacKinnon and others (2002, 2004), evaluated new and more powerful procedures to test indirect effects for these two large-scale experimental designs. This research, however, was limited to cases where the size of the indirect effect was assumed to be the same from site to site. Such an indirect effect is known as a fixed effect.

However, in the multisite trial, the indirect effect may be a random effect. That is, just like the effect of the treatment in this design, the size of the indirect effect may differ from site to site. If so, the indirect effect takes on a different expected value than in the fixed effect case and also has a different standard error. Kenny et al. (2003) presented statistical models for estimating and testing such random indirect effects. More recently, Bauer et al. (2006) provided an improved modeling procedure that can be used to test for random indirect effects and to identify whether the indirect effect depends on or is moderated by a site characteristic.

While the research literature has presented statistical models for both fixed and random indirect effects, nearly all of this literature focuses on either the fixed or random effect. That is, it is difficult to find a more comprehensive treatment of indirect effects for large-scale experimental designs. Similarly, virtually all of the research literature illustrates multilevel mediation analysis from either a hierarchical linear modeling (HLM) (Krull and MacKinnon, 1999, 2001; Pituch and Stapleton, 2008; Pituch et al., 2005, 2006) or a structural equation modeling (SEM) perspective (Cheung, 2007; Raykov and Mels, 2007). Yet, there are advantages and disadvantages for using each of these modeling approaches.

In this chapter, we present statistical models and testing procedures, both from the HLM and SEM approach, that can be used to capture the mediating effects of a treatment for the cluster-randomized and multisite experimental designs described above. In addition, we present models that can be used to test the indirect effect when this effect is fixed and random. By presenting both the fixed and random indirect effect cases in the same chapter, we hope that applied researchers will be able to easily distinguish when the indirect effect may and may not be a random effect. Such knowledge should enable researchers to use proper and more powerful statistical procedures for either case. Similarly, by presenting and highlighting the differences offered by the HLM and SEM approaches to multilevel mediation analysis, we seek to help researchers select and implement an analysis approach that is well suited to their experimental design.

The next section of the chapter presents mediation analysis via the HLM approach for the cluster-randomized design, which is followed by the HLM approach for mediation analysis for the multisite trial. After the HLM sections, the SEM approach to multilevel mediation analysis is illustrated. In this SEM section, we show how each of the models presented previously can be recast as multilevel structural equation models. Since most readers, we anticipate, are less familiar with the SEM approach, we present several figures to facilitate understanding of these models and provide Mplus syntax to help readers carry out the multilevel SEM analyses. Finally, the Discussion section compares and contrasts these two approaches.

THE CLUSTER-RANDOMIZED DESIGN

In the two-level cluster randomized design in which the final outcome of interest is an individual-level variable, two types of mediation designs are possible, depending on the level at which the mediator is measured. One possibility is to measure the mediator at the individual level. This design would be used when researchers believe that the key to impacting an outcome is by first changing individual behavior. For example, in teacher education research, this design may be used when a school-based professional development program is intended to improve the final outcome of teachers' ability to teach reading comprehension. But, in order to do so, this intervention must first impact teachers' knowledge of how students learn to read and how teachers can best help students read more proficiently. Note that since organizations (schools) would be randomly assigned to treatments in this design and the treatment variable, as presented below, is at the second or upper level of the statistical model, this design is known as the $2 \rightarrow 1 \rightarrow 1$ design. This notation indicates that the treatment is at the second level, (as all teachers within a given school receive either the treatment or control condition), the mediator (teacher knowledge) is at the first level, and the outcome (teacher skill) is at the first level. We will also refer to mediation in this design as *cross-level mediation*, because the treatment (at the upper level of the design) attains its effects via an individual-level mediator (at the lower level of the design).

A second possibility in the two-level cluster randomized trial is that the mediator is a variable that describes an attribute associated with an organization. Assume that, in the preceding example, the treatment will not work well until principals 'buy into' the reading strategies used by teachers. That is, the intervention must first affect principal support (the mediator) of the reading strategies used in the school, and principals who are more supportive of their school's reading strategies would be expected to encourage their teachers to use them more effectively in the classroom. Note that although the school principal is an individual, the values of this variable (principal support) cannot vary within a school, unless it is measured over time, as there is only one principal per school. Thus, this design is known as a $2 \rightarrow 2 \rightarrow 1$ design, because the treatment and mediator are school-level variables, while the outcome of interest (teacher skill) is at the individual level. We will refer to such a mediation model as *upper-level mediation*, because the school-based treatment effects are mediated by a variable at the upper level of the design. Note that *lower-level mediation*, in which the treatment, mediator, and outcome are all individual-level variables, or at the lower level of the data structure, will be covered later in the chapter under the multisite experimental design.

To illustrate the analyses suggested below for the cluster-randomized trial, the preceding examples will be used along with simulated data for the following hypothetical scenarios. In these scenarios, a school-based professional development program is implemented with the intention of improving teaching skill (the final outcome of interest). For the $2 \rightarrow 1 \rightarrow 1$ design, the hypothesized mediator is at the teacher level (teacher knowledge), while in the $2 \rightarrow 2 \rightarrow 1$ design, the hypothesized mediator is at the school level (principal support). For each design, a total of 40 schools are randomized to either a treatment (focused professional development) or a wait-listed control condition. We simulated data for 800 teachers for the 40 schools (20 teachers per school who have significant reading responsibilities). Scores for the mediator and outcome were generated from normally distributed populations. A dummy-coded variable is used to represent treatment condition, with a value of 0 representing the control and 1 representing the treatment schools. Readers interested in replicating the analyses shown below may contact the authors to request these data sets. In addition, we limit the presentation to results that are most relevant to answering the research questions. Other data analysis considerations, such as examining the data for outliers and assessing whether the statistical assumptions are reasonably satisfied, are not addressed.

For the illustration below, the following research questions are of interest:

1 Does the treatment work? That is, do teachers who receive the focused professional development foster better teaching skills than the control teachers? Such an expectation may be present if the intervention were thoughtfully developed and well executed.
2 Given that the teacher development program is effective, does the intervention attain its success through a mediating variable? For the 2 → 1 → 1 design, the hypothesized mediator is teacher knowledge, while in the 2 → 2 → 1 design, the hypothesized mediator is principal support. We also consider a design in which mediating variables are present at both the lower and upper levels. For each of the examples below, estimating and testing the direct and indirect effects of the treatment is a key study goal.

Cross-level mediation (2 → 1 → 1 design)

For this mediation design, the treatment is at the second level of the model and the mediator and outcome are at the first level. In order to estimate paths *a* and *b* of Figure 27.1, a 'separate-equations' approach can be used. As the name suggests, separate equations are used for the mediator and outcome to estimate the effects of interest. To estimate *path a* of Figure 27.1, the following level-1 and level-2 models are used:

$$M_{ij} = \beta_{0j} + r_{ij}, \tag{1}$$

$$\beta_{0j} = \gamma_{00} + \gamma_{01} T_j + u_{0j}, \tag{2}$$

where M_{ij} represents the mediator for a given teacher *i* in school *j*, and T_j is the dummy-coded treatment variable (1= treatment, 0 = control). Because there are no explanatory variables in equation (1), β_{0j} represents the mediator mean for a given school *j*, and r_{ij} is the deviation between a given teacher's score on the mediator and the corresponding school mean. At the school level, due to the dummy coding used for T_j, γ_{00} is the school mediator mean for control schools, and γ_{01} is the difference in mediator means between the treatment and control schools, or is path *a*. The u_{0j} term is a residual at the school level. Also, σ^2 and τ_{00} are the residual variances at the teacher and school levels, respectively.

To obtain an estimate of paths *b* and *c*', the outcome is modeled as a function of the mediator and treatment status. The level-1 and level-2 models are as follows:

$$Y_{ij} = \beta'_{0j} + \beta'_{1j} M_{ij} + r'_{ij}, \tag{3}$$

$$\beta'_{0j} = \gamma'_{00} + \gamma'_{01} T_j + u'_{C}, \tag{4}$$

$$\beta'_{1j} = \gamma'_{10}, \tag{5}$$

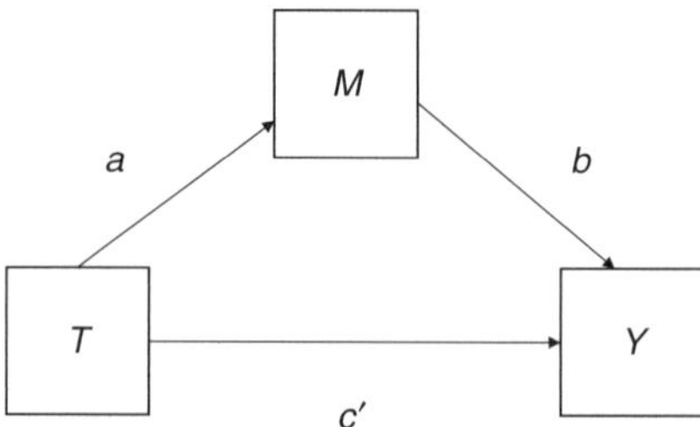

Figure 27.1 A basic mediation model

where Y_{ij} represents the outcome for individual *i* in school *j*, and M_{ij} and T_j are the same as defined above. Thus, γ'_{01} represents the impact of the treatment on the outcome, after controlling for the mediator (or path *c*' of Figure 27.1), and γ'_{10} represents the relationship between the mediator and outcome, controlling for the treatment (or path *b* of Figure 27.1). Note that, as explained in Pituch et al. (2010), group-mean centering should not be used in equation (3) for the mediator because path *c*' would not be estimated properly (it would remain the total or unmediated effect of the treatment). Thus, either no or grand-mean centering are good choices for the mediator in equation (3). Also, while we have modeled the relationship between the mediator and outcome as a fixed effect, a residual term may be added to equation (5) without altering the expression for the indirect effect. Further, σ'^2 and τ'_{00} are the residual variances at the teacher and school levels, respectively.

In this cluster-randomized experimental design, the indirect effect is a fixed effect. For the indirect effect to be a random effect, both paths *a* and *b* of Figure 27.1 must vary. However, path *a*, represented by γ_{01} in equation (2), is a fixed effect as it is at the highest level of the model. That is, there is no upper-level organization (such as district) across which this effect may vary. While path *b* may be modeled in this design as a random effect, by including a residual term in equation (5), the indirect effect is still regarded as fixed because path *a* cannot vary. Thus, in this model, the indirect effect takes the standard expression as the product of paths *a* and *b* and is:

$$\text{Indirect Effect} = (\gamma_{01})(\gamma'_{10}). \quad (6)$$

Illustration and results

Recall that in this $2 \rightarrow 1 \rightarrow 1$ example the treatment is the school-based professional development program designed to help teachers more effectively implement strategies used to teach reading. The mediator is a measure tapping the knowledge that each teacher has about how students learn to read, and the outcome is teacher skill at teaching reading strategies. To estimate the total effect of the treatment, we use equations (3) and (5), except that the mediator (M_{ij}) is not included in this analysis. Thus, equation (5) is also not used due to the exclusion of the mediator, and γ'_{01} now represents this total effect of the treatment on teacher skills. For this illustration, this treatment effect estimate is 0.404, with this effect being statistically significant ($SE = 0.123$, $p = 0.002$). Given that the standard deviation of the teaching skills measure is 1.17, the effect of the program is about 0.35 standard deviations, which is generally considered a nontrivial effect. Thus, these results support the idea that the professional development program helps improve teaching skills. Also, after including the treatment variable in the model, the teaching skill means vary across schools ($\tau'_{00} = 0.087$, $p < 0.001$), indicating the need to include a variance component at the school level.

To determine if the professional development program impacts teacher knowledge, as is expected, equations (1) and (2) are used. The results support the hypothesis that the professional development program impacts teacher knowledge as γ_{01}, or path a, is 0.687 and is statistically significant ($SE = 0.124$, $p < 0.001$). Given that the standard deviation of the teacher knowledge measure is 1.12, the treatment effect is equivalent to 0.61 standard deviations, indicative of a fairly strong treatment effect. To identify if teachers with greater knowledge also translate that into more skillful use of teaching strategies, equations (3)–(5) are used. As γ'_{10} is 0.414 ($SE = 0.036$, $p < 0.001$), teachers with more in-depth knowledge of using reading strategies are more skilled at implementing these strategies. Accordingly, the direct effect of the treatment (γ'_{01}) is 0.120, which is smaller in size than the treatment effect obtained previously and not statistically significant ($SE = 0.126$, $p = 0.348$).

To formally test the indirect effect of the professional development program on teacher skill, we use the PRODCLIN program (MacKinnon et al., 2007). This program obtains critical values from the distribution of the product of two normally distributed random variables to form a confidence interval estimate of the indirect effect. This product is generally nonnormally distributed, and this method that takes account of this nonnormality has outperformed methods that have been more commonly used to test for mediation for both single-level and multilevel mediation designs (MacKinnon et al., 2004; Pituch and Stapleton, 2008; Pituch et al., 2005, 2006). Briefly, in computing this confidence interval, the indirect effect is estimated and then the product of (a) the critical values mentioned above and (b) the standard error of the indirect effect is added to and subtracted from the estimated indirect effect. The Sobel (1982) standard error is used in this confidence interval, and this standard error is $\sqrt{a^2 o_b^2 + b^2 o_a^2}$, where a and b represent paths a and b, and o_a and o_b represent the standard errors of these paths.

For this example, the point estimate of the indirect effect (0.687×0.414) is 0.285, with the Sobel (1982) standard error equal to 0.057. The 95% confidence interval for the indirect effect provided by the PRODCLIN program is 0.177 to 0.401, supporting the presence of this effect in the population. Thus, there is support for the hypothesis that part of the impact of the professional development program on teacher skill is through increasing teacher knowledge. Further, in terms of standard deviations, the indirect effect is equivalent to 0.24 standard deviations (0.285/1.17) of the teacher skills measure, indicating an important indirect effect of the professional development program. Note that randomization of schools provides confidence in the causal inference associated with the total effect of the program on teacher skill. However, a correctly specified model is needed to provide a similar level of confidence for the causal claims associated with the direct and indirect effects of the program. Serious specification error, for example, the failure to include another important mediator, may introduce substantial bias in the estimates of the direct and indirect effects. In particular, given the use of grand-mean centering, the within-school slope associated with the mediator may be estimated with bias if the aggregate of the mediator has a different association with the outcome, as suggested in Raudenbush and Bryk (2002: 136). A mediation model that includes both a level-1 mediator and its aggregate that avoids this potential problem is treated later in this chapter.

Upper-level mediation (2 → 2 → 1 design)

In this cluster-randomized experimental design, schools are randomly assigned to treatments but the mediator is now measured at the school level. Thus, while the separate-equations approach can be used, the equation for the mediator is a single-level equation, with all the variables being at the school level. Thus, this equation is

$$M_j = \gamma_{00} + \gamma_{01} T_j + u_{0j}, \tag{7}$$

where M_j is the school-level mediator and T_j remains the dummy-coded treatment indicator variable (1 = treatment, 0 = control). Thus, γ_{01} is path a of Figure 27.1. Again, as in the cross-level mediation design, path a cannot be a random effect in this design because there is no upper-level unit across which this effect may vary. Thus, the indirect effect is a fixed effect. The typical ab product and Sobel (1982) standard error can then be used to estimate and test the indirect effect, as in the previous design.

Multilevel equations for the outcome are also needed to estimate paths b and c' of Figure 27.1. The first and second levels of this model are:

$$Y_{ij} = \beta'_{0j} + r'_{ij}, \tag{8}$$

$$\beta'_{0j} = \gamma'_{00} + \gamma'_{01} M_j + \gamma'_{02} T_j + u'_{0j}, \tag{9}$$

where Y_{ij} is the outcome score for student i in school j, and β'_{0j} represents the school mean for the outcome. At the second level of the model, the school-level mediator (M_j) and treatment variable (T_j) are included. Thus, γ'_{01} represents path b of Figure 27.1, and γ'_{02} represents path c'. In this mediation design, the fixed indirect effect is then

$$\text{Indirect Effect} = (\gamma_{01})(\gamma'_{01}). \tag{10}$$

Illustration and results

Recall that in this example the treatment is the school-based professional development program designed to help teachers more effectively implement strategies used to teach reading. For this example, the mediator is a measure tapping principal support for the reading strategies used in the school, and the final outcome of interest is teacher skill in implementing the reading strategies. To estimate the total effect of the program, we use equations (8) and (9), but, as in the previous example, omit the mediator from the model. As a result, γ'_{01} now represents the treatment effect, as the treatment variable is the only explanatory variable in the model. For this illustration, the estimate of this effect is 0.292 ($SE = 0.140$, $p = 0.040$), indicating that teachers in the professional development program develop greater teaching skill than control school teachers. Given that the standard deviation of the outcome across all 800 teachers is 1.10, this represents a fairly modest treatment effect of approximately one-quarter of a standard deviation. The variance of the school-level residuals is 0.144 ($p < 0.001$), indicating that, after controlling for the treatment indicator variable, the teacher skill means vary across schools.

To determine if principal support for the reading strategies used in schools is enhanced by the professional development program, we use equation (6). Principal support is positively impacted by the professional development, as γ_{01}, or path a, is 0.710 ($SE = 0.111$, $p < 0.001$). As the standard deviation of principal support is 0.50, this indicates a strong effect of the program on principal support. To identify if greater principal support is associated with more effective use of teaching strategies, equations (8) and (9) are used. Principal support is positively associated with teaching skill ($\gamma'_{01} = 0.573$, $SE = 0.184$, $p = 0.004$). The direct effect of the program (γ'_{02}) is –0.115 ($SE = 0.182$, $p = 0.532$), suggesting that no impact of the treatment remains after principal support is taken into account.

To estimate the indirect effects of the program on teacher skill, we use the PRODCLIN program. The point estimate of the indirect effect is 0.407, and the 95% confidence interval for this effect ranges from 0.144 to 0.714, indicating support for the indirect effect in the population. As such, this finding is consistent with the idea that the professional development program impacts teacher skill by first strengthening the support of principals for the reading strategies used in the school. Further, if the insignificant direct effect were dropped from the model, this implies that the total treatment effect is entirely indirect via principal support and is 0.407. This implied total treatment effect is about 37% of the standard deviation for teacher skill, suggesting a fairly strong impact of the professional development program on teacher skill via principal support.

Cross- and upper-level mediation (2 → 1 → 1 and 2 → 2 → 1 design)

One final mediation design considered here for the cluster-randomized trial combines aspects of the two previous models. Specifically, the design involves a level-1 mediator, such as teacher knowledge, but allows for the possibility that the aggregate of that variable (teacher collective knowledge) may also serve as a mediator. As indicated in Raudenbush and Bryk (2002), if the impact of a level-1 predictor (e.g. individual knowledge) on an outcome differs from the impact of the same but aggregated level-1 predictor (e.g. mean teacher knowledge) on the outcome, a contextual effect is said to be present. Below, we present a statistical model that can be used to test for the possible contextual effect associated with a mediator. The primary research question of interest we address is this: Does the collective knowledge of teachers in a school contribute any additional mediating effect beyond that contributed by individual teacher knowledge?

To incorporate the individual and group effects of a mediator, the following equations may be used. Equations (1)–(5) may be used with the exception that the mediator mean (mean teacher knowledge) is now added as an explanatory variable to equation (4). Thus, path c' is represented by γ'_{01} of equation (4). Note that there would be two estimates for path *a* in this example. One estimate is represented by γ_{01} in equation (2), which uses the individual teacher knowledge scores to arrive at the impact of the treatment on teacher knowledge. Another estimate of path *a* involves using the mean scores for the mediator (i.e. teacher collective knowledge) as the outcome and regressing these mean scores on the treatment variable. In this example, the estimates of both *a* paths are identical, because treatment and control means are identical when individual scores or cluster mean values of these scores are used as the dependent variable. Note, however, that if a cluster- or school-level measure of a mediator were not based on averaging individual scores (e.g. a school-level measure of group norms), then the estimates of the *a* paths would, in general, be different.

In addition to two estimates of path *a*, two estimates of the impact of the mediator on the outcome would be obtained. The first estimate involves the effect of individual teacher knowledge on the outcome, after controlling for mean teacher knowledge. We refer to this effect as path *b*, which is represented by γ'_{10} of equation (5). The second estimate is the effect of collective teacher knowledge on the outcome after controlling for the impact of individual teacher knowledge, or path *B*, which is captured by the new term (γ'_{02}) that would appear in Equation (4) due to adding the mediator mean to that equation. Thus, two indirect effects would then be present in this model: (γ_{01})(γ'_{10}) represents the indirect effect of the treatment through individual teacher knowledge, controlling for mean teacher knowledge and (γ_{01})(γ'_{02}) represents the indirect effect of the treatment through mean teacher knowledge, after controlling for individual teacher knowledge. Note, again, that path *a* cannot vary across organizations in this design because this effect is at the highest level (i.e. school) in this example. Thus, these indirect effects are fixed, and not random, effects.

ILLUSTRATION AND RESULTS

We use the same example as presented for the cross-level mediation design above. In that example, the effect of the treatment, without including any mediators, is 0.404 ($SE = 0.123$, $p = 0.002$) indicating that the professional development program improves teacher skills. Similarly, from this previous analysis, path a is 0.687 ($SE = 0.124$, $p < 0.001$), indicating that the treatment impacts teacher knowledge. As noted above, the same estimate and standard error were obtained when we regressed mean teacher knowledge on the treatment indicator variable.

To conclude the mediation analysis, equations (3)–(5) are used, with the exception that the mean teacher knowledge is now included as an explanatory variable in equation (4). Path b, linking individual teacher knowledge to teacher skill, is 0.426 ($SE = 0.037$, $p < 0.001$), and path B, linking mean teacher knowledge to that same outcome is –0.235 ($SE = 0.164$, $p = 0.159$). Thus, after controlling for individual teacher knowledge, there is no apparent impact of mean teacher knowledge on teacher skill. Since there is no contextual effect associated with mean teacher knowledge, we estimate and test the indirect effect of the training only for individual teacher knowledge. This indirect effect is 0.292 (Sobel $SE = 0.059$), and the 95% confidence interval estimate of this effect, as obtained by the use of PRODCLIN, is 0.183 to 0.412, providing support for this effect in the population. After including the two mediators in the model, the direct effect of the treatment on the outcome, or path $c' = 0.273$ ($SE = 0.164$, $p = 0.103$). Thus, the results support the idea that the impact of the professional development program on teacher skill is by increasing individual teacher knowledge and that teacher collective knowledge does not add any additional mediating effect to the treatment.

An important point about this analysis is the type of centering that is used for the level-1 or teacher-level mediator. Grand-mean centering was used for the example above, and the estimates of the paths involved in the mediation chain are identical to those obtained with the use of no centering. Note that group-mean centering of the level-1 mediator may also be used. When group-mean centering of a level-1 mediator is used in equations (3)–(5), along with the level-2 mediator added to equation (4), the estimates of paths b and c' are identical to those obtained with use of grand-mean centering. However, for these models, one key difference in the analysis results for group- versus grand-mean centering is the meaning and estimated value of path B. For group-mean centering, path B represents the relationship between the aggregated mediator and the outcome, controlling for the treatment, but not for the individual-level mediator. When we used group-mean centering for the level-1 mediator, the estimate of path B was 0.191 (SE = 0.16), which was not statistically significant, suggesting that the level-2 mediator cannot transmit any effect of the treatment to the outcome. In contrast, with grand-mean centering, path B represents the difference between the level-2 and level-1 slopes associated with the mediator (i.e. $0.191 - 0.426 = -0.235$), that is, the contextual effect. Note that the slope associated with the level-2 mediator obtained with group-mean centering (i.e. 0.191) can also be obtained with grand-mean centering by adding the level-1 and level-2 slopes associated with the mediator (i.e. $0.426 + -0.235 = 0.191$). Further, note that the indirect effect associated with the level-2 mediator via group-mean centering (i.e. aB) is $(0.687)(0.191) = 0.131$.

The indirect effect that would be obtained by multiplying paths *a* and *B* from the grand-mean centered analysis is (0.687)(–0.235) = –0.161. Note then that this indirect effect obtained via grand-mean centering is actually the difference between (a) the indirect effect associated with the level-2 mediator via group-mean centering and (b) the indirect effect associated with the level-1 mediator (i.e. 0.131 – 0.292 = –0.161).

While either grand- or group-mean centering can be used for this mediation analysis, group-mean centering of the level-1 mediator has a distinct disadvantage, which is the second primary difference in analysis results obtained with these centering methods. Specifically, path *a* linking the treatment to the level-1 mediator will always be equal to zero with group-mean centering, because all of the level-2 units (e.g. schools) will have the same mean for the mediator, with this mean being equal to zero. Thus, with group-mean centering, there can be no mediating link between the treatment, the level-1 mediator, and the outcome, as this indirect effect will always be equal to zero (because path *a* is zero). For this reason, grand-mean centering is a better choice, as it provides sensible estimates of path *a* as well as other parameter estimates and, as suggested by this example, allows for greater power to test indirect effects. It is important to remember, however, that with grand-mean centering, the slope estimate for the level-2 mediator represents a difference between the level-1 and level-2 slopes for the mediator. This parameter interpretation seems quite meaningful, as it addresses the question of whether the level-2 mediator adds something to the analysis beyond that provided by the level-1 mediator. If researchers were interested in obtaining an estimate of the slope associated with the level-2 mediator without controlling for the effect of the level-1 mediator, both group- and grand-mean centering, as indicated above, can be used to obtain this slope for the level-2 mediator. Use of group-mean centering may, however, facilitate obtaining the standard error for this slope, which is provided as a matter of routine in multilevel analysis software programs.

THE MULTISITE EXPERIMENTAL DESIGN

In the two-level multisite trial, participants are randomly assigned within organizations to the treatment conditions. In such a design, mediators and the final outcome would be measured at the individual or lower level of the model. Since the treatment variable distinguishes individuals within organizations, all the variables of interest are at the lower level. Thus, the mediation process that is studied in the multisite trial is known as *lower-level* mediation. In such a model, both paths *a* and *b* may vary across organizations. If so, the indirect effect is known as a random effect, which has a different expected value and standard error than the fixed indirect effect. If one or both paths do not vary across sites, then the indirect effect is a fixed one, and the expected value and standard error for this effect are the same as provided above for the cluster-randomized design. Below, we focus on random indirect effects but also consider the fixed effect case.

To illustrate the analyses suggested below for the multisite trial, the following example will be used. In this illustration, suppose that state education officials have designed an intervention to increase the likelihood that elementary school principals will remain on the job, that is, not self attrite. Accumulating evidence indicates that one of the key reasons why principals attrite, besides the long hours, is that they often do not feel, due primarily to time demands, that they play as important a role as they would like as an instructional leader in the school. Thus, state officials have developed an intervention designed to build principals' capacity to serve as an instructional leader in the schools, which includes specific advice to help them find ways in their schedule to allot more time to this role. While, in such a study, the ultimate outcome of interest would likely involve a direct measure of principal attrition, we assume that the state has requested a first-year evaluation of the program. As such, the outcome is a measure indicating the degree to which principals intend to remain on the job. The mediator is a measure of the degree to which principals feel that they are effectively serving as an instructional leader in the school.

Further, we assume that the state randomly selected 40 school districts to participate in the study. In order to meet the request of local school districts to have at least some of their principals participate in the program, the state has decided to use a multisite trial. That is, within each of the 40 school districts, 10 elementary school principals were assigned to the instructional leadership training program and 10 served as no-treatment controls. Thus, the state implemented a multisite experimental design, with a total of 400 principals assigned to the treatment program and 400 serving as controls, with principals nested within treatment groups that are 'crossed' with school districts.

For this illustration below, the following research questions are of interest:

1 Does the instructional leadership training program increase principals' intention to remain on the job? That is, is there an overall effect of the treatment?
2 Given that the training is effective, does the intervention appear to work by increasing the capacity of principals to serve as instructional leaders in the school? That is, is the treatment effect at least partially mediated? As in the previous illustrations, an important study goal is to estimate and test the direct and indirect effects of the treatment.

As in the previous examples, data were simulated to address these research questions. Scores for the mediator and outcome were generated from normal distributions and a dummy-coded treatment variable (with 1 = treatment and 0 = control) was used.

Hierarchical linear models for lower-level mediation ($1 \rightarrow 1 \rightarrow 1$ design)

Bauer et al. (2006) presented a multivariate HLM for lower-level mediation. We follow their approach here except that we use standard HLM notation for the model parameters. To use the multivariate approach, the data file must first be set up in a specific way. Table 27.1 provides a layout of the data set that fits the example used here. Note that Z_{ij} in Table 27.1 is a column in the data set that holds scores for the mediator and outcome, stacked within each principal i. The level-1 or principal-level model is then

$$Z_{ij} = S_{Mij}\beta_{1j} + S_{Mij}\beta_{2j}T_{ij} + S_{Yij}(\beta_{3j} + \beta_{4j}M_{ij} + \beta_{5j}T_{ij}) + r_{Zij}, \tag{11}$$

where S_{Mij} and S_{Yij} are dummy-coded variables indicating whether a line in the data file refers to the mediator or the outcome. Note that the products of (a) S_{Mij} and T_{ij}, (b) S_{Yij} and M_{ij}, and (c) S_{Yij} and T_{ij} must be included in the data file as each product serves as an explanatory variable in the model. Also, the model intercept has been removed from the equation. Finally, the level-1 residual variance is estimated as a function of another variable, such as variable *dv* in Table 27.1. Note that *dv* is a dichotomous variable with user assigned values, for example, 1 and 2, indicating that the variable represents the mediator or outcome.

Table 27.1 Example level-1 data file layout for multivariate analysis for lower-level mediation

District ID	*Prinicpal ID*	Z_{ij}^a	S_{Mij}	S_{Yij}	M_{ij}^b	T_{ij}^c	dv^d	$S_{Mij}T_{ij}$	$S_{Yij}M_{ij}$	$S_{Yij}T_{ij}$
1	1	M_{ij}	1	0	M_{ij}	1	1	1	0	0
1	1	Y_{ij}	0	1	M_{ij}	1	2	0	M_{ij}	1
1	2	M_{ij}	1	0	M_{ij}	1	1	1	0	0
1	2	Y_{ij}	0	1	M_{ij}	1	2	0	M_{ij}	1
1	3	M_{ij}	1	0	M_{ij}	1	1	1	0	0
1	3	Y_{ij}	0	1	M_{ij}	1	2	0	M_{ij}	1
1	4	M_{ij}	1	0	M_{ij}	0	1	1	0	0
1	4	Y_{ij}	0	1	M_{ij}	0	2	0	M_{ij}	1
1	5	M_{ij}	1	0	M_{ij}	0	1	1	0	0
1	5	Y_{ij}	0	1	M_{ij}	0	2	0	M_{ij}	1
1	6	M_{ij}	1	0	M_{ij}	0	1	1	0	0
1	6	Y_{ij}	0	1	M_{ij}	0	2	0	M_{ij}	1
.	.	.	.	.	.	.	.	.	.	.
N_k	N_{ij}	M_{ij}	1	0	M_{ijk}	0	1	1	0	0
N_k	N_{ij}	Y_{ij}	0	1	M_{ijk}	0	2	0	M_{ij}	1

[a] Z_{ij} holds scores for the mediator and outcome for each person.
[b] M_{ij} contains scores for the mediator, with the same values appearing in the proper place in column Z_{ij}.
[c] T_{ij} is a dummy-coded treatment indicator variable.
[d] *dv* is an indicator variable that is used to allow for separate level-1 variance estimates for the mediator and outcome.

Thus, by estimating the level-1 residual variance as a function of *dv*, separate variance estimates will be obtained for the mediator and outcome, as desired. At level 2, each of the regression coefficients are specified as random:

$$\beta_{1j} = \gamma_{10} + u_{1j}, \tag{12}$$

$$\beta_{2j} = \gamma_{20} + u_{2j}, \tag{13}$$

$$\beta_{3j} = \gamma_{30} + u_{3j}, \tag{14}$$

$$\beta_{4j} = \gamma_{40} + u_{4j}, \tag{15}$$

$$\beta_{5j} = \gamma_{50} + u_{5j}. \tag{16}$$

Thus, path *a* is γ_{20}, path *b* is γ_{40}, and path c' is γ_{50}.

Note that the single-level equation (11) may be used to form equations for the mediator and outcome by plugging values of 1 for S_{Mij} and 1 for S_{Yij}. To illustrate, when S_{Mij} = 1, equation (11) becomes

$$M_{ij} = \gamma_{10} + \gamma_{20}T_{ij} + u_{10j} + u_{20j} + r_{ij}, \tag{17}$$

and when S_{Yij} =1, then equation (11) becomes

$$\mathrm{Y}_{ij} = \gamma_{30} + \gamma_{40}\mathrm{M}_{ij} + \gamma_{50}\mathrm{T}_{ij} + \mathrm{u}_{30j} + \mathrm{u}_{40j} + \mathrm{u}_{50j} + \mathrm{r}'_{ij}, \tag{18}$$

where r'_{ij} is the residual variance for the final outcome of interest. With this alternate expression, it is relatively easy to recognize the parameters that represent the paths in the mediation process, as indicated above. Further, in equations (17) and (18), the residuals for the mediator and outcome are assumed to be uncorrelated. The advantages of specifying the residual variance, in equation (11) to be a function of variable *dv,* is that not only will the separate variances be estimated for the mediator and outcome, but also the residuals associated with these variables will be uncorrelated.

As indicated above, paths *a* and *b* may covary. The covariance of these paths is found in the variance-covariance matrix of the random effects at the upper-level of the model, which is the covariance matrix of the *u* terms in equations (12)–(16). This matrix is

$$\begin{pmatrix} \tau_{11} & & & & \\ \tau_{21} & \tau_{22} & & & \\ \tau_{31} & \tau_{32} & \tau_{33} & & \\ \tau_{41} & \tau_{42} & \tau_{43} & \tau_{44} & \\ \tau_{51} & \tau_{52} & \tau_{53} & \tau_{54} & \tau_{55} \end{pmatrix}, \tag{19}$$

where the covariance of paths *a* and *b* is represented by τ_{42}. As noted in Bauer et al. (2006) and Kenny et al. (2003), when paths *a* and *b* covary, the expected value of the indirect effect is no longer simply the product of the paths (*ab*), but is instead *ab* + the covariance of these paths. Thus, in this design, the expected value of the indirect effect, averaging across upper-level units (school districts) is

$$\text{Indirect effect } = (\gamma_{20})(\gamma_{40}) + \tau_{42}. \tag{20}$$

Note that if either path *a* or path *b* does not vary across organizations, then the indirect effect is a fixed effect and its expected value and standard error would be those typically used, as in the cluster-randomized trial presented earlier in this chapter. In this multisite design, values at or near zero for either τ_{22} or τ_{44} would be consistent with the specification of a fixed indirect effect. Also, given that the model has 15 variances and covariances that need to be estimated at the upper level of the model, estimation difficulties may arise, especially when the number of level-1 units, such as principals, is relatively small. These difficulties may force the user to fix τ_{22} or τ_{44} to zero, which would produce a fixed indirect effect.

Illustration and results

Recall that in this example the treatment is the instructional leadership program designed to boost the capacity of elementary school principals to serve as instructional leaders in their schools, thereby increasing their intent to remain on the job. The mediator is a measure tapping the confidence that elementary school principals have that they can effectively serve as an instructional leader. The final outcome of interest is a measure of the principals' intent to remain on the job, that is, to continue working as a principal.

To determine if the training program impacts principal's intent to remain on the job, we use a univariate HLM. This model includes only the outcome of interest and the treatment variable, both of which are included in the first level of the model. At the district level, we allow the level-1 intercept and treatment effect to vary across districts. Averaging across districts, the overall effect of the treatment is 0.631 ($SE = 0.112, p < 0.001$), indicating that after principals participate in the program they have greater intent to remain on the job. With a standard deviation of 1.63 for the intent measure, the treatment effect is fairly strong at about 0.39 standard deviations.

To determine if the effects of the training program are mediated by principal capacity to serve as an instructional leader, we use equations (11) through (16). Focusing on the key model parameters, the training program has a positive impact on instructional leader capacity, as path *a*, or γ_{20}, is 0.434 ($SE = 0.088, p < 0.001$). Given that the standard deviation for the capacity measure is 1.28, this impact of the training corresponds to 0.34 standard deviations, a fairly strong effect. Further, after controlling for treatment status, capacity is positively related to principal intent to remain on the job, as path *b* or γ_{50} is 0.551 ($SE = 0.078, p < 0.001$).

Thus, paths *a* and *b* of the mediation process are positive and statistically significant. These paths also vary across school districts, as the variances of path *a* and path *b*, respectively, are $\tau_{22} = 0.187$ ($p < 0.001$) and $\tau_{44} = 0.216$, ($p < 0.001$). Further, these paths covary, as this covariance, or τ_{42}, is 0.117 ($r = 0.592$). Using equation (20), we then estimate the indirect effect, averaging across districts, to be (0.434)(0.551) + 0.117 = 0.356. Given the standard deviation of intention, this indirect effect is relatively strong, equivalent to 0.22 standard deviations. Further, the direct effect (path *c*') of the treatment on the outcome is positive ($\gamma_{40} = 0.275$, $SE = 0.060$, $p < 0.001$), and this effect also varies across school districts ($\tau_{55} = 0.03$, $p = 0.032$).

Bauer et al. (2006) indicate that a confidence interval for the random indirect effect can be formed by using critical values from the standard normal distribution along with the standard error of the random indirect effect. For this multisite design, the standard error associated with this effect, as given in Bauer et al., is

$$\text{Standard Error} = \sqrt{b^2\text{Var}(a) + a^2\text{Var}(b) + \text{Var}(a)\text{Var}(b)} + \sqrt{2ab\text{Cov}(a,b) + \text{Cov}(a,b)^2 + \text{Var}(\tau_{ab})}, \tag{21}$$

where Var and Cov represent the sampling variances and covariances of the estimated paths *a* and *b* and the estimated covariance of these paths, τ_{ab}. For this illustration, the sampling covariance of paths *a* and *b* is approximately 0.003 and the sampling variance of τ_{ab} (or τ_{42}) is about 0.002. Plugging the relevant values into equation (21) gives the standard error of the indirect effect of 0.085. The 95% confidence interval for the indirect effect is then 0.190 to 0.522, providing support for the presence of the indirect effect in the population.

MULTILEVEL STRUCTURAL EQUATION MODELING

The focus of multilevel SEM, conceptually, is to parse out the within-cluster and between-cluster variance for each variable and then model within-cluster relations on the within-cluster variance components while simultaneously modeling between-cluster relations on the between-cluster variance components (Heck and Thomas, 2000; McDonald and Goldstein, 1989; Muthén, 1994; Stapleton, 2006). Therefore, it is critical for the researcher to carefully consider which relations to model at which level in the model.

As an example of this multilevel variance parsing, suppose we have an outcome of interest, teacher knowledge. There is variance in teacher knowledge attributable to clustering; perhaps some schools employ teachers who are more knowledgeable on average compared with other schools. Also, there is variance in teacher knowledge related to differences in individuals; teachers in the various schools are different from their own colleagues due to factors such as training and experience. Therefore, we can hypothesize that the variance in the teacher

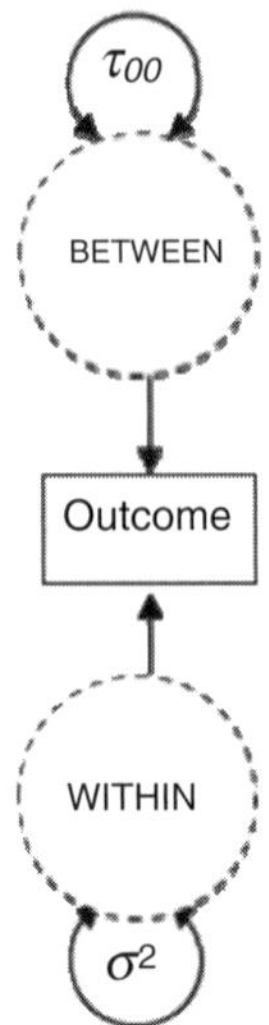

Figure 27.2 Variance parsing in a SEM framework

knowledge variable is comprised of some function of τ_{00} (between-school variance) and some function of σ_W^2 (within-school variance) as shown in Figure 27.2, with the between- and within-processes denoted as factors (shown with dotted lines to differentiate them from traditional latent construct factors). A researcher can then model relationships between variables with either the within-level variance or the between-level variance or with both.

SEM programs that can accommodate multilevel models (such as Mplus and LISREL) automatically do the variance parsing for the user. The Mplus analysis option, TYPE IS TWOLEVEL, and the LISREL SIMPLIS syntax, $CLUSTER, undertake the variance partitioning. As shown in Figure 27.3, using a treatment variable, a mediator, and an outcome, we have three measured variables (represented as boxes within the shaded region) and for each of the measured variables, we can choose to have the program parse the variability into within and between components. We then hypothesize relations among the 'constructs' represented by the dotted lines (currently shown as unrelated in Figure 27.3). Note that the shaded area is not accessible to the user; the user must specify only the 'within' model and the 'between' model to the SEM program.

To estimate parameters in the within and between models, the SEM program will calculate the sample between-cluster covariance matrix ($\boldsymbol{S}_B$) as well as the sample pooled within-cluster covariance matrix ($\boldsymbol{S}_{PW}$):

$$S_B = (J-1)^{-1}\sum_{j=1}^{J} n_j(\bar{y}_j - \bar{y})(\bar{y}_j - \bar{y})'$$

$$S_{PW} = (N-J)^{-1}\sum_{j=1}^{J}\sum_{i=1}^{n_j}(y_{ij} - \bar{y}_j)(y_{ij} - \bar{y}_j)'.$$

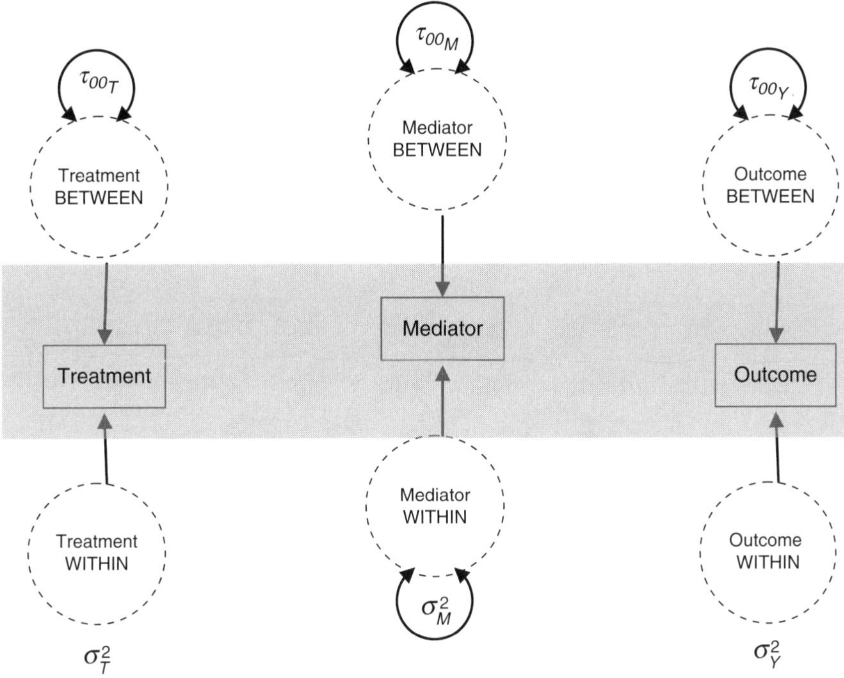

Figure 27.3 Conceptual variance parsing using SEM software

Then, the parameter estimates are determined to maximize the fit of these sample covariance matrices to the respective within- and between-implied covariance matrices ($\hat{\Sigma}_B$ and $\hat{\Sigma}_W$) defined by the hypothesized relations in the models. There may be perfect fit in one part of the model with poor fit in another. In most of the mediation designs examined in this chapter, model fit is not at issue given that the models are just-identified.

Using an SEM framework for cross-level mediation (2 → 1 → 1 design)

In this design, there are two dependent or endogenous variables (the mediator and the outcome), and one independent or exogenous variable (the treatment). Because the treatment is assigned at level 2, all of the variability in that variable must be defined as between-cluster variability, and thus, as shown in Figures 27.4(a) and (b), no within-group variability is modeled for treatment. The mediator, however, presents an interesting issue. When we are estimating path *a*, from the treatment to the mediator, that path can exist only at the between level of the model, and thus the mediator must be modeled to have between-cluster variability as shown in Figure 27.4(a). However, we hypothesize in the cross-level mediation design that the variability in the mediator is based on individual differences (it is a function of the effect of the treatment and differences in people and is not 'caused' by the cluster); therefore, when we model the effect of the

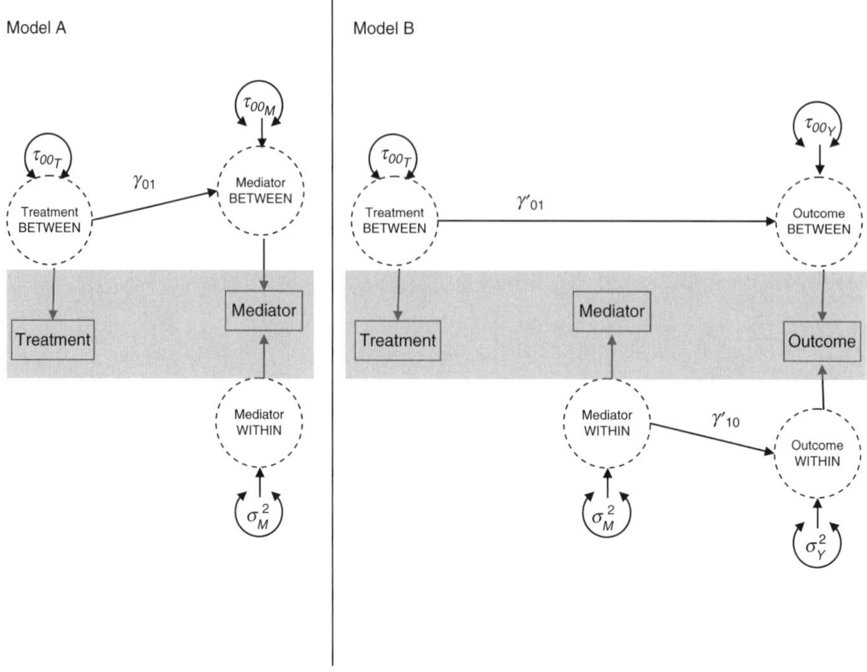

Figure 27.4 Cluster randomized with cross-level mediation (2 → 1 → 1 design)

mediator on the outcome (estimate path *b*), we model the mediator as having within-cluster variability only. In this case, it is necessary to split the full hypothesized model into two pieces (as shown in Figures 27.4(a) and (b)).

The model as shown in Figure 27.4(a) is specified using the following Mplus MODEL syntax:

```
MODEL:
  %WITHIN%
  %BETWEEN%
      M ON T;
```

Note that no relations are hypothesized at the 'within' level and thus no model is provided to Mplus in the %WITHIN% section. The model as shown in Figure 27.4(b) is specified using the following Mplus MODEL syntax:

```
MODEL:
  %WITHIN%
      Y ON M;
  %BETWEEN%
      Y ON T;
```

The maximum likelihood estimates match those obtained with HLM, but with slight differences in the estimated standard errors. The estimate of γ_{01}, or path *a*, is 0.687 with an estimated *SE* of 0.121 compared to 0.126 with HLM. From model 4(b), γ'_{10} is estimated as 0.414 with $SE = 0.036$, and γ'_{01} is 0.120 with a slightly different *SE* of 0.123 (compared to the 0.126 obtained with HLM). The estimates from these two models would then need to be input to a program such as PRODCLIN to obtain estimated confidence intervals for the mediated effect.

Using an SEM framework for upper-level mediation (2 → 2 → 1 Design)

In this design, all of the variability for both the treatment and the mediator is hypothesized to exist at the between level (as the variable values are associated with the cluster and not the individual). The model as shown in Figure 27.5 is hypothesized and can be specified in a single path model with the following model statements in Mplus:

```
MODEL:
  %WITHIN%
  %BETWEEN%
      M ON T;
      Y ON M T;
MODEL INDIRECT:
      Y IND T;
```

Again, note that no relations are posited to exist at the within-cluster level (the only parameter to be estimated at the within-cluster level is individual variability

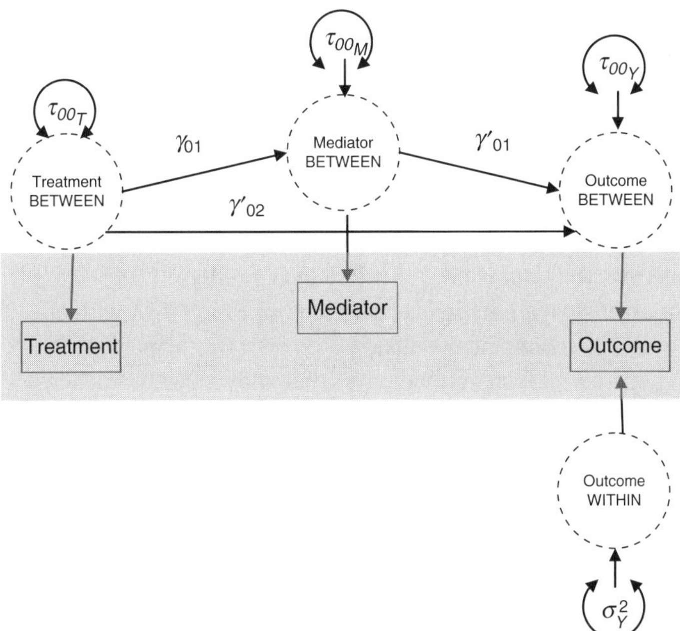

Figure 27.5 Cluster randomized with upper-level mediation (2 → 2 → 1 design)

in the outcome). Also note that a 'MODEL INDIRECT' statement requests Mplus to provide the estimated mediated effect and the standard error for that effect. The Mplus estimates of coefficients match those from HLM: γ_{01} , or path *a*, is 0.710 (*SE* = 0.108), γ'_{01} (path *b*) is 0.573 (*SE* = 0.178), and γ'_{02} (path *c'*) is –0.115 (*SE* = 0.176). In the indirect effects section of the output, Mplus provides the total indirect effect of 0.407, a Sobel (1982) standard error of 0.141, and a normal-based 95% confidence interval of 0.131 to 0.683. Note that the required parameter estimates can be input into the PRODCLIN program to obtain a somewhat more accurate interval estimate of the indirect effect.

Using an SEM framework for cross- and upper-level mediation (2 → 1 → 1 and 2 → 2 → 1 design)

In order to replicate the HLM estimates for the cross- and upper-level mediation design, an additional variable must be added to the model: the cluster average value of the mediator. In this design, the research question combines aspects of the 2 → 1 → 1 design (that hypothesizes that individual differences in the mediator is the causal mechanism) as well as the 2 → 2 → 1 design (that hypothesizes that there is a synergistic effect of having a higher mean value on the mediator). The model for this design is shown in Figure 27.6 and can be run in a single model in Mplus:

```
MODEL:
   %WITHIN%
         Y ON M ;
   %BETWEEN%
         AVE_M ON T;
         Y ON AVE_M T ;
```

The variables T and AVE_M are defined as 'BETWEEN' variables and the variable M is defined as a 'WITHIN' variable. By default, Mplus will use group mean centering for within-group variables and thus to force the use of group-mean centering, the command 'CENTERING = GRANDMEAN (M)' is used. The Mplus estimates of coefficients match those from HLM with only slight differences in the estimates of the standard errors: γ_{01}, or path *a*, is 0.687 (*SE* = 0.121), γ'_{10} (path *b*) linking individual teacher knowledge to teacher skill is 0.426 (*SE* = 0.033), and γ'_{02} (path *B*) linking mean teacher knowledge to that same outcome is –.235 (*SE* = 0.163). Finally, γ'_{0} (path *c'*) is 0.273 (*SE* = 0.160).

Using an SEM framework for lower-level mediation (1 → 1 → 1 design)

As shown in Figure 27.7, a lower-level mediation design includes a treatment variable that has no between-cluster variability (at each site, the same proportion of participants were assigned to the treatment and control conditions). Both the mediator and the outcome variable are hypothesized to vary across clusters, but

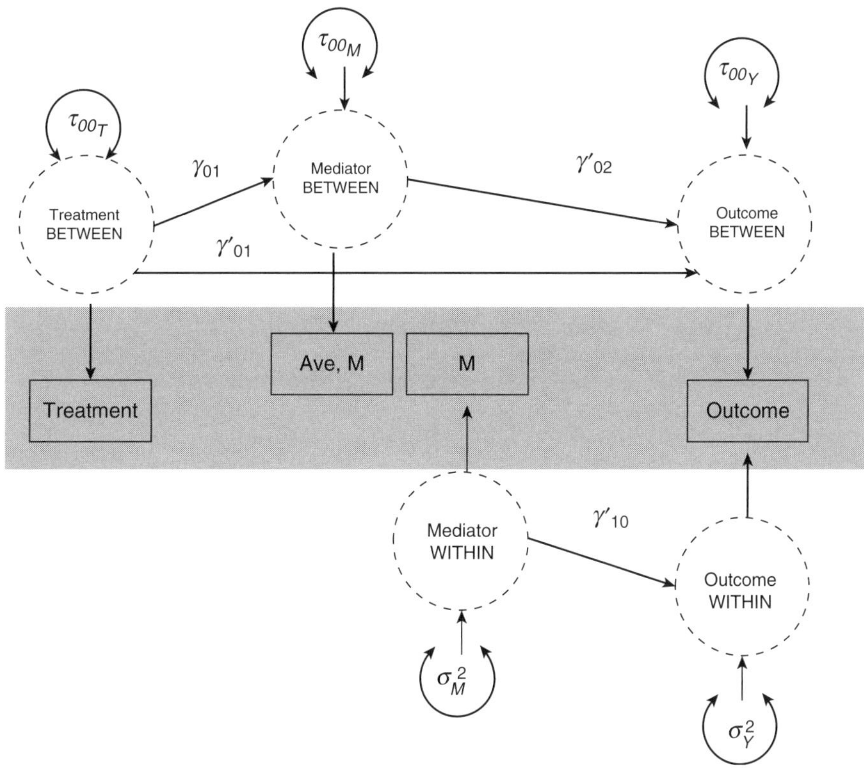

Figure 27.6 Cluster randomized with cross- and upper-level mediation ($2 \rightarrow 1 \rightarrow 1$ and $2 \rightarrow 2 \rightarrow 1$ design)

no relations are hypothesized between the cluster means of the mediator and outcome variable. Within clusters, the effect of the treatment on the mediator (path *a*), the effect of the mediator on the outcome (path *b*), and the effect of the treatment on the outcome (path *c*′) are allowed to vary across clusters and these random coefficients are symbolized by a black dot on the paths.

The Mplus statements to estimate this hypothesized model are provided as:

```
MODEL:
  %WITHIN%
        A | M ON T;
        B | Y ON M;
        CPRIME | Y ON T;
  %BETWEEN%
        A WITH B;
```

A regression statement that is prefixed with a '|' indicates that the effect is allowed to vary across clusters (represented as *u* in the equations presented in the HLM section) and the letter to the left of the '|' names the random effect. The 'A WITH B' statement specifies that the random components of the *a* and *b* paths are

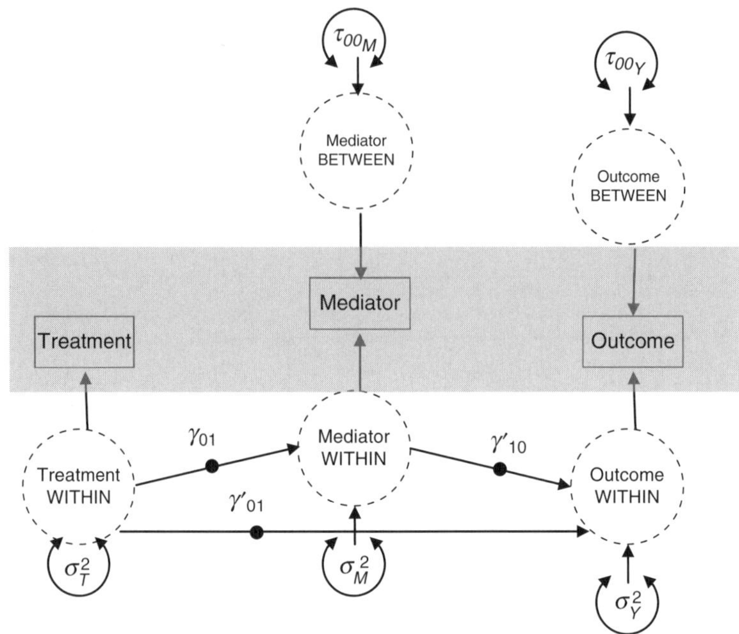

Figure 27.7 Multisite experiment with lower-level mediation (1 → 1 → 1 design)

assumed to covary. Note that, if desired, we could run a model that also allows the *a* and *b* random components to covary with the *c*' random component. When modeling with random coefficients, the MODEL INDIRECT command is not currently available with Mplus. Equations (20) and (21) can be used to estimate and test the indirect effect.

The estimates from this model are very similar to the HLM results presented earlier: γ_{01}, or path *a*, is 0.434 ($SE = 0.088$), γ'_{01} (path *b*) is 0.557 ($SE = 0.079$), and γ'_{02} (path *c*') is 0.268 ($SE = 0.062$). Additional parameters of interest in this model include the variability of path *a* across clusters ($\tau_{22} = 0.188$, $SE = 0.061$), the variability of path *b* across clusters ($\tau_{44} = 0.216$, $SE = 0.057$), the variability of path *c*' across clusters ($\tau_{55} = 0.050$, $SE = 0.047$), and the covariance of paths *a* and *b* ($\tau_{42} = 0.126$, $SE = 0.050$).

DISCUSSION

In this chapter, we have shown how multilevel mediation analysis may be conducted for some large-scale experimental designs using both the HLM and multilevel SEM framework. Both of these approaches are generally superior to a *single-level* analysis approach because the former approaches take into account the clustering or correlation of participants within sites and thus provide more accurate standard errors for the direct and indirect effects. Further, both the HLM and SEM approaches can be combined with modern testing approaches to provide for more powerful tests of indirect effects. In this chapter, we used the PRODCLIN program, primarily, to test indirect effects. This testing method takes into account the nonnormality of indirect effects, which results in more accurate confidence interval estimates of indirect effects and greater power than other methods. Although not shown here, both the HLM and SEM approaches may also be combined with resampling strategies, such as the bias-corrected bootstrap, which may offer a somewhat more powerful test of indirect effects. Although not illustrated in this chapter, both the HLM and SEM approaches can readily accommodate multiple mediators, which may arguably be realistic because experimental treatments, in general, may not attain their effects via one variable only. Further, it is apparent from our presentation, that the results using an HLM approach with software such as PROC MIXED in SAS, HLM, and MLwiN can yield equivalent estimates to those obtained via modeling path analyses in SEM software that can accommodate multilevel data.

Given that the HLM and multilevel SEM approaches provided similar results for the models we examined, one might ask whether either the HLM or SEM approach is preferred to the other. Each analysis we considered assumed the use of error-free measurements, that is, that the mediator(s) and outcome are measured with perfect reliability. SEM programs provide users with an option to take into account the impact of measurement error on analysis results, even when the variables of interest are measured with a single indicator. Hoyle and Kenny (1999) demonstrated that measurement error, if unaccounted for, may lead to underestimating the size of indirect effects. Further, their research showed that models that incorporate measurement error can greatly reduce this bias. If the mediator and outcome are measured with somewhat low reliabilities, then the multilevel SEM approach may be preferred over HLM.

In addition, SEM more readily allows for the use of multiple indicators to represent constructs of interest. For example, suppose for the upper-level mediation design ($2 \rightarrow 2 \rightarrow 1$) instead of having one measure of principal support for reading strategies, we might have three indicators of principal support taken from a questionnaire, an interview, or direct observation. These three indicators would be used to define the construct of principal support. Figure 27.8 shows how such a hypothesized mediation model could be set up in an SEM framework. Such latent construct extensions can be included in all the model designs discussed thus far, with latent constructs at the within-level, between-level or both, with the effects of measurement error taken into account when the paths involved in the mediation process are estimated. While the inclusion of a measurement model results in a more complicated analysis, this model provides for a sensible approach in handling the use of multiple indicators. Again, if a study is using multiple indicators to represent constructs of interest for the designs examined in this chapter, multilevel SEM would likely be preferred over the use of HLM.

HLM may be preferred over multilevel SEM when a study design involves three or more levels of data. For the cross-level mediation example presented in

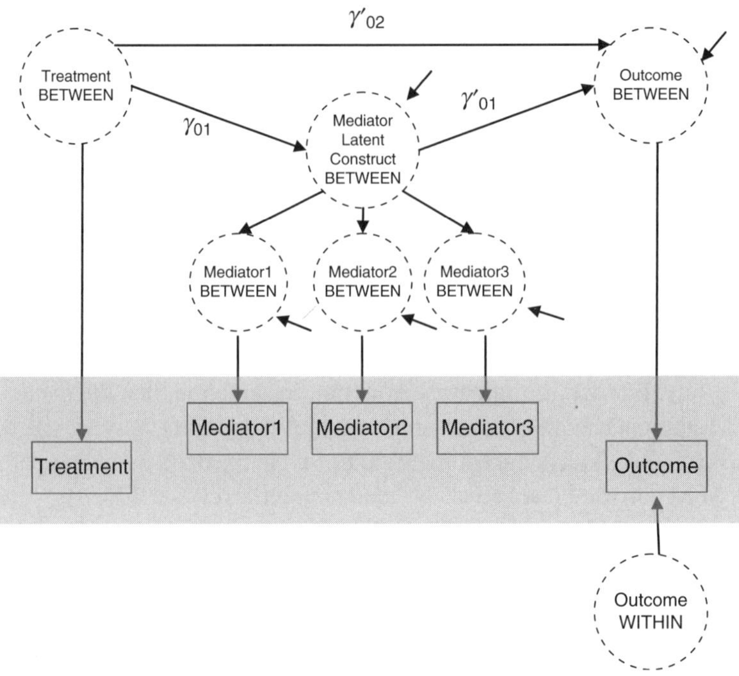

Figure 27.8 Cluster randomized with mediator as a latent variable ($2 \rightarrow 2 \rightarrow 1$ design)

the chapter, the professional development program, a school-based treatment, was designed to impact teacher knowledge of effective teaching strategies, which was hypothesized to lead to better teaching performance. Ultimately, however, the intervention would likely have a goal of impacting student achievement, via improvements in teacher skill. In such a design, three levels are present: students, teachers, and schools, and variability may be present at each of these levels. Thus, a three-level analysis model may be needed to provide for proper inference for the effects of interest. The HLM approach can be readily extended to three levels. Pituch et al. (2010) have shown how multilevel mediation analysis can be conducted for randomized field experiments that have three levels in the design. Although the extension to more than two levels of a SEM has been discussed and the matrix formulation provided (Skrondal and Rabe-Hesketh, 2004), current capability in SEM software supports analysis models with only a single nesting of data (thus a two-level model is all that can be accommodated). One exception is the latent growth model, wherein a three-level model, with individual repeated responses are considered level 1, is accommodated as a two-level multivariate model (Muthén, 1997).

Another design extension where multilevel mediation analysis could be conducted involves the use of repeated measures across time for the cluster-randomized or multisite trial. Repeated measures could be collected over time for the outcome, the mediator, or both. Experimental studies where the outcome is measured over time would focus on growth across time, and if specific mediating variables are responsible for the presumably greater growth in the treatment group. Studies where data are collected across time for both the mediator and outcome may address the question of whether greater growth in the mediator across time for a given treatment group is responsible for the greater growth in the final outcome of interest. Both HLM and multilevel SEM can be used for such analyses. The advantages mentioned above apply for these designs, with SEM facilitating representation of constructs with multiple indicators and HLM being more useful when additional levels are present in the data structure, such as student, class, and school.

A final design extension considered here is when the indirect effect or paths involved in the indirect effect are moderated by another variable. This design may be especially useful in evaluating the effects of an intervention, where one may hypothesize that treatment effects on the mediator and/or outcome may depend on, for example, initial status for these variables. Potential interactions may also be explored when, unexpectedly, no overall treatment or mediated effects are found. In either case, when path a or b is moderated by another variable, this implies that the indirect effect differs across subgroups and that the mediation process being examined does not generally hold across individuals or organizations. Such interactions within a mediation process may be modeled with either the HLM or multilevel SEM approach.

REFERENCES

Bauer, D.J., Preacher, K.J., and Gil, K.M. (2006). 'Conceptualizing and testing random indirect effects and moderated mediation in multilevel models: New procedures and recommendations'. *Psychological Methods,* 11(2): 142–63.

Borman, G.D., Slavin, R., Cheung, A., Chamberlain, A.M., Madden, N.A., and Chambers, B. (2005). 'Success for all: First-year results from the national randomized field trial'. *Educational Evaluation and Policy Analysis*, 27(1): 1–22.

Boruch, R.F. (ed.) (2005). 'Place randomized trials: Experimental test of public policy'. *The Annals of the American Academy of Political and Social Science,* 599.

Chatterji, M. (2004). 'Evidence on "what works": An argument for extended-term mixed-methods (ETMM) evaluation designs'. *Educational Researcher*, 33(1): 3–13.

Cheung, M.W.L. (2007). 'Comparison of approaches to constructing confidence intervals for mediating effects using structural equation models'. *Structural Equation Modeling*, 14(2): 227–46.

Donner, A. and Klar, N. (2000). *Design and Analysis of Cluster Randomization Trials in Health Research.* London: Arnold.

Eisenhart, M. and Towne, L. (2003). 'Contestation and change in national policy on "scientifically-based" education research'. *Educational Researcher*, 32(1): 31–8.

Finn, J.D. and Achilles, C.M. (1990). 'Answers and questions about class size: A statewide experiment'. *American Educational Research Journal,* 27(3): 557–77.

Heck, R.H. and Thomas, S.L. (2000). *An Introduction to Multilevel Modeling Techniques.* Mahwah, NJ: Lawrence Erlbaum Associates.

Hoyle, R.H. and Kenny, D.A. (1999). 'Sample size, reliability, and tests of statistical mediation'. In R.H. Hoyle (ed.) *Statistical Strategies for Small Sample Research.* Thousand Oaks, CA: Sage. pp. 195–222.

Institute of Education Sciences (2003). 'Identifying and implementing educational practices supported by rigorous evidence: A user friendly guide. Institute of Education Sciences', http://www.excelgov.org/evidence.

Judd, C.M. and Kenny, D.A. (1981). 'Process analysis: Estimating mediation in treatment evaluations'. *Evaluation Review*, 5(5): 602–19.

Kellam, S.G. and Langevin, D.J. (2003). 'A framework for understanding "evidence" in prevention research and programs'. *Prevention Science*, 4(3): 137–53.

Kenny, D.A., Kashy, D.A., and Bolger, N. (1998). 'Data analysis in social psychology'. In D.T. Gilbert, S.T. Fiske, and G. Lindzey (eds) *The Handbook of Social Psychology*, 4th edn. New York: McGraw-Hill. pp. 233–65.

Kenny, D.A., Korchmaros, J.D., and Bolger, N. (2003). 'Lower level mediation in multilevel models'. *Psychological Methods*, 8(2): 115–28.

Krull, J.L., and MacKinnon, D.P. (1999). 'Multilevel mediation modeling in group-based intervention studies'. *Evaluation Review*, 23(2): 144–58.

Krull, J.L., and MacKinnon, D.P. (2001). 'Multilevel modeling of individual and group level mediated effects'. *Multivariate Behavioral Research*, 36(2): 249–77.

MacKinnon, D.P. (2008). *Introduction to Statistical Mediation Analysis.* New York: Lawrence Erlbaum Associates.

MacKinnon, D.P., Lockwood, C.M., Hoffman, J.M., West, S.G., and Sheets, V. (2002). 'A comparison of methods to test mediation and other intervening variable effects'. *Psychological Methods*, 7(1): 83–104.

MacKinnon, D.P., Lockwood, C.M., and Williams, J. (2004). 'Confidence limits for the indirect effect: Distribution of the product and resampling methods'. *Multivariate Behavioral Research*, 39(1): 99–128.

MacKinnon, D.P., Fritz, M.S., Williams, J., and Lockwood, C.M. (2007). 'Distribution of the product confidence limits for the indirect effect: Program PRODCLIN'. *Behavior Research Methods*, 39(3): 384–89.

McDonald, R.P. and Goldstein, H. (1989). 'Balanced versus unbalanced designs for linear structural relations in two-level data'. *British Journal of Mathematical and Statistical Psychology*, 42(2): 215–32.

Mosteller, F. (1995). 'The Tennessee study of class size in the early grades'. The Future of Children. *Critical Issues for Children and Youth*, 5(2): 113–25.

Murray, D.M. (1998). *Design and Analysis of Group-randomized Trials.* New York: Oxford University Press.

Muthén, B.O. (1994). 'Multilevel covariance structure analysis'. *Sociological Methods and Research*, 22(3): 376–98.

Muthén, B.O. (1997). 'Latent variable modeling with longitudinal and multilevel data'. In A. Raftery (ed.) *Sociological Methodology.* Boston: Blackwell Publishers. pp. 453–80.

Olson, D.R. (2004). 'The triumph of hope over experience in the search for "What Works": A response to Slavin'. *Educational Researcher*, 33(1): 24–6.

Pituch, K.A. (2004). 'Textbook presentations on supplemental hypothesis testing activities, nonnormality, and the concept of mediation'. *Understanding Statistics*, 3(3): 135–50.

Pituch, K.A. and Stapleton, L.M. (2008). 'The performance of methods to test upper-level mediation in the presence of nonnormal data'. *Multivariate Behavioral Research*, 43(2): 237–67.

Pituch, K.A., Stapleton, L.M., and Kang, J.Y. (2006). 'A comparison of single sample and bootstrap methods to assess mediation in cluster-randomized trials'. *Multivariate Behavioral Research,* 41(3): 367–400.

Pituch, K.A., Murphy, D.L., and Tate, R.L. (2010). 'Three-level models for indirect effects in school- and class-randomized experiments in education'. *Journal of Experimental Education*, 78(1): 60–95.

Pituch, K.A., Whittaker, T.A., and Stapleton, L.M. (2005). 'A comparison of methods to test for mediation in multisite experiments'. *Multivariate Behavioral Research*, 40(1): 1–23.

Plewis, I. and Hurry, J. (1998). 'A multilevel perspective on the design and analysis of intervention studies'. *Educational Research and Evaluation*, 4(1): 13–26.

Raudenbush, S.W. and Bryk, A.S. (2002). *Hierarchical Linear Models: Applications and Data Analysis Methods*. 2nd edn. Thousand Oaks, CA: Sage. (1st edn, 1992.)

Raudenbush, S.W. and Liu, X. (2000). 'Statistical power and optimal design for multisite randomized trials'. *Psychological Methods*, 5(2): 199–213.

Raykov, T. and Mels, G. (2007). 'Lower-level mediation effect analysis in two-level studies: A note on a multilevel structural equation modeling approach'. *Structural Equation Modeling*, 14(4): 636–48.

Skrondal, A. and Rabe-Hesketh, S. (2004). *Generalized Latent Variable Modeling: Multilevel, Longitudinal, and Structural Equation Models*. Boca Raton: Chapman and Hall.

Sobel, M.E. (1982). 'Asymptotic confidence intervals for indirect effects in structural equation models'. In S. Leinhardt (ed.) *Sociological Methodology*. Washington, DC: American Sociological Association. pp. 290–312.

Stapleton, L.M. (2006). 'Using multilevel structural equation modeling techniques with complex sample data'. In G.R. Hancock and R. Mueller (eds) *A Second Course* in *Structural Equation Modeling*. Greenwich, CT: Information Age Publishing. pp. 345–83.

Tate, R.L. and Pituch, K.A. (2007). 'Multivariate hierarchical linear modeling in randomized field experiments'. *The Journal of Experimental Education*, 75(4): 317–37.

Varnell, S.P., Murray, D.M., Janega, J.B., and Blitstein, J.L. (2004). 'Design and analysis of group-randomized trials: A review of recent practices'. *American Journal of Public Health*, 94(3): 393–9.

What Works Clearinghouse (2005). 'WWC study review standards'. *Institute of Education Sciences*. http://w-w-c.org

Author Index

Page numbers ending with the letter 'n' refer to names in Notes at the end of the chapter

Subject Index

Page references to Figures or Tables are in *italic* print. Page numbers with 'n' following refer to Notes